Lincoln's First Crisis

Adapted from *The War with the South* by Robert Tomes (New York, 1862). Drawing by J. R. Chapin. Engraving by R. Dudensing.

Lincoln's First Crisis

Fort Sumter and the Betrayal of the President

William Bruce Johnson

STACKPOLE
BOOKS

Guilford, Connecticut

Published by Stackpole Books
An imprint of The Rowman & Littlefield Publishing Group, Inc.
4501 Forbes Blvd., Ste. 200
Lanham, MD 20706
www.rowman.com

Distributed by NATIONAL BOOK NETWORK

British Library Cataloguing in Publication Information available

Library of Congress Cataloging-in-Publication Data available

Names: Johnson, William Bruce, author.
Title: Lincoln's first crisis : Fort Sumter and the betrayal of the
    President / William Bruce Johnson.
Description: Guilford, Connecticut : Stackpole Books, [2020] | Includes
    bibliographical references and index. | Summary: "'Lincoln's First
    Crisis' covers four of the most consequential months in American
    history: December 1860 through April 1861. In this thoughtful, careful
    reassessment, Johnson reconstructs the beginning of the Civil War, when
    Lincoln bested his rivals and established himself as commander in chief,
    doing so on his own political, moral, and military terms that helped lay
    the foundation for meaningful Union victory"— Provided by publisher.
Identifiers: LCCN 2019050526 (print) | LCCN 2019050527 (ebook) | ISBN
    9780811739405 (cloth) | ISBN 9780811769365 (epub)
Subjects: LCSH: Lincoln, Abraham, 1809–1865. | United States—Politics and
    government—1857–1861. | United States—History—Civil War,
    1861–1865—Causes. | Secession.
Classification: LCC E440.5 .J668 2020 (print) | LCC E440.5 (ebook) | DDC
    973.7092—dc23
LC record available at https://lccn.loc.gov/2019050526
LC ebook record available at https://lccn.loc.gov/2019050527

∞™ The paper used in this publication meets the minimum requirements of American
National Standard for Information Sciences—Permanence of Paper for Printed Library
Materials, ANSI/NISO Z39.48-1992.

Contents

"Our Stormy-Browed Sister"

The Palmetto Republic

On November 5, 1860, South Carolina governor William Gist predicted that the next day's presidential election would be won by Abraham Lincoln, a candidate with no support in the Cotton South, leading a Republican Party that was "fatally bent upon our ruin."[1] Despite this and similarly dire warnings by other state leaders, many Charlestonians were observed to be "jubilant" upon news of Lincoln's victory, since now the only way to avoid the Republicans' predicted onslaught was to proceed with an initiative that the radical "fire-eaters" had been urging for a decade: secession from the United States. "The streets bloomed with palmetto flags," it was said, and the air was "charged with electrical feeling," as speakers happily addressed a crowd as "Citizens of the Southern Republic."[2]

Gist called for a special convention to prepare for the state's formal withdrawal, predicting that other slave states would soon follow. On November 17, an estimated twenty thousand people attended a gala featuring the "Miserere" from *Il Trovatore*, played as a requiem for the Union. Prominent citizens resigned their federal positions: Andrew Gordon Magrath as district judge, William Colcock as customs collector, James Conner as district attorney, and Robert Gourdin as head of the grand jury. In Washington too, South Carolinians began to vacate their congressional and administrative posts, and officers in the army and navy resigned their presidential commissions.[3] British envoy Lord Lyons informed the Foreign Office that while "the bulk of the southern people desire to cling to the Union so long . . . as their influence in Congress is sufficient to protect them" from the new regime, the resignations of South Carolina's congressional delegation would immediately diminish that influence. The en masse departures from Washington and Charleston's ironic pleasure at Lincoln's election were therefore of a piece: the more Carolinians stripped themselves of power in the federal government, the more they could allege what Governor Gist had called a "consolidated despotism" of free states arrayed against them, so that eventually (as Lyons noted) not just South Carolina and "three or four more of the violent little States" that had threatened withdrawal for a decade but also the entire South would "consider it necessary, in self-defence, to secede."[4] Senator James Henry Hammond (D/SC), a statesman of superior talent, joined the exodus from Washington but did so not with joy but with foreboding, having in mind the Japanese, "who when insulted rip open their own bowels."[5]

Seventy-three years earlier, shortly after the Constitutional Convention adjourned, James Madison informed Thomas Jefferson that South Carolina would be likely to adopt the new Constitution because the four delegates it had sent to Philadelphia, among that state's "weightiest characters," were returning home "unanimously zealous" in its favor.[6] This proved correct. In May 1788, a state ratification convention met in Charleston at the Exchange on East Bay Street and voted approval by a convincing margin of 149–73. The Constitution included several provisions to protect wealth generally and slaveholding particularly, and thus the ratification effort was led by "planters," those owning twenty or more slaves.[7] While Article VII of the Constitution specified that state conventions like the one held at the Exchange were the appropriate means for ratifying, the document did not provide a mechanism by which a state might unilaterally rescind its ratification or otherwise withdraw from the Union. Nevertheless, Governor Gist and secessionists in South Carolina's legislature believed they could avoid being characterized as mere "rebels"—a term they disliked because it suggested lawbreaking and violence—by invoking a similar convention to rescind the commitment their grandfathers' generation had made. If, as Carolinians had said for decades, the Constitution was a confederation of sovereign states, then any state could exit the Union if it employed the same mechanism provided in Article VII for entrance.[8]

By December 6, 1860, the date set for choosing delegates to the state's secession convention, the momentum for withdrawal was so great that Unionists, already marginalized and dispirited, took themselves out of consideration.[9] Alfred Huger, for instance, a wealthy slaveholder, a Princeton graduate, and a reputable official long involved in public service, had been approached to participate but declined. Thirty years earlier, Huger had been elected to a similarly "official" convention tasked with determining whether the state should "nullify" the federal tariff statute within its borders, a procedure that—like secession—was not provided for in the Constitution. Upon arrival, Huger had found that he and others who opposed nullification were mere window dressing, the agenda having been controlled from the start by those committed to violating this federal law in the name of state rights.[10] Huger sensed that in the secession convention, too, there would be no substantive debate, the outcome never in doubt.[11]

As the state secession convention drew near, most South Carolina Unionists fell silent. Henry William Ravenel, a botanist accustomed to close observation, noted in his journal that he could find no one who opposed withdrawal.[12] Benjamin Franklin Perry, coeditor of the *Greenville Southern Patriot* and *Mountaineer*, was one, however, as were the wealthy planter Wade Hampton, the aging attorney James Louis Petigru, and his friend Alfred Huger. "Would old Mr. Alfred Huger, who had been postmaster, it seemed, forever, resign" his federal appointment—the Reverend A. Toomer Porter asked—as so many others had done? "No, he would not lose his head as the rest of us had, he would wait and see" how Lincoln conducted himself in office.[13] Mary Boykin Chesnut, wife of resigning U.S. senator James Chesnut Jr., from her bedroom in Charleston could hear in the dining room below the after-dinner speeches of her husband and his friends, a gathering from which she, as a woman, was excluded. One speech she liked so much in "voice, tone, temper, sentiments & all" that she asked a relation who the speaker was, to be told that it was Alfred Huger.[14] His speech had unquestionably been a poignant one, since he had been born in the 1780s, had known people involved in fighting the Revolution and forming the Union, and would still openly admit his admiration for the United States.[15] When in 1850/1851 secession was urged as the appropriate reaction to Northern initiatives to deny slaveholders the right to settle in the federal territories of the West, Huger warned against it. And when in the late 1850s many Carolinians called for withdrawal rather than participation in an 1860 election that the Republicans might well win, he repeated that warning.[16]

While South Carolina had been since nullification times the spearhead of secessionism, no one knew or seemed to care what its slaveless yeomanry knew about the possible consequences of withdrawal, even though they would be called upon as foot soldiers in any armed conflict.[17] "Whoever waited for the common people," state legislator A. P. Aldrich told Senator Hammond, "when a great move was to be made. We must make the move & force them to follow."[18] For nearly a generation, the political elite had recited four themes:

Alfred Huger by Alexander H. Emmons, ca. 1850. Courtesy Old Exchange Building, Charleston, SC, gift of Captain and Mrs. Anthony Huger Malcom Edwards.

(1) the Constitution is a compact created by sovereign states; (2) the slave states have always abided by it while (3) the free states have repeatedly violated it; and (4) in response to such violations, any state is privileged to withdraw. These propositions had been repeated so often that no one questioned their accuracy, nor did families without slaves publicly question why they should send their sons into harm's way to preserve a system from which they derived only minimal benefits: the knowledge that unskilled manual labor was "below" them because it was reserved for blacks, a sort of "equality" with slaveholders by virtue of white skin and a universal voting franchise among white males, and the hope of becoming slaveholders if only slave importations from Africa could be reinstituted to bring prices down.[19]

On December 20, as word spread across Charleston that the Ordinance of Secession had been signed, "men hugged each other in the streets" and "ran hither and thither to hear what next."[20] At the corner of Meeting and Broad Streets, "the chimes of old St. Michael's rang merrily at intervals all the afternoon. Fire companies . . . paraded the streets, noisily jingling their bells, and one continually met members of the Vigilant Rifles, the Zouaves, the Washington Light-Infantry . . . hurrying in a state of great excitement to their headquarters." Understatement would not do. Laurence Keitt, having resigned from Congress to serve in the secession convention, proclaimed, "We have carried the body of this Union to its last resting place, and now we will drop the flag over its grave."[21] "Palmetto branches were borne in triumph along the streets" and "bales of cotton were suspended on ropes stretched from house to house." One was inscribed "THE WORLD WANTS IT," a verity proven by the succession of profitable years that had made slaves so expensive, even if South Carolina had long since lost its place as the center of American cotton production, and Charleston as cotton's preferred port of exit to the factories of New England and Europe.[22]

Huger and his good friend Petigru were both born just prior to the Constitution's adoption. Hearing the bells as he walked on Broad Street, the aging Petigru asked a friend, "Where's the fire?" to be told, "There is no fire; those are the joy bells ringing in honor of the passage of the Ordinance of Secession." Petigru replied, "I tell you there is a fire; they have this day set a blazing torch to the temple of constitutional liberty and . . . we shall have no more peace forever." To another he commented, "I have seen the last happy day of my life."[23] According to family lore, Petigru called South Carolina "too small for a republic, too large for an asylum."[24] Another friend, Perry, told a delegate that he had been trying to prevent the state's withdrawal for thirty years but would now join everyone in "going to the devil."[25]

In 1850, Robert Barnwell Rhett had been appointed to fill the Senate seat left vacant by the death of John C. Calhoun but quit in 1852 after no one would join him in his demand for the state's unilateral withdrawal. Since then, he had continued preaching secession in the pages of his family's *Charleston Mercury*. Now denying the common claim that the state's decision to withdraw had been caused by Lincoln's election, Rhett asserted that it had been roiling since nullification times—a phenomenon his intemperate rhetoric had done much to bring to this point.[26] An observer noted that after nightfall on December 20, "an illumination of the principal business streets by means of blazing tar-barrels produced a strong and bodeful light."[27]

"In Our Blindness"

Francis Pickens had arisen to national notice by being John C. Calhoun's kinsman, although they had their differences and a time came in the 1840s when Pickens came to think his own political skills superior to those of Calhoun, who had repeatedly tried and failed to be president.[28] A veteran of five terms in Congress, Pickens had just served as President James Buchanan's minister to Russia.[29] Passing through Washington in mid-November 1860 on his return to South Carolina (where he would soon succeed Gist as governor), Pickens met privately with another Carolinian, William Henry Trescot, then serving as assistant secretary of state, a position Buchanan allowed Trescot to retain even after he publicly declared himself a secessionist. Also present was another disloyal federal official, Secretary of War John B. Floyd of Virginia.[30] Although Pickens had been five thousand miles away, he had formed an opinion (Floyd noted in his diary) that "disunion was inevitable" and that "the time had come for decisive measures" because the Republicans' "malignant hostility" would result in an invasion of the South.[31]

While Unionism was seemingly moribund in South Carolina, reliance upon the protections afforded slavery in the Constitution had been sufficiently widespread that in 1859, Tennessee, Kentucky, North Carolina, and Georgia sent to Congress nineteen members of the so-called Opposition Party, its platform being to save the Union by preserving slavery in the slave states without demanding its western expansion.[32] In the 1860 presidential election, John Bell of Tennessee, heading the successor Constitutional Union Party, garnered 591,000 votes, less than the 848,000 obtained by the rump (Southern) Democratic candidate John C. Breckinridge of Kentucky but sufficient to show appreciable Southern support for the Union.[33] And while South Carolina prophesized Republican aggression, the Republicans' 1860 platform promised to protect "the right of each State to order and control its own domestic institutions according to its own judgment exclusively."[34] If the party's radical, abolitionist wing nevertheless proposed a bill in Congress to emancipate Southern slaves, they did not have the numbers to pass it. Nor would Lincoln, upon assuming the presidency, ever sign it, having repeatedly said that the Constitution did not empower him or Congress to end slavery in any state.[35]

In the unlikely event that Lincoln, upon taking office, chose to repudiate his prior pledges and bowed to the ultras in his party, the South could ignore any new antislavery statute because the Republicans would have no immediate means of enforcing it. Southerners could then seek from Chief Justice Roger Taney's Supreme Court—and would assuredly obtain—a suitably proslavery ruling. While the *Weekly Mississippian* asserted that the justices of the Supreme Court were old and that Lincoln would replace them with abolitionists, Lincoln had never voiced such an intention, and in any event the slave states could block any such effort by remaining in the Union.[36] Ultimately, then, the only available means to end Southern slavery was by an emancipation amendment to the Constitution. Although in the late 1840s Calhoun and Rhett had warned that this, too, would come, it was not reasonably in prospect.[37] Under Article V of the Constitution, such an amendment would require ratification by three-fourths (i.e., twenty-five) of the states, so that the fifteen slave states—merely by remaining in the Union—constituted an absolute and perpetual barrier. Nor would free states, if they ever achieved the three-fourths threshold (and that would require a Union totaling sixty states), proceed to ratify such an amendment, since the vast majority of Northern whites would not abide a massive influx of ex-slaves who, as "citizens," would be able to move about and seek employment as they liked.[38]

The Constitution not only insulated slaveholders from the disaster they predicted but also provided a clear path to ending the North/South crisis. Just prior to Lincoln's inauguration, two-thirds of both houses of Congress, pursuant to Article V, proposed a last-ditch affirmation of intersectional goodwill: a constitutional amendment guaranteeing slavery—permanently and irrevocably—in the slave states. Lincoln in his inaugural declared that he had no objection and forwarded the amendment to the governors, thus eliminating this crucial rationale for secession and in effect inviting the seven slave states that had already seceded to reconsider.[39] Prospects for passage were excellent; if the 1860 election had included a referendum on whether the federal government could end slavery in the South, the "ayes" would have amounted to not more than 5 percent of the Northern population, perhaps less than half that. An objective Southern press would have headlined the proposed amendment, as well as the high likelihood that it would be ratified, resolving the crisis. Instead, this extra guarantee of slavery's perpetuity was ignored, and Lincoln's inaugural speech, the embodiment of forbearance and Unionism, was characterized across the South as a cynical declaration of war.

Pickens, owner of eighty-two slaves, did not grasp that by withdrawing upon Lincoln's election without waiting to monitor his conduct in office, South Carolina was relinquishing in advance the privileges and benefits afforded slaveholders in the Constitution, the document that slaveholders had referred to for decades as the foundational source of their protection. When in 1850/1851 Rhett urged secession as an appropriate response to the free-soil movement in the West, Perry thought withdrawal "the most fatal blow which slavery could receive," since "nothing could . . . tend more" to the accomplishment of the abolitionists' "wicked purposes."[40] Representative William W. Boyce (D/SC) had agreed that secession would doom slavery, adding that "in our blindness," God would have "made us the instruments of its destruction," a prophetic comment with which the most famous of the abolitionists, William Lloyd Garrison, would surely have agreed.[41] While Garrison fervently desired dissolution so that Northerners would no longer be implicated in the Southern sin, he would observe in 1857 that no clear-eyed slaveholder could favor it.[42] And future Confederate vice president Alexander Stephens of Georgia, echoing Perry, wrote that slavery was "much more secure in the Union than out of it," adding that Lincoln—Stephens's friend since they both served as Whigs in the Thirtieth Congress—would "administer the Government . . . safely" for the slave states.[43] But the issue of whether slavery was better protected within or outside the Union—*the* crucial question facing every South Carolinian (whether a slaveowner or not)—was never subjected to rigorous, objective examination, either in the legislature or in the press.[44] Such a discussion would have revealed and exacerbated the fault lines between the planters and the "common people" and—since the planters had always been in control—they inculcated the sense that support for withdrawal was overwhelming.

Bellona, the Goddess of War

On the day South Carolina seceded, James Buchanan was in Washington attending a wedding. Sara Pryor, wife of Representative Roger Pryor (D/VA), noticed how much the president had aged in a few months, having provoked the enmity of both North and South in his mishandling of the territorial dispute between pro- and antislavery elements in Kansas. When word wafted in from the entry hall that South Carolina had just withdrawn, Mrs. Pryor leaned down and whispered the news to the seated Buchanan, who fell back in his chair, grasped its arms, asked for his carriage, and left.[45]

The nullification crisis had begun in 1829, when South Carolina informed Congress that it considered the promanufacturing tariff passed in 1828 not just oppressive but also unconstitutional, and it would thus not permit the collection of federal tariffs in the state's ports.[46] Violence seemed likely against customs collector James R. Pringle and his clerks at the Exchange.[47] Before state militiamen could act, however, Pringle, a committed Unionist from a distinguished local family, directed a Revenue cutter to overtake and board a vessel that was attempting to evade payment, thus maintaining federal authority offshore. President Andrew Jackson, meanwhile, threatened an invasion and the summary hanging of the state's leaders for violating a federal law. The crisis was then resolved in Congress by a negotiated tariff reduction.[48]

Lewis Cass of Michigan, Jackson's secretary of war in the 1830s, witnessed his aggressive reaction to the nullifiers' threats, including his ordering Major General Winfield Scott to send reinforcements to the small Union garrison there, along with an instruction to prepare ordnance for an expedition to Charleston on short notice.[49] Jackson's aggressive strategy worked brilliantly, causing Calhoun and the others to back down, even while claiming that they had won because some tariff rates were reduced. Cass would move on to a distinguished career in the Senate, becoming in 1857 Buchanan's secretary of state. In light of his experience under Jackson, Cass recommended that Buchanan react to South Carolina's new threats by again reinforcing the understaffed Union facilities in Charleston. When Buchanan in December 1860 rejected that advice, Cass resigned.[50] When on December 20 news of "sesech" (as it was popularly called) reached Cass, tears rolled down his cheeks. "It is all over!" he said. "The people in the South are mad; the people in the North are asleep. The president is pale with fear."[51]

The Pryors departed the wedding for the Washington home of a prominent Southern couple. In her 1904 memoir, Mrs. Pryor chose not to provide the relevant name so that she might quote—without breaching decorum—the extraordinary comments made that evening by her unidentified hostess. David Dixon Porter, a lieutenant in the U.S. Navy, had come to the same home to get a sense of Southern reactions to the momentous news. The hostess told him, "South Carolina has seceded, and . . . we will have a glorious monarchy, and you must join us." "And be made Duke of Benedict Arnold?" Lieutenant Porter quipped. "Nonsense!" she replied, "we will make you an admiral. . . . Would you have us tamely submit to all the indignities the North puts upon us, and place our necks under their feet?"[52] In his own reminiscence of that night, published in 1885, Porter would refer to his host as "a distinguished Southern gentleman" and his hostess as "a magnificent woman, greatly esteemed in Washington society for her genial manner, and admired for her wit and intellect." Privately, he noted that his host and hostess had been Senator Jefferson Davis and Varina Howell Davis of Mississippi.[53] Louisa Rodgers Meigs, wife of Porter's friend Montgomery Meigs, described Mrs. Davis as Bellona, the goddess of war, "her face and eyes . . . pregnant with storm and cloud."[54] Up in Boston, the physician-poet Oliver Wendell Holmes wrote of South Carolina, "She has gone,—she has left us in passion and pride,— / Our stormy-browed sister, so long at our side!" Herman Melville, pro-Union and antislavery, wrote ominously of a "tempest bursting from the waste of Time / On the world's fairest hope linked with man's foulest crime."[55]

"And the Peacemaker Be Forever Blest"

William Henry Seward of New York, elected to the Senate in 1849, established himself as the most adroit and articulate of the few abolitionists in the federal government. A powerful force in the Whig Party, in 1852 he advised (some said puppeteered) General Winfield Scott in the revered soldier's run for the presidency that year. But when Scott suffered an electoral loss of 254–52, proving so inept as a candidate as to speed the Whig Party toward its eventual demise, Seward helped found from its fragments the new Republican Party. When he declined being its presidential candidate in 1856, on advice that Republican moderates would reject his abolitionist record, the nomination went to John Frémont, a former military officer and explorer unburdened by recorded political views.[56]

While Frémont cut a broad swath across New England and the North, the Democracy's candidate, James Buchanan of Pennsylvania, unequivocally proslavery, swept the South. In 1858, Seward, on the floor of the Senate, accused Buchanan of conspiring with Chief Justice Roger Taney's Supreme Court in the *Dred Scott* decision, construing the Constitution as mandating the right of slaveholders to settle in the federal territories of the West.[57] In October of that year, as the Republicans' likely presidential nominee for 1860, Seward proclaimed in Rochester an "irrepressible conflict" between slavery and freedom.[58] Receiving wider coverage than the "House Divided" address given by the lesser-known Abraham Lincoln some months before, Seward's speech was construed in the South as bellicose, the *Memphis Daily Appeal* deeming it "incendiary and traitorous."[59] The New Orleans–based *De Bow's Review* called Seward "by far the ablest" but also "one of the most dangerous" leaders of a political party commonly equated by Southerners with the abolitionists. Mary Todd Lincoln, from a Kentucky slaveholding family, reportedly called him "that Abolitionist sneak."[60]

Rhett and other fire-eaters who for years had been soliciting support for secession were delighted to see Seward's harsh antislavery rhetoric make their task easier.[61] In October 1859, the abolitionist John Brown's raid on the federal arsenal at Harpers Ferry, Virginia, a failed attempt to trigger a widespread slave insurrection, proved to be a windfall for secessionists.[62] Southern statesmen and journalists had so demonized the abolitionists for three decades that it came as no surprise that Brown had been funded by three of the movement's leaders: Gerrit Smith, Theodore Parker, and Thomas Wentworth Higginson. Following Brown's trial and execution in Virginia, Abraham Lincoln, considering a run for the presidency, told an audience in Kansas that although he agreed with Brown that slavery was wrong, "that cannot excuse violence, bloodshed, and treason."[63] But Thoreau, Emerson, and other esteemed Northern intellectuals treated Brown not as a messianic butcher but as a martyred saint, thereby pushing untold numbers of erstwhile Unionist Southerners into the secessionist camp.[64] William Lloyd Garrison was also blamed for Brown's raid, despite Garrison's long-standing and clearly articulated doctrine of nonviolence. A young Virginia girl thought the raid God's vengeance for the treatment of Harriet Beecher Stowe's character Uncle Tom.[65] And while no one could prove any involvement by Senator Seward, fire-eaters could now reasonably claim that the Republicans' antislavery rhetoric had legitimated Brown's action and perhaps even incited it. Among those reportedly present at Brown's execution was John Wilkes Booth, who was in Virginia rehearsing a play. A Republican credibly noted that Harpers Ferry would make it impossible to forge alliances with anyone in the South.[66]

Years before, Garrison had come close to being lynched by a Boston mob, and when in 1837 journalist Elijah Lovejoy was shot in Alton, Illinois, many Northerners believed it was "just" to kill someone holding abolitionist views, particularly after he was warned not to publicize them.[67] Thousands of abolitionists, including Seward's wife Frances, saw their issue as Brown had seen it: as a moral absolute, and because Seward was in fact not a moral crusader but a "consummate tactician"—as William Henry Brisbane told fellow abolitionist Carl Schurz—he should not get the nomination because "we cannot always know where we shall find him on all points."[68] As Brisbane predicted, once the Republican Convention was in prospect, Seward abandoned his firebrand rhetoric and spoke in the Senate of conciliation with the South and then distributed tens of thousands of copies of the speech to show delegates and their constituents that he would be a sound and evenhanded president with no impulse either to interfere with slavery in the South or to advocate equality of the races in the North.[69] Seward's idea for solving the sectional crisis was to allow South Carolina and—if they wished—other cotton states, to "go in peace," since this would mollify the border states (Missouri, Kentucky, Maryland, northern Virginia, and Delaware) and the Middle South (Arkansas, Tennessee, southern Virginia, northern Louisiana, and North Carolina), thus ensuring their loyalty to the Union. Another thought was that the irascible leadership of some cotton states would treat a flat denial of the right to secede as a provocation, while simply admitting that right could prompt them, or their constituents, to weigh the decision on the merits—and stay.[70]

Seward had toured Europe and the Holy Land in the summer of 1859, meeting major statesmen and crowned heads, and then arrived home as the odds-on favorite for the Executive Mansion.[71] Virginia fire-eater Edmund Ruffin wrote that while he did not know whether the "wily" Seward or the "obscure and coarse" Abraham Lincoln would emerge as the Republican nominee, in either case the party intended to impose "complete subjection . . . and ruin" on the South.[72] Representative Schuyler Colfax (R/IN) was among those believing that the threat of withdrawal was and had always been posturing to extract concessions, stating months before the Republican Convention that nothing had happened in the Thirty-Sixth Congress except that "our Southern friends have dissolved the Union forty or fifty times."[73] Lincoln called secessionism a "game of bluff," predicting that the crisis would subside once its perpetrators saw that the North would not be intimidated and that thousands of federal appointments (as postmasters, customs collectors, lighthouse keepers, and so on, not to mention judges and prosecutors) would be awarded to those who remained loyal.[74] When someone like Senator Louis Trezevant Wigfall (D/TX) declared that the South was not just posturing, his views might be discounted because he often spoke recklessly and was reputed to have transformed disagreements into duels.[75] But Wigfall had grown up in South Carolina, and Lincoln knew nothing about the state.

Although Southerners viewed the Republicans as monolithically abolitionist, in fact they included a spectrum of beliefs, including radicals who desired "a violent destruction of the slave power; perhaps by war, perhaps by a slave insurrection," and conservatives who hoped "to keep the slave power more effectually under control, until its power for harm should be gradually exhausted, and its whole fabric gently and peacefully sapped away."[76] Henry Adams, who wrote this description, did not believe that Seward in the Senate, or his own father Charles Francis Adams in the House, was betraying fundamental Republican values by proposing a conciliation whose purpose was to keep the Upper South in the Union. If Virginia and other slave states remained loyal, eventually the people of the cotton states—so the theory went—would lose confidence in the secessionists and seek reinstatement.[77]

Seward's campaign managers arrived at the Chicago convention with a trainload of two thousand supporters called "irrepressibles," a term the newly conciliatory Seward would rather have forgotten, even as some abolitionists (such as James S. Pike of Horace Greeley's *New-York Tribune*) continued to back Seward because of the antislavery record he had now discarded as inconvenient.[78] Representative James G. Blaine (R/ME) sensed among Seward's acolytes an "air of dictation" likely to offend undecided delegates.[79] Greeley told Connecticut newspaperman Gideon Welles that Seward would win because he had "debauched" the convention, a harsh term that lacked moral force when uttered by Greeley, an erstwhile Seward stalwart embittered because he had received no share of the political spoils controlled by Seward's political advisor, Thurlow Weed.[80] The managing editor of Greeley's *Tribune*, Charles A. Dana, wrote that he and others went to Chicago not to nominate anyone in particular but only to defeat Seward.[81]

Abraham Lincoln, his one term as a Whig congressman long forgotten and his reputation outside Illinois due primarily to his published debates in a losing effort to unseat Democratic senator Stephen Douglas, had spoken brilliantly at New York's Cooper Union just two days prior to Seward's conciliatory Senate speech, thereby suddenly becoming a viable competitor on Seward's home turf.[82] In a list of presidential aspirants including Representative Edward Bates of Missouri and Senators Salmon P. Chase of Ohio and Simon Cameron of Pennsylvania, Lincoln was emerging in an enviable position: as a common second choice.[83] As the convention opened, skilled Cincinnati journalist Murat Halstead, with access to sources beyond those relied upon by New York newsmen, reported a growing belief that Lincoln would prevail.[84]

Although Virginia was a slave state, the yeomanry of its western counties supported a Republican newspaper and even sent Republican delegates to Chicago. Thought earlier to be solidly pro-Seward, the delegates instead split on the first ballot, with Lincoln garnering fourteen against a mere eight for Seward. This result was a harbinger. Lincoln took the nomination, his victory ascribed to: (1) a negative perception of the New York political machine controlled by Seward and Weed; (2) brilliant floor management and crowd manipulation by Lincoln's campaign strategists; and (3) the realization that to win in November the Republicans would need in Indiana, Pennsylvania, and Illinois one whose antislavery credentials were either less well known or perceived to be less radical than Seward's.[85] "Success rather than Seward" had been a blistering slogan.[86] Years later, Charles Francis Adams Sr., Seward's close friend, wrote that this "veteran champion" of reform "was set aside in favor of a gentleman . . . little known by any thing he had ever done"—the same phenomenon by which the mediocre James K. Polk obtained the presidency while it was denied to the brilliant Henry Clay simply because Clay's positions were familiar to all and thus disapproved by some.[87]

Southern politicians, newspaper editors, and citizens largely ignored the centrist views Lincoln had voiced at Cooper Union and in the published collection of his earlier debates with Douglas, choosing instead to paint him as an abolitionist ideologue indistinguishable from Seward at his most extreme.[88] Seward made matters worse when, campaigning on Lincoln's behalf, he assured antislavery audiences in the North that candidate Lincoln "confesses the obligation" of Seward's "higher law" and "avows himself . . . a soldier on the side of freedom in the irrepressible conflict," in essence suggesting that Lincoln would be a doctrinaire follower of positions Seward had once asserted but now ignored.[89] Seward's descriptions, carried in Northern newspapers, were then (not surprisingly) widely reprinted in the South.[90] As the presidential election approached, a Southern congressman wrote to Assistant Postmaster General Horatio King, "Men like myself, who for a lifetime have fought the extreme ultraisms of the South and the mad fanaticism of the North, will not permit Abe Lincoln's banner, inscribed with 'higher law,' 'negro equality,' 'irrepressible conflict' and 'final emancipation,' to wave over us."[91] After the November 1860 election, one way for Southerners to demonize Lincoln was to predict that he would be the mere rail-splitting figurehead in an abolitionist administration controlled by Seward.[92] Charleston postmaster Alfred Huger, in a letter to Kentucky-born postmaster general Joseph Holt, wrote as if Seward—not Lincoln—were the president-elect.[93] Howell Cobb, owner of one thousand slaves, told fellow Georgians that because the so-called Black Republicans had declared an "irrepressible conflict," war could not be avoided unless Seward and company softened their rhetoric. Come Inauguration Day—Cobb added—the South would be in the abolitionists' clutches.[94] Southerners who suggested waiting to see what Lincoln did in office were increasingly dismissed as fools, cowards, or traitors.

Representative John A. Gilmer (Opposition/NC), a Southern Unionist, implored Lincoln to express his views on slavery so as to "quiet, if not satisfy," all "reasonable minds." So, reportedly, did Supreme Court Justice John A. Campbell of Alabama, on advice from Montgomery Blair, who had argued Dred Scott's case. Alexander Stephens gave similar advice, as did Representative Thomas Corwin (R/OH), who noted an "excitement" in the

South bordering on "madness."[95] But Lincoln instead chose guidance from two experienced journalists, Gideon Welles and William Cullen Bryant, who advised that because Southern newspapers had no tradition of pluralism or evenhandedness regarding slavery, anything Lincoln said would be willfully misconstrued in order to generate more rancor against him, even as ultra Republicans would see any attempt by Lincoln to placate the South as betraying their support.[96] While Lincoln indicated having neither the constitutional authority nor the personal desire to disturb slavery in the Southern states, he communicated these sentiments confidentially via letters to persons he felt he could trust.[97] As he told the editor of the *Louisville Journal*, "I have *bad* men . . . to deal with, both North and South," men eager to "seize upon" any statement as a basis for "new misrepresentations—men who would like to frighten me, or, at least, to fix upon me the character of timidity and cowardice."[98]

Seward, meanwhile, ignoring his own fiery speeches on Lincoln's behalf before the election, now urged the president-elect to mitigate the glaring sectionalism of his mandate (he had won all eighteen of the free states but only two of 996 Southern counties) by seeking out Southern Unionists as cabinet officers. Lincoln tried, but none would accept. Although Thurlow Weed had undoubtedly consulted Seward before launching in his *Albany Evening Journal* a trial balloon in favor of the conciliation policy Seward had espoused prior to the Republican Convention, so tart was the reaction of radical Republicans that Seward chose to disavow it.[99] On December 3, 1860, however, as other leading members of Congress joined Seward in discussing whether they could prevent a North/South collision, he complained privately to Weed that some ultra Republicans were as intractable as South Carolina's fire-eaters.[100]

Lincoln had confidentially offered Seward the position of secretary of state, informing another contender for the post that this was necessary to keep the Republican Party intact (i.e., to make Seward an ally rather than an adversary), even if Seward's abolitionist past would make resolution of the North/South issues more difficult.[101] Weed traveled to Illinois to meet with Lincoln on December 20, intending to foist on this provincial a cabinet of pro-Seward men, only to find that Lincoln would have none of it. After Lincoln stressed to Weed that he would be flexible on issues other than that of free soil in the West, Seward became Lincoln's agent in the Senate's "Committee of Thirteen," one of several groups formed to resolve the North/South crisis. In this he was apparently ineffective, Georgia senator Robert Toombs later recalling that Seward "refused every overture," exhibiting a "sullen" and "persistent obstinacy that I have never yet seen surpassed." Toombs telegraphed to Atlanta, "All is at an end. North determined. Seward will not budge an

William Henry Seward, 1861. Charles D. Fredericks & Co. Senate Collection, Office of the Senate Curator #38.00275,001.

inch. Am in favor of secession."[102] On the night of December 13, half the congressional caucus of the cotton states declared that "all hope of relief in the Union" was "extinguished" and that "the honor, safety, and independence of the Southern people" required a Southern Confederacy.[103]

On December 22, Seward was pulled into a large gathering at New York's Astor House and invited to speak extemporaneously. The audience was well oiled, perhaps also the speaker, who characterized the momentous step South Carolina had just taken as "humbug."[104] Seward advised Lincoln that in his view the border states would remain in the Union if the Republicans abandoned their rhetoric about a free-soil West and instead acquiesced in the proposal of Senator John J. Crittenden (Am./KY) to override *Dred Scott* by constitutional amendment, dividing the territorial West into free and slave regions by reinstituting and extending the Missouri Compromise of 1820, the congressional statute that the Kansas-Nebraska Act had repealed and *Dred Scott* had struck down as having been void ab initio.[105] Seward added, however, that even this major concession would not stop Georgia, Alabama, Mississippi, and Louisiana from following South Carolina's lead.[106]

The Constitution, unlike the earlier Articles of Confederation, was ordained not by the states but by "the People," providing them with rights and obligations paramount to their state rights and obligations. On January 12, in a two-hour speech to Senate colleagues and a crowded gallery, Seward urged that no state could absolve its people from their allegiance to the Union, nor could a state's secession dissolve the Union, absent "the voluntary consent of the people of the United States, collected in the manner prescribed by the Constitution," presumably meaning the amendment process set forth in Article V, requiring the consent of three-fourths of the states.[107] But the tough abolitionist rhetoric of a decade before was gone. As in the weeks prior to the Republican Convention a year earlier, Seward mimicked Lincoln by saying that slavery in the Southern states was protected by the Constitution. "I have thought it my duty," he subsequently told Senate colleagues, "to hold myself open and ready for the best adjustment which could be practically made," believing that the various points of conflict would eventually "subside and pass away" if the crisis could be appropriately managed in the near term, a task he found himself uniquely capable of accomplishing even if he started with the handicap of being distrusted both by Southerners who doubted his conversion from abolition to conciliation and by abolitionists who were convinced of the change and thus now felt betrayed.[108]

Although Seward had confidentially accepted Lincoln's cabinet offer, he had failed to ask the president-elect to comment upon the text of his Senate speech beforehand, apparently concluding that while Lincoln remained intransigent regarding a free-soil West, he would not reasonably object to a public pledge of conciliation by the man still widely perceived as the head of the Republican Party—a pledge that accorded with Lincoln's stated views.[109] Radical Republicans were displeased with Seward's speech, Carl Schurz noting that whatever Seward might think privately, he had "no right on his own responsibility to compromise the president's future policies."[110] When Seward's wife, still a committed abolitionist, privately criticized her husband's conciliatory tone, he responded that he had to counter Senate Republicans who never uttered one word "to disarm prejudice and passion" or "encourage loyalty" (an accusation appropriately aimed at many of Seward's own earlier speeches).[111] Representative Corwin, writing to Lincoln of the utter failure of the House committee he had chaired to resolve the growing crisis, echoed what Seward had said about the Senate equivalent, calling the extreme Republicans "practical fools . . . quite as mad" as the fire-eaters.[112]

While Seward had sworn in his January 12 speech that no concession would surrender Republican principles, he promised to enforce the Fugitive Slave Act of 1850, a statute that made federal officials the enforcement agents of slaveholders seeking presumed runaways.[113] This declaration utterly repudiated Seward's earlier recommendation that right-thinking citizens should violate the statute (and thus the Constitution's enabling provision: Art. IV § 2 cl. 3) in service of a "higher law."[114] Now—theoretically—Seward would stand by and watch if his own wife (whose basement kitchen in Auburn, New York, was a stop on the Underground Railroad) were apprehended and prosecuted under the act. Salmon Chase, an unreformed antislavery radical who (much to Seward's chagrin) would soon be joining Lincoln's cabinet, considered Seward's Senate speech a fraud, as did the leading Massachusetts radical, Senator Charles Sumner.[115] Senator Ben Wade (R/OH) commented, "If we follow such leadership" as Seward's, "we will be in the wilderness longer than the children of Israel under Moses." While Garrison agreed with Schurz and Wade that Seward had sold out his antislavery principles, some stalwart abolitionists, among them James Russell Lowell, founder of the *Atlantic Monthly*, chose to remember Seward as he had once been.[116] The abolitionist poet John Greenleaf Whittier, similarly, confessed himself unable to censure in Seward's new policy "what was nobly meant," adding that if Seward could save the Union from "a baptism of blood, upon thy brow / A wreath . . . / Woven of the beatitudes, shall rest, / And the peacemaker be forever blest."[117]

2

"A Standing Menace"

In 1853, in an initiative interpreted by some as the federal government's display of its imperial grandeur, by others as an emblem of its sincere recognition of Charleston's importance as a source of tariff revenue, a huge new customhouse was begun several blocks north of the Exchange. Because Charleston was an alluvial city situated between two rivers, the building's massive weight required a fortune in supportive work to prevent its sinking into the sediment. Work halted because of the state's secession, leaving "immense blocks of the glistening stone" scattered on the ground. "Will you complete it?" *Times* of London correspondent William Howard Russell asked. "I should think not," a secessionist replied, since, as a new republic, South Carolina will "lay on few duties . . . what we want is free-trade. . . . The Yankees have plundered us with their custom-houses and duties long enough."[1]

While tariff rates were in fact low by historical standards and had been approved by Southern congressmen, secessionists commonly sought to bolster their cause by reciting old sources of resentment as if they were still current. Thus, thirty years after Pringle's bold fulfillment of the Constitution he had sworn to uphold against the nullifiers, his successor, W. F. Colcock (who, like Pringle, was the product of a distinguished local lineage), would resign his federal appointment in order to start collecting duties (at lower rates) for the state. Andrew Magrath, who similarly ignored his federal oath and resigned as Charleston's federal judge in order to become South Carolina's secretary of state, told Colcock that if any incoming ship questioned his authority, he should cite as legal precedent a formal opinion of the Buchanan administration to the effect that American ships entering any Peruvian port controlled by rebels should obey whatever laws they imposed locally, and not those issued by the national government in Lima.[2] Either Magrath believed the Peru policy to be persuasive precedent or he could find nothing better.[3]

Even before South Carolina formally seceded, Buchanan's attorney general, Jeremiah Black, asserted that the federal government does not engage in unconstitutional conduct against a state by merely enforcing authority assigned to it by the Constitution, even if special legislation would be required to collect duties outside Charleston Harbor. Senator Andrew Johnson (D/TN) agreed.[4] Some noted that while collections could be made offshore by the Revenue cutter *Harriet Lane*, it could not function there for long because it would burn half of its ten-day coal supply in traveling from the North and obviously would be refused replenishment locally.[5] However, the legal and logistical issues were unimportant in comparison with the federal policy to be vindicated. While a president could claim for a time that a local disturbance made tariff collections impossible, if he simply stopped trying to collect duties in a particular port, he would violate his sworn constitutional obligation to see that the tariff laws were uniformly obeyed. At that point, some foreign merchants would divert dutiable goods to what had become a low-duty port, thus triggering a drop in federal revenue. This, plus creditors' concerns about a national tariff system no longer under control, would drive up interest rates on federal borrowings at a moment when the Union might need substantial funds to finance a civil war against those in the state impeding tariff collection.[6] The North-to-South shift in foreign tonnage would also result in South-to-North smuggling of foreign goods on which no U.S. duty had been paid, along an extensive and porous border. This would turn thousands of merchants, traders, draymen, and factors into opportunistic violators of the tariff laws, stimulating a disrespect for federal law and necessitating a massive increase in federal law enforcement.[7] To complete the circle of problems, in the weeks after South Carolina's secession, dozens of New York importers asserted that if President Buchanan failed to collect tariff duties in the state because it had purported to secede, they would retaliate by evading duties in New York and other Northern ports.[8] As James Madison had warned during the nullification crisis, life without the Constitution would be like life before it, with commercial "rivalships, collisions, and animosities" kindling "the passions which are the forerunners of war."[9]

If South Carolina were to sustain its independence, it would be obliged to interfere with the collection process by a forced boarding of *Harriet Lane*, the drawing and possible firing of an officer's pistol, and maybe even a naval engagement in which the cutter and/or its assailant would be sunk, leaving the state to explain to the world that its conduct had been justified by U.S. policy vis-à-vis Peruvian rebels. But this time the dispute over tariffs did not ripen into a crisis, as both sides focused upon another indicium of federal authority in Charleston.

The Third System

In addition to customhouses, post offices, and courts, federal facilities within states had always included forts, navy yards, arsenals, lighthouses, and mints. The burning of Washington in 1814 brought home to President Madison the inadequacy of the nation's coastal defenses, and he proceeded to ask Congress for "the immediate extension and gradual completion of . . . works of defense, both fixed, and floating, on our maritime frontier."[10] In 1816 the War Department instituted a Board of Engineers for Fortifications, headed by Simon Bernard, formerly a senior engineer under Napoleon, tasked with devising a near-term plan for coastal defense while also becoming a permanent body of expertise for purposes of long-term strategic planning. Working with the army's chief engineer, Colonel Joseph G. Totten, and with Navy Captain J. D. Elliott (after two other senior engineers refused to work under the command of a foreigner), Bernard devised a master plan for stepped construction over several decades at a projected cost of $18 million.[11] The three would visit dozens of potential sites along the Atlantic and Gulf Coasts. Over the following decades, Congress, on the board's recommendation, would fund the construction or renovation of forty-two forts, integral components of what would be called the "Third System," with substantially more spent in the South than the North. The Corps of Engineers, meanwhile, would control the new military academy at West Point and secure many of its top students.[12]

A fundamental premise was that harbored cities were best defended by forts sufficiently armed and garrisoned to teach potential belligerents that any attempt to destroy the city and/or its commerce would be at a prohibitive cost to the invading fleet. However, neither the framers of the Constitution nor succeeding generations of citizens wanted the large military establishment that would be necessary to garrison these forts permanently (an estimated sixty thousand men in the early 1850s), even if, as the board asserted, a much larger force would be necessary to defend harbored cities that lacked these edifices.[13] In addition, the emergence of steamships, ironclads, rifled ordnance, and other technological advances, coupled with published studies of what actually succeeded and what failed in seacoast battles in Europe and elsewhere, caused some forward-thinking strategists to declare fortification theory—and the forts themselves—obsolete.[14] Periodic debates between the army (led by Totten) and the navy regarding whether U.S. coasts were best defended by fortifications or ships did nothing to advance congressional funding for either.[15] Thus, with the huge capital costs already spent and the forts at or near completion, additional congressional funding for the necessary completions, garrisons, and armaments became fitful.[16] Some forts would lie vacant, others staffed by a single caretaker.

In Charleston, the federal government owned five military properties. Near the western end of Sullivan's Island stood Fort Moultrie. Completed in 1809 as part of the so-called Second System of coastal defense, then occasionally renovated to accommodate a war garrison of three hundred, it had in place in the weeks before Lincoln's election a few dozen men from the First Artillery Regiment, led by eight officers.[17] Castle Pinckney, constructed in 1808–1811 on a marshy island nearby called Shute's Folly, presented a low-slung, semicircular bastion. Designed for a war complement of one hundred firing from one tier, it was sometimes inhabited by one widower sergeant and his daughter, his task being to keep the navigation beacon burning. Fort Sumter, on an artificial island in the mouth of Charleston Harbor, was almost equidistant from Fort Moultrie on Sullivan Island to its northeast, Fort Johnson on James Island to

Fort Moultrie, with Charleston in the distance. *Harper's Weekly* (November 17, 1860).

Fort Sumter at sunrise. *Harper's Weekly* (January 26, 1861).

its southwest, and Morris Island to its south. Designed for 650 men and 135 guns, it had as yet no artillerymen but 150 construction workers under one officer.[18] The buildings composing Fort Johnson were uninhabited and not maintained. And in the city itself was the Charleston Arsenal.

Fort Moultrie was positioned to fire upon enemy vessels as they crossed the 2,700 yards of water between it and Sumter. An example of time-honored fortification theory, its low profile presented a minimal target profile. Its fifty-six guns, positioned on barbette platforms to be fired over parapets from an open tier atop the fort, included cast-iron "columbiads" of eight-inch bore, capable of firing fifty-pound shells (a.k.a. bombs, as in Francis Scott Key's "the bombs bursting in air") as far as 3,900 yards, far enough to reach not only incoming warships but also Fort Sumter, in an intended partnership of overlapping coverage. Moultrie's armament also included cannons firing thirty-two-pound solid iron balls from a bore of 6.41 inches, and others with a bore of 5.82 inches firing twenty-four-pound balls.[19] Because the fort's walls were only fifteen feet high and blowing sand had accumulated around the edifice to form a natural glacis, it was vulnerable to an escalade assault by foot soldiers, whether from the water or town.[20] In addition, any sharpshooter or artillerist could position himself in or behind one of the houses or on one of the high sand dunes nearby and direct unobstructed volleys into the fort, thus impeding operation of the ocean-facing cannons on the exposed tier.[21]

Back in November 1832, before President Jackson sent warships with orders to defend Fort Moultrie and Castle Pinckney against the nullifiers, he had assigned Major General Winfield Scott the delicate task of preparing for armed conflict without provoking it.[22] The choice of Scott was apt. A Southerner (from Virginia), he knew the people of South Carolina, having practiced law in Charleston before joining the army. Facing the difficult task of protecting U.S. interests without inflaming locals, Scott wrote to a nullifier in the state legislature, William C. Preston:

> You have probably heard of the arrival of two or three companies at Charleston, in the last six weeks. . . . The intention simply is, that the forts in the harbor shall not be wrested from the United States. . . . [President Jackson], I presume, will stand on the defensive—thinking it better to discourage than to invite an attack . . . in order to gain time for wisdom and moderation to exert themselves in . . . Washington, and in the state house in Columbia. From humane considerations like these, the posts in question have been, and probably will be, slightly reënforced.[23]

So deftly did Scott control the situation (naval historian Alfred Thayer Mahan later wrote) that "a stay which began with taking precautions against possible fire-ships from the city, ended in a series of balls and general exchanges of courtesy between officers and citizens."[24]

In subsequent decades, Scott would rise to the rank of brevet lieutenant general and general in chief of the U.S. Army, the nation's most senior warrior. As the possibility of a civil war grew, Alfred Huger, who with Petigru, Joel Roberts Poinsett, and B. F. Perry had observed firsthand Scott's handling of the nullifiers in 1832 and knew of his role in a border dispute with Canada in 1839, asked Petigru to prevail upon Scott to intervene.[25] Scott reportedly advised that "South Carolina should be treated like an 'erring sister,'" meaning that it should be allowed to withdraw from the Union peacefully, with the hope that with respectful treatment it could eventually be persuaded to return.[26] Later, with the Civil War's ravages amply demonstrated, Petigru asserted that if Scott's "erring sister" idea had been instituted, secession "would have died a natural death."[27]

On September 29, 1860, Ulysses Doubleday wrote to Abraham Lincoln, enclosing several letters from his brother, Captain Abner Doubleday (West Point '42) of Auburn, New York, then stationed at Fort Moultrie. The cover letter recited that because Abner was a Republican, Charlestonians viewed him with suspicion and may have been opening his outgoing mail. Ulysses further observed that "the desire to secede . . . has always been rampant in Charleston," but "if the forts were properly manned," secession would fail.[28] On October 29, with no knowledge of Doubleday's letter, General Scott wrote to President Buchanan and to Secretary of War John B. Floyd. "From a knowledge of our Southern population," Scott wrote, "it is my solemn conviction" that Forts Moultrie and Sumter in Charleston, Forts Pickens and McCree in Pensacola, and several other facilities should be garrisoned immediately lest they be seized by locals.[29] Scott asked Floyd—a fellow Virginian—to have the commanders in Charleston, Pensacola, and Fort Monroe in Virginia prepare defenses, adding that reinforcement by regulars was impossible because only five companies (485 men and fifteen officers) were within reach of these outposts.[30] Attorney General Black reportedly urged the immediate dispatch of a force strong enough to deter "any attempt at disunion." As indicated above, Lewis Cass concurred.[31]

By mid-November, however, it was apparent that neither Buchanan nor Floyd would even acknowledge receiving Scott's memorandum.[32] On November 24, with South Carolina's secession convention still a month off, Robert Barnwell Rhett warned President Buchanan that if he sent more troops, South Carolina's withdrawal from the Union would be a "bloody" affair.[33] President Jackson (and Rhett had been among the nullifiers Jackson had stared down) would have answered that attempts at intimidation would be unavailing. But Buchanan, with no similar impulse, reportedly told Floyd that if Charleston's several forts were overrun "in consequence of our neglect to put them in defensible condition it were better for you and me both to be thrown into the Potomac with mill stones tied about our necks." Here was a classically Buchanan-esque perspective, describing what must be done not with a view of doing it, but rather of predicting the dire consequences to himself upon failing to do so.[34]

Major Robert Anderson

A prudent military officer assigned to a state threatening to declare its independence, commanding a fort utterly unsuited to repel a land assault, and observing men in the streets outside apparently preparing such an attack, would have ample reason for concern. That officer, Major Robert Anderson, having arrived in mid-November 1860 to command the artillerymen in Charleston, desired not only to secure a defensible position but also to avoid provocative incidents between his men and locals. Secretary Floyd had removed the prior commander because he had ordered the transfer of muskets and ammunition to Fort Moultrie from the Charleston Arsenal.[35] South Carolina now placed state militiamen outside that building, falsely stating that this arrangement was to protect against a slave insurrection.[36]

In removing Anderson's predecessor, Floyd had favored local feeling over the defense needs of soldiers under his command. Formerly Virginia's governor, Floyd apparently hoped that Charleston would construe his appointment of Anderson as a friendly gesture, in that Anderson was from Kentucky, had married a Georgian, had owned slaves, and had served in Charleston before.[37] His father was a colonel in the Revolutionary War, his mother a cousin of Chief Justice John Marshall of Virginia. As a West Point graduate (class of '25), Anderson was a comrade and friend of many Southerners, including the Kentucky-born Jefferson Davis (class of '28). Another officer noted that if qualifications for commanding Charleston's forts included "a boundless partiality for the South" and "hatred and contempt" for Northerners, then "few better than Major Anderson can be found."[38] Union officers at Fort Moultrie would receive so many invitations to mingle in local society that acceptances had to be limited to maintain readiness. Anderson's hosts at such gatherings assumed that if either Kentucky or Anderson's adopted state of Georgia seceded, he would forthwith resign his U.S. commission and join some Southern militia.[39] Among those who became Anderson's close friends—perhaps introduced by Alfred Huger—was Robert Newman Gourdin, a lawyer, merchant, and member of the Charleston City Council who had resigned as head of the federal grand jury upon Lincoln's election and would become a delegate to the state's secession convention. Anderson, although commanding a Union garrison in a state about to secede, assured Gourdin that he was committed to keeping the South from initiating hostilities.[40]

Despite Anderson's declared Southern affinities, as a war-vetted officer he had no interest in a friendly capitulation—on his own authority—of the indefensible Fort Moultrie. On November 23, he asked his superiors in Washington to dispatch reinforcements forthwith, since an attempt to overrun his garrison was "apparent to all" and "nothing . . . will be better calculated to prevent bloodshed" than a Union presence substantial enough to make it "madness and folly to attack us"—essentially the position Winfield Scott had taken.[41] On November 28 and again on December 1, Anderson pressed his request. "The question for the Government to decide," he wrote, is "whether when South Carolina secedes, these forts are to be surrendered." If so, "I must be informed of it, and instructed what course I am to pursue." But if instead they were to be defended, either reinforcements or warships were required without delay.[42]

Lewis Cass and Jeremiah Black urged reinforcement, while Scott explained to Buchanan that he and President Jackson had convinced Charlestonians that this was not synonymous with aggression.[43] Floyd, however, reportedly declared that "he would cut off his right hand before he would sign an order to send re-enforcements," while also telling Assistant Secretary of State W. H. Trescot to spread the word among Trescot's Charleston friends that Floyd would not let the forts capitulate.[44] Buchanan chose Floyd's advice, and on November 29 Trescot (with how much direct involvement from Buchanan is unclear) arranged with South Carolina governor William Gist that if Buchanan sent no reinforcements, local forces would not attack.[45]

In his initial letter requesting more troops, Anderson asked his superior, Colonel Samuel Cooper, adjutant general of the U.S. Army, to keep the request utterly secret, since if word got out and reached Charleston, locals would immediately attack. Anderson's letters of November 28 and December 1 crossed with two by Cooper, who advised Anderson that henceforth he should communicate only with Cooper or Floyd, not with anyone else in the War Department. While in subsequent weeks other high officials in the army and navy would similarly instruct subordinate officers in the field to limit their contacts because of suspected disloyalty among clerks, here the instruction was perfidious, in that both Floyd and Cooper would themselves prove to be disloyal, their apparent purpose being to limit what loyal personnel knew of Anderson's plight and his requests for help.[46] Cooper, denying Anderson's request for troops, did not mention the Trescot/Gist agreement, instead stating, "It is believed, from information thought to be reliable, that an attack will not be made on your command," adding that if that proved incorrect, "your actions must be such as to be free from the charge of initiating a collision."[47] Thus, while Anderson had made clear that his command was in an indefensible position, all Cooper would say was that if an attack came, Anderson's primary duty was to prove that he had not provoked it.

One of Anderson's officers, Assistant Surgeon Samuel Wylie Crawford, M.D., of Pennsylvania, heard from a Charleston friend that within fifteen days South Carolinians would take over the unfinished Fort Sumter, from which they could then fire upon Fort Moultrie, a decidedly inferior installation. Anderson so informed Colonel Cooper.[48] On December 6, Anderson told

Floyd that Charleston's mayor and several prominent citizens had asserted that "the forts *must be theirs* after secession," then two weeks off.[49] The aging James Louis Petigru, having been informed that an attack was imminent, came to Fort Moultrie for a "final visit." Anderson's second-in-command, Captain Doubleday, observed tears rolling down Petigru's cheeks as he expressed "the deep sorrow and sympathy he felt for us in our trying position," while deploring "the folly and the madness of the times."[50]

Unionists hoped to hear something constructive or encouraging from the lame-duck Buchanan in his yearly message to Congress, to be issued December 3. Buchanan, knowing that one or more slave states would secede in response to Lincoln's election, summoned his friend Edwin M. Stanton to the White House for advice. Years later, Stanton recalled telling the president that this was a great opportunity for him to "show the Country a grand example of the teachings of the Jackson School in which we were educated." President Jackson, who while in office was commonly addressed with the honorific "General Jackson," had spoken credibly of the coercive violence he was pleased to invoke to quell unconstitutional conduct, reportedly putting the nullifiers on notice that "if a single drop of blood shall be shed" in South Carolina "in opposition to the laws of the United States, I will hang the first man I can lay my hand on engaged in such treasonable conduct, upon the first tree I can reach." It was a threat that would not have been considered hyperbole by Calhoun and others familiar with Jackson's meting out of summary justice in the Seminole Wars.[51] Buchanan (in Stanton's recollection) answered that because in the early 1830s he had been minister to Russia and therefore did not know the issues in the nullification crisis, Stanton should draft for him "the arguments against the rights of Secession and Nullification." Buchanan also found it "very hard" that he was not being allowed to "finish my term of office in peace, at my time of life."[52] Stanton, after submitting his memorandum on secession and nullification, assured friends that Buchanan's message would be a strong one.

On December 1, a New York periodical, perhaps to give Buchanan backbone, reprinted Jackson's Proclamation against the nullifiers and one of Daniel Webster's anti-nullification speeches.[53] These had no effect, however, several journalists later writing that no state paper had been "more eagerly looked for" than Buchanan's December 3 message, nor did any "more entirely disappoint."[54] Buchanan adopted part of Stanton's memo, and thus his recitation of why secession is unconstitutional was articulate and confident. But Buchanan had also asked for advice from his attorney general, Jeremiah Black, and embraced Black's view that while the federal government might invoke force to protect one of its forts within a state's borders, nothing could be done to coerce a state that had chosen to withdraw, since "the power to make war against a state" was "at variance" with the Constitution's "whole spirit and intent."[55] That thought had been voiced by Madison, Hamilton, Tocqueville, and even Jackson himself in his farewell address—despite the palpable threat he had made against the nullifiers several years before.[56] Abraham Lincoln would give the idea deference in his first inaugural.[57] From Buchanan, however, a refusal to stand up to South Carolina seemed an irresponsible and fearful "après nous le déluge." Seward facetiously summarized Buchanan's position to be as follows: "it is the duty of the president to execute the laws—unless somebody opposes him—and . . . no State has a right to go out of the Union—unless it wants to." Seward's friend and fellow Republican Charles Francis Adams, descendant of two presidents, trained in the law office of Daniel Webster, and now representing Massachusetts in the House, thought Buchanan's position "timid and vascillating," while Petigru privately called it "shuffling, insincere and shabby."[58] Buchanan had always misjudged the fire-eaters, believing that they would respond collegially to his repeated efforts at appeasement, when in fact they saw these as weakness, whetting their appetite for further insults to federal authority.[59]

"Tangible Evidence of . . . a Hostile Act"

Fort Moultrie was generally considered an attractive posting, not just because of its proximity to Charleston but also because perhaps a hundred fashionable families maintained verandaed summer houses near the fort or rented accommodations at the Moultrie House hotel, leading William Tecumseh Sherman, a lieutenant there in 1842, to comment that army officers "were sought after, and hospitably entertained."[60] Anderson's predecessor commonly opened the fort and its surroundings to locals, going so far as to bring an eight-man regimental band. An officer noted that "the principal and only general amusement among the people is to come into the garrison and listen to the Band . . . each evening."[61]

In this pleasant atmosphere, the garrison had included a number of wives and children. But now, one officer's wife wrote to her sister, "the Charlestonians are erecting two batteries, one just opposite us, at a little village—Mount Pleasant—and another on this end of the island. . . . In this weak little fort, I suppose President Buchanan and Secretary Floyd intend the Southern Confederation to be cemented with the blood of this brave little garrison. Their names shall be handed down to the end of time." The *New York Times* published her letter, to great effect among Northern readers whose collective sympathy and patriotism were being gradually awakened by the isolated garrison's plight.[62] Anderson wrote to his wife that she and their young child should not come, since locals were showing a "romantic attachment" to Fort Moultrie, talking of Colonel William Moultrie's "gallant defense" of the predecessor, palmetto-log fort on the site in 1776, when he matched its thirty guns against two British frigates and six sloops of war mounting—collectively—nine times that number.[63]

On December 8, apparently pursuant to the standstill agreement Trescot had reached with Gist, five South Carolina congressmen, all of them about to resign and depart, met with Buchanan, voicing their "strong convictions that neither the constituted authorities, nor any body of the people of the State of South Carolina, will either attack or molest" the federal forts pending secession and the arrival in Washington of representatives commissioned by the state to negotiate the terms of its separation. This promise had, however, two conditions: (1) that Buchanan send no reinforcements and (2) that the several facilities' "relative military status" would "remain as at present," meaning that Anderson would not transfer any men from Moultrie to Sumter.[64] Buchanan later recalled responding that because their "strong convictions" did not constitute a guarantee, he could not be absolutely bound by the two conditions but must be left free to exercise his discretion, adding that any negotiation with state commissioners would be Congress's responsibility, not his. In Buchanan's recollection, they agreed. In their own later recall of the meeting, William Porcher Miles and Laurence Keitt admitted that Buchanan did make that objection but also recalled that as they were leaving the meeting, Buchanan promised not to act without notifying them.[65] On December 17, Horace Greeley's *Tribune* published a facetious editorial, widely reprinted, noting "a rumor . . . derived from responsible sources at Washington, to the effect that *President Buchanan is insane!*"[66] General Scott advised Buchanan and Floyd that Moultrie should be immediately reinforced and Sumter garrisoned. When Buchanan replied that this would be premature because South Carolina had not yet held its secession convention, Scott replied that once the state seceded, its agents would cut the telegraph wires from Washington so that Buchanan could no longer order Anderson to transfer his troops across Charleston Harbor.[67]

Floyd and Cooper, having rejected Anderson's repeated pleas, decided not to issue him written orders, instead dispatching Brevet Captain Don Carlos Buell (West Point '41), assistant adjutant general to Colonel Cooper, to convey oral instructions to Anderson.[68] Buell—perhaps doubting the fidelity of

Cooper and/or Floyd, or perhaps wishing merely to protect himself and/or Anderson from false charges of disobeying oral orders whose content might later be disputed—decided to commit the instructions to writing after all:

> You are carefully to avoid every act which would needlessly tend to provoke aggression; and for that reason you are not, without evident and imminent necessity, to take up any position which could be construed into the assumption of a hostile attitude. But you are to hold possession of the forts in this harbor, and if attacked you are to defend yourself to the last extremity. The smallness of your force will not permit you, perhaps, to occupy more than one of the three forts, but an attack on or an attempt to take possession of any one of them will be regarded as an act of hostility, and you may then put your command into either of them which you may deem most proper, to increase its power of resistance. You are also authorized to take similar steps whenever you have tangible evidence of a design to proceed to a hostile act.

Buell also told Anderson that while he did not himself have authority to order him to transfer his men to Fort Sumter, he personally considered doing so a military necessity, in that evidence of local activity left no doubt that if Anderson did not seize the fort, others would.[69]

Anderson and Scott were close friends. Anderson's older brother had been Scott's classmate at the College of William & Mary, and Anderson's wife Eliza was the daughter of Scott's friend.[70] Anderson had been Scott's aide-de-camp during the forced migration of the Cherokees across the Mississippi and then served under Scott in New York as assistant adjutant general. In the war with Mexico, Scott had paid Anderson the highest military compliment, saying (as Anderson happily confided to his wife) that "he wanted me in the trenches with him."[71] Prior to arriving at Charleston in November, Anderson had consulted with Scott, who advised that while Floyd had frozen him out of the decision-making process, his own view was that Anderson might need to transfer his garrison to Fort Sumter.[72]

On December 19, Anderson wrote to his former pastor, Richard B. Duane, that Moultrie could not be defended. "In a position, so full of responsibility and apparently so entirely cut off from all prospect of human relief," he noted that "were it not for my firm reliance upon and trust in our heavenly Father, I could not but be disheartened; but I feel that I am here in the performance of a solemn duty, and am assured that He who has shielded me when death claimed his victims all around me will not desert me now. . . . Pray for me and my little band."[73] Two days later, Anderson noted in his diary that the Carolinians would seize Fort Sumter and from there prevail against him, that in vain had he asked the War Department either to garrison Sumter or to destroy the armament and powder already in place there, and that he could not fathom the administration's inaction.[74] When an intrepid militiaman from Massachusetts, having followed the crisis in the newspapers, wrote Anderson a letter volunteering to come and help, Anderson repeated what he had said to Duane: that Fort Moultrie was indefensible.[75]

Upon returning to Washington, Buell handed Floyd a copy of what he had written out. Although Floyd's sole concern had been that Anderson do nothing provocative, the order gave Anderson permission to move his men whenever he saw "tangible evidence of a design" by the Carolinians to "proceed to a hostile act." Since such evidence had been blatant and ubiquitous for some time, the order essentially gave Anderson permission to move immediately—directly contrary to what Floyd actually wanted. Many years later, Buell dared tell a historian that the operative language was entirely his own, and not, strictly speaking, authorized by Floyd at all, written "to protect Major Anderson and the authority of the Government against injury and ridicule" because "the people of Charleston, and even the State authorities themselves," had in Buell's opinion already determined "to seize Fort Sumter at an opportune moment." Thus, the "plain effect" of Buell's wording "was to make Major Anderson the judge of the evidence of such a design, and throw upon him the responsibility of a failure to anticipate the execution of it."[76] Buell, apparently aware that Floyd was a negligent administrator, also told the historian that Floyd probably did not bother to read it, "even when the copy was laid before him by his chief-clerk."[77] Buchanan either missed or had no objection to the passage giving Anderson discretion to move (his account of an earlier conversation was that he insisted upon maintaining options), but he noticed that the order also required Anderson, if attacked, to fight to "the last extremity," a death sentence that would stimulate Northern wrath against both the South and the administration. Buchanan thus instructed Floyd to forward immediately to Anderson an amendment striking "last extremity" and in its place giving Anderson discretion to surrender to a superior force. Floyd made the change but still failed to notice that his order gave Anderson discretion to transfer his garrison to Fort Sumter at any time.[78]

Governor Francis W. Pickens, elected just prior to South Carolina's secession after two years as President Buchanan's minister to Russia, by letter expressed to Buchanan a desire to garrison a small contingent of local militiamen in Fort Sumter, on the stated rationale that its mere possession by

Governor Francis W. Pickens, December 1860. Courtesy of the Charleston Museum, 2007.26.27c.

local forces would (like the posting of a local guard at the arsenal) quiet the public mind. By this time, although Buchanan had substantially burnished Pickens's political standing by a prestigious posting to the court of the tsar of Russia—a post Buchanan himself had once held—Pickens's official letters to Buchanan lacked the respect due to any president, much less one who had accorded the writer such patronage. Pickens went so far as to tell Buchanan that if he refused this request to garrison a federal fort with state soldiers who had been involved in planning an attack on another federal fort (Moultrie), "I cannot answer for the consequences."[79] From Pickens, recently swept into office by the power of the fire-eating Rhett family and their *Charleston Mercury*, his letter plainly meant "I *will not* answer for the consequences."[80] This threat merited an immediate and tart response. Alternatively, if Buchanan believed that he and South Carolina's congressmen had come to a binding agreement, he could have responded that Pickens's letter plainly violated that agreement and that he would (in a Jacksonian way) hang the first Carolinian who entered Fort Sumter. Instead, on December 20, the day South Carolina seceded, Buchanan drafted a response indicating that as president he lacked the authority to hand over a federal fort to local militias—as if to say that if he had the authority, he would hand it over.[81]

Before Buchanan could sign and send this feeble response, Assistant Secretary of State Trescot arranged to have Pickens formally withdraw his letter.[82] First, it violated the standstill agreement, and therefore, if Buchanan were the kind of statesman to exploit an adversary's mistake, Pickens's letter released Buchanan from his undertaking not to transfer men from Moultrie to Sumter. Second, once Buchanan communicated to Pickens that he had no authority to give up the federal forts in Charleston, it would be fruitless to negotiate with Buchanan further for the turnover of the forts. Since Buchanan had repeatedly shown palpable weakness as a negotiator, Trescot undoubtedly wanted him to continue in that role. With Pickens's letter withdrawn, things remained as they had been.[83]

Earlier, before Anderson had arrived in Charleston, he had consulted in New York with Captain George W. Cullum (West Point '33). Thoroughly familiar with Charleston, Cullum had told him to request four companies of men for Sumter, another company for Castle Pinckney, and recruits to make up two full companies at Moultrie.[84] A reported majority of enlistees were immigrants, many of them Irish, Germans, and Poles.[85] Captain Edward O. C. Ord (West Point '39) of the Third Artillery at Fort Monroe, Virginia, sent Anderson a note indicating that foreign-born enlisted men at Fort Monroe were being offered $50 to $55 a month to desert the Union army and join Southern militia. Since Anderson's garrison included a number of foreign-born men, Ord wished to warn him, adding that he personally would be "much gratified" if Anderson abandoned the outdated Fort Moultrie, indefensible against shells timed to explode above the fort, in favor of the essentially impregnable Fort Sumter.[86]

John G. Foster (West Point '46), brevet captain of the U.S. Army's elite Corps of Engineers, was responsible for the construction work of 150 carpenters and masons at Sumter and a smaller crew at Moultrie. Some were local, while others were brought from Baltimore, among them dozens of foreign-born. A South Carolina militiaman demanded that Anderson produce a list of these laborers, asserting that among them were men to be conscripted for military duty in South Carolina's new army. As Floyd and Cooper well knew, at any moment locals might seize Sumter and "overawe and control" a workforce whose collective loyalty to the Union was problematic.[87] But when Anderson asked Cooper for instructions, he was told that if in fact these workmen were subject to being drafted by South Carolina, he should "cause them to be delivered up." Cooper was thus ordering Anderson to disrupt the construction of defenses necessary to repel an attack at the hands of local forces by allowing these workers to quit and join those forces in the attack. Anderson, undoubtedly appalled, did the only thing within his authority: make a clear record, by letter, of what he had just been ordered to do. In sane times, under competent and loyal leadership, that record would have subjected Cooper to charges—at a minimum—of gross dereliction of duty, or worse.[88] Foster, meanwhile, not under Anderson's command, urged him to transfer his men to Sumter before locals seized it.[89] Thus, five career officers—Buell, Scott, Cullum, Ord, and Foster—had each voiced to Anderson the necessity of this move.

Foster, seeing that if Sumter was attacked, those construction workers who were loyal would need weapons to fend off locals, managed to obtain from the arsenal forty muskets. Floyd, hearing of this, summarily ordered their return.[90] In a bow to local feeling similar to his appointment of Anderson, Floyd gave command of the Charleston Arsenal to Colonel Benjamin Huger (West Point '25), a kinsman of Alfred Huger and of the Pinckney family, whose ancestors included heroes of the Revolution.[91] When Anderson himself approached the arsenal to obtain arms and ammunition, Colonel Huger declined, explaining to his friend and West Point classmate that South Carolina volunteers stationed nearby had forbidden such transfers.[92] At the secession convention, a resolution was offered that the garrisoning of or mounting of guns at Fort Sumter or Castle Pinckney "must be regarded . . . as an overt act of hostility."[93] Anderson told Colonel Cooper that locals would seize Fort Sumter the moment they began to doubt that President Buchanan would relinquish it voluntarily, adding that locals had stationed a steamer between Moultrie and Sumter to block any move across the harbor. Anderson then added that he could—if so instructed—evade that steamer, transfer his garrison, and from Sumter provide cover for any Union effort to bring in supplies or reinforcements.[94] This was on Anderson's part a desperate and ill-considered request. Because Buell's written order had already afforded him discretion to make the move, to request permission was to undermine authority he already had.

3

"An Act of Gross Breach of Faith"

AT THE SECESSION CONVENTION, STATE ATTORNEY GENERAL ISAAC W. Hayne proposed that three commissioners be appointed to negotiate with President Buchanan "for the delivery of the Forts, Magazines, Light Houses, and other real estate, and all appurtenances thereto, within . . . South Carolina." Rather than compile a combined dollar value to be paid to the United States for its real and personal property within South Carolina's borders, delegate Andrew Magrath, who had resigned his position as federal judge, proposed that a study establish the value of not only all federal property within the state but all federal property everywhere and—consistent with the secessionist position that the Union was a confederation of sovereign states—from that computation establish the proportionate share to which South Carolina would be equitably entitled, much as when a corporation is dissolved and each shareholder receives his portion of the entire corpus of equity assets, once all debts are paid.[1] By proposing that valuation method, Magrath may have had in mind that since South Carolina, unlike many other states, had never lobbied Congress for federally financed "internal improvement" projects such as the Cumberland Road, a comparison of federal expenditures within South Carolina with those in states that had sought and obtained major infusions of federal largesse might now support an argument that South Carolina had somehow been chronically shortchanged.[2] If, then, the state's presumed "share" of the national infrastructure were proposed as an offset to what it should pay the federal government for the purchase of the few federal facilities constructed within the state, Magrath could have had no doubt that South Carolina would be not a debtor but a substantial creditor of the United States, thus enhancing its bargaining position on all issues.

On the day South Carolina seceded, Jefferson Davis hinted to fellow senators that the president could not reinforce any federal fort because the

Constitution envisioned them only to defend against foreign threats from the sea, not to engage in hostilities against their host state.[3] Two days later, the secession convention appointed the three commissioners—Robert W. Barnwell, James L. Orr, and James H. Adams—to negotiate with President Buchanan the turnover of the federal assets.[4] With the secession convention meeting in closed session, Magrath, having been asked to report on whether the federal government's continued possession of Forts Sumter and Moultrie, Castle Pinckney, and the arsenal was consistent "either with the honor or safety" of South Carolina once secession occurred, concluded that because the defense of the United States no longer applied as a reason for such possession, the federal government no longer had a right to these assets.[5]

Although W. H. Trescot was an undisguised secessionist, Buchanan apparently had not seen this as an intrinsic conflict of interest in a senior federal diplomat. This left Trescot free to resign whenever he wished, and he chose this moment. "Oh for an hour of Jackson," the *Springfield Republican* observed.[6] Now a sort of de facto minister for his native South Carolina in its dealings with Washington, Trescot received from Governor Pickens a telegram asking whether he thought Anderson might attempt to occupy Fort Sumter.[7] Trescot asked Floyd, who saw so little likelihood of such a move that he saw no need to issue Anderson a special order to stay where he was, adding that Buell's memorandum forbade any such transfer. Floyd's reading of that document was plainly mistaken. Trescot, who had accompanied Buell on his visit to Anderson and therefore must have read Buell's memorandum, either similarly failed to understand that it gave Anderson discretion to act or was promised by friends that the pro-Southern Anderson would never attempt such a thing.[8] Trescot therefore saw "no rational ground for anticipating premature difficulty" concerning the commissioners' negotiations to purchase Union assets.[9]

"To Prevent the Effusion of Blood"

Anderson wrote to his wife on December 24, "Would that I could be with you [on] Christmas, but I shall be very busy <u>attending to my duty</u> on that day." Assuming that Anderson inserted the underlining in his original letter (we have only a transcription), he was hinting something significant while avoiding any explicit statement, following rumors that although Alfred Huger's federal post office was still functioning, the Carolinians were steaming open the garrison's letters. Further:

I trust that something may soon recur by the Divine assistance which will show you His power and relieve your anxiety. I earnestly pray that I may by His blessing be the humble instrument of doing something that may benefit our beloved country. . . . The general opinion now is that they will take Ft. Sumter and then they can soon drive me from [Fort Moultrie]. . . . I would have to make the best terms I could for my little band—a humiliating position indeed for me to be placed in! I will strive to find out what is my duty, and with God's help will act <u>fully</u> up to it.[10]

This, too, was brimming with suggestion.

In order to avert suspicion among locals that he might attempt a covert move to Fort Sumter, Anderson accepted Captain Foster's invitation to dine in Moultrieville on Christmas Day.[11] A private under Anderson's command wrote to his father in Ireland that the major had prepared the fortifications in Moultrie "with such unparalleled vigor that our opponents soon became thoroughly convinced that he intended to make a desperate stand in the position he then held, and the duty of watching us was performed with a laxity corresponding to the strength of their conviction. So completely did our Commander keep his own counsel, that none in the garrison officer or soldier ever dreamed that he contemplated a move."[12] Further to hide his intentions, Anderson had equipment needed for Sumter's guns transferred to Fort Moultrie, presumably suggesting that any Carolinian force taking Fort Sumter would be deprived of needed equipment. He then planned to have the garrison's forty-five wives and children deposited in three boats and sent across the harbor to Fort Johnson, as if to put them out of harm's way in expectation of an attack on Moultrie, when in fact this would place them only 2,425 yards west of Fort Sumter. The man in charge was instructed that he should spend time appearing to look around for suitable quarters among Fort Johnson's dilapidated buildings but should not actually unload anyone or anything from the boats. If he heard two guns fired from Fort Moultrie, he was to take his passengers and cargo to Fort Sumter. Because of rain, the operation was postponed from Christmas Day to December 26.

On that day, it was resolved in the secession convention that Governor Pickens inform delegates of the condition of Forts Moultrie and Sumter and Castle Pinckney, "the number of guns mounted and ready for service in each," what changes had been made since the day of secession, and "whether he has any assurance that said Forts and Castle shall not be reinforced."[13] Pickens had posted armed steamers near Sumter and instituted land-based surveillance of

Moultrie commencing at 9:00 each night.[14] Monitoring this protocol, Anderson chose to commence the transfer just after nightfall on December 26, when his men, with their uniform coats off so they might appear as workers, rowed the mile from Moultrie to Sumter, thus establishing a garrison of about seventy enlisted men, nine officers, and—that attribute of earlier times—the regimental band. Moultrie then fired the two guns to summon the women and children.[15] The transfer was audacious, no less so for being militarily necessary, since it was undertaken contrary to the known wishes of Anderson's military superiors. At 8:00 p.m., Anderson wrote to Colonel Cooper, "I have the honor to report that I have just completed, by the blessing of God, the removal to this fort of all of my garrison," a move he declared necessary "to prevent the effusion of blood." He also wrote to his wife, assuring her that now "the whole force of S. Carolina would not venture to attack us," a conclusion supported by the theory that a large fortress, even if understaffed and undersupplied, is nevertheless impregnable against a larger, better-equipped land force.[16]

The situs of Fort Sumter was nationally historic. It was upon this shoal, varying in depth with the ebbs and flows but occasionally appearing above the surface at slack low water, that the twenty-eight-gun frigate HMS *Actæon* had run aground in June 1776 during the attack on William Moultrie's fort across the harbor. The British burned the ship to avoid its capture, and while three of its guns would be found and recovered in 1867, twenty-five guns and other artifacts remain beneath Fort Sumter or the ever-shifting sands.[17] Since the shoal was perfectly placed to defend the harbor, in 1770, six years prior to *Actæon*'s loss, the British royal governor had suggested building a fort by "laying stone ballast for two or three years."[18] In 1826, with Bernard and Totten's "Third System" of coastal defense under way, the Army Corps of Engineers picked this shoal as the situs of a fort.[19] In 1828, Congress finally passed an initial appropriation of $25,000, and work began.[20] Totten shipped from New York and New England over a number of years some 109,000 tons of granite quarry scrap as well as rough-cut and cut stone. Workers, including twenty-one slaves, progressed slowly, primarily because of the subsistence to be expected when constructing a heavy edifice on sand in a harbor with powerful and sometimes fierce tidal currents through the harbor mouth, subject also to hurricanes and nor'easters. By December 1834, however, the perimeter foundational granite emerged as an atoll two feet above low water. Walls were then set down on the atoll, followed by an artificial island of about 2.5 acres, including an esplanade and wharf.[21]

In 1837, Charleston members of South Carolina's house of representatives complained to the federal government that "the constant inroads of the

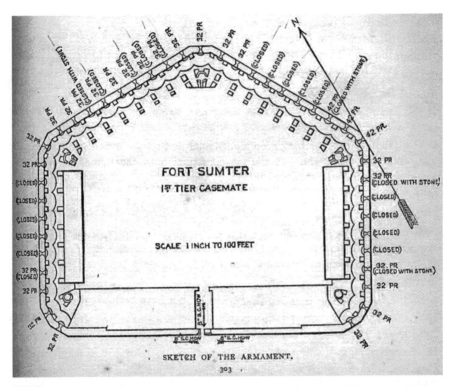

Diagram of Fort Sumter indicating placement of guns circa April 12–13, 1861. *War of the Rebellion: A Compilation of the Official Records of the Union and Confederate Armies*, Ser. 1, vol. 1 (Washington, 1880).

sea, since the laying of the foundation of Fort Sumter, are rapidly wearing away the Western portion of Sullivan's Island [although 2,700 yards away], causing alterations in the channels" and tending to impair the harbor's safety.[22] Although the long granite wharf had been built for fully loaded supply ships with deep drafts, Sumter's artificial island and its wharf had so changed the harbor's currents that the docking area was subjected to deposition and by the mid-1850s was too shallow to accommodate these vessels. After three decades of intermittent, ambivalent commitments by the federal government, the fort remained unfinished in the summer of 1858, when it became the unhappy holding pen for Africans extracted from a "slaver" intercepted for violating U.S. law. In a horrific statistic typical of the Middle Passage, one-third (160) had reportedly died on the way, and thirty-eight more passed while in federal custody there.[23]

Sumter was a so-called truncated hexagon, with one salient facing northeast to oppose ships attempting to enter the harbor.[24] Among the shortcomings of Moultrie and other low-slung forts from the older, "Second System" of American coastal defense was that they could not concentrate massive firepower for the few minutes that an enemy vessel was within close range.[25] Accomplishing this task required multistory forts from which several tiers of guns could fire simultaneously.[26] The walls built on Sumter's foundation, rising forty-eight feet above low water, were made of various materials, primarily 7.5 million "Charleston greys," clay bricks fired predominantly by slaves in local kilns. Totten tested materials to show their comparative ability to withstand attack by different ordnance and applied several different formulations of concrete, including "tabby," a combination of sand and oyster shells from which the salt had been washed, combined with the lime extracted from the shells by burning, using a technique devised by Totten.[27] Sumter's great height accommodated three tiers of guns, the lower two in casemates. The fort's thick walls, with iron-shuttered embrasures of Totten's design, protected artillerists from solid shot hitting the exterior, and barrel vaulted arches kept them protected from the collapse of masonry at higher levels.[28] On the top, terreplein level, however, were the guns of heaviest gauge, and their crews were unprotected. Although substantial construction work had been done, when Anderson, his men, and their families arrived on December 26, Foster's workmen had mounted only fifteen of 135 guns.

When Anderson departed Moultrie, he left Foster behind with instructions to disable or destroy its armaments, and as Charlestonians awoke on the morning of December 27, they saw smoke rising from burning gun carriages.[29] Additional supplies were rowed over from Moultrie (without opposition, apparently), and at noon the Stars and Stripes went up Sumter's flagpole. A young Charlestonian described Anderson's conduct in her diary as "stealing away in the darkness like a thief." Rumors spread that Anderson intended to counter such charges of cowardice by pledging to defend Sumter to the last man.[30] Some said Anderson was aiming Sumter's guns at the city and would open fire. The *Charleston Courier* declared that he "has achieved the unenviable distinction of opening civil war between American citizens, by an act of gross breach of faith," as if locals had not themselves been readying an attack.[31] At the secession convention, a resolution was submitted "to take immediate possession of Fort Moultrie and Castle Pinckney and to make the necessary

President James Buchanan and his cabinet, circa 1859. From left: Jacob Thompson, Lewis Cass, John B. Floyd, the president, Howell Cobb, Isaac Toucey, Joseph Holt, and Jeremiah S. Black. By Matthew Brady. Library of Congress LC-BH8277-537.

preparations" for the "recapture" of Fort Sumter (although South Carolina had never owned or possessed it) or for its destruction.[32] The *National Republican*, a Washington newspaper commenced following Lincoln's election, fairly gloated, writing that "the Nullifiers" (a term of snide historical disapprobation) were in "an agony of rage" over Anderson's "masterly movement," while President Buchanan now found himself "foiled in his plan of leaving Major Anderson so weak as to be unable to resist attack." Buchanan "divides his time between crying and praying," wrote Henry Adams—a singularly unattractive portrait of a chief executive and commander in chief.[33]

In a major scandal apparently attributable to Floyd's incompetence, he had become embroiled in the unlawful extraction of $870,000 from the Indian Trust Fund. On December 27, the scandal hit the front pages.[34] While presidents of even middling backbone would at this point have had Floyd escorted out and perhaps held pending charges, Buchanan did nothing. Scrambling to salvage himself, Floyd suddenly became a man of principle, demanding of Anderson by telegram that he explain why he had transferred his garrison.

Anderson replied, "I abandoned Fort Moultrie because I was certain that . . . if attacked, the garrison would never have surrendered without a fight."[35]

On December 28, Greeley's *Tribune* announced that the Union was gradually reinforcing Fort Sumter.[36] The story, although incorrect, may have derived from overheard rumors, for on that day, two months after Floyd first rejected General Scott's proposal to reinforce the Southern forts, Scott asked Floyd to reinforce Sumter immediately with 150 recruits from New York, supported by one or two warships.[37] Pickens, perhaps informed of the story, wrote to Anderson that any attempt at reinforcement or resupply would be opposed. Anderson immediately forwarded the letter to Colonel Cooper.[38]

When Floyd (not surprisingly) ignored Scott's request, rumors spread of Scott's imminent resignation.[39] Senator-Elect Salmon Chase (R/OH) begged him not to leave at a time when all the administration's actions were marked by "imbecility, or treason, or both."[40] Senator Seward quipped that it might be a good thing if Buchanan forced Scott to resign and "disavowed and cashiered" Anderson, since these radical acts would be enough to wake the North from its lethargy. "Screw 'em up to the war pitch," Seward said, "and the south will learn some manners."[41] For the legendary Winfield Scott to resign, either under demand from Buchanan or in protest of Buchanan's policies, would be a catastrophic blow for an administration already crumbling. Scott, no stranger to politics, may have spread the resignation rumor himself in order to intimidate the president into finally accepting his advice. Although Scott undoubtedly despised both Buchanan and Floyd, duty and self-regard suggested that he stay, since Floyd had been disgraced and was within hours of departure, and soon Buchanan, too, would be gone, relinquishing command to a new president under a mandate for aggressive change.

Floyd directed Anderson to return to Fort Moultrie because he had violated "the solemn pledges of the Government," an apparent reference to Buchanan's alleged promise to South Carolina congressmen in early December. When Governor Pickens informed Anderson that Buchanan had promised that no transfer would occur, Anderson responded that while his own sympathies lay entirely with the South, he had never been informed of any such promise.[42] While there is no reason to doubt Anderson, and in any event the mixed reports of Buchanan's conversation with the congressmen did not amount to "solemn pledges of the Government" as claimed by Floyd, here was a serviceable opportunity for Floyd to appear virtuous. "But one remedy is now left us," Floyd declared to Buchanan, "by which to vindicate our honor" and which, "in my judgment, can alone prevent bloodshed and civil war," and that was for Buchanan to permit Floyd to order Anderson to withdraw his garrison not just from Fort Sumter but from Charleston altogether.[43] Having made this written request to Buchanan, Floyd could now conveniently point to the president's refusal to let him order Anderson out of Charleston as his stated reason for resigning.[44]

"One True Man"

South Carolina's three commissioners had arrived in Washington on December 26 and scheduled a meeting with Buchanan for 1:00 p.m. on December 27 to discuss the disposition of the forts and other federal assets. Upon being informed of Anderson's move, however, they peremptorily canceled. Pickens had undoubtedly hoped to make all the necessary preparations for an attack upon Fort Moultrie so that when the commissioners sat down with Buchanan, they could extort from him a tacit recognition of South Carolina's independent status. Anderson's move foiled that plan. The commissioners now delivered to Buchanan a letter (reportedly drafted for them by Trescot) stating that while South Carolina could "have taken possession of the forts in Charleston harbor" at any time, it had not done so because of the "pledges" Buchanan had allegedly made to South Carolina's congressmen. Repeating essentially what Floyd had said, the commissioners urged Buchanan to order the "immediate withdrawal" of Anderson's men from South Carolina since, "under present circumstances, they are a standing menace which renders negotiation impossible."[45] The secession convention, in secret session, entertained a resolution by Magrath calling Anderson's transfer from one federal fort to another "an act of hostility." Pickens informed the convention that the move constituted "a direct violation of the distinct understanding" reached in Washington, "bringing on a state of war," an ambiguous phrase meaning either that a state of war now existed or that war was now inevitable if no corrective action was taken.[46] On December 30, the state seized the Charleston Arsenal, containing twenty-one thousand muskets, rifles, carbines, pistols, and field guns, valued collectively at $500,000.[47] The Union had possessed four military facilities on December 26; it now possessed one, albeit the only one that could be defended.

Edwin M. Stanton, just appointed attorney general, arrived late to his first cabinet meeting, where he and his allies—Jeremiah Black (who had become secretary of state following Cass's resignation) and Postmaster General Joseph Holt—heard Floyd, backed by Navy Secretary Isaac Toucey of Connecticut, Interior Secretary Jacob Thompson of Mississippi, and Treasury Secretary Philip F. Thomas of Maryland, declaim against Anderson's "Act of War." With

Buchanan "as pale as a sheet," Stanton later recalled, "it was a fight over a corpse."[48] Stanton began forwarding inside information to Seward regarding cabinet deliberations, to prepare him and President-Elect Lincoln. Seward sent to Lincoln in Springfield a letter marked "private," unsigned, and employing another senator's franking privilege, knowing that Lincoln would recognize its authorship by Seward's (execrable) handwriting. "It pains me to learn," Seward observed, "that things . . . are even worse" within Buchanan's cabinet than he had thought, with the president "debating day and night . . . whether he shall not recall Maj. Anderson & surrender Fort Sumter."[49] Horatio King, assistant postmaster general and staunchly Unionist, wrote to New York City postmaster John A. Dix, "Disunion men are raising heaven and earth to get the president to degrade Major Anderson."[50] "Never did a government stoop so low," James Russell Lowell would write, "as ours has done, not only in consenting to receive these ambassadors from Nowhere [referring to the three commissioners], but in suggesting that a soldier deserves court-martial who has done all he could to maintain himself in a forelorn hope, with rebellion in his front and treason in his rear."[51] Anderson wrote to his wife, "You have seen that the president and Sec'y [Floyd] disclaim what I have done—be perfectly easy on that score. I never felt my confidence in God more perfect than it now is. He will guard me through the storm which now impends." Further, "I can justify my course _fully_ before any tribunal I may be brought before. . . . If the Government had reasons for my not taking the step, they should have communicated them to me. Even if the Gov't does not endorse my action I am _sure_ it was right."[52] Alfred Huger, meanwhile, would try to defuse North/South tensions by, among other things, maintaining contact with two Kentuckians in Washington: Postmaster General Holt and Robert Anderson's brother Larz.[53]

Floyd's sudden resignation brought Scott out of his self-imposed reclusiveness, reportedly commenting that he hoped to "save the Country, if the Administration would let him."[54] On December 30, Scott asked Buchanan for a secret reinforcement of Fort Sumter, this time by 250 recruits, to be transported by a sloop of war and cutter.[55] Orders were issued by the War and Navy Departments to transport reinforcements on the screw sloop _Brooklyn_, docked in Norfolk, but Buchanan on December 31 directed that these orders be held in abeyance.

Buchanan met with Stanton, Holt, and Black—the nucleus of what would soon be his new, Unionist cabinet—and then drafted a response to the commissioners' demand for Anderson's withdrawal. Black thought it so weak that he reportedly threatened to resign if Buchanan sent it. "The forts in Charleston Harbor belong to this Government," Black advised, "and can not be given up," adding that while a fort "might be surrendered to a superior force," that would not happen because Sumter was impregnable. Since, in Black's view, the Union was constitutionally *obliged* to stay in Charleston, and Sumter afforded the protection by which it *could* stay, the administration must not utter "the remotest expression of a doubt" about the "perfect propriety" of what Anderson had done. By taking the strongest of the three forts in the harbor, Black wrote, Anderson had done "everything that mortal man could do to repair the fatal error" committed by the administration "in not sending down troops enough to hold *all* the forts" and thus "saved the country . . . when its day was darkest."[56] Black, like the departed Lewis Cass, recommended that Anderson be immediately reinforced. General Scott, of the same view and justifiably concerned that Buchanan still toyed with the idea of evacuation, requested a meeting, but he was told that the president would have no time to meet until he finished his response to the Southern commissioners.[57]

While numerous secessionists were quitting their federal positions and departing Washington, Senator Wigfall saw fit to stay on, the better to insult the government at close quarters while also monitoring its secrets and passing them to friends in his native South Carolina.[58] A stranger to restraint in words or action, the veteran of as many as eight duels, Wigfall put a British visitor in mind of "the eye of the Bengal tiger" in the Regent's Park Zoo. He had tried to enlist Floyd in a plot to kidnap Buchanan, which presumably would make Vice President Breckinridge, a Kentuckian, the nation's chief executive.[59] (Floyd, under pressure from his personal scandal, had declined.) Soon word spread that Floyd's replacement would be Postmaster General Holt, a Unionist Kentuckian described by Senator Toombs of Georgia as a "bitter foe" of Southern rights.[60] Wigfall telegrammed to Charleston, "Holt succeeds Floyd. This means war. Cut off supplies from Anderson and take Sumter soon as possible."[61]

The draft letter Buchanan had shown Black must have been exceedingly feeble, since the substitute he did send to the commissioners was itself anemic. They had demanded proof that Buchanan had not himself ordered Anderson to move, and Buchanan, rather than simply say that his word as president was sufficient, instead sought to assure them that "Major Anderson acted upon his own responsibility, and without authority." As proof, he gave them Buell's memo, presumably because it contained no direct order to occupy Sumter.[62] If Buchanan had reread it carefully, however, and apprised himself of what Anderson had written about the Carolinians' preparations for battle, he would have seen that the memo—which became an order once it was approved by

Buchanan's secretary of war—in fact authorized Anderson to move if he saw evidence of hostile intent, and such evidence was copious.

If Buchanan had released the Buell memo not just to the commissioners but also to the press, and then laid out what Anderson had previously reported to his superiors regarding the Carolinians' preparations to attack him in an indefensible position, he could have placed the commissioners at a serious disadvantage in the eyes of the nation and the world. Despite ample experience in diplomacy, however, Buchanan now had no sense of how a situation could be exploited. He had shown some earlier signs of audacity—for instance, the recklessly bold suggestion in 1854 that the United States simply take Cuba from Spain. But now a U.S. president was handing a putative enemy an internal order so as to exculpate himself and place blame on a besieged army officer under his command. The commissioners, for their part, apparently read the order more carefully than Buchanan had, for they summarily dropped the issue of whether Anderson's move was justified. Instead, on January 1, they delivered another highhanded letter, this one asserting that by refusing to order Anderson's return to Moultrie, Buchanan had breached his alleged agreement with the congressmen and thus had made war inevitable, adding that Floyd, a Southerner, had the sense of honor to resign in protest.[63]

In responding, Buchanan could have denied making any such promise to the congressmen, while deriding the commissioners for ascribing any sense of honor to Floyd. He could have exploited their sudden silence regarding whether Anderson's move was militarily justified by characterizing it as their tacit admission that Anderson had only reacted appropriately to an imminent threat. He could then have claimed personal credit—retrospectively—for Anderson's move by proclaiming that it was in response to the particular wording of an order that ultimately came from him. But he instead let this opportunity, too, slip away, making no response to the January 1 letter other than to return it with a curt statement that he declined to accept it.[64] The progress of secessionism in other states was from this moment based upon the assumption, never proven by the congressmen who met with Buchanan, nor disproven by Buchanan, that Anderson's move was "without authority" and in violation of an undertaking Buchanan had made.[65]

With an impulse solely to distance himself from Anderson, Buchanan apparently had no sense that a chain of command requires responsibility and deference not just *from* subordinates but also *to* them, particularly a subordinate in a difficult and isolated situation. Nor was Anderson an unknown factor. As Scott would have been pleased to recount, he had shown extraordinary courage in Mexico, remaining at the head of a column in the bloody battle of Molino del Rey, despite the bullet wound in his shoulder that gave him a noticeable and permanent stoop.[66] Buchanan's mediocrity had left the North without a hero, and Anderson, with a slave-state background, personified loyalty to the Union, courage, and finesse in the presence of a local hostile force, while staring down treachery, fear, and incompetence in his superiors. Even before he transferred to Sumter, *Harper's Weekly* informed Anderson that its subscribers were requesting illustrations of him and his men.[67] Now—writers for *Harper's* would observe—praises for Anderson "were upon all lips which did not mutter treason."[68] Letters arrived at the fort from well-wishers and

Major Robert Anderson, circa 1861, by Matthew Brady. MOLLUS-MASS Coll. 2:53, U.S. Army Mil. Hist. Inst.

Union officers at Fort Sumter, February 8, 1861. Seated (from left): Captain Abner Doubleday, Major Robert Anderson, Assisant Surgeon Samuel W. Crawford, Brevet Captain John G. Foster. Standing: Brevet Captain Truman Seymour, First Lieutenant George W. Snyder, First Lieutenant Jefferson C. Davis, Second Lieutenant Richard Kidder Meade, First Lieutenant Theodore Talbot. By George S. Cook. MOLLUS-MASS Coll., V26, p. 1252, U.S. Army Mil. Hist. Inst. Not included is Lieutenant Norman Hall, who had not yet returned from Washington.

from those seeking his autograph or a lock of his hair.[69] Wall Street stocks reportedly rose in contemplation of what seemed—at last—resolute action.[70] Boston attorney Leverett Saltonstall wrote to inform Anderson that he had just been toasted at a dinner, it being "indeed refreshing, in these sad days of demagogues, traitors, fanatics, idiots, and rascals in high places, to see one true man."[71] A hack poet wrote, "In storm and tempest, dauntless still and calm; / Honored by men, by loyal women loved, / The pride and boast of all thy countrymen, / The Cynosure of all eyes, still unmoved."[72]

Soon no article about Anderson and his men was publishable if it lacked the word "gallant." The January 7 *Hartford Courant* noted that "salutes in honor of the gallant Major were fired on Boston Common, Saturday noon, and in Philadelphia, on Saturday evening, five thousand persons met and heartily approved Anderson's course, and called on the president to sustain him, declaring all persons who wage war against the United States to be public enemies."[73] The House of Representatives, amid substantial acrimony from Southerners still present, resolved by 124–53 "that we fully approve of the bold and patriotic act of Major Anderson . . . and of the determination of the president to maintain that fearless officer in his present position."[74] "Anderson's movement was masterly," Elizabeth Blair wrote on January 9, "& has made him now the Hero of the day. . . . Yesterday there was nearly as many guns fired in his honor as that of Genl Jackson—whose spirit is now invoked daily for the protection of the Country."[75] The invocation of Jackson had special meaning to the Blair family, since Elizabeth's father, Francis P. Blair Sr., had been Jackson's trusted advisor, and her brother Montgomery, one of Dred Scott's lawyers, was Jackson's de facto godson.

The primary issue in the growing crisis was that of attributing blame, with each side contemplating what might provoke the other to fire first. On January 19, the abolitionist *Chicago Daily Tribune* opined that the "hope for freedom in this crisis does not rest with the North. If the South Carolinians would only make a determined assault upon Fort Sumter, level its walls to the sea, and slaughter its gallant commander and all his men—then perhaps the North would arise in vindication of the Constitution and laws, and teach the South that this country and government were not made wholly for slaveholders." Henry Adams, writing to his brother Charles, thought that what fellow Republicans needed was "a little bit of a fight" in which the Union got beaten, so as to "put the South in the wrong." The grandson of John Quincy Adams and great-grandson of John Adams, Henry carried good political genes but was at this time limited in experience to Harvard College and the grand tour. Thus, in his view, if Anderson "and his whole command were all murdered in cold blood" (Adams's puerile notion of "a little bit of a fight"), it would be "an excellent thing for the country, much as I should regret it on the part of those individuals."[76] Anderson's highest calling—apparently—was as a martyr in the Union cause.

Anderson's wife met with Buchanan and demanded that he dispatch reinforcements, arguing with such vehemence that Buchanan—ever the self-declared victim—took offense at the wife of an army officer pleading with him to save her husband's life. Eliza Bayard Clinch Anderson, a Georgian, was so distraught by the president's refusal to help that she sought the advice of Major Anderson's good friend, Jefferson Davis, only to find that Davis, about to resign his Senate seat and destined later to order the cannonade against her husband's garrison, was in no position to assist her.[77]

Burning Effigies

Like Wigfall, Trescot believed that Buchanan's appointment of Holt indicated war. Sending a telegram to the fire-eating ex-congressman William Porcher Miles to that effect, Trescot added that reinforcements would be sent aboard *Harriet Lane*, a Revenue cutter with a draft Trescot thought shallow enough to cross the sandbar outside Charleston Harbor. Southern newspapers published a rumor that *Harriet Lane* had already departed its slip in Jersey City, though its orders were not (according to the rumor) to aid Fort Sumter, but rather to collect customs duties outside Charleston Harbor.[78]

As Trescot prepared to leave Washington, Jeremiah Black reportedly said to him, "You beat us all the way through, and came very near carrying your last point; but fortunately our last card was a trump," a metaphor Trescot took to mean that in the end the Unionists in Buchanan's cabinet collectively convinced the president that he had more to fear from their threatened resignations and Northern backlash than he did from the Southerners he had repeatedly tried—and failed—to placate. Buchanan looked at the decision before him as a personal curse, commenting to a friend, "If I withdraw Anderson from Sumter, I can travel home to Wheatland [his home near Lancaster, Pennsylvania] by the light of my own burning effigies."[79] Stanton, perhaps to show Buchanan that the public might still rally behind resolution, surreptitiously invented with Representative Daniel E. Sickles (D/NY) a "spontaneous," "grass-roots" set of positive telegrams to the White House, along with a newspaper campaign and even a cannon salute to Buchanan as "a second Jackson."[80] But the North would never forgive Buchanan's attempt in 1857 to intimidate congressional Democrats into passing a proslavery constitution for Kansas against the wishes of the vast majority of settlers there.[81] And now Floyd's "principled" departure signaled the end of whatever support Buchanan had once grudgingly received from the South.[82]

The federal government—Jefferson Davis argued on the Senate floor— was allowing Anderson "to make war" against South Carolina, which had presented (and here Davis either lied or was grossly misinformed) no threat to him at Fort Moultrie. If, Davis urged, Buchanan had only ordered Anderson to return to Moultrie, Sumter would have remained as it had been, unoccupied by state troops, and "peace would have spread its pinions over this land, and calm negotiation would have been the order of the day."[83] Since Pickens had already threatened Buchanan if he failed to permit state troops to occupy Sumter, Davis was again misinformed or lying. Nor, as a tactical commander who had seen death at close quarters, would Davis have done other than his friend Anderson had done. Further, negotiations would have remained "calm" only if the Union troops left South Carolina.

At Trescot's suggestion, Senator Robert M. T. Hunter (D/VA) told Buchanan that if Anderson would return to Fort Moultrie, his safety would be guaranteed.[84] Buchanan was apparently being asked to order Anderson to relinquish an impregnable fortification recently attained and go back to one that was indefensible, and to do so not with a view to any permanent presence there but merely as a condition for South Carolina returning to the negotiating table. It was the kind of proposal one would never make to a reasonably resolute leader. Davis told a friend that Buchanan's "weakness has done as much harm as wickedness would have achieved."[85] It was, sadly, one of the few observations on which North and South could agree. Even if Buchanan had accepted Hunter's proposal (and he well might have, if still under the sway of the Southerners in his cabinet), conciliatory gestures mean little when offered by a leader perceived as unsteady, cynical, or mendacious, and Buchanan had exhibited all three traits.[86] But now he was at the mercy of a staunchly Unionist cabinet that—over the dissent of Interior Secretary Thompson—approved Scott's suggested reinforcement initiative.[87] Senator Hunter reportedly told Trescot that Buchanan had now "changed his ground and will maintain it to the last extremity," adding that Governor Pickens would do well to block the harbor entrance by sinking old derelict vessels. Buchanan, bowing now to cabinet Unionists as he had once bowed to the likes of Floyd, fearing the worst, observed, "It is now all over."[88]

"We Owe to John B. Floyd"

Floyd so combined incompetence and disloyalty that instances of one were sometimes ascribed to the other. In August 1859, he had received two anonymous letters from two different sources requesting that he send soldiers to Harpers Ferry because John Brown, known as messianically violent after butchering several proslavery settlers in Kansas, was going to instigate an armed slave insurrection. Floyd took no action, thereby opening himself to later allegations (though groundless) that he had wanted the slave revolt to go forward in order to galvanize Southern hatred of the North.[89] In a similar vein, Captain Doubleday later wrote that even if Floyd in the conduct of his office never went so far as to "make regular arrangements to have us all massacred," it was nevertheless true that "his orders and mode of procedure tended to that end."[90] In the anonymous *Diary of a Public Man* (1879), an extraordinary mix of "insider" facts and speculations, journalist William Henry Hurlbert would speculate that Floyd had consciously suggested Anderson's transfer to Sumter, since it was likely to lead to a conflict that would cause Floyd's home state of Virginia to join South Carolina in secession.[91] And an admirer of Anderson would claim that a "controlling" reason behind Anderson's move to Fort Sumter was not the likelihood of an imminent attack upon Fort Moultrie, but rather an order by Floyd to Captain Foster to mount Fort Sumter's guns "immediately," which necessarily meant that Floyd and his friends in Charleston—protestations to the contrary notwithstanding—wanted the fort to be fully equipped when locals seized it.[92] And although Floyd apparently neither sought nor obtained any personal gain from his involvement with the Indian Trust Fund scandal, it was difficult for most observers to believe that mere incompetence could have gotten him in so deeply.

Floyd's refusals to answer Anderson's reinforcement pleas never resulted in charges of dereliction of duty, although journalists charged treason. But other facts suggest that he had been—as Seward told Lincoln on December 29—"arming the South" against the Union he was sworn to protect.[93] On November 19, former Georgia Supreme Court justice Henry L. Benning, urging his state's secession, had said, "From the best information I can obtain, there is now a larger proportion of the public arms and munitions at the South than at the North."[94] On December 31, four days after the Indian Trust Fund scandal broke, the House standing Committee on Military Affairs undertook to examine not only "the condition of the forts, arsenals, dock yards, &c. . . . and whether they are supplied with adequate garrisons" (the issue Floyd and Buchanan had refused to address when requested by Scott two months earlier) but also "how, to whom, and at what price" muskets and ordnance had been distributed in the previous year.[95] On January 9, the House resolved to appoint a select committee to investigate, among other things, "whether any officer of this Government has . . . entered into any pledge . . . with any person . . . not to send reinforcements to the forts of the United States in the harbor of Charleston," and what "demand for reinforcements of the said forts has been made, and for what reason such reinforcements have not been furnished."[96] Even a cursory investigation would identify Scott's reinforcement recommendation of late October, its rejection by Floyd and Buchanan, and then Anderson's increasingly urgent requests for reinforcements in November and December, flatly refused by Floyd and Cooper.[97] On January 26, the House also appointed a committee "to inquire whether any secret organization hostile to the Government of the United States exists in the District of Columbia; and if so, whether . . . any employés or officers of the federal government, in the executive or judicial departments, are members thereof."[98]

These two probes were not rigorous and did not result in trials for malfeasance. Two significant facts did, however, emerge. First, because most armament manufacturers were located in the North, quantities of muskets, rifles, and artillery were commonly forwarded from these to various federal facilities and state militias in the South. On the day South Carolina seceded, Floyd tried to ship seventy-seven cannons to one fort in Mississippi and another in Texas. Since neither fort was near enough to completion to receive them, these shipments were clearly being made to place these guns in secessionist hands. And while secessionists did soon take over both forts, the cannons never arrived, Floyd's order having been canceled by his successor, Joseph Holt.[99] Second, a statute permitted the War Department to sell off weapons and ordnance "which . . . shall appear to be damaged, or otherwise unsuitable for the public service." Under that authority, Floyd had sold to "sundry persons and States" some 31,610 muskets at a paltry $2.50 each. The House Committee on Military Affairs concluded that only by "a very liberal construction" of the statute could such sales be deemed appropriate.[100]

The majority and minority of the House's select committee issued their respective reports on February 21. With the congressional session and Buchanan's administration both coming to an end in just eleven days, nothing could be accomplished.[101] If the times had not been out of joint, and if Buchanan had even a few months left in office, Floyd's misconduct, when added to every other irregularity in Buchanan's administration, would undoubtedly have triggered broader and more sustained congressional inquiries, followed by criminal referrals.[102] Decades later, for example, a former aide to General Scott wrote that Floyd had purposely "scattered" army units to render them unavailable to garrison Southern forts and that Scott could not personally bring in troops from these 198 "remote posts" without Floyd's assent, which he would not give.[103] While some demanded Floyd's prosecution, significant evidence would be derived from admissions he had made to congressional committeemen prior to his departure from Washington, and by law that evidence could not then be used in any subsequent trial against him.[104] In light of that problem, Robert Ould, U.S. district attorney for the District of Columbia, asked that all charges against Floyd be dropped.[105] When Virginia later joined the seceded states, Ould would resign and become the Commonwealth's assistant secretary of war, undoubtedly receiving many handshakes for his refusal to indict. So numerous had Floyd's problems been, however, that a prosecution could have been mounted even without the inculpatory statements he had made to Congress.

Given Floyd's various dealings in arms, his refusal to entertain Scott's requests to redeploy troops, and his "principled" resignation because Buchanan would not order Anderson back to Fort Moultrie, secessionists would ignore the scandal that actually drove him from office and view him as a hero. Shortly after Lincoln took office, the *Atlanta Confederacy* editorialized:

> But for the foresight and firmness and patriotic providence of John B. Floyd, in what stress and peril would the cotton States be floundering this day! He saw the inevitable doom of the union, or the doom of his own people. For many months past, from his standpoint, he had an expanded field of vision. . . . The North had the heavy guns, the light arms, the powder and ball, just as the North had everything else that belong to the common Government. How quietly [at Floyd's direction] were men shifted from our soil who might have been here to-day to murder us at Abraham Lincoln's order. How slender the garrisons became in Southern forts which were made for us and belong to nobody else, but which a savage enemy now chafes and rages to get possession of. Who sent 37,000 stand of arms to Georgia? How came 60,000 more prime death-dealing rifles at Jackson, Mississippi? . . . We owe to John B. Floyd an eternal tribute of gratitude.[106]

Floyd had been treated upon his homecoming to Virginia as a moral exemplar, and he said in a speech, "I undertook so to dispose of the power in my hands, that when the terrific hour came, you . . . and all of you, and each of you, should say, 'this man has done his duty.'"[107]

Floyd would be commissioned a brigadier general in the Confederate army, where his military career against the Union would be marked by incompetence and cowardice.[108] But the Cotton South chose to ignore all this, and at his death in 1863 (reportedly from typhus and jaundice contracted in the field), it was for disloyal activity as a member of Buchanan's cabinet that he was most admired, so much so that even the appropriate, ministerial acts of arms distribution in which he engaged were looked upon retrospectively as clever schemes to arm the South. The obituary carried in John Moncure Daniel's *Daily Richmond Examiner* and the *Baltimore Examiner* went so far as to declare that "the Southern Confederacy would not and could not be in existence" but for Floyd's conduct as Buchanan's secretary of war.[109]

4

Crossing the Bar

THE U.S. NAVY WAS COMPOSED OF OLD SHIPS UNDER SAIL, SHIPS REFITTED to combine sail with steam propulsion by paddle wheel, and a new generation of screw-driven ships with or without ancillary sails.[1] If Buchanan, under pressure from Unionists in his cabinet, decided to accede to Scott's plan to reinforce Fort Sumter, naval squadrons deployed in the Pacific, the East Indies, Africa, Brazil, and the Mediterranean—about twenty-eight vessels in all—would be irrelevant, given the time necessary to notify them, bring them home, and prepare them. Several dozen ships lay in domestic ports but were unfit for service. Just as Floyd was accused of scattering troops to the western frontiers, so would Navy Secretary Isaac Toucey be denounced for rendering numerous vessels unavailable.[2] A president could, of course, order that far-flung ships be brought home and/or that ships not ready for service be made ready. Once word got out—as it immediately would—a president might say, as Scott had said in Charleston in the 1830s, that having assets nearby and ready was not the same as committing them to battle. Buchanan, however, had no impulse to prepare for conflict and/or to give the secessionists pause by a show of strength. Nor, of course, would he ask Lincoln or Seward—his political enemies—whether they wanted ships ordered to return from abroad.

Toucey did have available the Home Squadron, eighteen vessels, including screw and side-wheeled steamers as well as several sailing ships. Alfred Thayer Mahan deemed this latter category "substantially worthless," although some were under consideration for conversion to steam.[3] "Home" was only a relative term, in that its jurisdiction spread from Newfoundland to Brazil, and at this juncture three of its ships were at Veracruz in Mexico, three were some-where off Cuba policing the slave trade, and three would soon be departing for Pensacola in the Florida Panhandle, home to several federal installations.

USS *Brooklyn* [ca. 1890s]. Library of Congress, LC-D4-20166.

Brooklyn was at Norfolk, while the twin-screw sloop of war *Pawnee*, displacing 1,533 tons, was moored at Philadelphia.

In 1858, Secretary of War Floyd had retained James St. Clair Morton, a brilliant army engineer who had for a time worked on Fort Sumter, to study how harbor fortifications might best be employed against substantial attacks. Given Floyd's other conduct, his motives may have been questionable. In any event, Morton had advised that while the U.S. Navy had no vessels capable of traversing the sandbar outside Charleston's bar in combat, two federal agencies under the aegis of the Treasury did: the U.S. Revenue Marine and the U.S. Coast Survey, comprising together five or six vessels.[4] The Revenue cutter *Harriet Lane*, drawing ten feet of water, was advanced in design and highly maneuverable, called by Lieutenant David Dixon Porter "the best craft we have . . . of her size."[5] The commander of a South Carolina militia brigade, James Simons, told Governor Pickens that if the Union wished to send reinforcements to Fort Sumter, the navy would likely appropriate *Harriet Lane* from the Treasury, and since Morris Island's defenses were so far composed of only three 24-pound cannons, manned not by experienced artillerymen but by cadets from the local military school (the Citadel), *Harriet Lane* "will steam by at fourteen knots per hour, and in fifteen minutes the reinforcements will

Revenue cutter *Harriet Lane*. *Harper's Weekly* (March 13, 1858).

be landed" at Fort Sumter.[6] Simons added that his supply and communication lines were all within the range of Fort Sumter's guns, while Fort Moultrie (as Anderson could have told him) was "untenable" against fire from Sumter and would fall "after a very short and bloody contest." Augustus Baldwin Longstreet, president of South Carolina College, agreed with Simons, urging local forces not to fire upon the cutter if it entered the harbor, since their "few worthless shots" would invite Sumter to fire upon Moultrie, leaving "hundreds of our sons . . . buried in its ruins," the survivors to await "the wrath of the United States upon our devoted city! . . . Let the first shot come from the enemy," Longstreet implored; "burn that precept into your hearts."[7]

No captain would enter unfamiliar waters unless they had been reliably sounded and charted to give him a comfortable margin. While naval warfare was known to schoolchildren as epochal broadside encounters by massive ships-of-the-line off coasts with exotic names, actual experience was more varied. In August 1855 near Kulan, China, two launches and a cutter lowered from the side-wheel steam sloop USS *Powhatan* engaged and defeated piratical war junks in a bay too shallow to accommodate *Powhatan's* twenty-feet, nine-inch draft.[8] Although Britain's Royal Navy was universally known for its victory off Trafalgar, its success in the Crimean War (1853–1856) stemmed in large part from a totally different form of naval engagement in which, after a frustrating year employing vessels too large to enter the relevant bays and estuaries, W. H. Walker's small, screw-driven gunboats were used to good effect.[9] Lieutenant David Farragut had requested permission from the U.S. Navy to visit Crimea in order to ascertain whether the array of vessels used, including one drawing only six feet, eight inches of water and capable of making seven knots per hour while carrying a sixty-eight-pound and a thirty-two-pound gun as well as two twenty-four-pound howitzers amidships, exhibited features Americans might imitate. Although Farragut, a brilliant tactician, might have gleaned and imparted much useful information regarding the new shallow-draft steamers, the navy refused to finance the trip.[10]

For decades, the United States and Great Britain had shared the responsibility of intercepting unlawful shipments of slaves from Africa and Cuba into Southern ports. When in the 1850s the United States accused the British of boarding U.S.-flag ships in search of hidden slaves, the British replied that such boardings were necessary because slave ships commonly carried U.S. flags and raised them in order to avoid inspection.[11] With unlawful boardings still in memory from the War of 1812, Stephen R. Mallory (D/FL), chairman of the Senate Naval Affairs Committee, and Thomas S. Bocock (D/VA), chairman of the House counterpart, initiated legislation to obtain smaller vessels to protect Southern ports from possible interventions by British warships.[12] Because the British boats "draw but six and a half feet of water," Mallory urged, they "can enter the very smallest harbors in our country. Are we not to build vessels to follow them in?" (suggesting that this ally against the slave trade was a putative enemy). Mallory asserted that no U.S. man-of-war had entered the port of Charleston since 1832, implying that small British craft could wreak havoc there (with Fort Sumter still under construction) as U.S. Navy ships—their drafts too deep to transect the bar outside Charleston Harbor—looked on helplessly from offshore.

In his report of December 1, 1856, Toucey's predecessor as navy secretary, James C. Dobbin of North Carolina, recommended the construction of small-draft sloops, each fitted out with a formidable fifteen to twenty guns and capable "of entering such ports as New Orleans, Savannah, and Charleston" in order to defend harbors "inaccessible to the larger class of heavier draught."[13] In June 1858, Congress passed, and President Buchanan signed, a bill calling for the speedy construction of seven screw sloops with drafts not to exceed fourteen feet, combining "the heaviest armament and the greatest speed compatible with their character and tonnage," as well as one side-wheel steamer with a draft under eight feet "for service in the China seas," with a combined appropriation of $1.2 million.[14] Between August 1858 and December 1860, the U.S. brig *Dolphin* (with a draft of thirteen feet) and the screw steamers *Mohawk* (fourteen feet), *Wyandotte* (fourteen feet), and *Crusader* (twelve feet, six inches) captured nine slavers, Toucey having urged that the Gulf of Mexico should "swarm with these floating fortifications."[15] Nevertheless, the money for the June 1858 bill was not appropriated within the twelve months allowed, and in June 1860, Senator Mallory, chairman of the relevant appropriations committee, introduced a new bill to construct seven steam sloops under fourteen feet in draft "to be employed in the suppression of the slave trade."[16] Mallory, a substantial slaveholder who in less than a year would employ his maritime expertise as secretary of the Confederate navy, knew that the Republicans were likely to win the November election and that the likely reaction of slave states would be secession. At a time when many slaveless Southerners wanted to reopen the slave trade to drive down slave prices, Mallory's motivation in wanting shallow-draft vessels built and stationed in Southern ports to police the slave trade—like the motivations of Floyd and Toucey—might well be questioned.[17] On February 21, 1861, with Mallory, Jefferson Davis, and dozens of other Southerners no longer in Washington and armed conflict likely with the newly formed Confederate States of America, Congress, seeing that any conflict would involve harbors, again ordered the speedy construction of seven sloops with drafts not exceeding fourteen feet.[18]

"Now Rolls a Dangerous Breaker"

Comparing the several seventeenth- and eighteenth-century depictions of Charleston's harbor with modern maps, it is impossible to know how much the seeming distortions should be ascribed to the vagaries of primitive cartography, and how much the configuration of the seashore actually changed.[19] In the decades between 1776 and 1861, Sullivan's Island, a "verdureless sandrift" whose southwestern face forms one side of the harbor's mouth, had been dramatically transformed by hurricanes and gales, one of which had obliterated what was left of the primitive palmetto-and-sand fort defended by William Moultrie during the Revolution, as well as its "First System" replacement from the 1790s.[20] By the 1830s, the sea had reclaimed perhaps 250 yards of beach and so encroached upon the third Fort Moultrie (dating from 1809) as to initiate its demise. But then Captain Alexander H. Bowman of the Army Corps of Engineers built a jetty system that reversed the erosion, so that by the time Major Anderson arrived in November 1860, it was not the ravages of seawater but the aggregation of sea- and wind-borne sand that encroached.[21]

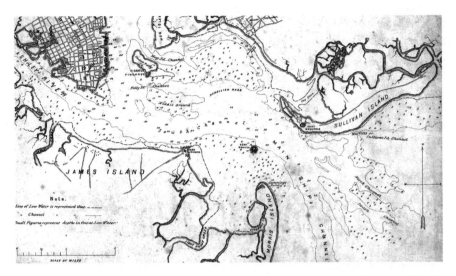

"Plan of Charleston Harbor, and Its Fortifications" (detail). Compiled by Eliot & Ames, 1861. Library of Congress G39124.C4_1861.E5.

More dramatic still had been the transformations at the southern lip of the harbor mouth, where a storm obliterated the inlets separating Morrison, Cumming's, and Middle Bay (a.k.a. "Coffin") Islands, thus forming an aggregated landmass named not by combining syllables from all three constituents, but rather by excising two letters from the smallest, thus verbally yielding: "Morris Island."[22]

Most of the sand that made up the bar outside Charleston Harbor was deposited by waves and storms from offshore.[23] In 1770, the bar reportedly lay twelve feet deep at low tide, while in 1851 the figure was 10.7 feet.[24] The latter measurement was an average of innumerable soundings taken, and would not account for the many shoals that brought the bar in places much closer to the surface—suddenly after a storm, or gradually, and for unpredictable intervals. It was commented in 1857 that a large ship drawing fifteen or twenty feet might easily cross the bar on one day, "and on the next, after a storm from the eastward, the sand is up to the very throats of the buoys."[25]

It was an era of substantial investigations of oceans, currents, and tides, much of it by indefatigable U.S. Navy specialists.[26] Tidal inflows from and outflows through the mouth of the harbor were said in one estimate to average 3.65 billion cubic feet per each ebb tide.[27] By the 1850s, decades of this action, combined with various gales, hurricanes, and swells, had so scoured the southern tip of Sullivan's Island and the northern tip of Morris Island as to widen the harbor mouth by no less than three-fourths of a mile. As with all littoral activity, the situation at any given moment was the net result of the fluctuating relative strength of various complementary and contrary forces.[28] The bar, with its northern extremity near Sullivan's Island, paralleled Morris Island and then curved slightly westward before reaching Folly Island. As of 1860, the bar varied in width from 3.5 miles due east of Fort Sumter to only half a mile east of Lighthouse Inlet.

The bar was commonly transected by four to six channels, with the depth of each varying between twelve feet and thirteen and a half feet at mean low tide, subject to disappearance and reemergence.[29] An 1836 navy study identified four channels, three of which were not navigable by large vessels. Harbor pilots told the naval commissioners that the recent erection of the foundation for Fort Sumter in the harbor mouth had already caused a considerable deepening of the channel moving through the mouth of the harbor just north of the fort. While this new scouring of the bottom apparently spent its force just outside the harbor mouth without actually cutting into—much less forming a new channel transecting—the sandbar, "the effect of so much power," they speculated, if aided by dredging machines, might someday make for a fine harbor entrance. As things were, the fourth channel then in existence, the so-called Main Ship Channel, was deep enough for the passage of large vessels but was subject "to great changes from heavy gales." Among these changes, it had been "entirely removed from its former site" by the extraordinary processes constituting littoral drift, which over the course of the prior twenty years had gradually caused it to shift to the south a reported half a mile, so that "where formerly passed in security ships of seventeen and eighteen feet draught of water, now rolls a dangerous breaker" over sands just below the surface. In 1831, the shoreline opposite what was then the western outlet of the Main Ship Channel was chosen as the site of a fixed-range beacon to guide ships approaching the channel's eastern opening from seaward. By 1850, however, littoral drift had moved the channel 320 yards south of the beacon, another twenty-six yards in the following year.

The task of the commissioners in the naval study, pursuant to a Senate resolution, had been to study ports south of the Chesapeake for the purpose of choosing a site for a navy yard, their criteria including a "sufficient depth of water to permit free access, at any state of tide, for the heaviest class of ships of war." A long list of prominent Charlestonians submitted to the Senate Committee on Naval Affairs a petition urging that their city be awarded the yard, its advantages including a harbor that was "already strongly fortified."

Two of those on the list, Alfred Huger and James Louis Petigru, could high-light the city's alleged loyalty to the Union by pointing to its recent defeat of the nullifiers, a defeat more accurately ascribed to President Jackson's threats, to Congress's internal negotiations, and to work by Huger, Petigru, and their comrades. But the Main Ship Channel's depths had been variously reported, one observer believing that its seaward entrée was 10.6 feet at mean low water, but decreased to a mere 8.7 feet during the ebb phase of spring tides, making it undependable.[30] Moreover, contemplating that the Main Ship Channel would likely be blocked altogether by some future storm, the commissioners thought "that a new, more convenient, and perhaps deeper channel" could be carved out by placing obstructions in the path of the outgoing tidal current, so as to direct all of the tide's force narrowly. The commissioners determined, however, that neither this nor the other channels across the bar would admit vessels drawing more than eighteen and a half feet, and even ships of that size would need "the aid of steam, a good tide, and smooth water," thus causing the sandbar to disqualify Charleston as the situs for a federal navy yard. John C. Calhoun, the nullifiers' intellectual leader, would now urge that federal money be withdrawn from "internal improvements" he thought useless, such as the Cumberland Road, and instead be applied to protection of the "long maritime frontier," beginning with $95,000 for a dry dock at Pensacola, which he saw as "all-important for the protection of Southern interests."[31]

In 1857, U.S. Army engineers built a new range beacon on the mainland, just opposite what was now the western terminus of the Main Ship Channel. A formidable 102 feet from base to lantern, with a focal plane 133 feet above mean sea level, the beacon was visible in clear weather from twenty nautical miles out. From the seaward side of the bar at night but in fair weather, a local pilot could thus locate the eastern entrance to the Main Ship Channel by lining himself up with the beacon and then follow the buoys in place the length of the passage. On December 20, 1860, the day South Carolina seceded, Raphael Semmes of Alabama, secretary of the federal Lighthouse Board, announced that the federal government had no authority to maintain lighthouses on the coast of South Carolina "against her will," a statement that would have mystified the framers of the Constitution.[32] South Carolina seized the tower and beacon, dismantled its advanced Fresnel lens, pulled up all buoys marking this and the other channels transecting the bar, and withdrew the familiar lightship formerly moored at Rattlesnake Shoal, off the northern end of Sullivan's Island.[33]

While the sandbar had once cost Charleston its bid to become a base for the U.S. Navy, it was now the city's best defense against that navy. Governor

Pickens asked Charleston's harbormaster and three pilots how a large vessel might—with no guidance—nevertheless negotiate one of the several channels, and whether such ingress could be blocked by sinking stone-laden hulks in those channels. They replied (although others would disagree) that vessels drawing up to sixteen feet could enter the harbor via the Sullivan's Island Channel, also known as Maffitt's Channel, and that planting obstacles to block the channel would not work.[34] As all observers understood, flooding and ebbing currents, when intensified by gales and outflows of the Cooper, Wando, and Ashley Rivers, could scour many tons of lightly packed sand and silt in just hours and might entomb a stone-laden hulk in tons of newly deposited sand while cutting a new channel around it. Such transformations had already been noted by the Revenue cutter *Gallatin*, the vessel formerly employed by President Jackson to challenge the nullifiers, while that vessel was taking soundings. Although Maffitt's Channel had remained fairly stable for decades, in the ebb phase of spring tides, when the moon, earth, and sun are particularly aligned, its clearances could decrease by two feet. *Gallatin's* commander, U.S. Navy lieutenant John N. Maffitt (in whose honor this passage was named by appreciative Charlestonians), had found it in 1852 "full of lumps" because of sand accreting around buoy moorings. Since their attendant buoys had long since become untethered and swept away by storms, the moorings could not easily be retrieved so that tidal currents could again pass unimpeded and keep the channel clear.[35] A "New Middle" (a.k.a. "Coast Survey") Channel had emerged and was identified in 1850, although its discoverer noted that when a small vessel foundered several hundred yards to its north and then drifted southward and dropped to the channel floor in February 1851, a six-foot shoal of sand formed around the wreck.[36] The North Channel had been preferred by the Northern coasting trade in happier days, but a natural bulkhead of fine sand athwart its eastern, ocean-side mouth afforded it a mere eight feet at mean low water, decreasing to six feet during the worst springtide conditions. Because it was narrow and shoaled, it could be negotiated only by marking it with buoys, and Governor Pickens had removed them.

Each channel, then, presented a bad gamble for a ship of size attempting an unconsented transection of the bar.[37] Launches and boats of light draft as used in Crimea might cross the bar at will, day or night, without searching for a channel.[38] Gustavus Vasa Fox, a retired navy officer with substantial experience in the coasting trade, would write that "at high water and smooth sea the bar is perfectly accessible to vessels drawing . . . seven feet of water," although the U.S. Navy could not make the approach because steamers of such light draft had not yet been built.[39] A common tidal increase of five feet from low to high water would accommodate somewhat larger vessels if they negotiated one of these passageways at the flood, but that would require good timing and some luck.

It had been axiomatic that in an exchange of fire between warships and shore batteries, with each side firing an equal number of guns of equivalent gauges, the batteries would prevail.[40] The captain of a warship large enough to engage Charleston's shore batteries as they were in January 1861 would need to consider the risks of attempting to transect the bar through one of the channels, since running aground on the bar would doom any vessel as a stationary target.[41] Knowledgeable pilots, if asked, would have said that only the Main Ship Channel might be located and used without navigational aids. A vessel successfully transecting the bar that way would then turn to starboard and parallel Morris Island for its entire four-mile length. Because Pickens had removed the south-facing beacon built behind and above Fort Moultrie, this could not be accomplished on a moonless night. And as any adverse ship approached the harbor entrance from the south, either during the day or by moonlight, it would encounter fire from the guns now being placed along Morris Island and at Cumming's Point upon its northern tip. If, to avoid these defenses, the intruder instead chose the narrow and shoal-ridden Maffitt's Channel, it would pass the batteries on Sullivan's Island at close quarters. With batteries thus on both the southern and the northern lip of the harbor entrance, each only thirteen hundred yards from its center, any ship that got that far and turned into the harbor would be fired upon from both sides and by whatever armed vessels the Carolinians brought to bear.[42]

Star of the West

Governor Pickens had spies in a number of ports, and the outfitting of *Brooklyn* in Norfolk triggered heightened vigilance. This screw sloop, launched in 1858, displaced 2,532 tons and drew sixteen feet, three inches, with a ship's complement commonly at 335.[43] Although its draft could be reduced to perhaps fifteen feet by carrying less coal, this was still much too deep to try negotiating a channel across the bar, either stealthily at night or in daylight under fire.[44] Thus, General Scott, in choosing *Brooklyn* as part of a plan to reinforce Fort Sumter, apparently intended to position that ship east of the bar with its nine-inch guns providing coverage for entry by a lighter vessel.[45]

Although James Simons had thought his South Carolina brigade unprepared, General Scott may have received reports that the Carolinians' batteries were multiplying and would fire to good effect. He may have come to believe that *Brooklyn*, despite its many guns, could not from outside the bar disperse the vessels that would assail *Harriet Lane* as it entered the harbor. In any event, Scott scrapped the *Lane/Brooklyn* plan, choosing instead on January 2, 1861, to hire a two-decked, side-wheeled passenger steamer: *Star of the West*. Seward's political advisor, Thurlow Weed, apparently helped in what would have been a delicate negotiation: chartering a commercial vessel (at $1,250 per day) to engage in a military operation from which it might well not return. Under the plan, the steamer would file official papers in New York to clear a coastal cruise ending at New Orleans (its usual destination), but this time, instead of civilian passengers, it would covertly board two hundred recruits from a steam tug off Staten Island, who would be hidden below deck as the vessel approached Charleston.[46] Just why Scott opted for stealth is unclear. When Buchanan later asked Toucey, he could answer only that he supposed Scott had been convinced by unidentified "advisers outside of the Administration." Buchanan guessed that the idea of using a civilian vessel came from Gustavus Fox, the ex-navy man who had often cruised Carolina's waters as an officer on passenger vessels.[47]

On Saturday, January 5, Pickens's agent in Norfolk sent a telegram: "*Brooklyn* still at navy-yard, now 5 P.M., and no steam"—meaning that the ship was not preparing to depart. That agent apparently talked to locals or to crew members that weekend, and on Monday, January 7, stated that *Brooklyn* would probably move across the mouths of the Elizabeth and James Rivers to have additional guns mounted at Hampton Roads (it would soon have a formidable twenty-five) but that its destination was probably not Charleston.[48] In New York a few days before, any curious person who might stroll along the Warren Street quay or offer a round of drinks in any nearby tavern frequented by stevedores would come to know that boxes being stowed on *Star of the West* were addressed to Fort Sumter. Monday's *New York Times* announced that three hundred marines had boarded a tug at Governor's Island on Saturday night and proceeded to New York's Lower Bay, where they were transferred to the outbound *Star of the West*. The ship was thus "already on her way to Charleston" to relieve "the gallant Major Anderson," its arrival off Charleston to be early Tuesday morning, January 8. The report was accurate enough. The ship had thrown off its lines about 5:00 p.m. on Saturday, hove to in the Lower Bay and took on 200–250 members of the Ninth Infantry, and then crossed the bar off Sandy Hook by 9 p.m.[49] Bradley S. Osbon of the *New York World*, a journalist of substantial maritime experience including cutlass encounters with Chinese pirates, had allegedly been invited to cover the operation, only to find when he arrived at the wharf that the vessel had departed early. William

Conan Church of the *Evening Post* was more fortunate and would thus enjoy exclusive coverage.[50]

On Tuesday, William Tecumseh Sherman, a retired military officer from Ohio who had become superintendent of the new Louisiana State Seminary of Learning and Military Academy (the predecessor of Louisiana State University), gathered from New Orleans papers that Buchanan had refused to reinforce Anderson. He reacted with disgust, noting that he would never serve such a timid government.[51] Greeley's *Tribune* that day regurgitated what the *Times* had broken the day before.[52] Senator Wigfall in a telegram told Governor Pickens that the ship "may be hourly expected off the harbor."[53] An informer ferreted out and passed on to Pickens the fact that behind the charter Weed had negotiated was General Scott—a long-time friend of Senator Seward.[54] On January 9, Pickens ordered a militia officer to hide "three hundred picked Riflemen" below decks on the steamer *Marion* and prevent the *Star of the West* from effecting the reinforcement.[55] On January 10, Pickens's spy in Norfolk reported that *Brooklyn* had left under sealed orders from Washington.[56] The next day, Pickens received word from a spy in Washington that *Brooklyn* was "due at Charleston now."[57]

Scott had chosen to live in New York, with no clear chains of command between him and the various administrative and logistical staffs working in Washington.[58] On January 5, the day *Star of the West* left New York, Scott in a handwritten memorandum had told Lieutenant Colonel Lorenzo Thomas, assistant adjutant general, that Major Anderson should be advised of the relief effort and instructed that if South Carolina's batteries opened fire upon any vessel appearing to bring reinforcements or supplies, he was authorized to "silence such fire."[59] This dispatch, instructions to a local commander regarding an operation to begin imminently that would likely involve many deaths and undoubtedly start a civil war, was sufficiently important to merit timely and secure delivery—either by hand or by multiple means. Yet the document never reached Anderson.[60] Whether the failure was due to negligence by Thomas (who was duly promoted thereafter), or to disloyal or merely incompetent elements in the War Department, or to some disruption of communication en route, was never revealed.

Since Sumter had only a small fraction of the artillerymen for which it was designed, its commander might well have requested from his superiors hundreds of additional men. But Major Anderson, having repeatedly asked Floyd for help a month before, and having then infuriated locals with a secret transfer to Sumter that neither Floyd nor Buchanan would support, concluded that Carolinians would not now tolerate any reinforcement effort. On

January 6, unaware that a relief effort had in fact departed New York the night before, Anderson wrote to Scott that local batteries would make entry by any Union ship "dangerous and difficult," while the men and assets he already had could hold Fort Sumter "against any force which can be brought against me." Nor, Anderson added, did reinforcements make sense if Buchanan's policy was (as newspapers had suggested) evacuation.[61]

On January 8, one of the newspapers delivered to Anderson's garrison reported that *Star of the West* would arrive that night with reinforcements. This might reasonably have suggested within the fort a preparation for battle, or at least a meeting among officers to decide how to respond if the ship did appear. Apparently Anderson convened no such meeting. Newspapers often published unsubstantiated rumors that would prove to be groundless, and perhaps Anderson could not believe that Washington would attempt reinforcement (1) with a civilian vessel and (2) without notifying him.[62]

Scott now attempted to abort the operation. It had required secrecy, and South Carolina now knew at least as much as the *New York Times* had revealed.[63] Second, on the night of Saturday, January 5, after *Star of the West* left New York, intelligence arrived to the effect that a heavy battery had been erected on Morris Island "which would probably destroy any unarmed vessel."[64] Third, Scott now had in hand Anderson's January 6 letter stating that he neither needed nor wanted help. But *Star of the West* was at sea, and Scott had failed to include in his plan any midcourse rendezvous (with *Brooklyn* or otherwise) to effect a last-minute adjustment or cancellation.

A steam voyage from New York to Charleston commonly took sixty hours. A dispatch to Greeley's *Tribune* telegraphed from Washington correspondent James S. Pike on January 8 and published on January 9 speculated that because Charleston remained quiet, the reinforcement had already occurred.[65] *Star of the West* had in fact run ahead of schedule and on January 8 had stopped for several hours some seventy miles northeast of Charleston, where the soldiers passed the time fishing. Resuming its journey and extinguishing its lights, it arrived off the Charleston bar at 1:30 a.m. on January 9. Before dawn, Lieutenant Charles R. Woods, unaware that South Carolina knew everything, ordered the troops below.[66] Captain John McGowan brought on deck the provisions for Anderson's garrison, believing that if his vessel was disabled near Sumter, he still might complete the mission with his six lifeboats.[67] Although McGowan had previously commanded a Revenue cutter and knew how to track smugglers through shoaled waters in the dark, he and Walter Brewer, the New York pilot he had retained for this operation, also knew that the draft of his vessel made it impossible for him to mimic the evasive tricks of lighter craft. McGowan wrote, "We proceeded with caution, running very slow and sounding" until about 4:00 a.m., when the vessel, with a draft of twenty-four feet, six inches, hove to in twenty-seven feet of water to await daylight. At Fort Sumter, men at reveille espied a ship at anchor off the bar, some concluding that Washington had decided upon a peaceful withdrawal and had thus provided commercial transportation.[68] While there had been no prior consultation with Sumter about navigation (or anything else), McGowan, seeing a beacon through the haze and knowing that locals had extinguished all other lights, concluded that it emanated from Fort Sumter and "after getting the bearings of it we steered to the S.W." to locate the Main Ship Channel.[69]

The new South Carolina Coast Police had purchased suitable small craft to cruise the bar and the harbor mouth, commanded by men who had recently resigned commissions in the U.S. Navy or had been students at Annapolis.[70] *General Clinch*, a small South Carolina side-wheeled steamer laying off the bar, saw *Star of the West* and signaled with one blue and two red lights. When McGowan, not knowing the local code, failed to respond, *General Clinch*, with a draft of less than nine feet, crossed the bar, steamed ahead in the Main Ship Channel, and began firing alarm rockets.[71] At 7:00 a.m., at ebb tide and in weak January light, *Star of the West* successfully transected the bar and turned to starboard to steam parallel to Morris Island toward the harbor entrance. Soon it attracted a shot across the bow from the masked battery on Morris Island, about eleven hundred yards distant. Fired at an angle of less than five degrees by cadets of the Citadel commanded by their superintendent, Major P. F. Stevens, it ricocheted across the water but spent its force and fell short.

Star of the West flew a U.S. flag from its flagstaff and, following the first shot, hoisted a U.S. ensign at the fore. A second shot skipped off the ocean one hundred yards short and then flew "clean over our vessel, aft, nearly on a line with the head of a sailor, but, luckily, a little above it." Another shot from the cadets' first gun ricocheted across the surface of the sea and fell short, while a fourth bounded and hit the hull abaft the fore-rigging and two feet above the waterline, just below the mate taking soundings.[72] Although Woods's men, hidden below, had mattresses with which to seal any hole, the ball's energy was too spent to break through the hull. Another reportedly hit the stack.

Fort Sumter was a mere 1,210 yards from Cumming's Point at the northern tip of Morris Island, from where Carolinians could fire both at Sumter and at ships navigating the Main Ship Channel and entering the harbor.[73] Sumter and Fort Moultrie, 1,820 yards apart, were positioned to offer overlapping firing zones against hostile ships, and while neither was designed

Star of the West fired upon by batteries on Morris Island and Fort Moultrie as depicted in *Frank Leslie's Illustrated* (January 19, 1861).

or intended to fire upon the other, each was in range of the other's guns of larger bore. Since only a fortnight had passed since Anderson had ordered the disabling or destruction of armament at Moultrie, it could now bring to bear against *Star of the West* only one operative weapon. Its two shots missed, the closer splashing half a mile short.[74]

When the vessel was less than two miles from both Sumter and Moultrie, two steamers emerged from Moultrie's wharf, one of them towing an armed schooner. Having not received Scott's notice (which de facto replaced Floyd's month-old order to remain on the defensive), Anderson did not know that he could open fire. In a quickly convened meeting in Sumter's laundry room, five of Anderson's officers stated that the flag was being insulted and Sumter must intervene. Five referred to Floyd's order and warned that to engage was to start a war. Anderson, breaking the tie, ordered his men to stand down.[75]

Star of the West turned about and retraced its route, taking another hit in its starboard quarter, for a total of either two or three hits out of some seven to seventeen shots reportedly fired. One of McGowan's officers wittily noted that the Charlestonians' hospitality exceeded his expectation in that "they gave us several balls."[76] On Morris Island, the cadets' performance had been sufficiently creditable that they could call themselves the "Star of the West Battery." Now the retreating vessel was again out of range, touching bottom two or three times as it transected the bar, attaining open water at 8:50 a.m.[77]

"A Magnet of Great Power"

The cannon fire had been audible and visible ashore. Anna Brackett, a teacher from Massachusetts preparing her lesson plan in Charleston's new Girls' High and Normal School, "heard the report of the first gun . . . and lifted my head to listen, with a great fear at my heart, and an effort to persuade myself that the sounds were only the effect of my excited imagination as they came and came again."[78] Catherine Edmondston noted in her diary:

> As we were dressing we suddenly heard the report of a heavy gun! Followed by another! . . . The expected re-inforcements for Sumter doubtless! . . . "Is she struck?" No! Oh she comes! Another! And another, whilst Sumter opens her Port Holes and slowly runs out her cannon, prepared for instant action. Now a heavy gun from Fort Moultrie! Will Sumter respond? No! Not yet! Another from Moultrie! How with Sumter now? Still silent! The vessel turns slowly. Is she struck? No one can tell, but slowly, reluctantly as it were, almost with a baffled look, the Steamer retreats down the channel.[79]

Suddenly the fashionable area of Charleston waterfront known as the Battery was "thronged with people . . . straining their eyes or looking through glasses out at Sumter, whose bristling front was surmounted with cannon, her flags waving defiance."[80] The January 10 *Charleston Courier* proclaimed that "the first gun of the new struggle for independence, (if struggle there is to be,) has been fired, and federal power has received its first repulse," while the Rhett family's *Mercury* urged that the state "has wiped out half a century of scorn and outrage." Others proudly used the word "revolution," thereby consciously associating the state's conduct with its patriotic victory over another oppressive imperial power eight decades before.[81]

Sullivan's Island now "swarmed with Charleston soldiery who were busily engaged in building batteries and placing in position cannon and mortars. . . . Thousands of negroes were detailed from the plantations" to build "sand batteries, bristling with guns." Fort Moultrie had generally been considered an attractive posting. And now, with all officers being local or Southern, the scene became "a magnet of great power" drawing "crowds of ladies . . . from the city in every steamer." Dress Parade at sundown each day was attended by hundreds, followed by "the pleasure of promenading with the lovely young dames of Charleston on the wide, firm beach." "Dashing young cavaliers . . . who scorned the Yankee scum," Whitelaw Reid later noted,

> rushed madly into the war as into a picnic. Here the boats from Charleston landed every day cases of champagne, *patés* innumerable, casks of claret, thousands of Havana cigars. . . . Here, with feasting, and dancing,

and love making, with music improvised from the ball room . . . the young men who had ruled "society" at Newport and Saratoga, and whose advent North had always been waited for as the opening of the season, dashed into revolution as they would into a waltz. Not one of them doubted that, only a few months later, he should make his accustomed visit to the Northern watering places, and be received with the distinction due to a hero of Southern independence.[82]

After this jubilation at victory in the first clash, however, the city showed signs of concern. "If a door slammed, we stopped talking, and looked at each other; and if the sound was repeated, we went to the window and listened for Fort Sumter. . . . Women trembled at the salutes which were fired in honor of the secession of other States, fearing lest the struggle had commenced and the dearly-loved son or brother in volunteer uniform was already under the storm of the columbiads" (the wide-bore iron howitzers of significant lethality).[83] A Northern visitor sensed in Charleston a new air of sobriety. The "dandified suits and superb silks" of prior years had disappeared; now the fashionable were buying nothing new "because the guns of Major Anderson might any day send the whole city into mourning." Patricians "discharged their foreign cooks and put their daughters into the kitchen."[84]

"Maj. A's Heart Is Not with His Duty"

Anderson advised Pickens that "an unarmed vessel bearing the flag of my Government" had been attacked, and if Pickens failed to disclaim responsibility, Anderson would consider it an act of war and retaliate against local shipping.[85] Pickens, undoubtedly wondering whether Anderson actually believed this, asserted that the vessel carried troops and that President Buchanan had been on notice that any reinforcement attempt would be looked upon "as an act of hostility." Pickens, although often verbally reckless, had also been a diplomat, and he undoubtedly chose that term over Anderson's "act of war" because if the head of one nation (which he considered himself to be) accuses another of an "act of war," the consequences may be difficult to contain. As to Anderson's threat to retaliate, Pickens dismissed that as an attempt by the United States to treat South Carolina as "a conquered province," an allusion to what had been for decades the major rationale for secession: that the North had unconstitutionally rejected the sovereignty of states.[86]

Anderson wrote to a friend that he had been "sorely tempted" to open fire, but "my defenses were just then in such a condition that I could not have opened the war," a fortunate happenstance because his silence preserved "the chance of having matters settled without bloodshed."[87] This statement was disingenuous. After he saw the *New York Times*, if his guns were not ready, that was his choice. And even if there had been no newspaper report, once *General Clinch* (named for Anderson's father-in-law) fired signal rockets, a bugle call to general quarters at Fort Sumter was required. That Anderson and his officers met in the laundry room to discuss their options—even after the Southern firing had begun—would suggest that there was still time to load and fire some rounds, and Catherine Edmondston reported seeing Sumter's iron shutters opened and its guns run out. Anderson had previously told Charleston friends that he would do his utmost to avoid war. Because he chose not to engage, the Civil War did not begin that morning. Although a month earlier Southerners had characterized Anderson's move to Sumter as an act of aggression, some within Sumter were now troubled by his passivity. Captain Foster had been observed leaving the laundry room meeting "smashing his hat, and muttering something about the flag, of which the words 'trample on it' reached the ears of the men at the guns."[88] If even one of Anderson's guns had fired, perhaps Captain McGowan on *Star of the West*, rather than being nonplussed by Sumter's silence, might have completed his approach.

Anderson continued to monitor with field glasses and report to Washington the ongoing construction of batteries. Abner Doubleday, second in rank to Anderson, later conjectured that as Anderson's adopted state of Georgia prepared to secede, Anderson appeared to confine his efforts to securing the fort against attack, ignoring provocation as if he "desired to become a spectator."[89] A committed Unionist from upstate New York, Doubleday had spent months with Anderson during this siege, voicing bitter criticism in letters to his family and later in his memoir. As he told his brother Ulysses, steamers carrying soldiers and guns constantly passed Sumter toward Morris Island; yet Anderson, despite Doubleday's repeated requests, refused to tell Governor Pickens to stop these obvious war preparations. On January 15, Ulysses Doubleday took the extraordinary step of forwarding to President-Elect Lincoln a letter Abner had written to his wife, its contents summarized by Ulysses as alleging that the garrison's situation "grows more critical, thanks to the vacillation and incompetency of Mr. Buchanan and Maj. Anderson." Ulysses added, "All this could have been prevented. Depend upon it Maj. A's heart is not with his duty."[90] Anderson had apparently confided to his close Charleston friend Robert Gourdin that if Kentucky seceded, it would "influence" his "decision" as to what to do, although he did not clarify what he meant.[91] By one rumor, Anderson had transferred his garrison not to attain a more viable defense but to bide his time while his native Kentucky decided whether to secede. If it did—so the rumor went—Anderson would surrender.[92] Just how—theoretically—a disloyal commander could surrender an impregnable fort, manned by loyal soldiers with a second-in-command who already distrusted him, the rumormongers did not suggest.

Since Anderson had standing orders to act strictly on the defensive, received no new orders concerning *Star of the West*, and knew that by opening fire he would start the war, his decision not to engage, a decision concurred in by half his officers, was not disloyal.[93] Still, Anderson neither demanded that Pickens stop preparing for war all around him nor asked Floyd or his successor, Holt, to do so.[94] He may have felt that it would not be productive, since Pickens would undoubtedly reply that the batteries were only for defensive purposes, necessitated by: (1) Anderson's aggressive move to Sumter, in breach of President Buchanan's promise to maintain the status quo, and then followed by (2) a deceptive attempt at reinforcement. Pickens would in any event refuse, and neither Anderson nor the administration was apparently willing to enforce such a demand.

Anderson repeatedly told his Charleston friend Robert Gourdin that the Union should evacuate Sumter, an unusual admission by the fort's commander to an avowed secessionist. Not that Anderson was admitting to a likely enemy—openly or tacitly—any wavering in his own personal sense of duty. It was indicative of the fractious times that while dozens of other officers foreswore their commissions and would soon fight the Union they had once pledged to defend, this Southern officer's sense of duty to the Union, unmovable despite the perfidy (e.g., Floyd, Cooper) and incompetence (e.g., Buchanan, Scott) of his superiors, would be continuously and deeply questioned, even by his second-in-command. Doubleday was not alone in predicting that Anderson was about to change sides. But when Anderson was informed by another officer serving elsewhere that he would (in the common parlance) "go with his state," Anderson reportedly replied, "The selection of the place in which we were born was not an act of our own volition; but when we took the oath of allegiance to our Government, it was an act of our manhood, and that oath we cannot break."[95] An assistant to Scott described Anderson as "rigorously temperate and moderate" and "as honest and conscientious as it is possible for a man to be."[96]

"Anderson Could Have Put Us Out"

Scott would later complain that Navy Secretary Toucey had "forced" him to lease *Star of the West* by refusing him use of *Brooklyn* or any other warship.[97] Toucey was a convenient target because he was already under investigation by a congressional committee for aiding the secessionists. But this particular charge, first memorialized in a note by Scott to Lincoln and Seward, lacks credibility. From the start, the reinforcement urged by Scott and Holt had the support of President Buchanan. The moment Scott asked for *Brooklyn*, Toucey ordered that it be made ready.[98] Scott, upon deciding to abort, had Toucey on January 7 issue an order for *Brooklyn* to depart Norfolk and either intercept *Star of the West* at Charleston or, if it did not arrive in time to stop the attempted penetration of the harbor, provide whatever support it could from beyond the bar.[99] Thus, while *Brooklyn* had been made available to Scott as an integral part of the operation, he instead called upon it only in a last-minute act of desperation.

Brooklyn received Toucey's orders on the morning of January 9 and left Norfolk at 11:20 a.m., its captain unaware that the incursion had in fact been attempted two hours before and that *Star of the West* was already on a northern heading. The two ships would pass mutually unobserved. When *Brooklyn* arrived off Charleston on January 12, a schooner advised that the *Star of the West* incursion had failed and it had left, adding that South Carolina had now sunk five hulks to block several of the channels across the bar.[100] Among these was an old slaver that had been seized and docked at Custom House Wharf, now weighted with stone recently seized from the United States (undoubtedly Massachusetts granite for the unfinished Custom House).

Pickens sunk no hulk in Maffitt's Channel, leaving it open for approved commercial traffic.[101] A few days later, the passenger steamer *Columbia*, departing Charleston on its regular mail schedule to New York, was unable to use the Main Ship Channel because of the sunken hulks. Attempting to exit via Maffitt's Channel, it ran aground. After tugs failed to dislodge it, a decision was made to disembark the passengers to the beach.[102] When one of them, a Northerner, wandered near Fort Moultrie, a South Carolina lieutenant admitted to him that during the *Star of the West* incident "Anderson could have put us out in a short time, if he had chosen."[103] Although Anderson had left a supply of twenty-four-pound shot at Fort Moultrie, the harbor mouth had been protected only by the few guns Anderson had failed to destroy and three 24-pounders mounted on an earthwork on Morris Island. There was not one battery aimed at Sumter, and in all of Charleston there was less than twenty thousand pounds of powder, enough for no more than three hours' firing.[104]

Bradley Osbon, the New York journalist who had missed the chance to be aboard *Star of the West*, confirmed that "a very small quantity of powder was in the Charleston forts at this time, and had Major Anderson been properly advised he would have opened with his powerful guns under cover of which the *Star of the West* might have come safely to port." Osbon, a former drifter/adventurer who had lectured on places he had seen and scrapes he had gotten into, then made the extraordinary allegation that "it was never intended that she should do so. The expedition ended precisely as had been planned by those who cajoled the president and abetted secession at Washington."[105] Osbon owed to his readers—but failed to provide—real proof for what he was alleging. In an initiative plagued by a succession of avoidable mishaps, it is possible that each could have been engineered by disloyal persons within the administration. And the mission might well have succeeded, despite all the other mistakes, if Anderson had only received the order to fire upon those assailing the vessel. With respect to that problem, as with the others, one could not rule out conscious sabotage by traitors, although it seems clear that General Scott and staff failed to take the prudent step of having Anderson's orders delivered by multiple means.

While the *Star of the West* venture had risked all-out war, neither Scott nor Holt nor Buchanan left any evidence of having grasped that plain fact. While Captain McGowan averted war by turning about, the *New York Times* called his decision cowardly, suggesting that he should have proceeded under fire even if Sumter's guns remained silent.[106] The charge was an outrageous libel, absent evidence that McGowan had been ordered to reach Fort Sumter or die trying. From McGowan's perspective in that moment, having narrowly avoided being hit going in, and with Fort Sumter silent, aborting the incursion was rational. Yet Scott, after falsely alleging that he had been forced to use a civilian vessel because Toucey had failed to give him a warship, told Lincoln and Seward that the men and supplies "might have landed" but for what he called McGowan's "imbecility."[107]

"Strictly on the Defensive"

If one believed that South Carolina's secession was constitutionally privileged, then the new nation-state had defended itself against invading foreign troops concealed in a passenger ship. If one believed that secession was unconstitutional, then firing upon any identified U.S. vessel—civilian or military—was treasonous, the Constitution (Art. III § 3) defining "Treason" as, among other things "levying War against" the United States. The *New York Sun*'s January 11 headline read, "Civil War Begun!"[108] The New York legislature resolved that "treason, as defined by the Constitution . . . exists . . . and . . . the insurgent State of South Carolina, after seizing the post-office, custom-house, moneys, and fortifications of the federal government, has, by firing into a vessel ordered by the Government to convey troops and provisions to Fort Sumter, virtually declared war" on the Union. New York thus tendered to President Buchanan "whatever aid in men and money he may require to enable him to enforce the laws and uphold the authority of the federal government."[109]

Jacob Thompson, while still Buchanan's secretary of the interior, had accepted a formal assignment from his home state of Mississippi to visit North Carolina in order to persuade that state to secede. Most presidents would have reacted by firing him and perhaps jailing him, particularly after Thompson was implicated in Floyd's Indian Trust Fund scandal. But Buchanan did nothing. Thompson had informed South Carolina's Augustus Baldwin Longstreet to expect *Star of the West*'s arrival at Charleston and then resigned his cabinet post. Like Floyd, he claimed to be taking a principled stand, asserting that the *Star of the West* operation violated what Thompson alleged to be a decision by Buchanan's cabinet not to send reinforcements. Thompson then traveled home. Arriving at the depot in Oxford, Mississippi, he told an admiring audience that it had been his telegram to Longstreet that had put South Carolina troops on alert, "and when the *Star of the West* arrived, she received a warm welcome from booming cannon, and soon beat a retreat. I was rejoiced . . . that the concealed trick, first conceived by General Scott, and adopted by Secretary Holt, but countermanded by the president when too late, proved a failure." Like Floyd, Thompson was comfortable telling constituents back home what he had done for them, in derogation of his sworn duties as a federal official. When Holt charged that the information Thompson had passed to Longstreet had been obtained in confidence while Thompson was a cabinet officer, Thompson ignored having bragged about that very fact in his speech at the depot, instead telling Holt that the *Star of the West*'s departure from New York with troops hidden on board had been published in a newspaper and thus was no longer confidential.[110]

Representative Charles Francis Adams noted in his diary that Buchanan had purged himself of secessionist influences, hosted numerous Republicans at a presidential reception, and was now so open to Republican sentiment that Seward, though not in the cabinet, seemed to be "the guiding hand at the helm."[111] Like most of Adams's comments about his friend Seward, this went too far. Buchanan had no interest in helping the incoming administration, and, with his one military initiative against secession botched, he was unlikely to try anything else in the waning weeks of his presidency. This afforded South Carolina time to improve its own military posture, to purchase ordnance pursuant to the appropriation approved in the secession convention, and to welcome in Charleston forces from other seceded states.[112] But Buchanan's new treasury secretary, John Adams Dix, wished to set a new tone. When informed that Revenue cutters (including one in Charleston) were being handed over to or expropriated by Southern forces, Dix sent a subordinate to New Orleans to order the cutters there and at Mobile to depart for New York.[113] The commander of the Mobile cutter, however, a Georgian, had already resigned and given his vessel to locals. The captain of the New Orleans cutter was still in possession, but, in connivance with the disloyal customs collector there, he refused to comply with Dix's order. Dix telegraphed a subordinate that "if any one attempts to haul down the American flag" on the cutter, "shoot him on the spot." Dix refused to show the telegram to Buchanan before sending it, lest the president think it too provocative. It was intercepted by Southern authorities, and the captain and customs collector successfully turned the vessel over to Louisiana, which—though still a member of the Union—accepted it.[114] If by 1861 more shallow-draft vessels had been built and delivered to Southern ports for use by federal officials (whether to police the slave trade or to protect against imagined coastal predations by similar British craft), the Confederacy would have had, in effect, if not a ready-made navy, at least a ready-made coast guard. As things were, it had a mere handful of such seized Union vessels.

Most Northern newspapers had been so appalled by Buchanan's myriad failures to act that they were loath to criticize now that he had finally ordered something done—even if it miscarried. But the British envoy in Washington, Lord Lyons, wrote what thousands were probably thinking when he told the foreign secretary that the fiasco tended "to make the Government and the Army objects of ridicule."[115] Holt, rather than apologize to Anderson for the administration's failure to notify him of a major operation in which he was to play an active role, instead expressed the government's "great satisfaction . . . at the forbearance, discretion and firmness with which you have acted, amid the perplexing and difficult circumstances in which you have been placed." If the batteries opening fire had been those of a foreign nation, Holt observed, it would have been Anderson's duty to return fire. As things were, he instead faced "highly-inflamed" passions in a U.S. state and was thus correct to stand down.[116] But an order *had* been issued to open fire. Because he did not receive it, Anderson was now being praised for not doing on his own what the government had in fact instructed him to do. Holt also lavishly praised Anderson for his move to Fort Sumter two weeks earlier—the first Washington official to show support. Perhaps Holt merely wanted to communicate fulsome praise so as to avoid receiving from Anderson (or, worse, reading in some newspaper) sharp words regarding the stillborn expedition and the humiliating, passive role Anderson and his men had played in it.

Holt stated, "You will continue, as heretofore, to act strictly on the defensive" and "to avoid, by all means compatible with the safety of your command, a collision with the hostile forces by which you are surrounded." Anderson might have asked that the missing order be reissued so he could engage if any other ship appeared under a U.S. flag. He might also have insisted that his superiors answer a series of "what-if" questions for contingencies that must have come to his mind constantly. But he remained passive, content to remain "strictly on the defensive" without any positive orders to engage in specified circumstances. Perhaps he so distrusted his superiors' competence and/or loyalty that he preferred the same complete personal discretion that brought him to Sumter. When, on February 16, Anderson did ask what to do if—as seemed likely—the Confederates' new ironclad barge, the so-called Floating Battery, was brought closer to Fort Sumter (thus indicating that it was preparing to fire), Secretary of War Holt responded that this was a hard question.[117]

On January 10, New York newspapers reported that *Star of the West* had been attacked and that Fort Sumter had not opened fire.[118] That night in Washington, Henry Adams saw General Scott at a dinner party. Since Adams found Scott "pompous as usual," presumably the general was not humiliated by news of his operation's utter failure. Scott's assistant, Lieutenant Colonel Erasmus Darwin Keyes, opined that if, as reported, the Carolinians had fired upon reinforcements headed for Fort Sumter, it would be appropriate for Anderson to retaliate by bombarding downtown Charleston. In making this reckless suggestion, Keyes did not contemplate that Anderson, who had refused even to fire upon military batteries and vessels that had attacked a civilian vessel flying the U.S. flag, would rather die than participate in such a thing. In 1832, Anderson had witnessed in the Bad Axe Massacre the carnage that results from murky and disputed negotiations, incompetent political appointees, and the senselessness of actions leading to reactions, followed by escalations, and so forth. His conduct in the Seminole War resulted in his being brevetted to captain. During the war with Mexico—a conflict widely seen as a mere land grab by the United States—he had written to his wife that "no more absurd scheme could be invented for settling national difficulties than the one we are engaged in—killing each other to find out who is in the right."[119] He subsequently moved Congress, with General Scott's encouragement and funding, to establish a home for old and incapacitated soldiers.[120]

If drivel about Anderson's killing civilians in downtown Charleston could be voiced by Lieutenant Colonel Keyes, an officer of substantial experience in a position of substantial discretion, little better could be expected of the naive

Henry Adams. "I am utterly delighted with the course of things down there," he wrote, hoping that "they've hurt some one on the *Star of the West*," since this "puts them so in the wrong that they will never recover from it. Then it will raise the North to fever heat and perhaps secure Kentucky" for the Union.[121] But if the Carolinians' firing upon a civilian vessel put them "in the wrong," their blameworthiness was substantially mitigated by Scott's use of subterfuge. A public announcement that Sumter's soldiers would be peaceably reinforced, followed by the arrival of those reinforcements standing on the deck of an unarmed vessel, would have been far more effective in putting Carolinians "in the wrong." By choosing deception, Scott had unwittingly conceded that the Union lacked constitutional authority to reinforce one of its installations.

Scott had also unwittingly emboldened the most impetuous Southern leaders, since they could exploit this ruse, like Buchanan breaking his alleged promise not to transfer men to Fort Sumter, as a typically underhanded Northern trick, akin to the story—often repeated in the South—of the Yankee commercial traveler who peddled junk cuckoo clocks to gullible Southern yeomen.[122] "Southerners," British journalist W. H. Russell observed, "regard New England and the kindred states as the birthplace of impurity of mind among men and of unchastity in women—the home of Free Love, of Fourierism, of Infidelity, of Abolitionism . . . a land saturated with the drippings of rotten philosophy, with the poisonous infections of a fanatic [i.e., abolitionist] press; without honor or modesty."[123] Washington lawyer Montgomery Blair wrote to his wife's brother-in-law, retired navy officer Gustavus Fox, "The real cause of our trouble arises from the notion generally entertained at the South" that Northerners, "factory people and shopkeepers," were inferior. "Rebellion," Blair wrote, springs from "pride which revolts against submission to supposed inferiors."[124]

"It Is Our Duty to Hold Our Position"

Lieutenant Adam J. Slemmer, like Major Anderson a former instructor at West Point, commanded a small band of eighty-three Union officers and men at Fort Barrancas in Pensacola Harbor. On January 9, 1861, he received in the mail from General Scott a January 3 order to "do the utmost in your power to prevent the seizure of either of the forts in Pensacola Harbor by surprise or assault."[125] Scott's message was intercepted and read by secessionists—perhaps in Florida, perhaps by a disloyal clerk back in the War Department—because on January 9, the day it was delivered to Lieutenant Slemmer, Stephen R. Mallory, in Washington, telegraphed to Florida governor Madison Perry that "Federal troops are said to be moving" on the two seaboard installations at

Lieutenant Adam J. Slemmer, U.S. Army. Library of Congress LC-DIG-cwpb-05155.

Pensacola previously unoccupied by Union troops: Fort McRee and Fort Pickens.[126] Because Pensacola had three other federal facilities—the navy yard at Warrington (its construction having been urged by John C. Calhoun in 1840), the Barrancas Barracks, and Fort Barrancas itself—Scott's mention of "either of the forts" and Mallory's mention of the two vacant seaboard forts could only mean that Slemmer, who had once served at Fort Moultrie, was about to reprise what Anderson had done in Charleston by moving his garrison to a more defensible but previously unoccupied facility, one that commanded the inferior position previously held, in an assemblage of fortifications designed to do battle only with an intruding fleet.[127] Since Mallory was at this time a U.S. senator (D/FL), his telegram was disloyal.[128]

On January 9, the same day Slemmer received word from Scott, the commandant of the Pensacola Navy Yard, Commodore James Armstrong, received from Navy Secretary Toucey a January 3 order, evidently coordinated with Scott's, to meet with and cooperate with Slemmer and "be vigilant to protect the public property."[129] The next day, Slemmer spiked the guns at Forts Barrancas and McRee, threw substantial supplies of powder into the

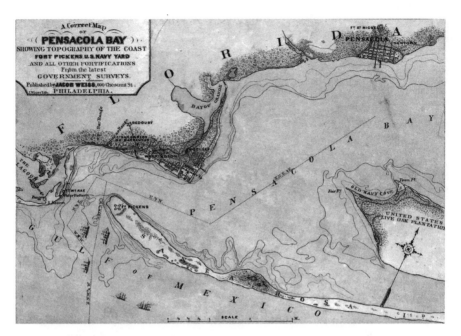

Map of Pensacola Bay by Jacob Weiss (undated), showing routes to avoid sandbar at harbor mouth. Library of Congress g3932p.cw0119000.

bay, and removed himself and his men to the more defensible Fort Pickens. Sited at the western end of Santa Rosa Island, it had been designed by Totten and Bernard with walls forty-five feet high and twelve feet thick. Constructed intermittently between 1828 and 1853 using granite shipped from the North and then named for the grandfather of South Carolina's incumbent governor, Fort Pickens could both command the harbor mouth and, given sufficient supplies, ordnance, and men, withstand a land siege of substantial duration.[130]

Under Armstrong's command of the frigate *United States* in 1843/1844, seaman Herman Melville witnessed 163 floggings. His novel of the voyage, *White-Jacket*, played a significant role in Congress banning the practice in 1851.[131] Armstrong now refused to cooperate with Slemmer, either by having his men join in occupying the fort (designed for a war garrison of 1,260) or by moving any of the navy yard's assets there, or by destroying those assets so they could not fall into enemy hands. Instead, several days later he allowed Florida and Alabama militiamen to seize the navy yard without a fight.[132] If Armstrong had resisted, the Civil War would have started there. He would later tell a U.S. Navy court convened against him in Washington:

Rhapsodic depiction of Fort Pickens with Fort McRee across the harbor mouth at right, from a sketch by Catharine Rogers Gilman, wife of Lieutenant Jeremiah H. Gilman. *Harper's Weekly* (February 23, 1861).

> This was the first time in the history of our country that hostility to the Government ever appeared in armed force, organized under State authority and acting under the forms of law. . . . From the commencement of these difficulties [President Buchanan's] messages and the whole tone of public opinion . . . spoke but one voice—that civil war should be avoided at all cost, and that the spilling of blood in such a strife would obliterate forever all hope of restoring the Government to its integrity. . . . To condemn this act of mine would be to reprobate the whole course of the Government.

While Buchanan's conduct over the prior few months gave color to such a defense, the court found Armstrong culpable.[133]

With the Confederacy not yet formally organized, its interim leaders instructed Florida and Alabama forces to proceed across the harbor and take Fort Pickens. On January 15, two former Union officers arrived and demanded Slemmer's surrender. One of them, Colonel William H. Chase (West Point '15) of the Florida militia, had helped construct the fort. He said,

"I have come to ask of you young officers, officers of the same army in which I have spent the best and happiest years of my life, the surrender of this fort. . . . Fearing that I might not be able to say it as I ought . . . I have put it in writing and will read it." He pulled the surrender demand from his pocket and began to read, but his eyes welled up with tears, and he handed it to another former Union officer, Captain Ebenezer Farrand, who had recently quit the U.S. Navy following thirty-eight years of service. Farrand claimed to have weak eyes (they were reportedly watering) and had to hand the message to a third officer to recite.[134] The next day, Slemmer responded, "It is our duty to hold our position until such a force is brought against us as to render it impossible to defend it, or until the political condition of the country is such as to induce us to surrender the public property in our keeping to such authorities as may be delegated legally to receive it."[135]

On January 21, Scott and Toucey ordered USS *Brooklyn*, just returned from the fiasco in Charleston, to transport several hundred troops under Captain Israel Vogdes to Pensacola, but not to disembark the men unless Fort Pickens came under assault by local forces.[136] Senators Mallory of Florida and Slidell of Louisiana, backed by Jefferson Davis, L. T. Wigfall, and others, proposed to Buchanan a local truce in which they would not attack Fort Pickens in return for his promise not to disembark any of the Union forces being sent there. Buchanan agreed, thus forgoing a reinforcement that would have yielded him wide praise in the North and vindicated the principle of maintaining Union facilities. Buchanan and Toucey also assured them that the South would not attack Fort Pickens so long as Buchanan was in office, while also warning that Republicans wished to "force a conflict between the Federal Government and the seceding states" before the March 4 inauguration so Lincoln would not be blamed. Meanwhile, Davis and the others had confidentially informed Florida's governor that possession of Fort Pickens "is not worth one drop of blood to us" and that—more important—for the South to initiate bloodshed "may be fatal to our cause."[137] Although by this time Southerners put no faith in any promise by Buchanan not to reinforce a fort, in this instance they did not care, since they as yet had no navy for which Pensacola could be a base, and upon assembling one they could avail themselves of Mobile, a large, protected port only sixty-four miles to the west. Thus, what they gave Buchanan in the bargain was a promise not to do what they had no intention of doing.[138]

On January 29, Toucey and Holt, with Scott's approval, telegraphed a dispatch to Lieutenant Slemmer reciting the terms of the truce.[139] On February 6, Navy Captain Samuel Barron arrived from Washington with instructions that Union warships should remain at least two miles offshore.[140] That day

Brooklyn arrived off Pensacola, followed by *Sabine*, a fifty-gun frigate.[141] Both were informed of the truce.

Fort Pickens contained many cannons but had not been garrisoned since 1851 and needed substantial repair, being—like Fort Sumter—a monument to Congress's fitful execution of the strategic vision of Totten and Bernard decades before.[142] Fifty-seven embrasures lacked not just cannons but also the protective metal shutters Totten had designed, and their openings were just seven feet above the wide ditch surrounding the edifice, affording any amphibious force easy access. Since entry might be by stealth, Slemmer kept half his men awake and ready every night, rendering them perpetually fatigued. In addition, Vogdes, after a brief inspection, found "the guns and carriages and implements . . . all old, and nearly unserviceable," with "no ammunition for the columbiads, no cartridge bags for them, nor flannel to make any. In fact, had it been the intention of the Government to place the fort in the state to render its defense impossible, it could not have been done more efficiently," the latter perhaps an allusion to Floyd.[143]

While the two sides had agreed to a standstill truce, it was "at will," requiring of the South no prior notice of attack and of the Union no prior notice of reinforcement. So long as the fort was not under attack, reinforcement and resupply would be easy. First, the Union soldiers and supplies were already offshore. Second, although there had been a massive commitment to surround Fort Sumter, Southern forces had not taken positions on Santa Rosa Island, so that the men and supplies could be landed on the Gulf beach without coming under direct Confederate fire. Waiting for a Confederate attack made little sense. While the truce allowed one of the Union ships, *Wyandotte*, a shallow-draft sloop formerly used in policing the slave trade, to remain in the harbor, and it could signal to the Union ships offshore if it saw the Southerners commence an amphibious assault from across the harbor, the attackers could land, enter the fort's embrasures, and overwhelm Slemmer's small garrison before any of the ships could arrive and disembark men, making their presence offshore useless.[144] In addition, since the truce required the ships to remain too far offshore to anchor and they were obliged to conserve fuel, southeasterly gales periodically blew them far away (in one instance almost to Mobile). So the Confederates, if they had wished, could have waited for such an occurrence to attack.[145] Thus, since Vogdes saw "all of the advantages of the present [truce] . . . on the side of the seceders," he urged his superiors in Washington to let him end the truce immediately and land enough soldiers, marines, and sailors to bring the garrison to four hundred men.[146]

5

"A Point of Pride"

THE MEMOIRS OF PRESIDENT BUCHANAN AND GENERAL SCOTT WOULD record much mutual bickering. Scott would write that he had had high confidence in one experienced navy man's proposed plan to resupply Fort Sumter, only to find that it was stymied by an alleged truce Buchanan had entered into with several Southern leaders regarding Charleston, Fort Pickens, and New Orleans. Buchanan vociferously denied the existence of such a truce, and in fact Scott was mistaken. Aging, corpulent, gouty, rheumatic, and dropsical, still carrying within him two bullets from the War of 1812, Scott had chosen to be out of touch with political Washington by maintaining his headquarters in New York. While he was prone to portray Buchanan's missteps as failures to take his advice, for the *Star of the West* episode the president had placed himself completely in Scott's hands—much to his regret.

On January 8, 1861, Buchanan bemoaned to Congress that federal forts and arsenals had recently been seized by locals in states that had not yet seceded, while "our small army has scarcely been sufficient to guard our remote frontiers against Indian incursions."[1] Scott, construing this as an allegation that these facilities were lost because he had understaffed or misdeployed his army, decided to give his October memorandum to the *National Intelligencer*, thus letting the public know that he had recommended reinforcement and that Buchanan and the disgraced Floyd had ignored him.[2] Federal ground forces were in fact minimal (a mere 16,367 men) and scattered across seventy-nine posts, with 183 of 198 companies in the western frontier, a few of the others bordering Canada.[3] But for this Scott was not to blame. Since Thomas Jefferson first warned against maintaining a standing army of the kind Great Britain had maintained against the colonists, the public had favored a policy of keeping a small force, joined as necessary by volunteers to be trained by a permanent cadre of West Point officers.[4] This officer corps, those with

87

Lieutenant General Winfield Scott, detail of photo of Scott and staff by Matthew Brady (September 6, 1861[?]). National Archives NA 524907.

knowledge of artillery, infantry, and engineering as well as the establishment and maintenance of good order, was now being depleted by the resignations of men who, obliged to choose between their sworn duty to the Union and their obligations at home, opted for the latter.[5]

With no cipher system in place, telegrams passing between Washington and Fort Sumter were not secure, making mail in sealed envelopes, moving through Alfred Huger's post office, the primary means of communication—even after the state's secession.[6] Although Abner Doubleday thought that his mail was being opened, Anderson assumed that even after his friend Huger ceased being a sworn federal employee under criminal sanction for opening mail, he would continue to consider sealed letters sacrosanct. To avoid taunt-ing between Union troops going to the post office and local troublemakers, Anderson and Huger set up a transfer point at the derelict Fort Johnson on James Island.[7] Governor Pickens several times demanded a halt to Sumter's mail and periodically cut off food purchased under contract from local sources. When Benjamin Huger asked his cousin Alfred to prevail upon Pickens to have these services resumed, Pickens at first complied; then he fluctuated between treating Anderson's garrison as representatives of a foreign power with which South Carolina was not at war and as a noxious enemy within the state. As Pickens understood, insofar as the mail was blocked, among the let-ters that would not be delivered might be one containing an evacuation order.[8]

On January 11, sensing that the *Star of the West* debacle afforded him a negotiating advantage, Pickens demanded Anderson's surrender. When Anderson referred him to Buchanan, Pickens dispatched South Carolina attorney general Isaac W. Hayne to Washington to revive the negotiation abandoned by South Carolina's three commissioners in protest over Ander-son's move to Sumter.[9] In Washington, Hayne first obtained a sense of things from Jefferson Davis and L. T. Wigfall. Although Pickens had apparently instructed Hayne (a fire-eater who had been an official at the nullification convention in 1832) to be aggressive with Buchanan, Davis urged that Ander-son's "little garrison . . . presses on nothing but a point of pride" and that if Pickens and Hayne merely waited, in a month "we shall . . . be in a condition to speak with a voice which all must hear."[10] Anderson, knowing that his friend Robert Gourdin was to accompany Hayne to Washington, asked that Gourdin meet with General Scott, with Senator Crittenden, and with Ander-son's brother Larz, with a view to developing some compromise.[11]

Hayne proposed that if Buchanan promised not to attempt reinforcement again, Sumter would have uninterrupted food, fuel, and communication with Washington by mail and messenger.[12] On its face, Hayne's offer seemed too generous, since: (1) Buchanan already stood accused of breaking a similar gentlemen's agreement not to transfer Anderson to Sumter, (2) keeping the garrison supplied with food would put off the day when Anderson's men would be forced to evacuate peacefully or face starvation, and (3) the timorous Buchanan, having just failed badly in one reinforcement effort, would not soon be undertaking another. However, Buchanan was now under pressure from Unionists in his cabinet, telling Senator Clement Claiborne Clay Jr. (D/AL)—presumably for dissemination—that he would not withdraw from Sumter and that if South Carolina's leaders attacked, "on them would rest the exclusive responsibility of commencing civil war."[13] Henry Adams took away from an interview with Larz Anderson that if South Carolina blocked communication and cut off food from local sources, Buchanan's reaction would be to resupply the garrison "at any price and at all hazards."[14] Writing through Holt, Buchanan now had the wherewithal to tell Hayne that while Major Anderson had not actually asked for reinforcements "and feels quite secure in his position," if reinforcements became necessary, "every effort will be made to supply them."[15] A week later, ignoring Davis's prior request not to pressure Buchanan unilaterally over what was only a "point of pride," Pickens and Hayne again demanded that Buchanan order Sumter's evacuation, something Buchanan had already refused to do.[16]

On January 23, Pickens told Davis that South Carolina would abide formation of the Confederacy and join a collective effort against Sumter, but only because the state did not yet have all assets in place to attack. If the other states did not act within two weeks, he added, South Carolina would proceed unilaterally.[17] The next day an anonymous Carolinian sent General Scott a letter confiding that if Anderson refused to surrender, South Carolina might be ready to attack within ten days.[18] The state was repeating the role it had played in 1832/1833 and again in 1850/1851—that of the hotspur, pressuring other slave states to act collectively by presenting them with credible threats of abrupt independent action that might force these states to join in on South Carolina's terms, thus perhaps undermining collective security. During nullification, no state had joined South Carolina either in its plan to disobey and disrupt a federal law or in the additional threat voiced by some that if the federal government refused to give up collecting tariff duties, South Carolina would secede. The crisis of 1850/1851 had yielded a somewhat greater willingness by some states to follow South Carolina if it chose to withdraw, and now some states were actually doing so. Pickens urged that the first initiative of a Confederate government would be to assess the seceded states for men and money and to elect a commander in chief "so that we can present to the world a military organization strong enough [to] give internal confidence amongst ourselves, & . . . show our opponents that we are ready for action."[19]

Adieus

Anderson now commanded eighty-six officers and men and forty loyal workers in a fort designed for 650. Scott took the position that when in October 1860 he first recommended reinforcement, it would have been feasible for unarmed transports to deposit the six hundred men and equipment required to bring Fort Sumter to full capacity, but now this was impossible without assembling an amphibious force to assault the Southern artillery batteries. Assessing Anderson's reports of the Carolinians' strength, Scott now said he would need five thousand regulars and twenty thousand volunteers.[20] In December the entire army had been composed of only 16,367 officers and men, and this number was now dramatically reduced by Southern departures. Moreover, the gathering and training of such a force would be known immediately and preempted by an attack upon Fort Sumter.[21] Stephen Douglas told the Senate that no attempt would be made to reinforce Fort Sumter because no such force could be raised before Sumter ran out of food.[22]

William Tecumseh Sherman noted privately that "Anderson should be reinforced if it cost ten thousand lives, and every habitation in Charleston."[23] Anderson had not yet evacuated the garrison's twenty-one wives and twenty-five children. Because Carolinians would shun the personal dishonor and public disgrace that would result from firing upon them, any attack would be preceded by a demand for their removal, and that had not yet come. Anderson, knowing that to refuse such a demand would in effect be to use the women and children as shields, would of course comply. Until such a demand was made, keeping the dependents aided morale but depleted the fort's food supplies, thus bringing more quickly the day of a peaceful (if abject) surrender. But Anderson chose in late January to order the dependents' evacuation, thereby eliminating voluntarily the most significant obstacle to a bloody engagement and the beginning of a war Anderson had wanted to avoid. Perhaps Anderson's hopes for a peaceful conclusion to the siege had waned when it appeared that Buchanan's only ambition—following the *Star of the West* misadventure—was to maintain the status quo until Sumter became Lincoln's problem. If the annihilation of his force was in prospect, a commander under siege and with no hope of relief would rather send wives and children home himself rather than wait for a demand, the receipt of which would tell the men and their dependents—while still together—that the men were to die not long after saying good-bye.

The women and children were sent by boat to Charleston to await the vessel taking them north. While there, locals reportedly terrified them by swearing that an attack would commence shortly after their departure.[24] On Sunday, February 3, as their ship steamed past Sumter and exited the harbor, the garrison "fired a gun and gave three heart-thrilling cheers as a parting farewell to the dear loved ones on board, whom they may possibly never meet again this side the grave. The response was weeping and 'waving adieus' to husbands and fathers—a small band pent up in an isolated fort, and completely surrounded by instruments of death, as five forts could be seen from the

Muzzle smoke from cannon salute to wives and children departing for New York, February 3, 1861, as depicted in *Frank Leslie's Illustrated* (February 23, 1861).

steamer's deck with their guns pointing towards Sumter."[25] Following their departure, Anderson continued to observe through field glasses the periodic arrival of new Southern militias, as slaves and their masters built what would become nineteen separate batteries positioned to fire smoothbore and rifled heavy guns at Sumter and at any relief vessels. Mailing reports of these dire developments to Washington each day, Anderson nevertheless continued to maintain that he wanted neither reinforcements nor (even) food.[26]

Fee Simple

On January 30, Representative John H. Reynolds (Anti-Lecompton D/NY) issued a report stating that U.S. statutes do not cease to be in effect in a state that has purported to secede and whose federal officers have all resigned, nor does the federal government thereby forfeit title to its assets therein.[27] If, as South Carolina maintained, secession was constitutionally permissible, then Reynolds's conclusion regarding the ongoing viability of federal statutes was certainly incorrect. The status of federal real and personal property, however, involved additional considerations. While South Carolina had indicated a willingness to negotiate the value of and pay for everything it wanted or had already taken, Holt on February 6 told Hayne that a president could no sooner sell Fort Sumter to South Carolina than he could sell the Capitol to Maryland, which had once owned the land on which it stood.[28]

The analogy was apt. The Constitution (Art. I § 8) empowers Congress to exercise "exclusive" jurisdiction over the district transferred by states to become the seat of government, with "like Authority over all Places purchased by the Consent of the Legislature of the State in which the Same shall be, for the Erection of Forts." While a president, as commander in chief under Article II, may order soldiers to occupy or vacate a fort, retake it from a foe, or defend it "to the last extremity," the fort itself, like the District of Columbia, remains under congressional control.[29] Madison wrote in *Federalist* 43 that "the public money" spent on forts "and the public property deposited in them, require that they should be exempt from the authority of the particular State," with "all objections and scruples" voiced by a state "obviated" by obtaining the state's concurrence at the time the property passes hands to the federal government.[30] A federal court wrote in 1855, "When land has been purchased by the United States for military or other purposes" with the state's consent, the state no longer owns the property nor has any jurisdiction over it. That being so, it "cannot be sold" without Congress's permission.[31]

When South Carolina's three commissioners arrived in December, they may or may not have understood that while they might negotiate with President Buchanan (and, of course, they refused to do so in protest over Anderson's transfer to Sumter), only Congress was constitutionally authorized to transact any sale. Senator Hunter of Virginia, being apprised of the constitutional language quoted above, assumed that Congress by resolution might delegate to President Buchanan responsibility to sell to the Southern states not just Sumter but all the federal facilities they had seized or intended to seize. Apparently believing that Buchanan sufficiently feared war that he might commit to such transactions, Hunter proposed a resolution whereby Congress authorized the president to agree with any state to return federal property therein to state ownership, with each state "paying for the value of the same if destroyed or injured" by its own act.[32] Thus, Hunter's provision, not a model of draftsmanship, was both extortionate and unwittingly comical, suggesting that if South Carolina applied to President Buchanan to deed back Fort Sumter but then reduced the fort to rubble, the state would pay the full value of what it had destroyed.

Whatever support Hunter's proposal might have enjoyed in Congress was diminished by the many Southern resignations. Nor, even if it had passed, was it likely to work, in that Buchanan would undoubtedly advise that Congress could not evade its own constitutional responsibilities by delegating them to him.[33] In any event, Hunter's proposal went nowhere. Meanwhile, Christopher Memminger, a leader in South Carolina's secession convention and now in Montgomery, Alabama, to monitor the formation of the Confederacy there, advised that the new entity was not in fact formulating plans to attack Sumter. (Jefferson Davis had, after all, thought it only a "point of pride.") South Carolina—Memminger advised—should therefore proceed alone.[34] Governor Pickens told Brigadier General R. G. M. Dunovant to prepare an attack lasting forty-eight hours, the duration he thought necessary to force Anderson's capitulation.[35]

Rebellion affords rebels certain "powers." Because, however, they are obtained by force rather than legal process, they are not denominated "rights," a distinction recognized since Thucydides. When British colonists rebelled in the 1770s and arrogated British forts, courthouses, post offices, and the like, it was by the British military capitulation, well before any treaty, that the Americans came to own these assets.[36] But South Carolina, deeming secession not a rebellion but a constitutional privilege, characterized itself as owner of these assets by operation of law, as part of its reversion to the complete sovereignty it had allegedly enjoyed prior to ratifying the Constitution in 1788. In its view, it was offering payment as a matter of comity—"fairness"—between sovereigns, for assets the federal government had left behind. Holt countered that because the Constitution did not allow secession, federal ownership of Fort Sumter was "complete and incontestable," adding that by seizing federal properties and threatening to seize others, South Carolina was engaged not in negotiation but in extortion.[37]

Holt here missed an additional basis for federal ownership of Sumter, one of particular salience because it remained valid even if one accepted the view that secession was constitutional. In 1794, Congress enacted a law authorizing the president to direct the construction and garrisoning of fortifications in Charleston and elsewhere, while permitting South Carolina and other designated coastal states to cede land to the federal government for the purpose.[38] In 1805, South Carolina's legislature granted to "the United States of America, all the right, title and claim of this State" in several sites, including Castle Pinckney and the five acres of marsh around it, five acres on Sullivan's Island for Fort Moultrie, and "a portion of the sand bank marked C, on the south easternmost point of Charleston, as delineated on . . . [a] plan [by Johann Christian Senf] of Charleston harbor, not exceeding two acres." This law further provided that if the United States failed within three years to "repair the fortifications now existing thereon" or build others "and keep a garrison or garrisons therein; in such case this grant or cession shall be void and of no effect."[39] The United States failed to build on the shoal, much less complete a fort and install a garrison, thus voiding the deed.

In November 1832, in the midst of the nullification crisis, Joel Poinsett, a staunch Unionist, reported to President Jackson that Fort Sumter "is just appearing above water and . . . ought to be driven on as rapidly as may be[,] for at a crisis like this the possession of such a position would render us very secure."[40] The Union's possessory authority was suddenly questioned when one William Laval claimed ownership of the shoal and (therefore) of the artificial island that the federal government had caused to emerge above it. Laval was not a random citizen presenting an unrecorded and overlooked old deed but a well-known nullifier who was comptroller general in the administration of Governor Robert Young Hayne, a kinsman of Isaac Hayne.[41] Because Governor Hayne was also a committed nullifier and nullification was far from over, Laval's claim of ownership was only a ploy to block, or at least impede, the construction of a federal fort at the mouth of Charleston's harbor, to embarrass a federal government that by this point had not just prevailed over but also humiliated the nullifiers.[42] A committee of the South Carolina legislature, itself controlled by disgruntled nullifiers, ignoring the Constitution and the statutory precedents, declared itself unable "to ascertain by what authority the [federal] government have assumed to erect" Fort Sumter. Nevertheless, it then formally ceded the fort to the federal government, while promising to examine Laval's claim.[43]

In 1841, the state's new governor, John Peter Richardson II, a Unionist, following appropriate resolutions of the legislature, executed a document to "grant, cede, and convey, unto the United States of America, all that part . . . of a certain bank, or shoal of land [comprising] one hundred and twenty-five acres: together with all and singular the rights, members, hereditaments, and appurtenances to the said premises . . . to have and to hold . . . unto the said United States of America, forever."[44] This grant, perpetual and absolute, added no proviso that it would be void or voidable if South Carolina ever purported to secede from the United States. Since that very issue had been part of the recent nullification crisis, kept current in 1841 not just by Laval's mischievous legal challenge but also by South Carolina's vociferous reaction to petitions then being submitted to Congress to emancipate slaves in the District of Columbia, the state might well have insisted upon a caveat that the grant would be void if South Carolina withdrew from the Union. But it did not do so. If it was an oversight, it was South Carolina's oversight. More likely, Governor Richardson and his advisors intentionally avoided such a contingency because Congress would not have taken kindly to such provocative language at a time when talk of nullification and secession was still in the air.[45] The deed to Fort Sumter, "forever," was a gesture of amity, in the nature of a treaty but executed as a real estate document.[46]

The United States (the Supreme Court opined in 1845) could acquire land from a state by deed, and its rights in such land were those set forth in the deed, including political dominion, limited only by the terms of the Constitution itself.[47] Although a state might void its own deed to any private grantee by an appropriate declaration of eminent domain, South Carolina had no such power when it deeded land for a federal fort, in that the Constitution (Art. I § 8) renders Congress's power over forts "exclusive."[48] As argued by Representative William Lowndes (R/SC) during the marathon debate on "internal improvements" in 1817–1818, "to deny to the General Government the common rights of purchase and of contract, was to impute to the Constitution" a "gross defect" it did not have.[49] In 1820, Representative Charles Pinckney (D-R/SC) introduced a resolution to study "restoring to all the States the jurisdiction of all the territory ceded by them for forts and arsenals," but solely to prevent criminals and debtors from evading state process and to stop duelists from evading his state's antidueling law by simply rowing to the federal reserve. That is, Pinckney, formerly a delegate to the Constitutional Convention, was not attempting to have ownership of forts revert to the states.[50]

In *United States v. Chicago* (1849), the city desired to lay out streets on land that was part of Fort Deerfield, a federal property. The Supreme Court thought it "our duty to support the general government in the exercise of all which is plainly granted to it and is necessary for the efficient discharge of the great powers entrusted to it by the people and the states. The erection of forts belongs to one of those powers."[51] Thus, so long as South Carolina's 1841 grant qualified as a "purchase" (the word used in the Constitution), the state divested itself of all ownership and jurisdictional rights over Fort Sumter "forever."[52] And if the Union still owned the fort, then the state could not limit or terminate access without violating the common-law principle that one who exercises access for several decades has established a perpetual easement for that purpose.[53]

Andrew Magrath, serving as a delegate to the secession convention, proposed a study of local property claimed by the United States, "how acquired; and whether the purpose for which it was so acquired, can be enjoyed by the United States after the State of South Carolina shall have seceded."[54] Several days later, with the secession convention meeting in secret session, Magrath stated that he would not be able to report on "the purposes" for which the federal government acquired Forts Sumter and Moultrie, Castle Pinckney, and the arsenal without first obtaining "exact information" contained in "the grants, deeds, or other modes in which they have been obtained."[55] Whether Magrath, an accomplished attorney and former federal judge, failed to search the relevant recordation office, or did search it and, finding the 1841 deed to Fort Sumter detrimental to his state's cause, ignored it, is unknown. If the contemplated seizure of the fort and ouster of Anderson's men, goals consuming so much rhetoric, were suddenly perceived to be contrary not only to the Constitution but also to a deed signed as recently as 1841, men for whom consistency and transparency (that is, "honour") were paramount values would suddenly need to hide from a major issue and shift to a new set of arguments for why the Union had no right to stay.[56]

The 1841 document, competently utilized by the Union, would have plainly established its legal right to remain in Fort Sumter, irrespective of the state's claim that it had withdrawn itself from U.S. jurisdiction. With the deed in hand and fully exploited in speeches and newspapers, the Confederates would have been forced into a posture that Davis and the others wanted to avoid: being mere rebels, lawbreakers. Any Union official talking to the South's European trading partners would thus be justified in saying something like "They signed a real estate agreement and decided to dishonor it the moment it no longer suited them, exactly as they did with the Constitution. They do not abide by their promises." The Union could also have submitted the issue to the Supreme Court. While the Court had demonstrated a radically proslavery bias in numerous decisions, most famously *Dred Scott*, it had shown no bias in favor of secession. Indeed, *Dred Scott* may be viewed as the Court's last-ditch attempt to hold the nation together. A case brought to decide whether the United States still owned the fort, despite the host state's purported secession, would undoubtedly have established that its ownership remained legally intact.[57] Secessionists could, of course, say that while the Court had jurisdiction over certain matters of constitutional interpretation, a state's secession was not one of them, since the states (so the argument went) created the Constitution itself.

"The Crisis Was Actually Passed"

Hayne, offended by Holt's February 6 letter rejecting his evacuation demand, told Pickens that he would consider his assignment in Washington a "disgrace" to his state and a source of personal "shame" if Sumter remained in Union hands "one moment longer" than necessary.[58] Hayne now wrote directly to Buchanan, who found the letter so offensive that his response (as with similar insults by the commissioners a month earlier) was not to accept it.[59] John Tyler of Virginia, a Unionist and a former U.S. president, volunteered to act as intermediary, but Hayne and other fire-eaters by this point saw no value in further talk.[60] Although Lincoln and Seward had by turns indicated commitments to conciliation, Representative Roger Pryor (D/VA) falsely charged that Republicans "obdurately reject all overtures . . . and avow a purpose to employ all the resources of Government for the subjugation of the retiring States," thus precipitating a civil war.[61]

On Monday, February 4, as representatives of what would soon be the Confederacy met in Montgomery, a "Peace Convention" gathered in the dance hall adjacent to Willard's Hotel, down the hill from the White House. Among 133 delegates from fourteen free-labor states and from seven of the slave states that had not seceded were one former president (Tyler), six former cabinet officers, nineteen former governors, and sixty-four ex-members of the Senate and House.[62] While some had hopes for this so-called Old Gentlemen's Convention, Gideon Welles, a Republican and former Free-Soil Democrat, thought all such attempts at a reasonable compromise doomed, driven by "concessions . . . to conciliate and satisfy" secessionists "who were determined not to be satisfied."[63]

Across the river, Virginia's voters were choosing delegates to a secession convention to begin February 13 in Richmond. In 1788, South Carolina had been firmly in favor of ratifying the Constitution, although Virginia's backing was much in question. Now, however, the result in South Carolina's secession convention had been unanimous, while a majority of Virginians had voted for the Unionists Bell and Douglas in November, and most of the delegates chosen to meet in Richmond were either definite or tentative Unionists, thus confirming Seward's comment to Lincoln several days earlier that the situation in Virginia was encouraging.[64]

On the afternoon of Tuesday, February 5, Charles Francis Adams Jr. was skating on Jamaica Pond near Boston when he noticed a "throng of skaters flocking together" on the far side, shouting and cheering. Someone—Adams soon gathered—had arrived with a newspaper suggesting that Virginia (given its delegate choices, apparently) would remain loyal to the Union. "The tears almost stood in my eyes; and I skated off to be alone," Adams wrote, "for I realized that the crisis was actually passed."[65] Signs of strong and even dominant Unionism had also appeared in Tennessee, Arkansas, Missouri,

North Carolina, Kentucky, Maryland, and Delaware, first by their votes for Unionists in the elections of 1858 and 1860, then by secession conventions that resulted in lopsided pro-Union votes, and in some instances by popular or administrative refusals even to call for such conventions.[66] If Virginia and these other states remained loyal, the Confederacy about to be formed by the citizens of the cotton states—comprising a mere 10 percent of the nation's whites—might be short lived.

Edmund Ruffin, although considered a secessionist troublemaker in his native Virginia, was quite at home in conversation with the denizens of the Charleston Hotel. If the Union sent reinforcements to Charleston (he had noted in his diary), or if any local forts were in federal hands when Lincoln took office on March 4, "they will be ... taken at any cost."[67] On February 9 in Montgomery, a congress of South Carolina, Georgia, Florida, Alabama, Mississippi, and Louisiana formed a "Constitution for the Provisional Government of the Confederate States of America," borrowing heavily from the U.S. Constitution although indicating that they were in fact "restoring" it to what it originally was, while inserting expressly what they thought was impliedly there: that the member states retained their sovereignty.[68] Many who had known Jefferson Davis in Washington were relieved that negotiations would now be with him as the Confederation's provisional president rather than the impetuous Rhett, Hayne, or Pickens. Toombs, meanwhile, had unwittingly taken himself out of contention by appearing tipsy at several social gatherings in Montgomery.[69] Three days later, South Carolina's executive council, in the spirit of brinksmanship developed by Pickens, announced to the Confederacy that it had "exhausted all attempts to acquire the peaceful possession of Fort Sumter" and was now obliged to adopt sterner measures. This was untrue, since diplomatic measures were far from exhausted, and if the state no longer wanted to talk, it would have the fort simply by waiting for its food to run out. Although the South Carolina flag, having flown over Charleston's post office for several months, was now joined by a Confederate flag, the *Charleston Courier* opined that by rights it was the state flag that should be raised over Sumter once that bastion was attained.[70] Pickens told Howell Cobb of Georgia, formerly Buchanan's treasury secretary and now the Confederacy's interim president pending Davis's arrival in Montgomery, that Fort Sumter must fall and, whether accomplished by the state or the Confederacy, it must occur before March 4.[71] The date was crucial, Pickens urged, because Buchanan had neither the stomach nor the forces to respond adequately to such an attack, while Lincoln had the stomach and could gather the forces but would be less likely to respond militarily if Sumter fell before he took office.[72]

Pickens, perhaps reacting to indications of strong Unionism in Virginia and Maryland, told Baltimore customs collector J. Thomason Mason that it would be a great mistake to believe that peace could be maintained if these two states reacted to General Scott's "pouring in federal troops" to defend Washington by remaining "neutral." Pickens would have both states view Scott's military buildup—in reaction to rumors that Southern hostiles intended to storm the city and/or to kidnap or assassinate Lincoln on Inauguration Day— as nothing short of "the deepest degradation," as if neither should tolerate an attempt by the nation's most senior military officer, a Virginian, to ensure the transfer of authority spelled out in the Constitution. If, as Pickens hoped, Southern forces seized Washington immediately, Lincoln would need to find a new venue for his inaugural, while resident ambassadors would recognize the Confederacy as the nation's legitimate government because it had seized the capital, and "Maryland and Virginia would be the great manufacturing states of the Union, and thus draw off much of the capital now vested in manufactures at the North."[73]

Thus wishing to press these slave states into military action on behalf of a Confederacy they had not yet joined, Pickens also continued to threaten that Confederacy, telling its Provisional Congress on February 13 that South Carolina had a sovereign's right to "control . . . a military post within its limits." This comported with the new Confederate Constitution, providing that each state was "sovereign and independent" and thus could wage war alone.[74] Again it was urged that an attack should precede Lincoln's inaugural, this time on the premise that General Scott would not dare redeploy troops to Charleston until Lincoln was safely installed in office.[75] Pickens grasped that an impulse stronger and broader than national community with the North was the slave states' sense of collective self-interest. If South Carolina carried out Pickens's threat to attack Sumter, Virginians would see that—even if they vehemently disagreed with that action—federal forces would come across their land, an invasion they would have to either allow or oppose. Even if the federals did not confiscate slaves, slaves would escape. Thus, the protection of Virginia's sovereignty as well as its "property" required solidarity with the cotton states. John Tyler, understanding that Virginians would react in that way, told Pickens, "Do not attack Fort Sumter."[76]

L. T. Wigfall argued that talk of a North/South war was "twaddle," since the sudden disappearance of Southern cotton would cause Northern factory workers and idle merchant seamen to riot and put Senator Seward's head on a pole.[77] On the evening of December 28, 1860, just after Major Anderson moved to Fort Sumter, James Chesnut Jr., the first U.S. senator to resign following Lincoln's election, was walking along Charleston's Battery and met Anthony Toomer Porter, Episcopal priest of the Church of the Holy Communion. To Porter's comment that "we are at the beginning of a terrible war," Chesnut, recently a delegate to the secession convention, replied, "Not at all. There will be no war, it will be all arranged. I will drink all the blood shed in the war."[78]

Chesnut's flippant optimism soon faded, however. In a secret session of the Confederate Provisional Congress in Montgomery on February 12, seeing a unilateral attack on Fort Sumter by South Carolina as a real possibility, he joined another member in stating that this would severely strain the cohesion of the new Confederate States of America.[79] Christopher Memminger, whose perspective had similarly changed as he took on the duties of Confederate secretary of the treasury, assured Pickens that there was "nothing degrading to the honour of the State" in abiding the Confederacy's determination, in that Anderson's garrison (as Davis, too, had said) "disturbs no one."[80] Even William Lowndes Yancey, who had wanted to "precipitate the cotton states into a revolution," now counseled restraint.[81]

To preempt South Carolina and establish its own legitimacy, the Confederation's Provisional Congress resolved to obtain Sumter "by negotiation or force, as early as practicable."[82] Those still hoping for a compromise (although none of the Confederate states had sent a delegate to Tyler's Peace Convention) were encouraged when Davis appointed as new commissioners to deal with Washington three men of probity who were unlikely to reprise the gratuitous insults of their South Carolina predecessors. André Bienvenue Roman, a former Louisiana governor, had sided with President Jackson against the nullifiers and, more recently, had opposed Louisiana's secession (albeit unsuccessfully). John Forsyth was editor of the *Mobile Register* and former U.S. minister to Mexico, and Martin J. Crawford of Georgia had just resigned from Congress. Although their ostensible task was to negotiate a price for federal assets with an estimated collective value above $6.5 million, more crucial were two additional marching orders: (1) obtain recognition for the Confederacy and (2) instill the feeling in Washington that secession was a fait accompli, rendering any effort at reintegration "utterly hopeless."[83] Once the Union "recognized" the Confederacy, even if only informally by agreeing to settle accounts, the threat of war would evaporate, freeing the Confederacy to pursue lucrative trading relations abroad. Although Great Britain and France had both outlawed slavery and the slave trade, any lingering moral scruples would soon give way (so Montgomery wagered) to the constant need for raw cotton, coupled with the benefit of selling manufactured goods to a wealthy new agricultural nation with minimal tariffs.[84] On March 1, Confederate secretary of war Leroy Pope Walker of Alabama notified Pickens that Jefferson Davis, with a distinguished career as an army officer and then as the Union's secretary of war, "assumes control of all military operations in your State," thus effectively depriving South Carolina of the sovereign authority that for thirty years it had claimed to have been trampled upon by the Union.[85]

"A Small Party Slipping In"

Holt's February 5 letter to Hayne informally terminated the de facto standstill period initiated when Anderson told Pickens to send a representative (Hayne) to Washington to negotiate.[86] While Anderson asked superiors not to mount the major amphibious invasion that would be required to overtake and destroy the Southern batteries arrayed against him, at this moment he did not reject "the little stratagem of a small party slipping in."[87] Inserting a few dozen men would not materially solve any fundamental problem but would have great symbolic value, exploiting the national pride that had been ignited by Anderson's daring move in December, and the national sympathy attendant upon his besieged status, by showing once more that a deft operation by a small and brave band of Union men (at least one with planning and execution superior to Scott's *Star of the West* initiative) could outwit and even humiliate an overwhelming Confederate force.

On February 4, the *New York Times'* Washington dispatch had reported the reinforcement of Sumter by four hundred troops lowered from *Brooklyn* in small boats with muffled oars. Although the tactic was sound and had been discussed, the report was mistaken. Vermont's *Burlington Free Press* reprinted the *Times'* story, placing it next to another that reported (correctly) that *Brooklyn* was off Pensacola. Either the editors had failed to notice—while setting type and reading proofs—that one of these accounts had to be false or they thought it unnecessary to point out inconsistencies between contiguous columns, considering their paper more as a forum than an arbiter.[88]

Not that readers would fail to notice the incongruity, since Anderson's situation and pluck had by now riveted Northerners. In New York, the aging son of Alexander Hamilton proposed a secret plan to reinforce Sumter with four hundred artillerists from New York's militia, to be financed by him and two other men of means, on the premise that since it was without the government's knowledge, South Carolina could not legitimately consider it an act of war. But the commander of the state's militia insisted that General Scott must be informed, and on January 1, Scott, indicating that he had discussed the proposal with President Buchanan, directed that it be abandoned.[89] The army and navy received various other relief plans over the transom, as when Nantucket fishermen proposed using whaleboats to be launched at night from a schooner they had already chartered for the purpose.[90] And Elias Hasket Derby III of Boston, with experience in both steamships and railroads, told Buchanan, Scott, and Toucey that the navy could "protect the gallant Anderson and the honor of our country without the effusion of blood" by cladding a light-draft steamer with two layers of 5/8-inch boiler iron, three inches apart, which Derby argued would withstand even thirty-two-pound balls while approaching Sumter. Heavier iron cladding for the three *Dévastation* class ships had proven very effective in the Crimean War, yielding in 1859 the first oceangoing ironclad frigate, *Gloire*.[91] Derby's particular formula was worth testing. But neither service branch took notice, having failed to grasp that *Dévastation* and *Gloire* had revolutionized naval warfare.

Gustavus Vasa Fox had attained the rank of acting midshipman in 1838, graduated Annapolis in 1841, and was commissioned a lieutenant in 1852. His commands had included a mail steamer owned by Marshall O. Roberts, who had already placed another of his ships, *Star of the West*, in harm's way on

Gustavus Vasa Fox. MOLLUS_MASS Coll. 7:322L, U.S. Army Mil. Hist. Inst.

the Union's behalf. In the early 1850s, Fox was second officer on the high-speed luxury liner *Baltic* between New York and Liverpool, also serving on other steamers plying routes from New York to Havana, New Orleans, and Panama.[92] After nineteen years' service, Fox granted his wife's request that he quit the sea and managed a fabric mill in Massachusetts. Finding that occupation infelicitous, he sought out Roberts, who advised that command of *Star of the West* at Charleston would have been his for the asking if Roberts had known of his interest.[93]

Wishing to head a new relief mission to Charleston, Fox now met in New York with George W. Blunt, an expert in lighthouses and seacoast piloting whose family had been publishing since 1796 the standard guide to U.S. harbors. The 1857 edition provided detailed descriptions of Charleston's harbor and its approaches, currents, and tides, although its convenient exposition of the colors and patterns of the various beacons, buoys, lights, and ranges, as well as the location of the light ship and bell boat, had become useless when Governor Pickens removed all these navigational aids.[94] On a clear day or a moonlit night, a knowledgeable pilot could be guided by the relative positions of the spires of St. Michael's (at 32°46′33″ lat., 79°55′38″ long.), St. Philip's, and the Circular Church, along with the fixed white beacon from the depleting oil lamp at Fort Sumter itself.

Although Fox might enlist vessels from the Revenue Marine, Coast Survey, or Lighthouse Board, none was of so shallow a draft as to cross the bar. An alternative of lighter draft was the standard harbor tug, which also featured speed and maneuverability, although all tugs were in private hands. Blunt thus discussed Fox's ideas with Charles H. Marshall, a substantial maritime owner whose early experiences had included hauling cotton from Charleston to Liverpool, and with Russell Sturgis, owner of several tugs who formerly had been a marine surveyor. Since they and Blunt served on a commission regulating navigation issues within New York Harbor, they knew about negotiating shoals, transferring cargo between ships and lighters, maneuvering tugs, and so forth—even if they knew nothing about performing these functions under fire.[95]

View of entrance to Charleston Harbor looking west from the bar (detail). Jacob Weiss, circa 1860/1861. Hagley Museum and Library.

Blunt also contacted General Scott, who on February 6 heard Fox's proposal to send to Charleston: (1) two shallow-draft tugs; (2) the side-wheel Revenue cutter *Harriet Lane*, capable of fourteen knots and carrying three 9-inch guns and a 4.2-inch Parrott rifled gun; (3) the twin-screw sloop of war *Pawnee*, equipped with eight 9-inch guns; and (4) a steamer such as *Baltic* to transport the reinforcements and supplies from New York.[96] The squadron would rendezvous off the Charleston bar in daylight, at which time Fox would survey the local defenses. Neither *Harriet Lane* nor *Pawnee*, drawing ten feet and eleven feet, respectively, would risk transecting the bar.[97] Rather, they would remain on its seaward side, from where they could fire upon Southern vessels, aided substantially by Fort Sumter, which would be at much closer range. Fox did not propose to engage the batteries at Cumming's Point and Fort Moultrie. Rather, after nightfall and at two hours before high water, the two New York tugs, each carrying half the reinforcements and provisions, would transect the bar on the rising tide and make the approach to Fort Sumter in the dark, hoping either to evade detection altogether by the land batteries or simply to avoid being hit, all the while keeping "within relieving distance of each other."[98]

Fox's proposal was put on hold. Preparation for any operation would quickly be known, thus ending the settlement discussions still pending in Congress and in the Peace Convention, while destroying the Unionists' hopes in Virginia and obliging the Confederacy's three representatives in Washington to cancel all negotiations.[99] Moreover, Buchanan, disappointed by Scott's prior effort, understood that a second failure would define his presidency as incompetent and leave as his legacy the outbreak of a civil war. The safe alternative was thus quietly to await Lincoln's inaugural. On February 9, Fox left Washington.[100]

A competing plan, using not tugs but open boats and oarsmen, was proposed to Scott and Toucey by Commander James H. Ward, a former executive officer of the U.S. Naval Academy and the author of *A Manual of Naval Tactics* (1859).[101] On February 20, several weeks after a Cincinnati newspaper published—and other papers republished—a false rumor that such an incursion had actually been made, Scott wrote to a subordinate in New York to ask Ward to ready his squadron.[102] Rumors quickly circulated, and by February 22 the *Charleston Mercury* predicted a stealthy reinforcement.[103] But Captain Ward, too, had been ordered to stand down.[104]

Fox, writing to his brother-in-law Montgomery Blair, criticized Ward's competing proposal because it required rowing 546 barrels of provisions and two hundred recruits in open boats across the bar and into the harbor, a total of five miles, in cold weather and at night. In conditions of bad visibility but calm seas at night and a rising tide, boats with muffled oars were more likely than steam-powered tugs to evade detection.[105] But because the boats were so slow, if they were spotted, they would be within range of shore batteries for an unacceptable thirty minutes. And because Ward's plan did not provide for eliminating Confederate vessels, these would be prowling the harbor entrance and could sink the boats by ramming, firing solid shot, or, if they got within two hundred yards, firing "canister" (essentially a large shotgun shell).[106] From farther out, they might try spherical case shot or "shrapnel," a thin metal sphere containing one-ounce lead musket balls (eighty in the twelve-pound boat howitzer, 175 in the twenty-four-pound). Set with a two-second fuse and correctly charged and aimed, the spherical case would burst 150 yards distant, spreading the pellets over an area of 150 yards.[107]

On March 3, a Southern observer in New York sent a letter indicating "positive information" that the incoming Lincoln administration, in consultation with Commodore Samuel L. Breese of the Brooklyn Navy Yard, was going to reinforce Sumter "immediately and secretly." According to the correspondent, an order had been issued on March 2 to transport 125 men on the U.S. Navy screw steamer *Crusader*, to leave port either on Inauguration Day or the next day in contemplation of a night incursion.[108] Southern leaders apparently took their correspondent's account seriously, for on the evening of March 4, inauguration night, Anderson noted that they posted four guard boats instead of the regular two.[109]

6

"Hold, Occupy, and Possess"

"My Head for a Football"

Although Seward had borne his nomination defeat with dignity, he described to his wife his next appearance in Washington as that of "a leader deposed by my own party in the hour of organization for decisive battle."[1] Soon, however, to the old assurance he now added a certain cockiness, telling the minister from Bremen that in the United States real power is held not by the president but by the leader of the ruling political party, which Seward still considered himself to be.[2] At a dinner at Stephen Douglas's home in February 1861 attended by Senator Crittenden, Supreme Court Justice John A. Campbell of Alabama, and French minister Henri Mercier, Seward gave a toast. "Away with all parties, all platforms of previous committals," he declared, "and whatever else will stand in the way of the restoration of the American Union!"[3] Since Lincoln's election had been unequivocally a matter of party and platform, Seward was here rhetorically repudiating not merely the Republican Party he had helped build, and of which he considered himself the head, but also the president whose administration he—although a defeated competitor—had been invited to join.[4] As the *New York Times* commented several weeks later, Lincoln faced a crucial and tumultuous choice for his inaugural address and first days in office: stay with the 1860 Republican platform on which he had successfully run, or abandon it in favor of Seward's notion of a conciliatory agenda dedicated to keeping the Upper South and border states in the Union.[5]

Seward took these liberties because he "thought Lincoln a clown, a clod, and planned to steer him by . . . indirection, subtle maneuvering" and "crooked paths. He would be Prime Minister; he would seize the reins from a nerveless President; keep Lincoln separated from other Cabinet officers" and hold "as few Cabinet meetings as possible," all with a view to averting war and saving the fractured Union, regardless of what Lincoln and his constituents wanted.[6] Although Lincoln had not only won the nomination from Seward but also showed Thurlow Weed that he was no pushover, Lord Lyons, the British envoy in Washington, reported to his superiors in London that Seward "seems to take it for granted that Mr. Lincoln will leave the whole management of affairs to him."[7] If the North/South crisis "is not satisfactorily settled within sixty days after I am seated in the saddle, and hold the reins firmly in my hand," Seward told Charles S. Morehead of Kentucky during Tyler's Peace Convention, "I will give you my head for a football."[8]

In the early spring of 1861, Henry Adams was serving as secretary to his father, Representative Charles Francis Adams. Not yet twenty-three, Henry was looking for a hero when (as happens) his father seemed no longer to merit that role. Whether Seward "is ever made President or not," Henry now wrote, "he never will be in a more responsible position than he is in now," the "virtual ruler of this country." With "that cool wisdom and philosophical self-control, so peculiar to his character," Seward had convinced his young admirer that all depended upon the loyalty of the Upper South and border states and that Seward's self-appointed task was to achieve "a firm alliance with the Unionists of Virginia and Maryland, to check the evil while there was yet time."[9] Gideon Welles, fifty-eight years old and not similarly in search of someone to idolize, had reasons accumulated over the years to distrust Seward, later describing him as ready "to acquiesce in almost any change of the fundamental law to get over a temporary difficulty."[10] While that accurately characterized Seward's political pragmatism, here the "temporary difficulty" Seward faced was nothing less than the unraveling of the Union and the likelihood of a civil war.

Because at this time 2,650 British mills purchased from the United States over six hundred million pounds of cotton per year (77 percent of total British consumption), the American crisis, with a Union blockade of Southern ports likely, was of crucial interest to Lord Lyons.[11] Seward sought to assure him (and Lyons forwarded the comments to London) that "the evils and hardships produced by Secession" will within a few months "become intolerably grievous to the Southern States," and then, as those states become assured of Lincoln's peaceful intentions, "the conservative element . . . now kept under the surface by the violent pressure of the Secessionists, will emerge with irresistible force," so that in elections to be held in the seceded states in November 1861, Unionists will prevail and proceed to unwind secession. At that point (Lyons told his superiors), Seward will "place himself at the head of a strong Union party" with tendrils in the South as well as the North, something neither Lincoln nor Stephen Douglas had attained.[12] Seward's theory for avoiding a civil war was thus tied to his own ambition to attain the presidency after all, by abandoning and displacing the sectional Republican government of which he was about to be second-in-command.

Senator Crittenden's proposed amendments to the Constitution purported to be permanent—that is, they included language providing that they could never be repealed. They could not possibly be approved as a package in Congress because the Republicans (already a majority in the House and, following Southern resignations, in the Senate as well) vehemently opposed one key element: the expansion of slavery. Another element, the guaranteed permanence of slavery in the Southern states, sponsored by Seward in the Senate (as carved out from Crittenden's package) and repeatedly endorsed by President-Elect Lincoln, might be enough to keep within the Union those slave states of the Upper South that had not yet seceded.[13] Seward (like the amendment's House sponsor, Thomas Corwin) saw the ultra Republicans as obstructionist.[14] Privately over brandy, Seward assured Justice Campbell that the provision would safeguard Southern slavery for fifty years, adding that he had become its sponsor at some risk to himself, since if he pressed it too publicly, Republican ultras might pressure Lincoln to withdraw his cabinet offer.[15] Seward undoubtedly said this to portray himself as the South's champion at this crucial moment, and it was certainly true that from the time ultras first heard that Seward, an apostate abolitionist, would be Lincoln's premier, they urged the president-elect to reconsider.[16]

Further attempting to portray himself as the South's best hope, Seward mischaracterized Lincoln's position as more antislavery than it was. The constitutional amendments proposed by Senator Crittenden and by the Peace Convention both permitted the expansion of slavery into the West.[17] Because Lincoln and other Republicans had made clear that they would not permit such expansion, both proposals were defeated.[18] Lincoln had also said, however, that Congress could not impose emancipation in the slave states because that was not among the powers enumerated in Article I, section 8.[19] Because Corwin's and Seward's proposed constitutional amendment perpetuating slavery in the South did not address slavery in the West, it passed both chambers by the required two-thirds.[20] Its supporters included two of every five Republicans because Lincoln—willing to compromise on everything but slavery extension—had said he would happily sign it. Upon taking office, he did so, and forwarded it to all governors.[21] While this deprived slaveholders of their fundamental argument that the Republicans intended to end slavery in the South, the initiative was soon neglected, North/South relations being no longer amenable to a long-term, constitutional solution.[22]

Lincoln chose for the powerful position of treasury secretary Salmon Chase of Ohio, who had competed against Lincoln and Seward for the Republican nomination and whose supporters had tried to unseat Seward from the cabinet. Because of Chase's impressive and long-standing antislavery credentials, his appointment undercut Seward's conciliation agenda as well as his claim of being "in the saddle."[23] Two other anti-Seward men, Montgomery Blair and Gideon Welles, were rumored to be under consideration for cabinet posts, suggesting a cabal headed by Lincoln to keep Seward in check.[24] Seward reacted on March 2, just two days prior to the inaugural, by suddenly rescinding his acceptance of Lincoln's cabinet offer.[25] Concerned about powerful enemies in a cabinet he had once expected to fill with men beholden to him, Seward apparently wagered that Lincoln would panic and accord Seward extraordinary authority rather than risk the public embarrassment of his departure even before Lincoln was sworn in. Seward may also have pondered that no president since Jackson had won two terms, and Lincoln, seemingly a bumbling amateur, was likely to fail. If, then, Seward simply stayed clear of the inevitable disaster, he might spend his time forming his new "Union Party" and the 1864 nomination would be his. It was a scenario partially predicted in a futuristic novel published in June 1860 by the multitalented secessionist Edmund Ruffin.[26]

Lincoln, however, chose not to beg Seward to stay, instead calling Seward's bluff by letting it be known that he could find a replacement.[27] Then, just prior to leaving parlor no. 6 of Willard's Hotel to deliver his inaugural speech, Lincoln dashed off a note asking Seward to reconsider. Seward, startled (if not chastened) by this tangle with a man he still underestimated, spoke with the new president that night and reaffirmed his acceptance.[28] A journalist for the *New York Herald* asked Lincoln what news he might take back to its editor, James Gordon Bennett. "You may tell him," Lincoln replied, "that Thurlow Weed has found out that Seward was not nominated at Chicago."[29]

"The Government Will Not Assail You"

In December 1860, a newspaper reported (incorrectly) that President Buchanan had sent an order to Major Anderson to surrender Fort Moultrie if it came under attack. When the article was mentioned to President-Elect Lincoln, he testily responded that if Buchanan had issued such an order, "they ought to hang him!"[30] On the same day, Lincoln told a confidential source in the army, "If the forts fall, my judgment is that they are to be retaken." Although General Scott had no official or personal relationship with Lincoln, he had sent him a copy of his October memorandum urging reinforcement of the Southern forts, perhaps to show the president-elect that the crisis derived from Buchanan's failure to take Scott's advice. Lincoln on December 21 secretly asked Scott through an intermediary to begin preparations to "hold or retake the forts, as the case may require, at and after the inauguration."[31] On Christmas Eve, Lincoln wrote to Senator Lyman Trumbull (R/IL), "If our friends at Washington concur, announce publicly at once" that the Southern forts "are to be retaken after the inauguration."[32]

The instruction was indicative of the president-elect's naïveté, in that any such announcement would have fairly invited secessionists to isolate Fort Sumter (forcing it to be starved out), to take Fort Pickens immediately, and to install there, in the ten weeks remaining before Lincoln took office, ordnance and artillerymen sufficient to render it and the navy yard unassailable. This situation would force the newly installed president either to back down from his prior public commitment to retake Union properties or to carry out expeditions that were sure both to start a civil war and to do so with dramatic Union defeats, thereby squandering—perhaps irrevocably—the national goodwill he would need to defeat secessionism and maintain the Union. But his suggestions to Scott and Trumbull went nowhere and Lincoln continued, as before, to say almost nothing concerning his proposed policies. Then, on February 11, speaking in Indianapolis on his way to Washington, he asserted that it would not be "coercion" if the federal government were to hold the forts it still had, retake those that had been taken, collect tariff duties, or withdraw mail service from areas "where the mails themselves are habitually violated."[33] By thus using hypotheticals and disjunctives, declaring not what he was going to do but what it might be proper to do, Lincoln gained accolades from Northern audiences while avoiding preemptive countermeasures in the South.

When drafting his inaugural speech in Springfield, Lincoln had in hand the Constitution, Jackson's Proclamation against the nullifiers, Webster's "Second Reply to Hayne," and Henry Clay's major speech urging the Compromise of 1850.[34] A friend, the prominent Illinois lawyer Orville H. Browning, recommended deleting any suggestion that federal properties already seized by the Confederates would be retaken. A better strategy, Browning urged, would be an attempt to resupply and reinforce Fort Sumter, since this would induce South Carolina to open fire, thereby justifying the federal government in "repelling" Southern "aggression."[35]

Seward in late January had told Lincoln that the several facilities lost at Pensacola that month must be retaken but then reversed himself, suggesting (as Browning did) that Lincoln expunge from the inaugural any commitment to reclaim properties already seized. While Seward admitted that Republican radicals would be displeased, he had already dismissed such men as "reckless."[36] In the cover letter accompanying his comments, Seward was not reluctant to talk down to the president-elect, informing him that "only the soothing words which I have spoken [e.g., his January 12 speech] have saved us and carried us along thus far," something "every loyal man, and, indeed, every disloyal man in the South, will tell you."[37] Seward was thus claiming personal credit for the South's having not yet attacked Sumter, a claim contradicted by correspondence showing that Sumter had not been under immediate threat only because neither South Carolina nor the Confederacy was ready.[38]

Lincoln's draft inaugural now stated that, in accordance with the powers and responsibilities granted him under Article II, he would "hold, occupy, and possess the property, and places belonging to the government."[39] As things stood on March 4, 1861, this entailed keeping four facilities federally occupied: Fort Sumter, Fort Pickens, Fort Taylor at Key West, and the unfinished Fort Jefferson on Garden Key in the Dry Tortugas, seventy nautical miles west of Fort Taylor.[40] L. T. Wigfall, still in the Senate despite his strident secessionism, asked why the Confederates should not seize these assets rather than "sit quietly" until General Scott ordered their reinforcement.[41]

After 11:00 a.m. on March 4, with Buchanan's failed presidency in its final minutes, Secretary of War Holt told Buchanan of a February 28 dispatch just received from Anderson indicating that any Union relief effort would require no fewer than twenty thousand trained soldiers.[42] Now, as in early February, Anderson and Scott both well knew that no such force could be raised before the garrison ran out of food.[43] Buchanan's response to Holt was that this was "a matter for the new Administration."[44] In the moments before the inaugural, Buchanan took Lincoln aside. "I was waiting with boyish wonder and credulity," Lincoln's assistant secretary John Hay later wrote, "to see what momentous counsels" would be imparted. Buchanan proceeded to tell Lincoln "many intimate details of the kitchen and pantry," adding that the water from the well on the right was better than the one on the left. Lincoln displayed "that weary, introverted look of his, not answering," and when Hay later mentioned the conversation, Lincoln "admitted he had not heard a word of it."[45] If Buchanan had instead consumed these moments by handing over Anderson's dispatch, perhaps Lincoln would have altered his speech by reverting to

Seward's suggestion of making no commitment to hold Fort Sumter and the other assets still in federal hands. As things were, Lincoln voiced his pledge to "hold, occupy, and possess" Fort Sumter, unaware of just how little time he had to fulfill that verbal commitment or renounce it as impracticable.[46]

While practical and logistical problems dogged Lincoln's intention to retain vestiges of federal authority in the South, he did have—and used—the moral high ground: "In *your* hands, my dissatisfied fellow countrymen," he told the Confederates in his inaugural,

> and not in *mine*, is the momentous issue of civil war. The government will not assail *you*. You can have no conflict, without being yourselves the aggressors. *You* have no oath registered in Heaven to destroy the government, while *I* . . . have the most solemn one to "preserve, protect, and defend" it. . . . We are not enemies, but friends. . . . Though passion may have strained, it must not break our bonds of affection. The mystic chords of memory, stretching from every battle-field, and patriot grave, to every living heart and hearthstone, all over this broad land, will yet swell the chorus of Union, when again touched, as surely they will be, by the better angels of our nature.[47]

At a meeting on the evening of March 7, several Southerners asked Lincoln to construe the meaning of his inaugural. He reportedly responded, "It meant peace."[48] Not surprisingly, radical Republicans saw the inaugural's conciliatory tone (Lord Lyons noted) as "an abandonment of principle."[49] Southern newspapers, meanwhile, found in the speech not one syllable to praise.[50] Some had hoped to spot in it—the Charleston correspondent of Greeley's *Tribune* noted—"a provocation for extreme action," only to be crestfallen by its "calm and dignified" timbre.[51] While any objective reader would find that solemnity encouraging, the *Richmond Enquirer* construed it as "the cool, unimpassioned, deliberate language of the fanatic, with the purpose of pursuing the promptings of fanaticism even to the dismemberment of the Government with the horrors of civil war."[52] The *Charleston Courier* and *Mercury* vied with each other in describing the speech's supposed belligerence.[53] John M. Daniel's *Richmond Examiner*, not to be outdone, called Lincoln "an ugly and ferocious old Orang-Outang from the wilds of Illinois," a "creature whom no one can hear with patience or look on without disgust."[54] Roger Pryor called Lincoln "a feculent excrescence of Northwestern vulgarity."[55] Justice Campbell, feeling no sense of deference to a coordinate branch of the government he had sworn to defend and by which he was still employed, called Lincoln's speech "a beastly thing," "wanting in statesmanship . . . and . . . dignity & decorum . . . an incendiary message . . . calculated to set the country in a blaze."[56] Alfred Huger, having been introduced to Anderson by their mutual friend Robert Gourdin, told Anderson that the inaugural left "no hope" of averting war.[57] A friend commented to Chase, "The wiser and kinder you are" to slaveholders, "the more foolish they will be, and the surer to fight and be destroyed."[58]

On March 5, Lincoln's first full day in office, Holt sent him Anderson's February 28 dispatch saying that the garrison's food would run out in a few weeks.[59] Seward wrote to his wife, "Fort Sumter in danger. Relief of it practically impossible."[60] Holt failed to mention Anderson's dispatch of December 26 wherein he notified his superiors that he had "about four months' supply of provisions."[61] While the receipt of such information would have immediately prompted a competent secretary of war to record in his February calendar that a decision was necessary regarding the garrison's fate, the secretary at that time was Floyd, engulfed in scandal, and Floyd and his calendar (if he kept one) were gone. Others in the Buchanan administration were aware of the food problem, in that Larz Anderson, after visiting his brother in mid-January, reported back to Buchanan and Scott, undoubtedly letting them know (as he let Henry Adams know) that the garrison could "hold out two or three months, though not with comfort."[62] But no one before now had informed Lincoln.

A Circle of Fire

On Christmas Day, 1860, one day before Major Anderson's move to Fort Sumter, Alfred Huger asked his cousin Benjamin Huger to consider leading South Carolina's new military force.[63] Benjamin had been Anderson's classmate at West Point and with him wrote *Instruction for Heavy Artillery* (1851), which would be used by both sides in the Civil War.[64] Like Anderson, Huger was a highly decorated veteran of the Mexican conflict under General Scott, who thought him "an officer distinguished by every kind of merit." His greatest military achievement, the capture of Veracruz after three weeks of shelling, suggested his suitability to lead the effort against the "impregnable" Fort Sumter.[65] But on January 3, 1861, he responded to Alfred:

> Maj A[nderson] and myself went to West Point together 40 years [ago] and have been comrades in the Army from that day to this, & I am now to . . . make war upon him & his sixty men!! . . . My first counsel would

be, not to attack or molest Majr. Anderson's command. In such times of excitement . . . where the State is first in a movement dependent upon the public opinion and sympathy of other [Southern states] for its success, the great element, to allow the development of this public opinion, is time. To gain this time, you want to keep every thing as quiet as possible, & make delays if necessary . . . and not to commit any act tending to civil war, which none of us may see the end of.[66]

On February 22, after Colonel Huger repeatedly declined, Jefferson Davis summoned Pierre G. Toutant Beauregard to command all Confederate forces at Charleston.[67] The very model of the "dashing" Southern officer, Beauregard could trace his lineage to Tider the Young, who had commanded one of the Welsh revolts against Edward I in the thirteenth century before escaping to France and changing his name to Toutant, to which the mellifluous "Beauregard" attached in the seventeenth century by marriage. General Scott and Colonel Joseph Totten had both admired his incisive and daring work in Mexico.[68]

General Pierre G. Toutant Beauregard. By Matthew Brady. National Archives NA 525441.

In November 1860, President Buchanan and Secretary Floyd, pursuant to the same pro-Southern policy that assigned Major Anderson to Fort Moultrie and Colonel Huger to the Charleston Arsenal, had appointed Beauregard as superintendent of the United States Military Academy at West Point. He accepted but stated that he would resign if—as seemed imminent—his native Louisiana left the Union. Floyd's replacement, Joseph Holt, deprived Beauregard of that option by summarily removing him. Beauregard arrived in Charleston on March 1 in a new Confederate uniform bearing the brass and stitched indicia of a brigadier general. He met with Governor Pickens at the Charleston Hotel and then inspected the several batteries around Charleston Harbor. "Among the privates there," an approved biography recorded, "were planters and sons of planters, some of them the wealthiest men of South Carolina, diligently working, side by side with their slaves. . . . Numerous were the plans—each 'infallible'—suggested by these high-spirited gentlemen, for taking the formidable work which loomed up majestic and defiant in the distance."[69] The Southerners had gathered not just a new and growing provisional army but also dozens of iron and bronze guns, howitzers, and mortars, many of them from federal forts and arsenals recently seized.[70] Beauregard's plan was to construct a "circle of fire" with Fort Sumter at its center, "in accord with the principles of gunnery; that is to say, near enough to Fort Sumter to do it the greatest possible damage, and yet far enough away to be almost beyond range of its fire."[71] With human and material resources vastly superior to Anderson's, Beauregard also enjoyed the double benefit of spreading his assets around this circumference with everything aimed at the center, while Anderson had the double disadvantage of being that communal target while aiming at diffuse peripheral assailants.

General Scott, like most observers, thought Seward the intelligence of the new administration, Lincoln the gawky figurehead.[72] The administration had several topics to consider, Scott told Seward. Should it:

- halt and reverse secessionism by abandoning the Republican platform in favor of allowing slavery to expand into the West;
- do nothing, and within sixty days watch Maryland and Virginia secede, thereby making Washington a Union enclave isolated within "a foreign country," requiring "a permanent garrison of at least thirty-five thousand";
- collect duties outside the ports of seceded states, or close and blockade such ports;
- conquer the seceded states by raising a well-disciplined army of three hundred thousand men, more than a third of whom will be lost to "skirmishes, sieges, battles, & southern fevers," at a total cost of at least $250

million, followed by heavy garrisons in the defeated states that would be required "for generations"; or

- forget these other considerations and simply "say to the seceded States—wayward sisters, depart in peace!"[73]

Seward, who had been Scott's political advisor for a decade, had been suggesting the last alternative. If, as Seward would have anticipated, the cabinet would find each of Scott's other choices unacceptable, he could construct and carry out a plan under the last option.[74]

While most believed that Unionism would be affirmed in the Upper South and border states if Lincoln voluntarily abandoned Charleston and Pensacola, this step would not by itself amount to letting the wayward sisters depart in peace, since he would also need to give up attempting to collect customs duties anywhere in the Cotton South and then passively wait and hope that Seward's notion of an eventual reintegration would occur—all the while fighting off an impeachment effort by Republicans who would legitimately feel betrayed. If instead Lincoln gave up the forts but attempted to collect duties outside Charleston Harbor, that effort would be resisted and lead inevitably to an incident, which in turn might cause the loyal slave states to join their fellow slaveowners, making them neither friends nor neutrals but enemies at the border of Pennsylvania.

Virginia was pivotal. When in October 1860 General Scott recommended to Buchanan and Floyd the reinforcement of Southern forts, he issued copies to various fellow Virginians, endorsed with the words "If Virginia can be saved from secession, *she* may save the Union."[75] Bordering on several free-soil states as well as the nation's capital (to which it had once donated a portion of its northeast corner), Virginia avoided the insularity by which the cotton states convinced themselves that free-labor states were distant, malevolent entities with incompatible values.[76] It had played an unparalleled role in the founding of the republic and in providing brilliant presidents.[77] It was large and rich. Its substantial cities and towns did business with the North. It was home to a million whites, among them fifty-two thousand slaveholders, with 491,000 slaves—more than any other state. It had two hundred thousand white males of military age and would be invaded by a Northern army moving south. With counties west of the Blue Ridge dominated by slaveless yeomen, it had openly debated emancipation and had maintained a mix of free- and slave-labor systems.[78] As its tobacco fields gave up their nutrients, it sold its excess slaves "down the river" to the expanding Cotton South, and if a time came when seceded states reopened the importation of slaves from Africa, the value of

Virginia's inventory would plunge.[79] In December 1860, John Pendleton Kennedy, author of the widely read *Swallow Barn*, a novel of Virginia plantation life, wrote that secessionists should look to the Upper South for guidance, since without it, "no confederacy of Slave States . . . can possibly be formed" that would be "at all worthy of respect and consideration as an independent power."[80]

Virginia's secession convention began on February 13. On February 27, Lincoln met for two hours with George W. Summers, a delegate from the western part of the state, reportedly telling him (although this is disputed) that if the convention concluded with a pro-Union vote, he would evacuate Fort Sumter.[81] A few days later, however, Lincoln promised in his inaugural to retain the Southern forts. Radical Republicans intended to hold him to that promise, while Summers and other Unionists apparently saw Sumter's abandonment as a condition of Virginia's loyalty.[82] Seward advised Lincoln that not just Virginia but all the border states could be secured if he appointed Judge Summers to the Supreme Court.[83] Lincoln declined.

Seward met with a close friend, William Gwin, who subsequently reported to the Southern commissioners in Washington that Seward wanted to retain Virginia's loyalty by "moderation and justice" pending the seceded states' reintegration but swore to "crush" Jefferson Davis and Robert Toombs, both of whom he had known well in the Senate. A report of Seward's comments was forwarded to Toombs, universally known as the only real fire-eater in the Confederate cabinet, who undoubtedly showed it to Davis.[84] For all Seward's public talk of conciliation, an effort in that direction required—at a minimum—an understated, uniform, trustworthy diplomacy of which he seemed incapable.

"All Else Is Easy"

Lincoln, apprised of Sumter's food crisis and undoubtedly concerned about the unacceptable alternatives laid out in General Scott's list, now had three choices:

- evacuate Fort Sumter and thereby repudiate an inaugural promise just made, while urging in mitigation that the withdrawal was *not* a peace offering to the South (thus destroying the only value the withdrawal would have had there) but a military necessity;
- gather what forces he could in an effort to reinforce the garrison, either by stealth or openly, thereby starting the war and losing additional slave states; or

- deliberate and weigh the options pending the few weeks available until Anderson's men ran out of food, knowing that every day the Confederates would be mounting more artillery and gathering more troops in opposition to any relief effort.[85]

Among the dozens of unsolicited proposals to relieve the garrison were a submarine to transport reinforcements and a balloon to drift over and drop supplies within the walls.[86]

Buchanan, home in Pennsylvania, asserted that he had decided against relieving Fort Sumter because of the huge force requirements noted in Anderson's February 28 dispatch, leaving as the only alternative "to let the Confederate States commence the war" against Fort Sumter's small garrison, while authorizing Anderson to capitulate if overwhelmed.[87] On March 11, Anderson wrote to his former pastor in New Jersey that while he was surprised that Lincoln had not yet made up his mind whether to abandon or reinforce Fort Sumter, he understood that decisions entailing a probable cost in lives were difficult to make and that Lincoln, once he deeply considered the matter, would extract the garrison.[88] But Anderson had mentioned an alternative to a massive attack: a small incursion that required no amphibious assault because the batteries might be circumvented by stealth.[89] Buchanan had heard competing incursion plans from Ward and Fox but rejected them as impracticable, given reports of guard boats at the mouth of the harbor. Captain Henry Julius Hartstene, former commander of *Pawnee*, had resigned his U.S. commission and now commanded the Confederate naval forces at Charleston.[90] Hartstene contacted Russell Sturgis in New York to ask about purchasing two tugs, although Sturgis, a staunch Unionist, declined.[91] Gustavus Fox, unaware that Hartstene had already obtained tugs from Savannah, told his brother-in-law Montgomery Blair, about to be appointed as Lincoln's postmaster general, that the chances of successfully reaching Fort Sumter by tug would naturally be decreased if Hartstene was similarly equipped.[92]

Holt, in his March 5 memorandum to Lincoln, revealed that "an expedition has been quietly prepared . . . under the supervision of General Scott, who arranged its details," and "is ready to sail from New York on a few hours' notice for transporting troops and supplies to Fort Sumter." Because Washington was filled with disloyal people, the new Confederate government received word of this Union naval squadron.[93] Although Scott may have had several shallow-draft steamers from the Coast Survey ready on ten hours' notice, it was unlikely that the new president on his second day in office would approve—sight unseen—a plan devised by the aging general responsible for the *Star of the West* fiasco.[94] And Scott told Lincoln that the plan he had in mind (i.e., Ward's) was no longer viable because of recent improvements in Confederate defenses, adding that Anderson saw no alternative to surrender.[95]

With Vice President Hannibal Hamlin's New England background came the right to choose a New Englander for the cabinet.[96] After consultation in the region, Hamlin opted against Seward designee Charles Francis Adams and instead picked Gideon Welles, a cofounder of the Republican Party in Connecticut. His support for Andrew Jackson in the 1830s had yielded him appointment as Hartford's postmaster, and he had once edited the estimable *Hartford Times*.[97] While this background suited him for postmaster general, that position went to Montgomery Blair, with Welles becoming navy secretary.[98] Welles now gathered senior naval officers—Commodores Silas H. Stringham and Hiram Paulding (Ret.) and Captains Charles Stewart and Francis Gregory (Ret.)—who approved Fox's plan to resupply Fort Sumter using fast, shallow-draft steam tugs.[99]

That plan, meanwhile, had evolved. In one variant, the tugs with a draft of six feet and speed of fourteen knots would convene at night east of the Charleston bar and then, two hours before high water, transect the bar on the rising tide. In several iterations, the tugs were to be three in number, the lead tug containing no troops, its sole purpose (and that of its dauntless captain and crew) being to draw fire. Each of the other tugs would carry half of the reinforcements, protected from gunboats firing canister, case shot, or shells by bales of cotton or hay soaked with water. Each tug would have a launch or boat trailing behind, to be used as a lifeboat if necessary. The tugs would enter the harbor at midchannel, thirteen hundred yards distant from Fort Moultrie and Cumming's Point and move rapidly at right angles to their lines of fire.[100] Each tug would be armed with "the heaviest howitzers" because—in Fox's view—"the vital point . . . is a naval force that can destroy" the Confederates' vessels and onshore batteries. Fox could not be seriously suggesting that three tugs fitted out with twelve- or twenty-four-pound boat guns could damage distant shore batteries; all they might reasonably discharge was solid shot or case or canister toward an oncoming vessel. "All else," he wrote, "is easy," a word he could not actually have meant.[101]

On March 5, with Holt's dire memo in hand and having in his inaugural pledged to retain the Southern forts, Lincoln reportedly told Scott not just to hold but also to reinforce all Southern forts still in Union hands.[102] It was an order Scott would have been delighted to receive four months earlier, although he now thought that any operation in Charleston required a massive amphibious force that could not be assembled in time. Regarding Pensacola, Scott informed Lincoln that a January truce required that reinforcements remain on *Brooklyn*, waiting offshore, unless Fort Pickens was attacked.[103]

7

"Mr. Seward Has Triumphed"

LINCOLN HAD EVERY REASON TO BE WARY OF SEWARD, THE DENIZEN OF NEW York politics who had thought the Republican nomination his by right, who bragged about being "in the saddle" in the administration, who made policy pronouncements without seeking Lincoln's concurrence, and who, on the eve of the inaugural, threatened to resign in an effort to intimidate the new president into granting him extraordinary powers. Welles later noted that while in these early days other cabinet officers committed themselves to understanding their own departments, Seward "spent a considerable portion of every day with the president, patronizing and instructing him, hearing and telling anecdotes" and solidifying his role as "the Premier,—as he liked to be called," while reducing Lincoln's involvement with other advisors by limiting cabinet meetings.[1] Seward on March 6 informed the Southern commissioners in Washington that "the president himself is really not aware of the condition of the country." One of them, Martin Crawford, passed on these comments to Confederate Secretary of State Toombs, adding that all of the cabinet were for peace except Chase and Blair, who were not influential.[2] Seward would have been Crawford's source for these skewed perspectives.

On March 9, in his first substantive cabinet meeting, Lincoln asked Scott how long Anderson could hold out if nothing was done and what Scott would need to resupply or reinforce him.[3] Scott had consulted with Totten, the architect of the nation's system of coastal fortifications, and with Captain Foster of the Corps of Engineers, who had been with Anderson at Sumter and had served with Anderson and Scott in the Mexican War.[4] Scott and Totten concurred with Anderson's view that Sumter must be evacuated because it was about to run out of food and could not be resupplied without a force of twenty thousand. Attorney General Edward Bates later recalled being astonished at this revelation.[5] A March 10 dispatch to the *New York Times* reported a "general impression" in Washington that the administration "has determined on withdrawing the troops from Fort Sumter," based upon Scott's view that any attempted reinforcement would entail "an immense loss of life."[6] Lincoln reportedly discussed the cabinet meeting with Stephen Douglas, who passed on to journalist William Henry Hurlbert the perspective that everyone but Blair wanted Sumter abandoned.[7]

The Southern commissioners telegraphed Toombs that "things look better" than the Confederate leaders had hoped for, since Anderson himself had counseled withdrawal and "good sources" now said that Fort Sumter "will be evacuated within . . . 10 days," with a growing perception in Washington that Fort Pickens, too, would be given up. Louis Wigfall reported to Jefferson Davis and General Beauregard that the cabinet's informal decision was for a withdrawal not in ten days but five.[8] Seward, in a "lively, almost in a boisterous mood," reportedly assured journalist Hurlbert that Fort Sumter would indeed be vacated quickly.[9] Well might a new secretary of state, believing that the Union could be saved only if the Upper South remained loyal, and that this required Sumter's abandonment, be delighted to hear military experts declare relief impossible, since any fellow cabinet officer who vociferously opposed voluntary abandonment as a gesture of conciliation would now be under pressure to accept it as a matter of military necessity.

On March 9 or 10, having apparently received no confirmation from Scott that appropriate plans were under way to reinforce Fort Sumter or Fort Pickens as orally ordered on March 5, Lincoln issued to Scott a written order to employ "all possible vigilance for the maintenance of all the places within the military department of the United States; and to promptly call upon all the departments of the government for the means necessary to that end."[10] On March 12, seven days after Lincoln's first request, Scott had his assistant adjutant general, Brigadier General Edward D. Townsend, issue an order to Captain Vogdes, still off Pensacola: "At the first favorable moment, you will land with your company, reenforce Fort Pickens, and hold the same till further orders."[11] Lincoln had apparently concluded that if Vogdes's men were transferred from *Brooklyn* to Fort Pickens, federal authority would be maintained in the South and his inaugural promise vindicated, even if Fort Sumter—as Scott and Anderson seemed to believe—could not be relieved without a huge invasion force that Scott did not have. Radical Republicans would be angry, but so long as his inaugural promise had been fulfilled at Pensacola, that anger could be contained by the excuse that Sumter's loss was Buchanan's fault. Nor was keeping Fort Sumter a military necessity, in that the ongoing collection of tariff duties—if desired—could be accomplished by Revenue cutters offshore, or Charleston could be blockaded by warships offshore.[12]

Fort Pickens had food sufficient to support Slemmer's small garrison through June 1861 but lacked arms and ammunition.[13] Vogdes, not knowing of the Scott/Townsend March 12 order to transfer his men, sent to the North a list of items that would be required to operate Fort Pickens when and if they did come ashore. After the items were assembled in New York and made ready for shipment, Scott, although under instructions from Lincoln to call upon all departments of the government for the means necessary to maintain the Southern forts, ordered that these supplies not be sent.[14]

Francis Blair, the Republican Party's most senior and experienced cofounder, sought and obtained an interview with Lincoln, warning him that if he ordered Anderson's withdrawal, the voters would reject the decision, the party would collapse, and Lincoln would probably be impeached. A surrender of Sumter, Blair urged, was "virtually a surrender of the Union," to be allowed only "under irresistible force," adding that negotiating with traitors was itself traitorous and that Lincoln should either explain to the public that Sumter could not be defended because of Buchanan's failures or declare that he would try to retain possession of the fort without provoking hostilities. While the senior Blair admitted to his son, the postmaster general, that he had spoken to Lincoln with a "zeal" approaching impertinence, his warnings (Gideon Welles later recalled) "touched a chord" in Lincoln.[15] A March 12 *New York Times* dispatch noted that while Scott and Secretary of War Simon Cameron favored abandonment, Lincoln, Chase, and Montgomery Blair were "strongly opposed" and were "constantly receiving remonstrances from . . . [Republican] radicals against the evacuation," some of these going so far "as to threaten political retribution" and the destruction of the Republican Party (as Blair Sr. had warned).[16] Whig newspaperman James Watson Webb told Lincoln that if he evacuated Sumter without military necessity, not one in a hundred "of our friends at the North" would approve.[17] "The rumor that the evacuation of Fort Sumter is contemplated," a constituent wrote to Gideon Welles, "throws a pall over the popular heart."[18] Seward, meanwhile, told Charles Francis Adams that Lincoln was about to order Sumter's abandonment but was given pause by the radical Republicans' "violent remonstrances."[19]

Scott on March 11 wrote out and gave to Secretary of War Cameron the evacuation order Scott hoped to send to Anderson.[20] That day, the Washington journalist and political strategist James Harvey, born in South Carolina, sent a telegram to his old schoolmate, Andrew Magrath, the former federal

Lieutenant General Scott's evacuation order to Major Anderson (March 11, 1861). Lincoln Papers, Library of Congress.

judge, now a member of that state's executive council, with a copy to the aging Unionist James Louis Petigru. It read, "Order issued for withdrawal of Anderson's command. Scott declares it military necessity. This is private."[21] Magrath asked for a confirmation. After speaking with Seward and Cameron, Harvey responded, "My information is direct and positive," Sumter's abandonment being delayed by "nothing but forms."[22]

Harvey's information did not remain private, in that a Washington dispatch went to the *New York Times* announcing that the battle of the Cabinet has been fought, and Mr. Seward has triumphed. The Cabinet has ordered the withdrawal of Major Anderson from Sumter, and thus [has] destroyed the hope of the Secessionists to cement in blood the destruction of the Union. . . . The Cabinet met at 11 o'clock and discussed the question until 2 P.M., when it was formally decided to withdraw the troops from Sumter on the ground that Mr. Buchanan had left the fort in a condition that rendered its reinforcement impossible without a greater sacrifice of life than the importance of the position would justify. The decision has been received by the radical Republicans with great disapprobation. Mr. Seward . . . thinks that if the people in the Cotton States have no cause to concentrate their animosity against the Government at Washington, it will soon develop itself against the Government at Montgomery.[23]

The story, so flattering to Seward and his theory of the crisis and its resolution as to resemble a press release, was also notable for ignoring the president entirely. The alleged withdrawal policy was unabashedly "Mr. Seward's policy" and had been ordered by "the Cabinet," as if the Constitution invested the executive power of the United States in a board of directors of which Seward was chairman and Lincoln just an ex officio member.

The construct was easy to accept because Seward had described Lincoln as weak, and Buchanan and similarly weak predecessors had let their cabinets rule them. Yet even the *National Republican*, an administration organ, announced in the same vein that the cabinet had decided to evacuate Fort Sumter "as a matter of conciliation to the border States" and because "yielding a point of pride to South Carolina . . . would satisfy the country generally" that the administration wanted peace.[24] The Southern commissioners in Washington reported to Montgomery a comment by Senator Crittenden that Scott "was also for peace and would sustain" Seward's conciliation policy, adding that Sumter's evacuation, if it happened, would be because of Scott's influence on Lincoln.[25] One of Anderson's officers, Samuel Wylie Crawford, M.D., wrote in his diary, "Papers again speak of our withdrawal as a certainty."[26] One of the commissioners, John Forsyth, wrote to Governor Pickens, "I confidently believe Sumter will be evacuated, and think a Government messenger left here yesterday with orders to that effect for Anderson."[27] Forsyth had perhaps heard about Scott's handwritten order of March 11, without knowing that it had neither been approved by Lincoln nor handed to a messenger for delivery to Anderson. Confederate leaders believed that with the cabinet inclined to withdrawal, the South should press its advantage by instructing the commissioners to concede nothing of value except in exchange for the Union's abandonment of both Sumter and Pensacola.[28]

The March 15 Cabinet Meeting

James Harvey reported to Magrath that while "great efforts" were under way to reconsider withdrawal, evacuation would ultimately prevail at the March 15 cabinet meeting.[29] Meanwhile, the cabinet member most vociferous against withdrawal, Montgomery Blair, telegraphed his brother-in-law, Gustavus Fox, to return to Washington and present his revised relief plan at that meeting.[30] With Generals Scott and Totten and Commodore Stringham in attendance, Fox laid out the proposed operation: place a warship outside the harbor and beyond the range of the shore batteries, its mere presence there being sufficient—Fox argued—to drive the Confederate ships away from the harbor mouth and back toward Charleston, thus leaving Fox's tugs free to proceed at night, subject to attack only by the shore batteries. Welles replied that the Confederate vessels would not retreat unless they were actually fired upon by the warship and/or Sumter. Once that happened, Welles noted, "will it not be claimed that aggressive war has been commenced by us upon the State and its citizens in their own harbor?"[31]

Scott again asserted that any operation required a massive amphibious landing to eliminate the batteries on both sides of the harbor entrance. Totten concurred.[32] Fox retorted that the question of passing batteries at night was a naval question, concerning which he had compiled a list of such successes, headed by Britain's shallow-draft paddle steamers and screw gunboats in the Crimean War.[33] Fox undoubtedly knew of that operation via the reports by *Times* of London correspondent W. H. Russell, reports that established Russell's reputation as the world's greatest war correspondent and yielded him the assignment of reporting the prospective U.S. civil war.

Crimea had also been studied by U.S. Navy commander John A. Dahlgren.[34] Among Dahlgren's major innovations in ordnance were rifled cannons, cannons varying their thickness over the length of the bore in parallel with the amount of explosive pressure exerted at each point, and a family of twelve-pound bronze howitzers placed on special carriages on the gunwale and aft on launches and boats, firing shot, canister, or a nine-pound shell up to one thousand yards, with well-trained crewmen capable of reloading and firing every six seconds.[35] Another was his fitting out the sloop *Plymouth* with a variety of guns so that sailors could learn their various characteristics in rolling seas.[36]

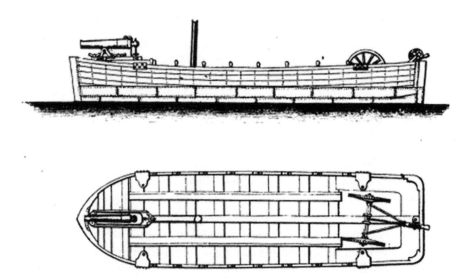

Views of a frigate launch. John A. Dahlgren, *Boat Armament of the U.S. Navy*, 2nd ed. (Philadelphia, 1856).

In China in August 1855, two launches and a cutter from the side-wheel steam sloop *Powhatan* were involved in the battle at Ty-ho Bay. Carrying a combined total of one hundred men and mounting twelve-pound Dahlgren howitzers, they and several similar British boats were towed to the mouth of the bay by a British steamer that was too large to enter and successfully fought piratical war junks in a brutal engagement.[37]

In Mexico in March 1847, Scott had commanded an amphibious landing of 8,600 troops, "a model for imitation," spearheaded by sixty-five flat-bottomed surf boats, each thirty-five to forty feet long with capacity for forty to forty-five men.[38] But this was at Collado, two and a half miles south of Veracruz and beyond the range of that city's guns. The present situation was thus not analogous, and Scott opposed this operation because in his view it required more than twice the number of men he had had there.

President Lincoln, for his part, knew about navigating shoals in the dark, having been a riverboatman. In 1849, Lincoln obtained a patent for bellows that, when strapped to the sides of a vessel and inflated, could so decrease the vessel's draft as to clear sandbars or, if stuck on one, get the vessel dislodged without having to increase buoyancy by throwing cargo (or ordnance) over-board.[39] Although a Charleston incursion with ample planning time might thus have included a direct and substantial contribution from a commander in chief with relevant expertise, no one now had the time to contemplate whether such contraptions might be scaled up and employed to lift Union warships over the Charleston bar. Lincoln, the least self-important and least self-revealing of men, apparently saw no need even to inform these experts about his relevant skill, instead commenting, "I know little about ships."[40] When Lincoln asked whether any high naval official would approve Fox's plan, Commodore Stringham voiced assent.[41]

Several days earlier, Douglas had introduced in the Senate a resolution demanding that Lincoln explain, among other things, whether the reason for keeping Forts Sumter and Pickens in federal hands was to coerce the return of South Carolina and Florida.[42] Lincoln, undoubtedly briefed concerning Douglas's initiative and aware that Douglas had specifically asked whether it was "wise" to retain Sumter and Pickens, proceeded to ask each cabinet member to provide, in writing, an opinion regarding whether, assuming it was possible to provision Fort Sumter, it was "wise" to do so.[43] Seward provided several solid reasons why it was unwise. First, any plan would become immediately known and Fort Sumter would be attacked before any expedition arrived, thus initiating war. Second, even if an incursion succeeded and some supplies reached Fort Sumter, the Union could not ultimately prevail there, because the Confederates would eventually reduce the fort to rubble and/or storm and overrun it. Sumter was not intended for a long siege by batteries of artillery and would ultimately either surrender or be sacrificed.[44] While the death of Anderson and his men would galvanize the North and ensure successful recruitment and ample material support, the symbolic value of their collective martyrdom was all any strategist could reasonably hope for in a battle Anderson could not win. Finally, even if the operation could be kept secret and every component worked as planned, the fort would have no utility because it could never be used to subjugate the city or state, much less the Confederacy. Thus—Seward advised—the Union "will have inaugurated a civil war by our own act, without an adequate object." He recommended using a naval force to collect tariff duties offshore but wanted Sumter evacuated. Cameron and Scott agreed.[45]

Attorney General Bates, from the border state of Missouri and, like Cameron, Chase, and Seward, an unsuccessful candidate against Lincoln, believed that any relief force would be wiped out.[46] Welles thought that the public, aware of the food issue, had already accustomed itself to Sumter's abandonment. Seward now had four cabinet members firmly behind evacuation: Cameron, Bates, Welles, and Interior Secretary Caleb B. Smith, a political hack who came in the bargain Lincoln's handlers had negotiated to win Indiana.[47] Chase, although a fervent antislavery radical, now hedged.[48]

This left Montgomery Blair. Soaking up as a child not only the political aperçus of his father but also the perspectives on executive authority held by President Jackson (who treated him as a son), Blair enrolled at West Point (at Jackson's urging), later becoming a prosecutor and premier appellate litigator, ultimately as lead counsel in *Dred Scott*.[49] Blair did not now espouse any particular military tactic to reach Fort Sumter, even that of his brother-in-law Fox. Nor did he reject any other, simply urging that something positive must be tried, at a moment when Southerners saw Northerners as "deficient in the courage to maintain the Government." Evacuation would not prevent war— Blair urged—but would instead "embolden" the Confederates, unless Lincoln also abandoned Fort Pickens, Key West, Tortugas, Hampton Roads, and all other indicia of federal authority in the South. The Confederacy, that is, would require a complete capitulation.[50]

"The Highest Assurances"

Back on March 11, the three Confederate commissioners had requested a face-to-face but unofficial interview with Seward to discuss recognition of their government and to negotiate the Confederacy's purchase of Fort Sumter and other assets. Seward declined, derisively characterizing these men to his wife as "ambassadors."[51] They then presented a formal request for diplomatic recognition, thus forcing Seward to: (1) recognize the Confederacy as a foreign power, (2) formally refuse their request and thus increase the chances of an attack upon Fort Sumter and/or Fort Pickens, or (3) negotiate with them— as they had requested—informally.[52] U.S. Supreme Court justice Samuel Nelson of New York suggested that he and Justice Campbell of Alabama act as intermediaries. Campbell, who had earlier discussed with his friend Montgomery Blair the possibility of brokering a peace, seemed a sound choice. Although he owned slaves and had written a series of proslavery articles, he had opposed nullification. He had asserted that "a State may dissolve its relation to the Union at its pleasure," but he "was not a patron or friend of the secession movement." His record overall was that of a Unionist, and of course he had not—like hundreds of others—resigned his federal position.[53] While Campbell had concurred in the Court's *Dred Scott* decision, Blair apparently did not hold this against him.[54]

In submitting his comments to Lincoln regarding evacuation versus reinforcement, Seward did not see fit to reveal that he was negotiating with the Confederacy and that any attempt at resupply or reinforcement would summarily terminate those conversations. Campbell had significant moral authority among Southern leaders, and Nelson had drafted the original majority opinion that Dred Scott remained a slave.[55] Campbell later recalled that Nelson had met with Seward, with Treasury Secretary Salmon Chase, and with Attorney General Edward Bates, telling each that, after research and consultation with Chief Justice Taney, he believed that the Constitution did not permit any coercive acts by the executive branch without appropriate enactments by Congress (which was not in session), adding that moderation would "inevitably lead to the restoration of the Union in all of its integrity." Seward reportedly "expressed gratification to find so many impediments" to coercion and wished there were more.[56]

On March 15, the day of the cabinet meeting, Seward invited Justices Nelson and Campbell to his office, where he warned them that he could not ask the cabinet to take the huge step of granting diplomatic recognition to the Confederacy when it was already under pressure (from Seward himself, among others) to give up Fort Sumter. Campbell here suggested a compromise: if Lincoln would evacuate Fort Sumter, the commissioners, in return, would temporarily suspend their demand for diplomatic recognition. Seward accepted, recklessly promising that Sumter would be vacated in less than the three days required for the commissioners to report the compromise by mail to Jefferson Davis in Montgomery.[57] Seward further promised that the administration would undertake "no measures changing the existing status of things prejudicial to the Confederate States," meaning that it would not reinforce Fort Pickens.[58] Even as he made this promise, Seward knew that Lincoln had already ordered that reinforcement.

Campbell and Nelson had no reason to doubt that Seward would deliver on his promises. Various newspapers—some perhaps at Seward's prompting, others merely repeating rumors—had already set the public expectation that Anderson's men would soon depart. Seward or anyone wishing to effect that result could say—truthfully—that Scott had already drafted the evacuation order. Justice Campbell, not holding Seward to his impulsive promise of three days, told Commissioner Crawford that he had "perfect confidence" in an evacuation "in the next five days." Crawford and Forsyth in turn assured Confederate Secretary of State Toombs.[59] Edwin Stanton advised the retired Buchanan that Anderson's withdrawal was "certain."[60]

A highly placed spy told Confederate secretary of war Leroy Walker that while the administration was promoting Sumter's evacuation as a peace initiative, that was window dressing because the garrison's food was running out.[61] On March 18, Greeley's *Tribune*, perhaps through its undercover correspondent in Charleston, Charles D. Brigham, reported a widespread expectation in South Carolina that Sumter would be evacuated on March 20.[62] Several Pennsylvania newspapers were displeased that Lincoln might quietly withdraw his inaugural promise, ignore his constitutional obligation to see that the laws are obeyed, and hand Sumter to the rebels.[63]

On March 21, Confederate vice president Alexander Stephens told a Savannah audience that abandonment was imminent.[64] While Unionists firmly controlled Virginia's pending secession convention, their strength stemmed from Seward's unequivocal promise that Sumter would be abandoned.[65] After Seward had an intermediary reassure Judge Summers, the latter, writing from Richmond, indicated that the evacuation "acted like a charm" for Unionists in the convention. Although the past tense suggested that Summers had accepted Seward's representation that removal was essentially a fait accompli, he then asked why it had not yet happened, adding that if Anderson remained, it would "ruin" the Unionist hegemony in Virginia.[66]

Seward knew how to manipulate newspapers. While the *Tribune*'s owner, Horace Greeley, was a personal enemy, that paper was a "rookery" of twenty-eight editors and 184 other employees, among whom Seward had friends with whom to plant a story.[67] When the rival *New York Times* suggested that there would be no evacuation, the *Tribune* reiterated that Scott had signed the relevant order and that it merely awaited the president's approval. Both assertions were true. It then added, "It is ascertained from a reliable source that Fort Sumter is to be evacuated to-morrow. The order has already gone forward."[68] Both of these assertions were false.

Beauregard notified the commissioners that Anderson's men had not left.[69] Justice Campbell sought out Seward, who apparently reassured him, and he in turn reassured the commissioners.[70] In Campbell's retelling, Seward said that the cabinet had passed a "resolution" mandating the withdrawal. No evidence exists, however, that the cabinet had passed a resolution to do anything, much less that Lincoln bound himself to accept it. While Seward would have the world believe that Lincoln had little authority over his cabinet, when Lincoln took office, numerous newspapers reported his view to be that "no votes will be taken in the Cabinet" and that he would, after consulting with its members, "take the responsibility of carrying out his line of policy irrespective of their opinions."[71] Campbell and Crawford, both statesmen of substantial national experience, should here have kept in mind a maxim Seward would later voice to his son: "There is but one vote in the Cabinet," the one "cast by the president."[72] Lincoln so strictly kept his own counsel, so carefully refused to show his hand even to close advisors, that as each day passed without Scott's evacuation order arriving in Charleston, Seward, with diminishing prospects of fulfilling an evacuation promise recklessly uttered, would now have Campbell blame Lincoln, whom Seward described as unable to focus on a crisis and resolve it.[73]

On March 20, Greeley's *Tribune* reported that an order had been sent to Pensacola to disembark the troops still waiting offshore.[74] Seward again assured Campbell, who again assured the commissioners, that neither Fort Pickens nor Fort Sumter would be reinforced.[75] They in turn forwarded to Toombs "the highest assurances that the delay in the evacuation of Fort Sumter shows no bad faith" and that Fort Pickens "will not be reinforced without notice to us." The note concluded, "We feel encouraged," an unwitting compliment to Seward's ability to neutralize adverse news. Forsyth told Pickens and Toombs that he had "faith" in Seward.[76]

8

A Sea of Troubles

The Revival of Fox's Plan

With administration officials divided on the merits of Fox's proposed expedition, it was decided that Fox should reconnoiter Charleston and report.[1] At a train stop northwest of the city, Alfred Huger boarded and recognized the man with whom Fox was talking, Isaac E. Holmes, who had served with Huger in the state legislature many years before. Huger "seemed much depressed" with the North/South crisis, although Holmes assured Huger—on the highest authority—that Sumter would be evacuated. Fox in a later memoir wrote that Holmes named the authority, but at that moment the train whistle blew, so Fox could not hear. That story is not credible: if some high authority had told Holmes that the administration intended to evacuate, that clearly meant that it did not intend to approve the operation Fox had proposed and which was the reason for this trip. Fox, that is, would have asked for the name.[2] In any event, the name he would have heard above the melodramatic whistle (if there was a whistle) would have been "Seward."

Arriving in Charleston, Fox sought out Captain Hartstene, his friend during their respective navy years, who directed him to speak with Governor Pickens. Although Pickens had decamped the state capital in Columbia and set up a makeshift governor's office at Charleston's city hall on Broad Street, he transacted much of his important business at the Charleston Hotel, his self-appointed roles including that of gatekeeper for all Northerners requesting to visit Sumter.[3] The official document Fox presented was a letter from Secretary of War Cameron to General Scott, stating that "the President requires accurate information in regard to the command of Major Anderson . . . and wishes a competent person sent for that purpose."[4] Such a letter would typically introduce an army officer with expertise in health, food rationing, and/or morale or discipline. As Hartstene would have told Governor Pickens, Fox had no such expertise and was not even in the Cameron/Scott chain of command, being a civilian and former navy captain with extensive experience in coastal navigation, including South Carolina. Despite the palpably false representation, Pickens let Fox proceed. Having undoubtedly gleaned that Seward wished to evacuate Anderson but that Lincoln was wavering, Pickens may have thought that Fox's actual assignment was to arrange that evacuation by a vessel. Nor did such visit involve risk, since Fox would be constantly chaperoned by Hartstene.

Fox arrived at Fort Sumter at 8:30 p.m., stayed for an hour and fifteen minutes, returned briefly to Charleston (where Hartstene introduced him to Beauregard), and boarded the train for Washington that night.[5] Hartstene later talked to a journalist, purporting to tell him verbatim what Fox said. Although the journalist's published account is faulty, several elements seem credible: First, Fox had told Anderson that the decision of whether to evacuate was Anderson's to make, and Anderson responded that if Fox would write that out on the authority of the president, the garrison would depart. Fox, perhaps nonplussed, replied that he was not authorized to issue such a writing (and certainly Lincoln gave him no such authority).[6] Second, Anderson stated that because he expected an evacuation order, he had not reduced his men from three-fourths to half rations, and that Fox could report that April 15, at noon, was the moment "beyond which he could not hold the Fort."[7]

From Pickens's perspective, this report would have been enough to justify his permitting the visit, since it now seemed clear that evacuation was imminent. But there was still the fact of Fox's expertise in coastal navigation, and when Hartstene admitted to Beauregard that he had left Fox and Anderson alone for a few minutes, Beauregard reportedly expressed concern that they had hatched some relief effort.[8] Since Fox had apparently promised Governor Pickens that no such discussion would occur, neither Fox nor Anderson—even years later—would admit that in the few moments alone they violated the condition Pickens had imposed.[9] But a substantive discussion was had. A stone quay extended twenty feet out from Sumter's gorge wall, met by the granite landing wharf extending 171 feet.[10] Anderson on March 22 wrote to Colonel Thomas in Washington, "I have examined the point alluded to by Mr. Fox last night. A vessel lying there will be under the fire of thirteen guns from Fort Moultrie, and Captain Foster says that at the pan-coupé, or immediately on its right—the best place for her to land—she would require, even at high tide, if drawing ten feet, a staging of forty feet. The Department can decide what the chances will be of a safe debarkation and unloading at that point under these circumstances."[11] And Fox, for his part, recalled that Anderson, like Scott, believed that no entry was possible without an amphibious assault on the batteries of Morris Island.[12]

That Beauregard was right to be concerned was manifested several days later, when accounts appeared in several Northern newspapers. It was as if Greeley's *New-York Daily Tribune* was present at Fox's debriefing in Washington:

> It is very well understood that he had a plan for introducing reënforcements, which had been submitted to members of the Cabinet, and was regarded as ... practicable but attended with the probability ... of [a confrontation], which constituted the chief objection to its adoption. He is perfectly familiar with all the approaches to the harbor of Charleston, having been long connected with the coast survey, and had practical experience as the commander of one of [William Henry] Aspinwall's steamers. . . . Capt. Fox is fully impressed with the courage, integrity and sincerity of Major Anderson, with whom, however, his communication was necessarily limited, as Gov. Pickens sent Capt. Hartstein, late of our Navy, as an escort with him to the Fort, who kept within earshot during most of the interview, or, at least, near enough to prevent any free communication.[13]

The *Boston Daily Courier* of March 29 announced, "One of the most sensible, prudent, and praiseworthy acts of the government of the United States, which has come under our observation, for a long time, is that of sending Captain G.V. Fox, formerly of Massachusetts, on a secret mission of observation to Fort Sumter, to ascertain and report, from actual personal inspection, the practicality of reinforcing that fortress."[14]

"A Fool's Paradise"

Lincoln, knowing few Southern leaders, had assumed that Seward's conciliatory strategy derived from extensive conversations with well-informed and influential people in the slave states.[15] While it seemed clear that the evacuation of Fort Sumter would encourage Virginia's Unionists, there was no guarantee that it would lead to the return of the cotton states. Instead, they might interpret it—and tell certain foreign powers to interpret it—as the Union's acquiescence in Southern secession. This in turn might lead to Confederate alliances with nations having ambitions regarding the vast western territories now owned by a dramatically reduced Union, defended by a tiny standing army, led by an officer corps sharply reduced by Southern defections. Then there was the question of a Confederacy expanded by so-called filibusters in the Caribbean and Central America. That is, once Seward was allowed to let the cotton states go, their impulse might well be not to begin the process of reintegration, but rather to consolidate, expand, and exploit, with a captive press predicting a rosy future if everyone just stayed the course.

With the political aspect of evacuation versus reinforcement dependent upon the accuracy of Seward's perceptions of the South, Lincoln decided on a test. First, he dispatched to Charleston his personal bodyguard, crony, and former Illinois law partner, Ward H. Lamon, with a letter of introduction by Montgomery Blair claiming that he was on post office business. While this was hardly a credible cover, it would allow Lamon to meet with Alfred Huger, thought to be a good source for gauging the likelihood of a Unionist revival.[16] Governor Pickens greeted Lamon at the Charleston Hotel, choosing not to question the postal credentials of someone known to be the president's body-guard, perhaps guessing that his real purpose was to give Lincoln—portrayed by Seward as weak willed—a degree of comfort concerning the wisdom or necessity of Seward's evacuation idea. "Nothing can prevent war," Pickens told Lamon, "except the acquiescence of the president . . . in secession, and his unalterable resolve *not* to attempt any reinforcement of the Southern forts."[17]

Lincoln also sent another Illinois friend, Stephen A. Hurlbut, his cover being a visit to his wife's sister. Hurlbut's primary contact would be the most renowned of the Unionists, James Louis Petigru, under whom Hurlbut had studied law many years before. Lincoln would not have known (because Hurlbut would have told no one) that when Hurlbut first appeared in Illinois back in 1845, he was on the run, having evaded (with Petigru's assistance) charges of forgery and embezzlement in Charleston. Hurlbut had been deeply admired by, among others, his young half brother, William Henry Hurlbert, who in later years would write the anonymous *Diary of a Public Man*, the trenchant pseudomemoir of life in Washington in 1860–1861. Perhaps it was the scandal driving his half brother to flee Charleston that caused William Henry Hurlbert to change the spelling of his last name. In any event, the black mark in Stephen Hurlbut's past was potentially significant, since Charleston's Unionists, already under pressure to remain discreet, might not have wished to voice their candid opinions to someone who was not only an emissary from a Republican president but also a man with a tarnished local reputation in a society in which unblemished honor was a paramount value. Although Hurlbut was invited to meet his old friend W. H. Trescot and a few other prominent citizens, some estimable men, including the Unionists Alfred Huger, Benjamin Franklin Perry, William Aiken, George S. Bryan, and Donald L. McKay, declined to receive him.

Since word had already spread in Charleston that Lamon was "a Lincoln hireling," he was thought to be at sufficient risk from local toughs that Governor Pickens issued him a special pass permitting him to travel—unmolested—the several blocks from the Charleston Hotel to Alfred Huger's post office in the Exchange.[18] Given what Huger had reportedly said to Fox on the train about the current status of Unionism, his advice to Lamon could not have been encouraging. Petigru, for his part, warned that "the whole people were infuriated and crazed," that "no act of headlong violence by them would surprise him," and that he seldom ventured from his house, believing that he was being watched.[19] When Hurlbut on March 27 returned to Washington with an eighteen-page report, Lincoln called for Seward to attend. "The sentiment of National Patriotism," Hurlbut urged, "always feeble in Carolina, has been extinguished . . . by . . . paramount allegiance to the State."[20] This news, of course, repudiated Seward's theory that Unionism had been suppressed but would reemerge. Charles Francis Adams Jr. later wrote that Seward had derived "what little knowledge he had" of the South from "unreliable" and "misinformed" sources who had left him "in a fool's Paradise."[21]

Governor Pickens had refused Hurlbut's request to visit Major Anderson but granted Lamon's, perhaps sensing that Lamon's actual agenda was to arrange the promised withdrawal.[22] Lamon and Anderson "remained closeted"—Sumter's physician, Dr. Samuel Wylie Crawford, wrote in his diary—for over ninety minutes, after Lamon stated that Lincoln "wanted more facts to substantiate his position in withdrawing us."[23] Anderson apparently voiced to Lamon his belief that he would not be allowed to evacuate without first surrendering. This was passed to Beauregard, who told Anderson that there was no such requirement.[24] Prior to departing for Washington, Lamon affirmatively announced to Pickens that evacuation was imminent.[25] This statement was consistent with Seward's promise to Justice Campbell—a promise now two weeks old. "In this, as in . . . everything else," one source told a journalist, "Mr. Seward . . . [repeating what the *New York Times* had declared two weeks before] has triumphed."[26]

"Our Happy Constitution"

While secessionists believed that King Cotton would secure all of the Confederacy's financial and political requisites with Great Britain, France, and

Germany, the yearly cycle of planting, growing, and harvesting had for decades depended upon banking and mercantile interests located in the North. Cotton planters, primarily through local factors, indebted themselves to Northern banks in order to buy additional slaves, new acreage, and seeds, and they retired at least part of the debt following the harvest, before or after the cotton arrived in Northern ports or at Liverpool, Le Havre, or Bremen. While an Alabaman once complained to Calhoun, "Financially we are more enslaved than our negroes," this was simply anti-Northern rhetoric; planters were naturally free to develop financing institutions locally or to make their own arrangements in Europe.[27] They had stayed with New York bankers because these provided the best terms and service.

In his postwar memoir, Jefferson Davis alleged that many Northern political leaders and commentators agreed that the slave states had the right to secede and that the Union had no right to coerce their return.[28] In the early spring of 1861, Southerners owed Northern banks, merchants, and businessmen between $150 million and $300 million, a debt that would be discounted, perhaps radically, perhaps triggering significant Northern bankruptcies if—as seemed likely—the debtor and creditor regions went to war.[29] As New York financiers fretted about whether secession might entail the repudiation of debts, they tried to convince their debtor/customers that they, too, were antiabolitionist.[30] August Belmont, a New York financier/politician with substantial connections in the South, told Southern commissioner John Forsyth that although New York's commitment to the Union was unsullied by base motives, if it looked only to its own interests, it would "cut loose" from promanufacturing tariffs and "Puritanical" New England and "open her magnificent port to the commerce of the world," so that "what Venice was once . . . New-York would ere long become to the two hemispheres."[31] Although Belmont rejected that dream, New York mayor Fernando Wood preferred the vision of a second Venice or Bremen, proposing that the city secede from the state and Union to protect its lucrative creditor/debtor arrangements with Southern planters.[32] There was talk of a new confederacy involving members from New England, the Middle Atlantic states (down to Norfolk), the Midwest, and the West Coast, in league with the South.[33]

European recognition of the Confederacy would mean to the Union the loss of millions of dollars in duties. That being so, the Union at this time might reasonably have chosen not to raise but lower tariffs in order to deprive Southerners of this particular incentive to break away.[34] But under the policies of Buchanan's former treasury secretary, Howell Cobb, the federal debt had increased steadily since the Panic of 1857, causing some to allege that Cobb, a Georgian, had purposely increased the deficit in order to deprive the Union of a war chest.[35] In any event, the federal government now needed revenue. While self-interest drove bankers and merchants involved in cotton to oppose the Republicans, Pennsylvania's coal, wool, and iron interests—ownership and labor—gladly supported the increased tariff duties Republicans promised, at a time when—for instance—it cost $45 to produce a ton of rails, which the British were selling for $41. If higher tariffs put extra pressure on the loyal slave states to quit and join their brethren to the South, Northern manufacturers above all wished to protect their profit margins, and Northern laborers their wages. On March 2, with Southern members largely departed, Congress passed the protective Morrill Tariff.[36] President Buchanan, about to retire to protariff Pennsylvania and with no vestigial desire to appease an ungrateful South, signed the bill. President-Elect Lincoln, with strong support from free workers (he had, of course, promised them the West), voiced his prospective support—giving Southerners one more reason to hate him.[37] While older Southerners might see here a revival of the casus belli for nullification thirty years before, youth could respond that debates about whether a state could nullify a discriminatory federal tariff law had become irrelevant because secession nullified *all* federal laws.[38] The *Charleston Mercury* called the Morrill law a great boon for the South because it fairly invited Europeans to trade directly with what would be a low-tariff Confederacy.[39]

Commissioner André Roman informed Toombs that much could be accomplished through discussions with foreign ministers in Washington. Roman told France's minister, Henri Mercier, that the commissioners' negotiations through Justice Campbell were likely to conclude with "a truce maintaining the present status . . . equivalent to a quasi recognition of our independence." Mercier replied that his own sources (presumably within the U.S. government) were of the same view.[40] The mere fact that the Confederacy had commissioners in Washington talking to the administration might help it convince Great Britain and France—where it had already sent envoys—to grant diplomatic recognition.[41] Mercier, wanting no break in the delivery of Southern cotton to French mills (fulfilling 90 percent of French requirements), mentioned a possible British/French entente cordiale recognizing the Confederacy, thereby putting pressure on Lincoln to do the same, while also impeding the Southern impulse for war.[42]

On February 28, 1861, about to depart as secretary of state, Jeremiah Black instructed U.S. ministers in Europe to prevent their respective host nations from granting the Confederacy diplomatic recognition, noting that since the points raised in Buchanan's December 3 message denying a right of secession had not been refuted, the government retained "constitutional juris-diction" over the seceded states—meaning that the Union would look with disfavor upon any nation that recognized the Confederacy or sought to evade U.S. duties.[43] On March 9, Black's successor, Seward, would have U.S. minis-ters tell their host governments that "the present disturbances had their origin only in popular passions, excited under novel circumstances of very transient character," and that the American people "still retain and cherish a profound confidence in our happy Constitution."[44] While a foreign government could understand Black's references to legal authority and power, no observer of North/South relations over the prior thirty years could see Seward's com-ments as more than whistling in the dark.

The March 29 Cabinet Meeting

Lincoln had been impressed by Francis Blair's hard-line advice but did not broadcast that fact to his cabinet. Seward told the commissioners that his conciliation policy was gathering strength in the cabinet and (as they related to the Confederate leadership on March 26) that he would "impress the pres-ident so strongly with his views that he will ultimately control him."[45] But such statements by Seward were contradicted by other sources. On March 20, the Confederates' most skillful spy in Washington informed Montgomery that despite the truce in Pensacola, Lincoln would soon transfer men from the ships offshore to Fort Pickens.[46] On March 29, Commissioners Crawford and Roman forwarded to Toombs a *New-York Daily Tribune* report that on March 14 a special messenger had been dispatched to Pensacola with an order directing the four hundred troops on *Brooklyn* to come ashore.[47]

On the evening of March 28, Lincoln hosted a dinner. One of the invi-tees, British journalist W. H. Russell, described another, General Scott, as the republic's personification of "the monarchical idea," the living man who absorbed "some of the feeling which is lavished on the pictures and memory" of General Washington. Scott arrived but then exited without appearing pub-licly, it being said that he was indisposed by one of his several ailments, which included chronic dysentery and dropsy.[48] After dinner, Lincoln asked his cabinet to linger. Scott had drafted a memorandum, perhaps a tardy response to Lincoln's March 15 request for opinions regarding Fort Sumter, which Lincoln now recited. "It is doubtful," Scott had written, "according to recent information from the South," whether a withdrawal from Sumter would itself keep additional states from seceding, particularly if such withdrawal were ascribed to military necessity rather than as a peace offering. And that would clearly be the Confederacy's reaction if the abandonment of Charleston were accompanied by reinforcement in Pensacola. However, "our Southern friends . . . are clear"—Scott urged—"that the evacuation of both the forts would instantly soothe and give confidence to the eight remaining slaveholding States, and render their cordial adherence to this Union perpetual."[49] While Lincoln in reciting this contained his anger at Scott's proposal, Montgomery Blair articulated what Lincoln was thinking: that Scott was not offering a *military* reason to abandon Fort Pickens but merely voicing a political opinion, something beyond his authority and competence.[50]

Not that Scott was a stranger to politics. Shortly after his deft handling of the Charleston reinforcement in the early 1830s, he began to entertain presidential ambitions. After he successfully led an army of fourteen thousand in the Mexican War, Mexicans who wanted the United States to annex their country offered him $1.25 million to be Mexico's president and oversee the transition.[51] Rejecting that honor from a vanquished foe, Scott hoped instead to follow the examples of Washington, Jackson, and Zachary Taylor by exploiting his martial prowess to fuel support for the presidency. To Whig strategists backing his candidacy in 1852, led by William Henry Seward, Scott had seemed a viable candidate in the North because, although a Virginian, he had not publicly praised the divisive Fugitive Slave Act.[52] But many Southern Whigs would not support Scott, in part because the abolitionist Seward would undoubtedly act as a sort of premier in any Scott administration, a role into which Seward had already insinuated himself under Taylor, another politically naïve general the Whigs had enlisted.[53] And if Southerners would not back Scott, neither would their partners among the New York merchants and bankers. While the popular vote was far from disgraceful (1.4 million, versus 1.6 million for Franklin Pierce) and Scott's personal campaign style was not an issue because candidates did not then "actively" seek the office, Scott's incompetence as even a passive contender may be judged by the fact that his speeches were published not by him but by Pierce. In the end, Scott garnered only 42 of 296 electoral votes, hastening the demise of a Whig Party that for eighteen years had helped hold the nation together by drawing support from all sections.[54]

While some generals would thereafter have retired or confined themselves to military matters, Scott included in his October 1860 memorandum to Buchanan and Floyd political speculations about how secessionism would turn the United States into not two but a number of regional confederations. Buchanan would later upbraid him for venturing such comments, even without knowing that Scott had distributed them in Virginia.[55] And while some presidential candidates who failed as badly as Scott did in 1852 might then change advisors, Scott would remain so abjectly under Seward's influence that historian Frederick Bancroft used the term "mesmerism."[56] Welles would write that with vanity being Scott's abiding weakness, Seward "contrived by flattery to infuse" into him the political views Seward wanted "commended to [Lincoln] when he made military inquiries."[57] While Lincoln himself had delivered several campaign speeches for Scott in 1852, this fact, even if known and remembered by Scott, would not have been sufficient grounds for Scott now to shift his allegiance from Seward to the new president.[58]

Two weeks before Lincoln's bitter recitation of Scott's memo, Scott had issued an order—at Lincoln's insistence—directing the troops off Pensacola to come ashore. If Seward, pursuant to his conciliation policy, now dared advise Lincoln to abandon Fort Pickens, he would be repudiating—and seen by Lincoln and the cabinet as repudiating—a momentous decision already made and a momentous order already issued, thus isolating Seward in a cabinet he had undertaken to dominate. Seward thus could have whispered the idea in Scott's ear, believing that Lincoln might entertain it if voiced by the legendary general in chief.[59] Whether this was the genesis of Scott's memo is unknown. But Seward, in the face of published speculation that an order to reinforce Fort Pickens had in fact been issued and was on its way, nevertheless assured the Southern commissioners that Pensacola would not be reinforced. And his credibility with them would be substantially enhanced if he could say that Scott had gone further by recommending that Pensacola be abandoned.[60]

The president had talked briefly to Scott before the dinner party, leaving him feeling "nettled [according to Scott's military secretary, Keyes] at the idea of having been considered tardy in making preparations to reinforce Fort Pickens."[61] Perhaps this, and neither indisposition nor Lincoln's rejection of unsolicited political advice, was the reason for Scott's sudden departure. Lincoln had every right to be furious. By reinforcing Fort Pickens, he could satisfy Republicans—and everyone loyal to the Union—that federal authority was being maintained, even as he bolstered Unionism in the slave states by abandoning Sumter.[62] In his March 4 inaugural, Lincoln had promised that the Southern forts would be held. While this would itself be enough to prompt an attentive senior officer to begin preparations, that did not happen. The next day, Lincoln ordered Scott to carry out this policy. That oral order was not carried out, obliging the president to issue the order in writing. And still, on March 28, there was no word that the reinforcement had occurred.

Stanton noted to Buchanan that "growls about Scott's 'imbecility' are growing frequent."[63] If Stanton thought these rumors worth forwarding to the ex-president, it was because Buchanan had been justifiably rancorous that Scott's bungling had cost him a chance for success in the *Star of the West* venture, the one risk Buchanan had actually dared to take to redeem his presidency. While Scott had tried to blame that operation's failure on Toucey, the reality would not have been lost on any intelligent observer, including Lincoln. Now, with no word from Fort Pickens, Scott, rather than come forward with a reasonable explanation for the inordinate delay, saw fit to recommend that the facility instead be abandoned, an idea that would serve Seward's secret agenda with the commissioners but which was directly inconsistent with the president's strategy, inaugural promise, and order. Not surprisingly, Lincoln had a sleepless night.[64] Well might Lincoln say (if Keyes's diary is to be believed) that if General Scott could not follow his orders, perhaps someone else could.[65]

On Friday, March 29, just hours after Lincoln had heatedly recited Scott's advice, he asked each cabinet officer to submit his views—without consulting with other members—regarding the Southern forts.[66] Welles, Chase, Bates, Blair, Caleb Smith, and Seward (who had witnessed Lincoln's reaction to Scott) all urged that Fort Pickens be reinforced, Seward distinguishing himself by adding that he had just the man, Army Captain Montgomery C. Meigs, to oversee the operation.[67] When Navy Secretary Welles reminded Seward that no new effort was necessary because a reinforcement order had already been signed and sent, Seward answered (Welles later recalled) that still more should be done. This was an odd comment, since no one had suggested that the marines and artillerymen who had been waiting on ships off Pensacola would be insufficient.[68] Perhaps Seward, even as he pressed conciliation with the Southern commissioners, wanted to prove his ardor to Lincoln and the cabinet. And by inserting his man, he would have control.

With regard to Fort Sumter, Seward reiterated that Confederate spies would know of any expedition in advance, that any relief effort would not only fail but also precipitate a war, and that Anderson's situation was in any event untenable. Blair (with a resignation letter in his pocket if Lincoln adopted Seward's position) asserted that South Carolina was heading the rebellion, and if the administration acquiesced there, "years of bloody strife" would follow.[69] Blair's resignation would humiliate Lincoln more severely than Seward's threatened departure just prior to the inaugural, because it would serve as the unfortunate answer to what had become the new president's defining issue: whether he would break his inaugural promise to hold the Southern forts.[70] Welles and Treasury Secretary Chase now backed Blair, while Attorney General Bates equivocated. Cameron, although his position as secretary of war logically required of him some extra measure of leadership on this issue, submitted nothing, perhaps not knowing which alternative could be more profitably exploited in his railroad business. And Caleb Smith, Seward's one remaining ally, added nothing of value.[71]

Seward apparently told Campbell—who told Crawford, who told Toombs—that Blair was "implacable" (which was true) but "alone" (which was false). The reports of Lamon and Hurlbut disproving Seward's views on Unionism in Charleston, followed by the reaction of Lincoln and his cabinet to Scott's suggested abandonment of Fort Pickens, followed by the March 29 cabinet meeting, all repudiated Seward's conciliation policy. Rather than admit defeat, Seward was reduced to lying to the Southerners about the cabinet's discussions, so that Commissioner Roman could report to Toombs that Seward's peace policy of abandoning both forts was in fact "every day gaining ground" and that this was being publicly disavowed because Lincoln needed to placate radical Republicans and feared a no-confidence vote in elections about to take place in Connecticut and Rhode Island.[72] Roman's missive to Toombs also reflected Seward's ongoing theme that Lincoln lacked the courage to order Anderson's withdrawal, while adding that Seward in the near future would meet with the commissioners face-to-face and propose a truce to last perhaps until Congress reconvened on December 2, 1861. Thus, any such proposal by Seward, if accepted, would have been a brilliant achievement, buying eight months for the fires of secessionism to burn out.

Following the cabinet meeting, Lincoln met privately with Fox, Welles, and Blair and issued orders to relieve Sumter.[73] An enclosure to those orders, reportedly by Fox, specified preparation of *Pawnee* at Washington and *Harriet Lane* at New York, along with—at Norfolk—*Pocahontas*, a former merchantman recently converted as a steam sloop, not included by Fox in his initial plan in early February.[74] Since *Pocahontas* drew twelve feet of water, it would not be crossing the bar but joining these other vessels at its eastern edge to apply suppressive fire.[75] Lincoln also ordered three tugs for the actual incursion and a transport to bring the troops from the North. Fox traveled to New York to meet with two substantial shipowners who had earlier shown an interest, Charles Marshall and W. H. Aspinwall, but found them (as he confided to Blair) "astonished" that the plan was still under consideration, believing that "the time has passed" and that "the people are reconciled" to abandoning Sumter and "making the stand" at Fort Pickens.[76] Lincoln would have no reason to tell Fox that he was tardily authorizing the Sumter operation because Scott had failed to secure Fort Pickens.[77] On March 31, Marshall backed out.[78]

By the end of the March 29 cabinet meeting, Seward would have known that his recommendation to abandon Sumter had not prevailed. Although

Lincoln chose not to inform Seward that he was meeting with Welles, Blair, and Fox to mount an operation, Seward's sources were numerous, and he found out that the president had decided to freeze him out of this epochal decision. If Seward had any hope of salvaging conciliation, he would need to keep telling Justice Campbell that an evacuation order had been agreed to by the cabinet and only awaited the president's signature, even though newspapers and spies would soon be finding out that Lincoln was instead preparing aggressive action.[79] Lincoln, having had no sleep on Thursday night after his distressing encounter with Scott, and understanding that his decision to have Fox proceed meant the start of the Civil War, had a bad night on Friday as well, with a migraine so severe that on Saturday, March 30, Mrs. Lincoln said he "keeled over" from the pain.[80]

"It Is Now Quite Certain"

The commissioners wrote to Toombs that they and Campbell still had complete faith in Seward's promise that Sumter would be evacuated and that Pensacola would not be reinforced without prior notice.[81] When Governor Pickens telegraphed Crawford to complain that Lamon had not yet returned to Charleston to oversee Anderson's withdrawal, Crawford on Saturday assured him that the evacuation had been agreed upon in the cabinet and was delayed only to get past the New England elections.[82] That evening Seward promised to address the commissioners' concerns on Monday, April 1.[83]

When Monday arrived, Seward told Campbell that Lincoln not only denied authorizing Lamon to arrange for Sumter's evacuation but also would have Lamon personally admit this fact to them. They declined, undoubtedly because of something else Seward said: that Lamon *was* in fact authorized to arrange Anderson's withdrawal, but—with elections imminent in Connecticut and Rhode Island—Lincoln would disavow it. Campbell relayed the conversation to Crawford, who assured Toombs that "the Cabinet and President had agreed" on the evacuation even before Lamon went to Charleston.[84] Further to assure Toombs of Anderson's imminent withdrawal, Crawford noted that the administration was about to float an $8 million bond issue, which Wall Street would not touch unless "fully persuaded" that Lincoln would pursue Seward's conciliation policy.[85]

The source for all of this was Seward. Whether Lamon went to Charleston with instructions from Lincoln to discuss evacuation with Anderson and Pickens, and whether, upon Lamon's return, Lincoln denied giving Lamon such instructions, are not independently verifiable. Lincoln may well have told Lamon that if tensions were high in Charleston, he could suggest that evacuation was imminent, simply to keep the Confederates from firing upon Fort Sumter before Lincoln received notice that Pensacola was secure. Upon receiving that notice, Lincoln could afford politically to abandon Sumter and send Lamon back to arrange it—just as Lamon had promised. But then nothing was heard from Pensacola. By March 29, three weeks after Lincoln first instructed Scott, he was forced to order relief for Sumter rather than risk the grave political humiliation of having Anderson surrender for lack of food because Lincoln had done nothing.[86] Thus forced to act, Lincoln would then have been obliged to deny the evacuation promises Lamon had made on his behalf, perhaps even telling Lamon that he would have to say that he had been confused or misspoke.

It may have happened that way, but there is a second possibility. While Lincoln's files contain no letter from Lamon to him reporting his reaction to the situation in Charleston, Seward's files contain a letter from Lamon to Seward, telling him that according to "the best lights that I can judge from, after casting around, I am satisfied of the policy and propriety of immediately evacuating Fort Sumter."[87] This policy of immediate evacuation was Seward's, not Lincoln's. There is no direct evidence that Lincoln ever told Lamon, or anyone, that he favored withdrawal, much less that Lamon should give promises of withdrawal to Major Anderson and Governor Pickens. Lamon was Lincoln's confidant and agent, not Seward's. A letter to Seward—rather than to Lincoln—makes sense only if Seward, prior to Lamon's departure from Washington on March 24, had insinuated to him that the president secretly favored evacuation and wanted Lamon to report his impressions back to Seward rather than to Lincoln directly, perhaps because a letter to Lincoln was more likely to be steamed open, perhaps so that Lincoln could—if necessary—plausibly deny any involvement in an evacuation initiative. Seward would have thought it important to have such a letter in hand because, insofar as the commissioners were losing confidence in him, he could show Campbell a missive from Lincoln's own agent indicating that all was just as Seward had represented. He could do the same with newspapers as necessary to continue their reporting that evacuation was certain.[88]

After notifying Seward that the policy of evacuation was sound, Lamon, perhaps believing that this was all Seward—and Lincoln—needed to know to issue the evacuation order, might then have misconstrued his own role in Charleston to be that of not merely monitoring local feeling but also laying the groundwork for carrying out that order. By promising both Major Anderson and Governor Pickens that evacuation was imminent, Lamon unwittingly put pressure on Lincoln to fulfill that promise. If the president gave in, Seward, who had been promising evacuation for weeks, would be vindicated, his strategy for peace achieved, his hegemony in the cabinet demonstrated, the loyalty of the Upper South better secured, and war—perhaps—averted.[89]

But Lincoln did not give in. The headline in Greeley's April 1 *Tribune* read, "Fort Sumter to Be Re-enforced . . . The Attack Left to the South." Although Greeley did not know that Lincoln had told Fox to proceed, and the article itself—unlike the headline—indicated that reinforcement had not actually been decided upon but was only under consideration, it was notable for discounting Lamon's evacuation promise.[90] On April 2, the *New York Times* reported that *Pawnee* had been ordered to Charleston, but only to evacuate Anderson's men.[91] The story might have been planted by Seward as further proof to the commissioners that evacuation was imminent. Or it could have been planted by Seward, or Welles, or Blair, as an "innocent" explanation for why *Pawnee* was suddenly being fitted out.

Lamon, informed that no evacuation order would issue, wrote two drafts of a letter to Governor Pickens, essentially worming out of the allegation that he had virtually promised withdrawal. "You will recollect," he wrote, that when he arrived,

> I told you that I had no special business with [Major Anderson], and was unauthorised by President Lincoln, that I had heard a great deal, and had seen many statements in the papers and I desired to go there and judge for myself. After visiting Sumter, I returned to your Head Quarters to pay my respects to you and then told you that I thought Sumter ought to be evacuated, that in my opinion it ought to be done[;] then I again told you however that that was my own opinion only. Then you remarked that ["]of course it is your opinion individually and no one is bound by it or responsible for it["] or something to that effect. I did think then that the Fort would be immediately evacuated and have seen nothing since to change that opinion. I yet believe it will be very soon.[92]

The phrase "told you that I thought Sumter ought to be evacuated" includes a number of cross-outs, suggesting on Lamon's part a reluctance, lack of assurance, and/or substantial care in choosing words. Why Lamon drafted such a letter, or at whose request, is unknown. Once sent, it might serve to mitigate charges likely to come from Pickens that Lincoln's personal agent promised evacuation to give Lincoln time to prepare a naval operation. But neither draft appears to have been finalized or sent.

A Modest Proposal

The results in the Connecticut and Rhode Island elections showed that the Republicans were losing ground.[93] The so-called wide-awakes, foot soldiers of the Republican Party, sufficiently militant to wear uniforms and be drilled by officers, would not be pleased to see compromise or Buchanan-esque inertia.[94] Lincoln's Illinois friend Gustave Koerner warned that German Americans were ready to fight secessionism but were fretting "under the present peace policy."[95] A Cincinnati Republican told Lincoln that if—as rumored—he evacuated both Southern forts, Cincinnati's municipal government would pass out of Republican hands. A New Yorker did not mince his words: "I voted for you thinking that in you the country would find a defender of its rights & honour. I am totally disappointed. . . . Give up Sumter, Sir, & you are as dead politically as John Brown is physically."[96]

Seward, having repeatedly failed to manipulate Lincoln, now engaged in a desperate effort. In a memorandum bearing the modest title "Some Thoughts for the President's Consideration," Seward leveled a number of outrageous accusations against Lincoln, among them that he had failed to articulate to the public any clear domestic or foreign policy and had allowed "the question before the public" to be slavery when it should be "union and disunion."[97] Seward implored Lincoln to shift the focus, suggesting that this could be accomplished by the simple expedient of abandoning Fort Sumter and reinforcing Fort Pickens.[98]

If in fact Lincoln in the first three weeks of his administration had stated no policy and had pressed a vehement antislavery agenda while saying nothing about preserving the Union, a desperate plea by a senior advisor to change public perception would have been reasonable. But Lincoln's policy *was* evacuation-cum-reinforcement, and his inaugural stated a policy of Unionism, not antislavery. Seward's criticism came with particular ill grace in that he had recommended that Lincoln omit from his inaugural any statement of policy with respect to maintaining Union facilities in the South, only to have Lincoln reject that advice and instead declare a policy of holding facilities still under Union control. Some who accused Lincoln of weakness in his first month were saying that he had succumbed to Seward's own "infatuated belief in the possibility of a peaceful solution and . . . fear of coercion."[99] In now reading Seward's reckless criticism, Lincoln would not have missed this hypocrisy.

The first month had included missteps suggesting weakness. Even before Lincoln arrived, the word in Washington (Henry Adams reported to his brother) was that Lincoln "is not a strong man."[100] On the trip from

Springfield before the inaugural, after Frederick Seward, at his father's urging, warned Lincoln that an assassination would be attempted during a change of trains at Baltimore, Lamon and others worked out a secret entrée to Washington, after which detractors, led by the *Baltimore Sun*, portrayed Lincoln as skulking into the capital wearing an outlandish disguise. On March 2, Louis Wigfall predicted on the floor of the Senate that such a weakling would not "look war sternly in the face" but instead withdraw from Charleston and Pensacola within a week or ten days of taking office.[101] Lincoln appeared to be drifting and ineffectual, holding few cabinet meetings (at Seward's suggestion) and spending most of his time with the thousands of patronage seekers who inhabited every hallway and staircase in search of the hundreds of positions to be secured by presidential appointment.[102] After the March 15 cabinet meeting, Lord Lyons, informed that Lincoln had polled his cabinet on the Sumter issue, told London that the mere fact of taking a vote showed on Lincoln's part a lack of personal decisiveness.[103] When Seward brought to the White House his friend Charles Francis Adams, upon whose skills as envoy extraordinary and minister plenipotentiary to London might hinge whether Great Britain allied itself with the Confederacy, Lincoln, "shabbily dressed," "uncouth" with "much-kneed, ill-fitting trousers, coarse stockings, and worn slippers," dismissed Adams's expression of thanks for the appointment by commenting that it was Seward, who had chosen him. "Then, stretching out his legs before him ... with an air of great relief as he swung his long arms to his head," he told Seward, "Well ... I've this morning decided that Chicago post-office appointment," as if somehow it were more important than the diplomatic burden this grandson of John Adams was about to assume.[104]

Since Lincoln had no reason to insult Adams, he may at this moment have been exhausted and unimpressive, his priorities simply confused. Experienced observers commonly thought Lincoln perpetually tired by the inordinate amount of time he committed to minor sinecures at a time of crisis. But his friend Leonard Swett, one of those who had masterminded Lincoln's nomination in Chicago, defended the endless hours with those seeking preferment by saying that Lincoln wanted all disputatious factions to get something, yet never enough to be satisfied, keeping them hungry for more, and thus unifying them all in being beholden to the man who had taken the time to listen to their parochial desires.[105]

Even if Swett was wrong and the time Lincoln spent on aspirants was wasted, he had clearly made the reinforcement of Fort Pickens an early priority and issued the requisite order to Scott without hesitation. Lincoln's seeming indecision regarding Fort Sumter derived not—as Seward told the commissioners—from personal weakness, but rather from Scott's failure to carry out Lincoln's Pensacola order. And now, not content to wait longer, Lincoln was sending ships to Sumter, a fact Seward knew when he wrote "Some Thoughts" (although he did not tell Lincoln he knew). Lincoln had thus made bold and significant decisions. True, he had kept his cards close, saying little publicly, or even to his cabinet, although leaks—real, fake, and mixed—were legion. Yet throughout he was weighing perilous choices in the face of inadequate and/or inconsistent information, mixed with the various, evolving views from advisors of questionable objectivity and/or competency and/or personal loyalty to Lincoln. But he was not doing nothing.

Seward's "Some Thoughts" memo included the outrageous suggestion that Lincoln commence a war with Spain and France over Caribbean issues, urging that this act would generate spontaneous national patriotism among Southerners and even suggest to them that in return for rejoining the Union they might get the grand prize they had always craved: Cuba, along with its huge inventory of slaves.[106] And while there were in fact issues between the United States and these two European powers, if Lincoln took Seward's advice and declared war on either, Southerners, rather than flock to defend the Union, might well ask these nations to recognize the Confederacy and even to sign alliances of mutual defense.[107] As a further insult, Seward suggested that the proposed war with major European powers, the evacuation of Charleston, and the reinforcement of Pensacola were all matters beyond Lincoln's ability and thus should be assigned to him.

The memo was disloyal, hypocritical, and contemptible. Seward had been engaged in negotiations with the commissioners without informing the commander in chief at whose pleasure he served. He had deprecated Lincoln to Campbell, knowing that he would pass on to Confederate leaders a view of Lincoln as weak and indecisive. And he had made reckless promises that were directly contrary to what Lincoln wanted, subsequently doubling down on those promises by lying to the Southerners about what was about to happen. Given all this, the memo seemed to be the product of an unaccustomed desperation at the prospect of being exposed at any moment.[108] With all of the memo's criticisms of Lincoln, it was as if Seward were projecting upon the tired, smiling, gaunt, and self-effacing president all the mistakes that an honest objectivity would have compelled Seward to see in himself.[109]

Lincoln at this point could reasonably have concluded that his secretary of state had lost possession of his faculties and must immediately resign and seek a competent neurologist.[110] Instead, he took Seward aside and—as if he were dealing with one of his boys for writing a bad word on the blackboard—he said that he disagreed.[111] For decades to come, Southerners would claim that Lincoln tried to lull them into believing that Sumter would soon be vacated, in order to trick them. The tone and substance of Seward's memorandum and Lincoln's response, however, demonstrate that Lincoln knew nothing of the confident promises Seward had made.[112] Washington was filled with true, false, and mixed rumors, and Lincoln, busy with infusing loyalty into would-be postmasters and lighthouse keepers, apparently never saw or heard enough to ask Seward why everyone was so sure Sumter would be abandoned when Lincoln had uttered not one word to that effect.[113]

The diction and syntax of "Some Thoughts" were so simple as to suggest that Seward intended it to be assimilated not just by Lincoln but also by the average newspaper reader. When Lincoln's secretaries in 1888 discovered and published the memo, they received a letter from James B. Swain, who in 1861 had been the *New York Times'* Washington correspondent. Swain recounted that Seward had asked to meet with *Times* editor Henry J. Raymond, a stalwart Seward supporter who had helped Thurlow Weed manage Seward's unsuccessful for the Republican nomination.[114] Raymond arrived in Washington at midnight on Sunday, March 31, and discussed with Seward, Swain, and Weed the memo Seward would be handing to Lincoln the next day. Pursuant to the plan developed at that late-night meeting, Seward would hand Swain the "Some Thoughts" memo after meeting with the president, along with Lincoln's expected acceptance, and these would be published in Tuesday's edition. (Presumably Raymond would first blue-pencil such things as Seward's suggestion to provoke a war with France and Spain.) That edition would also include an editorial by Raymond urging that Seward take over North/South negotiations. But on Monday, Raymond canceled everything, presumably on word that Lincoln had surprised Seward by rejecting his proposal.[115] In the end, all the *Times* had for its connivance in Seward's attempted takeover of presidential authority was a devastating editorial in the edition of Wednesday, April 3, stating that Lincoln had no policy to deal with secession.[116]

"Breakers Are Before Us"

Confederate forces could take Fort Pickens in an hour. If that happened, Lincoln's opponents would immediately remind the public that he had promised on March 4 to occupy the Southern forts and had inherited from Buchanan ships two miles offshore with reinforcements and guns, but then he failed to send them in. If, in addition, Lincoln did nothing in Charleston and Anderson abandoned Fort Sumter for lack of food, the outrage would rise to the level of impeachment initiatives. Since at that point Lincoln could no longer summon the popular will to oppose secession, the Confederacy would be peacefully established and be recognized by other nations.

Newspapers had so often reported Sumter's imminent abandonment that—as the British journalist W. H. Russell wittily remarked—the stereotype plates with the words "Evacuation of Fort Sumter" had worn out.[117] The *Mobile Mercury*, adapting a line from the poet Alexander Pope, asserted that "Fort Sumter never is, but always to be, delivered up."[118] When hearsay reached the commissioners indicating naval preparations in New York, Seward floated a rumor that they were in reaction to Spain's ambition to annex the Dominican Republic. When the newspapers rejected that explanation, Seward felt compelled to write down and hand to Campbell a note stating that "the president may desire to supply Fort Sumter, but will not undertake to do so, without first giving notice to Governor Pickens."[119] Campbell, instead of swearing to expose as fraudulent the past weeks' promises of imminent evacuation, or warning that the Confederate reaction to this radical change might well be to commence a cannonade immediately, naively asked Seward whether this note signaled a change in policy.[120] Seward answered that while Lincoln found withdrawal "irksome" and allowed people to fill his head with resupply schemes, none was likely to happen. Seward then left the room, indicating that he was going to confer with Lincoln. Upon returning, Seward affirmed that if Sumter was resupplied, it would be preceded by notice.[121]

Crawford and Roman conveyed to Governor Pickens their opinion that "the president has not the courage to Execute the [evacuation] order we know to have been agreed on in Cabinet" but instead "intends to shift responsibility upon Major Anderson by suffering him to be starved out."[122] Seward, undoubtedly their source, thus drew their attention away from his failed promises of withdrawal by again urging that the only obstacle to executing an evacuation order drafted by Scott and voted upon by the cabinet was a weak president, the only change being that he was now also charging Lincoln with cowardice, of treating Anderson as shamelessly as Buchanan had. On April 3, Fox confided, "My expedition is ordered to be got ready, but I doubt if we shall get off. Delay, indecision, obstacles. War will commence at Pensacola. There the Govt is making a stand" with "reinforcements, already ordered to land."[123] On the same day, Campbell wrote to Jefferson Davis, "I do not doubt that Sumter will be evacuated shortly, without any effort to supply it." With respect to Fort Pickens, Campbell told Davis, "I do not think there is any settled plan. . . . All that I have [from Seward] is a promise that the status will not be attempted to be changed . . . without notice," essentially the same promise that Seward had just made regarding Fort Sumter.[124] But Seward had simply exchanged one lie for another, at first saying Fort Pickens would not be reinforced, now saying it would not be reinforced without notice, when in fact the truce did not require notice and Lincoln had ordered reinforcement—without notice—weeks before. Seward wrote to his wife, "I am full of occupation, and more of anxieties. . . . Dangers and breakers are before us."[125] Although Seward did not have a maritime background, he had chosen a nautical metaphor—that of an imminent shipwreck.

Crawford and Roman, experienced public men, had been dispatched to Washington to exercise their independent powers of observation and judgment. Having accepted Seward's evacuation promises for some weeks, perhaps they now feared that, in forwarding to Confederate leaders news of Seward's sudden abandonment of those prior promises, the leaders might lose confidence in the commissioners for having been strung along. Seward himself helped to blunt the shock of the change by ascribing it to Lincoln's indecisiveness, a theme he had been developing for weeks. The commissioners would have their superiors accept that so long as Governor Pickens received no notice of resupply, they should do nothing, since the feckless president, by taking no positive action himself, would let Anderson's garrison simply run out of food, thus ending the crisis with a quiet capitulation on Anderson's responsibility, for a brilliant (if bloodless) Confederate victory over a predictable example of Northern incompetence.[126] This having been said, from the moment it emerged that Lincoln might not evacuate Sumter but would give notice prior to sending provisions, the Confederacy was hobbled. If it now opened fire upon Sumter, as Governor Pickens had repeatedly threatened, it could no longer excuse itself by saying either that the Union was refusing to negotiate or that the Union was about to send reinforcements (rather than just food and medical supplies). Therefore, by promising to provide notice, Lincoln—Seward's alleged weakling—had "positioned" the Confederacy and bought time.

9

Captain Meigs and Lieutenant Porter

Exile and Return

In suddenly advocating the reinforcement of Fort Pickens, Seward urged Lincoln to put in charge a junior army officer, Captain Montgomery Cunningham Meigs.[1] By graduating fifth in the West Point class of 1836, Meigs had qualified for the elite Corps of Engineers, eventually becoming the architect and chief engineer of the Washington Aqueduct, a complicated but elegant project to provide drinking water to the District of Columbia via a succession of diversions from the Great Falls of the Potomac in Maryland.[2] While this alone would be sufficient to define a career, Meigs also became supervising engineer on the expansion of the Capitol Building, where his objectivity and independence from political pork-barrel spending were protected by President Franklin Pierce's careful and conservative secretary of war, Jefferson Davis.[3] But when James Buchanan assumed the presidency, Meigs found himself under the thumb of a new and irresponsible superior, John Floyd, whose many shortcomings included awarding government contracts to unqualified cronies and lobbyists.[4] Meigs complained to Davis, now back in the Senate, and to Senator Seward, and to Georgia's Robert Toombs.[5] Failing to obtain satisfaction, Meigs took the extraordinary and ill-advised step of filing a formal protest of Floyd's conduct with Floyd's superior, President Buchanan.[6] Buchanan turned to Attorney General Jeremiah Black, who on July 31, 1860, issued a formal opinion holding that since decisions by a cabinet member are to be construed as decisions by the president himself, Meigs, subordinate to a cabinet member, had no right to appeal his decision to the president.

Not content with disposing of the legal point, Black added that Meigs had a grossly inflated perception of his own discretionary authority. "What right has he," Black wrote, "to anticipate that his superior officers will be guilty of blunders, extravagance, and fraud upon the public treasury?"[7] This superfluous insult to Meigs demonstrated that Black, the nation's highest law enforcement official, had no sense—either from comments by others or by personal intuition—that there might be substance to Meigs's complaints about Floyd, even if spoken out of turn. Meigs's allegations were, of course, prophetic, and Floyd would be engulfed in a scandal of "blunders, extravagance, and fraud upon the public treasury." But that exposure was still six months off. Floyd told Buchanan that if Meigs were not stripped of his authority on these two major Washington projects and "ordered away," Floyd would quit. Meigs was thus fired and exiled to the unfinished Fort Jefferson in Dry Tortugas.[8]

When passing through Pensacola on his way to career banishment, Meigs in November 1860 wrote to General Scott that "a few ardent, desperate men" could seize the several federal facilities there. Such a warning would by that point have come as no surprise to Scott, who had already asked Floyd and Buchanan—in vain—to protect the Southern forts.[9] Meanwhile, disputes between Meigs and the architect of the Capitol had caused that project to languish even before Meigs's dismissal. The many loose pieces of beautifully carved stone lying on the surrounding grounds became sad omens (someone observed) of the nation's "predetermined destruction." Herman Melville saw similar symbolism in the rust of the cast-iron superstructure of the dome, left uncompleted and spectral.[10]

On January 6, 1861, Louisa Rodgers Meigs joyfully wrote to her husband in exile, "Floyd has resigned" and "Scott is on the stage . . . fully sustained by Mr Holt . . . who is a firm Union man." While Mrs. Meigs declared herself "very anxious to see Genl Scott" to end her husband's exile, Scott had no time because he was "engaged morning noon and night" on what was later revealed as the *Star of the West* operation.[11] Holt soon ended Meigs's banishment and—at Meigs's insistence—formally reinstated him to direct the Capitol project, with one of those assigned to the project by Floyd when Meigs was fired now to suffer his own career banishment to the Tortugas. "It is like the movement of a tragedy of Euripides"—Meigs could now observe—in which "justice after long delay is meted out with equal scales to all the persons in the drama."[12] Meigs reached Washington in time to attend Lincoln's inaugural, observing that although the huge construction crane towering above the east portico of the Capitol may have been thought a bad portent, the crowd gave a general impression that at last "we have a government."[13]

Seward, who had tried to help Meigs in his travails many months before, appreciated that this officer brought a sophisticated and incisive perspective to logistical issues, uttered with a self-confidence as brash as Seward's own. On March 29, the day of the crucial cabinet meeting and Lincoln's secret agreement with Fox and Welles to resupply Fort Sumter, Seward brought Meigs to meet Lincoln regarding a new reinforcement effort at Fort Pickens. Lincoln started (Meigs later recalled) by asking whether he thought Fort Sumter could be relieved, the same question Lincoln had asked Fox.[14] Meigs, undoubtedly rehearsed by Seward, deflected the question, stating that Charleston "was a matter for the navy" since "it must be done by ships," and he could find suitable naval officers to discuss it.[15] The purported distinction was bogus, since a new expedition to Pensacola similarly involved ships. Meigs urged that the Confederates should be confronted in Pensacola Bay by *Powhatan*, but only if commanded by Lieutenant David Dixon Porter, whose junior rank (albeit of twenty years' duration) would not otherwise yield him such a billet. Lincoln, a veteran of innumerable civil and criminal trials, may have sensed that what he was hearing had been carefully scripted in advance. But, having still heard nothing definitive about the original order to reinforce Fort Pickens from ships just offshore, Lincoln indulged Meigs, perhaps sensing that if Fort Pickens or Fort Sumter were suddenly attacked in an "enfeebled condition," he could now say in his own defense that he was personally planning expeditions to both forts. Southern newspapers reported that *Brooklyn* and its reinforcements had departed its offshore position at Pensacola for Key West, suggesting to Lincoln (Meigs noted) that the order he had issued to Scott weeks before had simply "fizzled out."[16]

On the morning of March 31, Easter Sunday, Scott's longtime military secretary, Lieutenant Colonel Erasmus Darwin Keyes, perhaps to cheer up Scott after Lincoln and his cabinet had angrily rejected his suggested abandonment of Fort Pickens, expounded to Scott for thirty uninterrupted minutes the difficulties of transporting across Santa Rosa Island's wide beach the heavy ordnance necessary to defend that fort. Scott, seeing a chance to redeem himself with Lincoln via this new and strictly military rationale for not attempting to relieve Fort Pickens, told Keyes to go to Seward's house and repeat what he had just said. But Seward, having abandoned his conciliation theory once the cabinet went against him, was now leading the effort to send an armada to Pensacola and thus would not tolerate a military reason not to do it. Seward instead told Keyes to fetch Meigs, then on his way to Easter services. The two returned to Seward's house, where they were told to prepare and present to the president at 4:00 p.m. a new plan to reinforce Fort Pickens.[17] They set to work preparing, and although they arrived at the White House with five minutes to spare, Keyes later recounted that he had not had

Captain Montgomery C. Meigs, circa March 1861. Library of Congress LC-DIG-ppm-sca-07785. Lieutenant David Dixon Porter. Detail from photograph of U.S. commissioners for the first Japanese embassy to the United States, May–July 1860. Library of Congress LC-USZ62-22333.

the time to notify Scott of this crucial meeting. Over the next two hours Keyes and Meigs detailed their reinforcement plan to the president, while Scott, well pleased with Keyes's exposition a few hours before of why such a reinforcement was impossible, remained at home.

Lincoln, having spoken thus far only to very senior officers such as Generals Scott (age seventy-four) and Totten (age seventy-two), was pleased to hear the views of men—as he phrased it—who could still mount a horse. Following the presentation, Lincoln told Meigs and Keyes to obtain Scott's approval, but not out of respect for either the man or his opinions. Lincoln—in Meigs's retelling, as in Keyes's—was not reluctant to blame Scott for making this new initiative necessary. "Tell him," Lincoln now said, "that I wish this thing done and not to let it fail unless [Scott] can show that I have refused him something he asked for as necessary. I depend upon you gentlemen to push this thing through."[18]

Scott, when told of the meeting and of the aggressive plan discussed and decided there, must have been shocked at how utterly things had changed since the morning. Chastised for failing to carry out a presidential order to reinforce Fort Pickens, and then for volunteering strictly political reasons to abandon that facility altogether, Scott now reversed himself 180 degrees, proclaiming, "The great Frederick used to say that 'when the King commands, all things are possible!' It shall be done," as it was suddenly "of prime importance" not to abandon Fort Pickens but to effect "the immediate departure of a war steamer with instructions to enter Pensacola Harbor."[19] Undoubtedly fearful that Lincoln would request his retirement if he exhibited less than full-throated support, Scott summarily approved the Meigs/Keyes reinforcement plan without even questioning (as any prudent officer would) why ships should be dispatched to steam down the Atlantic, undoubtedly to be identified by Confederate spies even before their departure, without first ascertaining just what had happened to the troops and supplies that had been sent to Pensacola two months before. Scott could not mention this obvious threshold question, since he was to blame for having no answer. Better just to approve the new plan and flatter Lincoln with a comparison to Frederick the Great. Scott also directed Lincoln's attention to the October 1860 memorandum—first sent to Lincoln in December—wherein Scott had urged the reinforcement of the Southern forts.[20] While he did note that the difficulties had "quadrupled in the past month" because Confederate brigadier general Braxton Bragg, commander of Southern forces at Pensacola since early March, had reportedly gathered four thousand to five thousand men and had mounted guns at Fort McRee that could fire both at Fort Pickens and at relief ships entering the harbor, he failed to mention that this Confederate buildup had largely postdated Lincoln's original reinforcement order.[21]

A few days later, General Totten handed Secretary of War Cameron a memorandum elucidating why Fort Sumter and Fort Pickens should both be abandoned. Perhaps suggested by his fellow septuagenarian Scott just after Scott on March 28 had found his own advice rejected as merely political, Totten apparently did not know that Scott had suddenly reversed himself.[22] If Cameron ever passed the memo to Lincoln, it would have had no effect, since he had ceased taking advice from strategists who could no longer mount a horse.

"At Any Cost or Risk"

The Union had always benefited from the South's proud traditions of civic and military service. Just a few months earlier, of 4,470 federal civil servants and military officers, close to half—2,154—hailed from the fifteen slaveholding states, despite a much smaller combined white population than that of the free states.[23] In the five months following Lincoln's election, however, the military and civil ranks were rapidly depleted. Many became Confederate officers and employees, some at the specific invitation of Jefferson Davis.[24] Some replicated in the Confederacy the rank or title of the position they had left, bringing with them the relevant office forms and other materials they would need. Colonel Samuel Cooper, who had instructed Anderson to confine his communications to him and Floyd, resigned his commission on March 7 and nine days later assumed the same duties in a gray uniform.

On March 2, House Republicans censured outgoing navy secretary Toucey for accepting the resignations of twenty-nine Southern officers, since this immunized them from the courts-martial that would otherwise apply to those who waged war against the Union they had sworn to defend.[25] Between March 7 and March 23, another forty officers resigned from the U.S. Navy, with more resignations coming every day and a prospect that, as the ships Toucey had sent abroad eventually came home, a goodly portion of their officers would also resign their commissions and take up arms.[26] A Naval Academy teacher informed Welles that perhaps only five of the forty officers there were loyal, while cadet midshipmen openly wore blue cockades, a symbol of secession.[27] Maritime expert George W. Blunt told Montgomery Blair that two men on a ship docked in the Brooklyn Navy Yard "are in the habit of talking disunion and there is very good reason to believe that they are in the practice of furnishing information to the traitors."[28]

The War Department had been controlled for twelve years by pro-Southern men—Charles M. Conrad, Jefferson Davis, and John Floyd—keeping "the fountains of all power and patronage" with Southern officers (Lieutenant Colonel Keyes had complained to Seward), while "we of the north have been eternally kept down." It was a situation that Keyes's direct superior, General Scott, a Virginian, had apparently failed to rectify.[29] Some Southern officers, like civil employees and cabinet officers, chose not to resign even if they had abandoned their sworn allegiance, leading Frederick Seward to observe that in Washington, a Southern city, "all the departments contained many" who stayed only "to use their positions to give aid or information to the opponents of the Government."[30] Upon arriving in mid-March, William Tecumseh Sherman found the War Department a place of "open, unconcealed talk, amounting to high-treason," something neither Holt nor Cameron fixed.[31]

Meigs did not explain, and Lincoln never asked why, Lieutenant David Dixon Porter's participation was indispensable. If Lincoln had inquired, he would have found that Porter's expertise included navigating shoals, more valuable at Charleston than Pensacola. Undoubtedly Meigs's sole basis for requesting Porter's assistance in the Pensacola mission was that they were neighbors in Georgetown and Porter seemed to be, like Meigs, bold, brilliant (as each man's subsequent career would demonstrate), and impatient. Forty-eight years old and stuck at the rank of lieutenant, Porter shared with Meigs the frustration of a career stymied because a statutorily limited number of more senior positions were held by superannuated timeservers, there being no retirement or pension system.[32] Although the resignation of Southern officers and the likelihood of war suggested better times ahead for an ambitious junior officer, Porter had given up and volunteered to engage in a survey of the California coast, his bags already packed when Meigs showed up at his door and took him to Seward's office.

Seward asked whether he was familiar with Pensacola Harbor. Porter replied that he was. "Could it be possible then sir," Seward reportedly inquired, "to take a frigate in there, and save Fort Pickens from falling into the hands of the rebels?"[33] Seward's question assumed—quite contrary to fact—that the fort would soon be lost unless some dauntless officer fit out a sidewheeler in the North, steamed around the Florida Peninsula, and—sixteen hundred nautical miles and two weeks later—ran a gauntlet of 125 guns firing from Fort McRee, forty-four from Fort Barrancas, and eight from Barrancas Barracks, to save the imperiled Union fort.[34] Meigs had unquestionably briefed Porter regarding what Seward did and did not want to hear. If an ambitious junior officer is suddenly asked by a high government official to opine on the merits of a mission that is dangerous and likely to yield glory and preferment in a top-heavy bureaucracy, his response is a foregone conclusion. Porter replied that he would have no difficulty accomplishing the mission.

In Porter's *Naval History of the Civil War* (1886), its quasi-official status and purported objectivity created by the author's reference to himself in the third person, he wrote, "Those familiar with the early events of the Rebellion will remember that Fort Pickens was ... held ... with a handful of men" who were "preparing to defend it against a large force of Confederates."[35] In fact, those familiar with these events would know that a large Union force had waited offshore for two months and that an order from Scott to transfer that force was outstanding.

In order to obtain troops, Meigs and Porter spoke with Scott and his aide, Keyes. Although Scott had headed a masterful amphibious exercise in Mexico, his capacious military treatise did not recognize the existence of the navy, much less did it set forth protocols for how the two branches should cooperate in amphibious operations. Although Scott just days before had wanted to convince Lincoln of his enthusiasm for the Pensacola mission, paying Scott a visit, Porter later noted, "was very much like calling on a sick bear."[36]

On Monday, April 1, the day of Seward's "Some Thoughts" memorandum, Seward brought Meigs and Porter to meet with Lincoln.[37] In Porter's self-serving recollection of the conversation, it was Lincoln who framed the agenda. "Tell me," Lincoln allegedly asked, "how we can prevent Fort Pickens from falling into the hands of the rebels, for if [Lieutenant] Slemmer is not at once relieved there will be no holding it."[38] Porter thus had Lincoln imitate Seward by ignoring the threshold question of how to contact the ships already there or nearby and order them to offload their men and supplies, shifting to a question that ignored those ships or assumed that—contrary to orders and without notice—they had decided to return to the North.

The plan presented by Meigs and Keyes involved a clash of forces at the entrance to Pensacola Harbor, where Porter might go down in the history books (perhaps posthumously) alongside his father, Commodore David Porter, a hero of the War of 1812.[39] This proposed clash totally ignored what should have been the strategic objective: the successful reinforcement of Fort Pickens without a fight. If Meigs and Porter had been interested in bolstering the garrison so the fort would stand as a Union bulwark in the South (Lincoln's original goal), each would have volunteered to be a courier to deliver another copy of the order transferring men already nearby. While Confederate reports that *Brooklyn* had steamed to Key West might or might not be accurate, certainly no one in the room believed that the ships and men at Pensacola since early February were on their way home. Lincoln would have intuited that perhaps those men would get Scott's orders any day and take Fort Pickens, making the Meigs/Porter armada mere surplusage. If that armada had not yet departed from Northern ports, the operation could be canceled. If they had left, perhaps they would get the news when they stopped off at Key West, perhaps not. But what happened two weeks hence in Florida was unimportant. Lincoln's real purpose was to have a major operation to point to when—as was by now close to certain—he would be denounced for having done nothing to vindicate the Union.

Meigs and Porter, having thus secured the blessings of both Seward and Lincoln, remained at the White House, where, over the next several hours, they drafted the relevant orders for Lincoln's signature.[40] The first was for Porter:

> Sir: You will proceed to New York, and with the least possible delay assume command of any naval steamer available. Proceed to Pensacola Harbor, and at any cost or risk prevent any [Confederate] expedition from the mainland reaching Fort Pickens. . . . You will exhibit this order to any naval officer at Pensacola if you deem it necessary after you have established yourself within the harbor. . . . This order, its object, and your destination will be communicated to no person whatever until you reach the harbor.
>
> Abraham Lincoln
> Recommended: Wm. H. Seward.[41]

In phrasing this do-and-die command for the president's signature, Porter nicely positioned himself as a hero: steam into Pensacola's harbor, past a phalanx of Confederate batteries, and obtain front-page coverage in every newspaper in the United States and most European capitals, while also obtaining (perchance) a brevetted promotion in what would suddenly be a wartime navy. By directing himself to reveal the order to no one prior to entering the harbor, Porter could steam past the Union flotilla still waiting outside the harbor and take all the glory.[42] The order ignored that if the Confederates intended to attack, they would not wait for Porter's expected arrival to do so.[43]

The second order handed to Lincoln was one Porter could present at the Brooklyn Navy Yard to make local personnel snap to. It read:

> Lieutenant D.D. Porter will take command of the steamer *Powhatan*, or any other United States steamer ready for sea which he may deem most fit for the service to which he has been assigned by confidential instructions of this date. All officers are commanded to afford him all such facilities as he may deem necessary for getting to sea as soon as possible. He will select the officers who are to accompany him.
>
> Abraham Lincoln
> Recommended: Wm. H. Seward.[44]

This obliged all officers to help Porter, while enabling him to respond to any question or challenge to his authority by alluding to the other order whose contents he was not obliged to reveal. An ancillary order to the commandant of the Brooklyn Navy Yard, to be sent as a telegram, stated, "Fit out the *Powhatan* to go to sea at the earliest possible moment under sealed orders." Another, to be delivered by confidential messenger the next day, informed the commandant that Porter would relieve *Powhatan*'s commander, Captain Samuel Mercer, adding, "You will under no circumstances communicate to the Navy Department the fact that [*Powhatan*] is fitting out."[45]

Lincoln stated that this was "a most irregular mode of proceeding"—a navy operation with a navy ship commanded by a naval officer but to be hidden from the Department of the Navy and its secretary. But Porter, who months before had turned down Varina Davis's offer to become an admiral in her new navy, told Lincoln that some of the officers and clerks around Welles were disloyal.[46] No one had suggested that Welles himself should be personally briefed. When Lincoln noted that "Uncle Gideon," a somewhat odd figure of Puritan stock with an antique wig, would be miffed upon discovering Porter's secret naval operation, Seward promised to "make it all right" with Welles.[47] In fact, Seward had no such intention. Letting it be known around Washington that he considered Welles an inconsequential person who was unqualified to be navy secretary, Seward in fact harbored a stronger negative animus, since Welles, as head of Connecticut's delegation to the Republican Convention, had helped defeat Seward's nomination and had attacked Seward's "irrepressible conflict" speech.[48] Thurlow Weed had intrigued against Welles, snidely telling Lincoln that rather than appoint him, Lincoln should hang in the Navy Department a figurehead from the prow of a ship adorned with a wig and whiskers.[49]

By insisting that the operation be hidden from the Navy Department, Porter thus sealed for himself a special relationship with the president and secretary of state, neither of whom knew about military strategy and tactics, while immunizing himself from challenges by any superior official—military or civil—who had a perspective or priority at variance with the self-serving orders just handed to the president for signature. Lincoln's cabinet, as would be expected in matters of grave import, had heated debates about Fort Sumter but none about the wisdom of the Porter/Meigs initiative, because only Seward and Lincoln knew anything about it.

"What Have I Done Wrong?"

The last order submitted to Lincoln for signature that day required Captain Samuel Mercer to surrender command of *Powhatan*. The order ended, "Hoping soon to be able to give you a better command than the one you now

Gideon Welles. Library of Congress. Brady-Handy Collection. LC-USZ62-72777.

enjoy, and trusting that you will have full confidence in the disposition of the Government toward you." Since military orders do not typically inform the recipient that he is well liked, nor promise better things to come, Porter and/ or Meigs here surmised that a captain, when presented with an order stripping him of command and giving it to a lieutenant, might be sufficiently incensed to contact the Navy Department.[50] By sugarcoating the order, they bought Mercer's acquiescence and silence.

The side-wheel steam sloop *Powhatan*, with 3,765 tons' displacement and a ship's complement of 289, was heavily armed, commonly outfitted with one 11-inch gun capable of throwing a 135-pound shell, as well as ten 9-inch Dahlgren guns, five 12-pounders, and several armed launches, cutters, and boats. The vessel was historically noteworthy as the flagship of Admiral Matthew Perry's mission in 1853–1854 to open Japan to trade.[51] In late 1860, it and other ships of the Home Squadron were stationed at Veracruz, only 776

USS *Powhatan* during service in Asia, circa 1853–1855. National Archives NA 513000.

nautical miles from the maintenance facility at Pensacola. When news reached Washington that the facility had been turned over to local forces, some spoke of impeaching Secretary Toucey for keeping these ships at Veracruz far past their maintenance schedules, when they might have been in Pensacola Harbor in a position to fight off the assailants. Toucey might, of course, have answered that he kept them away from Pensacola for fear that they would be seized there. By now ordering *Powhatan* all the way to New York for long-overdue maintenance and repair, Toucey invited allegations that he did this to make the warship unavailable in the South, where it was needed.[52]

Meigs had first mentioned *Powhatan* to Lincoln on March 31 or April 1, having seen newspaper articles announcing that it had arrived in New York.[53] He and Porter, perhaps because they did not know how long the repairs would take, did not name *Powhatan* in one of their orders, but only "any naval steamer available," while saying in another, "*Powhatan*, or any other United States steamer ready for sea." Because Porter also had Lincoln issue an order that "under no circumstances" was anyone to "communicate to the Navy Department the fact that [*Powhatan*] is fitting out," Porter would not be conferring with or seeking information from Welles regarding the vessel's status. He therefore did not know that Welles, informed on March 28 that *Powhatan* needed an engine overhaul, ordered that its officers be detached, its crew discharged indefinitely, and its attendant marines transferred.[54]

On April 1, Lincoln asked Fox to return to Washington to work on the details of the Charleston mission.[55] At 4:10 p.m. that day, the Brooklyn Navy Yard received from Welles (presumably at Fox's urging) a telegram voiding his March 28 instruction to dismiss *Powhatan*'s officers and crew and ordering that the vessel be readied for sea immediately. At 6:30 p.m. the Yard received from Welles a second telegram: "Fit out the *Powhatan* to go to sea at earliest possible moment." These words were almost identical to those used by Porter and Meigs in the order submitted to Lincoln for signature.[56] And that order, also sent as a telegram, must have been sent from Washington around the same time, since it was marked "Rec'd" in the Brooklyn Navy Yard at 6:50 p.m., just twenty minutes later.[57]

It was unusual to receive from Washington orders for the immediate fitting out of a vessel that needed such extensive work as to send the crew home. In perilous times, with similar orders for the same vessel arriving not just from the Navy Department but also from the president himself, the conclusion was logical that an important initiative was suddenly in prospect. Given all that, no one at the Brooklyn Navy Yard would have imagined that the two orders, received from the secretary of the navy and from the president within twenty minutes, giving the same instruction in nearly identical language respecting the same vessel, were not for the same mission and that neither sender knew what the other was doing.

That evening, Welles was having dinner at Willard's Hotel when Lincoln's chief personal secretary, John G. Nicolay, appeared with a large package containing several naval orders signed by Lincoln, although Welles immediately concluded that Lincoln "could not possibly" have read them.[58] In one, Lincoln instructed Welles to relieve Commodore Silas Stringham of his administrative job, one that included working with Welles on a highly confidential basis in culling out disloyal officers.[59] Stringham, the order recited, was to proceed to Pensacola and should be replaced in this sensitive position by Captain Samuel Barron.[60]

Welles, although derided even by Lincoln as an unwittingly comic figure, was nevertheless an experienced public man. Recognizing Barron's name and believing him to be possibly disloyal, Welles proceeded directly to the White House and asked Lincoln, "What have I done wrong?"—meaning that no cabinet officer would have his authority so completely undermined except as a punishment. In response, Lincoln "expressed as much surprise as I felt, that he had sent me such a document," adding that Welles should simply disregard it if he liked.[61] Lincoln explained that Captain Meigs and a navy lieutenant named Porter had been at the White House all day regarding a project for Seward, and although Lincoln had "yielded" to it, Seward prepared the papers and Lincoln simply signed them, many "without reading,—for he had not time, and if he could not trust the secretary of state, he knew not whom he could trust."[62]

When Lincoln mentioned Porter's name, Welles responded that Porter and Barron were both "favorites" of Jefferson Davis.[63] Because Porter reacted to a growing possibility of civil war by obtaining a transfer to the Pacific, Welles doubted Porter's Union commitment.[64] And while Porter had himself told Lincoln that it was to avoid secessionist spies among naval personnel that no one—not even Secretary Welles—could know about his mission to Pensacola, now Welles, similarly believing that the department was rife with untrustworthy men, was suggesting that Barron, the man Porter tried to put in charge of determining who was and was not loyal, and perhaps Porter himself were among the traitors.

Seward had let it be known that he intended to "overawe and browbeat" Welles and Cameron as necessary to bring their respective departments "under his own control."[65] Seward thus would not have been reluctant to approve a lieutenant's plan to cut the secretary of the navy out of the chain of command, for no reason other than to demonstrate that he could do it. Since Seward grossly overestimated his own knowledge of the South and Southerners, he may have believed that by appointing Barron, a Virginian, he was helping to seal Virginia's loyalty.[66] He must have guessed that Welles would complain to Lincoln but had no idea that such complaint would be so well grounded—that is, Seward apparently neither knew who Barron was nor cared to know.

In the course of signing various orders that excluded Welles from a naval operation, Lincoln had reportedly been sufficiently concerned to say, "Seward, see that I don't burn my fingers."[67] Even now, however, with the mischievous Barron/Stringham order exposed, Lincoln would not reveal to Welles that Seward was in charge of a naval expedition. And Welles did not ask, much less did he tell Lincoln—as a more experienced and self-assured professional bureaucrat would have—that if the president would not trust him with knowledge of operations involving personnel and assets from his own department, perhaps it was best that he should resign.[68] If Welles had so stated, Lincoln would undoubtedly have confided in him everything he knew about Seward's project, including the names of the vessels chosen, and Welles would immediately have identified the conflict involving *Powhatan*. Instead, Welles did not make a fuss. "Whether Porter was prompted by any of his Rebel associates to intrigue for Barron," Welles later wrote, "I never ascertained." Welles could not have known that back when South Carolina seceded and Varina Davis had flippantly offered to make her friend Porter an admiral in a new Confederate navy, his response was that accepting such a post would make him a second Benedict Arnold.[69]

About Barron, Welles was dead accurate. It would emerge that at the time Seward and Porter tried to install Barron as Welles's confidential assistant for purging disloyal officers, Barron had already been issued a Confederate commission. Only then did he resign his Union commission and leave Washington, to be placed in command of Fort Hatteras on North Carolina's Outer Banks. On August 29, 1861, Barron was captured in the first Union victory of the war, which happened also to be that operational rarity: an amphibious operation combining warships (including the cutter *Harriet Lane*), transports, a tug, schooners, and surfboats. The Union officer to whom Barron surrendered his sword was Commodore Stringham, the man Porter had wanted Barron to replace.[70]

Seward had repeatedly invited the Southern commissioners to believe that Lincoln was spineless and in the end would let Anderson's garrison run out of food and abjectly surrender. But one of the Confederacy's highly placed spies in Washington gave Confederate secretary of war Leroy Walker a sense that in the wake of the March 29 cabinet meeting, Lincoln was in fact "pursuing a hostile and treacherous policy," with one source acquainted with naval officers saying Lincoln intended to reinforce both Pickens and Sumter, the latter perhaps including a movement against Beauregard's batteries from the rear "with infantry and field artillery, &c., while their ships press up the bay."[71]

10

Under Siege

A State for a Fort

In 1860–1861, 28 percent of Virginia's elite had no slaves, with only 23 percent owning twenty or more, its western districts being sufficiently antislavery to send delegates to the Republican Convention.[1] This contrasted sharply with South Carolina, where 90 percent of those who attended the secession convention were slaveholders, and of these almost half owned at least fifty, some more than one hundred.[2] On Tuesday, April 2, Lincoln told Seward that he wished to meet with Judge Summers or some other Unionist delegate to Virginia's secession convention, adding that (because Fox would soon launch a fleet to relieve Sumter) the meeting must occur by Friday, April 5. For several weeks, a court-martial had been convened in Washington to decide the fate of Commodore Armstrong arising out of his giving up Pensacola's navy yard. Seward called upon the Washington lawyer acting as judge advocate in that proceeding, Allan B. Magruder, to utilize several days' recess by fetching Summers from Richmond. Arriving there on April 3, Magruder met with Summers, who declined, although another Unionist delegate to the secession convention, John B. Baldwin, agreed to travel to Washington on the overnight train. Baldwin and Magruder presented themselves at Seward's office at 10:00 a.m. on Thursday, April 4, and Seward walked them over to the White House.[3]

As they arrived, Lincoln was meeting with several Republican governors who undoubtedly were urging him to reinforce Fort Sumter.[4] Following brief introductions, Lincoln searched around for a vacant room, brought Baldwin inside, and closed the door (thereby excluding Seward and Magruder). Five years later, Baldwin would tell a congressional committee what he said to the president: that to preserve Virginia's loyalty and avoid war, not only must he evacuate Fort Sumter and Fort Pickens, but he must also declare that he was doing so not from military necessity but as a peace offering. Lincoln refused, saying that Baldwin had come "too late," a charge that stunned Baldwin, since he had come on the first available train.

Several weeks earlier, on or about March 20, Lincoln had invited Judge Summers, the acknowledged leader of Virginia's Unionists, to discuss the crisis, only to find that Summers "hesitated, delayed, and finally refused to come."[5] And now, a second time, Summers had declined a presidential invitation, undoubtedly causing Lincoln to speculate that Summers thought Unionism in Virginia would become tainted by any contact with Lincoln. Given Summers's apparent attitude, Lincoln might reasonably have been reluctant to abandon two forts he had publicly promised to hold as a price for Virginia remaining in the Union, when the man leading the Unionist effort in Virginia would not even meet with him.[6]

In the two weeks since Summers's initial refusal, the prospects for concil- iation had deteriorated. Because Scott had failed to carry out Lincoln's order to reinforce Fort Pickens, Lincoln could not abandon Fort Sumter without invoking the anger of ultra Republicans, particularly after Francis Blair had strenuously reminded him of his mandate. Several cabinet members who had earlier advocated evacuation now—perhaps under pressure from constituents—wanted intervention. Hurlbut's visit to Charleston had proven that Seward was wrong about hidden Unionism there, and Seward's probity and judgment were now in question. Meanwhile, Baldwin, the man who came when Summers refused, was hardly one to instill confidence that Unionism in Virginia was other than paper thin. In the secession convention, Baldwin had asserted that if Lincoln did no more than attempt to provide food to Ander- son's men, he would be starting the Civil War.[7]

Lincoln, as if to scuttle the meeting, told Baldwin that he would not vacate Forts Sumter and Pickens unless Virginia's secession convention resolved to remain in the Union and then permanently adjourned. Baldwin responded that this was impossible: although Unionism at this point clearly had the upper hand in the convention, all hinged on Seward's promises of evacuation. If Unionists demanded that the convention end peremptorily before the status of Forts Sumter and Pickens was resolved, secessionist delegates—Baldwin warned—would call a new convention from which Unionist delegates would be systematically excluded, and Virginia would secede.[8]

In 1866, the same congressional committee that questioned Baldwin also examined another Virginia Unionist, John Minor Botts, Lincoln's fellow Whig in the Thirtieth Congress and a secret supporter in the 1860 election.[9]

Challenging Baldwin's entire account, Botts swore that on Sunday, April 7, Lincoln told Botts that he had offered Baldwin the evacuation of Forts Sumter and Pickens in return for Virginia's loyalty and that Baldwin had squandered a chance for peace simply by misunderstanding the offer. "Sir, he would not listen to it for a moment," Lincoln reportedly said of Baldwin. "He hardly treated me with civility."[10] Botts thus essentially charged Baldwin with missing the last clear chance to avoid the Civil War.

Among those corroborating Botts's account was another Unionist, George Plumer Smith, who later recounted that a few days after Virginia seceded, Lincoln told him that he had met with Baldwin and proposed that if the Virginia convention pledged the state's loyalty and then went home, he would evacuate Fort Sumter. Lincoln at that time swore Smith to secrecy, and when in January 1863 Smith asked Lincoln's secretary, John Hay, to have Lincoln confirm, Lincoln did so, while reiterating that the Lincoln/Baldwin conversation should remain a secret.[11] While this report would appear to substantiate Botts, if Baldwin had been shown the Smith/Hay correspondence, he would undoubtedly have said that it was accurate as far as it went but that it failed to include Baldwin's reply to the effect that the secessionists in the Virginia convention would never have allowed an interim loyalty vote to stand and then go home.[12] Baldwin's account is more intrinsically trustworthy. It is much more likely that Baldwin told Lincoln that no such bargain was possible than that he turned Lincoln down because he did not understand what Lincoln was offering. Lincoln would not have promised withdrawal from Fort Sumter without assurance of a binding pro-loyalty vote from Virginia, and it would have been clear to him by this point that the Virginians considered the withdrawal from Fort Sumter (and Fort Pickens) a condition for getting that vote.

Botts's account is also marred by significant factual errors. Among these, he testified that the Baldwin/Lincoln meeting took place on Friday, April 5, when other accounts indicate the morning of April 4.[13] Botts's dating error is significant, since it has Lincoln making a representation he could not have made. "You have recently taken a vote in the Virginia convention" (Botts has Lincoln telling Baldwin), where secession was rejected "by ninety to forty-five.... If you will go back to Richmond and get that Union majority to adjourn and go home without passing the ordinance of secession," Fort Sumter would be abandoned. Even if one indulges Botts's offering actual dialogue for a conversation that (1) took place five years earlier and (2) he did not himself attend, the fact remains that in Baldwin's testimony his discussion with Lincoln ended—at the latest—by 12:30 p.m. on April 4, and the encouraging

90–45 vote did not occur until that afternoon.[14] Because Botts testified against Baldwin in Congress, he heard Baldwin testify that he met Lincoln on April 4 and not on April 5. In the months that followed their conflicting testimony, Botts had ample time to check his facts prior to publishing a book in which he repeated his charges. But Botts remained adamant, making this crucial dating error not merely negligent but also willful.[15]

In the days following his discussion with Lincoln, Baldwin recounted its substance to colleagues, and his 1866 testimony was supported by several letters.[16] Some of these events were later described by the Virginia cleric and scholar Robert Lewis Dabney, with Baldwin his likely source. In this version, when Magruder first arrived in Richmond to fetch a Unionist to meet with Lincoln, he announced, affirmatively and unconditionally, that Seward had authorized him to say that Fort Sumter would be evacuated and that *Pawnee* would soon go to Charleston to retrieve Anderson's men.[17] This news clearly influenced the resounding 90–45 interim rejection of secessionism in the convention on the afternoon of April 4, a margin sufficient perhaps to convince a president (unaware of what Seward had allegedly promised) that Virginia would remain loyal. But by the time news of the 90–45 vote reached Washington, the Lincoln/Baldwin meeting had concluded. And although withdrawing Anderson would defuse the immediate tension, South Carolina's fire-eaters, harboring three decades of resentment, would not just celebrate a bloodless victory and retire to their plantations. While most Carolinians knew little about Fort Pickens, *its* abandonment would immediately become the sine qua non of keeping the peace. All the attributes of a new nation would be enthusiastically pursued, and since Lincoln would attempt to collect duties, sooner or later there would be an incident. Whatever his reasons, Lincoln chose not to relinquish a fort in the hope of keeping a state.

In 1868, two years after the Baldwin/Botts congressional hearings, Senator Garrett Davis (Unionist/KY) said that Lincoln "stated to me most distinctly" in a brief meeting in late April 1861 "that when Mr. Baldwin and one or two other gentlemen came [to Washington] from the Virginia convention he had made the proposition to Mr. Baldwin and his colleagues . . . that if the Virginia convention would adjourn without doing anything he would withdraw the troops from Fort Sumter."[18] Since Baldwin met with Lincoln alone, Davis may have been confusing several meetings. Lincoln had met with several other Virginians prior to his inaugural and reportedly discussed with them abandoning Fort Sumter in exchange for Virginia's loyalty. But nothing came of that meeting. And on April 8, after Virginia Unionists heard Baldwin's disappointing report of his meeting with Lincoln, three came to Washington to have Lincoln clarify his policy.[19] Meeting with them on April 12, Lincoln was no longer prepared to trade Fort Sumter for Virginia's loyalty, reportedly saying, "I can't understand it at all; Virginia wants to remain in the Union, and yet wants me to let South Carolina go out and the Union be dissolved, in order that Virginia may stay in."[20] The quotation, whether accurate or not, well summarized the view of a president who did not believe the Constitution allowed a state to secede. Nor could Lincoln by that point have offered a fort for a state, since, even as they spoke, Fort Sumter was under attack.

"Your Duty Both as Soldier & Christian"

Back on December 21, Floyd, at Buchanan's direction, had instructed Anderson that it was "neither expected nor desired that you should expose your own life or that of your men in a hopeless conflict" against "a force so superior that resistance would, in your judgment, be a useless waste of life." Thus, rather than "make a vain . . . sacrifice of your own life and the lives of the men under your command, upon a mere point of honor," Floyd urged that it will "be your duty to yield to necessity, and make the best terms in your power," exercising the "sound military discretion" operative in "an honorable, brave, and humane officer."[21]

By late January, a 360-degree survey from Sumter's parapets would reveal a superior and growing force to which resistance would be a waste of life.[22] Nevertheless, Anderson on January 28 wrote to his local friend, Gourdin, "If an attack is made . . . God willing, the Fort will fall into the possession of the state in such a condition that no flag can be raised on its walls. I am opposed to this shedding of blood, but if the strife be forced upon me, and we are overcome by numbers, not a soul will, probably, be found alive in the ruins."[23] He said the same to others, and his comments—although watered down—reached the press.[24]

While Anderson habitually referred to phenomena as indicative of God's will, in his letter to Gourdin he was employing words not of simple faith but of apocalypse. Anderson was too familiar with death to indulge in melodrama, too disciplined to engage in hyperbole, too honest to prevaricate. To an officer now focused solely upon the concepts of "Honor" and "Duty" that had defined his life, directions to do the easy thing, when issued by mediocrities like Floyd and Buchanan, could not have meant much, even if they were above Anderson in the chain of command.

Like Scott and countless other soldiers, Anderson was still subject to bouts of fever from his service in southern climates decades before. In late February, it was widely reported that he was suffering from pneumonia and

Fort Moultrie on Sullivan's Island, with summer houses and (at right) Moultrie House hotel, as seen from Fort Sumter through field glasses, February 13, 1861.

Fort Johnson as seen from Fort Sumter on February 13, 1861.

Cumming's Point and Morris Island as seen from Fort Sumter. Ironclad Battery under construction at center.

Sketched by Brevet Captain Truman Seymour. George B. Davis et al., *Atlas to Accompany the Official Records of the Union and Confederate Armies* (Washington, 1891–1895). The Cartographic Research Laboratory, University of Alabama.

was under the care of a Charleston physician.[25] After weeks of siege, under stress, ill, and undoubtedly depressed, he was making the best of the hand he had been dealt, letting it be known to the other side, unofficially but unequivocally, that if the Southerners attacked, he and his men would give them neither a victory in which they could take any pride nor a functioning fort with which to defend their harbor against Union ships in the months and years ahead. While the Carolinians' hunger to possess Sumter grew daily, no coolheaded leader—political or military—would wish to reap the whirlwind of Northern revenge and international obloquy that would follow the death of Anderson and his few dozen soldiers—less than a third of the men Leonidas commanded at Thermopylae.

Gourdin clearly credited Anderson's sincerity, for he replied, "I read this declaration with profound, unmitigated regret, for I cannot but regard such a determination [as] altogether inconsistent with your convictions of the right and wrong of this unhappy controversy and with your duty as a Christian man and a Christian soldier."[26] Gourdin was sufficiently concerned that within a few hours he wrote again: "If in obedience to a false conception of duty or of honor you sacrifice, recklessly and heedlessly, your own life, and the lives of others, what will be your record here, and hereafter?"[27] Gourdin contacted Alfred Huger, asking whether he should apprise South Carolina authorities. Huger replied that it was "absurd" for a man who obviously believed in God and had professed Southern sympathies to "shed blood in a cause not fortified in his own heart." Huger pointed out that Anderson had not sworn Gourdin to confidentiality, and even if he had, Gourdin was obliged "to your country & to humanity" to divulge Anderson's threat, in part because of the "Death & personal sufferings" that would result from withholding it.[28] Whether Anderson believed that his letter might be shared with authorities, or even intended that it would be, is not known.

Pierre Beauregard distinguished himself at West Point when Anderson taught artillery there, graduating second in the class of 1838.[29] After Beauregard took command in Charleston, the notes passed between the two were not just civil but also cordial, an ironic aspect of a martial culture in which men can exhibit actual affection even while squaring off to fight to the death. But the requirements of courtesy and sincere mutual regard could not paper over the reality, with both men knowing that soon they must (as in *Henry V*) "disguise fair nature with hard-favoured rage." In a letter marked by politeness, Beauregard asked Anderson, as a condition of his being allowed to evacuate in peace, not to destroy any of Fort Sumter's assets. Perhaps Beauregard had been apprised of Anderson's note to Gourdin; perhaps he knew of Floyd's order to fight to the last extremity and/or of President Buchanan's unequivocal cancellation of that order. Perhaps Beauregard had in mind that Anderson had destroyed assets at Fort Moultrie. Whatever Beauregard knew or did not know of Anderson's state of mind, he should have intuited that his beleaguered former teacher would not negotiate with him to surrender guns and ammunition (as Commodore James Armstrong had at Pensacola) in exchange for personal safety. Anderson in response declared himself "deeply hurt" by Beauregard's request, swearing, "If I can only be permitted to leave on the pledge you mention, I shall never, so help me God, leave this fort alive."[30] Beauregard, in passing the letter to Confederate secretary of war Leroy Walker, tried to smooth over the agitation evident in these remarks, describing

Anderson as "a most gallant officer, incapable of any act that might tarnish his reputation as a soldier."[31]

Anderson's bitter frustration is further shown in a letter written the next day to Lorenzo Thomas, just promoted to adjutant general at the rank of colonel. Enclosing his correspondence with Beauregard, Anderson noted that the Confederates "may have misunderstood a remark which I have made, viz, that if attacked, and I found that I could not hold possession of the fort, that I would blow it up, sacrificing our lives in preference to permitting ourselves to fall into their hands." Of course, Beauregard (and Gourdin, and Huger) had *not* misunderstood the remark, nor did Anderson here disavow it. The next sentence, though lightly veiled, must have given Thomas pause: "I hope," Anderson declared, "that the authorities here now understand distinctly that I shall give no pledges whatever. I shall do nothing which is not fully justified by the highest sense of honorable and straightforward dealing, and will not permit from any source any insinuation that I have acted in any other manner in the performance of my duty, &c., here."[32] Thomas might reasonably have wondered what Anderson meant by "any insinuation" from "any source." Surrounded by thousands of fellow Southerners, all of them led by a former student, Anderson had learned to expect nothing helpful or supportive from his own government, whether under the proslavery Buchanan or the Black Republican Lincoln, the latter rumored to want the blame for surrender placed on Anderson so none would be ascribed to him. A direct order from Buchanan not to permit a wasteful loss of life, several months old and neither reaffirmed nor replaced by the new commander in chief, seemed now to Anderson only a trick by which to scapegoat him for "surrendering." Anderson thus believed that he had nothing to fight for, or die for, or have his men fight and die for, but "Duty" and "Honor," which now seemed to require death in order to demonstrate their purity.

Beauregard attempted to make amends by having a gift delivered. In response, Anderson, referring to it as a "military irregularity," returned it with a temperate note: "Trusting that in a few days we shall be placed in a position which will be more agreeable and acceptable to both of us than the anomalous ones we now occupy" (an apparent reference to Lamon's expected return with an evacuation order). Beauregard apologized that the parcel had been accepted at the fort without Anderson's knowledge, "hoping that we may soon meet on the same friendly footing as heretofore."[33]

Anderson's family left to posterity some partial transcriptions of his correspondence. In letters sent just before and after his transfer from Moultrie, Anderson had assessed the situation objectively, giving an occasional assurance that his wife Eliza should not be unduly concerned for his safety. By March 4, so concerned was Anderson with her welfare that he wrote an extraordinary note to Alfred Huger: "Enclosed . . . 3 ct. stamp, due for my yesterday's mail. My poor wife, who is an invalid, becomes very uneasy when a failure of the mail makes her miss the recpt of my daily report. May I take the liberty of asking her to telegraph you in such cases? The newspaper stories, so recently and generally circulated, that I was ill, have made her very nervous about me." Anderson added that someone from the fort would report to Huger if in fact Anderson was too ill to attend to his duties, meaning that so long as Huger received no such report, he could advise Mrs. Anderson, upon inquiry, that all was well.[34]

Anderson's letters to his wife reveal his evolving perspective regarding the evacuation:

- March 26: "The Law partner of the president came down to see me yesterday, [saying] . . . that in his opinion this fort ought to be given up, and that the sooner it was done the better."
- March 29: "Another week nearly gone, and the order not yet received to give up. . . . It is a bitter pill for the new Administration to take, and I fancy, like the child with the nauseating dose, the longer it is deferred the harder it will be to take."
- March 31: "No special messenger has yet made his appearance. Gen. Scott will, I am sure let you know as soon as orders have been sent me."
- April 1: "How long will the authorities in Washington keep us in doubt—and your heart at its utmost tension . . . ? It is too bad. I am heartily sick of it. If they wish to shift the responsibility upon my shoulders then let them say so and I will act; but this giving out from day to day, from hour to hour that the order will soon be issued is trifling upon too important a question. . . . I have written to Gen Scott today, and shall also write an official letter showing the Dept. that it must come at once to some decision. . . . They must send us away or send us something to eat!"[35]

Anderson concealed from his wife his darker thoughts. After talking with Anderson alone for ninety minutes, Lamon described him as "deeply despondent," fully realizing "the critical position he and his men occupied" and apprehending "the worst possible consequences if measures were not promptly taken by the government to strengthen him."[36] So affecting was the impression that perhaps personal concern for Anderson played some role in Lamon's pushing so hard for evacuation. Upon returning to Washington, Lamon saw fit to tell one or more persons that Anderson had confided in him something highly disturbing, for on March 29, General Scott, who seldom communicated directly with Anderson, sent him an extraordinary note. "I have heard of your declaration to Col. Lamon," Scott wrote, "indicating a desperate purpose. I forbid it as your commander[,] it being against your duty both as soldier & Christian. Your friend, Winfield Scott."[37]

That Anderson had mentioned to Lamon—as he earlier had mentioned to Gourdin—a "purpose" sufficiently "desperate" that his general would "forbid it" as against his duty "as soldier & Christian" is further revealed in a distressed letter Anderson wrote to Scott on April 1, probably before he received Scott's letter or even imagined a direct, unsolicited communication from his commander in the Mexican War. In it, Anderson attempted to construct a historical background and excuse for the martyrdom he had now repeatedly

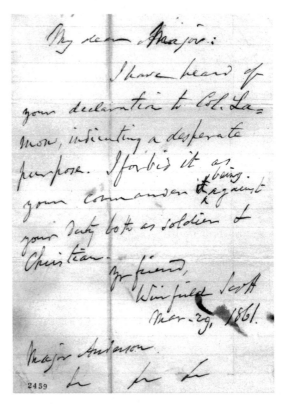

Scott note to Anderson (March 29, 1861). Robert Anderson Papers, vol. 11, Library of Congress.

proposed. "So great was the excitement in S. Carolina against this command, when I came into this Fort, and for weeks afterwards," he wrote, that if his garrison came under attack at that time, "not a soul would have been left alive." That is, he was here trying to transform his prior comments about a suicidal refusal to surrender into an observation about homicidal intentions on the part of the assaulting force. From this he segued to admitting having said "more than once, that, rather than let my garrison suffer that fate, I would blow up the Fort as they entered the walls, and all who might be in it," thereby killing some Confederates while depriving them of the chance to massacre its inhabitants. Anderson further admitted that the passage of time had not caused him to change his mind. "Cut off from all intercourse with my Government," he told Scott, "I have been compelled to act according to the dictates of my own judgment, and, had the contingency referred to, arisen, I should, after prayerfully appealing to God, to teach me my duty, have cheerfully and promptly performed it."[38] Nowhere in this message did he mention that the standing order from Buchanan and Floyd was to capitulate to an overwhelming force. Scott, apparently knowing nothing of that order, could not invoke it, although in essence he replicated it on his own authority.

Anderson's threat of martyrdom was, among other things, the card he could play against a Republican president who apparently desired to evade responsibility by scapegoating him, exactly what Buchanan would have done but for the Unionists in his cabinet. If Lamon or Scott communicated to Lincoln the growing evidence of Anderson's mental strain, Lincoln would have felt additional pressure—even after telling Fox to prepare a relief effort—to order an immediate evacuation rather than risk the self-annihilation Anderson had "cheerfully" promised. Any such catastrophic ending would be portrayed by Lincoln's political enemies as the result of choices Lincoln made—or failed to make—in the comfort of his office. To "stand up" to the rebels by launching a relief effort was one thing; to relegate the garrison to a losing battle against an overwhelming force was quite another. When the press found that an affirmative order of evacuation had already been drafted by Scott weeks before but that Lincoln failed to sign it, many in Congress, under pressure from outraged constituents, would undoubtedly demand impeachment proceedings. The administration would never recover.

The issue was already in the open. On March 22, the day Fox returned to Washington, the *Charleston Mercury* suggested that his object had been "to ascertain whether Major Anderson was in a temper to have his military prestige sacrificed upon the altar of Black Republicanism," the intention of "Lincoln and his pack" being "to leave [Anderson] to eat his last ounce of bread, and then to let loose the Northern howl" upon him for evacuating without having been specifically ordered to do so. The article was republished in the North.[39] In the Senate, Stephen Douglas alleged that Lincoln, fearful that a Republican ultra would charge him with having "backed down" by ordering Sumter evacuated, was secretly discussing with his advisors the two choices their failure to act had left in Anderson's hands: stay there "until he starves to death," or light "with his own hand . . . the match that blows him and his little garrison into eternity."[40]

Lincoln, knowing of Anderson primarily through the Doubledays' accusations of disloyalty, had never reached out to him with words of support, nor asked Scott to do so, despite numerous newspaper accounts of the garrison's sense of isolation. Anderson, as a young officer in 1832, had mustered Lincoln in and out of the Black Hawk War, but of those moments had no recollection, making clear to Gourdin that his only feeling for Lincoln was contempt.[41] It was Lincoln's very close friend and bodyguard Lamon who had promised Anderson that Sumter would be evacuated, only—at Lincoln's presumed insistence—to break that promise. Meanwhile, the silence of Cameron, Lincoln's secretary of war, amounted to a dereliction.

Whether apprised of Anderson's emotional state or not, Lincoln still entertained sufficient doubts about his loyalty (exactly the point upon which Anderson was now—quite superfluously—prepared to die) that Lincoln turned to Abner Doubleday's wife Mary, asking her to forward her husband's letters so that he might glean from them a deeper understanding. She complied, telling Lincoln that her husband had been "exceedingly cautious" in his letters after many were not delivered and others had apparently been opened and read. The letters she sent included nothing against Anderson and only reiterated what everyone already knew: that the food was running out.[42]

On April 3, *Rhoda H. Shannon*, a schooner out of Boston flying a U.S. flag, mistook Charleston for Savannah and was fired upon by the Confederates as it approached the harbor mouth. Anderson reported that the incident was over before his guns could be made ready and that he had complied with Holt's February 23 orders by acting "strictly on the defensive." Anderson here saw fit to add, "The remarks made to me by Colonel Lamon, taken in connection with the tenor of newspaper articles, have induced me, as stated in previous communications, to believe that orders would soon be issued" to evacuate.[43]

Pickens, wanting the garrison to depart—if possible—without being fired upon, and perhaps accepting that a principled person could prefer martyrdom if the only alternative was dishonor, concluded that Anderson might leave if he could be convinced that Lincoln had actually granted him the requisite authority. When Fox had told Anderson that he could leave on his own authority, Anderson showed great eagerness to do so but required written proof, which Fox could not give. Pickens now had in hand the April 1 dispatch of Commissioner Martin Crawford, someone Anderson knew and trusted. But Crawford had written, "My opinion is that the president has not the courage to execute the order, agreed upon in [the] Cabinet for the evacuation of the fort, but . . . intends to shift the responsibility upon Major Anderson, by suffering him to be starved out."[44] Because this was not by a Union official indicating presidential permission but only the opinion of a secessionist official indicating presidential weakness, Pickens chose not to show it to Anderson. Rather, on April 4, when one of Captain Foster's engineers, Lieutenant George W. Snyder, came over to Charleston, Pickens described the letter to Snyder as saying that Crawford had been "authorized" (by Seward, speaking for Lincoln) to say that "no attempt would be made to reinforce Fort Sumter with men or provisions," but Lincoln, rather than issue an order for Anderson's withdrawal, "would leave him to act for himself."[45] This characterization, while not suggesting an affirmative presidential order, did indicate a presidential grant of discretion.

Perhaps Anderson sensed that Pickens was misrepresenting Crawford's dispatch, or perhaps what Snyder related did nothing to alter Anderson's belief that a cowardly and incompetent president, having promised in his inaugural to hold Fort Sumter, only to find that too difficult, would rather give Anderson the "discretion"—and, thus, the blame—for giving it up. On April 5, Anderson wrote to Colonel Thomas in Washington, summarizing Commissioner Crawford's reported view that Lincoln was leaving the decision to him. "I cannot but think," Anderson wrote,

> that Mr. Crawford has misunderstood what he has heard in Washington, as I cannot think that the Government would abandon, without instructions and without advice, a command which has tried to do all its duty to our country. I cannot but think that if the Government decides to do nothing[,] which can be construed into a recognition of the fact of the dissolution of the Union, that it will, at all events, say to me that I must do the best I can, and not compel me to do an act which will leave my motives and actions liable to misconception,

meaning that if he was forced to surrender on his own authority, he would be publicly accused (even if no food was left) of allowing his pro-Southern sympathies to prevail over his sense of duty and loyalty.

Demonstrably, this was an accusation Anderson found so intolerable that he would rather die—and have his men die with him—than hear it uttered. Further:

> I am sure that I shall not be left without instructions, even though they may be confidential. After thirty odd years of service I do not wish it to be said that I have treasonably abandoned a post and turned over to unauthorized persons public property intrusted to my charge [as Armstrong did in Pensacola]. I am entitled to this act of justice at the hands of my Government, and I feel confident that I shall not be disappointed. . . . Unless we receive supplies I shall be compelled to stay here without food [i.e., starve], or to abandon this post very early next week.[46]

The letter was forceful, pleading, but dignified and self-possessed—showing appropriate signs of frustration but not desperation, much less irrationality.

Several days later, Anderson noted, "My letter of the 5th should reach Washington this afternoon and an answer can well be returned by Wednesday [April 10]. I shall take no step until ample time . . . has been given—shall remain a day or two after we have eaten our last crust of bread (of pork we have an ample supply) and no orders having then been received, I shall be compelled to act. I shall do it calmly, quietly, prayerfully, in the full consciousness that I am doing what is right, and shall do it without thinking whether it will meet with the popular favor or not."[47] His allusion to "popular favor" suggested that he now contemplated evacuation, since resisting to the death would yield substantial popular favor. "I wonder," he told his wife Eliza, "if any man was ever before placed in such a position. . . . I have written very plainly and very strongly to Washington" insisting upon "orders of some kind. I shall remain here so long as my provisions last, hoping until the last hour that my orders may come; and, if none arrive, I shall then do that which I trust, God will, after my turning to him for guidance, put it into my heart to do."[48] That last comment was undoubtedly intended to be taken (and was taken) by his wife as an allusion to voluntary surrender. But if the same letter had been sent to Scott, Lamon, Gourdin, or Alfred Huger, they would have interpreted it more ominously.

The December 21 order "to yield to necessity, and make the best terms in your power" indicated that Anderson could share that instruction with the other officers at a time of "close necessity."[49] Since this was such a time, Anderson could have reviewed with his officers the several orders by Floyd and Holt, as well as Buell's memorandum, and—collectively and consensually—they could have discussed their options. They had voted on what to do about *Star of the West*, and, under siege since December and with death now an option, they had certainly earned the right to participate in deciding what to do. But Anderson instead assumed the entire burden himself. The garrison's medical officer recorded in his diary, "The Major is very greatly depressed in Spirits, and today told me he thought of taking down our flag. Without supplies[,] without encouragement we are left to ourselves, and the greatest depression prevails among us."[50] On April 8, Anderson reduced his men from three-fourths to half rations.[51]

Commissioner Crawford's prediction that Lincoln lacked the will to do anything was incorrect, and on April 4, the day Lincoln told Fox to proceed, Lincoln drafted and Cameron signed and mailed to Anderson a letter stating that an expedition was being readied and that if the garrison could sustain itself until April 11 or 12, the ships, "finding your flag flying, will attempt to provision you, and, in case the effort is resisted, will endeavor also to reinforce you. You will therefore hold out if possible till [their] arrival."[52] *Times* of London correspondent William Howard Russell wrote in his April 5 dispatch, "No matter what reports may appear in the papers or in letters, distrust them if they would lead you to believe that Mr. Lincoln is preparing . . . to abandon what he has."[53] While Lincoln might earlier have worried that Anderson would surrender out of disloyalty, he now specified to Anderson that "whenever, if at all, in your judgment, to save yourself and command, a capitulation becomes a necessity, you are authorized to make it," essentially reiterating the Buchanan/Floyd order from December (of which Lincoln may have known nothing). Lincoln added that he did not wish "to subject your command to any danger or hardship beyond what, in your judgment, would be usual in military life." While intended to be sympathetic, this statement was—in the circumstances—laughable, since Anderson and his command had long since surpassed those thresholds of danger and hardship. Scott, perhaps sensing that Lincoln had been shown or might be shown Anderson's several letters of complaint, told Lincoln that while Anderson "showed some nervous irritability," this condition undoubtedly arose "from particle sickness"—microorganisms from old campaigns—coupled with "long confinement & a sense of neglect," although he was "an officer of the highest honor, valor, patriotism & morals."[54]

II

"Sail On, O Ship of State!"

Sail on, O ship of State!
Sail on, O UNION, strong and great!
Humanity—with all its fears,
With all the hopes of future years,
Is hanging breathless on thy fate!

—Henry Wadsworth Longfellow,
"The Building of the Ship"

AT ANY TIME A TELEGRAM OR A COPY OF A SOUTHERN NEWSPAPER MIGHT arrive at the White House indicating that Scott's order to reinforce Fort Pickens had at last been received on *Brooklyn* and its troops had been transferred. But if that transfer did not take place, the reinforcement that Meigs, Porter, and Seward were organizing would not appear off Pensacola before April 15, designated by Anderson as the day he would exercise his discretion if reinforcement, resupply, or a Confederate attack did not occur earlier. Seward, having repeatedly promised Justice Campbell that Fort Pickens would not be reinforced, must have considered that when the Confederates learned that this promise was broken, either by the transfer of men already offshore or by the departure from Northern ports of Seward's new effort, they might withdraw their permission to let Fort Sumter's garrison evacuate voluntarily, publicly ascribing the change to Seward's mendacity.

The novice president had been ill served; things did not need to be in such disarray. If (1) the March 12 order had provided that the transfer of men from *Brooklyn* to Fort Pickens should take place at a designated time—say, 4:00 a.m. on March 25—and (2) the order was correct in form and thus mandatory upon those involved, and (3) the means chosen to deliver the order ensured that it would arrive in time, then Lincoln could have arranged with Governor Pickens for the evacuation of Fort Sumter at, say, 4:00 p.m. on March 24, so that Major Anderson and his men would be safely at sea by the time news was telegraphed to Charleston of what had taken place in Pensacola, six hundred miles away. Lincoln would thus have adroitly fulfilled his inaugural promise of maintaining a federal outpost where it was feasible, while also extracting heroic soldiers from harm's way at an outpost that was surrounded by an overwhelming force planning to attack, and which served no military purpose. Following such a coordinated effort, the president would have been applauded for his acumen as well as his audacity, and while the fire-eaters would have claimed to have been victimized by a "typical" Yankee trick, the world would have applauded the maneuver.

No one offered such a coordinated solution, or any other. Lincoln, a brilliant trial lawyer, would become a superior military thinker, but that would take time. Scott had lost his strategic and tactical edge and was making fundamental blunders. While Meigs and Porter had the intelligence, imagination, and daring to devise such a coordinated plan, Seward had set their parameters so narrowly as to render their conceptual talents irrelevant. In addition, Seward himself had spent so much time prevaricating and so little time engaged in creative thinking as to have become a mere ad hoc improviser. Welles was being frozen out by Seward, Meigs, and Porter. And Cameron was useless.

The Brooklyn Navy Yard

Scott did not award command of the land portion of the Pensacola venture to Meigs, but rather to Colonel Harvey Brown (West Point '18).[1] As secretary of state, Seward had access to the funds necessary to finance the Pensacola venture without congressional scrutiny and proceeded to hand Meigs a bank order for $10,000, of which Meigs gave Porter $1,000 to expedite the work on *Powhatan*.[2] When Porter arrived at the Brooklyn Navy Yard the next morning, he presented Lincoln's orders to the executive officer, Commander Andrew Hull Foote. Although one of the several documents Porter had written to himself called for "any naval steamer available," the other to take "*Powhatan*, or any other United States steamer ready for sea," the two orders he drafted to Foote—one delivered by telegram, one by messenger—were specific and mandatory: "Fit out *Powhatan* to go to sea at the earliest possible moment."[3]

Foote and Welles, descendants of Puritans and products of strict Yankee households, had been close friends at the Episcopal Academy at Cheshire,

Connecticut. As a young sailor, Foote had committed himself to God, making him an enthusiastic participant in the naval effort off Africa against the slave trade. Shortly after Welles's cabinet appointment, Foote had come to Washington to renew their friendship, and now he had to weigh that against a presidential order forbidding him to inform Welles of the Seward/Porter project and its conflicting requisition for *Powhatan*.[4] Porter had told Foote that if he dared say anything to Welles, "the President will consider it high treason, and you will lose the best chance you ever had in your life" in a top-heavy navy where it was difficult to distinguish oneself for purposes of elevation in grade and rank. If he must contact anyone, Porter added, it should be Seward or Lincoln. Foote chose to let the glaring *Powhatan* issue rest.[5] On April 2, Foote told Welles that *Powhatan* could be ready by April 6.[6] The next day, he stated that the officers and crew were being retrieved and it could depart April 5.[7]

Foote's conscience apparently nagged at him, and he suggested to Welles that something was amiss, albeit doing so in a periphrastic manner that might slip by disloyal Navy Department clerks and/or exculpate himself from a subsequent charge of willfully violating a presidential order. "Captain Meigs has called on me," he wrote, "with a letter showing his authority from the Government to have certain preparations made and things placed on board vessels soon to go to sea, about which you are familiar; but as the orders do not come direct [from you], I make this report."[8] Welles knew that Seward had a secret project, that Meigs was involved, and that Lincoln wanted him to stay clear of it. He certainly would have been alarmed if Foote had mentioned that one of the "vessels soon to go to sea" pursuant to Meigs's project was *Powhatan*—the vessel Fox had reserved—but Foote did not mention it. And although Welles could read in the April 4 *New York Times* that *Powhatan*, "to the astonishment of every one," had been ordered to be fitted out immediately despite its need for substantial repairs, he had no reason to doubt that the order referred to was his own.[9] Foote now telegraphed Welles that *Powhatan* "will drop down off the Battery at daylight [on April 6] and wait your orders."[10] Not to mention Porter's intention to take the ship was, in the circumstances, a deceit by Foote, albeit immunized by Porter and Meigs.[11]

The Departure of the Union Squadron(s)

That evening, Welles telegrammed Foote, "Delay the *Powhatan* for further instructions," and then sent a second telegram indicating that if a certain junior officer did not return to *Powhatan* by April 7, he should be replaced.[12] This second message, otherwise unimportant, showed that Welles, who had

Secretary of State Seward and his son, Assistant Secretary of State Frederick Seward, 1861. Seward House Museum, Auburn, New York.

repeatedly told Foote to rush, had now decided not to order *Powhatan*'s departure on April 6.[13] Foote informed Porter, also telling him (for the first time, apparently) that Welles had also requisitioned *Powhatan*.[14] Porter's initial reaction (Meigs wrote in his diary) was "despair," threatening to leave for the California coastal survey after all.[15] But then he invented a reason to ignore Welles's order, telling Foote that it was a fake, perhaps drafted by a disloyal clerk in Welles's office to sabotage their crucial mission to save Fort Pickens.[16] Meigs, less ready to defy Welles's instruction, much less call it a fake, telegraphed Seward for help.[17]

Seward apparently could see no way to ignore Welles and send Porter and *Powhatan* on their way, and so on April 5, after 11:00 p.m., he and his son Frederick knocked on Welles's door at Willard's Hotel.[18] Despite the late hour, the three decided that they must consult the president and headed up the hill to the White House. Lincoln was still working. Upon being advised of an apparent conflict regarding *Powhatan*, Lincoln said he could not remember Welles requesting that vessel. Earlier in the day, Welles had issued an order to Captain Mercer placing him in overall command of a naval squadron at Charleston composed of *Powhatan*, *Pawnee*, *Pocahontas*, and *Harriet Lane*.[19]

Upon looking at that order, Lincoln (Welles later wrote) "then remembered distinctly all the facts, and, turning promptly to Mr. Seward, said the *Powhatan* must be restored to Mercer, that on no account must the Sumter expedition fail." Seward protested that his own expedition was just as important and might fail without *Powhatan*. Lincoln (again, in Welles's recollection) responded that the Pensacola operation "could wait . . . and . . . directed Mr. Seward to telegraph and return the *Powhatan* to Mercer without delay." Seward "suggested the difficulty of getting a dispatch . . . to the [Brooklyn] Navy Yard at so late an hour, but the President was imperative that it should be done."[20]

Welles later noted that Lincoln "took upon himself the whole blame" for the confusion, adding that Lincoln "never shunned any responsibility and often declared that he, and not his Cabinet, was [at] fault for errors imputed to them, when I sometimes thought otherwise."[21] If Lincoln erred, it was forgivable. On March 29, the day the majority of the cabinet rejected Seward's conciliation plan and Lincoln met with Welles, Fox, and Blair to prepare an expedition to Charleston, a memorandum (probably by Fox) named *Pocahontas* and *Pawnee* but not *Powhatan*, because Welles had just decommissioned it for repairs.[22] Nor did Fox's prior proposals to Lincoln (and, earlier, to Buchanan) mention *Powhatan*, since Fox would have known from newspapers that it was not ready for sea duty. But then Welles, just days after decommissioning the vessel, apparently decided—perhaps at Fox's urging—that its substantial firepower was needed at Charleston.

Meigs, when called upon years later to defend Seward's role in all this, stated that it was he himself, not Seward, who first suggested to Lincoln, on either March 31 or April 1, that *Powhatan* (despite, apparently, its need for repairs) go to Pensacola.[23] Although Welles on the afternoon of April 1 suddenly ordered it to be fitted out for Charleston, the record does not reveal that he told Lincoln of the change.[24] Lincoln's only "error," then, was to have heard Welles, on April 5, list several ships that Mercer would command at Charleston and not remember that one of them was *Powhatan*. A number of navy ships bore Indian names, five of them with Indian names beginning with "P."[25]

Porter's biographer would observe that although Porter, Seward, and Meigs all knew that their decision to hide the Pensacola expedition from Welles had been "in the highest degree irregular," they could see that Lincoln had himself excluded Welles from their first confidential meeting at the White House.[26] That biographer, himself a naval officer, thought Seward "the real culprit," fully exploiting "the president's inexperience in executive business." But Seward was unaware of any conflict prior to the evening of

April 5, when he received from Meigs a febrile telegram that forced him to reach out to Welles at his hotel. On the way to the late-night meeting with Lincoln, Seward admitted (Welles later recalled) that, "old as he was, he had learned a lesson from this affair, and that was, he had better attend to his own business and confine his labors to his own Department."[27] But Seward was not sincerely contrite, only embarrassed, perhaps hoping that if he apologized in the few minutes available before meeting with the president, Welles would not in Lincoln's presence accuse Seward of deviousness, and Lincoln would not rebuke Seward for failing to notify Welles of what he was doing—as he had promised. Given Seward's desperate failures of recent days, including his failed palace coup and his secretive and unsuccessful negotiations with the commissioners, Seward had ample reason to feel vulnerable to accusation. April 5's *New York Herald* proclaimed that "the leading members of the Administration charge upon Mr. Seward the whole blame of the present state of affairs. They assert that but for his dilatory policy and revengeful course towards all whom did not advocate his interests at Chicago, Mr. Lincoln would have pursued a very different course."[28]

April 6

Newspapers recorded in detail the preparations on *Powhatan* and the steam transport *Atlantic*, including the calibers of guns and shells strewn about the decks pending stowage, while further noting that some Dahlgren guns were meant to be placed on the gunwales of open launches. Lieutenant John C. Tidball, about to embark on *Atlantic*, noted that reporters swarmed around Pier 41 on the East River "prying for threads of items which they could weave" into a "plausible theory" as to the ship's destination and purpose.[29] Among the ordnance were parts of a large shipment assembled earlier in response to a requisition by Captain Vogdes at Pensacola, but which General Scott had unaccountably held up since March 21.[30] The *Richmond Daily Dispatch* stated that on Friday, April 5, some thirty-seven thousand shells (a figure presumably not arrived at by guessing) lay on New York wharves, as well as "a large number of gun-carriages, each . . . directed to 'Capt. Vogdel [*sic*], United States Army, Fort Pickens, Fla.'"[31]

While New York officials were beginning to monitor telegrams conveying military information to the South, communication between spies in Washington and Confederate leaders was easier, in that some local telegraph operators were secessionist, and telegrams could be hand-carried across the Potomac to Virginia and wired South from there.[32] Since two different expeditions had been mounted at cross-purposes, piecemeal information gleaned in Washington and New York served to obfuscate just as effectively as any disinformation a more adept administration might have sought to spread. Greeley's *Tribune*, in the formatting of the time, headed one column with fourteen headlines in various typefaces, with the various stories following seriatim as separate paragraphs. Among the headlines was "Fort Sumter to Be Provisioned," while two others, "The Great Gulf Expedition / Sailing of the *Powhatan* and *Atlantic*," set contiguously, suggested that the *Tribune* knew the destination of these particular ships to be the Gulf rather than Charleston.[33] But the underlying articles themselves indicate no such knowledge. The *New York World* stated that *Powhatan* would not be ordered to Pensacola, not because Lincoln had ordered it to Charleston (a fact that was not publicly known) but because other ships were already at Pensacola.[34] The commissioners admitted to Toombs that they did not know where the departing ships were going.[35]

Meigs, not knowing that Lincoln the night before had ordered Seward to return *Powhatan* to Mercer, wrote in his diary:

> Had to go to the Navy Yard to endeavor to save the *Powhatan*. This did twice, and I succeeded in taking her[,] though written orders from Secretary of the Navy to send her to help reinforce Sumter ... were in the yard. I took the ground that Capt. Mercer had been relieved by orders signed by the President, that she was promised to our expedition, was a necessary and most important part of it ... that no man, [navy] secretary or other, had a right to take her, and that [Welles] could not do it as I was by the President made responsible and told not to let even the Secretary of the Navy know that this expedition was going on.[36]

By Foote's schedule, *Powhatan* was to throw off its lines at 1:00 p.m. The *Richmond Dispatch*, having gathered that the vessel was originally to have left the previous evening, posted a stringer on the waterfront who advised that the vessel had been "merely awaiting orders, for during the day two sealed packets were received by the commanding officer [Mercer], and immediately upon the receipt steam was got up," with the moorings unfastened at 2:00.[37] The *Dispatch*'s report was wrong in one regard. While *Powhatan* did receive two packages and upon their arrival it did get up steam and cast off, they were not sailing orders authorizing that departure, but rather additional instructions from Welles *not* to depart. It was upon receiving these that Mercer, Meigs, and Porter met, discussed them, and jointly decided to disobey them. Having not yet received the telegram Lincoln had ordered Seward to send in the late-night meeting of April 5, directing Porter to return *Powhatan* to Mercer, they purportedly considered themselves justified in disregarding all other orders, reverting to the initial order (drafted by them) carrying Lincoln's signature.[38]

Foote later wrote to Welles, "The *Powhatan* sailed at 2:45 this afternoon, just before Mr. Seward's telegram reached me."[39] Seward's telegram thus reached Foote's office at 3:00 p.m., fifteen hours after the president ordered that it be sent, and two hours after *Powhatan* had been scheduled to leave. The inference is amply justified that Seward delayed sending the telegram so that it would not arrive in time to carry out the president's order redirecting *Powhatan* to Charleston.[40] Foote, undoubtedly fearful of a later rebuke if he made no effort to pursue *Powhatan* to deliver Seward's telegram, now sent a subordinate on a fast steamer.[41] By chance, *Powhatan*'s progress from the navy yard had been slow, taking an hour to get up steam in the East River prior to crossing to Staten Island, where it disembarked Captain Mercer, disguised as a civilian so no spies ashore would see that *Powhatan* was under a new command. All this took two and a half hours, with Porter hiding in the captain's stateroom.[42]

Foote's lieutenant caught up with *Powhatan* and handed Porter the telegram: "Give the *Powhatan* up to Captain Mercer. Seward."[43] An officer may be immunized from the charge of disobeying an order if it contains some insufficiency, and Seward, by signing the order in his own name rather than in Lincoln's, had given Porter an excuse to disregard it. Technically, Seward was not even in Porter's chain of command, and in any event a prior order by the president superseded Seward's order, as it did Welles's.[44] Thus, yet again claiming superior authority in the presidential order he had himself drafted (in Seward's presence), Porter now wrote a response to Seward: "I received my orders from the president and shall proceed and execute them."[45]

Before directing Foote's lieutenant to return to the Brooklyn Navy Yard, Porter had the ready wit to compose a record that would paint his decision to ignore Seward's order as a heroic act. Since *Powhatan* was not yet at sea, it began with a lie:

At Sea, April 6, 1861

Dear Captain [Foote]: The telegram [by Seward] you sent me afforded me no comfort; on the contrary, [it] burdened me. Still, the president says nothing and I must obey his orders; they are too explicit to be misunderstood. I got them from his own hand. He has not recalled them. . . . [I] am sustained by my sense of duty and will leave the rest to that kind

Providence which has never deserted me in very trying circumstances. Will you please forward the enclosed dispatch to the secretary of state?[46]

Under the facts thus alleged, no panel of inquiry, and indeed no newspaper reader, would impugn a navy lieutenant who had just volunteered for an allegedly perilous mission, because he was obliged to follow not only his president but also a "kind Providence" that had "never deserted" him in "trying circumstances." Foote forwarded the message to Seward. Years later, Foote joked to Porter that for what he had done in essentially hijacking *Powhatan* in the face of adverse orders, he "ought to have been tried and shot."[47]

Porter's reference to a "kind Providence" that had "never deserted" him helped to deflect attention from the fact that he claimed to be operating under an order handed him by the president, yet asked Foote to forward his message not to Lincoln but Seward. A telegraph slip dated April 6 at 11:17 a.m.—that is, several hours before *Powhatan's* scheduled departure—sets forth a message by Porter addressed to President Lincoln: "The Secretary of the Navy has issued an order in conflict with yours of the first april and this complicates matters seriously. The original destination of the *Powhattan* has been changed[.] Shall I or shall I not carry out your original order delivered in presence of Capt. Meigs[?]" Any such telegram would have been sent through Foote's office; yet Foote, in his several messages to Washington, makes no mention of it. The accounts later published by Lincoln's two secretaries do not refer to it, nor does it appear in the *Official Records of the Union and Confederate Navies*. The record reveals no response from Lincoln. The slip itself was not among Lincoln's papers, but rather in the files of Seward, who was not the addressee.[48] The inference is reasonable that the telegram slip was written out (probably long after 11:17 a.m. on April 6) to make a record—a false record—either at Seward's direction or with his approval, to indicate that Porter, in the face of inconsistent orders from the president and Welles, did what any reasonably prudent officer would have done in the circumstances as he understood them, by asking the president for clarification and—after receiving no response—continuing to accord the president's original directive priority over Welles's. In a chronology so fabricated, the failure of the officer's telegram to get through to the president—ascribed perhaps to disloyal elements in the sending or receiving telegraph offices, or otherwise—would naturally be beyond that officer's control. And since accusatory memoirs and adverse congressional investigations continued well after the war, Seward would never have reason to discard this fabricated "evidence" of Porter's good faith. Hence its survival in Seward's files after his death.[49]

Telegram slip addressed to President Lincoln, dated April 6, 1861. Seward Family Papers, Addition. Courtesy of the Dep't of Rare Books and Special Collections, University of Rochester Library.

Porter now appeared on deck as *Powhatan*'s commander "and gave orders to go ahead fast. In an hour and a half," he later wrote, "we were over the bar" off Sandy Hook and "discharged the pilot." Steering south for an hour, he then turned due east "to throw any pursuers off our track (for I was determined to go to Fort Pickens)."[50] Porter, that is, so desired to evade any further instructions from superiors that he would for a time even head due east, slightly delaying his sought-after rendezvous with destiny. Foote's lieutenant, returning to the Brooklyn Navy Yard, said that Porter "desired me to express his regrets" that Seward's dispatch "came to his hands . . . too late to change his plans, inasmuch as" Meigs and his men "had already gone to sea."[51] This was untrue, in that Meigs and his men would not depart New York on *Atlantic* until the following morning.[52] But Porter, if necessary, many months later, in any inquiry, could say he believed that *Atlantic* had already gone and that not to follow it would leave it vulnerable in Pensacola.

The *National Republican*, under an April 6 dateline, reported that Meigs and the mechanics he had used in Washington had "left for parts unknown" on *Atlantic* with longboats lashed to its deck, leaving Confederate analysts to wonder what Meigs and his construction workers intended to build and where they intended to build it.[53] The *Richmond Daily Dispatch*, however, noted that these "mysterious boats" were "evidently built for speed"—that is, "to be used in reinforcement of Fort Sumter." Discussed in the same article—with evident fascination—was a steam hoist used to lift seventy-three horses on board.[54] Horses, plainly irrelevant to any stealthy, nighttime approach to Fort Sumter by tugs or launches, suggested either an amphibious landing on Charleston's beaches by cavalry or light artillery or else some other destination more amenable to mounted assault, perhaps the mouth of the Brazos in Texas.[55] The April 10 *Charleston Mercury* similarly concluded that *Atlantic* could not be headed either to Sumter or to Pickens because light artillery "would be quite useless" at either place. Meigs wrote that "nobody, not even . . . my old instructor in engineering" (famed West Point professor Dennis Hart Mahan), could believe that horse artillery might be employed within the confines of a fort. But Meigs in fact intended to deploy horse-drawn artillery at strategic points around Santa Rosa Island, to be used as mobile redoubts, applying Professor Mahan's theory that a fort's defenses could include mounted light batteries positioned within hailing distance.[56]

Scott's military secretary, Lieutenant Colonel Keyes, had been working with Meigs and Porter. Remaining behind to supervise the loading of two other ships for Pensacola, he wrote to Seward on April 7, "Captain Meigs received a telegram to stop a certain vessel. Fortunately, it came too late," since "its execution would have struck our enterprise between the horns."[57] The telegram referred to was Seward's, and Keyes knew it was Seward's. In nevertheless choosing "*a* telegram" rather than "*your* telegram" and otherwise avoiding specifics, Keyes was amateurishly attempting to disguise what he actually meant: "You will be happy to know that your telegram arrived too late to stop our enterprise." Keyes's reaction to Seward's telegram was thus the same as Porter's. Seward, characterized by Welles as "a very decisive and emphatic opponent" of Sumter's relief, refused to carry out—and in fact obstructed—Lincoln's orders. Since Seward could not seriously have believed that Porter would have—two weeks hence—the decisive battle he hoped for in Pensacola, the remaining inference is that Seward wanted the Sumter expedition to fail.[58]

Like Porter, Meigs wrote a self-protective letter, to be deposited in the post office at *Atlantic*'s first port of call, Key West. Although nothing in it required or suggested that he should record the time of day, he wrote at the top 2:30 p.m., thus leaving a record (perhaps a false record) that he wrote it prior to seeing Seward's telegram. In this letter, addressed to Seward, Meigs named two of the vessels (*Atlantic* and *Illinois*) about to depart for Pensacola; yet he did not name *Powhatan*, instead referring to it generically as "a war steamer." Like Keyes, Meigs appears to have been nervously reluctant to admit knowing where *Powhatan* was and was not going, since this might later be pieced together with extrinsic evidence he could not control, to support charges. Yet, like Keyes, he felt compelled to acknowledge the scheme in which they had all participated. "When the arrow has sped from the bow," he wrote, "it may glance aside, but who shall reclaim it before its flight is finished?"[59] By this oddly gnomic metaphor, Meigs was perhaps suggesting that, once *Powhatan* departed New York for Pensacola, Seward's last-minute telegram might have "glanced" it but had not been enough to redirect the vessel to Charleston. Since by this expression Meigs intended to amuse Seward, he, like Keyes,

U.S. Mail Steamship *Baltic*, 1852. N. Currier. Library of Congress LC-DG-ds-00792.

apparently understood that Seward's reaction to Porter's refusal to obey his telegram would have been not shock or anger but satisfaction.

A pro-Southern writer, noting New York's lucrative financial relations with the South, wrote that when "the expedition" steamed down the harbor and out of the narrows, "crowds looked on with a gloomy curiosity, foreboding evil. Not a cheer was raised—not a gun was fired. The fleet steamed away in silence, and no voice said, God speed."[60] In fact, the departures of ships, reflecting the haste and confusion with which two operations were mounted, were too piecemeal to be viewed as a fleet departing New York. *Pawnee*, commanded by Stephen C. Rowan, left Washington on Sunday, April 7, under orders to stop at Norfolk for supplies. *Uncle Ben*, a Lake Erie tug previously brought to New York City via the Erie Canal and the Hudson River at Fox's request, reportedly left that evening. *Harriet Lane* left on the eighth, *Pocahontas* on the tenth.

Baltic, a 2,700-ton wooden passenger and mail steamer, was known for its record-breaking Liverpool–New York crossings in 1851 and 1854, averaging 12.91 and 13.04 knots, respectively.[61] Fox, who at that time had been

Stowing supplies on *Baltic* (April 8, 1861) for expedition to Charleston. *Harper's Weekly* (April 20, 1861).

its chief executive officer, had now leased the ship from W. H. Aspinwall to bring supplies, sixteen open boats, and the troops he would try to land at Fort Sumter if the initial resupply effort was opposed. With Fox aboard, *Baltic* cast off at 5:00 p.m. on Monday, April 8, but failed to clear the bar outside New York Harbor, forcing it to anchor off Sandy Hook until the morning tide of Tuesday, April 9.[62] New York's sandbar was not a problem for *Yankee*, Russell Sturgis's new, four-hundred-ton tug, drawing only eight feet. As Fox was now informed, a third tug designated for the venture, *Thomas Freeborn*, chartered by Sturgis, was unlikely to leave New York because the owner, captain, and crew "all backed out upon suspicion of going under fire."[63]

"The destination of the ships," the *New York Times* noted in its April 10 report, whether Pensacola, or Charleston, or Texas, or all three of them, "continues to be the theme of conjecture." British correspondent W. H. Russell told Seward that if he would reveal where the ships were going, Russell could discreetly add it to his dispatch to London, the contents of which would do no harm because the information would not arrive back in the United States for a month.[64] Although Seward habitually did favors for journalists in order to exact favors in return, he declined, perhaps because, like Keyes and Meigs, he did not wish to be on record as knowing where *Powhatan* was and was not headed.

Senator Stephen Douglas, hearing on credible authority that the Confederates were about to attack Fort Sumter, informed Gideon Welles. Now aware that Seward had diverted *Powhatan* elsewhere, Welles—perhaps merely to discomfort Seward—asked Douglas to advise Seward of the imminent attack. Douglas, although unaware that Seward had just deprived the operation of its largest warship, told Welles that talking to Seward would be a waste of time, since he and Weed had treated the whole North/South crisis as some kind of party issue they were used to dealing with in New York.[65]

"At the First Favorable Moment"

"In Important Cases . . . Send Messengers"

In a memo to Seward, Meigs on April 1 had referred to a March 27 report by a senior engineer at Pensacola, Major Zealous B. Tower, indicating that before *Brooklyn* departed Pensacola for Key West, it had transferred its troops to the frigate *Sabine*.[1] This meant that the troops were still just off Pensacola, rendering the Meigs/Porter expedition superfluous. The memo was marked "Private & Confidential" and—not surprisingly—neither Seward nor Meigs showed the report to Lincoln, who might then have called off their operation.

Tower's report indicated that when and if instructions came to transfer troops from the ships offshore to Fort Pickens, the officer responsible for the transfer would be Henry A. Adams, a navy captain. This presented a significant issue of interservice protocol, since the March 12 transfer order was signed by an army officer under Scott, and Captain Adams, upon receiving it, would know that to honor it would be to violate the January truce, which had been signed by Adams's superior in the navy chain of command, Secretary Toucey. Although Scott independently received and reviewed Tower's March 27 report, it apparently did not stimulate in him or his staff any sense that his March 12 transfer order—when and if it arrived—might be viewed as technically deficient.

Lincoln's sense that the transfer order had "fizzled out" was perhaps an overreaction derived from Scott's failure to accomplish this simple but crucial assignment, upon which depended Lincoln's entire strategy for avoiding war while fulfilling his electoral mandate. Undoubtedly mindful that asking for the legendary general's resignation would reveal a severe disarray in his administration, Lincoln suppressed his sense of frustration and politely asked Scott to start making "short, comprehensive daily reports . . . of what occurs in [your] Department, including . . . the receipt of intelligence." Having read Tower's memo, Scott, in the first of his daily summaries, unceremoniously informed Lincoln that the troops were still off Pensacola.[2] Scott was well aware of Lincoln's anger. As an experienced strategist, he might by now have intuited that Lincoln had conditioned his evacuation of Fort Sumter—and thus his hopes to avert war—upon the transfer at Pensacola and that Lincoln's recent decision instead to resupply Sumter had been necessitated by Scott's failure. If he had not mishandled the *Star of the West* operation, federal authority would have been established in Charleston and Sumter's garrison would not be now running out of food. And if—as was very likely—Fox's effort was met with resistance, the commencement of the war would in some sense be Scott's fault.

Perhaps it was with this dire consequence of his failure to transfer troops in mind that Scott saw fit to include in his first daily report an exculpatory explanation for that failure. The March 12 order, he wrote,

> was issued by me . . . & in *duplicate*, about the middle of March, & the two copies were dispatched by two naval vessels from New York. No previous safe conveyance had presented itself in that month. The mail & the wires had, some time before, been turned against us, & we could not, without great hazard, employ officers as dispatch bearers. Major Towers [*sic*] was stopped this side of Pensacola, & Lieuts. Prime & Saunders captured & placed on parole.[3]

Lincoln asked for neither backup documentation nor corroboration for these statements. If he had done so, he would have found Scott's explanation totally unsatisfactory, so much so as to require Scott's resignation.

For telegraph messages that the Confederates would allow, communication with Pensacola was rapid.[4] Scott was, of course, correct that one could not send by telegraph a significant, secret military order to transfer reinforcements, thereby terminating a North/South truce.[5] But there were two other means of communication. On January 3, Scott had written a confidential letter to Lieutenant Slemmer to "do the utmost in your power to prevent the seizure of either of the forts in Pensacola Harbor by surprise or assault." Mailed that day or the next, Slemmer received it (still sealed) six days later.[6] The January 29 truce provided that communication between Washington and the Union officers in Pensacola was "to be kept open and unobstructed."[7] The Confederacy had set up a postal service using the federal system as a template, and although the mailing of letters between North and South was not a seamless process, a procedure was in place, and the truce allowed Union officers to pick up and deliver mail at the Pensacola Navy Yard, now in Confederate hands. But if Scott believed that mail would be tampered with despite Confederate undertaking to the contrary, in the truce the federal government also retained the right "freely to communicate" with the local Union force "by special messenger."[8]

In explaining to Lincoln why he refused to deliver the transfer order by messenger, Scott appears to have forgotten this important provision of the truce. Indeed, his recollection of the truce was altogether muddled. On March 5, the day Lincoln first ordered him to reinforce the Southern forts, Scott told Lincoln of "some thing like a truce established between [President Buchanan] & a number of principal seceders—here, in So. Carolina, Florida &c—which truce or informal understanding included Ft. Pickens."[9] The January 29 document was not "something like a truce" but a truce, not "informal" but formal, and included specific language allowing the delivery of orders by messenger.[10] With Townsend, Keyes, and other senior staff members to assist Scott, it is astounding that none of them knew of the communication method available for rapid and secure communication at a time of grave crisis or—if they did know—that they chose not to employ it, knowing that this would delay the transfer by weeks.[11]

Later, Scott gave a different, yet equally flawed, account of the truce. In the autumn of 1862, in one of his retrospective quarrels with Buchanan, he claimed not to have seen the terms of the truce until March 25, having thought it a quasi armistice negotiated at the Washington Peace Convention and thus void once that convention ended. Buchanan, in response, quoted a memorandum by Holt dated January 29, 1861, indicating that he had shown the truce document to Scott, who "expressed himself entirely satisfied with it."[12] Scott, perhaps like Shakespeare's Polonius, was unaware that his acuity had diminished, a dangerous attribute in someone who was supposed to provide not just unassailable military advice but also institutional continuity between outgoing and incoming administrations under the threat of war.[13]

In his April 1 note, Scott told Lincoln that he did not attempt the option of using messengers because "we could not, without great hazard, employ officers as dispatch bearers." If in fact Confederates did stop Union couriers moving between Washington and Pensacola, it would have been a plain violation of the truce and therefore grounds for complaint by Seward with the Confederate commissioners. Upon telegraphic notice from the commissioners, Montgomery would undoubtedly have resolved the problem immediately, since not to do so would be to invite Northern and European newspapers to report that the Confederates had cut off Fort Pickens from outside contact. Since this act would be in violation of a written truce, it might easily be seen as a provocative act putting the South in the wrong and meriting a military response. But because Scott had forgotten the language of the truce, and because his staff officers—whether because of incompetence or otherwise— failed to remind him, he would be in no position to insist upon a truce-based privilege of using couriers or to protest their being stopped en route.

As evidence that he could not have sent the transfer order by messenger, Scott told Lincoln that Lieutenant Frederick E. Prime, Lieutenant John S. Saunders, and Brevet Major Tower had all been stopped. However, Lieutenant Prime was arrested on January 13. Since this was before the truce, the incident is irrelevant on that basis alone. In addition, Prime was not a courier traveling from Washington with a message, but rather arriving from New Orleans on other business. Additional evidence indicates that Union messengers to and from Washington were at this time traveling unimpeded, even before the truce expressly guaranteed that right.[14]

Because the alleged incident regarding Lieutenant Saunders, like that involving Lieutenant Prime, occurred before the truce, it, too, was not pertinent. Moreover, if the incident Scott refers to regarding Saunders is the one for which records have survived, it involved Saunders's delivery of two sealed packages. They were not intercepted or confiscated en route but duly delivered to Commodore Armstrong. It was Armstrong, already under arrest by the Confederates, who voluntarily handed them over (along with the whole Pensacola Navy Yard) to his captors.[15]

Back on January 4, Scott ordered Brevet Major Tower to Pensacola, advising him, "If the telegraphic wires be in operation, report often; but both the wires and the mail may be under hostile control. In important cases, therefore, send messengers."[16] Whatever the incident was regarding Tower, he, too, was no courier. A highly skilled engineer, first in the West Point class of 1841, Tower does not appear to have been impeded from delivering anything, but only from living within Fort Pickens, since Confederate general Braxton Bragg asserted that if Tower bunked there overnight, he would be deemed a prohibited "reinforcement" within the meaning of the January 29 truce.[17] Tower authored the March 27 report while there and obviously had no difficulty bringing it north himself for Scott and Meigs to review.[18] Thus, Scott included Tower as an example of why messengers could not be used between Washington and Pensacola when Tower himself had just arrived in Washington from Pensacola with a message.

Nor does Scott's note to Lincoln accurately recite his handling of the transfer order Lincoln had instructed him to send. Lincoln in his inaugural embraced the view Scott had previously expressed to him several times: that the Southern forts should be held. Yet when Lincoln told Scott on March 5 to protect Southern assets, Scott did nothing. Why is unknown. Perhaps he thought the time for reinforcement had passed and believed Lincoln might simply forget his own instruction. Perhaps Scott and/or his staff officers let the matter drift through incompetence.[19] Perhaps Seward, with his allegedly mesmeric influence on Scott, instructed him to go slowly, in that a precipitant reinforcement of Fort Pickens would violate Seward's promises and ruin his conciliation plan, the only chance (so Seward believed) to avoid war.[20] In any event, when Lincoln found that Scott had done nothing, he instructed him to issue a written order.

Scott's assistant, Townsend, did not draft the written transfer order until March 12. In his April 1 note, Scott wrote that he placed duplicate copies of this order on two ships. Clearly he wished to show Lincoln that he exercised an abundance of care—as when an officer directs that an important message should be delivered by two couriers on two different routes, or by a courier and via the mail. If Scott in January had employed two means to deliver his message to Anderson, Fort Sumter would have joined the fight and *Star of the West* might have successfully landed troops. But Scott had failed to take that precaution then. Further, his present statement about duplicate transfer orders for Pensacola was false.

The two relevant vessels were the USS *Crusader* and the USS *Mohawk*.[21] On March 11, presumably after Lincoln first complained that Scott had failed to carry out his wishes regarding the Southern forts, the commander of *Crusader* received a letter from Welles stating that a messenger would soon appear who should be conveyed "with all practicable despatch" to the USS *Brooklyn*, "supposed to be" off Pensacola, and then proceed to protect U.S. authority at Key West.[22] On March 12, Welles told the executive officer of the Brooklyn Navy Yard, his friend Commander Foote, that one of the two vessels would be required for a different mission: to convoy a transport to Texas.[23] Enclosed with the letter was a communication from General Scott, undoubtedly relating to his March 12 order to Vogdes to transfer his men to Fort Pickens.[24] It was decided that *Mohawk* would go to Texas and *Crusader* would carry Scott's order to Pensacola.

Although the order carried a date of March 12, on March 13 Foote advised Welles that neither the messenger nor the order had arrived.[25] On

March 14, *Mohawk* left New York for Texas. While its captain could have been instructed to take a detour and stop at Pensacola first, or to deposit the order at Key West on the way, he received no such instruction and *Mohawk* was not carrying the order when it left New York, because the order had not arrived from Washington in time for its scheduled departure.[26] Later in the day on March 14, Foote told Welles that *Crusader* had its steam up and was ready to depart for Pensacola but was still awaiting Scott's order. Welles apparently looked into the matter and ascribed the delay to some unspecified error in the War Department.[27] Not until noon on March 16 did the order reach *Crusader*, and it departed.[28]

Commander Foote apparently sensed that the order might be inadequate to its purpose. Knowing, however, that *Crusader* had been waiting for several days, he chose not to delay it further and did not suggest to Welles that perhaps he should issue a navy order because the transfer of men would need to be accomplished by naval officers. Rather, after letting *Crusader* depart, Foote wrote to Welles that although Welles had not himself issued any order, "I concluded it to be your intention that the *Crusader* should proceed immediately to sea."[29] As with the letters Foote would write to Welles regarding *Powhatan*, he seemed less interested in articulating a possible problem requiring an immediate solution than in protecting himself if something went wrong. And Welles apparently did not know enough about the protocol of orders to ask his old friend what point he was trying to make.

As Scott knew, travel by steamer between New York to Pensacola took two to three weeks, so that by choosing that delivery method, the order would not arrive until the end of March or early April. Given that fact, and knowing that Anderson's food supply was running low, Scott should have so advised Lincoln, who would then have demanded some faster method. But Scott said nothing about delivery and Lincoln seems not to have asked, apparently assuming—incorrectly—that Scott would naturally use the most expeditious means available.

Crusader traveled 1,045 nautical miles down the Atlantic coast and arrived at Key West on March 25, where it was halted by a boiler leak, still 460 nautical miles short of Pensacola. Since Scott had not provided for duplicate delivery, the order might have stayed there for days or even weeks. But because the Union squadron off Pensacola was running short of supplies, *Brooklyn* traveled to Key West. It was *Brooklyn*'s chance arrival there on the morning of March 26, as reported by Southern newspapers, that had led Lincoln to conclude that the reinforcement effort had "fizzled out." *Brooklyn* took the order, loaded supplies, and returned to Pensacola, arriving late on March 31.

Thus, twenty-six days after Lincoln first told Scott what he wanted, and only because *Brooklyn* had left its assigned station, the order was delivered.[30]

Back in early February, Captain Vogdes told Captain Adams that while Adams, a naval officer, "must be governed" by instructions from the Navy Department, Vogdes had been "led to believe" that the instructions given Adams by the navy did include an order "to cooperate" with Vogdes, an army officer, "in the defense" of the fort.[31] Army and naval officers were not formally obliged to cooperate. General Scott's multivolume discourse on army tactics provided punctilious accounts of relations among different army ranks but never mentioned the word "navy."[32] As Vogdes and Adams contemplated their interservice problem, in mid-March an intra-army conflict emerged, when Lieutenant Slemmer suddenly questioned Captain Vogdes's asserted authority to command not just the troops he had brought on *Brooklyn* in early February but also those Slemmer had aggregated at Fort Pickens before *Brooklyn* arrived. The purpose of the January 29 truce was to preserve the status quo by barring Vogdes's men from leaving the ships and entering the fort, in return for which the Confederates would not attack. Slemmer construed that truce (in which he was named and which bore the signature of his superior, Secretary of War Holt) quite strictly, believing that it barred Vogdes not only from transferring his own men to the fort but also from assuming command of Slemmer's men inside. That interpretation comported with General Bragg's view that even one additional man inside the fort constituted a "reinforcement," in violation of the truce.

On March 17, Vogdes had sent a complaint to Washington indicating that the intra-army conflict Slemmer had posed also constituted a challenge to Vogdes's authority to seek the cooperation of Captain Adams of the navy. That is, Vogdes was concerned that when and if an order came from General Scott to transfer Vogdes's men to Fort Pickens, Slemmer might well say that the order violated the truce, which had been signed by Secretary of War Holt, who was above Scott in the army chain of command. Captain Adams of the navy, if advised of Slemmer's interpretation, might take the position that—having received from the navy no appropriate orders himself—he would not cooperate with Captain Vogdes by directing his sailors to lower the boats.[33] This command conflict apparently so troubled Vogdes that a few days later, without having received a response from Washington, he wrote directly to Scott, finding it "indispensable" to have "a perfect understanding between the troops and the naval forces."[34]

Assuming that Vogdes had sent his letter to Scott by special messenger, it would have arrived within three days and should have triggered in Scott four ideas. First, the March 12 order directed an army officer, Vogdes, to transfer troops from ships to a fort, when positioning the ship, lowering the boats, rowing the troops to shore, and possibly exchanging fire with Confederate shore batteries were navy responsibilities, requiring a naval order. Since, further, the January 29 truce was signed by Navy Secretary Toucey, presumably any order contravening the truce should be signed either by Navy Secretary Welles or by President Lincoln. Third, Scott's March 12 transfer order was not signed by a secretary of war or a president, thus putting in doubt whether two army officers, Vogdes or Slemmer, were obliged to follow it if doing so violated a truce signed by Secretary of War Holt, above Scott in the chain of command. Finally, assuming Vogdes's letter to Scott had been delivered by special messenger, it should have made Scott realize that this means of delivering orders worked.

Scott's March 12 order had directed Captain Vogdes to reinforce Fort Pickens "at the first favorable moment." Vogdes received it when *Brooklyn* returned from Key West on the night of March 31 and presented it to the senior naval officer off Pensacola, Captain Adams, who refused to honor it.[35] Captain Adams was married to a Louisianan and had sufficient Southern sympathies to have hosted the local Confederate commander, General Bragg, for dinner on one of the Union ships. Adams's three sons would follow his two brothers into the Confederate service, and he would later note to the British journalist Russell that in any battle he might be firing at one of his own children.[36] But Adams's refusal to obey Scott's order was not motivated by a Southern bias. Rather, the January 29 truce forbidding the transfer of troops had been agreed to by Adams's superior, Navy Secretary Toucey, and by Scott's superior, War Secretary Holt. Adams, a career naval officer who had enlisted as a midshipman during the War of 1812, now wrote to Welles, explaining that he must abide by the truce signed by his and Scott's superiors. He added that Scott's order "was of old date [March 12] and may have been issued without a full knowledge of the conditions of affairs here."[37] Adams must have been baffled by Scott's choice of the slowest possible means of delivery for this crucial communication when the truce allowed messengers. And he must also have been disturbed by the order's lack of a reference to the truce it was dramatically violating. One slip of paper, appropriately authored by the president or Welles, and appropriately worded with indicia of reliability (e.g., "notwithstanding the truce entered into"), could have been delivered to Adams from Washington in three days, by March 15, and the transfer from *Brooklyn* would have been completed overnight, freeing Lincoln to offset the South's anger by announcing the evacuation of Fort Sumter. Instead, Fort Pickens was still not reinforced, and Lincoln thus could not abandon Fort Sumter.[38]

Although Scott had failed to use a messenger to deliver his March 12 transfer order, Captain Adams availed himself of a navy messenger to inform Welles that he had refused Scott's order. The messenger arrived at Welles's office on the afternoon of April 6, just as *Powhatan* was leaving New York.[39] Welles, although undoubtedly appalled by Scott's error, chose not to notify Scott that his March 12 order had finally arrived but was technically deficient. Scott would soon know, however, because Captain Vogdes, as concerned as Adams, had dispatched an army messenger to Washington.

In forwarding to Lincoln the news that the transfer had still not taken place because of this interservice issue, Scott neither acknowledged the deficiency in his order nor promised to make things right forthwith, but rather became indignant, telling the president, "I have no time to comment on this extraordinary conduct."[40] Since Lincoln could see that not one but two messengers had just arrived speedily from Pensacola, Scott's explanation for choosing delivery by ship could now be construed as either grossly negligent or mischievous, and ample grounds for forcing Scott's retirement. Welles, meanwhile, handed his order to another navy courier, Lieutenant John L. Worden, and told him to proceed immediately to Pensacola by train, adding that on the way he should memorize the order and then destroy it. Worden did so, and while Southern authorities—despite the truce—questioned him (without detaining him) en route, by that point he had no paper to be confiscated and read.[41]

Several months later, Lincoln would tell Congress that Captain Adams had refused to carry out Scott's March 12 order because of "some *quasi* armistice" of the Buchanan administration that Lincoln's cabinet at the time knew only by "vague and uncertain rumors."[42] The Senate in response unanimously resolved to ask Lincoln for information, "if not incompatible with the public interest," regarding "the character" of this "*quasi* armistice." Lincoln referred this request to Welles, who invoked the executive privilege, thus disabling the Senate from asking why Scott failed to make clear to Lincoln every element of the truce (even down to its provision allowing messengers).[43]

The Courtesy of Proper Notice

Seward apparently favored providing prior notice to South Carolina of an attempt to resupply Sumter as a courtesy—that is, to smooth the sharp transition from his promises of evacuation. Welles and Chase, too, wanted a notice issued, not as a courtesy but so that if war came, it would have been started by the Confederates' attack upon a Union attempt—previously announced to them as such—to provide food (only) to Anderson's men.[44] The Southern commissioners in Washington told Toombs and Beauregard that Lincoln would act like a coward and strike without notice.[45]

On the afternoon of Saturday, April 6, aware that the transfer had still not taken place at Pensacola, Lincoln drafted and Cameron signed a formal notice to Governor Pickens that "an attempt will be made to supply Fort Sumter with provisions only, and . . . if such attempt be not resisted" by local forces, no effort would be made "to throw in men, arms, or ammunition."[46] Skillfully worded, the notice provided no specifics, leaving the Confederates to guess whether the resupply attempt would be by day or night—in the open or secret—or by warship, tug, commercial passenger vessel, or open twenty-man launch, armed or unarmed, thus generating the kind of speculation that impedes collective action.[47] Although they might estimate when the squadron would arrive, this was to be derived from reports of when the several ships left their Northern ports, not from anything Lincoln's "notice" told them. Lincoln chose not to inform Scott of this extraordinary gesture of giving an enemy prior knowledge of an intended action.[48]

On April 7, Campbell asked Seward if, even with ships already at sea, Seward would reiterate assurances previously made. Seward scribbled, "Faith as to Sumter, fully kept. Wait and see."[49] Some would later assert that Seward was here falsely renewing his promise that Sumter would be evacuated.[50] But all Seward meant—and all Campbell took him to mean—was that any Charleston operation would be preceded by notice.[51] By promising to keep faith only "as to Sumter," Seward let Campbell infer that Fort Pickens might well be reinforced—and without notice. Although Lincoln saw a strategic benefit in giving the Confederates prior notice of the Sumter expedition, he did not intend similarly to play by the Marquess of Queensberry rules at Pensacola. Conflict *somewhere* seemed at this point inevitable, and Seward may have felt—as a matter of strategy and/or to maintain his own reputation—that the conflict should begin with a preemptive strike by the Confederates at Pensacola, something Seward's cryptic note to Campbell fairly invited. From the moment the Confederates attacked there, whatever happened at Fort Sumter might be seen as merely derivative, thus making Seward's prior promises to evacuate Fort Sumter—and his failure to fulfill those promises—irrelevant, a minor footnote in the commencement of the Civil War.

After the *Richmond Dispatch* reported Vogdes's name and address on supplies being loaded on ships in New York, Brigadier General Samuel Cooper, now adjutant and inspector general for the Confederacy after resigning the same position in the Union, telegraphed General Bragg at Pensacola: "The Government at Washington have determined to reenforce Fort Pickens, and troops are now leaving for that purpose."[52] Bragg must have wondered why Lincoln had decided to send troops from New York when he already had ample reinforcements two miles offshore. Jefferson Davis had told Bragg that while somehow getting the Union to open fire on his troops would bring the Upper South into the Confederacy, the Union would hold back from doing so for that reason.[53] But keeping Pensacola quiet also had value for the Confederacy. First, Davis, Wigfall, Mallory, and Slidell had all sought the January 29 truce because they did not think Fort Pickens "worth one drop of blood."[54] Second, a military victory at Charleston was virtually certain because the Confederacy had committed its assets there. This arrangement left little for Bragg. British journalist W. H. Russell, experienced in tactical matters, reported that Pensacola's thirteen batteries, spread in an arc of 135 degrees, supposedly had eighty guns targeting Fort Pickens, but included among them were only five large-bore siege guns. Nor was the total gun count trustworthy, since the batteries to the right and left of Fort Barrancas were mounted (someone said) with faux cannons made of tree trunks.[55] Russell saw ammunition sufficient for only one day, and Bragg complained to Montgomery that he had not enough cartridge bags nor flannel, nor money to buy these supplies in Mobile.[56] So shoddy had been the casting of cannonballs that an overflow of liquid metal from the molds hardened as protruding flanges, rendering each ball not only inaccurate as a projectile but also hazardous to the gun and to those firing it. Even if Bragg had had more assets, he could not eliminate the Union ships offshore. Since the terms of the truce allowed only one Union ship, *Wyandotte*, inside the harbor, it was the only one within range. Bragg had no navy to engage the others, nor even to frustrate any landing of men from those ships on the ocean-side beach of Santa Rosa.[57]

In early March, Montgomery had instructed Florida, Alabama, Mississippi, Georgia, and Louisiana to send troops to Pensacola, and by mid-April there were a reported four thousand to five thousand men in various states of training.[58] Given the lack of relevant siege armament and ammunition, in Bragg's view the only feasible method to capture Fort Pickens was by bringing men across the harbor in boats for an amphibious landing, obtaining entry—either in secret or by coup de main—using makeshift ladders to reach any of the fifty-seven unsealed embrasures located a mere seven feet above the ditch surrounding the fort, all with a view of securing Slemmer's capitulation before Vogdes's troops could arrive from offshore.[59] But Montgomery continued to consider Fort Pickens worthless, and on April 8 he instructed Bragg not to initiate such an assault.[60]

Lincoln's resupply notice for Fort Sumter was to be delivered to Governor Pickens by two government couriers. They left Washington at 6:00 p.m. on Saturday, April 6, under instructions that if when they arrived at Charleston the Union flag still flew over Sumter, they were to seek out the governor and recite the notice. If, however, Sumter was under attack or had already fallen, their assignment was over because peaceful resupply was no longer possible. The April 7 dispatch of *New-York Tribune* correspondent James S. Pike announced to the North—and to Southern papers that chose to carry his story—that the president's message to Governor Pickens would be "conclusive," "calm," and "firm," positive attributes no Southerner would ever ascribe to Lincoln.[61]

On the same southbound train was Lieutenant Worden, traveling to Pensacola with Welles's order to reinforce Fort Pickens, although the three men, surrounded by Southern passengers, did not discuss their respective assignments. The three arrived at Charleston at 6:00 p.m. on Monday, April 8. Worden continued on his journey, while the other two, establishing that the distant Sumter was not under attack, found Governor Pickens and recited the notice: "An attempt will be made to supply Fort Sumter with provisions only, and . . . if such attempt be not resisted" by local forces, "no effort to throw in men, arms, or ammunition, will be made, without further notice, or in case of an attack upon the Fort." Pickens took a copy and, calling in Beauregard, read it to him.[62]

Lieutenant Worden arrived at Pensacola around midnight on April 10 and presented himself at Bragg's headquarters. Having destroyed Welles's order en route, upon inquiry he assured Bragg that he had "only . . . a verbal message of a pacific nature," and Bragg, without demanding specifics, granted him permission to visit with Captain Adams offshore. Because of adverse winds, he could not reach Adams's ship until midday on April 12.[63] He recited Welles's order, and Adams prepared the transfer, which commenced after sundown that night, over a month after Lincoln had first ordered it. Bragg's men heard signal guns fired by the transports and at 9:00 p.m. saw unusual lights at Fort Pickens, but they neither opposed the operation nor (by some reports) even knew that it had occurred until morning.[64] An entry in the log of the Union ship *Sabine* evidenced the hoisting out of a cutter and launches in aid of the operation, noting that by 6:30 a.m. on April 13, the garrison had grown from 83 men to 282. The *Charleston Mercury* would later report that the Union had made the transfer because a local schoolteacher sent a letter to a local newspaper stating that the Confederates were going to attack the following night.[65] Welles, crediting such hearsay, could feel proud that he— unlike the hapless Scott—had lost no time in dispatching a messenger with a technically sufficient order, so that the transfer took place at the last possible moment before the fort would have been lost.[66] But no attack had actually been planned.

After Captain Adams heard Welles's message, he told Worden to return to Washington. Passing through Montgomery on April 13, Worden was detained.[67] As Adams should have understood, the transfer of men voided the truce, including its provision for the safe passage of messengers. On or before April 16, still confined, Worden provided a written statement indicating that before he left Washington, Welles informed him that under the terms of the truce "I would have no difficulty in making the communication to Captain Adams," further alleging that when he arrived at Bragg's headquarters on April 11, Bragg had assured him that he would be able to return to Washington provided that he and Captain Adams did not violate the truce. "I remarked that I knew nothing of the agreement he mentioned." Although Worden repeated Bragg's words when he met Adams offshore, Adams (according to Worden's statement) did not tell him that the transfer violated a truce and therefore Worden would not be able to return to Washington. Worden further alleged that he never asked Welles, or Bragg, or Adams, for the substance of the agreement.[68] All of this appears to have been truthful, in that Welles's order—memorized by Worden and recited to Adams—called for the transfer of the troops to shore, arguably a move "of a pacific nature" if one did not know that such transfer violated a truce.[69] Eventually released via a prisoner exchange, Worden would command *Monitor* in its engagement with *Virginia* (a.k.a. *Merrimack*).

Bragg had been Robert Anderson's student at West Point and fellow officer in Mexico. His fame derived from "A little more grape, Captain Bragg," an understated and pseudo-polite order falsely ascribed to General Zachary Taylor during a furious clash. This became the title of a patriotic song whose popularity helped lift Taylor into the presidency.[70] Bragg's lack of assets at Pensacola, a constant theme in his correspondence with Montgomery, suggested to some a personal lack of *l'entreprise audacieuse*, since for weeks he clearly had sufficient men and assets to take Fort Pickens.[71] Since, however, Montgomery had thought Fort Pickens worthless, and since South Carolinians would have been furious to hear that the war with the Union had been initiated elsewhere, Bragg was perhaps the right commander for Pensacola. In any event, with Fort Pickens's garrison now a multiple of what it had been just a day before, the opportunity for seizure had passed. Slemmer was now pleased to yield command to Vogdes, and when Bragg, undoubtedly crestfallen, asked them why they had chosen to violate the truce, they responded that the transfer order had come from Washington.[72] "Twice," they might have added.

"If Something Is Not Done Pretty Soon"

The South seldom discussed the daunting odds it now faced in terms of both industrialization and mere numbers. Robert Mills (architect of the Washington Monument), William Gregg (founder of South Carolina's renowned Graniteville), and writers in *De Bow's Review* had long urged a Southern commitment to manufacturing to achieve economic independence. Such advice was largely ignored by the planter elite, however, and the states that had just seceded contained only 5 percent of the combined industrial capacity of the thirty-three pre-secession states.[73] The South's iron production was 6 percent of the North's, its capacity for firearms 3 percent.[74] For six decades, the percentage of the Southern workforce engaged in agriculture had remained at 80, while in the North that figure had dropped from 70 to 40. A quarter of Northerners now lived in urban areas, versus only one Southerner in ten.[75]

The South had a stellar officer class, many of them trained in the needed specialties at West Point, Annapolis, the Citadel, or the Virginia Military Institute. Between 1847 and 1861, Southerners had been secretary of the navy for nine years and secretary of war for eleven, and of course one of the latter, Jefferson Davis, would be entrusted with husbanding the Confederacy's resources.[76] W. T. Wigfall, born in South Carolina and with a long personal history of turning quarrels into duels, suggested that the Southern warrior tradition would count for much in offsetting the North's superior industrial capability.[77] But William Tecumseh Sherman, whose military postings had included Charleston, wrote that Southerners had underestimated not only the North's industrial capacity but also its commitment. "If your people will but stop and think," he urged, "they must see in the end that you will surely fail."[78] While Wigfall had predicted that once cotton ceased arriving at Northern mills, workers would rebel and Northern industrial capability would be hobbled, that was bluster.

Because secession initiatives surrounding the Compromise of 1850 had come to naught, there was a sense that this time the tide had to be taken at the crest. When South Carolina seceded in December 1860, Mary Boykin Chesnut observed that its people had "exasperated and heated themselves into a fever that only bloodletting could ever cure—it was the inevitable remedy."[79] In the weeks that followed, the torchlight parades, fireworks, and stump speeches betokening the initial enthusiasm began to fade. The man South Carolina sent to Florida to promote secession there admitted that his state had catapulted itself into unilateral withdrawal rather than abide what other states might do, for fear that "public feeling" would "subside," that the state would lose its "spirit of adventure," and that other states, viewing it as backing down, would themselves lose "the courage necessary to concurrence."[80] The *Mobile Mercury* accused the South of "sinking into a fatal apathy" in which "the spirit and even the patriotism of the people is oozing out" under a "do-nothing policy" toward Sumter. "If something is not done pretty soon, decisive," the newspaper declared—either Anderson's voluntary evacuation or his expulsion—the South "will become so disgusted with the sham of Southern independence that the first chance the people get at a popular election, they will turn the whole [secession] movement topsy turvy" (exactly the outcome predicted by Seward).[81] A facetious Northern visitor suggested that those predicting an imminent clash of arms, like the cultist Millerites who had prophesized that the world would end on October 22, 1844, should admit an erroneous computation and request an extension of time.[82]

"Bleeding Kansas" and Harpers Ferry were constantly cited as the newest examples of Northern aggression against an innocent South. On April 8, a passenger steamer was on its daily rounds from Fort Johnson to the other Confederate batteries around Charleston Harbor. As it passed within six hundred yards of Fort Sumter, one of its passengers, Edmund Ruffin, seeing artillerymen on Sumter's upper tier loading a cannon, hoped they would open fire. "I greatly coveted the distinction & éclat which I might have acquired," he noted in his diary, if even one passenger were thus killed or injured, since he would thus have been a witness to the event that drew his beloved Virginia and perhaps most of the other slave states into the Confederacy.[83] However, Confederate Secretary of State Toombs, formerly a vocal fire-eater, seemed suddenly to lose his commitment, reportedly saying on April 9 that opening fire upon Sumter "is suicide . . . and will lose us every friend at the North," the wanton striking of a hornet's nest from which "legions now quiet will swarm out and sting us to death."[84] But nagging doubts about precipitant violence might be overcome by initiating that violence. On April 11, Davis met in Montgomery with Secretary of War Leroy Walker and Alabama newspaperman and legislator J. G. Gilchrist to discuss attacking Sumter. When Walker voiced some reluctance, Gilchrist retorted, "Sir, unless you sprinkle blood in the face of the people of Alabama they will be back in the old Union in less than ten days."[85]

Back on February 22, Lincoln had stated in Philadelphia that the government "will not use force, unless force is used against it." In his inaugural he said, "In *your* hands, my dissatisfied fellow countrymen, and not in *mine*, is the momentous issue of civil war. The government will not assail *you*. You can have no conflict, without being yourselves the aggressors."[86] While such declarations of nonaggression meant nothing in the cotton states, through these iterations, coupled with the particular wording of his notice to Governor Pickens, Lincoln wished to establish a record. While the free states did not at this juncture exhibit the coherence necessary to prosecute a war of scale and duration, near unanimity could be obtained in an instant if the Confederates initiated an attack against Anderson's "gallant" men or fired upon an attempt to supply them with food.

The wording of Lincoln's notice left the Confederates with several unattractive choices. First, if they could see tugs or hand-oared boats approaching the harbor mouth, they might stop them for inspection and, upon finding only food, let them proceed. While the Confederates could thus show the North and the world a certain humanity, allowing Anderson to extend his stay would undermine the legitimacy of secession and disappoint pent-up Southern demands for a resolution. After what Hurlbut and Lamon had both told Lincoln, he could guess that the Confederates would find this option unacceptable.[87]

An alternative was to stop the vessels as they attempted to enter Charleston Harbor and demand their return to the fleet. Fox addressed a letter to Governor Pickens and entrusted it to Captain Daniel Jackson, an experienced harbor pilot who was to be in one of the shallow-draft vessels attempting entry. The letter stated, "The U.S. Govt has directed me to deliver a quantity of provisions to Major Anderson . . . due notice of which has probably been given to you by special messenger from Washington. . . . If your batteries open fire it will be upon an unarmed boat, and unarmed men performing an act of duty and humanity." Fox told Captain Jackson to hand the letter to anyone opposing his entry and, if entry was still refused, to return to the fleet.[88]

The third alternative available to the Confederates was not to approach but simply to open fire on the tugs or boats. Fox told Captain Jackson, "If you are fired upon going in, turn back at once." That is, the tugs or open boats were not supposed either to continue with the initial resupply effort under fire or to return fire.[89] Only in the second, contested phase, then—the attempt to insert men and arms as well as food—did the Union intend to fight its way in. Because Lincoln's notice did not say whether the first boats would be fitted out with small cannons, whether the crews would be armed, or whether they would retreat if challenged, Pickens and Beauregard knew nothing of Fox's instructions to Jackson. If, then, Beauregard and Pickens chose to open fire and sank the boats or tugs, a copy of the letter Captain Jackson had carried would undoubtedly appear in newspapers, thereby rendering the Confederates dramatically blameworthy in the eyes of Northerners who as yet had no quarrel with the South, and of Europeans needed as customers and political allies. Lincoln's plan was in this regard masterful.

Southerners had no reason to trust Lincoln's statement that the vessels would contain only food. As Jefferson Davis later pointed out, Scott in January had chartered *Star of the West*, a civilian passenger vessel, in order to hide soldiers below deck, while Seward and Lamon had repeatedly promised the evacuation of Sumter, only to have Lincoln break that promise.[90] In Charleston, Emma Holmes, in her early twenties, wrote in her diary that "the constant talk of evacuating the fort" and the visits by Lamon and Fox were "only attempts to blind and beguile us," and now Lincoln and others "seek to throw the onus of opening the war on us."[91] Edward A. Pollard of the *Daily Richmond Examiner* would later write that although the expedition was promoted as conveying "provisions to the starving garrison," it did include war vessels and warriors and thus was "evidently designed to provoke a collision," Lincoln's notice being only "the artifice by which the federal government, having deceived the South" repeatedly, now "induced it" to start the war.[92]

An additional option available to the Confederates was to fire upon Fort Sumter before the fleet arrived. Although Emma Holmes thought that the conflict had commenced with Lincoln's dispatch of warships, the first shot fired would commonly be designated as the initial act of war. On April 5, Russell, a seasoned war correspondent, wrote that the popular reaction in the North and West to "an attack on the forts while the United States flag is floating over them" would be as useful to Washington as "the effect of abandoning the forts or tamely surrendering them would be hurtful."[93] Although the Confederacy did not offer leadership positions to fire-eaters like Wigfall, Yancey, Pickens, Ruffin, and the Rhett family, it did feel the pressure applied by such men because of the verbal damage they could do.[94] If Jefferson Davis, with extensive experience in both war and politics, chose to wait for an attempted incursion, he could position the Union as the aggressor and thus be more sure of support from slave states that had not yet seceded, as well as European trading partners. But that would be disadvantageous tactically since, as Wigfall reminded him, the Confederates would then be fighting both Fort Sumter and the fleet.[95] And that fleet might be formidable, perhaps comprising all the vessels, troops, ordnance, and horses that had left Northern ports. After all, it made no sense for the Union to send a substantial force to Pensacola when one was already there.

A second reason to fire upon Sumter before the fleet arrived was that killing men in open boats or unarmed tugs, in an operation Lincoln would later characterize as "giving . . . bread" to a "few brave and hungry men," would yield substantially greater negative publicity.[96] While Sumter was undermanned, it was built to withstand cannonades and could return fire, supporting some notion of a "fair fight," even if such fight was bound to end in a Confederate victory, whether by surrender under fire, destruction of the fort, or starvation. Third was the perceived likelihood that some or all of the other slave states would embrace the Confederacy even if it did fire first. Fourth, as Captain Hartstene of the Confederate navy had indicated, darkness and low visibility meant that a resupply effort might actually succeed. If that happened, Anderson's men could conceivably stay in the fort so long as the new shipment of food lasted. This would leave the Confederates with a choice. They could engage in a perpetual shelling, which might be viewed as an unfair slaughter or might not yield capitulation, while depleting their scarce supplies of ordnance and powder. Or they could call a halt to that shelling, thereby tacitly admitting that Anderson had withstood the siege and that the Union had therefore prevailed, which would cause current and would-be adherents of secession to lose heart. Or they could engage in an amphibious assault on Fort Sumter, with many deaths on both sides but a clear moral victory for the North. In response to Wigfall's suggestion to fire on the fort before any fleet arrived, Davis wrote that he had come to the same conclusion.[97]

The exact words of Lincoln's notice should have been forwarded to Montgomery, lest crucial nuances be lost. Instead, Beauregard summarized it: "An authorized messenger from President Lincoln just informed Governor Pickens and myself that provisions will be sent to Fort Sumter peaceably, or otherwise by force."[98] This made Lincoln's notice seem more bellicose than it actually was, denying cautious men like Davis the opportunity to ponder and parse its intentional subtleties and ambiguities. While Lincoln's couriers had declared themselves unauthorized to accept any response, Davis could reach Lincoln by telegraph (and might have improved the Confederacy's posture by doing so). He might have written, for instance, that Confederate vessels would stop any incoming Union vessels, without firing upon them, and direct them to turn back, while adding—for good measure—that by launching an armada,

Lincoln had betrayed the withdrawal repeatedly promised by Seward and Lamon. Whatever happened after that—even if a few supplies got through—Davis could proclaim that the Confederacy justifiably felt deceived by the Union's bad-faith negotiations and had done everything it could to avoid war. This would suggest to otherwise neutral Northerners as well as foreign governments that the Confederates, to the degree that they were "rebels," were so only after attempting every peaceful means to protect their right to secede.

When the Southern commissioners first appeared in Washington on March 12, Seward chose not to reject the credentials they formally presented as representatives of a new government, since doing so might trigger in Montgomery a sense that he had left no alternative to war. On April 7, knowing that Union ships were leaving port, the commissioners demanded Seward's formal rejection, which he issued the next day.[99] The commissioners thereupon cut out Campbell and on April 9 wrote directly to Seward: "Your refusal to entertain [our] overtures for a peaceful solution," as well as "the active naval and military preparations of [your] Government, and a formal notice to the commanding General of the Confederate forces in the harbor of Charleston that the president intends to provision Fort Sumter by forcible means, if necessary, are viewed . . . as a declaration of war against the Confederate States; for the president of the United States knows that Fort Sumter can not be provisioned without the effusion of blood. [We] accept the gage of battle thus thrown down."[100] Thus, like Beauregard, they utterly ignored Lincoln's subtlety, making him out to be the reckless aggressor described by countless Southern journalists and statesmen. A year later, Pickens, summarizing the background of the war to South Carolina's senate, characterized Lincoln's notice as indicating "an utter want of manliness and straight-forward conduct."[101]

13

"We Have the Honor to Notify You"

Armamentaria

By one count, artillery seized from sixteen Union forts and arsenals totaled 1,262 muzzle-loaded cannons. Of these, Beauregard now had almost fifty aimed at Sumter.[1] On James Island were two installations, including Fort Johnson's three 24-pounders and a battery of four 10-inch mortars.[2] Morris Island's three batteries had three 8-inch columbiads, six or seven 10-inch mortars, and two 42-pounders with a bore of seven inches. At Cumming's Point was a new 3.5-inch Blakely rifled gun. Manufactured by Fawcett, Preston & Co. of Liverpool, it had been donated by Charles K. Prioleau, a Liverpool resident with Charleston roots, and reportedly carried a plaque saluting the state's December 20 secession. This remarkable weapon could drill a twelve-pound rifled projectile twenty inches into a fortress wall, versus only eleven inches for a sixty-four-pound solid shot from a smoothbore eight-inch columbiad. And it could be accurately aimed at an open embrasure.[3]

Near Cumming's Point was the Ironclad Battery, sometimes called the "Stevens Iron Battery." It was designed not by the inventors (R. L. and E. A. Stevens) of an ironclad warship commonly called the "Stevens Battery," but rather by one Clement Hoffman Stevens, a cashier in the Planters and Mechanics Bank, upon the suggestion of the belletrist William Gilmore Simms. Fabricated with heavy pine timbers, protected vertically by sandbags, and plated by dovetailed, riveted railroad iron, angled up from the side facing Fort Sumter at forty-three degrees, it presented a smooth, inclined surface, which Sumter's shots would hit obliquely. To maximize the skidding effect, it was said that grease had been spread on the surface of the plates. Reportedly

Ironclad Battery (left) and tents (right) at Cumming's Point, as seen from Fort Sumter. February 19, 1861, sketched by Brevet Captain Truman Seymour. George B. Davis et al., *Atlas to Accompany the Official Records of the Union and Confederate Armies* (Washington, 1891–1895). The Cartographic Research Laboratory, University of Alabama.

Ironclad Battery and others under construction at Cumming's Point on Morris Island, with Fort Moultrie's flag across the harbor. As depicted in *Frank Leslie's Illustrated* (March 30, 1861). Library of Congress LC-USZ6-1912.

the first ironclad fortification ever built, it housed three 8-inch columbiads in three embrasures protected by iron shutters.

On Sullivan's Island and on Mount Pleasant on the mainland directly behind it, Beauregard had strategically placed, among other assets, seven 8-inch columbiads.[4] There he also had five 32-pounders, with a range of 1,922 yards using solid shot; four 24-pounders with a similar range; six 10-inch mortars firing shells; two 8-inch seacoast howitzers; and a 9-inch Dahlgren shell gun.[5] Fort Moultrie, combining newly purchased assets with guns crippled by Anderson but now rehabilitated, had thirty-eight weapons, among them three 8-inch columbiads, two 32-pounders, and four 24-pounders.[6] To its east, guarding the entrance to Maffitt's Channel, was a battery composed of an 8-inch howitzer, two 32-pounders, and two 24-pounders. West of Moultrie, situated on the area of Sullivan's Island closest to Sumter, was an Enfilade Battery, first revealed on April 8 when Beauregard collapsed the summer house that had hidden it from view. Composed of two 24-pounders and two 32-pounders, it could ricochet shot along the barbette tier of Sumter's right and left flanks. This, coupled with the shells and case shot exploding above the fort, would make it impossible for Anderson's men to operate the heavier-gauge guns mounted there.[7] Other ordnance was already aimed and ranged from various positions on Sullivan's Island to converge at Sumter's wharf, where any Union vessel that somehow avoided destruction prior to reaching it would be destroyed while attempting to unload.[8]

Although the Confederate navy was one-tenth the size of the Union's, it had already developed several remarkable inventions.[9] Major J. H. Trapier and Captain John Randolph Hamilton had constructed a gigantic Floating Battery from iron plating, the same precious commodity used at Cumming's Point. Armed with two 42-pounders and two 32-pounders, it could be moved close to Fort Sumter to achieve maximum accuracy and penetrating power. Some discussed possibly running it aground upon a shoal between Cumming's Point and James Island in order to pound Sumter's comparatively weak rear wall. A forty-two-pound shot with a service charge of ten and a half pounds had an initial velocity of 1,620 feet per second. At five hundred yards from its target, it could penetrate forty-three inches of multilayered, seasoned oak (the standard test, of course, being the ability to penetrate wooden hulls). But the Confederates chose instead to moor the Floating Battery behind a seawall at the western end of Sullivan's Island.[10] Although a forty-two-pound shot had a reported range of up to 2,805 yards at an elevation of ten degrees and only two thousand yards lay between the Floating Battery's mooring and Fort Sumter, at that distance the penetrating power was reduced by two-thirds, to

Floating Battery designed by J. R. Hamilton and J. H. Trapier. Photo by Alma A. Pelot for Jesse H. Boiles (ca. April 11, 1861). Nelson Atkins Museum of Art 2005.27.462.

fifteen inches of seasoned oak.[11] By deciding not to place the Floating Battery close to Sumter to optimize its tactical advantage, Beauregard may have been weighing the benefits and risks not of firepower but of public perceptions. Anderson's men were surrounded by land batteries and could not possibly prevail. The Confederacy, an agrarian economy with only a small fraction of the North's industrial power and technology, wanted the North and the world to recognize its industrial innovations.[12] By positioning the Floating Battery in shallow water far from Sumter, Beauregard eliminated the risk that Anderson's guns—subject to the same calculus of impact and accuracy that suggested using the Floating Battery at close quarters—could severely damage this prize invention or even sink it, thereby embarrassing the Confederacy while yielding Anderson's men substantial acclaim in an inevitably hopeless contest. Better to allow the Floating Battery to be photographed, sketched, and described, and then given a merely ancillary role at a safe distance.

Sumter's garrison was too small to man all the artillery pieces that could be mounted, nor were there enough breech sights, gunner's levels, quadrants, and other equipment to use all the guns that could be manned.[13] On December 27, the day after Anderson's transfer from Moultrie, mischievous persons spread rumors in Charleston that he intended to fire at the city. While killing noncombatants was something no one who knew Anderson could imagine, in February his subordinates unwittingly bolstered that threat. When elevated to 39°15', a ten-inch columbiad could fire a 102-pound shell 2.74 miles, a 125-pound ball over 3 miles, but these ranges could be expanded by upending the gun and planting it in the ground as a mortar. Some of Anderson's men, perhaps with too much time on their hands, had dug a trench in the parade ground and positioned a columbiad as a mortar aimed at Charleston and then loaded it with two pounds of powder (a fraction of the standard shell charge of twelve to eighteen pounds) to see how far the shell would go. "The gun was fired, and the eyes of the garrison followed the shell as it described its graceful curve in the direction of the city. By the time it reached the summit of its trajectory," however, it became apparent that either the charge had been far greater than two pounds or (more likely) the men had forgotten that because of the much sharper parabola of a mortar shell's trajectory, they should have used a lighter charge. Now "fears were entertained," someone later noted, "that the shell would reach the city, or at least the shipping near the wharves." Suspense grew as the projectile neared the end of a flight that took half a minute, traveling three miles.[14] "Fortunately it fell short, and did no damage beyond scaring the secessionist guard-boat then leaving the wharf for her nightly post of observation."[15] While there were no further range-testing experiments, everyone was sufficiently impressed by positioning columbiads as mortars that four 8-inch columbiads were placed in a trench in the parade ground, braced in position at the breech and chase by timbers so as to deliver—close to vertically—a sixty-four-pound shot to test the impact resistance of the Ironclad Battery at nearby Morris Island, or a fifty-pound explosive shell to scatter ground troops.[16]

"I Ought to Have Been Informed"

On March 29, Montgomery had told Beauregard to bar all further visits to Fort Sumter by emissaries except upon the presentation of written orders to be reviewed by him, along with an undertaking that there were no additional oral instructions.[17] When receipt of Lincoln's notice to Governor Pickens ended all hope of an evacuation order, Confederate war secretary Walker wrote that the mails "must be stopped" and the fort "completely isolated."[18]

Anderson, like many brave people, had experienced a personal crisis, which had now passed. Not yet knowing that Union ships were on their way, he noted:

> I confess that since Col. Lamon's visit—he spoke so positively of our being withdrawn—I became impatient at the delays in Washington, but I have now forced all that back, and shall quietly await whatever may come. I pray that no attempt will be made now, when it is alas too late, to throw in either provisions or men. It will be a needless and disgraceful sacrifice of life. No force we can raise will be able to force an entrance, and a vessel placed alongside of our walls would be under such a heavy fire that it would not be possible to unload her.[19]

From Scott's mistakes, Lincoln had learned the importance of redundant delivery. On April 6, the same day Lincoln dispatched two couriers to deliver his notice to Governor Pickens, he ordered that the Lincoln/Cameron April 4 letter, previously mailed to Anderson to notify him of the expedition, should also be delivered by hand.[20] The courier arrived, but Governor Pickens refused to let him proceed. On April 8, one of Pickens's staff came to Alfred Huger's post office in the Exchange, seized Fort Sumter's outgoing mail, and laid it out before Pickens, Beauregard, and Magrath.[21] Magrath refused to open anything, commenting that as a federal judge he had sent people to prison for doing so. Pickens conquered his own reluctance and opened a letter by Major Anderson to Colonel Thomas in Washington, written earlier that day. It happened to be in response to the Lincoln/Cameron April 4 letter, which had arrived in Anderson's April 7 mail, just before Huger was told to stop all deliveries.[22] Thus, while Pickens had stopped the courier carrying a backup copy, the mailed original had gotten through.

Anderson's correspondence always comported with the niceties of military courtesy, such as "I have the honor to report," "I am, very respectfully, your obedient servant," and so forth, a standard of gentility that rendered even more stark Anderson's present statement to his superior: "I ought to have been informed" of Lincoln's intention to send help, he wrote, so he could have argued against it. Asserting that the operation directly contravened Lamon's promise to the Confederates to evacuate the garrison, Anderson did not know—because Lincoln and Cameron had failed to tell him—that the operation would not in fact be a surprise because Governor Pickens was being notified.[23] Anderson's letter ended, "We shall strive to do our duty, though I frankly say that my heart is not in the war which I see is to be thus commenced."[24] The observation was consistent with all Lincoln had learned about Anderson from the Doubledays.

Before forwarding the letter to Huger for mailing to Colonel Thomas, Anderson had recited it to his officers, thereby revealing to them his own feeling about the peril in which they would soon be engaged.[25] Given the harshness and bitterness with which Anderson criticized the decision of his commander in chief to mount an expedition, and his obvious inability to have it called off, Anderson asked the intended recipient of his letter, Thomas, to destroy it after reading it, rather than handing it to Cameron and Lincoln. But Thomas would not be in a position to destroy the letter because he would never receive it. While Pickens and Beauregard might release the purloined letter to the press, and thus gain for the Confederacy some marginal benefit by way of anti-Lincoln publicity, doing so would be to admit having stolen it, in an era when such conduct was not openly acknowledged. Since Lincoln had provided notice of the expedition, Pickens could hardly say that the theft could be justified by the letter's having revealed a "secret" invasion.[26]

Beauregard told Anderson that his outgoing mail had been seized. Because Lincoln and Cameron did not inform Anderson that they were telling Pickens what they intended, Anderson now feared that if his April 8 letter was opened, it would reveal the plan and thus put many lives at risk. He thus demanded that all mail be returned to him, still sealed. Beauregard refused, stating as his reason that Fox had engaged in "treachery" by falsely promising Governor Pickens that he would not discuss military matters. Anderson could have little doubt that it was by opening his letter that Beauregard had absolute proof of Fox's "treachery."[27]

"If You But Strike a Blow"

As James Madison and countless others had articulated through the decades, the slave states were naturally allied against free states. While it was commonly said in early 1861 that any attempt to coerce the return of any seceded state would trigger slave-state solidarity, coercion was not narrowly defined as an attack by Union forces.[28] Rather, as Seward explained to Charles Francis Adams, merely maintaining a federal fort within a seceded state, cut off and surrounded by a vastly superior force, was deemed by Southerners to be "coercive."[29] And while few Northerners could have believed that an attack upon a small Union garrison by an overwhelming Confederate army would actuate cohesion among slave states, Virginia Unionist John Baldwin had reportedly told Lincoln at the White House that "if there is a gun fired at Sumter—I do not care on which side it is fired—the thing is gone . . . as sure as there is a God in heaven. . . . Virginia herself, strong as the Union majority in the Convention is now, will be out in forty-eight hours."[30]

In 1916, Charles Francis Adams Jr. wrote that Seward's plan to keep Virginia loyal so that the Lower South would eventually return was wrong-headed and doomed to fail.[34] Adams did not explain his basis for that belief, and since Seward's plan was thwarted by Lincoln, whether it was ab initio "wrongheaded" was never squarely tested. But a tipping point was at hand. J. B. Jones, a Virginian living in New Jersey, read about the departures of ships from Northern ports and decided to return home. On April 10, torrential rains from a gale offshore destroyed so many bridges that a local newspaper quipped that Stafford County had in effect "seceded."[31] Jones's train finally approached Richmond, where, three hundred miles from such Unionist enclaves as Clarksburg, Wheeling, and Morgantown, people were "more and more excited" and "pretty nearly unanimous" for immediate secession, sufficiently so that if the pending convention continued to be pro-Union, in "opposition to the popular will," Jones predicted "startling revolutionary measures" by a "People's Spontaneous Convention" of the kind Baldwin had darkly predicted to Lincoln, its measures perhaps to include "arrests and executions" of Union-ists.[32] South Carolina secretary of war David F. Jamison, invited to address Virginia's pending secession convention, provided a complete inventory of the armaments and regiments in position around Charleston Harbor, so as to leave delegates in no doubt as to which side would win the impending battle.[33]

Further to tighten the bond between the two slave states, recently resigned Virginia congressman Roger Pryor traveled to Charleston and on April 10 (Sara Pryor later recalled) "delivered to an immense and enthusiastic audience, a most impassioned and vehement speech."[35] This must have been for Mrs. Pryor an epochal moment, since it had been she who in December had whispered in President Buchanan's ear during a wedding party that South Carolina had left the Union. "Gentlemen," her husband now proclaimed to his Charleston audience,

> I thank you . . . that you have at last annihilated this accursed Union [applause], reeking with corruption, and insolent with excess of tyranny. Thank God, it is at last blasted and riven by the lightning wrath of an out-raged and indignant people. [Loud applause] . . . For my part, gentlemen, if Abraham Lincoln . . . to-morrow, were to abdicate . . . and . . . give me a blank sheet of paper to write the condition of reannexation to the defunct Union, I would scornfully spurn the overture. [Applause] . . . Proclaim to

the world that upon no condition, and under no circumstance will South Carolina ever again enter into political association with the abolitionists of New England. [Cries of "Never!" and applause]

Pryor promised that if only the forces gathered around Charleston would open fire upon Fort Sumter, "just so certain as to-morrow's sun will rise upon us, just so certain will Virginia be a member of the Southern confederacy. We will put her in *if you but strike a blow*."[36] Some months before, he had reportedly said that if a U.S. president used force to prevent any state from seceding, he would personally stab the president to death if necessary.[37]

"I Will Await the First Shot"

Confederate Secretary of War Walker told Beauregard to demand Anderson's evacuation prior to any attempted resupply and, upon his refusal, to attack. Beauregard informed the commissioners that the battle was imminent.[38] Governor Pickens promised Commissioner Forsyth that any resupply attempt would be resisted "at every cost," telling Jefferson Davis that he was doubling the steamboats at the harbor mouth.[39] Captain Hartstene, who had acted as chaperone-cum-monitor during the visit of his friend Gustavus Fox, ordered the armed steam tug *Lady Davis*, the passenger side-wheeler *General Clinch*, and his own flagship, *Gordon*, to watch for Union ships, instructing a subordinate to cruise as far as Bull's Bay each morning (twenty-three miles up the coast) to watch for vessels offshore and then return to patrol slowly all night between the anchorage off the Moultrie House and the *Clinch*, stationed at the Swash Channel.[40] Beauregard agreed that the likeliest approach was through the Swash Channel, telling the commander on Sullivan's Island on April 10 that a reinforcement attempt might well happen that night, employing barges.[41]

Beauregard anchored several hulks in the harbor mouth, to be set alight if any federal vessel approached, and he had also ordered from New York four Drummond lights.[42] Invented in England to increase the accuracy of land surveys and then installed at London's Covent Garden and other theaters for an intensity of stage lighting far beyond what was possible with candles or oil, they were commonly called "lime lights" because they produced intense illumination when jets of oxygen and hydrogen ignited as they together passed over a surface of lime. Placed on either side of the harbor mouth, these were to be aimed at any intruder the moment it was identified, and immediately all available guns were to open fire.[43] Hartstene and Beauregard thus did not

Steamer passing Ironclad Battery at Cumming's Point as seen from Fort Sumter, February 13, 1861. Sketch by Brevet Captain Truman Seymour. George B. Davis et al., *Atlas to Accompany the Official Records of the Union and Confederate Armies* (Washington, 1891–1895). The Cartographic Research Laboratory, University of Alabama.

intend to stop vessels for inspection or questioning, but to destroy them. On April 11, a witness noted, Confederate guard boats "sailed on the outskirts of the harbor, scanning the horizon for the first sign of Lincoln's men of war."[44]

Despite the daily rounds of reconnaissance, the small steamers patrolling the harbor mouth, and the redundant sources of illumination, Hartstene feared that he would nevertheless miss small Union vessels transecting the bar and entering the harbor mouth at night and that Anderson's gunners could and would sink Confederate vessels the moment the engagement began. On the night of April 10/11, he and Wigfall thus arranged for two rafts carrying pine to be anchored near the southwest side of the fort, with fires to be maintained on them so that "the guns may see to fire upon a party disembarking" at Sumter's wharf.[45] If Hartstene had considered that these fires would also backlight Fort Sumter and Morris Island, and thereby help the Union squadron navigate, he apparently decided that this risk was outweighed by the fires' value in revealing vessels that had evaded the defenses at the harbor mouth, his greater concern.

The Revenue cutter *Harriet Lane* was named for President Buchanan's niece, the dedicatee of the popular ballad "Listen to the Mocking Bird."

Hattie Lane had served (brilliantly, by all accounts) as her bachelor uncle's hostess, both when he was minister in London and then as president. Nathaniel Hawthorne described her as "extremely self-possessed and well poised, without affectation or assumption, but quietly conscious of rank, as much so as if she were an Earl's daughter."[46] Rumors circulated of a possible match with Washington's most eligible bachelor, Lord Lyons, the British envoy. The vessel christened in her name, with a complement of ninety officers and crew, was fit for royalty, having been chosen as the Prince of Wales's vessel during his visit to the United States in the autumn of 1860.[47] In its present voyage to Charleston, it brought along B. S. Osbon, the by-now-famous reporter for the *New York World*. Osbon, who missed coverage of the *Star of the West* incursion, had covered the royal visit and befriended the cutter's captain, John Faunce, who ended up giving him a berth as the only reporter in the Union squadron.

Harriet Lane departed New York Harbor under instructions to steam south for twelve hours before opening sealed orders, which included hauling down from the masthead the Treasury Department pennant and ensign and hoisting in their stead the flags of the Union and U.S. Navy. Upon hearing that they were about to go into battle against the Confederates at Charleston, some of the crew blurted out mutinous talk to the effect that they had not signed on as warriors. Captain Faunce replied:

> I appreciate your surprise and point of view. Still, as your commanding officer, I will say right here and now that every man must do his duty and obey orders implicitly, *or, by God, he will never have a chance to see a gun fired in action!* My orders are to take the ship to Charleston and to report to the senior officer, and I'm going to do so if I have to bury half of this ship's company on the way. Go forward, now, and do your duty like good Americans.

He then turned to the boatswain and snapped "Pipe down!" with the ensuing whistle thus formally dismissing the men. While Osbon noted some further muttering when the men retreated to their end of the vessel, "by midnight all hands were about their work cheerfully."[48]

Charleston lies 632 nautical miles from New York. All the way down the coast, every vessel, regardless of departure time and destination, encountered the same fierce northeasterly gale.[49] It blew *Atlantic* one hundred miles off course, an experienced officer telling Meigs that he had never seen a heavier sea except off the Cape of Good Hope.[50] On April 10, somewhere off Georgia, the horses on *Atlantic* were so tossed about that several died.[51] As *Harriet Lane* passed Cape Hatteras, "loaded with coal as we were, we wallowed through the billows that broke over us continually," Captain Faunce related, "threatening to end our part of the expedition right there. At one time it was thought . . . we should be obliged to throw some of our guns overboard."[52] Faunce rejected that option, and this cutter, designed not for braving major gales in open water but for speed and maneuverability close to shore, "proved to be an excellent sea boat" and proceeded with its armament intact.

In the afternoon and evening of Thursday, April 11—Emma Holmes noted in her diary—"spectators of every age and sex" thronged the Battery on Charleston's waterfront, "anxiously watching and awaiting with the momentary expectation of hearing . . . cannon opening on the fort or on the fleet which was reported off the bar."[53] At 3:30 p.m., Colonel James Chesnut Jr. and two other aides-de-camp to General Beauregard arrived at Sumter in a small boat, informing Anderson that if the garrison departed, it would be provided safe passage. At 4:30, Anderson, following consultation with his officers, rejected that proposal. While guessing that Beauregard had intercepted his April 8 letter objecting to the Union attempt to help him, Anderson probably also concluded that Beauregard did not have Lincoln's April 4 letter to him, which had made clear that Anderson was not permitted to evacuate because he was obliged to await the fleet and join the ensuing battle. As Chesnut, back in the boat, began to shove off, Anderson said, "I will await the first shot, and if you do not batter us to pieces we will be starved out in a few days." Chesnut, intuiting that this was more than idle banter, asked Anderson whether he could quote it to Beauregard. Anderson said he could.[54]

A forced evacuation for lack of food would have occurred earlier if the Confederates had cut off all local supplies just after the *Star of the West* incident. If the garrison had reached the bottom of the larder in, say, the third week of March, Anderson and his men would now be at home, and even radical Republicans would be loath to blame Lincoln for failing to resolve a crisis that came to a head just as he took office but was caused by the prior administration's errors. But because the Confederates had not been ready, militarily or politically, and because Seward repeatedly persuaded them that voluntary evacuation was an imminent certainty, it made sense for them to keep the negotiations friendly by not cutting off all food. These factors so prolonged the Sumter crisis as to make it Lincoln's responsibility.

Because Anderson believed that Beauregard had intercepted his letter and from that source knew that a fleet was coming, Anderson in his "starved out" proposal could not have intended to trick his former student into agreeing to wait passively for Anderson's food to run out, only to find warships off the bar.

But perhaps no ships would come. When a report of seven vessels off Charleston proved false, Edmund Ruffin of Virginia, whose years of vocal secessionism South Carolina had recognized by giving him a place of honor at its secession convention, noted in his diary that Lincoln's notice of an expedition headed for Charleston "was but another of the government lies for systematic deception," with the actual destination Pensacola or Texas.[55] Anderson also had no faith in Lincoln's word, the alleged fleet possibly being just one more "pretence."[56] If Lincoln wanted to label the Confederates as aggressors, one way to do so would be to have them believe that a fleet was on its way, so that they might decide to open fire on the fort before the expected fleet arrived. But no fleet need actually appear on the horizon. And if that was Lincoln's plan, he would not inform Anderson that the expedition was a hoax; it would be necessary that Anderson also believe that a squadron was coming, since this deprived him of the option of surrendering voluntarily because his food had run out. Thus, Lincoln, who had already contravened Lamon's and Seward's promises of imminent evacuation, might once more be playing Anderson and his men as pawns. Or the expedition might have been originally bona fide and then aborted by Lincoln, as Scott had tried to abort the *Star of the West* operation, because the element of secrecy was lost. Or, given the tremendous gale, some of the vessels could have been damaged, sunk, or diverted, perhaps scuttling the operation. In any of these scenarios, Anderson's men would soon run out of food—just as he told Chesnut. Thus, Anderson lost nothing—not even his reputation for honesty—by a veiled suggestion to Beauregard that he not initiate hostilities but merely wait for the food to run out.

Beauregard forwarded Anderson's "starved out" comment to Montgomery.[57] The threshold reaction undoubtedly was that Anderson, erroneously believing that the Confederates knew nothing of the approaching federal ships, was trying to trick them. But on the off chance that Anderson's proposal might be bona fide, and having never abandoned the hope of a peaceful, voluntary evacuation, the Confederates wrote him a message: "If you will state the time at which you will evacuate Fort Sumter, and agree that in the mean time you will not use your guns against us, unless ours shall be employed against Fort Sumter, we will abstain from opening fire upon you."[58] The message had been carefully crafted; it would require Anderson to refrain from firing upon the Confederates even if they were sinking Union ships off the bar or Union tugs or boats approaching the fort.

Beauregard received the proposal and gave it to Colonel Chesnut for delivery. Around the time Anderson had given Chesnut his "starved out" comment on Thursday afternoon, one of the Confederate pilot boats had spotted

Harriet Lane heave to some miles east of the bar. By 7:30 that evening, word of its presence had spread among the Confederates.[59] Thus, when rowing out to Sumter and giving Anderson the Confederates' proposal at 1:30 a.m. on Friday, April 12, Chesnut knew that at least some portion of the Union fleet had arrived. Accompanying him this time was Virginia's Roger Pryor. Having given a rabidly anti-Union speech, Pryor was invited to participate in the late-night negotiation with Anderson, apparently in order to enhance his status when he returned home to urge Virginia's secession.

As Pryor, Chesnut, and two other officials waited, Anderson expended almost two hours in private discussion with his officers. The major question would have been whether Anderson could or would sign a promise not to fire except if his fort was fired upon, when abiding by such a promise would mean doing nothing as Union soldiers and sailors died attempting entry into the harbor. But Assistant Surgeon Crawford's account of the meeting includes no mention of the imminent arrival of Union ships, as if Crawford did not wish to record the arguments for and against making a written undertaking one did not intend to honor. Crawford did record his medical opinion that men could survive two days on water but did not mention that the moment of crisis was not near at hand because the fort still had many barrels of pork.[60] Still, Chesnut had been misleadingly told that the food would run out soon, and Washington had been falsely told that this would happen on April 15.[61] If, because of adverse weather, or logistical problems, or because the whole expedition was only a feint, no resupply and/or relief effort was evident by noon on April 15, it was unlikely to occur at all. It would be reasonable for a commander, thus isolated and with no chance of winning an exchange with the batteries surrounding him, to conclude that he should take down his flag—with honor—at the date and time he had previously specified.

At 3:00 a.m. on April 12, *Baltic* reached the designated rendezvous point, ten miles east of the Charleston lighthouse.[62] A few minutes later, Chesnut and his colleagues, having waited in Sumter's guardhouse, passed word to Anderson that they would wait no longer. Anderson appeared and handed Chesnut a note for Beauregard: "Cordially united with you in the desire to avoid the useless effusion of blood, I will . . . evacuate Fort Sumter by noon on the 15th instant, and . . . I will not in the mean time open my fires upon your forces unless compelled to do so by some hostile act against this fort or the flag of my Government by the forces under your command."[63] By adding "or the flag of my Government," Anderson sought to keep himself free to act if the Confederates opened fire upon any Union vessel. Anderson then added two additional conditions: that he would consider himself free to fire if, prior to noon on the fifteenth, he received either "additional supplies" or "controlling instructions from my Government." As Anderson and Chesnut both knew, "additional supplies" were due imminently. The Confederates' proposal had been a test to see whether Anderson would lie, and he would not, but he would employ slippery words to compose a counteroffer he considered honorable.[64]

Chesnut construed Anderson's answer as a rejection that need not be taken back to Beauregard, and thus at 3:20 a.m. he wrote, "We have the honor to notify you" that General Beauregard

> will open the fire of his batteries on Fort Sumter in one hour from this time.
>
> > We have the honor to be, very respectfully,
> > Your obedient servants, [etc.][65]

Chesnut, Beauregard, and Jefferson Davis understood—from Lincoln's notice—that by commencing an attack on Fort Sumter they would free the gathering Union fleet not just to resupply but also to reinforce Anderson's garrison.

"Like the Wings of a Fire Fly"

On Friday, April 12, between 4:25 and 4:30 a.m., on James Island, Roger Pryor was offered the chance to light the first fuse, an honor undoubtedly bestowed as an additional means to bind Virginia to the secessionist cause. Pryor declined, evincing an unwillingness to trigger the commencement of death by a signal mortar, despite his flamboyant insults to the Union just a day before. The honor of the first signal shot thus went to a lieutenant under the command of Captain George S. James.[66]

With a service charge of ten pounds and an elevation of forty-five degrees, a ten-inch seacoast mortar could project an exploding shell of almost one hundred pounds up to 4,250 yards, a multiple of what was required to reach Sumter. Charged, then, following the computation of the appropriate combination of powder and angle to give the appropriate trajectory, the slow-moving mortar shell "went curving over in a kind of semi-circle, the lit fuze trailing behind, showing a glimmering light, like the wings of a fire fly," until it burst about a hundred feet above the fort ("right over our heads," a private

Signal shell bursting above Fort Sumter at 4:30 a.m. on April 12, with muzzle smoke visible from mortar on James Island, at left. As depicted by T. R. Davis from Ironclad Battery. Clarence C. Buel and Robert U. Johnson, eds., *Battles and Leaders of the Civil War* (1884–1887; New York, 1887), vol. 1.

wrote home), its remains falling with a "crashing noise, in the very centre" of the fort's one-and-a-quarter-acre parade ground.[67] The Confederate batteries had arranged to fire two minutes apart with "the round of all the pieces & batteries to be completed in 32 minutes, & then to begin again."[68] By 4:50 a.m., "all the batteries and mortars which encircled the grim fortress . . . were in full play against it," each solid shot evidenced by a muzzle flash and then impact, with shells and case shot "capering through the air like a shower of meteors on a frolic."[69]

Within the fort, the enlisted men were at their best. "The thrill that ran through our veins at this time was indescribable," an Irish private noted. "The stern defiant look on each man's countenance plainly told that fear was no part of his constitution." Instead, "something like an expression of awe crept over the features of everyone, as battery after battery opened fire and the hissing shot came plowing along leaving wreck and ruin in their path." The Confederates had spared nothing to make this a glittering display of Southern military superiority, the better to impress Pryor, other visitors, and all of Charleston.

Anderson had bricked up most of the ports of the middle tier and barred his men from the exposed top tier with its large-bore columbiads, concentrating them in the lowest tier, where they could operate four 42-pound and twenty-three 32-pound guns out of casemates. With a reported sixty guns now mounted, officers decided that they would concentrate fire with three guns bearing on Cumming's Point, four aimed at Fort Moultrie, six at the other batteries on Sullivan's Island, and four aimed at Fort Johnson's two batteries.[70] Anderson had used flagstones and other materials to cover the interior opening of the casemates, thus protecting the artillerists from shell fragments and case shot from explosions just above the parade ground, as well as the shards of brick and stone and splinters of wood released when cannonballs overshot the exterior and hit the interior wall opposite.[71] By one report, Anderson's men at 5:30 returned two shots at Fort Moultrie, although others said that Sumter remained silent. At 6:30 a drizzle began. Edmund Ruffin had been concerned that Anderson would not return fire, since this "would have cheapened our conquest." Thus, when at a few minutes past 7:00 Sumter began to respond, Ruffin found it "gratifying," while others thought it "almost a relief," for "a worthy foe disdains one who makes no resistance" and "gallantry ever admires gallantry."[72]

Captain Doubleday's initial target was the Ironclad Battery near Cumming's Point, twelve hundred yards distant. Most of the thirty-two-pound balls (a local journalist reported) were aimed too high and thus "whizzed above the battery" on their way to the marsh beyond, where, hitting the water at a low angle, they ricocheted over the surface, "tearing up vast masses of the sea-weed, and giving a terrible fright to hundreds of the sea-fowl, which rose in every direction."[73] An aide to Beauregard later wrote, "Few artillerymen, without actual experience, have any idea of the difficulty of aiming a gun during a bombardment," even after achieving great accuracy in practice. Smoke envelopes both the battery firing and the target, its constantly changing density causing a constantly changing distortion from variable refraction, a literal example of Clausewitz's fog of war.[74] This problem, perhaps combined with a paucity at Fort Sumter of elevating screws, pintle bolts, and other equipment required for fine tuning, may account for Doubleday's inaccuracy. And for those shots that did make contact, the Iron Battery's novel design worked perfectly. Many bounced off "like hail-stones," said one observer, or, said another, "like marbles thrown on the back of a turtle." Some shattered on impact, and none penetrated the railroad plating.[75]

Anderson's men, unaware that the Confederates had already dismissed as impracticable the idea of an amphibious Confederate assault against this island fortress, had cleverly adapted the various available materials to fabricate grenades and other weapons to be hung or dropped from the protruding parapets. Regarding Sumter's return of fire, among items in short supply were cartridge bags to hold the explosive powder. Lieutenant R. K. Meade, a West Point–trained engineer, taught the men how to fabricate these, employing flannel and wool from shirts and blankets, hand-stitched with the fort's few needles. But because the fort had no weight scale, the likely distance and force of each projectile was to be guessed by the size of each makeshift bag.[76] By the middle of the first day, Anderson had expended such a high percentage of his inventory of seventeen hundred bags that he limited the firing to two guns aimed at Morris Island, two at Fort Moultrie, and two at the Enfilade and Floating Batteries to the west of Fort Moultrie, with an occasional shot at James Island.[77]

By dawn on Friday, April 12, *Harriet Lane, Baltic,* and *Pawnee* were at the rendezvous point.[78] Fox, with nineteen years at sea, had already surmised that because of the gale, neither of the tugs would arrive and improvisation would be required.[79] *Uncle Ben,* it was later found, had sought shelter in Wilmington, North Carolina, where it was seized by secessionists.[80] *Yankee,* its smokestack torn off by the gale, had been driven as far south as Savannah. Although a vessel with such a name would have been a decided prize, it avoided capture and found its way north to Norfolk by April 14, without attempting to join Fox's group.[81] Captain Faunce reportedly stared to the west and commented, "For God's sake . . . I hope they don't expect us to take these big vessels over the Bar," although there is no record of anyone suggesting that particular improvisation.[82]

After 7:00 a.m. on Friday, *Baltic* (with Fox aboard) and *Harriet Lane* steamed west from the rendezvous point to the bar, "to execute my orders," Fox noted, "to carry provisions to Fort Sumter," perhaps by lowering one or more of *Baltic's* sixteen boats.[83] As they neared the bar, however, Fox "observed that war had commenced," thus negating any hope of resupply without reinforcement.[84] While Fox only heard the cannonade after 7:00, Sumter had been under barrage since 4:30. Osbon, a passenger on *Harriet Lane,* would write that at 4:30, still out at the rendezvous point, he was startled from his bunk by "the boom of a gun."[85] A veteran of the lecture circuit prior to taking up journalism, he may have been fictionalizing so as to invoke an "eyewitness" feeling. But it may have been Fox who fictionalized his account of hearing that cannonade only when close to the shore, to show that he was not out at the rendezvous point waiting, but close in and just about to risk his life on an incursion in an open boat, even without *Powhatan* or the tugs, at the moment the Confederates robbed him of that chance by opening fire.

The passenger and mail steamer *Nashville* now appeared out of the mist with no colors showing. As it steamed toward the Union ships, Captain Faunce, misidentifying it as the Confederate steamer *Isabel,* ordered a shot across its bow, thus making a U.S. Revenue Marine vessel the first Union ship to open fire in the Civil War. *Nashville* raised a U.S. ensign to the peak of its gaff and was allowed to pass.[86] Because several other commercial vessels had accumulated nearby, choosing to remain offshore rather than be mistaken for combatants, Beauregard, through field glasses in inclement weather, might well have beheld what appeared to be a substantial Union fleet.[87]

The same wind that may have muffled the cannonade to a witness some miles east of the bar had apparently afforded mainland residents to the west a livelier sound.[88] Anna Brackett, a teacher from the North, was "twenty miles away, in one of the beautiful homes where we had been so often welcome guests, and on coming down to breakfast found anxious faces and much excitement among the servants, who reported that they had heard firing all the night in the direction of Charleston. We ate breakfast almost in silence." By another account, the cannonade could be heard as far as Pineville, twice that distance from Charleston. And a woman claimed to have heard the guns in Columbia, more than one hundred miles away.[89]

In Charleston itself, after months of distemper among those who did not deem patience a virtue, many were suddenly as festive as in the weeks after Lincoln's election—or at least wished to appear so. A journalist saw

> lights flash magically from the windows of every house, and in the twin-kling of an eye . . . an agitated mass of people are rushing towards the water-front . . . in the wildest stage of excitement. Grave citizens, whose dignity under ordinary circumstances is unimpeachable, are at the top of their speed, dressing while they run, and sending up explosive "hoorays" as if they must have a safety-valve for their enthusiasm or be suffocated. There are men *sans* coat, women *sans* crinoline and children in their night-gowns. The "Battery" . . . is a conglomeration of *déshabille* in every style, and the mysteries of the feminine *toilette* are revealed. . . . With faces pale, hair unkempt and eyes sharpened by the strange fascination of the scene, the impassioned multitude stand by the hour, peering into the darkness and reading the progress of the fight by the flashing of the guns.[90]

By evening, Jacob Cardozo recalled, "the east and south battery were crowded with beautiful women, and the long array of gay carriages and music and con-versation blended their attractions . . . as they took their way for nearly a mile in succession" while watching the battle's "gilded" and "brilliant" spectacle.[91]

Near Fort Moultrie, Reverend A. T. Porter, chaplain of Charleston's historic Washington Light Infantry, noted that as cannon shots from Fort Sumter hit the beach and ricocheted, onlookers treated it as a game and

View of Sumter bombardment from Charleston housetops, showing several women overwhelmed, as depicted in *Harper's Weekly* (May 4, 1861).

chased them. When Reverend Porter and friends ascended the tower of the fashionable Moultrie House hotel for a better view of the action, Sumter's artillerists, seeing through their field glasses human movement in the tower 1.4 miles distant, decided that it was being employed as an observation post. After several shots hit the tower, Porter and the others "scrambled out."[92]

The First South Carolina Volunteers under Colonel Johnson Hagood, with constituent units from the Barnwell, Orangeburg, and Colleton Districts, had arrived by train in two battalions, the first at 10:00 p.m. on April 11, the second just before dawn on April 12, having been summoned to defend against a possible amphibious landing. Hagood's men assembled at Charleston's fashionable Racecourse and then proceeded east where they witnessed the bombardment. From Morris Island, Hagood saw Sumter's flagstaff "shot away, and its fall was greeted with enthusiastic cheers by the regiment. These had scarcely subsided when one generous fellow called out, 'Hurrah for Anderson, too,' and more than one voice responded to his call."[93]

Before word of the battle reached Lincoln, he began to inform concerned Virginians that if the Confederates tried to drive U.S. forces from the Southern forts "either by assault or starvation" and "a collision of arms" resulted, "I shall hold myself at liberty to re-possess, if I can, like places which had been seized" prior to his having taken office. This statement, more aggressive than his inaugural, was rendered outdated by the Confederate attack and was thus replaced with "If, as now appears to be true, in pursuit of a purpose to drive the United States authority from these places, an unprovoked assault, has been made upon Fort-Sumter, I shall hold myself at liberty to re-possess, if I can, like places," and so forth, and to "repel force with force."[94]

In the early afternoon of April 12, around the time that Lieutenant Worden, six hundred miles away at Pensacola, was telling Captain Adams to transfer his men from the ships to Fort Pickens, a Confederate diarist recorded seeing *Pawnee*, *Baltic*, and *Pocahontas* (a misidentification, since that vessel had not yet arrived) off the Charleston bar. An inhabitant of Sumter later wrote that the men saw "several of the vessels of the fleet beyond the Bar" dipping their flags. Anderson ordered someone to dip Sumter's flag in recognition, a dangerous assignment because "shells were bursting in every direction" over the exposed parade ground. Sergeant Peter Hart, a veteran of the Mexican War, had been in January a New York City policeman when Mrs. Anderson found him and delivered him to the fort with instructions to keep her husband from harm.[95] Hart expanded his assignment when, seeing the flag halfway down, the halyard perhaps severed by case shot or a shell fragment, he "rushed out through the fire to assist in getting it up." Shortly after Hart reraised the flag, the halyard was cut again, but it was now so twisted and intertwined that the flag would not fall.[96]

Anderson might have burned one or two signal fires on the barbette tier to help vessels navigate their way in. He did not, perhaps because this would expose to shelling anyone trying to light the fires, perhaps because he did not wish to do anything to aid an incursion he believed would fail and result in superfluous deaths. Although several columbiads had been set in the parade ground as mortars, Anderson did not employ them, some saying that the constant shelling would not allow the men to expose themselves long enough to load. After the lighter shots from Sumter's casemates proved to be—at best—glancing blows against the inclined roof of the Ironclad Battery, Anderson might well have tried to crack the railroad plating by using these makeshift mortars. Incrementally more effective than the eight-inch columbiads already aimed in that direction would be the ten-inch columbiad, although this was still aimed toward Charleston, having never been repositioned. Thus did Anderson deprive himself of the one weapon most likely to prevail over Stevens's novel structure and the Confederate inventiveness it represented, apparently not wishing to kill enemy soldiers in a battle he could not win.[97]

Major William H. C. Whiting, an engineer who graduated first in the West Point class of 1845, had sat passively by in the first months of 1861 as Southerners took over Union forts he could have defended. Thereafter resigning and donning a Confederate uniform, he found himself on April 12 on Morris Island, under orders from General Beauregard to "strengthen the force protecting the batteries" on the island's southern end, it being Beauregard's guess that any amphibious landing would occur there. By 2:30 that afternoon, however, Beauregard had decided that a landing was unlikely and reverted to the conviction that reinforcements would come in boats or barges through the Swash Channel. Beauregard then added, "Anderson says he has only provisions for four days, so let us keep the ball in motion."[98]

On the night of April 12/13, as "the rain fell in torrents, and the wind howled weird-like and drearily among the sand hills," the Confederates kept the fires "brightly blazing" to detect boats or tugs. "The Heavens were obscured by rain clouds," someone said, making the scene "as dark as Erebus," although the Confederates' "pyrotechnic display" was "truly grand," the "yellow glare" illuminating the darkness "for miles around."[99] As many Confederate eyes focused upon the glowing harbor mouth, sentinels walked the nether beaches in the dark, drenched by the gale and wondering whether the occasional lightning might starkly reveal Union soldiers emerging from the surf.[100] Captain Hartstene opined that the sea was too rough for either an entrance to the harbor or an amphibious landing, while Whiting thought the night so dark that perhaps a boat or two had already slipped through, since he thought he saw an increase in the number of men on Sumter's parapets.[101] At 10:00 on Friday night, a Confederate diarist noted, "Tide going down, no signs of fleet, miserable cowards. Anderson has just signaled them. They answer but remain inactive, calmly gazing at the battle; the execrations of our men are loud against them."[102]

Despite the rain, wind, and poor visibility, the Confederates had by now so perfectly gauged the range of their seventeen mortars that a high proportion of shells and case shot exploded over Sumter's parade ground. If Anderson had not taken the precaution of removing all flagstones, any shells or case shot that failed to explode in the air, or shells fitted with percussion fuses to explode on impact, would on landing have turned the stone into lethal jagged missiles darting toward the men in the casemates. Instead, these rounds dug into the sand before exploding, reminding one soldier of earthquakes. The cannonade had reached its climax around 10:00 p.m., and while "all the streets were thronged with people full of excitement and enthusiasm" most of the night, a citizen observed, "the discharges of cannon gradually diminished as the sun rose. All the clouds which rendered the night so dark and dismal disappeared as the day began to break, while the air became most beautiful, balmy and refreshing."[103]

From the eight-inch columbiads on Sullivan's Island had come some forty "hot shots," sixty-four-pound balls superheated in a furnace prior to being loaded so as to ignite anything flammable where they landed. These started fires, as did exploding shells, particularly those with percussion fuses.[104] In the early morning of Saturday, April 13, Sumter's officers' quarters, with innumerable exposed wooden surfaces and containing furniture, bedding, and clothing, started to burn out of control. Smoke drifting into the casemates became so thick that men could breathe only by lying on the floor, their faces covered with wet cloths. The fire also threatened the magazine, from which barrels of powder were quickly rolled out and dumped in the harbor, while others were placed in the casemates and covered with wet blankets to avoid ignition by the burning debris blowing about.[105]

Sealed Orders

Before Porter and Meigs departed New York Harbor for Pensacola, they informed Captain Mercer that Welles's April 5 order giving Mercer command of *Powhatan* at Charleston was void because the president's April 1 order, earlier in date but from a higher authority, instructed Mercer to relinquish command of *Powhatan* so it could be used for their secret mission.[106] But there was a problem. While Lincoln's order told Mercer to "consider yourself detached" from command "of your ship," Welles's order also gave Mercer flag command of the entire squadron at Charleston and instructed him to "put yourself in communication" with Fox at Charleston "and cooperate with him to accomplish and carry into effect" the object of the expedition. The duty to exercise flag command and to offer one's services to the authority in overall charge is personal. Lincoln's order required only that Mercer detach himself from his ship; with regard to his flag duties, the order was silent—that is, it was the ship Lincoln needed, not Mercer.[107] On April 5, the day Welles issued Mercer his orders, Welles issued coordinate instructions to Captain Faunce of *Harriet Lane*, Commander S. C. Rowan of *Pawnee*, and Commander J. P. Gillis of *Pocahontas* to "report to Captain Samuel Mercer, of the *Powhatan*," ten miles east of Charleston, and "should [Captain Mercer] not be there, you will await his arrival."[108] If, therefore, Mercer did not arrive, these officers were ordered to do nothing on their own. And while Lincoln's April 1 order did not bar Mercer from contacting the Navy Department for clarification, it made clear that *Powhatan*'s new mission was confidential, and Porter and Meigs would have reminded Mercer that the better command Lincoln had promised him in that order would be withdrawn if Mercer violated confidentiality.

On April 6, before *Powhatan* departed New York, Porter had deposited Mercer at Staten Island, from which he made his way back to the Brooklyn Naval Yard. Having no reason to doubt that Rowan, Faunce, Gillis, and Fox expected him off Charleston and would not proceed until he arrived, Mercer knew that *Harriet Lane* had not yet departed New York, and he could thus exercise flag command by accompanying Captain Faunce on that vessel. Mercer chose not to go, however. Further, apparently wishing to avoid a personal meeting with Captain Faunce in which he would, of course, need to say *something* about the changed circumstances, he instead had someone deliver to Faunce an envelope containing the April 5 order Welles had issued to Mercer to command *Powhatan* and the squadron at Charleston. With it was a confusing, prolix letter by Mercer that would suggest, when read alongside Welles's coordinate order to Faunce himself, that nothing had changed, so that Faunce and the other officers should await Mercer and *Powhatan* off Charleston.[109]

Harriet Lane arrived at the rendezvous on the afternoon of April 11. *Baltic*, with Fox aboard, arrived at 3:00 a.m. on April 12, and Rowan on *Pawnee* around dawn, whereupon Faunce lowered a boat from *Harriet Lane* and delivered to Rowan, the senior officer present, the envelope Mercer had given him, containing Welles's April 5 order to Mercer to take command at Charleston, while also showing him Welles's April 5 order to Faunce himself.[110] Rowan, whose orders were identical to Faunce's, had the same reaction: that Mercer was in command, that he was coming on *Powhatan*, and that Rowan and Faunce should not proceed until he arrived.[111] When Fox boarded *Pawnee* and asked Rowan whether he would now commence the attempted resupply effort, Rowan replied that his orders required him to await *Powhatan* ten miles to the east, while adding that he would prepare and arm *Pawnee*'s launch and one of its cutters for Fox's use.[112] It was at this time that Fox, not similarly under orders to await Mercer, took *Baltic* close to the bar and (by his recollection) found that the moment for resupply had passed because the Confederates were firing upon Sumter, the triggering event to change the operation from resupply to resupply and reinforcement.[113] Finding an incursion impossible at this point, Fox returned to the rendezvous point and throughout the night of April 12/13 "made signals for *Powhatan* . . . in the driving rain and northeast wind," sure that the ship would soon arrive because it had left New York several days before *Baltic*.[114]

While the Union commanders must by this point have guessed that the Confederates considered them cowards, Welles's orders left them no discretion to attempt an incursion before Mercer arrived.[115] While the time most propitious for an incursion on April 12 was on an incoming tide that would crest between 7:00 and 8:00 p.m., that time came and went.[116] Rowan fulfilled his promise to Fox, in that *Pawnee*'s abstract log records that between 4:00 and 6:00 a.m. on April 13, its crew "hoisted out [a] launch and placed the howitzer and ammunition boxes in her preparatory for an expedition."[117] At 8:00 a.m., however, Fox came aboard *Pawnee* for a strategy meeting in which it was decided that no attempt should be made because no launch or boat, even if lightly loaded, could avoid being swamped in the heavy sea.[118]

Fox later wrote that in the course of this meeting he "learned for the first time that Captain Rowan had received a note from Captain Mercer . . . stating that the *Powhatan* was detached by order of 'superior authority.'"[119] Back on April 7 in New York, Mercer had apparently written a letter to the "Senior Naval Officer Off Charleston Harbor," who (in Mercer's absence) was Rowan. In it, Mercer stated, "Captain John Faunce will present to you when he meets you . . . a copy of instructions which I received from the Department for my guidance, while I was in command of . . . *Powhatan*. That vessel having been diverted from the service off Charleston by superior authority, and another officer placed in command of her, I have only to send you a copy of my instructions for your guidance."[120] This second letter, then, plainly indicated that no one should await either *Powhatan* or Mercer because neither was coming.

Although Fox and Rowan both later discussed what happened at this morning April 13 meeting, neither ever mentioned just how that letter came to appear. Why it did not surface earlier is unknown, nor is it known through whose hands the letter passed between Mercer's writing it on the seventh and Fox's seeing it at this meeting on the thirteenth.[121] Presumably Faunce handed to Rowan on April 12 whatever Mercer had given him. Because this letter states that Faunce "will present to you when he meets you" the order by which Welles gave command to Mercer, presumably Mercer did not put this explanatory letter in the envelope he had delivered to Faunce back in New York but expected and intended that the senior naval officer would receive it by some other means.[122]

The "superior authority" would have been Seward, for whom delayed, forged, and "misplaced" communications were standard tricks. Lord Lyons wrote to his government on April 9 that because an expedition to relieve Fort Sumter constituted a "complete defeat" for Seward's policy of conciliation, it was surprising that Seward had not resigned, as senior ministers did in Westminster when policies they advocated were rejected by the government they served. Lyons added, however, that Seward may have had hopes "of prevailing in the end, and even of causing the orders already given to the Commanders of the Expedition to be modified."[123] Lyons did not set forth what—if any—factual basis he had for that comment, although clearly the "orders already given" by Welles were "modified" by Mercer, following a meeting with Seward's subordinates Porter and Meigs. In an unpublished memoir, Fox wrote, "Notwithstanding the earnest desire of the President to reinforce and provision Fort Sumter, Mr. Seward seems to have been under obligations to oppose the attempt." Further, "as Major Anderson's supplies would be utterly exhausted on the 15th of April[,] every effort was made by some strong hand to delay the expedition until its supporters must give it up."[124]

The "strong hand" Fox referred to would also have been Seward. He had the bravado to keep Fox in misguided expectation of *Powhatan's* arrival, and his agents, Porter and Meigs, had the bravado to spell out for Mercer in New York the patriotic necessity of his cooperation and the professional reward promised by Lincoln if he cooperated. However, the only evidence of Mercer acting other than obtusely is the disappearance and reappearance of his letter explaining that he and *Powhatan* were not coming. The letter might have been included in the envelope Mercer gave to Faunce and Faunce handed over to Rowan on April 12, and then Rowan failed to notice it until the next day. Or Mercer placed it in a separate envelope, and Faunce forgot about it until the thirteenth. Conceivably, Mercer could have entrusted the letter to a friend on *Harriet Lane*, telling him that it should appear only if the incursion was rendered impossible and Fort Sumter was about to capitulate. Fire was visible from Fort Sumter on the clear morning of the thirteenth, the letter appeared at the meeting that morning, and Sumter raised a white flag at 1:00 p.m.[125] But there is no direct proof that Mercer consciously helped sabotage the mission.

The letter was obviously significant, and Rowan later commented that it "astonished Fox" because he believed it "crippled the expedition."[126] The latter conclusion was true in the sense that if Faunce had the letter and handed it to Rowan in their meeting at dawn on April 12, Rowan would have understood that no one should be waiting for Mercer and *Powhatan*, and he would have told Fox that, rather than spending the night signaling for *Powhatan*, he should improvise whatever effort he could with the assets available.

Whatever happened that morning, neither at the moment the letter was read nor in Fox's later recollections nor in reports by Rowan and Faunce was there any accusation against anyone for possessing the letter without revealing it to those dutifully complying with their orders not to relieve Sumter without Mercer and *Powhatan*.[127] The letter was never deeply scrutinized, or cited in recollections, or published in compilations. It survives only in one known copy and in portions quoted by Fox from memory.[128] Whether what happened resulted from negligence or from an intention to cripple the operation (a potentially capital offense), the question became unimportant, because the failure to resupply or reinforce Fort Sumter was "overdetermined"—that is, caused by multiple and overlapping factors. The tugs did not arrive, and the sea was too rough for open boats, so that Fort Sumter was in extremis before any of the attendant officers' potential improvisations (e.g., to commandeer an ice schooner, whose cargo might keep it afloat after being hit) could be carried out.[129] Thus, why Fox was not informed shortly after Faunce arrived that neither *Powhatan* nor Mercer was coming, and why Mercer did not come on *Harriet Lane* and assume command, and why Seward's telegram to New York redirecting *Powhatan* to Charleston arrived so late, while together forming circumstantial evidence of a criminal conspiracy, became moot points.

14

"We Have Humbled the Flag of the United States"

"This Was War, with All Its Glories, Its Terrors, Its Uncertainties"

On Saturday morning, Anna Brackett rushed down to the Battery. "The sun rose cloudless and bright on one of the April days which are like the June days of New England. . . . It was believed that the firing had ceased—why, no one could tell." Soon it was decided that because the wind had shifted and was now coming from the west, they could hear no reports from guns but could still see the smoke emitted as each cannon fired. Emma Holmes noted the same phenomenon. A witness thought he saw three small boats coming in from the direction of *Harriet Lane*. A woman with opera glasses agreed, while "another, incredulous, [said] they are nothing but waves."[1]

Most soldiers who had stood in the driving rain of Friday night on Morris Island to repel a possible amphibious attack were by the morning of the thirteenth so spent that their commander, Major Whiting, asked Beauregard to bring in one thousand to twelve hundred replacements.[2] Colonel Hagood's men had bivouacked and several fainted from exposure and lack of food. But then (Hagood noted) the "tempestuous weather" of Friday night had given way to "a lovely April day," with "Negroes . . . busily at work in the fields" and "the air . . . vocal with birds," with the spring vegetation a month more advanced than in the inland region where his men lived. "Contrasting strangely with this lovely rural scenery," he wrote, "the roar and reverberation of the distant bombardment called attention to the doomed fortress in the bay." The column of smoke from the officers' quarters, dramatically visible to Hagood on James

Island, could also be seen by the Union squadron ten miles offshore, misinterpreted by some as Anderson's signal to the ships to approach.[3] This smoke, Hagood wrote, when coupled with "the lurid flash from the portholes shooting out low down" a "level column of smoke over the water," and "the bursting of the shells over the fort, marked by light puffs of smoke, slowly fading out into fantastic wreaths," gave one "the consciousness that this was war, with its glories, its terrors, its uncertainties."[4] Reverend Porter, observing the burning fort from Sullivan's Island, noted, "I witnessed then a scene that I doubt was ever equaled. The gallantry of the defense struck the chivalry of the attackers, and without a command every soldier mounted the parapet of every battery of the Confederates and gave three cheers for Major Anderson."[5]

While the Confederate batteries had prearranged their targeting and sequencing, ongoing communication by messenger was no easy matter, since the batteries on Morris Island and James Island were separated from the northern batteries by the harbor, and from each other by two miles of salt marshes transected by creeks. Wigfall, out of egotism and/or gallantry but caring nothing for the chain of command, had slaves row him from Cumming's Point to Sumter and, with no authority from Beauregard, climbed through an open embrasure requesting to negotiate with Major Anderson. "We stubbornly refused him admittance for a while," a soldier wrote, "but he begged so hard, exhibited the flag he carried and even surrendered his sword, that at last we helped him in." Wigfall had noted that the fort's flag was down, although by the time Anderson appeared, it was up again. Wigfall arranged the terms with Anderson; then he found Beauregard and misstated them as "unconditional surrender," something Anderson would have died rather than accept.[6] At 1:30 p.m., Governor Pickens issued a telegram to Montgomery indicating that Fort Sumter had raised a white flag.[7] At 2:30, *Pawnee* lowered a boat with a view to making contact with Anderson and arranging the evacuation, but when the boat came within a half a mile of Cumming's Point, that battery fired two shells, which fell short. When it came closer to the shore, "the surf running high, several officers came down the beach and warned the boat off, shouting that Major Anderson had surrendered unconditionally."[8] No other Union vessel—large or small—either had crossed or would cross the bar. Charles Francis Adams Sr., not yet departed for London as U.S. minister there, wrote that the firing upon Fort Sumter, following the failed "eleventh hour" relief effort by Lincoln, constituted "a perfect verification" of his friend Seward's view that Lincoln had squandered the opportunity of withdrawing Anderson's men earlier, when he could have claimed that he was doing so "magnanimously" and not—as was about to happen—by necessity. That is,

"Mr. Lincoln," with whom "nothing seems to proceed from a real conviction of a systematic plan adequate to the emergency," has "plunged us into a war."[9]

Beauregard sorted out the confusion Wigfall had caused, offering Anderson the same liberal terms he had presented before the battle began, excepting only the privilege of saluting his flag. Anderson replied that it would be "exceedingly gratifying to him, as well as to his command, to be permitted to salute their flag, having so gallantly defended the fort under such trying circumstances, and hoped that General Beauregard would not refuse it, as such a privilege was not unusual." Beauregard complied, telling his own men that he did so "to show our magnanimity to the gallant defenders who were only executing the orders of their Government."[10]

"The Appearance of an Old Ruin"

In the battle, fourteen Confederate batteries had reportedly fired more than 2,300 solid shot and more than 950 shells and case shot, suggesting either that Beauregard intended to batter the fort rather than kill its inhabitants or that he used what he had and was relatively short on shells (or fuses). In any event, after more than 3,300 firings, with most rounds reaching their target, and up to six fragments flying from each shell, and eighty musket balls from each twelve-pound spherical case shot, and uncounted splinters and shards flying about from hits by solid shot, Anderson's garrison suffered in the thirty-four-hour barrage not one fatality.[11] This was due to a paucity of men in a thick-walled facility designed for ten times their number; Anderson's decision not to use the exposed barbette level or the guns set as mortars in the exposed parade ground; and the removal of flagstones from the parade ground and their use to protect the casemates.[12]

Although Sumter fired something approaching one thousand rounds, no Confederates died, a statistic that is more impressive because of the numbers present.[13] By one report, on April 14 they had 2,625 on Morris Island, 1,720 on Sullivan's Island, and another 2,650 in and around Charleston.[14] An aide to Beauregard ascribed the absence of Confederate deaths to Anderson's confining his artillerymen to the lowest of the fort's three tiers, which also confined them to using smaller-bore guns.[15] The upper-tier columbiads might well have destroyed several of the batteries, while an extensive use of shell and case shot might have killed some foot soldiers and/or artillerymen guarding Morris Island, without achieving any tactical or strategic objective. Although Confederates composed songs and poems suggesting that the victory involved courage and skill, an objective summation would be that dozens of young and inexperienced gunners received thirty-four hours of target practice while (technically) "under fire," making them seasoned warriors.[16] Although the engagement's full significance was thus attained by both sides via pyrotechnics without carnage, Isaac Hayne, with some gloating, sent to his former nemesis, Joseph Holt, and to President Lincoln, a telegram proclaiming that "Fort Sumter has surrendered & not a Carolinian hurt," as if the Union should be humbled by Anderson's not inflicting a few meaningless deaths.[17] And a Southerner seated next to British visitor W. H. Russell in Norfolk's Atlantic Hotel complained that he was not "quite content about this Sumter business" because "there's nary one killed nor wounded."[18]

When Captain Hartstene steamed out beyond the bar to arrange Anderson's evacuation, a newspaperman accompanying him reported that they boarded *Powhatan* and met with its captain, John P. Gillis. The reporter, subjected to ample hearsay to the effect that *Powhatan* would be there, apparently misread the name of the vessel as he approached. Several days later, the Charleston *Courier* reported that *Powhatan* had been there and that it and the entire fleet was under the command of David Dixon Porter.[19] Hartstene brought Captain Gillis to Fort Sumter, which he found "a complete wreck . . . its shattered battlements" and "tottering walls" presenting "the appearance of an old ruin."[20] A local journalist, walking into the fort on Sunday, April 14, to cover the hastily prepared transition ceremonies, said it was "as if the Genius of Destruction had tasked its energies to make the thing complete, brooded over by the desolation of ages," giving Anderson's men "the satisfaction of leaving it in a condition calculated to inspire the least possible pleasure to its captors."[21] While Anderson had once thought that this result also required the garrison's self-destruction, that turned out not to be true.

In the closing ceremony consented to by Beauregard, the seventeenth of a planned hundred-gun salute went awry, some ascribing the explosion to an airborne ember from the smoldering officers' quarters, others to a clumsy Union artilleryman who ignored the swabbing protocol before reloading. Since only wool or silk cartridge bags were assured of complete incineration upon firing, perhaps the use of cotton was responsible. In any event, this gunner inflicted mortal wounds on himself and another, the first deaths of a war whose military and civilian casualties are even now not fully tallied.[22] Anderson cut the salute short at fifty and included in the ceremony the burial of the hapless artilleryman in a parade ground pockmarked by exploded mortar shells and hiding at least ten that had failed to explode. (The second man would die later in a local hospital.) The mishap so extended the day's schedule that the fort's formal transfer into Confederate hands did not occur until 4:00

Fort Sumter, April 15, 1861. Confederate seven-star flag and staff raised by derrick previously employed by Union to hoist cannons to terreplein level. Columbiads set as mortars aimed south, toward Cumming's Point. Furnace building at center used to heat shot aimed at wooden ships and structures. Parade-ground stones pulled up and piled in front of casemates. Enlisted men's barracks burned out. Attributed to Alma A. Pelot or George S. Cook. Library of Congress LC-DIG-ppmsca-32284.

p.m., when, "amid deafening cheers and with an enthusiastic salute from the guns of all the batteries around the harbor, the Confederate and the Palmetto flags were hoisted side by side, on the damaged ramparts of the fort."[23]

Governor Pickens spoke from the balcony of the Charleston Hotel. "We have had a great many delicate and peculiar relations," he urged, since the state's secession of December 20. "We took the lead in coming out of this old Union" and now "have humbled the flag of the United States . . . before the glorious little State of South Carolina."[24] Pickens would have his listeners believe themselves a collective David, even if, by any objective standard, they and the vast collection of state and Confederate forces encamped for miles around were more akin to a collective Goliath. The aged James Louis Petigru, as on the day of secession and back in the nullification era, found himself "in the midst of joy . . . one does not feel," telling his sister that "we are on the road to ruin."[25] The siege had begun prior to the existence of the Confederacy, and although South Carolina wanted now to pay for (and thus "own") the bombardment, the Confederacy declined and booked this first success as a collaborative effort.[26] Up in Richmond, "when the news came that the 'Stars and Stripes,' that never fell before in the face of an enemy, had been lowered" at Sumter, "a delirium of joy seized the Disunionists," who "turned out by thousands . . . shouting the war cries of secession."[27]

Because of the tragic delay in the departure ceremonies, Anderson's men missed the receding tide and had to wait outside the fort as the Confederates wandered around their new prize and held their gala. Beauregard, "prompted," his biographer wrote, "by the feeling of delicacy which so distinguishes all his social and official relations," chose not to attend, so that he might not meet Major Anderson, "his former friend and professor, now his defeated foe, lest his presence, at such a juncture, might add to the distress and natural mortification of a gallant officer."[28]

As *Isabel* took Anderson and his men out through the harbor mouth and across the bar to be transferred to *Baltic*, Confederate soldiers at Cumming's Point "lined the beach, silent, and with heads uncovered." Beauregard, reporting this, was quick to add that "upon the lips of all" who thus paid homage to Anderson were "expressions of scorn at the apparent cowardice of the fleet in not even attempting to rescue so gallant an officer and his command."[29] Petigru "felt for poor Anderson, deeply abandoned as he was to an obscure fate, to serve as a sort of stepping stone to a conflict in which he could reap no honor and left without a friend to stand by him and his few followers while the fleet looked upon his distress with careless eyes."[30]

"And so ended," *Punch* of London wittily noted, "the first (and we trust the last) engagement of the American Civil War."[31] Others, closer to the scene, were similarly optimistic. "The general impression now," Florida novelist Ellen Call Long would have a character recite, "is that the federal government, realizing that the South is in earnest, will let us depart in peace; and as this is the first, so it will be the last blow struck to secure independence."[32] L. T. Wigfall's wife wrote to their daughter, "I trust in God, this business will end. Heaven has favored our side, and we are all grateful to a Kind Providence."[33] The history of the prior six months, culminating in this exchange of fire, was something akin to a duel among gentlemen, starting with brooding hostility, followed by accusations of dishonest or disreputable conduct, followed by a ritualistic violence in which the accumulated tension is released, the anger dissipated, and the antagonists' status as "gentlemen" maintained. Everyone, a Confederate veteran later wrote, "thought that the battle of Fort Sumter would be the only battle, though why we thought so I cannot conceive."[34]

Before departing, some of Anderson's officers were interviewed by journalists. The image of starving men fighting to the last cartridge and last morsel had dramatic power, and one officer so argued, although a credible defense could have been mounted for several more days. Captain J. G. Foster later wrote that the men could and would have "cheerfully fought five or six days, and if necessary much longer, on pork alone, of which we had a sufficient supply."[35] Although the Confederate barrage had destroyed three of the ten-thousand-gallon water cisterns, the remaining one was far from empty. An aide to Beauregard concluded that Anderson "should not have surrendered" but rather should have waited for the fleet to act.[36] This was unfair. It is true that if Wigfall had never stepped into the fort requesting its surrender, the blaze would have burned out, the garrison could have carried on for a few days, and, with the storm ended, Fox surely would have tried an approach. Anderson had been obliged by the Lincoln/Cameron letter to wait for the ships, but the honor derived from enduring a thirty-four-hour barrage had earned him the right to spare the lives of Fox's reinforcements, of his own men, and of the Confederate adversaries by raising a white flag. For Unionists everywhere, Anderson had vindicated federal authority, even while relinquishing the asset whose only value was as a symbol of that authority.

Fox, like Porter, had hungered for renown, telling his wife that "Anderson's fame will be nothing to mine if I succeed."[37] Because he did not succeed, his task became that of transporting Anderson and his men to New York. Fox described Anderson during the voyage as "weak physically" and "prostrated mentally," while the journalist Osbon, also on board, found Anderson's spirit "broken." Fox claimed that Anderson asked him, and Osbon claimed that Anderson asked *him*, to prepare for his signature a telegram to Secretary of War Cameron, to be handed to the telegraph boat before *Baltic* entered New York Harbor. It read:

Steamship Baltic, off Sandy Hook,

April 18, 1861, 10:30 A.M., via New York

Having defended Fort Sumter for thirty-four hours, until the quarters were entirely burned, the main gates destroyed by fire, the gorge walls seriously impaired, the magazine surrounded by flames, and its door closed from the effects of the heat, four barrels and three cartridges of powder only being available, and no provisions remaining but pork, I accepted terms of evacuation offered by General Beauregard (being the same offered by him on the 11th instant, prior to the commencement of hostilities), and marched out of the fort on Sunday afternoon, the 14th instant, with colors flying and drums beating, bringing away company and private property, and saluting my flag with fifty guns.

Robert Anderson
Major First Artillery, Commanding.[38]

Other participants would negotiate substantial publishing contracts for detailed accounts of their involvement in Fort Sumter. Anderson's would have been—by far—the most lucrative, and among the most articulate. Yet this telegram, written not by him but for him, would be his only published account.

"No Candid Man"

On Saturday, April 13, the last day of fighting in Charleston, Justice Campbell angrily wrote to Seward that when he volunteered to act as an intermediary, he had pledged to the Southern commissioners that he would "communicate information upon what I considered as the best authority," and they had relied upon him to determine "the credibility of my informant." Those commissioners now felt abused and, as "no candid man" could deny, Seward's "equivocating conduct" and "systematic duplicity" regarding the evacuation of Fort Sumter was—Campbell urged—the "proximate cause" of the Confederate attack.[39]

"Proximate cause" is a term from tort law, implying that but for Seward's false promises of evacuation, the Confederates would not have attacked and war would not have ensued.[40] This was untrue. The Confederates opened fire to stop Lincoln's attempt at resupply. While Campbell and Roman accused Seward of stringing them along so Lincoln could prepare his expedition, Seward flatly opposed what Lincoln was doing, going so far (the evidence strongly suggests) as to deprive the expedition of its flagship, in contravention of the president's clear directive.[41] For several weeks, Seward had believed—irresponsibly but sincerely—that he could impose his will on Lincoln and other cabinet members. Newspapers—with or without Seward's connivance—lent verisimilitude to his promises. And while Campbell (and the same was true of Roman) charged Seward with negotiating in bad faith to play for time, delay had always been the South's strategy. In December 1860, as his constituents champed at the bit for action, Governor Pickens voiced dismay at how unprepared Charleston was militarily. On January 13, Jefferson Davis expressed the hope that Pickens had "diligently employed" the time being consumed by negotiations over Sumter by solidifying the harbor's defenses and preparing to capture the fort.[42] Five weeks later, Davis told Pickens that war was inevitable but that the South was not prepared and had "little capacity for speedy repair of past neglect."

When Beauregard, a skilled artillerist, arrived on March 1, the batteries and troops were still not ready.[43] On March 6, the day the Confederate Congress formed an army and navy and called for one hundred thousand volunteers, Commissioner Crawford wrote to Confederate Secretary of State Toombs, "I have felt it my duty under instructions from your Department as well as from my best judgment to adopt and support" Seward's policy of maintaining peace, even if "his reasons and my own . . . are as wide apart as the poles." Crawford, that is, saw Seward as "fully persuaded that peace will bring about a reconstruction of the Union, whilst I feel confident that it will build up, and cement our Confederacy, and put us beyond the reach either of his arms or of his diplomacy."[44] Two days later, Crawford and Forsyth noted, "It is well that [Seward] should indulge in dreams [of peace and reintegration into the Union] which we know are not to be realized."[45]

The commissioners received piecemeal reports of what transpired in the meetings of Lincoln's cabinet, in part from Seward (through Campbell) and from newspapers, Washington hearsay, and spies, with each providing a mix of accuracy, falsehood, and invention.[46] On March 14, they told Walker that while Lincoln's cabinet was fiercely divided, "the outside pressure in favor of peace grows stronger every hour. Lincoln inclines to peace, and I have now no doubt that General Scott is Seward's anxious and laborious coadjutor in the same direction." They believed they could make Seward their unwitting agent in keeping the cabinet from opting for war. After Seward's initial refusal to meet with them directly, they served upon him what they described to Walker as an "official bombshell": a demand for diplomatic recognition. In Forsyth's view, the mere delivery of the document put Seward off balance so that he "has already had to beg for time," presumably fearing that at any moment the commissioners could intimidate him by cutting off negotiations and demanding that he either recognize them as ambassadors of a foreign government, and thereby recognize peaceful secession, or refuse their credentials, leaving no alternative to war. From Forsyth's viewpoint, Seward needed to stall for time because "since the 4th of March two of the Republican illusions have exploded—first, that it was very easy to re-enforce the forts, and second, that they could collect the revenue on floating custom-houses at sea." Thus, "never was [an] Administration in such a dilemma. The only question . . . with them [is] which of its two horns had it better be impaled over": trying to reinforce the forts or trying to collect tariff duties from cutters offshore. In any event, the commissioners were in no rush, "playing a game in which time is our best advocate."[47]

While thus pleased with themselves for their supposed manipulation and intimidation of Seward (whom they dared call "a coward"), the commissioners nevertheless assured Toombs on March 26 that they would not press the issue of diplomatic recognition until the Confederacy was fully prepared to react to nonrecognition by commencing the war.[48] Montgomery was still not ready on April 2, Toombs telling the commissioners that if Seward asked for more time—regardless of the reason—they should consent to it. Thus, while the administration "continues to follow its present vacillating and uncertain course, neither declaring war nor establishing peace, it afford[s] the Confederate States the advantages of both conditions, and enables them to make all necessary arrangement for the public defence, and the solidifying of their Government, more safely, cheaply, and expeditiously, than they could, were the attitude of the United States more definite and decided." The commissioners' assignment was thus "to play with Seward" and his hopes for peace, in order to "delay and gain time until the South was ready" to commence the war.[49]

Forsyth undoubtedly wanted to instill in the Confederate leaders a sense not only that he and the two other commissioners had Seward and Lincoln just where they wanted them but also that Lincoln and the men around him were weak. Forsyth went so far as to write that the members of Lincoln's cabinet "believe, and we encourage the pleasant thought, that in case of war their precious persons would not be safe in Washington. With prudence, wisdom, and firmness we have the rascals 'on the hip'"—that is, under control.[50] In Forsyth's view, the "great danger" was that "from ignorance of the true state of things in the South," Lincoln's cabinet "may blunder us into a war when they really do not mean it," as if one side should be blamed for a war because it underestimated the other side's thirst for one.

Diplomats, like generals, should not underestimate their adversaries. The commissioners did themselves and their cause no favors by belittling Seward, an experienced and guileful lawyer/politician, or Lincoln, whose character they constructed from Seward's disparagements. It would be observed that Seward "thought he understood the South, and what was still more important, human nature."[51] It is apparent that he "played" the Southerners he was dealing with, while allowing them to believe that they were "playing" him. But Jefferson Davis, with ample prior acquaintance with Seward in the Senate, knew better.[52] While Seward repeatedly said that the administration intended to evacuate Fort Sumter, and Campbell and the commissioners believed him, Davis told Governor Pickens that he had no "sanguine hope that the enemy would retire peaceably from your harbor."[53] On March 15, Walker told Beauregard, "Give but little credit to the rumors of an amicable adjustment. Do not slacken for a moment your energies."[54] On April 2, Walker confided that Montgomery "has at no time placed any reliance on assurances by the Government in Washington in respect to the evacuation of Fort Sumter, or entertained any confidence in the disposition of the latter to make any concession or yield any point to which it is not driven by absolute necessity."[55]

When Seward ignored Campbell's April 13 letter demanding an explanation, Campbell on April 20 repeated the demand. Again, none was forthcoming.[56] Campbell resigned from the Supreme Court on April 25, later becoming the Confederacy's assistant secretary of war, a ministerial/clerical post he claimed to have accepted only "to be of use in mitigating the evils" of war if and when the possibility of peace was broached.[57] His tenure as intermediary between Seward and the Confederacy, however, would suggest that he was ill suited for such a task.

On May 11, Edwin Stanton, always looking for Washington rumors that might redeem Buchanan, told the ex-president that the Seward/Campbell negotiations "will some day, perhaps, be brought to light, and, if they were as has been represented to me [perhaps by Campbell or one of the commissioners], Mr. Seward and the Lincoln Administration will not be in a position to make sneering observations respecting any negotiations during your Administration."[58] That day, Jefferson Davis saw fit to release to the press Campbell's two accusatory letters to Seward, observing later that "the crooked path of diplomacy can scarcely furnish an example so wanting in courtesy, in candor, and directness, as was the course of the United States Government toward our Commissioners in Washington."[59] The *Nashville Union and American*, under the heading "Lincoln's Treachery," urged that "the records of history, except in the most barbarous ages or nations, furnish no instance of such falsehood, baseness and treachery" as when Seward promised Campbell to "keep faith as to Sumter" even as Fox "was at Fort Sumter planning to reinforce it."[60] While the Confederate leaders had not in fact relied upon Seward's promises of evacuation, Campbell's allegation that Seward and Lincoln had duped the Confederates in this regard was accepted in the South, some going so far as to tie their conduct to Anderson's nocturnal transfer.[61] When Anderson "violated the agreement to 'preserve intact the military status' by moving from Moultrie into Sumter," a Southerner later wrote,

> and Mr. Seward violated his solemnly-plighted word to the Confederate commissioners by attempting to reinforce and provision Sumter, and thereby convert it into a fortress for the subjugation of Charleston [an allegation for which there was no evidence]—"the first gun" had been virtually fired by the United States Government, and the reduction of the fort was as purely an act of self-defence and self-preservation as is to be found in all history.[62]

As against the charge that "the Confederate states began the war by firing upon Fort Sumter," Jubal Early responded that "if those states had the right to withdraw from the Union and the United States had no right to resist or coerce them[,] then the attempt to maintain a garrisoned fort was an act of war . . . patiently borne with, for nearly three months after the secession of South Carolina." Early added that "the threat to supply Fort Sumter indicated a purpose of war," although the "threat" voiced by Lincoln was to maintain the Union's presence—peacefully.[63]

Davis and others therefore rejected the suggestion that Lincoln was unaware of Seward's activities. If, after all—Davis urged—Seward had acted without Lincoln's knowledge, the publication of Campbell's two accusatory letters would have caused Lincoln to fire him.[64] Thus, it was said that Lincoln tricked the three commissioners, stalling them while preparing his expedition.[65] But, unknown to Davis, Lincoln had multiple grounds for ousting Seward. By instead retaining him, Lincoln did not condone—much less connive in—Seward's style of conducting public office. Rather, he undoubtedly wished to avoid the political catastrophe of admitting such disarray in his administration, one that would cause some to allege that Lincoln's failure to control Seward caused the war.[66] Nor was it likely that Seward, for his part, would quietly retire in disgrace. Having often alluded to the 1864 election, he, Weed, and various friends could eventually shape a story in which he had been the brilliant strategist of peace and Lincoln the naïve rail-splitter who incompetently stumbled into war.

The *National Republican*, not surprisingly, chose not to publish Campbell's accusation letters, purporting to find them "too long and too dull" to reprint for their readers and too lacking in substance to analyze.[67] Seward remained silent, but Thurlow Weed issued in the *Albany Evening Journal* what amounted to a response. If Seward "were at liberty to reply to ex-Judge Campbell," Weed wrote, "revealing all that passed between them on several occasions," not only would Seward be in the clear, but Campbell's reputation for candor would itself be tarnished.[68]

In any event, Lincoln apparently chose not to punish Seward; both must have thanked God for an outcome in Charleston that, although it did not avert war, positioned the Union well. Nor were Seward's misadventures predictive of his future loyalty and contributions. As he told his wife in mid-May, "It is due to the president to say, that his magnanimity is almost superhuman."[69] By June, he had settled into a supportive role, telling her, "Executive skill and vigor are rare qualities. The president is the best of us; but he needs constant and assiduous cooperation."[70] This was something a president might reasonably expect from his secretary of state.

15

"Wavering Hearts Were Turned to Iron"

BLAIR TOLD LINCOLN THAT FOX FELT BETRAYED BY THE UNANNOUNCED reassignment of *Powhatan*, and on May 1 Lincoln sought to comfort him:

> The practicality of your plan was not, in fact, brought to a test. By reason of a gale, well known in advance to be possible and not improbable, the tugs, an essential part of the plan, never reached the [rendezvous]; while, by an accident for which you were in no wise responsible, and possibly I to some extent was, you were deprived of a war vessel, with her men, which you deemed of great importance to the enterprise.[1]

To look squarely at an operation in which virtually everything had gone wrong and say of it that its underlying plan "was not, in fact, brought to a test" was a verbal triumph, exceeding even the description of *Powhatan*'s disengagement as an "accident."[2] Lincoln went so far as to say that the tugs' absence due to a gale was "not improbable," while not stating explicitly that because of this gale, *Powhatan*'s absence was irrelevant because Fox's mission would have failed anyway.

Lincoln could not admit to Fox the obvious fact that the operation had turned out splendidly by falling apart. Such a statement might well have made Fox think that Lincoln had led a conspiracy to divert *Powhatan*, using Fox as a pawn in a game where actual entry into the harbor was neither expected nor desired, only the appearance of enough ships beyond the bar to make the Confederates fire first and thus start the war.[3] But the fact remained that all the talk about the feasibility and risks of resupplying and/or reinforcing Fort Sumter, all the grave and reasonable doubts expressed by Seward and others about whether even a successful operation would improve or worsen the Union's overall posture, and then all the work Fox put in to prepare an expedition in which he and others were prepared to sacrifice their lives, had turned out to have highest value by failing, with not one vessel, one warrior, or one box of hardtack entering the harbor.[4]

Years later, Major Anderson's nephew, Lieutenant Colonel Thomas M. Anderson, undoubtedly following conversations with his uncle, wrote that Lincoln "must have known" that Fox's expedition of two hundred men, "mostly recruits, and the absurd naval force . . . would fail as it did fail."[5] Henry Villard went so far as to declare that Lincoln's strategy *required* that Fox fail.[6] It is true that Scott, Totten, Ward, Seward, and others had entertained grave doubts about Fox's prospects. But the record reveals no evidence that Lincoln knew, desired, or intended that the expedition miscarry.[7] Although he would later become a superior military strategist, as of March 29, less than one month in office, Lincoln had mistakenly relied heavily upon Scott and Seward. When both men failed him, he fell back on his own strategic intuition.[8] He gave Fox everything he requested, and when he was told that Fox had been deprived of *Powhatan*, he ordered that it be returned. While gales in that region at that time of year were "not improbable," Lincoln obviously could not know in advance that during the week chosen—the last week that could have been chosen—a gale of Homeric ferocity would eliminate the two tugs that actually departed New York and render impossible entry by open boats.[9] And he could not know that *Powhatan*—contrary to his order to Seward—went elsewhere.

It was said that whenever Napoleon considered an officer for promotion, he would ask, "Is he lucky?" Although Napoleon's notion of luck may have been simple Corsican superstition, he would also have discerned that some shape their own luck by adroitly identifying the likelihood and weight of the relevant risks and benefits and placing their bets accordingly. Villard called the failed operation an "act of Providence for the right cause." While the fleet's departure from the North

> was the signal for the rebel attack on Sumter, its miscarriage caused the fort's surrender. But it was the very striking down of the United States flag by rebel guns that led to the bursting of the patriotic hurricane that swept away all dissensions, all partisan enmities, all fear, all apathy. It has been claimed that Lincoln deliberately planned the whole move in sure expectation of its marvellous effect, but this may well be doubted.[10]

James Russell Lowell also found it "good-luck" that the government "had a fort which it was so profitable to lose."[11]

Holt spoke with Anderson in May, thereafter describing him to Buchanan as "thoroughly loyal, & if he ever had any sympathy with the revolutionists—which I am now far from believing—I think the ferocious spirit in which the siege & cannonade of Sumter were conducted crushed it out of him." Anderson seemed to Holt satisfied that everything had been "providential—that the course pursued had been the means of fixing the eyes of the nation on Sumter & of awakening to the last degree its anxieties for its fate, so that . . . its fall proved the instrumentality of arousing the national enthusiasm & loyalty."[12] Lincoln's initial call-up on April 15 for seventy-five thousand recruits, while triggering the angry secession of additional states, was oversubscribed by fifteen thousand.[13] Anderson became an excellent rallying point for volunteers. "Our Union banner still shall wave," ran a typical poetic salute, "Each bar in bold relief, / If we but dare defend our flag / Like Sumter's gallant chief."[14] Ruth N. Cromwell's war song "Our Union and Our Flag" recited that "when first those starry folds . . . received the traitor's murderous fire . . . wavering hearts were turned to iron."[15] Congress upon reconvening would pass a statute permitting the president to summon any and all state and federal forces to suppress a "rebellion" against the federal government.[16]

"A Cheap Price to Pay"

To Anderson the gods had allotted five months of fearful expectation in which to reveal his stoic heroism while expending every effort—in vain—not to start a war at Charleston. Despite everything he had been through, the army, under the negative influences of Floyd, Buchanan, and Lincoln, had seen no reason to promote him even to lieutenant colonel, some saying that this was—after all—a small garrison at a time (prior to April 12) of "peace." Now it gave him military command in his native Kentucky and jumped him to brigadier general. That state, declaring neutrality on May 20, would be no sinecure for a spent warrior, in that factions continued to wage pitched battles. In October, reportedly because of ill health, Anderson relinquished the post to William Tecumseh Sherman.[17] In 1863, unsuitable for a wartime command, Anderson retired.

Unlike Anderson, David Dixon Porter had expended every effort (also in vain) to start a war, so that his own heroic fame might be established. Porter would be one of Anderson's few detractors, writing in his journal, "Although [Anderson's] sympathies may have been for the Union, and his determination strong to defend his flag, yet he went into the business without the heart of a truly loyal man. . . . When the true story of that affair is known . . . Anderson will not be recognized as one of the heroes of the war."[18] These allegations were groundless and unfair. Porter's ego was undoubtedly bruised by the universal adulation accorded a modest, soft-spoken, and brave officer, and no negative "true story" ever emerged. Despite Abner Doubleday's abiding resentment of Anderson, the worst thing he could say was that neither the Carolinians' firing upon *Star of the West* nor their subsequent buildup of assets around Sumter would cause Anderson to attack. If, either in Fort Sumter or while later researching his memoir, Doubleday had uncovered better evidence with which to impugn his superior officer's integrity, he would have provided it. A much more accurate prophecy than Porter's of how Anderson would later be viewed is found in a letter from Anderson's friend Alfred Huger, written on April 14, 1861, the day Anderson and his men left. "May I beg to be presented to Mrs Anderson and also to assure you both," Huger wrote, "of the feeling you have excited in my mind, never to be erased until I cease to reverence truth and to honor those who worship at her altars!"[19]

Lincoln had for months doubted Anderson's loyalty, while Anderson had made no secret of his contempt for Lincoln. Advised that Anderson was bitter, Lincoln on May 1 penned a "purely private and social letter," saying he would be "much gratified" if Anderson would visit the White House "at your earliest convenience, when and where I can personally testify my appreciation of your services and fidelity, and perhaps explain some things on my part which you may not have understood."[20] Anderson could not know that the reason Lamon's promise to evacuate Sumter went unfulfilled was not betrayal by Lincoln, but rather the failure of Anderson's old friend, General Scott, to secure Fort Pickens.[21] While Lincoln would never reveal a subordinate's error in order to excuse his own seeming ineptitude or trickery, perhaps Lincoln wished merely to assure Anderson that he had never intended to let Anderson take the blame for surrendering. But Anderson continued to bear a solemn, soldierly grudge, and he chose not to accept this "purely private" offer by his commander in chief.

The letter Anderson had written to Washington to protest Fox's expedition, intercepted and opened by Governor Pickens, would not be revealed until the war's end, by which time Anderson's stature as the war's first and one of its most revered heroes had been so long secure that it could not be undermined by a revelation that he had vehemently opposed an administration initiative that—although a failure—would burnish his own reputation to the level of apotheosis.[22] Anderson's fellow Southerners would find solace in the letter, Jefferson Davis commenting that it "fully vindicates Major Anderson from all suspicion of complicity or sympathy with the bad faith of the Government which he was serving."[23]

Anderson's nephew later wrote that the Lincoln administration "showed nothing but doubt and vacillation in regard to the Sumter question up to the time of the fall of the fort. Evidently all it cared for was a show of force on the part of the garrison, and a proof of aggression on the part of the rebels."[24] While he wrote this as a criticism, some might say that this was exactly what was called for. By the time (1882) Thomas Anderson wrote, records were available providing a much fuller picture of the decision-making process and the difficulties Lincoln faced. But he instead chose to record what his uncle had bitterly uttered in the privacy of his family, having considered himself at Sumter "a sheep tied watching the butcher sharpening a knife to cut his throat."[25]

That Robert Anderson had refused Lincoln's invitation to hear Lincoln's side of things suggests that he would have disbelieved anything Lincoln said. Thomas Anderson suggested that Lincoln "intended to sacrifice" the garrison "for moral effect"—that is, he accused Lincoln of believing both that the Confederates would open fire on Fort Sumter and that the barrage would be lethal. Edward Pollard, a progenitor of the romanticized view of the Civil War as a "Lost Cause" of states' rights, would say that Lincoln had calculated in advance

the result and the effect, on the country, of the hostile movements which he had directed against the sovereignty of South Carolina. He had procured the battle of Sumter; he had no desire or hope to retain the fort: the circumstances of the battle and the non-participation of his fleet in it, were sufficient evidences, to every honest and reflecting mind, that it was not a contest for victory, and that "sending . . . provisions to a starving garrison" was an ingenious artifice to commence the war that the Federal Government had fully resolved upon, under the specious but shallow appearance of that government being involved by the force of circumstances, rather than by its own volition, in the terrible consequence of civil war.[26]

Anderson's nephew further asserted that while in the end the administration was "happy" to see the men "get off with their lives," if they "had perished, it would have been a cheap price to pay for the magnificent outburst of patriotism that followed. Indeed it might have been better if they had."[27]

These latter sentiments were inappropriate and unfair insofar as they suggested that Lincoln had casually discounted Anderson's men as expendable.

If Scott had efficiently delivered the transfer order to Fort Pickens, Lincoln would have ordered Sumter's evacuation. Later, in sending the ships, it was not Lincoln's purpose to have the garrison martyred, even if Anderson himself in his darker moments had threatened exactly that. It is true that Scott and others would have advised Lincoln that Anderson would not raise a white flag simply because of overwhelming odds, and therefore some quantum of men would likely die. Lincoln would have understood that the only way to guarantee no loss of life—including Anderson's own life—was to order an evacuation, and Lincoln—because of his own reasonable assessment of the entire picture in the wake of Scott's failure—had rejected that option. But Lincoln would also have been told by competent authority that Fort Sumter, even if severely undermanned, could not be toppled by bombardment. While he may or may not have been told that wooden quarters could be burned, that conflagration proved to be a convenient moment for surrender, and not the cause of surrender. In the end, Lincoln gambled with soldiers' lives (as presidents must) and won, at the price of *no* battle deaths.

"Master of the Situation"

Southerners, having never granted Lincoln one favorable inference on any topic, now claimed that he had tricked the South into firing the first shot. Many Northerners were prepared to agree. On April 18, the *Pittsburgh Gazette* declared that "Mr. Lincoln, with admirable sagacity, kept [Fort Sumter] for five weeks in a weak and helpless condition, and suffered the impression to go abroad that he was unable, or afraid, to retain or strengthen it. He next let the impression get abroad that he was about to do something for it," when Jefferson Davis, "in order to gain the inside track," initiated the attack and "thus ran blindly into the trap" Lincoln had set for him. The journalist, that is, only a few days after Sumter fell, interpreted the previous five weeks as entirely puppeteered by a brilliantly intuitive commander in chief.[28] Sun Tzu, the ancient author of *The Art of War*, could not have recited a better strategy for an isolated command facing an overwhelming force.

In 1858, challenging incumbent Stephen Douglas's bid for reelection as Illinois senator, Lincoln in a series of debates had forced Douglas to take positions that made him unattractive to Free-Soilers and Republicans. Although Lincoln narrowly lost to Douglas, two years later Douglas would fail to secure the Northern Democratic presidential nomination and Lincoln would be in the White House.[29] Leonard Swett had ridden with Lincoln the eleven thousand square miles of central Illinois that made up the Eighth Judicial Circuit, trying some one thousand cases against or beside him.[30] Reflecting upon his friend in 1866, Swett noted the widely held belief that Lincoln was "a frank, guileless, and unsophisticated man," when in fact, "beneath a smooth surface of candor," apparently declaring "all his thoughts and feelings," Lincoln "handled and moved men remotely as we do pieces upon a chess-board." Adept in the art of being underestimated, Lincoln told "all that was unimportant," Swett observed, "with a gushing frankness, yet no man ever kept his real purposes closer, or penetrated the future further with his deep designs." It was said that in trials he argued his adversary's case better than his adversary could, the latter misconstruing Lincoln's voluntary concessions and admissions as naïveté, only then to wake up "in a ditch."[31]

Swett saw Lincoln as a profound analyst from whom not only Sun Tzu but also Hegel and Marx might learn, "the whole world" being to him "a question of cause and effect." Lincoln's whole political life was

a calculation of the law of forces and ultimate results. . . . He believed the results to which certain causes tended; he did not believe that those results could be materially hastened or impeded. . . . He believed . . . that the agitation of slavery would produce its overthrow, and he acted upon the result as though it was present from the beginning. His tactics were to get himself in the right place and remain there still, until events would find him in that place. This course of action led him to say and do things which could not be understood when considered in reference to the immediate surroundings in which they were done or said.[32]

Karl Marx wrote in October 1861 that for months the North "had quietly looked on" as the secessionists took assets and insulted the Union flag. Finally, to avoid letting Anderson give up peacefully for lack of food, and to avoid the constitutional resolution Lincoln mentioned in his inaugural, the secessionists "resolved to force the Union government out of its passive attitude by a sensational act of war, and *solely for this reason* proceeded to the bombardment of Fort Sumter."[33] While most observers would say that the secessionists engaged in "a sensational act of war" *despite* the fact that it would force the Union out of its passivity, Swett's Lincoln might have said that he wanted above all to awake the North from its passivity, and the secessionists' decision, undertaken voluntarily, to engage in "a sensational act of war" was bound to have exactly that result.

In October 1863, Swett urged Lincoln to checkmate potential rivals for the coming Republican nomination with a bold stroke: recommend a constitutional amendment to end slavery. Lincoln—in Swett's telling—replied, "I have never done an official act with a view to promote my own personal aggrandizement, and I don't like to begin now." Nor was there any need to do so, at least for a man of destiny, since success lay in taking the tide of inevitability at the crest. "I can see that emancipation is coming," he said. "Whoever can wait for it will see it; whoever stands in its way will be run over by it."[34] In that sense, Lincoln did not (as the schoolchildren's adage has it) "free the slaves," but rather saw that the slaves would be freed.

Lincoln later told his friend Orville Browning that "all the troubles and anxieties of his life had not equaled" the time when all of his cabinet members but Blair were for voluntarily abandoning Fort Sumter.[35] At the March 15 cabinet meeting at which Blair alone urged intervention, Lincoln stated no views. Only after the cabinet's collective position had shifted on March 29 and the formidable Seward had been marginalized did Lincoln tell Fox to proceed. Years later, Lincoln's secretaries wrote:

> When he finally gave the order that the fleet should sail he was master of the situation; master of his Cabinet; master of the moral attitude and issues of the struggle; master of the public opinion which must arise out of the impending conflict; master if the rebels hesitate or repent, because they would thereby forfeit their prestige with the South; master if they persisted, for he would then command a united North.[36]

The secretaries' perfect hindsight, mixed with idolatry for their sainted ex-employer, might here be credited, since they had been the president's intimates at this crucial moment. Although Lincoln had no egotistical compulsion to explain to anyone the depths of his strategic thinking, Hay and Nicolay in the first week of April 1861 observed a neophyte who waffled and then suddenly and deliberately committed all of his chips at what turned out to be the right moment in the game. And, in an irony that would have pained Fox considerably, it was with the loss of Fort Sumter that Lincoln's antecedent "troubles and anxieties" disappeared. What Fox saw as a personal disaster, Lincoln saw as a suitable resolution of a crisis. Fox got over his resentment sufficiently that on May 9 he accepted Lincoln's offer of chief clerk of the Navy Department and was elevated on July 31 to assistant secretary of the navy, a post invented for him and which he performed with great skill and energy.[37]

"The First Successful Military Expedition of the War"

Gideon Welles and John Nicolay both later commented that neither Lincoln nor anyone in his cabinet had read or knew the substance of the January 29 truce concerning Pensacola.[38] If Scott had remembered it when Lincoln first told him on March 5 to reinforce the Southern forts, Scott would presumably have pointed out that the reinforcement of Fort Pickens would violate that truce, making this point a factor in the deliberative process. Welles, whatever he might have known of the truce prior to April 6, received that day a quick lesson when the bedraggled courier Lieutenant Gwathmey arrived in his office to explain why Captain Adams had refused to execute the transfer order issued by Scott over three weeks earlier. By this time, however, Welles also knew that within a few days the expedition to Charleston would render irrelevant any nice questions about honoring or breaking a local armistice in Pensacola.

If Captain Adams had honored and carried out General Scott's March 12 order when he (finally) received it, some Confederate leaders might have considered attacking Fort Pickens so they could announce that the war had been started by the Union's violation of a negotiated truce. But General Bragg professed to lack assets, Davis and others thought Pensacola strategically worthless, and South Carolina would resent seeing the war commenced in Florida. Alternatively, the Confederates could have opened fire on Fort Sumter, asserting that the Union's violation of the truce in Pensacola constituted a declaration of war to which the attack on Sumter was only a response. As things were, the transfer of Union soldiers from the ships to Fort Pickens, delayed until the night of April 12–13, had little impact on the Confederate leaders because it had been preempted by the cannonade at Charleston at 4:30 the previous morning. Although the successful transfer finally vindicated Lincoln's promise to "hold, occupy, and possess" Southern forts, what would otherwise have been publicized as a bold and significant achievement was buried, ironically, under the huge wave of positive publicity Lincoln received following news from Charleston, where—in contrast with Pensacola—his reinforcement effort had utterly failed.

On the afternoon of April 13, as Fort Sumter was surrendering five hundred nautical miles to the north, *Atlantic* stopped off at Key West on its way to Fort Pickens.[39] Meigs was here notified that *Brooklyn* had come from Pensacola several weeks before to obtain supplies, had picked up Scott's March 12 transfer order, and had returned to Pensacola. This news reasonably meant that the transfer had already taken place, rendering Meigs's expedition super-fluous.[40] Meigs could not know that the original order was not carried out because it contained a technical flaw, nor could he know that a messenger had delivered a new, technically adequate order on April 12 and that the transfer had thus just occurred. Nor could he know that Sumter had been attacked, was evacuated, and was now in Confederate hands.

Before proceeding to Pensacola, *Atlantic* stopped at Fort Jefferson on Tortugas, the largest of the Third System forts, built to accommodate 450 guns. Because Colonel Harvey Brown had guessed that Pensacola—rather than Tortugas or Key West—was the likeliest situs for any initial battle in the Gulf of Mexico, he had *Atlantic* take aboard several howitzers and mortars to provide to Captain Vogdes. Several had just been delivered *to* Tortugas *from* Pensacola, because Captain Vogdes—for his part—had guessed that it was Tortugas where they were most needed, and he had asked *Brooklyn* to drop them off on its way to Key West.[41]

Meigs knew Tortugas, having been exiled there by Floyd. "My friends," Meigs noted in his journal, "seemed glad to see me. Some of the laborers and mechanics not only welcomed me on shore, but came off to express their feelings. They said their hearts grew large in their breasts when they saw me upon the boat. As they went off, they gave three cheers for Captain Meigs, with a good will and loud voices. Many volunteered to go with me, said they would stand by me, and die by me, but I had enough."[42] By "I had enough," Meigs meant that he and Colonel Brown had already taken aboard some twenty slaves and an overseer to do the considerable work required at the long-neglected Fort Pickens. At some earlier time of amicable relations between the Union and the state of Florida, the masters of these slaves had contracted with the federal government—at what were reportedly "very remunerative prices"—to construct federal forts. Some slaves were said to be beneficially owned by Stephen Mallory, who, after resigning from the U.S. Senate on January 21, had helped to negotiate the January 29 truce for Florida.[43]

Several slavemasters, upon hearing that their human "property" had been transferred to Fort Pickens, complained that this was not within the ambit of their contract with the federal government and therefore constituted slave stealing. Their assertion eventually came across the desk of Secretary of State Seward, who construed the contract to allow the government to transfer slaves from Tortugas to work on Fort Pickens, adding that naturally the masters would be paid for the work their slaves performed there.[44] Thus, although by the time of Seward's decision hostilities had commenced, he honored the Union contract to pay slaveholders in the seceded state of Florida, for the

Off-loading horses on Santa Rosa Island with Fort Pickens in distance, April 16, 1861, as depicted in *Harper's Weekly* (May 25, 1861).

work of their slaves in preparing a federal fort within that state, so it could do battle with the seceded state and its slaveowners.

On the afternoon of April 16, ten days and sixteen hundred nautical miles from New York, *Atlantic* approached the Union ships anchored off Pensacola. Since the transfer of men from *Brooklyn* to Fort Pickens had taken place four days earlier and without opposition, Meigs at 9:00 p.m. began transferring *Atlantic*'s 450 warriors to shore without waiting for *Powhatan*, due the next day.[45]

During *Powhatan*'s fitting out in New York, a newspaper reported that the materials brought aboard included some British pennants.[46] At midday on April 17, *Powhatan* arrived off Pensacola disguised as a British mail ship, with gun portholes painted over and belching the appropriately sooty smoke of British bituminous coal, rather than clean-burning Pennsylvania anthracite. It anchored off Santa Rosa Island, its disguise at first fooling even some of the Union men.[47] In their planning back in Washington, Porter and Meigs had envisioned bringing *Powhatan* across the bar and through Pensacola's narrow harbor mouth, running the gauntlet of guns arrayed at Forts Barrancas and McRee and along the beach between them. If the shore batteries were fooled by its disguise, or fired but failed to sink or disable it, *Powhatan* could then anchor at the far end of the harbor, beyond the range of those batteries but ready to discourage or harass any attempted amphibious assault on Fort Pickens by men in boats moving across the harbor.[48] Since, however, Fort Pickens was now fully manned, the Confederates would not launch such an attack.

In a loving memoir of his father, under whom he served from age eleven, Porter would write that Commodore David Porter had to buck ungrateful superiors in order to serve his country, and although Americans no longer praised nor even remembered the naval heroes of the War of 1812, the navy then "had on its rolls . . . gallant spirits who would have rivaled the fame of Blake and Nelson, had the opportunity been offered them."[49] And so here was the son's opportunity to make his dead father proud. As Meigs well knew, Porter had in hand a presidential order to proceed "at any cost or risk." Among the self-serving elements Porter had drafted into that order was a provision whereby he was not to report to or consult with any naval officer already at Pensacola until "after you have established yourself within the harbor," meaning that no one could intervene to stop him.[50] For ten days Porter had been contemplating his coming resplendence—perhaps in death—in vindicating the Union cause, no matter how quixotic the means.

Meigs, fearing that "no man on earth could stop Porter bent on an act of desperate gallantry and devotion," knew that if any local officer approached Porter and tried to appeal to reason and common sense, Porter would respond with what had worked to perfection before: that he had an order from the president and was going to obey it.[51] Meigs received a note from Colonel Brown stating that Bragg's "elaborate range of batteries" and the "wretched condition" of Fort Pickens's defenses required that Porter do nothing to provoke the Confederates, Brown's sole task being to continue moving supplies ashore to render Fort Pickens impregnable.[52]

Porter, comfortable that because of his order, signed by Lincoln, he could disregard the protests of Brown and Meigs, began to take *Powhatan* through the harbor mouth to engage the enemy.[53] Meigs was in the harbor on *Wyandotte* (the one Union ship General Bragg had permitted to be there) and gave repeated signals identifying himself and instructing Porter to stop. When Porter ignored him, Meigs steered *Wyandotte* to cut across *Powhatan*'s course, as Confederate artillerymen passively watched a Union warship challenge what might or might not be a British mail ship. Porter finally reversed engines and Meigs managed to give him Colonel Brown's letter and endorsed its propriety.[54] Porter, upon being informed that a naval engagement would be counterproductive and aware that Meigs himself would not be impressed by his invocation of presidential authority, chose to write to Brown asking for his consent to proceed at the earliest possible opportunity: "In looking carefully over the orders of the president in relation to my entering the harbor, I find them so imperative that they leave no margin for any contingency that may arise."[55] But Meigs would have already informed Brown that Porter did not need to look at the orders too carefully, since he had written them. Porter acquiesced, while adding that he and his crew remained "ready to sacrifice themselves on the altar of their country," this thwarting of his venture being (he later told a friend) "the great disappointment of my life."[56]

In September 1865, Meigs would proclaim that his and Porter's mission to Pensacola had been "the first successful military expedition of the war."[57] But the war had started in Charleston in the early morning of April 12. That night came the war's first successful Union operation: the transfer of Vogdes's troops from *Brooklyn* to Fort Pickens. But this event occurred several days before Meigs or Porter arrived, the transfer being no "expedition" only because the ships had been nearby for several months. The only other "expedition"— Fox's—had, of course, been a military failure. The gale off Charleston had made the resupply and reinforcement efforts there impossible, thus rendering *Powhatan*'s absence irrelevant. But here, too, the ship proved to be useless. Captain Adams noted to Secretary Welles that he would rather have had one "steamer of light draft—5 or 6 feet—that could carry supplies or reinforcements up to the very walls of Fort Pickens" than a dozen ships of *Powhatan*'s size.[58] Thus, the Meigs/Porter "expedition," while "successful," was militarily meaningless. No newspaper, not even the *National Republican*, made anything of *Powhatan*'s arrival at Pensacola.[59]

The peaceful transfer of men, ordnance, supplies, and horses would continue, and Fort Pickens would soon have 1,262 men, along with an attendant naval squadron of *Brooklyn*, *Sabine*, *Wyandotte*, *Atlantic*, *Powhatan*, and other ships, totaling an additional force of over two thousand, all in defense of a facility in which the Confederates had taken no interest.[60] Weeks later, on May 23, Porter rather pitiably wrote to Meigs, "If we want to have a fight here, we will have to fire the first shot. The other party won't begin."[61]

Conclusion

"You No See the House Afire?"

On April 13, with the barrage of Fort Sumter at its height, Mary Chesnut noted:

> Not by one word or look can we detect any change in the demeanor of these negro servants. Laurence sits at our door, as sleepy and as respectful, and as profoundly indifferent. So are they all. They carry it too far. You could not tell that they hear even the awful row that is going on in the bay, though it is dinning in their ears night and day. People talk before them as if they were chairs and tables. And they make no sign. Are they stolidly stupid or wiser than we are, silent and strong, biding their time?[1]

Johnson Hagood, who had commanded the First South Carolina Volunteers, later wrote of his troops' excitement on April 13 when, from James Island, they witnessed the barrage of Fort Sumter at its height, with smoke rising from the burning officers' quarters. One soldier, undoubtedly for the entertainment of the others, shouted to "an aged negress" who was "patiently delving with others in a field by the roadside." "Old woman," he asked, "what's the matter over yonder?" She responded, "You no see the house afire?" Hagood commented that clearly this slave, a "type of her class . . . did not take in fully the magnitude of the occasion." Hagood, too, was a "type" of his "class": the plantation owner. Although he told this story for the amusement value of deriding the old woman's ignorance and obliviousness, in this Shakespearean scene it was she, not he, who had taken in fully the magnitude of the occasion.[2]

On April 18, British journalist W. H. Russell visited General Beauregard as he arranged to return Sumter to its status as a defensive facility against seaborne invaders. That evening, Russell attended a dinner party hosted by the British consul Robert Bunch. "One very venerable old gentleman" named Alfred Huger, he wrote, was particularly desirous to speak:

> He formerly held some official appointment [i.e., postmaster] under the federal government, but had gone out with his state. . . . He was not happy at the prospect before him or his country. "I have lived too long," he exclaimed; "I should have died 'ere these evil days arrived." What thoughts, indeed, must have troubled his mind when he reflected that his country was but little older than himself; for, he was one who had shaken hands with the framers of the Declaration of Independence. But though the tears rolled down his cheeks when he spoke of the prospect of civil war, there was no symptom of apprehension for the result, or indeed of any regret for the contest, which he regarded as the natural consequence of the insults, injustice, and aggression of the North against Southern rights.

Russell noted that only one person present, "a most lively, quaint, witty old lawyer named [James Louis] Petigru," continued to dissent from "the doctrines of Secession; but he seems to be treated as an amiable, harmless person, who has a weakness of intellect or a 'Bee in his bonnet' on this particular matter."[3]

Although Beauregard had told Russell that it would be "madness" for the Union to return to Charleston and attack, by December 1862 it was clear that the Union would do so. The South Carolina poet Henry Timrod wrote, "Dark Sumter, like a battlemented cloud, / Looms o'er the solemn deep," while "Old Charleston looks from roof, and spire, and dome / Across her tranquil bay," as it had in April 1861. "In the temple of the Fates / God has inscribed her doom." Awaiting that outcome, the city's "maidens . . . Seem each one to have caught the strength of him / Whose sword she sadly bound."[4] Others would say that in fact it was the men who caught strength from the women. Back in February 1861, a visitor to Charleston asked a young lady whether she was concerned that her fiancé might soon be going off to fight. She responded that "no woman of Carolina would for a moment tolerate a coward." The visitor thought that while local women may not have originated secessionism, they "perfected" it.[5]

On June 20, 1863, with Union ships engaged in a blockade of Charleston Harbor, Esther Alden wrote:

> In spite of the war every one is so bright and cheerful, and the men are so charming and look so nice in their uniforms. We see a great many of them,

and I have been to a most delightful dance in Fort Sumter. The night was lovely and we went down in rowing boats. It was a strange scene, cannon balls piled in every direction, sentinels pacing the ramparts, and within the casemates pretty, well-dressed women, and handsome well-bred men dancing, as though unconscious that we were actually under the guns of the blockading fleet. It was my first party, and the strange charm of the situation wove a spell around me; every man seemed to me a hero—not only a possible but an actual hero! One looks at a man so differently when you think he may be killed to-morrow! Men whom up to this time I have thought dull and commonplace that night seemed charming.[6]

Fort Sumter would host no more dances. Twenty days later, on July 10, 1863, Union troops would land on Morris Island, as it was feared they might two years before. On July 11, and again on July 18, Union forces would attack Battery Wagner, the extraordinary sand fortress, a kind of organic gray monster constructed by the Confederates not far from where a battery of local cadets had once opened fire upon *Star of the West*.[7]

Johnson Hagood would later secure a permanent (if minor) place in history, in the recollection of a Union officer who was captured by the Confederates following that July 18 attack:

I saw Colonel [Robert Gould] Shaw, of the Fifty-fourth Mass. (colored) regiment lying dead upon the ground, just outside the parapet. A stalwart negro man had fallen near him. . . . The Colonel had been killed by a rifle shot through the chest, though he had received other wounds. Brigadier-General [Hagood], commanding the Rebel forces, said to me: "I knew Colonel Shaw before the war, and then esteemed him. Had he been in command of white troops, I should have given him an honorable burial. As it is, I shall bury him in the common trench, among the negroes that fell with him."

This Hagood considered a fitting gesture of opprobrium for the brave and experienced officer, age twenty-five, his body already stripped down to his drawers, his watch stolen.[8] The war had for decades been craved and then initiated by Johnson Hagood and the "types" of his "class." Hundreds of thousands of people died on each side, and now Hagood had unwittingly offered the war's defining moment, what in the end it was "about," and what about it was noble and ignoble. His order to bury Shaw "with his 'niggers'"—the term he probably used and which was commonly used in retellings—showed, "in a flash of light," Henry Cabot Lodge wrote, "the hideous barbarism of a system which made such things and such feelings possible."[9] As with his anecdote of the old slave woman, Hagood's perspective, so assured and self-convinced, would outlive and shame him.[10]

Colonel Shaw, however, needed no redemption. When his father heard of an effort to disinter his son so that he could be accorded the honors appropriate to an officer, he wrote, "We can imagine no holier place than that in which he lies, among his brave and devoted followers, nor wish for him better company."[11]

Thomas Low Nichols, from New Hampshire but staunchly pro-Southern, wrote of the North's "war of hatred and revenge against people who asked only for independence and peace."[12] A Northern partisan, by contrast, would write that Charleston "intentionally provoked the indignation of our people, and made it cowardice not to punish her for her insolence, to say nothing of her treason."[13] A Northerner recounted that because some of the older blacks, having "never heard their masters mention the name of a Yankee" except with a profane adjective, "have been praying for years, 'O Lord! Bress, we beseech thee, and speedily bring along de comin' of de *dam* Yankees.'"[14] The city would be subjected to periodic bombardment from late 1863 through most of 1864. While Fort Sumter was reduced to rubble, the Confederate garrison never surrendered. Instead, in February 1865 Confederate forces abandoned Charleston, thus depriving General William Tecumseh Sherman, with his philosophy of total war, of any reason for further devastation.

When on February 18 Union occupiers approached,

> the wharves looked as if they had been deserted for half a century—broken down, dilapidated; grass and moss peeping up between the pavements, where once the busy feet of commerce trod incessantly. The warehouses near the river, the streets as we enter them, the houses, and the stores, and the public buildings—we look at them and hold our breath in utter amazement. . . . Ruin, ruin, ruin . . . staring at us from every paneless window.[15]

Many of the white marble blocks of the Custom House still lay scattered, just as when work stopped at secession, although others had reportedly been used to sink a derelict slaver in the harbor mouth. A Northern visitor, noting the paucity of young men and the prevalence of young women dressed in black, thought of Longfellow's prophetic poem "Retribution" (1846): "The mills of God grind slowly, yet they grind exceeding small."[16]

Charleston's Exchange Building from the north, circa 1865. Library of Congress LC-DIG-cwpb-03006.

As the war wound down, President Lincoln approved an order that the retired Robert Anderson should travel to Fort Sumter and at noon on Friday, April 14, 1865, hoist again the flag he and his men had saluted and lowered four years before.[17] As reported that day in the *National Republican*, also invited was Abner Doubleday, another of the six officers at Sumter who had become generals.[18] One of Lincoln's secretaries, John Nicolay, would attend the event, as would Gideon Welles's son.[19]

Following the ceremony, a gala was held at the Charleston Hotel, from whose balcony Governor Pickens had once derided the Union. Among those now toasting Anderson was Joseph Holt, who had replaced John Floyd as President Buchanan's secretary of war. "It is not uncommon for organizations

Arrival of General Anderson and other dignitaries at flag-raising ceremony at Fort Sumter, April 14, 1865. Library of Congress LC-DIG-cwpb-0270.

in treason or in crime," Holt said, "to commit mistakes in the selection of agents to accomplish their work; and no man in all history committed a greater mistake than Floyd" in selecting Anderson—simply because of his Southern background—to command Fort Sumter.[20] Anderson had hated Lincoln, but he now raised a glass to "the man who, when elected President of the United States, was compelled to reach the seat of government with an escort, but who now could travel all over our country with millions of hands and hearts to sustain him."[21]

Elsewhere in the April 14 *National Republican* was an advertisement by Ford's New Theatre at Tenth Street near Pennsylvania Avenue for the last performance of Miss Laura Keane in Tom Taylor's play *Our American Cousin*.[22] "Mr. Lincoln liked the theatre not so much for itself," a Washington newspaperman had observed, but "because of the rest it afforded him. I have seen him more than once looking at a play without seeming to know what was going on before him. Abstracted and silent, scene after scene would pass, and nothing roused him until some broad joke or curious antic disturbed his equanimity."[23] He had loved reciting Shakespeare, particularly *Richard II*: "Let us sit upon the ground, / And tell sad stories of the death of kings."[24]

Lincoln kept a file labeled "Assassination," which by late March 1865 contained eighty items. On April 11, two days after the surrender at Appomattox Court House, and four days before Ford's Theatre, the president recounted to Ward Lamon and to Mrs. Lincoln a disturbing dream:

> I retired very late. I had been up waiting for important dispatches from the front. I could not have been long in bed when I fell into a slumber. . . . I soon began to dream. There seemed to be a death-like stillness about me. Then I heard subdued sobs, as if a number of people were weeping. I thought I left my bed and wandered downstairs. There the silence was broken by the same pitiful sobbing, but the mourners were invisible. I went from room to room; no living person was in sight, but the same mournful sounds of distress met me as I passed along. It was light in all the rooms; every object was familiar to me; but where were all the people who were grieving as if their hearts would break? I was puzzled and alarmed. What could be the meaning of all this? Determined to find the cause of a state of things so mysterious and so shocking, I kept on until I arrived at the East Room, which I entered. There I met with a sickening surprise. Before me was a catafalque, on which rested a corpse wrapped in funeral vestments. Around it were stationed soldiers who were acting as guards; and there was a throng of people, some gazing mournfully upon the corpse, whose face was covered, others weeping pitifully. "Who is dead in the White House?" I demanded of one of the soldiers. "The President," was his answer; "he was killed by an assassin!" Then came a loud burst of grief from the crowd, which awoke me from my dream. I slept no more that night; and although it was only a dream, I have been strangely annoyed by it ever since.[25]

Lincoln last drew breath at 7:00 a.m. on Saturday, April 15. Among those present at 516 Tenth Street was Brevet Major General Montgomery Meigs, who applied his talent for imposing order on chaos by stationing himself at the front door to decide who could and could not enter. Meigs had become one of Lincoln's most trusted advisors.[26] So had Seward. A co-conspirator of John Wilkes Booth had tried to kill Seward at Rodgers House, his residence on Lafayette Square, and in the process severely injured Seward's son Frederick. By the time newspapers were issuing second editions on April 15, the secretary of state was expected to recover, although Frederick remained close to death for several days.[27]

John Nicolay, returning from the ceremony in Charleston, would first hear of Lincoln's death from the pilot who boarded to navigate the Chesapeake. "Nicolay tossed in his berth, crying out in sorrow that he had killed the president by going away. He meant, of course, that if he had been in Washington and with the president, Mr. Lincoln might not have been shot."[28] Lamon, who had long served as a personal bodyguard, was not at Ford's Theatre because Lincoln had dispatched him to Richmond.

On September 13, 1865, at noon, delegates assembled in the Baptist church in the ruined city of Columbia, to repeal South Carolina's Ordinance of Secession. Among them was Alfred Huger, "over eighty years of age," a Northern visitor reported, but "tall, and not much bent," with

> a face indicative of great force and strength of character. . . . The scene was in the highest degree dramatic,—the venerable old man standing between the platform and a table, with a supporting hand on each, and speaking in the most impassioned manner, with a clear, resonant voice that easily filled the whole church; every member of the Convention sitting with strained attention; the galleries bending over in silence, the better to see and hear; a clerk standing near the feeble Huguenot Carolinian to pass the glass of water while he spoke, and reach for him his staff when he had concluded.

South Carolina, Huger said,

> is my mother; I have all my life loved what she loved, and hated what she hated; everything she had I made my own, and every act of hers was my act; as I have had but one hope, to live with her, so now I have but one desire, to die on her soil and be laid in her bosom. If I am wrong in everything else, I know I am right in loving South Carolina,—know I am right in believing that, whatever glory the future may bring our reunited country, it

can neither brighten nor tarnish the glory of South Carolina. . . . And now, no matter . . . what there is to endure and to forget, let us all do our duty as becomes her children, counting it our chiefest honor to stand by her in evil report as well as in good report.

Also present was ex-governor Francis Pickens, described by a Northern attendee as "a battered old wreck" with "round and piggish eyes," his "bristly iron-gray moustache and chin whiskers" setting up "a very peculiar and notice-able contrast" with his brown wig. Having experienced "swift repentance," he spoke with a meek voice and "eats his humble pie with some ostenta-tion," being "specially solicitous that nothing shall be done to offend . . . His Excellency the President of the United States." This image put the Northern observer in mind of Pickens's speech just after the capitulation of the Union garrison in April 1861, in which he declared that "the glorious little State of South Carolina" had "humbled the flag of the United States."[29]

Notes

Chapter 1: "Our Stormy-Browed Sister"

1. *Journal of the Senate of South Carolina* (Columbia, 1860), 9–10.
2. *Cleveland (OH) Daily Leader* (11/17/1860) 4; McClintock (2008) 15–16; Wooster (1969) 55n; Brackett 946; Victor 46; Schultz 225–26.
3. See, for example, Morrison 126–28. Seventy-nine percent of officers from the Lower South quit the U.S. Army, a figure that would have been higher but for those who remained because of Northern ties. In the border states, only 27.4 percent quit. Skelton 356–57, 445nn19–20. Some West Point classes (it is unclear how many) were assigned *View of the Constitution of the United States of America*, wherein William Rawle asserted that secession was implicitly permitted in the Constitution, although not favored. In 1844, *Elements of Moral Science* by Brown president Francis Wayland became West Point's foundational ethics text, but with Wayland's antislavery paragraphs (widely read in other editions) omitted. Skelton 170–71.
4. Richard, Lord Lyons/Lord John Russell (11/12/1860), Barnes and Barnes 2; Gist (11/5/1860), *Journal of the Senate of South Carolina* (Columbia, 1860), 9–10. See also Crawford (1896) 12–14; George S. Boutwell, *Reminiscences of Sixty Years in Public Affairs* (New York: McClure, Phillips, 1902), 1:252; Detzer 14; A. Porter 118; Freehling (2007) 399–402.
5. J. H. Hammond/Marcus S. M. Hammond (11/12/1860), *The Hammonds of Redcliffe*, ed. Carol Bleser (1981; Columbia: University of South Carolina Press, 1997), 88; Chauncey S. Boucher, "South Carolina and the South on the Eve of Secession, 1852 to 1860," *Wash. U. Studies* 6/2:81, 121–25 (4/1919). See also [William Grayson], *Letters of Curtius* (Charleston, 1851), 10; *Appeal to the State Rights Party of South Carolina*, ed. Maxcy Gregg (Columbia, 1858), vi–viii; Faust; Jon L. Wakelyn, *Confederates against the Confederacy* (Westport, CT: Praeger, 2002), 3; L. Anderson 84–86; Merchant 142; Genovese 101; Freehling (2007) 27–34.
6. Madison/Jefferson (10/24/1787), Madison 10:205, 218. Madison had heard one of those delegates, Charles Cotesworth Pinckney, pledge to support the Constitution "with all his influence." (9/17/1787), Elliot 5:558.
7. (7/23/1787), Farrand 2:95; Elliot 4:338–41. Pinckney later assured South Carolina legislators that Congress could never pass an emancipation law because section 8 of Article I enumerates Congress's powers, and the emancipation of slaves was not one of them. (1/17/1788), Elliot 4:286. The provisions directly and indirectly dealing with

slavery are noted in, for example, Paul Finkelman, *Slavery and the Founders* (Armonk, NY: M.E. Sharpe, 1996), 3–7. Regarding such ratifying conventions, see, for example, Noah Webster, "On Government" (1788), *Collection of Essays and Fugitiv[e] Writings* (Boston, 1790), 49, 51–57; Hamilton, *Federalist* 40; Gordon Wood, *The Creation of the American Republic* (1969; New York: Norton, 1972), 306–43; H. J. Powell, "The Original Understanding of Original Intent," *Harv. L. Rev.* 98:885, 906–7 (1985).

8. "Act to Provide for the Calling of a Convention of the People of This State" (11/13/1860), *Convention Journal* 459. The narrator of the anonymous *Diary of a Public Man* (1879) purported to have had on December 28, 1860, a conversation with James L. Orr, one of three men sent by South Carolina to negotiate with President Buchanan the terms of the state's withdrawal, in which Orr saw "no constitutional reason why the Federal Government should refuse to recognize" his state's independence, since the federal government could not have been formed without its concurrence. The narrator dismissed the argument as absurd. [Hurlbert] (1945) 27–28.

9. See, for example, Schultz 228–29; L. Anderson 90–95.

10. While the method for choosing delegates to the nullification convention was not on its face discriminatory against Unionists, few wished to be part of a convention that seemed to them skewed in advance. See "An Act to Provide for the Calling of a Convention" (10/26/1832), *SLSC* 1:309.

11. McCarter Journal, 1860–1866 1:20, Lib. Cong. call no. MMC-1932; *Charleston Courier* (11/28/1860) 3; id. (11/30/1860) 1; Lillian A. Kibler, "Unionist Sentiment in South Carolina in 1860," *J. South. Hist.* 4/3:346, 360 (8/1938).

12. (11/16/1860), Ravenel 39. See also *Globe* (24/1) App. 287 (1/21/1836).

13. A. Porter 118–19.

14. (2/18/1861), Mary Chesnut, *The Private Mary Chesnut*, ed. C. Vann Woodward and Elisabeth Muhlenfeld (New York: Oxford University Press, 1984), 4 (emphasis omitted). Compare Chesnut, *Diary from Dixie*, ed. Isabell D. Martin and Myrta Lockett Avary (1905; New York: D. Appleton, 1906), xxvi, *and* Mary Chesnut, *Mary Chesnut's Civil War* ed. C. Vann Woodward (New Haven, CT: Yale University Press, 1981), 3–4.

15. Huger/Joseph Holt (11/27/1860), *Holt Papers* 26:3447–3447a, Lib. Cong. See also Huger/Holt (12/4/1860), id. 26:3454; S. Channing 282–83; Ford.

16. Huger/Rep. William Porcher Miles (D/SC) (5/13/1851), Huger (1851); Huger/Miles (12/12/1859, 6/1/1860), *Miles Papers*, folder 31. See also Huger/Miles (4/4/1860), id.; Huger/Miles (11/28/1859), id. folder 21; Huger/J. J. McCarter[?] (10/4/1856), *Huger Papers*, box 3, pp. 13, 17.

17. See, for example, Joseph Sitterson, *The Secession Movement in South Carolina* (Chapel Hill: University of North Carolina Press, 1939), 138; Eric Foner, "The Causes of the American Civil War" (1974) in Foner, *Politics and Ideology in the Age of the Civil War* (New York: Oxford University Press, 1980) 15, 28–29.

18. (11/25/1860) quoted in S. Channing 6.

19. See, for example, Ronald Takaki, "The Movement to Reopen the African Slave Trade in South Carolina," *S.C. Hist. Mag.* 66/1:38 (1/1965).

20. A. Porter 118. See also Quigley 108–9.

21. Brackett 946; W. F. G. Peck, "Four Years under Fire at Charleston," *Harper's Monthly* 31:358 (8/1865); E. Adams 2:2–7; Keitt quoted in John A. Logan, *The Great Conspiracy* (New York, 1886), 115. See also Merchant.

22. See, for example, William Gregg, *Essays on Domestic Industry* (Charleston, 1845), 18; Ulrich B. Phillips, *History of Transportation in the Eastern Cotton Belt to 1860* (New York: Columbia University Press, 1908), 355; Craven (1932) 75–76; Tom Downey, *Planting a Capitalist South* (Baton Rouge: Louisiana State University Press, 2006), 69–91; Rachel Klein, *Unification of a Slave State* (Chapel Hill: University of North Carolina Press, 1990), 257–58; Petty 86; Freehling (2007) 20; J. Van Deusen 182–219; Freehling (1994) 167; A. G. Smith, "The Old Order Changes" (1958), *Perspectives in South Carolina History*, ed. Ernest Lander and Robert Ackerman (Columbia: University of South Carolina Press, 1973), 95, 99–101; Lacy K. Ford Jr., *Origins of Southern Radicalism* (New York: Oxford University Press, 1988), 215–17, 244–80. In every year between 1821 and 1860, South Carolina's exports were a multiple of its imports. J. Van Deusen 332. In 1820, South Carolina's 170,000 bales per year made up more than half U.S. production, and the dollar value of Charleston's exports exceeded that of New York's. Beginning in the 1830s, thousands of South Carolinians moved to Alabama, Louisiana, Mississippi, Arkansas, and Texas and set up plantations. Petty 233; Charles Sydnor, *The Development of Southern Sectionalism 1819–1848* (Baton Rouge: Louisiana State University Press, 1948), 23. By the 1850s, Charleston's 320,000 bales constituted less than 10 percent of U.S. production. Charles F. Kovacik and John J. Winberry, *South Carolina* (1988; Columbia: University of South Carolina Press, 1989), 91–92. Mississippi, meanwhile, had become a prodigy, expanding its cotton production so rapidly that by 1860 its 1.2 million bales compromised 20 percent of the world's supply. Bradley Bond, *Political Culture in the Nineteenth-Century South* (Baton Rouge: Louisiana State University Press, 1995), 54. See also R. R. Russel, *Economic Aspects of Southern Sectionalism* (Urbana: Southern Illinois University Press, 1924), 199. Regarding the decline of Charleston as a port due to advances in navigation, see *Lord Wrottesley's Speech in the House of Lords . . . on Lieut. Maury's Plan*, 2nd ed. (London, 1853), 17.
23. Petigru/Susan Petigru King (11/10/1860), Petigru 361, 364; Petigru quoted in L. A. Kibler, "Unionist Sentiment in South Carolina in 1860," *J. Southern Hist.* 4/3:346, 365 (8/1938).
24. William Shepard McAninch, "Petigru College," *S. Carolina L. Rev.* 49:531, 539n91 (1998). See also Sean Wilentz, *Rise of American Democracy* (New York: Norton, 2005), 945n5; Ford, 415n98; A. Porter 116.
25. B. Perry (1883) 16; M. Klein 326; Nevins (1950) 2:325–26. See also Halleck 161–209; Stampp (1950) 71–73; Schultz 40.
26. E. McPherson 18, Elliot G. Storke, *Complete History of the Great American Rebellion* (Auburn, NY, 1863–1865), 1:36, F. Moore (1861–1866), Supp. vol. 1:44. See also George Bancroft/Dean Milman (8/15/1861), M. A. Howe, *Life and Letters of George Bancroft* (New York: C. Scribner's Sons, 1908) 2:133, 135; Rhett 7, 51; Barney (1972) 91–95; Thomas S. Goodwin, *Natural History of Secession* (New York, 1864), 152–57.
27. Brackett 946.
28. See, for example, Calhoun 20:xiv.
29. Buchanan had thought sufficiently of Pickens to have designated him at one point as his successor, before Buchanan's unpopularity made his political preferences irrelevant. Edmunds (1967) 174–90.
30. See, for example, William Henry Trescot, *The Position and Course of the South* (Charleston, 1850), [3], 14; Genovese 79–81.

31. (11/10, 11/1860), "Private Diary of Secretary Floyd," Pollard (1867A) 794–96; *Charleston Courier* (12/18/1860); Wooster (1969) 55n. See also *Confederate Congress* 1:160, 162; Edmunds (1967) 202–3; Edmunds (1970) 27–28.

32. See, for example, *Sister States, Enemy States*, ed. Kent Dollar, Larry Whiteaker, and W. Calvin Dickinson (Lexington: University Press of Kentucky, 2009); Brian D. McKnight, *Contested Borderland* (Lexington: University Press of Kentucky, 2006), 14–21.

33. Following the 1860 election, the *Alexandria Gazette* opined that since Breckinridge could not possibly have won the presidency, his supporters should instead have backed Bell, who called for adherence to the Constitution and the negotiation and compromise of all issues. (11/8/1860) 2. See also *Library of Original Sources*, ed. Oliver Thatcher (New York: University Research Extension, 1907), 9:207; *Nashville Republican Banner* (1/26/1861); R. R. Russel, *Economic Aspects of Southern Sectionalism* (Urbana: Southern Illinois University Press, 1924), 238–39. Regarding the persistence of grassroots Unionism even after the war began, see Margaret M. Storey, "Civil War Unionists and the Political Culture of Loyalty in Alabama, 1860–1861," *J. South. Hist.* 69/1:71 (2/2003). See also Barney (1974); Quigley 114–16; Peter B. Knupfer, *The Union as It Is* (Chapel Hill: University of North Carolina Press, 1991), 1–22.

34. *National Republican Platform* (Chicago [1860]), para. 4. Lincoln would quote it in his first inaugural. Basler et al. 4:262, 263.

35. See, for example, Speech at Galesburg (10/7/1858), Basler et al. 3:207, 231 ("The right of property in a slave is distinctly and expressly affirmed in the Constitution of the United States. Therefore, nothing in the Constitution or laws of any State can destroy the right of property in a slave"). The *New York Times* published extracts of Lincoln's speeches indicating that he would not interfere with slavery where it already existed, and while the *Richmond Enquirer* excerpted the article and other Southern papers carried it, its dovish message did not dissuade the *Enquirer* from warning that "submission to Black Republican rule" would be both "degrading" and "dangerous." (11/10/1860) 2; *Nashville Union and American* (11/16/1860) 2 cols. 1–2. See also Beard and Beard 2:24–25, 38–39.

36. (11/28/1860) 2.

37. See, for example, John C. Calhoun, "Address of the Southern Delegates in Congress, to Their Constituents" (2/1/1849), Calhoun 26:225; *Globe* (29/2) App. 246 (1/15/1847) (Rep. R. B. Rhett, D/SC); Cleo Hearon, *Mississippi and the Compromise of 1850*, Pubs. Miss. Hist. Soc. 14:7, 39 (1914); Herman V. Ames, *John C. Calhoun and the Secession Movement of 1850* (Worcester, MA: American Antiquarian Society, 1918), 10–12; Holt (1999) 386–87.

38. See, for example, *Globe* (36/2) 408 (1/16/1861); Gienapp (1996) 79, 85; William W. Freehling, *The South vs. the South* (New York: Oxford University Press, 2001), 37–39; Freehling (2007) 15; Paul Finkelman, "Cost of Compromise and the Covenant with Death," *Pepp. L. Rev.* 38:845, 846–47 (2011); Amar (2001) 1114–16.

39. See chapter 6, notes 14–21 and accompanying text.

40. Perry (12/11/1850), Perry (1887) 111, 123.

41. Boyce/J. P. Richardson, *Washington Daily Union* (6/4/1851) 3 cols. 3–4. Garrison, a child of the Second Great Awakening and comfortable with biblical prophecies of the apocalypse, had warned a Fourth of July audience in 1837 that unless God is "faithless in

the execution of his threatenings" (something Garrison would have found unthinkable), disunion was "in the womb of events." (7/4/1837) quoted in Massachusetts Abolition Society, *True History of the Late Division in the Anti-slavery Societies* (Boston, 1841), 8.

42. *Proceedings of the State Disunion Convention* (Boston, 1857), 41. Since Garrison had learned that slaveholders were not to be persuaded that they were engaged in "a heinous sin against God," he no longer attempted to engage them, although he continued to believe that while the Union could whip the South "into subjection," "deluge her soil with blood," and "extort" her allegiance "at the cannon's mouth," doing so would be meaningless because it would not "conquer her spirit." *Liberator* (2/15/1861) 3. But see Fredrickson 41–42. See also Alvan Stewart, *Writings and Speeches of Alvan Stewart on Slavery*, ed. Luther R. Marsh (New York, 1860), 56; *Globe* (36/2) 768 (2/6/1861).

43. Stephens/J. Henly Smith (7/10/1860), Phillips 486, 487; Stephens (1910) 61, 172. See also Stephens (11/14/1860), Stephens (1866) 694, 696, Stephens (1868–1870) 2:278; Stephens (1/1861), E. McPherson 20, 25; Hodge 4–5. Upon becoming vice president of the Confederacy, Stephens would take the opposite position in his famous "Cornerstone" speech. (3/21/1861), Stephens (1866) 718. See also Trescot (1850) 15–16; Jon L. Wakelyn, *Confederates against the Confederacy* (Westport, CT: Praeger, 2002), 20–21; Quigley 54.

44. Regarding the knotty issue of who in the slave states voted for the secessionist Breckenridge or the Unionist Bell, see, for example, Schultz 162–63, 196–99; Seymour Martin Lipset, *Political Man*, rev. ed. (Baltimore: Johns Hopkins University Press, 1981), 373–84. Yeoman farmers and poor "sandhillers" of the middle of the state exercised their traditional commitment to the Democratic Party by voting for Breckinridge (and not Douglas). See, for example, William Montgomery in *Wheeling (VA) Daily Intelligencer* (4/24/1861) 1; W. E. Smith, *The Francis Preston Blair Family in Politics* (New York: Macmillan, 1933), 1:469–73; T. Barnes 2:259–60; Margaret Storey, "Civil War Unionists and the Political Culture of Loyalty in Alabama, 1860–1861," *J. South. Hist.* 69/1:71, 83–84 (2/2003); Forrest McDonald, *States' Rights and the Union* (Lawrence: University Press of Kansas, 2000), 187–89; McClintock (2008) 31–38; Denton (2009) 20–21; W. T. Sherman/John Sherman (6/1/1860), Thorndike 83, 84; Stephens (11/14/1860), Stephens (1866) 694, 696; J. T. Headley, *The Great Rebellion* (Hartford, CT, 1863–1866), 1:38–39; Nevins (1950) 2:224; Freehling (2007) 338–39; Potter (1976) 167–70, 502–4. See also Victor 135–36; Herndon (2016) 369; Seward/C. F. Adams Jr. (4/10/1861), *Foreign Relations* 71, 72; Faulkner 3–4; Mark A. Graber, *"Dred Scott" and the Problem of Constitutional Evil* (New York: Cambridge University Press, 2006), 159–71; R. W. Fogel, *Without Consent or Contract* (New York: Cambridge University Press, 1989), 381–87; Peter Knupfer, "James Buchanan, the Election of 1860, and the Demise of Jacksonian Politics," Birkner 146. But see Wooster (1962) 20.

45. S. Pryor (1909) 153–55; C. K. Rogers/Emeline Rogers Divver (1/6/1861), Abbott and Puryear 19. See also P. Klein 375; Furgurson 17–18.

46. "South Carolina Protest," *Register* (20/2) 53 (2/10/1829); [John C. Calhoun], *Exposition and Protest* (12/19/1828) (Columbia, SC, 1829).

47. *Register* (21/1) 78–79 (1/27/1830).

48. Proclamation (12/10/1832), Richardson (1897–1903) 2:640, 650; Parton 3:284–85, 465–69; Act of 3/2/1833, ch. 55 § [1], 4 Stat. 629.

49. Jackson/Cass (10/29/1832), Jackson 4:483; Jackson/Cass (12/17/1832), id. 4:502; Curtis 2:399; Klunder 77–80.

50. Buchanan/Cass (12/15/1860), Buchanan (1908–1911) 11:60; Nicolay and Hay (1917) 2:392–93; Curtis 2:397–401; Buchanan quoted in Lawrence A. Gobright, *Recollection of Men and Things at Washington* (Washington, 1869), 248; Victor 79–80; Klunder 304–8; George C. Gorham, *Life and Public Services of Edwin M. Stanton* (Boston, 1899), 1:115. Cass apparently attempted to rescind his resignation, but Buchanan refused his readmission. Buchanan memorandum (12/17/1860), Buchanan (1908–1911) 11:67; Curtis 2:399–400; P. Klein 372.

51. *Newbury (VT) Aurora of the Valley* (12/22/1860) 2; Cass quoted in Benson John Lossing, *Pictorial History of the Civil War in the United States* (Philadelphia, 1866–1868), 1:141. See also Frank B. Woodford, *Lewis Cass* (New Brunswick, NJ: Rutgers University Press, 1950), 323–30.

52. S. Pryor (1904) 113. See also Joan E. Cashin, *First Lady of the Confederacy* (Cambridge, MA: Belknap Press of Harvard University Press, 2006), 92–95.

53. D. Porter (1885) 9; *Porter Journal* 42–47. See also Welles (1960) 2:255–56; Richard S. West Jr., *The Second Admiral: A Life of David Dixon Porter 1813–1891* (New York: Coward-McCann, 1937), 72. Varina Davis's own two-volume biography of her husband does not mention the episode.

54. Louisa Rodgers Meigs/Montgomery C. Meigs (1/3/1861), *Meigs Papers* Reel 7, Lib. Cong.

55. Oliver Wendell Holmes, "Brother Jonathan's Lament for Sister Caroline," *Complete Poetical Works of Oliver Wendell Holmes* (1887; Boston: Houghton Mifflin, 1910), 153; Herman Melville, "Misgivings" (1860), *Battle-Pieces and Aspects of the War* (New York, 1866), 13. See also Howard R. Floan, *The South in Northern Eyes* (Austin: University of Texas Press, 1958).

56. *Harper's* 5/28:544 (9/1852); Blaine 1:101–6; "The Political Parties of the Day" (10/21/1856), W. Seward (1884–1890) 4:276, 280–81; *"The Dangers of Extending Slavery"* [10/12/1855] *and "The Contest and the Crisis"* [10/19/1855]: *Two Speeches of William H. Seward* ([Washington?], [1856?]); A. G. Riddle, *Life of Benjamin F. Wade* (Cleveland, OH, 1886), 188; Holt (1999) 263, 730–55; Robert F. Dalzell Jr., *Daniel Webster and the Trial of American Nationalism 1843–1852* (Boston: Houghton Mifflin, 1973), 247–88; Mitchell 94–98; Rothschild 122.

57. *Globe* (35/1) 939, 941 (3/3/1858); Ratner and Teeter 50–59; Richard W. Sewell, *House Divided: Sectionalism and Civil War, 1848–1865* (Baltimore: Johns Hopkins University Press, 1988), 56–62; Freehling (2007) 109–22; Fehrenbacher (1978) 312–15, 473–74; James F. Simon, *Lincoln and Chief Justice Taney* (New York: Simon & Schuster, 2006), 155–56; Harold M. Hyman and William M. Wiecek, *Equal Justice under Law* (New York: Harper & Row, 1982), 178–79. All but the two dissenters were Democrats. Substantive contacts between Buchanan and two of the justices before the opinion was written, published by Buchanan to show that the decision did *not* derive from improper pressure applied by him, are in Buchanan (1908–1911), 10:106–8n. See also Varon 566–67; Nevins (1950), 1:91, 108–12; J. McPherson (1988) 173, 178–79; Daniel Farber, *Lincoln's Constitution* (Chicago: University of Chicago Press, 2003), 10; Beard and Beard 17–19.

58. "The Irrepressible Conflict" (10/25/1858), *New-York Daily Tribune* (11/9/1858) 6. See also W. Smith 1:428; Holt (1999) 983; M. L. Wilson, "The Repressible Conflict: Seward's Concept of Progress and the Free-Soil Movement," *J. South. Hist.* 37/4:533 (11/1971); Robert Oliver, "William H. Seward on the 'Irrepressible Conflict,'" in *Antislavery and Disunion, 1858–1861,* ed. Jeffery J. Auer (New York: Harper & Row, 1963), 29; Sumner 6:188. Two years earlier, Seward had spoken of "an ancient and eternal conflict between two entirely antagonistic systems of human labor . . . as old as the republic itself, although it has never ripened before." "The Political Parties of the Day" (10/21/1856), W. Seward (1884–1890) 4:276, 279.

59. *Memphis Daily Appeal* (11/19/1858) 2; id. (11/11/1858) 2; John Wise, *End of an Era* (Boston, 1899), 116–17. See also James Scovel, "Personal Recollections of Abraham Lincoln," *Lippincott's Monthly Mag.* 44/2:244, 247n (8/1889); J. H. Adams (1856), *London Quart. Rev.* 101/202:178, 192 (4/1857); Lincoln speech in Chicago (7/10/1858), Basler et al. 2:484, 491. Lincoln repeated the idea in his debates with Douglas.

60. Piatt 31.

61. "Presidential Candidates and Aspirants," *De Bow's Rev.* 19/1:92, 102 (7/1860); Nevins (1950) 1:412–13.

62. John Underwood of upstate New York formed a company to help Northern farmers immigrate to northwest Virginia where, by yeoman-like example and discussion with locals, they might lead the Commonwealth to free-soil status. Several hundred families moved to the first enclave, Ceredo on the Ohio River, but in short order locals' reaction to Brown's raid drove them out. Patricia Hickin, "John C. Underwood and the Antislavery Movement in Virginia, 1847–1860," *Virginia Mag. of Hist. & Biog.* 73/2:156 (4/1965). See also W. C. Davis 77; Hammond/R. F. Simpson (11/22/1860), *Hammond Papers* Reel 15.

63. (12/3/1859), Basler et al. 3:497, 502.

64. See, for example, Mitchell 117–21; Henry David Thoreau, "Plea for Captain John Brown" (1859), *Writings of Henry David Thoreau* (Boston, 1893), 10:197; Ashworth 2:126; Schultz 190–92; Barney (1972) 121–22; Gregory Eiselein, *Literature and Humanitarian Reform in the Civil War Era* (Bloomington: Indiana University Press, 1996), 17–48.

65. Constance Cary Harrison, *Recollections Grave and Gay* (1911; New York: C. Scribner's Sons, 1912), 42.

66. *Rise and Progress of the Bloody Outbreak at Harper's Ferry* ([New York?], [1859?]), 4–8; Trefousse 129–30. Seward, Lincoln, and other Republicans publicly criticized Brown's raid and considered it highly destructive of Unionist feeling, and the Republican platform included a strong anti-Brown comment. Yet not even a congressional investigation would quell Southern conspiracy charges. See, for example, P. Klein 335–37; Freehling (2007) 208–21; Donald Reynolds, *Texas Terror: The Slave Insurrection Panic* (Baton Rouge: Louisiana State University Press, 2007), 116; G. Van Deusen (1947) 243–44; Abrahamson 3–16; Nevins (1950) 2:104–12; G. G. Glover, *Immediate Pre–Civil War Compromise Efforts* (Nashville, TN: George Peabody College for Teachers, 1934), 9–10; Fredrickson 42–50.

67. See, for example, *Southern Argus* (12/26/1837) 1; *Vermont Telegraph* 38 (11/29/1837).

68. Brisbane/Schurz (2/7/1859), William Henry Brisbane Papers Reel 2, *Wisconsin State Hist. Soc.* See also Gienapp (1987) 191.

69. *Globe* (36/1) 910, 912–13 (2/29/1860); Nevins (1950) 2:181–83.

70. See Abraham Oakey Hall, *Horace Greeley Decently Dissected* (New York, 1862), 34–36; Guelzo 34.

71. See, for example, Hendrick 28; G. Van Deusen (1947) 243; Henry Hall, *History of Auburn* (Auburn, NY, 1869), 533. Weed assured the public that the purpose of Seward's European trip had not been to secure the blessing of British abolitionists.

72. [Edmund Ruffin], *Anticipations of the Future, to Serve as Lessons for the Present Time* (Richmond, VA, 1860), viii–ix. See also Allen E. Buchanan, *Secession* (Boulder, CO: Westview, 1991), 99.

73. Colfax/Hannah Matthews (1/15/1860), O. J. Hollister, *Life of Schuyler Colfax* (New York, 1886), 151n1. See also Francis Lieber/G. S. Hillard (10/23/1856), Lieber 290.

74. Piatt 30; Bridges 40–44; C. G. Miller, *Donn Piatt* (Cincinnati, OH, 1893), 136.

75. See, for example, *Globe* (36/1) 1301 (3/22/1860); Richard Edwards/Andrew Johnson (2/11/1861), A. Johnson 4:271; Robertson 11.

76. H. Adams (1910) 676.

77. See, for example, T. Barnes 2:307–9; Crofts (1989) 217–21; Crofts (1979); Duberman 252–55. See also Williams C. Wickham/Scott (3/11/1861), *Lincoln Papers*.

78. (5/20/1860), James S. Pike, *First Blows of the Civil War* (New York, 1879), 515, 517; Halstead 140–41. See also *Memoirs of Gustave Koerner 1809–1896*, ed. Thomas McCormack (Cedar Rapids, IA: Torch, 1909), 2:85; Julian 178–80; Welles (1959–1960) 2:17–18; Welles (1925) 19; R. White 322–29; Hearn (2010) 9–18.

79. Blaine/W. P. Fessenden (5/16/1860), Francis Fessenden, *Life and Public Services of William Pitt Fessenden* (Boston: Houghton Mifflin, 1907), 1:112; Halstead 123, 129, 132, 141–42. See also T. Barnes 2:261–73; Green 52–62; Egerton 136–43; Brown 188–90.

80. Greeley contributed substantially to Republican success in the 1856 elections by publishing a documentary history of the Kansas question: *History of the Struggle for Slavery Extension or Restriction in the United States* (New York, 1856). See also Mitchell 101–2. Regarding Weed, see, for example, Nichols 2:211–21.

81. "Welles, Gideon. Diary (extracts) 1860–62" Folder, p. 2, *Nicolay Papers*; Charles A. Dana, *Recollections of the Civil War* (1898; New York: D. Appleton, 1913), 3–4. See also Goodwin 80, 215–16, 241–42.

82. (2/27/1860), Basler et al. 3:522.

83. L. E. Chittenden, *Personal Reminiscences 1840–1890* (New York, 1893), 382; Guelzo 122–24; Nevins (1950) 2:185–88.

84. Halstead 122. See also *Three against Lincoln*, ed. William B. Hesseltine (Baton Rouge: Louisiana State University Press, 1960). Greeley's influence was so strong that some incorrectly thought he had "sprung" Lincoln on the convention. See, for example, Charles Godfrey Leland, *Memoirs* (New York, 1893), 236–37.

85. See, for example, Lothrop 194–97; Green 21; W. Smith 1:481–86, 501, 505; Catton and Catton 221–24; Denton (2009) 19–20; Denton (2014) 43; Greeley (1893) 34; Herndon and Weik 3:471; Crofts (1989) 216; J. M. Forbes/Nassau William Senior (6/18/1860), Forbes 1:183; Isaac Hill Bromley, "What Caused the Defeat of Mr. Seward," R. Wilson 275, 279–80; Leonard Swett/Joseph H. Drummond (5/27/1860), id. 292; Carl Schurz, *Reminiscences of Carl Schurz* (New York: McClure, 1907), 2:176–86, 211–12; James A.

Hamilton, *Reminiscences of James A. Hamilton* (New York, 1869), 453; Ratner and Teeter 85; Huston 241–44; E. Foner (1970) 210–15.

86. Halstead 142, 145–52; *The American* 4/112:391 (9/30/1882); Henry Wilson (1872–1877) 2:692; Julian 177; Hearn (2010) 4. See also Blaine 1:165–69; H. White 102–7; J. Sherman 199–202; Nevins (1950) 2:4, 52, 176–77; W. Smith 1:472–73; Holt (1978) 215–16; Denton (2009) 11–20; Isaac Hill Bromley, "What Caused the Defeat of Mr. Seward," R. Wilson 275, 289; Nevins (1950) 2:234–35, 248–50; G. Van Deusen (1947) 251–52; Reid 220–28; J. McPherson (1988) 215–21.

87. Charles Francis Adams Sr., *Address on the Life, Character and Services of William Henry Seward* (Albany, NY, 1873), 22–23. See also (3/31/1861), C. F. Adams Sr.

88. *Political Debates between Hon. Abraham Lincoln and Hon. Stephen A. Douglas* (Columbus, OH, 1860). An exception to the Southern blackout was the Republican *Daily Intelligencer* of Wheeling, Virginia (3/3/1860) 1.

89. Speech in Bowdoin Square, Boston (8/14/1860), *Appleton* 450. Further,

> For the first time in the history of the republic the slave power has not . . . the power to terrify or alarm the freeman so as to make him submit . . . and compromise. It rails now with a feeble voice, as it thundered in our ears for twenty or thirty years past. With a feeble and muttering voice they cry out that they will tear the Union to pieces. (Derisive laughter.) Who's afraid? (Laughter and cries of "No one!") They complain that if we will not surrender our principles, and our system and our right—being a majority—to rule, and if we will not accept their system, and such rules as they will give us, they will go out of the Union. Who's afraid? (Laughter.) Nobody's afraid. . . .

Minnesota (9/18/1860), *The Campaign of 1860* (Albany, NY, 1860), 9, 15 (emphasis omitted).

90. *Globe* (31/1) App. 260, 263–65, 268 (3/11/1850) (Seward). See, for example, *Keowee Courier* [Pickens Court House, SC] (9/8/1860) 1; *Nashville Patriot* (8/23/1860) 2. See also "The Doctrine of the 'Higher Law,'" *South. Lit. Messenger* 17/3:130 (3/1851); William Hosmer, *The Higher Law* (Auburn, NY, 1852), 176.

91. (11/5/1860), H. King (1872) 404. See also Guelzo 107–12.

92. See, for example, [William D. Porter], Tract No. 2, *Mr. Douglas and the Doctrine of Coercion* (n.p., [after 8/25/1860]) 18; Clingman quoted in Clement A. Evans, "Civil History of the Confederate States," Evans 1:247, 332. Senator Trusten Polk (D/MO) claimed that Lincoln "was the first man of his party to enunciate the dogma that there is an irrepressible conflict." *Globe* (36/2) 356 (1/14/1861).

93. Seward, Huger wrote, "had caused infinite pain by his continued assault . . . upon our property. . . . I, born in the Union, but before the Constitution, am fated to outlive these noble institutions! What have I done to Mr. Seward, to sanction what he is now doing to me?" Huger/Holt (11/27/1860), *Holt Papers* 26:3447, 3447a. See also Ollinger Crenshaw, *The Slave States in the Presidential Election of 1860* (Baltimore: Johns Hopkins University Press, 1945), 106. Huger was born in 1788, after the Constitution was drafted but before it was ratified.

94. Cobb (12/6/1860), Phillips 505–10. Some would find a certain allusive wit in applying "Black" to "Republican" since another despised movement, socialism, had been led by the *Red Republican*, a British magazine whose publishing credits included *The Communist Manifesto*. It was "no great mistake"—a Columbia, South Carolina, newspaper opined—to think "Black Republicans are negroes," since "they love each other desperately." *Southern Daily Guardian* quoted in *Daily Federal Union* [Milledgeville, GA] (12/2/1860) 2. See also Pollard (1862) 34–35; *Abraham Lincoln's Record on the Slavery Question* (Baltimore, [1860]); *Speech of Hon. Roger A. Pryor of Virginia, on the Principles and Policies of the Black Republican Party* (Washington, DC, 1859).

95. Gilmer/Lincoln (12/10/1860), *Lincoln Papers*; Corwin/Lincoln (12/19/1860), id.; Campbell (1874) 28; Stephens/Lincoln (12/30/1861), Stephens (1866) 151, 153. In 1862, a proslavery Kentuckian, presenting the Southern case to the British, wrote that Lincoln could have avoided secession if only he had said that he would do what he could to preserve the Union, that he would faithfully execute the Fugitive Slave Act of 1850, and that he would abide by the Constitution and federal laws as interpreted by the Supreme Court. Shaffner 408. Lincoln in fact had repeatedly said all these things, even that he would abide by *Dred Scott* while working for its eventual reversal. See, for example, Basler et al. 2:398, 401, 403, 3:522, 543–46.

96. See, for example, Bryant/Lincoln (6/16/1860), *Lincoln Papers*; Welles/Lincoln (12/10/1860), Welles (1925) 7; Welles (1924) 71; Lightner 149–56.

97. In a "For your eyes only" letter to Alexander Stephens, Lincoln wrote, "Do the people of the South really entertain fears that a Republican Administration would, *directly, or indirectly*, interfere with their slaves . . . ? If they do, I wish to assure you . . . that there is no cause for such fears." Lincoln/Stephens (12/22/1860), Basler et al. 4:160. See also Inaugural (3/4/1861), id. 4:262, 265–70; Crofts (1989) 215–53; Weed 1:615.

98. Lincoln/George Prentice (10/29/1860), Basler et al. 4:134, 135; Charles Maltby, *The Life and Public Services of Abraham Lincoln* (Stockton, CA, 1884), 163. Even the committed abolitionist senator Charles Sumner (R/MA) denied that the Constitution allowed the federal government to interfere with slavery in the states. Sumner/A. P. Brooks (9/9/1860), *Works of Charles Sumner* (Boston, 1874), 5:269.

99. See, for example, Hendrick 132–35; Daniel Crofts, "Secession Winter: William Henry Seward and the Decision for War," *NY Hist.* 65/3:229, 238 (7/1984); Mark J. Stegmaier annot., H. Adams (2012) 93n6; W. Cooper (2012) 67; Nevins (1950) 2:393–94.

100. T. Barnes 2:308.

101. Lincoln/Seward (12/8/1860), Basler et al. 4:148; Bates (12/16/1860), Bates 164–65; Hearn (2010) 27–28. See also (12/31/1860), id. 171; Hendrick 111–12; Chase/J. T. Trowbridge (3/19/1864), Warden 364–65.

102. Toombs 1880 interview, F. Seward (1891) 486; Kirwan 378–82; Duberman 233–35; Trefousse 144. See also (1/2/1861), C. F. Adams Sr.; R. White 360–61; Holt (1999) 983–84; Hearn (2010) 28–29; Stephenson 112–15. The Committee of Thirteen abandoned its deliberations after December 31. Clement A. Evans, "Civil History of the Confederate States," Evans 1:247, 346. See also William J. Cooper Jr., "The Critical Signpost on the Journey toward Secession," *J. South. Hist.* 77/1:3, 9–11 (2/2011); Gamaliel Bradford Jr., "Robert Toombs: A Confederate Portrait," *Atlantic* 112:208 (8/1913).

103. E. McPherson 37; Ulrich B. Phillips, *Life of Robert Toombs* (New York: Macmillan, 1913), 205.

104. Quoted in Bancroft (1900) 2:8.

105. Act of 3/6/1820, ch. 22 § 8, 3 Stat. 545, 548; *Annals* (16/1) 427 (2/17/1820). See also Act of 3/3/1820, ch. 19, 3 Stat. 544. The Missouri Compromise was impliedly repealed by the package of legislation collectively known as the Compromise of 1850. Act of 9/9/1850, ch. 49, 9 Stat. 446; Act of 9/9/1850, ch. 50, 9 Stat. 452; Act of 9/9/1850, ch. 51, 9 Stat. 453; Act of 9/16/1850, ch. 60, 9 Stat. 462; Act of 9/20/1850, ch. 63, 9 Stat. 467. It was then expressly repealed in the Kansas-Nebraska Act. Act of 5/30/1854, ch. 59 §§ 14, 19, 32, 10 Stat. 277, 282–84, 289. Two years later, the Supreme Court in *Dred Scott* declared the Missouri Compromise void in its inception because in its view the Constitution gave Congress no authority over slavery in U.S. territories. Scott v. Sandford, 60 U.S. (19 How.) 393, 455, 487–91, 528–29 (1857). Senator Crittenden proposed to overturn that ruling by reintroducing the Missouri Compromise not as a mere statute but as a constitutional amendment. See, for example, *Sen. J.* (36/2) 49 (12/18/1860); *Globe* (36/2) 114 (12/18/1860); Sen. Committee Rpts. No. 288 (36/2) (12/31/1860) 3; Crittenden 2:233, 377.

106. Seward/Lincoln (12/26/1860), *Lincoln Papers*. Two years before, William Yancey of Alabama had told Virginia's Roger Pryor that a confederacy of cotton states would benefit if the Upper South remained in the Union, because it would provide a long buffer zone against abolitionism. Then, if secession prospered, "in time Virginia, and the other border States that desired it, could join the southern confederacy, and be protected by the power of its arms and its diplomacy." (Ca. Aug. 1858), *Non-Interference by Congress with Slavery in the Territories: Speech of Hon. S. A. Douglas of Illinois, in the Senate, May 15 and 16, 1860* (n.p., n.d.), 26.

107. *Globe* (36/2) 341, 343 (1/12/1861). See also Reid 257. The Constitution is silent on the issue of secession, a silence having led some to assert that it did not allow an unconsented withdrawal, others to say that the Constitution is a confederation created by sovereign states from which any could withdraw, and still others to maintain that withdrawal is an intrinsic right of any government by consent. Compare Senator Daniel Webster (Anti-Jacksonian/MA) in his debate with Senator Robert Young Hayne (Jacksonian/SC), *Register* (21/1) 80 (1/27/1830) with William Rawle, *View of the Constitution of the United States of America* (Philadelphia, 1825), 289–92.

108. *Globe* (36/2) 657 (1/31/1861). See also (1/25/1861), C. F. Adams Sr.; P. Foner 253.

109. See, for example, Seward/Lincoln (12/28/1860), *Seward Papers* Reel 60; Hendrick 136–37; Burlingame (2008) 1:720–22; Goodwin 285; Foreman 65. As additional cotton states seceded, Seward became convinced, as he told Lincoln, that "every thought that we think ought to be conciliatory[,] forbearing and patient." Seward/Lincoln (1/27/1861), *Lincoln Papers*.

110. Schurz/Margarethe Schurz (2/4/1861), *Intimate Letters of Carl Schurz 1841–1869*, trans. and ed. Joseph Schafer (Madison: State Historical Society of Wisconsin, 1928), 242, 243. See also G. Van Deusen (1967) 242–43; Hans L. Trefousse, *Carl Schurz: A Biography* (Knoxville: University of Tennessee Press, 1982).

111. W. H. Seward/Frances Seward (1/18/1861), F. Seward (1891) 496, 497 (emphasis deleted).

112. Corwin/Lincoln (1/16/1861), *Lincoln Papers.* See also (1/11, 12, 14/1861), C. F. Adams Sr.

113. Act of 9/18/1850, ch. 60, 9 Stat. 462.

114. *Globe* (31/1) App. 260, 263–65, 268 (3/11/1850). Although Seward had professed to hate the statute, when the opportunity came to cut off funding for its enforcement, he absented himself. *Globe* (32/1) App. 1102–1125 (8/26/1852).

115. See, for example, Francis Fessenden, *Life and Public Services of William Pitt Fessenden* (Boston: Houghton Mifflin, 1907), 1:121–22; Chase/Seward (1/10/1861), *Seward Papers* Reel 61; Hearn (2010) 33–38; Rothschild 157–222; Sumner/J. M. Forbes (1/13/1861), Forbes 1:186; Trefousse 152–53. See also David H. Donald, *Charles Sumner and the Coming of the Civil War* (New York: Knopf, 1960), 372–77; Elizabeth Blair Lee/Samuel Phillips Lee (1/17/1861), E. Lee 24, 25. Henry Adams would say that Seward and Sumner "would have disliked each other by instinct had they lived in different planets." H. Adams (1918), 102. See also Henry Adams/*Boston Daily Advertiser* (1/13/1861), H. Adams (2012) 107 and nn1–12; W. S. Thayer/J. C. Bancroft Davis (1/6/1861), Thayer 238; (1/15/1861), C. F. Adams Sr. See also Lincoln/Seward (1/19/1861), Basler et al. 4:176; McClintock (2008) 89–92, 166–67; Holzer 192–94; Crofts (1989) 217–19, 236. Cf. Bancroft (1894) 607–8.

116. Wade quoted in Ashley 4; Garrison, *Liberator* (3/16/1860) 2; id. (1/18/1861) 2; *Atlantic Monthly* 6:492, 499 (10/1860).

117. "To William H. Seward" (1861), *Complete Poetical Works of Whittier* (Boston, 1894), 332. See also H. Adams (1910) 685; Stahr 223–26.

Chapter 2: "A Standing Menace"

1. Russell (1863) 1:145; White/Philip F. Thomas (1/2/1861), "Seizure of Forts, Arsenals, Revenue Cutters, and Other Property of the United States" 81, *Select Committee Reports*; Ivan D. Steen, "Charleston in the 1850's," *S.C. Hist. Mag.* 71/1:36, 38–39 (1/1970); Whitelaw Reid, *After the War: A Southern Tour* (New York, 1866), 58.

2. Magrath/Colcock (1/29/1861), *Correspondence with the Collector* (Charleston, 1861), 8–10; Brauer 141–42, 147; Thomas Sergeant, *Constitutional Law* (Philadelphia, 1822), 325. Cf. C. F. Adams Jr. (1915) 202–3; Lyons/Russell (3/26/1861), id. 219, 220, 222.

3. Henry Raymond of the *New York Times* wrote that because federal statutes were the "supreme Law of the Land," customs laws triggered debts to the federal government by individual importers, regardless of whether their goods arrived in a state that had purported to secede from the Union. *NYT* (12/13/1860) 1, 2.

4. See (11/20/1860), *Att'y-Gen. Ops.* 9:517, 522–26 (Black); *Globe* (36/2) 134 (12/19/1860) (Johnson); *Globe* (37/4) 1457–59 (3/15/1861) (Senator Douglas).

5. See, for example, Welles (1959–1960) 2:43; Victor 167. See also Stahr 263–65.

6. See Richard Hofstadter, "The Tariff Issue on the Eve of the Civil War," *Am. Hist. Rev.* 44/1:50 (10/1938); Dabney 454–55; *Galveston (TX) Civilian and Gazette* (1/15/1861) 2; Nevins (1950) 1:197–98, 219–28; Ashworth 2:104–5.

7. See, for example, Rhett 36; *Globe* (37/4) 1440 (3/7/1861) (Sen. L. T. Wigfall).

8. See, for example, Rep. John Cochrane (D/NY), "Further Provision for Collection of Duties on Imports," Rpt. no. 59 (1/30/1861), *Select Committee Reports*; P. Foner 300–302; Brauer 147.

9. Madison/Mathew Carey (7/27/1831), https://founders.archives.gov/documents/Madison/99-02-02-2411.

10. *Seventh Annual Message* (12/5/1815), Richardson (1897–1903) 1:562, 566.

11. See, for example, Bernard et al./Calhoun (2/7/1821), *Am. State Papers* (Military) 2:305–13; M. A. Smith 6, 31–65; J. Moore (1981A) 5–15; W. H. Carter, "Bvt. Maj. Gen. Simon Bernard," *Professional Memoirs, Corps of Engineers* 5:21:306 (5/6/1913); Forest Hill, *Roads, Rails & Waterways* (Norman: University of Oklahoma Press, 1957), 6–15. Regarding Totten's significant role in planning and building fortifications, see Todd A. Shallat, "American Gibraltars," *Army History* (Winter 2008): 5, 13–15; David A. Clary, *Fortress America: The Corps of Engineers, Hampton Roads, and United States Coastal Defense* (Charlottesville: University Press of Virginia, 1990), 38–43; R. Browning 28–31; J. Moore (1981B) 14–16; Lewis.

12. See *Am. State Papers* (Military Affairs) 2:304–14; Totten (1851) 96–108; Totten/C. M. Conrad (11/1/1851), H.R., Exec. Doc. No. 5 (32/1) 42; M. A. Smith; J. Moore (1981A); J. Van Deusen 107–12; S. J. Watson, "Knowledge, Interest and the Limits of Military Professionalism," *War in History* 5/3:280, 284–85 (7/1998); Skelton 168–69, 292–93; Weaver 137; Lewis 37–66; R. Browning 3, 24–40; Robinson 85–129.

13. See, for example, J. Moore (1981A) 4; M. A. Smith 47, 125–32; Bernardo and Bacon 148–51; H. Wager Halleck, "Report on the Means of National Defence" (10/20/1843), Sen. Ex. Doc. 85 (28/2) 2, 7–10; Huntington 164–70, 193–226; Meneely 14–27.

14. See J. G. Totten et al., "Report on the Defence of the Atlantic Frontier" (5/10/1840), U.S. Cong., H.R. Ex. Doc. 92 (37/2) 81; Joel Poinsett/R. M. T. Hunter (5/12/1840), id. 78; Totten/Charles Gratiot (3/22/1836), id. 22, 23, 39; Lewis Cass/Andrew Jackson (4/7/1836), id. 2; "Memorial of Edmund P. Gaines" (12/31/1839), id. 173; [Alexander J. Swift], "Fleets versus Forts," *U.S. Mag. and Dem. Rev.* n.s. 13:577 (12/1843); J. G. Barnard, "Harbor Defence by Fortifications and Steam-Vessels," *South. Lit. Messenger* 11:25 (1/1845); Halleck 70, 155–209; Edmund Hunt, "Army Attack and National Defence," *Am. [Whig] Rev.* 4/2:146, 154–56 (8/1846). See also J. A. Dahlgren/C. M. Conrad (9/1851), U.S. Cong., H.R. Ex. Doc. 92 (37/2) 364; Report of S. F. Dupont (undated), id. 321; Totten/Conrad (11/1/1851), id. 232, 253–54, 289–90; Sen. Exec. Doc. 59 (36/1), Richard Delafield, "Report on the Art of War in Europe in 1854, 1855, and 1856" (6/16/1860) 18–51; John Scoffern, *Projectile Weapons of War and Explosive Compounds*, 4th ed. (London, 1859), 206–64; Bernardo and Bacon 162–63; M. A. Smith 179–99; Skelton 244–46; Paullin 205–76.

15. See, for example, Totten et al., "Report on the Defence of the Atlantic Frontier" (4/24/1840), "Permanent Fortifications and Sea-Coast Defences," H.R. Rep. no. 86 (37/2) 142, 143 (4/23/1862); *Assessment* III.01-2.

16. See, for example, M. A. Smith 162–68.

17. *General Regulations* 13; C. M. Conrad/Linn Boyd (12/11/1851), H.R., Exec. Doc. No. 5 (32/1) 20; Lewis 25–36.

18. Id. 20, 24–25; F. J. Porter/Cooper (11/11/1860), *OR* 1/1:70–72; Chester 50; Crawford (1887) 2; Crawford (1896) 2; Ryan 74; *Charleston Yearbook* 472–88; R. E. De Russy/John B. Floyd (11/8/1859), Sen. Ex. Doc. no. 2 (36/1) 392, 404–5.

19. Capt. A. H. Bowman (1/21/1842), Bache et al. 25–26; F. J. Porter/Col. Samuel Cooper (11/11/1860), *OR* 1/1:70; *HABS* 18; *Ordnance Manual* 34–35, 63–65, 387–88; Ryan 97n1; Gordon 3; Soady 165–66; *Field Manual for the Use of the Officers on Ordnance Duty*

(Richmond, VA 1862), 9–10; Lewis 33n35. Cf. Guernsey and Alden 33. Most smooth-bore guns were described not by bore diameter but by the weight of solid iron shot they fired, even if they also fired lighter projectiles: shells, canister shot, spherical case shot, and grapeshot. Hazlett, Olmstead, and Parks 23–24; Roberts 89–101; *Ordnance Manual*. See also Konstam 33–34. Totten conducted a thorough examination of the comparative effects on walls and embrasures of a forty-two-pound cannon using different charges of powder when firing: (1) a solid ball of forty-two pounds, versus (2) a canister containing twenty-seven larger to eighty-six smaller pellets weighing, with the canister, a collective forty-eight pounds; (3) spherical case shot, composed of 306 musket balls weighing, with the case, a collective thirty-nine pounds; and (4) grape, weighing 4.2 pounds per shot, a collective "stand" of nine comprising 51¼ pounds. Totten (1857) 44–167.

20. Totten had first noted this in his report of 1826. Although the concern was repeated verbatim in his reports of 1836, 1840, and 1851, apparently neither he nor the incumbent secretaries of war nor the House of Representatives considered it a priority. H.R. Rpt. no. 86: "Permanent Fortifications and Sea-Coast Defences" (37/2) 43, 101, 142, 193, 404 (4/23/1862).

21. [De Forest] 499; Crawford (1887) 63–64, 69–71; Crawford (1896) 5–6; Anderson/ Robert N. Gourdin (12/27/1860), id. 128. See also Anderson/Gourdin (12/29/1860), id. 129, 130; Hyde 15; H. Scott 284–99.

22. Alexander Macomb/J. P. Zanzinger (10/29/1832), *Register* (22/2) App. 198; Jackson/ Lewis Cass (10/29/1832), Jackson 4:483; Jackson/John Coffee (12/14/1832) id. 4:499, 500; William R. Nester, *The Age of Jackson* (Dulles, VA: Potomac Books, 2013), 126. Jackson's secretary of war, Lewis Cass of Michigan, a former army brigadier general, told Scott to "examine every thing connected with the fortifications" in Charleston Harbor and to use his discretion "to take such measures, either by strengthening these defences, or by reinforcing these garrisons with troops drawn from any other posts, as you may think prudence and just precaution require." Cass/Scott (11/18/1832), *Register* (22/2) App. 199. See also Peskin 86–87, 233–34; Elliott 275–85; M. Wright 66–67; Eisenhower 135–40.

23. (12/14/1832), W. Scott (1864) 1:239, 242; Mansfield 254; F. Moore (1862) 6, 9.

24. *Admiral Farragut* (New York, 1892), 73.

25. See, for example, W. Scott (1864) 1:512–57; Philip M. Hamer, *The Secession Movement in South Carolina, 1847–1852* (Allentown, PA: H. R. Haas, 1918), 54–56; Holt (1999) 101.

26. Scott would later pose this scenario as one of the unattractive alternatives available to Lincoln's new administration. Scott/Seward (3/3/1861), *Lincoln Papers*. See also Crofts (1977–1978) 362–66; *Mag. of Am. Hist.* 8/10:702 (10/1882).

27. This was later recounted in Huger/William Ravenel (6/24/1865), *Ravenel Papers*. The correspondence between Petigru and Scott is neither in the *Petigru Papers* nor in Winfield Scott's papers at the University of Michigan.

28. Ulysses Doubleday/Lincoln (9/29/1860), *Lincoln Papers*. See also Abner Doubleday/ Ulysses Doubleday (9/25/1860), Ulysses Doubleday/John G. Nicolay (11/18/1860), *Lincoln Papers*; *Auburn Citizen-Advertiser* (7/23/1964) 8; Detzer 38–41; Thomas Barthel, *Abner Doubleday: A Civil War Biography* (Jefferson, NC: McFarland, 2010), 57–58.

29. Scott, "Views Suggested by the Imminent Danger" (10/29/1860), *Lincoln Papers*, Victor 80, F. Moore (1861–1866) 1:122. See also Scott (3/30/1861), W. Scott (1862) 3; Totten/ Joseph Holt (1/10/1861), *OR* 3/1:34; Simon Cameron, "Report of the Secretary of War"

(7/1/1861), F. Moore (1861–1866) 2:229–30; Nicolay and Hay (1917) 2:339–43; E. Townsend 7, 249; P. Klein 187, 355; Elliott 676–77. A number of writers and cartographers employed the phonetic spelling "Sumpter." In the present work, these have all been silently corrected.

30. Scott/Floyd (10/30/1860), *Lincoln Papers*; [Buchanan] (1866) 99–105.

31. (11/9/1860), "Private Diary of Secretary Floyd," Pollard (1867A) 792.

32. Scott/Crittenden (11/12/1860), Crittenden 1:219. In a diary entry for a meeting of Buchanan's cabinet just after Lincoln's election, Floyd had written, "I expressed myself decidedly opposed to any rash movement" by the Union against South Carolina, "and against the idea of secession at this time . . . because I think that Lincoln's Administration will fail, and be regarded as impotent for good or evil, within four months after his inauguration." (11/9/1860), "Private Diary of Secretary Floyd," Pollard (1867A) 793; Trescot (1908) 532.

33. Rhett/Buchanan (11/24/1860), Buchanan (1908–1911) 11:5. See also Lincoln (2/11/1861), Basler et al. 4:194, 195.

34. Buchanan quoted in William Henry Smith, *Political History of Slavery* (New York: G. P. Putnam's Sons, 1903), 1:318; *New-York Daily Tribune* (1/16/1861) 4.

35. See H. K. Craig/Floyd (10/31/1860), *OR* 1/1:67, 68; Col. John L. Gardner/Craig (11/5/1860), *OR* 1/1: 68; F. C. Humphreys/Craig (11/10/1860), *OR* 1/1:69; Trescot (1908) 533; Order (11/15/1860), *Anderson Papers* vol. 8; Detzer 16, 27–28, 54–61; Catton 141–42; Gordon 4–5; Doubleday (1876) 13–14; E. Cooper 27, 29–30; Abner Doubleday/Ulysses Doubleday (9/23/1860), (9/25/1860), *Lincoln Papers*; Keyes (10/15/1860), Keyes 370; Austin 237; McClintock (2008) 15–18, 62.

36. F. C. Humphreys/Craig (11/12/1860), *OR* 1/1:72.

37. Trescot (1908) 533. Having obtained the slaves by marrying a Georgian, Anderson claimed that at this time he liberated them. See the anonymous pencil introduction (by John G. Nicolay) to *Anderson Diary*. See also Detzer 24. In a variant account, Anderson sold the slaves, but the buyer refused to pay, asserting that a pro-Yankee Union officer deserved no recompense. For another view on Anderson's replacing Gardner, see Ulysses Doubleday/Nicolay (11/18/1860), *Lincoln Papers*.

38. Lieutenant Colonel Erasmus Darwin Keyes (10/15/1860), Keyes 370; Jefferson Davis/Anderson (1/20/1850), Lawton (1914) 128.

39. See, for example, Dawson 37–40; [Hurlbert] (1879) 484–85.

40. Anderson/Gourdin (12/11/1860), Crawford (1887) 69. See also Freehling (2007) 390–91, 399; *The Gourdin Family*, comp. Peter Gaillard Gourdin, IV (Easley, SC: Southern Historical Press, 1980); Chalmers Gaston Davidson, *The Last Foray* (Columbia: University of South Carolina Press, 1971), 63–65.

41. Anderson/Samuel Cooper (11/23/1860), *OR* 1/1:74, 75. See also Ulysses Doubleday/Nicolay (11/18/1860), *Lincoln Papers*.

42. Anderson/Cooper (11/28/1860), *OR* 1/1:78; Anderson/Cooper (12/1/1860), *OR* 1/1:81. See also E. L. Anderson, *Soldier and Pioneer: A Biographical Sketch of Lt.-Col. Richard C. Anderson* (New York, 1879); Woodford 259–60; Doubleday (1876) 14.

43. Scott/Buchanan (12/15/1860), *Lincoln Papers*.

44. Trescot (1908) 533–36.

45. Trescot/William H. Gist (11/26/1860), Crawford (1887) 30; Gist/Trescot (11/29/1860), id. 31; Trescot (1908) 535–36.

46. Cooper/Anderson (11/28/1860), *Anderson Papers* vol. 8; Austin 239.

47. Cooper/Anderson (12/1/1860), *Anderson Papers* vol. 8, *OR* 1/1:82.

48. Crawford (1887) 65; Anderson/Cooper (12/9/1860), *OR* 1/1:89; Catton 151.

49. Anderson/Cooper (12/6/1860), *OR* 1/1:87.

50. Doubleday (1876) 56.

51. Jackson quoted in Parton 3:284–85, Currie 3:106n93. See also Jackson/Joel Poinsett (12/9/1832), Jackson 4:497, 498.

52. John C. Ropes memorandum (2/8/1870) 5–7, Horatio Woodman Papers, Ms. N-492, *Mass. Hist. Soc.*

53. *Pulpit and Rostrum* nos. 15 and 16 (12/1/1860).

54. Guernsey and Alden 21.

55. (12/3/1860), Buchanan (1908–1911) 11:7, 12, 16–19; Buchanan/Black (11/17/1860), id. 11:20–21n1; Black (11/20/1860), *Att'y-Gen. Ops.* 9:517, 523–25. See also Black (9/10/1883), Gwin and Coleman (1892) 91–92; Curtis 2:319; Victor 66; Guernsey and Alden 27–28; [William D. Porter], Tract No. 2, *Mr. Douglas and the Doctrine of Coercion* (n.p., n.d.), 13–15; Christopher Collier and James Lincoln Collier, *Decision in Philadelphia* (New York: Random House/Reader's Digest, 1986), 190–91. While proclaiming that he would "submit to Congress the whole question in all its bearings," Buchanan implied that this would be useless because in his view Congress too lacked authority to coerce a state to remain in the Union. See Currie 4:238–39.

56. Madison, *Federalist* 14, 45, 46; Madison (5/31, 6/8/1787), Elliot 5:140, 171; Madison/Jefferson (10/24/1787), Madison 10:205; Madison/Trist (12/23/1832), http://founders. archives.gov/documents/Madison/99-02-02-2650; Hamilton, *Federalist* 16, 22, 28; Tocqueville, *Democracy in America*, rev. ed., trans. Henry Reeve (New York, 1898), 1:499, 500; Jackson (3/4/1837), Richardson (1897–1903) 3:291, 297. See also Edmund Randolph, "Letter on the Federal Constitution" (10/10/1787), Elliot 1:482, 485.

57. Lincoln Inaugural (3/4/1861), Basler et al. 4:262. See also Seward/C. F. Adams (4/10/1861), *Foreign Relations* 71; Rhodes (1892–1906) 3:130–36; *Secession, State & Liberty*, ed. David Gordon (New Brunswick, NJ: Rutgers University Press, 1998); P. Klein 361–63.

58. Seward/Frances Seward (12/5/1860), F. Seward (1891) 480; C. F. Adams (12/4/1861) quoted in Duberman 227; Petigru/Jane Petigru (12/6/1860), Petigru 362, 363. See also (12/6/1860), Ravenel 42; Holzer 131–32. Senator Charles Sumner (R/MA) reacted by reciting to colleagues President Jackson's views on nullification. (12/10/1860), *Globe* (36/2) 32, Sumner 7:165; Jackson/Andrew Crawford (5/1/1833), Jackson 5:71, 72. F. Y. Klingsberg attempted to vindicate the speech in "James Buchanan and the Crisis of the Union," *J. South. Hist.* 9/4:455 (11/1943).

59. See, for example, *New-York Daily Tribune* (3/9/1857) 5; Victor 78; William Harris (1985) 48; Welles (10/1876) 437–38; Michael A. Morrison, *Slavery and the American West* (Chapel Hill: University of North Carolina Press, 1997), 188–90; Stampp (1990) 91–93, 105–6.

60. S. M. Bowman and R. B. Irwin, *Sherman and His Campaigns* (New York, 1865), 16.

61. Quoted in Moultrie.battlefieldsinmotion.com.

62. *NYT* (12/17/1861); Evert Duyckinck, *National History of the War for the Union* (New York, 1861–1866) 1:39.

63. *Anderson Diary.* This and other entries are transcriptions, not in Anderson's handwriting. See also Alexander Garden, *Anecdotes of the Revolutionary War in America* (Charleston, 1822), 8 ("considering himself pledged to give a proof to the enemy of American valour, [Moultrie] scorned the disgrace of relinquishing the post he had sworn to defend, and heroically prepared for action"); William Moultrie, *Memoirs of the American Revolution* (New York, 1802), 1:122–84; Edwin C. Bearss, *Battle of Sullivan's Island and the Capture of Fort Moultrie* (Washington, DC: U.S. Dep't of the Interior, Div. of History, Office of Archeology and Historic Preservation, 1968); Stokely 44; T. Anderson 5; *Charleston Yearbook* 478–81; Webb Garrison, *Amazing Women of the Civil War* (Nashville, TN: Rutledge Hill, 1999), ch. 9.

64. John McQueen et al./Buchanan (12/9/1860), *OR* 1/1:126; H.R. no. 88, "Relative to the Correspondence between the President and the Commissioners" (2/27/1861), 5–7, *Select Committee Reports; Appleton* 649–50, Nicolay and Hay (1917) 2:383. See also Tenney 4–5.

65. See, for example, Buchanan (on or after 12/10/1860), Buchanan (1908–1911) 11:56–57; Buchanan, "Answer to General Scott" (10/28/1862), id. 11:279, 290; "Statement of Messrs. Miles and Keitt," *Convention Journal* 498, 499–502; [Buchanan] (1866) 167–68; Curtis 2:376–80; Gorham 1:136–46; Guernsey and Alden 34–35; Merchant 144–46 and 224n55. Buchanan recalled that the meeting had taken place on December 8, that the memorandum he requested (dated December 9) was delivered to him by three of the members on December 10, and that two of the three, John McQueen and M. L. Bonham, called upon him again (without Miles, Keitt, or Boyce) and strongly assured him that no fort would be attacked pending resolution of negotiations. Buchanan (on or after 12/10/1860), Buchanan (1908–1911) 11:56–57. Edmund Ruffin recorded in his diary the gist of informed opinion among denizens of the Charleston Hotel. "Strong efforts have been made to induce the president . . . to reinforce the forts," Ruffin noted, "but he has declined. It seems to be the understanding that the forts are not to be reinforced; & if not reinforced, they will not be attacked, until their surrender to S.C. is finally refused" or until Lincoln's inaugural on March 4. (12/23/1860), Ruffin (1972–89) 1:514. See also H. King (1895) 162; Buchanan/Barnwell et al. (12/31/1860), *OR* 1/1:115, 116–17.

66. *New-York Daily Tribune* (12/17/1860) 4; *Chicago Tribune* (12/20/1860) 2; S. Pryor (1904) 113; Henry Adams/Charles Francis Adams Jr. (12/22/1860), H. Adams (1982–88) 1:211, 212. See also J. Sherman 204, 214.

67. G. Thomas (12/17/1860), *Crawford Papers* 1:46. See also Crawford (1915) item 452; Kielbowicz 97.

68. Buell/Crawford (1/12/1884), *Goodyear Collection* Box 1 Folder 3 vol. 1, item 20, pp. 11–12; Crawford (1887) 72; *General Orders* 1:20.

69. Buell/Anderson (12/11/1860), *OR* 1/1:89, 90; Buell/Crawford (1/12/1884), *Goodyear Collection* vol. 1, item 20, pp. 11–15; Crawford (1887) 72. See also Crawford (1915) [15]; "Mem. Left with me by Major Buell Dec 11/60," *Anderson Papers* 8:1842. A copy in a fine hand, probably Anderson's own, is in id. p. 1844.

70. Herbert Baxter Adams, *The College of William and Mary* (Washington, DC: Government Printing Office, 1887), 51; Lewis Collins, *Historical Sketches of Kentucky* (Cincinnati: J.A. & U.P. James, 1848), 169–70.

71. Anderson/E. Anderson (2/24/1847), R. Anderson (1911) 55, 56; F. Moore (1862) 215, 216; Detzer 18.

72. Elliott 678. See also Fitz-John Porter/Crawford (9/9/1887), Crawford (1915) item 371.

73. (12/19/1861), Crawford (1915) [2], *Goodyear Collection* vol. 1. See also Paltsits 717–18.

74. (12/21/1860), *Anderson Diary*.

75. Anderson/Edward W. Hinks (12/24/1860), *History of Essex County, Massachusetts* (Philadelphia, 1888), 1:363, *Hist. Mag.* (1/1872) 46. Hinks would have a distinguished career in the Civil War.

76. Buell/Crawford (1/12/1884), *Goodyear Collection* vol. 1, item 20, pp. 6–7. See also Buell/Crawford (2/18/1884), *Goodyear Collection* vol. 1, item 23 ("It was inserted because I clearly believed, that to wait for the <u>occurance</u> of the 'hostile act,' . . . would be to lose the opportunity to take it at all"); Crawford (1915) [17].

77. Buell/Crawford (2/4/1884), *Goodyear Collection* vol. 1, item 22, p. 3.

78. Floyd/Anderson (12/21/1860), Emory Upton, "Military Policy of the United States," Sen. Doc. no. 494 (62/2) (Washington, 1912) 226, Lawton (1911) [opp. 6]; *OR* 1/1:103; *OR* 1/1:119n; [Miles et al.] 9; D. P. Butler/[Anderson] (12/11/1861), Crawford (1887) 72–75; J. Davis (1938) 1:595; S. Jones 16; F. Moore (1861–1866) 1:13; T. Anderson 25–26, 29–30; Buchanan (1908–1911) 11:82; [Buchanan] (1866) 166–67; Stephen D. Engle, *Don Carlos Buell: Most Promising of All* (Chapel Hill: University of North Carolina Press, 1999), 53–63; Detzer 80–82; W. Cooper (2012) 114; P. Klein 376; McClintock (2008) 106–7; Catton 147–49.

79. Pickens/Buchanan (12/17/1860), Nicolay and Hay (1917) 3:2. See also Trescot (1908) 541; Curtis 2:383–84.

80. See Edmunds (1967) 205.

81. Buchanan/Pickens (12/20/1861), Buchanan (1908–1911) 11:71.

82. Trescot/Pickens (12/21/1860), Nicolay and Hay (1917) 3:7, 9; Pickens/Trescot (12/21/1860), Buchanan (1908–1911) 11:73; Catton 151–52; Crawford (1887) 83–88.

83. It does not appear that either Pickens or Buchanan believed that they were making an enforceable agreement. See, for example, Curtis 2:378n. Buchanan already had a reputation for vacillation rather than forthrightness, and Pickens was widely thought incapable of handling subtleties. See, for example, (1/31/1861), Ravenel 51–52. See also Buchanan memorandum (12/20/1860), Buchanan (1908–1911) 11:70; Meredith 49–52; Francis Pickens, Message No. 1 (11/5/1861), *Journal of the Senate of the State of South Carolina* (Columbia, 1861), 10, 20.

84. Cullum 1:350.

85. Skelton 262–64.

86. Ord/Anderson (11/26/1860), *Anderson Papers* vol. 8. Of seventy-three enlisted men under Anderson whose places of birth were traced, only thirteen had been born in the United States. See Goodheart 169.

87. F. J. Porter/Cooper (11/11/1860), *OR* 1/1:70, 72. See also Detzer 47–50.

88. Anderson/Cooper (11/28/1860), *OR* 1/1:78; Cooper/Anderson (12/14/1860), *OR* 1/1:92, 93. See also Anderson/Cooper (12/18/1860), *OR* 1/1:94.

89. Foster (1952). When, years later, one of Anderson's officers was writing a history and asked Buell for comment, he responded that Anderson did not reveal to him that he "had determined or intended to make the movement to Sumter" but did indicate "that he realized the importance of it." Buell/Crawford (2/4/1884), *Goodyear Collection* vol. 1, item 22.

90. Floyd/Foster (12/19/1860), *Anderson Papers* vol. 10; Trescot (1908) 539; Crawford (1887) 77–78; Woodford 261; Foster (1866) 6; Catton 150–51; E. Cooper 34; Rhoades 14–16.

91. See, for example, Benjamin Huger/Craig (11/20/1860), *OR* 1/1:74; Rhoades 10–11; Dorothy Kelly MacDowell, "Aristocratic, Patriotic Huger Family," *South Carolina Hist. Mag.* 40:22, 23 (Jan.–Feb. 1976); *Lowcountry Carolina Genealogies,* comp. Charlton deSaussure (Greenville, SC: Independent Publishing Platform, 1997).

92. See John G. Foster/F. C. Humphreys (12/18/1860), *OR* 1/1:97. See also draft of Buchanan/Pickett (12/20/1860), Buchanan (1908–1911) 11:72.

93. *Convention Journal* 66.

94. Anderson/Cooper (12/22/1860), *OR* 1/1:105.

Chapter 3: "An Act of Gross Breach of Faith"

1. (12/18, 19/1860), *Public Proceedings* 37, 38. See also Rhett 19.

2. Maria Pinckney had written that the East bribed the West with internal improvements and free land, and the West reciprocated by supporting import tariffs. *Quintessence of Long Speeches* (Charleston, 1830), 20. Between 1789 and 1860, federal expenditures for roads and canals were substantially greater in the North than in the South, in part because few Southerners lobbied for and some actually rejected offered funds. While some Southerners argued particularly against fortifications, $22 million was invested in fortifications in the South in this period versus $16.4 million in the North. J. Van Deusen 107–37, 335–36.

3. *Globe* (36/2) 155–56 (12/20/1860).

4. See, for example, Gist/Trescot (11/29/1860), Crawford (1887) 32; H.R. no. 88, "Relative to the Correspondence between the President and the Commissioners" (2/27/1861), *Select Committee Reports.* The author of *Diary of a Public Man* claimed to have had a conversation with Orr on December 28 about Anderson's move to Sumter and the constitutional propriety of secession. Hurlbert (1945) 27–29.

5. *Convention Journal* 64–65.

6. Reproduced in *Newbury (VT) Aurora of the Valley* (12/22/1860) 2. See also Andrew C. McLaughlin, *Lewis Cass* (1892; Boston, 1919), 341; Gwin and Coleman (1892) 87.

7. Pickens/Trescot (12/23/1860), Trescot (1908) 542. See also Gorham 1:117–20; Abner Doubleday/Ulysses Doubleday (9/23/1860), (9/25/1860), *Lincoln Papers.*

8. Trescot had been secretary to the U.S. legation in London in 1853 and wrote two scholarly books: *The Diplomacy of the Revolution* (New York, 1852) and *The Diplomatic History of the Administrations of Washington and Adams* (Boston, 1857). These credentials, along with his superior lineage and connections among Charleston's elite families, led Buchanan to appoint him as what came to be—given Lewis Cass's lack of suitable skills—the de facto secretary of state. See Curtis 2:399–400; Galliard Hunt in Trescot (1908) 528–30. That an expert on diplomacy could misconstrue a short document, particularly after witnessing its drafting and presentation, is surprising and lends some support to the later speculation that Floyd (and Trescot) wanted Anderson to move to Fort Sumter to give the South a good excuse to commence hostilities. But there is ample evidence indicating that Floyd and Trescot in fact wished to avoid that outcome.

9. Trescot (1908) 542; L. F. Lee/Montgomery Meigs (12/12/1860), *Meigs Papers* Reel 12.

10. (12/24/1861), *Anderson Diary*. See also Detzer 109–13; Nicolay and Hay (1917) 3:46.

11. Nicolay and Hay (1917) 3:45–46. See also JoAnn Smith Bartlett, *Abner Doubleday: His Life and Times* (Bloomington: Indiana University Press, 2009), 96.

12. John Thompson/Robert Thompson (2/14/1861), "A Union Soldier at Fort Sumter, 1860–1861," *S.C. Hist. Mag.* 67/2:99 (4/1966), Johnston; Lee and Chepesiuk 7.

13. *Public Proceedings* 86, *Convention Journal* 90–91.

14. J. G. Foster/R. E. De Russy (12/22/1860), *OR* 1/1:106; E. Milby Burton, *The Siege of Charleston, 1861–1865* (Columbia: University of South Carolina Press, 1970), 8–9; Foster (1952).

15. Anderson/E. Anderson (undated), Nicolay and Hay (1917) 3:47–48n; Jefferson C. Davis, "Charleston Harbor, 1860–1861: A Memoir from the Union Garrison," ed. James P. Jones, *S.C. Hist. Mag.* 62/3:148, 149 (7/1961).

16. Anderson/Cooper (12/26/1861), *OR* 1/1:2; Anderson/E. Anderson (12/26/1860), Lawton (1914) 6; François Gay de Vernon, *Treatise on the Science of War and Fortification* (1805), trans. John M. O'Connor (New York, 1817), 2:4–14 (italics omitted). See also A. H. Jomini, *Summary of the Art of War* (1836), trans. O. F. Winship and E. E. McLean (New York, 1854), 163–74; Foster (1952) 3; Ryan 32–33.

17. The three guns retrieved were eventually mounted by a veterans' group in St. Louis's Lafayette Park. Two other British vessels also ran aground but were successfully refloated. See David Lee Russell, *Victory on Sullivan's Island* (Haverford, PA: Infinity, 2002), 209; Matthew A. Russell and Submerged Cultural Resources Unit, *Fort Sumter National Monument Submerged Cultural Resources Survey* (Santa Fe, NM: Submerged Cultural Resources Unit, Cultural Resources Management, Intermountain Support Office, US National Park Service, 1998), 1–2; William Moultrie, *Memoirs of the American Revolution* (New York, 1802), 1:174–75; http://www.riverfronttimes.com/bestof/2000/award/best-monument-in-new-clothing.

18. William Bull (11/30, 1770), Merrens 254, 261.

19. "Revised Report of the Board of Engineers on the Defence of the Seaboard" (3/24/1826), H.R. Rpt. no. 86: "Permanent Fortifications and Sea-Coast Defences" (37/2) 23, 43 (4/23/1862).

20. Act of 3/19/1828, ch. 18, 4 Stat. 256.

21. See "Report on the Defence of Charleston Harbor" (1827), Record Group 77, Corps of Engineers, Entry 223, p. 2, National Archives, Washington, DC; *Assessment* III.02-1; T. S. Brown/Charles Gratiot (12/8/[1834]), *Am. State Papers* (Military Affairs) 5:464; F. Barnes (1962) 4.

22. *Acts and Resolutions of the General Assembly of the State of South Carolina, Passed in December, 1837* (Columbia, 1838), 52–53.

23. See *North Carolina Standard* (9/18/1858) 2; *Edgefield (SC) Advertiser* (9/22/1858) 2; Schultz 158–59.

24. See, for example, *HABS* 14–15. Totten and others chose the hexagonal shape because the pivoting range of the gun carriages and the size of the embrasure openings did not permit a traverse of more than sixty degrees. A 120-degree angle thus accommodated a full field of fire. Lewis 52.

25. See Lewis 21–25.

26. Marquis de Montalembert, *La Fortification Perpendiculaire* (Paris, 1776–78), 1:133–75, 2:158–71, 230, 3:59–88; Halleck 327–41; M. A. Smith 15–19.

27. *HABS* 10, 12; Joseph G. Totten, "Brief Observations on Common Mortars," *Essays on Hydraulic and Common Mortars* by C. L. Treussart et al. (New York, 1842), 227, 241; Totten (1857) 44–71; Denis A. Brosnan et al., "Characterization and Degradation of Cementitious Materials at Fort Sumter National Monument," paper presented at Am. Hist. Cement Conf. (3/31/2011) 1–2; Denis A. Brosnan, *Final Report: Forensic Analysis of Building Materials . . . Fort Sumter National Monument* (6/26, 2012) 5–16; *Assessment* V.3.01.1-20-21; J. Johnson 17–18; R. Browning 73; *Charleston Yearbook* 483–88. See also Stokely 14.

28. See, for example, Weaver 19–27; Konstam 18–20.

29. With regard to rendering ordnance unserviceable, see, for example, Roberts 21, 22; *Ordnance Manual* 32; Gibbon 77; *Field Manual for the Use of the Officers on Ordnance Duty* (Richmond, VA, 1862), 14.

30. See, for example, [De Forest] 497; Emma Holmes (2/13/1861), Holmes 2.

31. Quoted in F. Moore (1861–1866) 1:8; F. Moore (1862) 217. See also *Littleton Washington's Journal*, ed. Douglas Lee Giboney (N.p.: Xlibris, 2001), 180.

32. *Pickens Papers* Reel 2, *Convention Journal* 114; Crawford, *Fort Sumter Diary* (12/27/1860) 5; Pickens/David F. Jamison (12/28/1860), *OR* 1/1:252; *Confederate War J.* 1/2:10 (5/1893); (12/27 [1860]), (10/15/1860), Keyes 370, 371–72; Doubleday (1876) 126; Gibbon 443, 459; F. Moore (1861–1866) 1:9; Crawford (1887) 79–81; M. Klein 163–68.

33. *National Republican* (12/29/1860) 23; Henry Adams/Charles Francis Adams Jr. (12/18/1860), H. Adams (1982–1988) 1:208. See also Furgurson 23–25.

34. See, for example, *National Republican* (12/27/1860) 3; id. (12/28/1860) 2; "The Indian Bonds Defence of W. H. Russell," *NYT* (4/2/1861); Buchanan/Stanton (12/24/1860), Buchanan (1908–1911) 11:75; Victor 113–15; Auchampaugh (1923) 381–83; Nevins (1950) 2:371–74; Detzer 71–73; P. Klein 357, 377.

35. Floyd/Anderson (12/27/1860), *OR* 1/1:3; Trescot (1908) 543; Anderson/Floyd (12/27/1860), *OR* 1/1:3; Crawford (1887) 145–49. See also Dawson 46; T. Anderson 5–7; Stampp (1950) 76, 256; Buchanan (1908–1911) 12:200–210; M. Klein 149–50, 169. Although Anderson's telegram got through, the secession convention that day agreed to a resolution to take possession of Charleston's telegraph office and "prevent all communication between the city and Fort Sumter." *Pickens Papers* Reel 2, *Convention Journal* 114.

36. *New-York Daily Tribune* (12/28/1860) 6.

37. Scott/Floyd (12/28/1860), *Lincoln Papers*; Scott (3/30/1861), W. Scott (1862) 3, 5; Buchanan (10/28/1862), id. 11, 18–19.

38. Pickens (12/28/1860), *OR* 1/1:113; Anderson/Cooper (12/28/1860), *OR* 1/1:112.

39. Scott reportedly said that if Anderson were ordered back to Fort Moultrie, he would resign and command the local militia defending Washington from a Southern attack. *National Republican* (12/31/1860) 4. When the South read in newspapers the false report that Scott had resigned and would fight for Virginia, the city of Mobile gave him a hundred-gun salute. E. Townsend 4–6. See also Francis MacDonnell, "The Confederate Spin on Winfield Scott and George Thomas," *Civil War Hist.* 34/4:255 (12/1998).

40. Chase/Scott (12/29/1860), *Salmon P. Chase Papers*, ed. John Niven (Kent, OH: Kent State University Press, 1993–1998), 3:43.

41. Henry Adams/Charles Francis Adams Jr. (12/29/1860), H. Adams (1982–1986) 1:214, 215, H. Adams (1930–1938) 1:73, 74.
42. Ellison Capers, "South Carolina," Evans 5:7–9.
43. Floyd/Buchanan (12/29/1860), F. Moore (1861–1866) 1:10, Pollard (1867A) 799–800; [Hurlbert] (1879) 126–30.
44. Black/Charles R. Buckalem (no date) quoted in Auchampaugh (1923) 384.
45. Robert W. Barnwell, James H. Adams, James L. Orr/Buchanan (12/28/1861), *Convention Journal* 484.
46. *Convention Journal* 115; id. 121–22, May and Faunt 25. See also Pickens, Message No. 1 (11/5/1861), *Journal of the Senate of the State of South Carolina* (Columbia, 1861), 10, 21.
47. See, for example, John Cunningham/Frederick C. Humphreys (12/30/1860), "Seizure of Forts, Arsenals, Revenue Cutters, and Other Property of the United States," 89, *Select Committee Reports*; Humphreys quoted in H.R. (32/2), Misc. Doc. no. 12: "Defences of the Harbor of Charleston, and the Distribution of Arms," Holt/Stanton (1/3/1861); Crawford (1887) 1; Crawford (1896) 1.
48. John C. Ropes memorandum (2/8/1870) 8–9, Horatio Woodman Papers, Ms. N-492, Mass. Hist. Soc.
49. Seward/Lincoln (12/29/1860), *Lincoln Papers*.
50. King/Dix (12/31/1860), H. King (1895) 38.
51. "E Pluribus Unum" (2/1861), *Political Essays* (Boston, 1890), 45, 69–70.
52. Anderson/Eliza Anderson (12/27, 29/1860), *Anderson Diary*. He told his former pastor:

> Much has been said about my having come here on my own responsibility. Unwilling to see my little band sacrificed, I determined, after earnestly awaiting instructions as long as I could, to . . . [extricate] myself from my dangerous position. . . . The Governor of this State has interdicted all intercourse with the city except that of sending and receiving letters, so that you see we are quasi enemies. Were I disposed to declare myself independent of, to secede from, the General Government and retaliate, I could cut Charleston off from her supplies, but I will show [Pickens] that I am more of a Christian than to make the innocent suffer for the petty conduct of their Governor.

Anderson/Richard B. Duane (12/30/1860), Crawford (1915) [1]–[2].
53. See, for example, Huger/Holt (1/12/1861), *Holt Papers* 26:3519; Gourdin/Holt (1/27/1861), *Holt Papers* 27:3561; Gourdin/Anderson (12/17/1860), *Anderson Papers* 10:1852; Gourdin/Anderson (2/2/1861), id. 10:2231; Huger/Anderson (1/29/1861), id., vol. 13; Huger/Anderson (5/24/1861), id.; J. Davis (1861) 1:216; Larz Anderson/Holt [ca. early Feb. 1861], *Holt Papers* 27:3583; W. P. Anderson, *Anderson Family Records* (Cincinnati: Press of W. F. Schaefer, 1936), 56; Henry S. Foote, *A Casket of Reminiscences* (New York, 1874), 95.
54. Louisa Rodgers Meigs/Montgomery Meigs (1/6/1861), *Meigs Papers* Reel 7.
55. Scott/Buchanan (12/30/1861), *Lincoln Papers*; Buchanan, "Answer to General Scott" (10/28/1862), Buchanan (1908–1911) 11:279, 287.
56. Black, "Memorandum for the President on the Subject of the Paper Drawn Up by Him" (12/30/1860), J. Black 14, 15–16; Holt/J. Buchanan Henry (5/26/1884), Buchanan (1908–1911) 11:84; *NY World* (1/25/1870) 4; P. Klein 380–87.
57. Buchanan/Scott (12/30/1860), *Lincoln Papers*. See also (1/4/1861), C. F. Adams Sr.

58. See, for example, *Globe* (37/4) 1447–48 (3/11/1861).
59. Russell (1863) 1:154; Furgurson 22.
60. Toombs (1/1/1861), Phillips 528; Buchanan/Holt (12/31/1860), *OR* 3/1:21. Holt would later join the Union army and head the panel that tried those charged with conspiring to kill Lincoln.
61. Wigfall/M. L. Bonham (1/2/1861), *OR* 1/1:252; Walther 179–94. See also David S. Heidler, *Pulling the Temple Down* (Mechanicsburg, PA: Stackpole Books, 1994), 112.
62. Buchanan/Barnwell (12/31/1860), *OR* 1/1:115, 118. In several other sources, the letter bears a date of 12/30/1860. See, for example, *Convention Journal* 485. See also McClure (1892) 300–302; M. Klein 176; K. Williams 1:22.
63. Barnwell et al./Buchanan (1/1/1861), F. Moore (1861–1866) 1:14; J. Davis (1938) 1:597; Pollard (1862) 36; Pollard (1867A) 800n.
64. Buchanan/Jacob Thompson (1/9/1861), Buchanan (1908–1911) 11:100, 101; Buchanan, "Answer to General Scott" (10/28/1862), id. 11:279, 286–87; id. 12:162.
65. See, for example, Lathers 126.
66. Lawton (1911) 15.
67. *Harper's Weekly*/Anderson (12/18/1860), *Anderson Papers* vol. 10.
68. Guernsey and Alden 29.
69. See, for example, *Anderson Papers*; *Crawford Papers* 1:14; Paltsits 718.
70. Guernsey and Alden 35.
71. Saltonstall/Anderson (1/3/1861), H.R., Rpt. no. 441 (50/1) 1, 2 (2/14/1888). Regarding Saltonstall, see, for example, *Proceedings of the New-England Historical Genealogical Society* (Boston, 1896), 134.
72. J. H. Elliot, "Major Anderson" (2/1861), *Fort Sumter Memorial* xv. See also James Russell Lowell/Charles Nordhoff (12/31/1860), *Letters of James Russell Lowell*, ed. Charles Eliot Norton (Boston, 1904), 2:54, 56.
73. *Hartford Daily Courant* (1/7/1861) 2. See also Richard Arnold/Anderson (1/19/1861), *OR* 1/53:62.
74. *Globe* (36/2) 280–82 (1/7/1861).
75. Elizabeth Blair Lee/Samuel Phillips Lee (1/9/1861), E. Lee 20.
76. H. Adams/C. F. Adams Jr. (1/17/1861), H. Adams (1982–1986) 1:221, 224.
77. Elizabeth Blair Lee/Samuel Phillips Lee (1/9/1861), E. Lee 20, 22n7; E. B. Lee/S. P. Lee (2/12/1861), id. 36; [Miles et al.] 21–22.
78. See, for example, *Anderson (SC) Intelligencer* (1/10/1861) 1. See also id. (1/3/1861) 2; *Richmond Daily Dispatch* (1/3/1861) 1; *New-York Daily Tribune* (1/1/1861) 8.
79. Quoted in Trescot (1908) 552. See also V. Davis 2:55.
80. John Russell Young, *Men and Memories*, ed. May D. Russell Young (New York: F. T. Neely, 1901), 22–26; W. A. Swanberg, *Sickles the Incredible* (New York: Scribner, 1956), 110; *National Republican* (1/3/1861) 3; Frost 40. See also *Fremont (OH) Journal* (1/4/1861) 2; *Stroudsburg (PA) Jeffersonian* (1/3/1861) 2; Mark J. Stegmaier annot., H. Adams (2012) 74n6. Stanton and Sickles had previously demonstrated their collective skills in swaying perceptions, when Stanton saved Sickles from execution by inventing the "temporary insanity" defense.
81. See, for example, Buchanan (12/8/1857), Richardson (1897–1903) 5:436, 450–54; Buchanan/Nathaniel Taylor (8/15/1857), Buchanan (1908–1911) 11:117, 120; Buchanan (2/2/1858), id. 12:27.
82. Davis/Edwin De Leon (1/8/1861), J. Davis (1971–) 7:6.

83. [De Forest] 497; *Globe* (36/2) 306–8 (1/10/1861). Even after the war, some Southerners claimed that Anderson's belief that Fort Moultrie would be attacked was fanciful. See, for example, Jordan 39–40.

84. Trescot (1908) 545–46.

85. Id. 306; Davis/Edwin De Leon (1/8/1861), J. Davis (1971–) 7:6. See also *Globe* (36/2) 284 (1/9/1861).

86. See, for example, Charles Eugene Hamlin, *Life and Times of Hannibal Hamlin* (Cambridge, MA, 1899), 380. Some Southerners charged him with personally ordering Anderson's transfer, calling him "double-faced and treacherous, hardly allowing him the poor credit of being a well-intentioned imbecile." [De Forest] 497. Davis later reportedly remarked that if Buchanan had had the nerve to withdraw Anderson, "it would have been such a conspicuous act of conciliation" as to stall the secession effort then under way by additional slave states. Quoted in, for example, *NYT* (7/13/1881), *Life and Death of Jefferson Davis*, ed. A. C. Bancroft (New York, 1889), 145–46.

87. Jacob Thompson/Buchanan (1/8/1861), Buchanan (1908–1911) 11:100, Buchanan/Thompson (1/9/1861), id. 11:101; [Miles et al.] 20; Tilley 116–30; Buchanan (10/28/1862), W. Scott (1862) 11, 17; J. Black 19–20. See also Crawford (1915) item 455.

88. Trescot/Howell Cobb (1/14/1861), Trescot (1908) 546; id. 545–46; Hunter/Cobb (1/14/1861), Phillips 529, 530; Buchanan/Thompson (1/9/1861), Buchanan (1908–1911) 11:101; Trescot quoted in Catton 173.

89. Floyd testimony (3/5/1860), No. 278, Report of the [Senate] Select Committee on Harper's Ferry (36/1) 251; id. (1/16/1860) 71 (testimony of F. M. Arny); *Rise and Progress of the Bloody Outbreak at Harper's Ferry* ([New York?], [1859?]), 9–12; Benjamin F. Gue, *History of Iowa from the Earliest Times* (New York: Century History, 1903), 2:23–30; G. Van Deusen (1947) 243–44.

90. Doubleday (1998) 229.

91. [Hurlbert] (1879) 262. Cf. id. 485. See also Hurlbert (1945) 49, 80; Crofts (2010); Daniel Crofts, "A Fresh Look at 'Diary of a Public Man,'" *Civil War Hist.* 55/4:442 (12/2009); James G. Randall, "Has the Lincoln Theme Been Exhausted?" *Am. Hist. Rev.* 41/2:270, 277–78 and n27 (1/1936).

92. Gordon 13. See also Doubleday (1876) 57–58. Foster would immediately have told Anderson of his suspicions. See Otto Eisenschiml and E. B. Long, "The Big 'Ifs' at Fort Sumter," *Am. Mercury* 82:94, 98 (4/1956).

93. Seward/Lincoln (12/29/1860), *Lincoln Papers*.

94. In *Secession Debated*, ed. William W. Freehling and Craig M. Simpson (New York: Oxford University Press, 1992), 115, 130.

95. H.R., Committee on Military Affairs, Report no. 85: "Forts, Arsenals, Arms &c." [to accompany H.R. no. 1003] 2/18/1861 (36/2); Benjamin Stanton/Joseph Holt (12/31/1860), *OR* 3/1:21–22.

96. *Globe* (36/2) 295, 1096 (1/9, 2/21/1861); "Naval Force."

97. In addition, on January 3, Georgia militiamen, upon the order of their governor, had walked into Fort Pulaski, at the mouth of the Savannah River, and taken it from its solitary caretaker. Charles C. Jones, "The Seizure and Reduction of Fort Pulaski," *Mag. of Am. Hist.* 14/1:53 (7/1885); Ulrich B. Phillips, *Life of Robert Toombs* (New York: Macmillan, 1913), 215–16; Herbert M. Schiller, *Sumter Is Avenged* (Shippensburg, PA: White Mane, 1995), 4–5; Hendrickson 160–62.

98. *Globe* (36/2) 572 (1/26/1861). After testimony from numerous witnesses, and despite letters received by General Scott indicating that the government was under threat, the Select Committee of Five concluded that there was no "secret organization here or elsewhere hostile to the government." H.R., "Alleged Hostile Organization against the Government within the District of Columbia" (36/2) 2, 52, 53 (2/14/1861), *Select Committee Reports*. See also H. King (1872) 405–7.

99. Floyd/H. K. Craig (12/29/1859), *OR* 3/1:44; F. Moore (1861–1866) 1:10; H. K. Craig/Joseph Holt (1/18/18[61]), "Seizure of Forts, Arsenals, Revenue Cutters, and Other Property of the United States," 84–85, *Select Committee Reports*; Scott/Lincoln (1/4/1861), *Lincoln Papers*; *National Republican* (12/31/1860) 2; Totten/Holt (1/8/1861), *National Intelligencer* (1/18/1861) 3; Buchanan, "Answer to General Scott's 'Rejoinder'" (11/17/1862), Buchanan (1908–1911) 11:310, 313; Crawford (1887) 149–50, 213–17; H. King (1895) 122–25; Faulkner 53; E. McPherson 34–35; J. Black 12–13; [Buchanan] (1866) 186–87, 220–28; Gorham 1:85–90; William Wilkins et al./Buchanan (12/25/1860), *OR* 3/1:15; Totten/Holt (1/8/1861), *OR* 3/1:32; Reuben Davis, *Recollections of Mississippi and Mississippians* (Boston, 1890), 395; John Laird Wilson, *Battles of America by Sea and Land* (New York, 1878), 3:14; E. Cooper 27–40; Catton 174–76; Swanberg 21–116; E. Channing 284–88.

100. Act of 3/3/1825, ch. 93, 4 Stat. 127; H.R., Committee on Military Affairs, Report no. 85: "Forts, Arsenals, Arms &c." [to accompany Bill H.R. no. 1003], 2/18/1861 (36/2) 1–3; *Cincinnati Daily Press* (1/2/1861) 2; Buchanan/H. King (11/12/1861), H. King (1872) 408; Victor 115. But see Buchanan, "Answer to General Scott's 'Rejoinder'" (11/17/1862), Buchanan (1908–1911) 11:310, 313.

101. *Globe* (36/2) 1256–57 (2/21/1861).

102. Louisa Rodgers Meigs/Montgomery Meigs (1/6/1861), *Meigs Papers* Reel 7. But see Robert M. Hughes, "John B. Floyd—A Defence," *Tyler's Quart. Hist. & Geneal. Mag.* 2/3:154 (1/1921).

103. E. Townsend 8; Skelton 184.

104. See, for example, *Globe* (36/2) 294 (1/9/1861); *NYT* (2/13/1861); [Buchanan] (1866) 221–25; Doubleday (1876) 17n; Swanberg 168, 356n29; E. Cooper 39. See also Floyd/William Pennington (12/28/1860), *Globe* (36/2) 218.

105. *National Republican* (3/20/1861) 1; *NYT* (3/21/1861) 4; *NYT* (3/22/1861) 4.

106. (3/16/1861), *National Republican* (3/25/1861) 2. The *Mobile Advertiser* similarly commented, "We are much obliged to Secretary Floyd for the foresight he has thus displayed in disarming the North, and equipping the South for this emergency." Quoted in, for example, J. Sherman 170–71, Draper 1:544. Regarding Floyd, see also Ambler (1918) 161; J. M. Batten, "Governor John Floyd," *John P. Branch Hist. Papers of Randolph-Macon College* 4/1:5 (6/1913); Henry Tragle, *The Southampton Slave Revolt of 1831: A Compilation of Source Material* (Amherst: University of Massachusetts Press, 1971), 250–51.

107. *NYT* (1/21/1861). See, for example, *National Republican* (12/27/1860) 1; *NYT* (12/31/1860) 1; Elizabeth Blair Lee/Samuel Phillips Lee (1/9/1861), E. Lee 20; E. Cooper 33–39. See also *National Republican* (1/1/1861) 2; Jeremiah Black/Henry Wilson (ca. 2/1861), J. Black 245, 258.

108. See, for example, Thomas Riddle, "Reminiscences of Floyd's Operations in West Virginia in 1861," *South. Hist. Soc. Papers* 11/:92 (1883); "The Fall of Fort Donelson,"

NYT (2/18/1862); David G. Moore, *William S. Rosecrans and the Union Victory* (Jefferson, NC: McFarland, 2014), 15–20; Eicher 533; "Report of the War Department," H.R., "Report on the Treatment of Prisoners of War, by the Rebel Authorities," Rpt. no. 45 (40/3) 273, 277–86; Ould, "The Exchange of Prisoners," *Annals of the War Written by Leading Participants* (Philadelphia, 1879), 32, 50. But see Pollard (1867A) 801–7.

109. Quoted in F. Moore (1861–1866) 1:387, W. Scott (1864) 2:615–16; M. Wright 298; Shanks 184–85. Compare *Abington Virginian* (9/4/1863) 1; *Carolina Spartan* (Spartanburg, SC) (9/10/1863) 1; *New-York Tribune* (9/1/1863) 1; *Nashville Daily Union* (9/5/1863) 1; *Point Pleasant (WV) Weekly Reg.* (9/24/1863) 1; John Jay, "The Great Conspiracy, and England's Neutrality" (7/4/1861), *Littell's Living Age*, 3rd Ser. 14:323, 334–35 (7–9/1861); E. Townsend 8; Lyman Trumbull (3/3/1861), H. White 123, 130–31. But see R. M. Hughes, "John B. Floyd—A Defence," *Tyler's Quart. Hist. & Geneal. Mag.* 2/3:154 (1/1921).

Chapter 4: Crossing the Bar

1. Isaac Toucey, "Report of the Secretary of the Navy" (12/2/1859), *Globe* (36/1) App. 13; "Report of the Select Committee of Five," *Globe* (36/1) 1095 (2/21/1861); *Officers' Register* 104–6; Paullin 179–81. See also Bernardo and Bacon 180–83; Sondhaus 56.

2. See, for example, *Globe* (36/2) 1095, 1096, 1381 (2/21, 3/2/1861); Elizabeth Lee/ Samuel Lee (2/6/1861), E. Lee 32; "Naval Force" 5–6; Nevins (1950) 1:73; Kettell 187. When the Republican journalist Gideon Welles, Toucey's longtime political adversary in Connecticut, heard that the administration, following heated internal debate, would not order Anderson back to Fort Moultrie, Welles good-heartedly wrote to Toucey, "Whatever may have been our political differences . . . I cannot permit your conduct in sustaining Maj. Anderson, to pass without expressing my thanks to you. . . . In taking possession of Fort Sumter, that gallant officer has won the applause of men of all parties here [in Hartford]. . . . They, one and all, sustain the Administration for sustaining him." (1/3/1861), *Welles Papers/LC* Reel 18. Although Toucey thanked Welles for the compliment, Toucey had in fact been among those whispering in Buchanan's ear to order Anderson to vacate Fort Sumter. Toucey/ Welles (2/14/1861), *Goodyear Collection* Box 1, Folder 4, vol. 2, item 40. See also Welles (1924) 59. Welles's later reminiscence of Toucey is blistering. Welles/William Bartlett (undated), *Welles Papers/LC* Reel 26. See also Welles diary (7/2/1863), Welles (2014) 233, 234 and n6.

3. *From Sail to Steam* (New York, 1907), 34; Bernardo and Bacon 166–67.

4. See James St. Clair Morton, *Memoir on the Dangers and Defences of New York City* [9/30/1858] (Washington, 1858), iv, 34. See also *Coast Survey 1859*; H.R., *Message from the President of the United States*, Ex. Doc. no. 2 (35/2) 2:494, 524; [Chesney] 185. In addition, the Lighthouse Board's *Coeur de Lion*, given its intended use, drew a mere four feet, six inches of water.

5. Porter/G. V. Fox (3/11/1862), Fox (1920) 1:73, 84; Silverstone 41, 82, 187; Paine 69. Data on a number of U.S. war vessels are found in, for example, *ORN* 1/4:xv–xvi. Cf. Tucker (2011) 1:285.

6. Simons/Pickens (1/1/1861), Nicolay and Hay (1917) 3:119–21, quoted in Crawford (1915) item 397.

7. See, for example, Longstreet, *Anderson (SC) Intelligencer* (1/11/1861) 1; Longstreet, "Shall South Carolina Begin the War?" (1861), Oscar Penn Fitzgerald, *Judge Longstreet: A Life Sketch* (Nashville, TN, 1891), 128. See also "South Carolina Convention Adjourned," *NYT* (1/7/1861).

8. See *New-York Daily Tribune* (10/20/1855) 6; "The Naval Expedition against the Kulan Pirates," *U.S. Naut. Mag. & Naval J.* 3/3:190 (12/1855); Dahlgren (1856A) 172–81; William Graham (12/17/1850), id. 20; *DANFS* vol. 5; Clowes 6:389. The draft listed was when loaded. See Silverstone 24; Tucker (2011) 2:542. *ORN* 2/1:183 lists the draft as twenty feet, nine inches loaded, eighteen feet light. J. C. Dobbin/D. L. Yulee (12/17/1856) lists the draft at twenty feet, two inches. *Globe* (34/3) App. 175 (1/27/1857). *DANFS*, vol. 5, lists the draft as eighteen feet, six inches, Paine one inch less. Paine 133. See also Nevins (1959) 70n9.

9. See, for example, Preston and Major 19–22, 33–34. See also Sondhaus 5. Britain's success in Crimea with vessels drawing less than seven feet led to the construction of boats drawing four feet. William Howard Russell, *The British Expedition to the Crimea*, rev. ed. (London, 1858), 401, 512, 518–34; "The Gun-Boat Question Settled," *U.S. Naut. Mag. & Naval J.* 4/4:286 (7/1856); Clowes 6:427–28, 460, 484–85; G. A. Osbon, "The Crimean Gunboats," *Mariner's Mirror* 51/2:103, 104 (1965); id. 51/3:211 (1965). Regarding the British paddle box boat, see Andrew Lambert, "Looking for Gunboats," *J. Maritime Res.* 6/1:65 (6/2004).

10. Alfred Thayer Mahan, *Admiral Farragut* (New York, 1892), 98. Secretary of War Jefferson Davis, in contrast, ordered three officers to assess European military capability, and its application in Crimea, and each issued a report. See Sen. Exec. Doc. 59 (36/1), Richard Delafield, "Report on the Art of War in Europe in 1854, 1855, and 1856" (6/16/1860) v–vi, 18–61; Sen. Exec. Doc. 60 (36/1), "Military Commission to Europe, in 1855 and 1856: Report of Major Alfred Mordecai" (6/16/1860) 61–68; George B. McClellan, *The Armies of Europe* (Philadelphia, 1861). See also Durkin 97–98; Bernardo and Bacon 183.

11. See, for example, Clowes 6:392–93; *Report from the Select Committee on Slave Trade Treaties* (London, 1853), iv–viii, 74–75, 231, 258, 260; W. E. B. Du Bois, *The Suppression of the African Slave-Trade* (New York, 1896), 143–49, 161–63; Henry Wheaton, *Enquiry into the Validity of the British Claim to a Right of Visitation and Search* (Philadelphia, 1842), 4; Joseph T. Crawford/Earl of Malmesbury (5/9/1858), *Class B. Correspondence with British Ministers and Agents in Foreign Countries . . . Relating to the Slave Trade* (London, [1859]), 162; Crawford/Lord Napier (6/1/1858), id. 166; David Murray, *Odious Commerce* (Cambridge: Cambridge University Press 1980), 263–65; *Globe* (35/1) 2415 (5/26/1858). See also Matthew Mason, *Slavery and Politics in the Early American Republic* (Chapel Hill: University of North Carolina Press, 2006), 88.

12. See, for example, *Globe* (35/1) 2731–42 (6/7/1858); id. (36/1) 3108 (6/18/1860); id. (34/3) App. 175 (1/27/1857) (Sen. David L. Yulee, D/FL); Dobbin/Yulee (12/17/1856), id.; id. 271 (1/20/1857) (Sen. Alfred Iverson, D/GA); D. Porter (1886) 17.

13. Rpt. of the Sec. of the Navy (12/1/1856), *Globe* (34/3) App. 27, 29 (12/1/1856).

14. Act of 6/12/1858, ch. 153 § 6, 11 Stat. 314, 319. See also Durkin 61–62, 68, 86–88, 97–108.

15. Rpt. of the Sec. of the Navy (12/6/1858), Sen. Exec. Doc. no. 1 (35/2) 3, 8. See also Harold D. Langley, "Isaac Toucey," Coletta 303, 305–6, 316.

16. *Globe* (36/1) 3097, 3108–9 (6/18/1860).

17. Navy Lieutenant David Dixon Porter related a very different story: that as the likelihood of a civil war grew, Senator Mallory made sure that any ship approved for purchase or construction should be of too deep a draft to enter Southern harbors unassisted. Porter/G. V. Fox (7/5/1861), Fox (1920) 2:73, 76. Porter, who ascribed this account to Senator Jefferson Davis, was commonly a faulty witness, preferring entertainment and/ or self-aggrandizement to accuracy. In Porter's version, Mallory would go so far as to interfere with the design of ships already approved for construction by demanding that they be larger. This commonly meant that their steam engines and ancillary machinery, designed for the smaller vessel originally specified, ended up being "almost useless" when installed in what was suddenly a different class of vessel. Porter's account is inconsistent with the appropriations Mallory actually made and with Mallory's claim to have been a loyal Union man up until the time his state seceded. See Durkin 113.

18. Senator James Murray Mason (D/VA) charged that the request came at a time when the House was introducing a bill denying port-of-entry status to seceded states, suggesting that the vessels would be used to monitor blockade those ports. *Globe* (36/2) 844–53 (2/11/1861). The Senate nevertheless passed the provision, 30–18. Sen. J. (36/2) 215 (2/11/1861). It passed in the House and was signed into law by President Buchanan. Act of 2/21/1861 ch. § 9, 12 Stat. 147, 151. See also Sprout and Sprout 144–49; Karp 223–25.

19. See, for example, Sir Peter Parker, "Plan of the Attack of Fort Sulivan [*sic*], the Key of Charlestown" (1776); Antoine de Sartine, "Plan de la barre et du havre de Charles-Town" (1778); R. Cowley, "Charles Town, South Carolina, with a Chart of the Bars & Harbours" (1780); Joseph F. W. Des Barres, "Sketch of the Operations before Charleston" (1780), all in http://www.loc.gov/maps/. See also http://test.scmemory-search.org; https://scroom.files.wordpress.com/2010/07/city-of-charleston-historical-maps.pdf; C. F. Beautemps-Beaupré, *Practice of Nautical Surveying* (1808), trans. Richard Copeland (London, 1823); William Whewell, *Essay towards a First Approximation to a Map of Cotidal Lines* (London, 1833), 153–59, 172, 203–27.

20. See, for example, W. C. Redfield, *On Three Several Hurricanes of the Atlantic* (New Haven, CT: B. L. Hamlen, 1846), 24; Henry Piddington, *Sailor's Horn-Book for the Law of Storms*, 3rd ed. (London, 1860), 1–12, 168–76; Act of 3/20/1794, ch. 9 § 1, 1 Stat. 345, 346.

21. Capt. A. H. Bowman (10/11/1839, 1/21/1842), Sen. Ex. Doc. no. 1 (33/1) 168, 453, 456; *Charleston Yearbook* 478–79, 494–98; J. Moore (1981B) 18.

22. *Charleston Yearbook* 491; Wise 2; www.loc.gov/resource/g3913c.cws00132 /?r=0.401,0.719,0.211,0.129,0; Douglas W. Bostick, *The Morris Island Lighthouse* (Charleston, 2008), 14.

23. See, for example, M. J. Hancock et al., "Sandbar Formation under Surface Waves," *J. Geophysical Res.* 113/C7:1 (7/2008).

24. William Bull (11/30/1770), Merrens 254, 261; Maffitt in Bache et al. 16–21; *Charleston Yearbook* 495–99; *Appleton* 99. See also *Report of the Superintendent of the Coast Survey . . . During the Year 1852* (Washington, 1853), 80.

25. *Globe* (34/3) App. 272 (1/20/1857).
26. See, for example, Matthew Fontaine Maury, "Remarks on the Gulf Stream and Currents of the Sea," *Am. J. Sci. & the Arts* 47/1:161 (10/1844); Maury, *Lieut. Maury's Investigations of the Winds and Currents of the Sea* (Washington, 1851); Maury, *The Physical Geography of the Sea* (1855); Grady 93–97, 122–28.
27. L. F. Vernon-Harcourt, *Harbours and Docks* (Oxford, 1885), 1:173; W. M. Black, "Improvement of Harbors on the South Atlantic Coast," *Trans. Am. Soc. Civil Eng.* 29/7:223, 246 (7/1893).
28. Regarding the relationship between the velocity of the current and the nature of the particles carried and deposited, see, for example, Edward Forbes in *Proc. Royal Soc. of Edinb.* 3:474 (1857); D. S. Howard, "Formation of Bars in Rivers and Harbors," *J. Franklin Inst.* 66:73 (8/1858).
29. Q. A. Gillmore/A. A. Humphreys (3/9/1878), *Annual Report of the Chief of Engineers* (1878) 1:554–57.
30. Melancthon T. Woolsey et al., "Survey of Ports South of the Chesapeake" (12/20/1836), *Public Documents Printed by Order of the Senate of the United States* (24/2), vol. 2, doc. 194, pp. 2–3 (Washington, 1837). See also Act of 5/26/1824, ch. 166, 4 Stat. 48. 194; *American Almanac and Repository of Useful Knowledge* (Boston, 1830), 13–15; id. (Boston, 1860) 7; Henry Mitchell, *Tides and Tidal Phenomena* (Washington, 1868), 12. Compare the map, circa 1825, at www.loc.gov/resource/g3913c.cws00132/?r=0.401,0.719,0.211,0.129,0.
31. *Globe* (26/1) 521–22 (7/11/1840); id. (26/1) App. 368 (4/1/1840).
32. Three of Congress's powers enumerated in section 8 of Article I—"to regulate commerce with foreign nations, and among the several states," to build "forts, magazines, arsenals, dock-yards, and other needful buildings," and to "promote the general Welfare"—were almost universally considered sufficient to support congressional financing, construction, and staffing of such assets within states. See, for example, Act of 8/7/1789 ch. 9 § 2, 1 Stat. 53; Act of 7/22/1790, ch. 32, 1 Stat. 137; *Annals* (18/1) 1:1009 (1/13/1824) (Rep. P. P. Barbour, Crawf.-R/VA); "Act for Ceding to and Vesting in the United States the Light House on Middle Bay Island" (1/20/1790), *SLSC* 5:147; Hamilton/Benjamin Lincoln (3/10/1790), *Papers of Alexander Hamilton*, ed. Harold C. Syrett (New York: Columbia University Press, 1961–1987), 6:297; Currie 1:69–70.
33. Maffitt in Bache et al. 17–21; *Hunt's Merchants' Mag. & Commercial Rev.* 37:353, 492, 493 (10/1857); *Coast Survey 1855* 60; *Charleston Yearbook* 498; Robert Bunch/W. G. Romaine (1/3/1861), *Naut. Mag. & Naval Chron.* (2/1861) 103–4; W. W. Harllee/Pickens (3/26/1861), *Convention Journal* 533–34; George R. Putnam, *Lighthouses and Lightships of the United States* (Boston: Houghton Mifflin, 1917), 17, 100. See also Douglas W. Bostick, *The Morris Island Lighthouse* (Charleston, 2008); Alexander G. Findlay, *Description and List of the Lighthouses of the World 1861* (London, 1861), 129; John Purdy, *Memoir, Descriptive and Explanatory, of the Northern Atlantic Ocean*, 11th ed. (London, 1861), 99–100, 165. A condition of federal funding and maintenance of lighthouses, beacons, buoys, and public piers theretofore owned and maintained by the states was that the relevant states cede the facilities and land. Act of 8/7/1789, ch. 9 § 1, 1 Stat. 53, 54. See also "Act for Ceding to and Vesting in the United States the Light House on Middle Bay Island" (1/20/1790), *SLSC* 5:147.

34. S. C. Turner et al./Pickens (1/5/1861), Blair (1881) 361–62. They did not specify whether the sixteen-foot limit was for high or low tide. See also John L. Branch/L. M. Hatch (1/11/1861), *OR* 1/53:118; Soady 173–74; *Coast Survey 1859* 126, 139, 143, 169; *Coast Survey 1860* 134. *Appleton* 99 reported eleven feet for Maffitt's Channel.

35. Maffitt in Bache et al. 16–21. See also A. H. Bowman/Totten (1/29/1853), Sen. Ex. Doc. no. 1 (33/1) 461; Maffitt, "Letter to the Superintendent" (9/1855), *Coast Survey 1855* 155; *Coast Survey 1859* 126–27; *Coast Survey 1860* 60, 123; *Charleston Yearbook* 495–99; "Report of the Superintendent of the Coast Survey" (10/1849) 45, Sen. Ex. Doc. no. 5 (31/1); A. D. Bache, "Method Used in the Coast Survey Showing the Results of Current Observations," *Coast Survey 1851* 136; Bland Simpson, *Two Captains from Carolina* (Chapel Hill: University of North Carolina Press, 2012), 108–12; *Appleton* 99; Fenn Peck/Bache (3/17/1852), Sen. Ex. Doc. no. 1 (33/1) 460; W. M. Black, "Improvement of Harbors on the South Atlantic Coast," *Trans. Am. Soc. Civil Eng.* 29/7:223, 227–31 (1893); Allen M. Teeter, *Effects of Cooper River Rediversion Flows on Shoaling Conditions at Charleston Harbor, South Carolina*, Army Corps of Engineers Tech. Rep. HL-89-3 (2/1989) 1–11.

36. Maffitt in Bache et al. 21; Maffitt (1859) 698. See also Thomas Stevenson, *Design and Construction of Harbours*, 2nd ed. (Edinburgh, 1874), 238–39.

37. In addition to channels mentioned in the text, the Overall Channel was reported in the 1850 Coast Survey as blocked by a shoal of fine sand at its western mouth, there providing only six feet at mean low water. Lawford's Channel was reported by one authority as providing eleven feet at mean low water, by another as having provided twelve feet in 1817, but only seven feet by 1850. A third authority wrote in 1852 that so many shoals had developed in Lawford's Channel in the prior eighteen months that it had been abandoned by the Savannah steamers for which it had once been the preferred approach. *Appleton* 99; Bache et al. 18; Maffitt in Bache et al. 21–22. See also Robert Mills, *Statistics of South Carolina* (Charleston, 1826), 401. The Swash Channel, said to vary in depth from seven to ten feet, was subject to various vicissitudes. Maffitt in Bache et al. 16, 20; *Appleton* 99. Gustavus Vasa Fox later wrote that the Swash Channel had "no shoal spots less than nine feet at high water." Fox (2/24/1865), *ORN* 1/4:245–46; "Result of G. V. Fox's Plan for Reinforcing Fort Sumter," Fox (1920) 1:38.

38. Bache et al. 11, 14; Maffitt in Bache et al. 20.

39. See Fox, "Mem. for the Relief of Fort Sumter, by G. V. Fox," *Fox Collection* Box 14, Folder 10, Fox (2/6/1861), *ORN* 1/4:223, Fox (1920) 1:8.

40. See, for example, H. Wager Halleck, "Report on the Means of National Defence" (10/20/1843), Sen. Ex. Doc. 85 (28/2) 2, 17–76; Totten (1851) 5–6, 14–22.

41. See, for example, Rowena Reed, *Combined Operations in the Civil War* (Annapolis, MD: Naval Institute Press, 1978), 11; John Caldwell Tidball, *Manual of Heavy Artillery Service*, 2nd ed. (Washington, 1881), 38–39, 64–65, 347, 356.

42. Bache et al. 11; Maffitt in Bache et al. 20; John R. Spears, *History of Our Navy from Its Origin to the End of the War with Spain* (New York, 1899), 4:465–67.

43. See, for example, "Naval Force" 2–4, 18; Toucey, "Report of the Sec. of the Navy," *Globe* (36/2) App. 20, 22 (12/1/1860); Edgar Stanton Maclay, *History of the United States Navy from 1775 to 1898*, rev. ed. (New York, 1898), 2:159–60; Kenneth J. Blume and Spencer C. Tucker, "Navy, U.S.," Tucker (2011) 2:461. Cf. *Officers' Register* 111–19.

44. See Jeremiah Black/Scott (1/16/1861), *OR* 1/1:140, 142. See also *Globe* (36/2) 1095 (2/21/1861); Tucker (2011) 1:81; *ORN* 2/1:48. That *Brooklyn* had crossed the bar before was irrelevant because it had used a local pilot navigating one of the channels then designated by buoys and range dayboard markers. See, for example, *NYT* (1/10/1861).

45. Silverstone 35; *DANFS*.

46. Scott/A. H. Schultz (1/2/1861), *Holt Papers* Box 101, "Correspondence with Winfield Scott" File, *OR* 1/1:128; Scott (1/4/1861), appended to Buchanan/Scott (12/31/1860), *Lincoln Papers*; Gibson and Gibson 1:300; Weed/Lincoln (1/4/1861), *Lincoln Papers*; V. Jones 5, 7; Hendrickson 105.

47. Buchanan would write that Scott "had unluckily become convinced" by "a gentleman whom I forbear to name." [Buchanan] (1866) 190; "Answer to General Scott" (10/28/1862), Buchanan (1908–1911) 11:279, 288. See also Buchanan/Toucey (9/15/1865), id. 11:397; Toucey/Buchanan (9/18/1865), id. 11:398n1. Fox never suggested that he was Scott's source for the idea of using a commercial vessel, and Scott may have had no substantive contact with Fox prior to February, leaving unanswered who the "gentleman" was. See Scott/Fox (1/30/1861), *Fox Collection* Series I, Box 4, Folder 11.

48. "Naval Force" 4, 20; SC Executive Council minutes (1/5/1861), Blair (1881) 361; Buchanan/J. M. Mason et al. (1/10/1861), Buchanan (1908–1911) 11:103, 104; *ORN* 1/4:xv; *ORN* 2/1:48; Silverstone 35; *Appleton* 499. See also *ORN* 1/1:xv; *Globe* (36/2) 1095 (2/21/1861); Welles (1861) 235; George E. Buker, *Blockaders, Refugees, & Contrabands* (Tuscaloosa: University of Alabama Press, 1993), 1.

49. *NYT* (1/7/1861) 1; Charles R. Woods/Henry L. Scott (1/13/1861), *OR* 1/1:9. The *Times* story was reproduced in many newspapers, for example, *Hartford Daily Current* (1/8/1861) 2. See also (1/7/1861), C. F. Adams Sr.

50. Osbon 107; J. Perry 87–94.

51. *Home Letters of General Sherman*, ed. M. A. DeWolfe Howe (New York: C. Scribner's Sons, 1909), 190.

52. *New-York Daily Tribune* (1/8/1861) 4.

53. Wigfall/Pickens (1/8/1861), T. Anderson 39, 54–55. See also *Edgefield (SC) Advertiser* (1/9/1861) 2.

54. L. Q. Washington/Pickens (1/8/1861), Blair (1881) 363; "Jones"/Pickens (1/7/1861), id. 362; W. S. Ashe/J. L. Orr (1/8/1861), id. 363.

55. Pickens/Col. John Cunningham (1/9/1861) quoted in Crawford (1915) item 343. See also Pickens/D. H. Hamilton (1/9/1861), id., item 344.

56. The spy, not knowing about *Star of the West*, speculated that since no troops had boarded *Brooklyn*, a reinforcement of Sumter was not in prospect. Charles Harris/Pickens (1/10/1861), Blair (1881) 365.

57. L. Q. Washington/Pickens (1/11/1861), Blair (1881) 365.

58. Morrison 13–14.

59. Scott/Col. Justin Dimick (12/31/1860), *OR* 1/1:119; "Memoranda: Instructions to Be Sent by Colonel Thomas, in Writing, to Major Anderson" [undated], *Holt Papers* Box 101, "Correspondence with Winfield Scott" File; Scott/Lt. Col. Lorenzo Thomas (1/2/1861), *OR* 1/1:128; Thomas/Scott (1/4/1861), *OR* 1/1:130; Thomas/Charles R. Woods (1/5/1861), *OR* 1/1:131–32. See also Scott/Dimick [undated], *Holt Papers* Box 101, "Correspondence with Winfield Scott" File.

60. Thomas/Anderson (1/5/1861), *Lincoln Archives*; T. Anderson 31–32; Crawford (1887) 168–83; Keyes 372–73; Doubleday (1876) 101–5; K. Williams 1:26–27.

61. Anderson/Cooper (1/6/1861), *OR* 1/1:133.

62. Crawford (1/8/1861), *Fort Sumter Diary* 11–12. See also Detzer 43–44.

63. See, for example, Scott/William Walker (1/7/1861), *ORN* 1/4:220; Toucey/Walker (1/7/1861), id. Secretary of the Interior Jacob Thompson, a Mississippian, believed that it was Buchanan who aborted the operation. See note 103 below and accompanying text. It is difficult to believe that Buchanan, having been so reluctant to approve the mission, wished to proceed after being informed that the element of surprise was lost, even if Scott wanted to continue.

64. Holt/Jacob Thompson (3/5/1861), W. Scott (1862) 19–20; [Buchanan] (1866) 191; H. King (1872) 409; *NYT* (9/16/1865) 8.

65. *New-York Daily Tribune* (1/9/1861) 5.

66. Thomas/Woods (1/5/1861), *OR* 1/1:131.

67. *NY Evening Post* reproduced in, for example, *Central Wisconsin Independent* (1/24/1861) 1.

68. Chester 60–61; Detzer 152–63.

69. McGowan (1/12/1861), *NYT* (1/16/1861); *HABS* 13–14; Paine 168. See also Crawford (1915) item 433.

70. A. C. Garlington/Pickens (3/26/1861), *Convention Journal* 528, 530.

71. Silverstone 239. See also P. F. Stevens/D. F. Jamison (1/9/1861) quoted in Crawford (1915) item 436; Livia Hallam with James Reasoner, *Call to Arms* (Nashville, TN: Cumberland House, 2005), 10–15.

72. *NY Post* reproduced in, for example, *Central Wisconsin Independent* (1/24/1861) 1; H. M. Clarkson, "Story of *The Star of the West*," *Confed. Vet.* 21/5:234 (5/1913). Regarding ricochets, see, for example, Roberts 79–83. See also *Appleton* 663.

73. Crawford (1887) [474–75]; J. Johnson 17; Deed (11/22/1841), SC Dep't of Archives and Hist.

74. See James Heyward Trapier/Pickens (1/4/1861) quoted in Crawford (1915) item 458.

75. Foster (1866) 7.

76. *NY Post* reproduced in, for example, *Central Wisconsin Independent* (1/24/1861) 1; Woods/Henry L. Scott (1/13/1861), *OR* 1/1:9, 10; *Appleton* 662–63; H. Scott 64–65. A. B. Roman's version of the engagement was read and approved by Pierre G. T. Beauregard, who had reportedly spoken to Captain McGowan in New Orleans not long after the incident. Roman 1:27–28. Although that Union witness believed he heard guns of two different calibers fired from Morris Island, Robert Barnwell Rhett told Edmund Ruffin, "There were but three guns (24 pounders) at the sand battery on Morris's Island, & only one instrument for taking aim, which caused slow firing. But 7 shots were fired, of which 3 struck." (1/11/1861), Ruffin (1972–1989) 1:530. See also Dahlgren (1856B) 13–15, 29–37; T. Taylor 2:154, 177; Guernsey and Alden 40; Philip Katcher, *Confederate Artilleryman 1861–65* (Oxford: Osprey, 2001), 12.

77. McGowan/M. O. Roberts (1/12/1861), *NYT* (1/16/1861); J. Davis (1938) 1:291n. Several hours later, Governor Pickens met with the five other members of his executive council and decided not to initiate a pursuit. "A.B." (1/9/1861), Blair (1881) 363–64.

78. Brackett 947. See also U.S. Dep't of Educ., *Report of the Commissioner of Education* (Washington, 1868), 785–88.
79. (1/9/1861), Simpson, Sears, and Sheehan-Dean 189. Regarding Fort Moultrie's participation, see, for example, K. Williams 1:385–86n25.
80. Dickert 18.
81. *Charleston Courier* (1/10/1861), W. A. Harris 4, 23–25; *Mercury* (1/10/1858) quoted in Lossing 1:158; Crawford (1887) 188; M. Klein 192–204.
82. Powe 24; Whitelaw Reid, *After the War: A Southern Tour* (New York, 1866), 63.
83. [De Forest] 497; Halleck 280; Gibbon 58–59; Roberts 32; H. Scott 164–65; Katcher 55–61. See also Ripley 45–55, 71–85, 368–69.
84. [De Forest] 490.
85. Anderson/Pickens (1/9/1861), *OR* 1/1:134. See also *New-York Daily Tribune* (1/10/1861) 5; id. (1/11/1861) 5.
86. Pickens/Anderson (1/9/1861), *OR* 1/1:135. See also Pickens, Message No. 1 (11/5/1861), *Journal of the Senate of the State of South Carolina* (Columbia, SC, 1861), 10, 22.
87. *New-York Daily Tribune* (1/29/1861) 8.
88. Chester 61; T. H. Williams (1954) 15.
89. Doubleday (1876) 75.
90. Ulysses Doubleday/Lincoln (1/15/1861), *Lincoln Papers*.
91. Gourdin/Anderson (2/2/1861), *S.C. Hist. Mag.* 60/1 (1/1959) 10, 12. See also Hurlbert (1945) 80–91.
92. See, for example, [Hurlbert] (1879) 484–89; Rhodes (1892–1906) 3:326.
93. Senator John Crittenden later thought it worthwhile to assure Anderson that the secession of additional states in January was not triggered by his move to Fort Sumter. Crittenden/Anderson (2/12/1861), *Anderson Papers* 10:2283.
94. "Such leniency," Florida memoirist Ellen Call Long later wrote, "is inexplicable, unless your government condemns the whole proceedings as child's play, that will exhaust itself in one effort." *Florida Breezes; or, Florida, New and Old* (Jacksonville, FL, 1883), 309. Although some Unionists entertained this belief, neither Anderson nor Buchanan did.
95. Lawton (1911) 16–17.
96. Keyes 367–68. See also Crawford (2/3/1861), describing Anderson as "a sincere Christian, a frank, straightforward gentleman and soldier," worth "all the praise that has been showered upon him." Crawford (1915) item 101.
97. Scott endorsement of Holt/Lincoln (3/5/1861), *Lincoln Papers*; W. Scott (1862) 6; Scott, "Communicated to the Editors [of the *National Intelligencer*] for Publication" (10/21/1862), Buchanan (1908–1911) 11:293, 298; Toucey/W. A. Howard (1/24/1861), "Naval Force" 17, 19–20; McClure (1892) 297–98. Cf. [Buchanan] (1866) 189; Stanton/Buchanan (3/10/1861), Curtis 2:529.
98. Toucey/Charles McCauley (12/31/1860), *ORN* 1/4:219; Toucey/McCauley (1/3/1861), *ORN* 1/4:219; Elliott 684–85.
99. See Jefferson Davis/W. H. Trescot (1/11/1861), *OR* 1/53:118; [Buchanan] (1866) 191–92.

100. *Brooklyn's* captain, subsequently reporting all this to Toucey, added, "Considering this information reliable, and not deeming it necessary" for *Brooklyn* to lower one of its boats and send it over the bar, "which might have invited a shot from the numerous batteries that lined the shores, we put about" for Hampton Roads. W. S. Walker/Toucey (1/15/1861), *OR* 1/4:221; (1/13/1861) Ruffin (1972–1989) 1:533. Well into the war, Gustavus Vasa Fox would initiate the Union effort to block these same channels by buying twenty-four New Bedford whalers and filling them with seventy-five hundred tons of stone pulled from New England rural walls, making the so-called Stone Fleet. See *History of New Bedford*, ed. Zephaniah Pease (New York: Lewis Historical, 1918), 1:50–57; John Spears, *The Story of the New England Whalers* (New York: Macmillan, 1908), 334–35, 356, 390–93.

101. (1/9/1861), Blair (1881) 364. See also Wigfall/Pickens (1/8/1861), *OR* 1/1:253; Anderson/Pickens (1/9/1861), *OR* 1/1:134; Anderson/Cooper (1/6/1861), *OR* 1/1:133; Pickens/Anderson (1/9/1861), *OR* 1/1:136; Holt/Anderson (1/16/1861), *OR* 1/1:140; Anderson/Holt (1/21/1861), *OR* 1/1:143; W. S. Walker/Toucey (1/15/1861), *ORN* 1/4:221; Crawford (1887) 185–92, 200–201; Doubleday (1876) 107–8; http://markerhunter.wordpress.com/2011/01/10/uss-brooklyn-off-charleston/.

102. See, for example, S. W. Crawford (1/28/1861), *Fort Sumter Diary* 22.

103. [De Forest] 501. Pickens would soon declare martial law on Sullivan's Island, making such conversations less likely. Proclamation (2/9/1861), *Pickens Papers* Reel 2.

104. Roswell S. Ripley/ R. G. M. Dunovant (1/16/1861) quoted in Crawford (1915) item 381; D. F. Jamison/Pickens (3/25/1861), *Convention Journal* 518.

105. Osbon 108.

106. *NYT* (1/14/1861).

107. Scott endorsement of Holt/Lincoln (3/5/1861), *Lincoln Papers*.

108. *New York Sun* (1/11/1861) 2.

109. *OR* 4/1:60–61. While the role of judges is typically limited to trying cases or controversies between parties who come before them, Judge David Smalley of Vermont was sufficiently incensed by the firing upon *Star of the West* that, assigned to the federal circuit court in New York, he charged the sitting grand jury to investigate possible acts of treason by South Carolina. *In re* Charge to Grand Jury—Treason, 4 Blatch. Cir. Ct. Rpts. 518, 519, 30 Fed. Cases no. 18,270, 1032, 1033 (2nd Cir. 1861). Francis C. Treadwell of New York, an aging pro-Union attorney and gadfly, tried to file in the Supreme Court a sworn complaint demanding the arrest of leading secessionists as traitors. Those named included James Henry Hammond, J. W. Hayne, William Porcher Miles, James Chesnut, and Laurence M. Keitt of South Carolina; John B. Floyd and Roger A. Pryor of Virginia; Jefferson Davis of Mississippi; Robert Toombs, Martin J. Crawford, and Howell Cobb of Georgia; and L. T. Wigfall of Texas. This was a slapdash effort, and Chief Justice Taney summarily rejected it. Francis C. Treadwell, *Secession an Absurdity: It Is Perjury, Treason & War*, 2nd ed. (New York, 1861), 15–16.

110. Thompson, circa late Feb. 1861, *National Republican* (3/1/1861) 2; Thompson/Buchanan (1/8/1861), Buchanan/Thompson (1/9/1861), Buchanan (1908–1911) 11:100, 101; [Miles et al.] 20; Tilley 116–30; Buchanan (10/28/1862), W. Scott (1862) 11, 17; J. Black 19–20; Holt/Thompson (3/5/1861), W. Scott (1862) 19–20; H. King (1872) 409; H. King (1895) 96–99; "Reply of Mr. Thompson to Mr. Holt," *NYT* (3/19/1861); E. Cooper 41–49; Holt/Joshua Speed (5/31/1861), Holt, *The Fallacy of*

Neutrality: An Address by the Hon. Joseph Holt (New York, 1861), 15; Charles B. Dew, *Apostles of Disunion* (Charlottesville: University Press of Virginia, 2001), 30–32. See also *New-York Daily Tribune* (1/9/1861) 5; J. Cutler Andrews, "The Southern Telegraph Company, 1861–1865," *J. South. Hist.* 30/3:319, 323 (8/1964).

111. (1/15/1861), C. F. Adams Sr.

112. The financing is summarized in Edward Frost/Pickens (3/25/1861), *Convention Journal* 524.

113. Shortly after Anderson had transferred his men to Fort Sumter in December, Captain N. L. Coste of the cutter *William Aiken*, then in Charleston Harbor, hauled down the Revenue Service flag and volunteered his vessel and himself to the state. *Anderson (SC) Intelligencer* (1/3/1861) 2; *NYT* (1/9/1861); Foster (1952) 5; Hendrickson 89.

114. John Adams Dix, *Speeches and Occasional Addresses* (New York, 1864), 2:437–42, 446–51. Dix's letter is reproduced in, for example, Preble 399. A loyal seaman had been sufficiently impressed by Dix's order that he kept the Revenue flag and forwarded it. See David Richie in *Memoirs of John Adams Dix*, comp. Morgan Dix (New York, 1883), 1:374, 375. See also id. 1:370–71. (Between Cobb's resignation and Dix's appointment was the short tenure of Philip F. Thomas.)

115. Lyons/Russell (1/15/1861), Barnes and Barnes 20.

116. Holt/Anderson (1/10/1861), *OR* 1/1:136, Crawford (1887) 177; Holt/Anderson (1/16/1861), *OR* 1/1:140, Crawford (1887) 205. See also Dawson 186–90; Nicolay and Hay (1917) 4:22–23.

117. Holt/Anderson (2/23/1861), *OR* 1/1:182, Crawford (1887) 293 quoting Holt/Anderson (1/10/1861), Crawford (1887) 177 and citing Buell/Anderson (12/11/1860), *OR* 1/1:89. See also John Scoffern, *Projectile Weapons of War and Explosive Compounds*, 4th ed. (London, 1859), 365–70.

118. See, for example, *New York Sun* (1/10/1861) 2; *New-York Daily Tribune* (1/10/1861) 5.

119. Anderson/Larz Anderson (8/5/1832), *Massacre at Bad Axe*, comp. Crawford B. Thayer (n.p.: n.p., 1984), 292; Anderson/E. Anderson (3/8/1847), R. Anderson (1911) 70, 71. See also R. Anderson (1888). Anderson wrote to Gourdin, "I think an appeal to arms and to brute force is unbecoming the age in which we live." He told a churchman from rural Connecticut, "No one would more deeply deplore the shedding of blood than I should. I trust in God that time may now be gained, and that instead of resorting to the arbitrament of the sword, reason and good sense will regulate the action of those in authority." Anderson/Gourdin (12/11/1860), Crawford (1887) 69; "General Political Intelligence," *NYT* (2/14/1861); Dawson 1/3:144n; Faulkner 83.

120. Lawton (1914) 121–44.

121. H. Adams/C. F. Adams Jr. (1/11/1861), H. Adams (1982–1986) 1:220, 221, H. Adams (1930–1938) 1:78, 79.

122. See, for example, M. Adams 9–10, 27–28, 50; Welles (11/1870) 618; Parton 3:442–46; Ostaus 88; Potter (1976) 43; Richard N. Current, *Northernizing the South* (Athens: University of Georgia Press, 1983), 28–30; Adam L. Tate, *Conservatism and Southern Intellectuals 1789–1861* (Columbia: University of Missouri Press, 2005), 61–68; M. Adams 2–25; Stampp (1990) 27; Greenberg 130–31. South Carolina attorney general Isaac W. Hayne accosted President Buchanan with the "disguised and secret manner" with which the reinforcement had been attempted. Hayne/Buchanan (1/31/1861), Buchanan (1908–1911) 11:132, J. Davis (1938) 1:634, 638, *Correspondence and Other*

Papers Relating to Fort Sumter, 2nd ed. (Charleston, 1861), 28; Buchanan (10/28/1862), W. Scott (1862) 11, 22.

123. (4/30/1861), Russell (1861B) 3, 5; Potter (1976) 30–35. See also Hammond/Thomas Clarkson (1/28/1845), Hammond (1866) 114, 134.

124. Blair/Fox (1/31/1861), Fox (1920) 1:3, 4. See also Charles Francis Adams, *Some Phases of the Civil War* (Cambridge, MA: Harvard University Press, 1905), 17–19; Charles L. Woodbury, *Genealogical Sketches of the Woodbury Family* (Manchester, NH: J. B. Clarke, 1904), 185.

125. George W. Lay/Slemmer (1/3/1861), *OR* 1/1:334. Cf. Erben 214–15. See also W. W. Davis 61–64; Bearss (1957–1961) 36:127–28; Bearss (1989) 6–7; Bearss (1983) 510–11, 527; Scott/Zealous B. Tower (1/4/1861), *OR* 1/1:350; Mottelay and Campbell-Copeland 48–49.

126. *OR* 1/1:444. See also Bearss (1957–1961) 36:139.

127. See, for example, Weaver 158–70.

128. Mallory's state would secede on January 10, but he would not withdraw from the Senate until January 21.

129. Toucey/Armstrong (1/3/1861), *ORN* 1/4:5; Armstrong acknowledgment, id.

130. See, for example, C. M. Conrad/Linn Boyd (12/11/1851), H.R., Exec. Doc. No. 5 (32/1) 22; Slemmer/Samuel Cooper (1/8/1861), *OR* 1/1:333; Slemmer/Lorenzo Thomas (2/5/1861), *OR* 1/1:334, 336, 341; Erben 215–16; Henry Walke/Toucey (2/4/1861), *ORN* 1/4:78, 79; Halleck 70–73; *NYT* (2/5/1861); Weaver 158–63; W. W. Davis 74–86; J. Tidball 117–18; J. Gilman 27–28; *OR* 3/1:48; Nicolay and Hay (1917) 3:163; Bearss (1983) 55–97; Robinson 97–98; Cecil B. Hartley, *Heroes and Patriots of the South* (Philadelphia, 1860), 269–87; Mottelay and Campbell-Copeland 45.

131. Melville's narrator, White-Jacket, has grown so to hate the practice that when Captain Claret is about to flog him for an offense he did not commit, he contemplates killing Claret, even at the cost of his own life. Herman Melville, *White-Jacket* (1850; Boston, 1892), 260–65. Whether and to what extent the fictional Claret is Armstrong is unsettled. See, for example, S. R. Franklin, *Memories of a Rear-Admiral* (New York, 1898), 18–20, 64–69; Seitz 25n; Howard Vincent, *The Tailoring of Melville's White-Jacket* (Evanston, IL: Northwestern University Press, 1970), 47. The squadron commander, Commodore Thomas ap [= son of] Catesby Jones, using *United States* as his flagship, was subsequently relieved of command, and Congress, under the influence of Melville's novel, banned flogging. *Globe* (31/1) 2057–61 (9/28/1850); Myra Glenn, "The Naval Reform Campaign against Flogging," *Am. Quart.* 35/4:408 (Autumn 1983); Paullin 231–34.

132. Cannons thus turned over included three 10-inch and twelve 8-inch columbiads, twenty-four 42-pounders, thirty-four 32-pounders, and seventy-five 24-pounders. Josiah Gorgas (4/20/1861), *OR* 4/1:227; Ryan 34–35, 53–54; Henry Walke, *Naval Scenes and Reminiscences of the Civil War in the United States* (New York, 1877), 4–7; Bearss (1983) 503–10; Paullin 217–18.

133. See, for example, Armstrong statement (2/20/1861), *ORN* 1/4:48, 51; court findings (2/20/1861), *ORN* 1/4:47; Welles, Navy General Order (4/24/1861), *ORN* 1/4:53. See also testimony of Armstrong (1/25/1861), "Naval Force" 57–93; Johns 25–28; Bearss (1957–1961) 36:126–33; W. W. Davis 75–77. Regarding the more egregious Twiggs case in Texas, see, for example, Victor 453–56; Texas v. White, 74 U.S. (7 Wall.) 700, 723–24 (1869).

134. J. Gilman 30–31. See also J. J. Dickison, "Military History of Florida," Evans 11:14–15.
135. J. J. Seibels/T. Lomax (1/13/1861), *OR* 1/52 Pt. II:7; [De Forest] 503; J. H. Gilman/ William H. Chase (1/16/1861), *ORN* 1/4:63.
136. Toucey/W. S. Walker (1/21/1861), *ORN* 1/4:66; Toucey/James Glynn et al. (1/21/1861), *ORN* 1/4:67; Lorenzo Thomas/Justin Dimick (1/21/1861), *OR* 1/1:351; Thomas/ Vogdes (1/21/1861), *OR* 1/1:352. See also Crawford (1915) items 453 and 454.
137. Slidell/Perry (1/18/1861), *OR* 1/1:445. See also William H. Chase/V. M. Randolph (1/21/1861), *ORN* 1/4:211; Mallory/Slidell (1/28/1861), *OR* 1/1:354; Mallory/ Chase (1/28/1861), *ORN* 1/4:213; A. B. Moore/William M. Brooks (1/28/1861), *OR* 1/1:445, 446; Tilley 15–31; Chase/Randolph (1/30/1861), *ORN* 1/4:213, 214; Scott (3/30/1861), W. Scott (1862), 3, 8; [Buchanan] (1866) 215–16; Bearss (1989) 7–10, 18; Chadwick 249–51; Stanton/Buchanan (7/16/1861), Stanton 481. See also Johns 42–44; Nevins (1950) 1:78.
138. See Albert Castel, "The Bombardment of Fort Sumter," in *Battle Chronicles of the Civil War*, ed. James M. McPherson (New York: Macmillan, 1989), 1:23, 36; Flower 99–100.
139. Holt, Toucey/Glynn, W. S. Walker, Slemmer (1/29/1861), *Welles Papers/NYPL* Box 3 Reel 2, *OR* 1/1:355; Holt/Slemmer (1/29/1861), *OR* 1/1:355; S. R. Mallory/Chase (1/29/1861), *ORN* 1/4:213; Bearss (1983) 524–26; *Fox Collection* Series I, Box 4, Folder 11.
140. See S. R. Mallory/V. M. Randolph (1/28/1861), *ORN* 1/4:212; Mallory/Slidell (1/28/1861), *OR* 1/1:354; William Chase/Randolph (1/28, 30/1861), *ORN* 1/4:212, 413.
141. Vogdes/Lorenzo Thomas (2/7/1861), *OR* 1/1:357; Erben 220; Buchanan (10/28/1862), W. Scott (1862) 11, 16–17; Crawford (1887) 401; [Buchanan] (1866) 215; "From Fort Pickens," *NYT* (4/2/1861); Silverstone 128.
142. J. Moore (1981A); S. J. Watson, "Knowledge, Interest and the Limits of Military Professionalism," *War in History* 5/3:280, 302–6 (7/1998); Bearss (1983) 489–90; Totten (1857).
143. Vogdes/Thomas (2/7/1861), *OR* 1/1:357; Seitz 31–32. The ordnance included several large-bore columbiads, one 8-inch seacoast howitzer, several 42- and fourteen 32-pounders, twenty-five 24-pound howitzers, seven 12-pounders, six field pieces, and twenty-two thousand pounds of powder.
144. Randolph/Chase (1/30/1861), *ORN* 1/4:214. See also *Globe* (36/1) 3068 (6/16/1860) (Senator Mallory).
145. H. A. Adams/Toucey (2/19/1861), *ORN* 1/4:85; Vogdes/Adams (4/13/1861), *ORN* 1/4:116; Bearss (1983) 529–30.
146. Vogdes/Thomas (2/7/1861), *OR* 1/1:357; Bearss (1983) 489–90. See also Dennis Hart Mahan, *Summary of the Course of Permanent Fortification* (Charleston, 1862), 339–49; R. Browning 40–41, 63–66; Johns 44.

Chapter 5: "A Point of Pride"

1. (1/8/1861), *Globe* (36/2) 294–95 (1/9/1861); [Buchanan] (1866) 291, 294.
2. Scott, "Views Suggested by the Imminent Danger" (10/29/1860), F. Moore (1861–1866) 1:122; Scott/Floyd (10/30/1860), id. 1:123; *National Intelligencer* (1/18/1861), Buchanan

(1908–1911) 11:301. Scott asserted by way of excuse that Floyd, now back in Virginia as the secessionists' hero, had so misstated the relevant history that he felt obliged to set things straight. See also Scott, "Rejoinder of Lieutenant-General Scott to Ex-President Buchanan" (11/12/1862), id. 11:304, 306; E. Townsend 249, [Buchanan] (1866) 287; Buchanan (10/28/1862), W. Scott (1862) 11, 17–18; id. 6; McClure (1892) 303. Buchanan later called Scott's decision to publish the memorandum a "violation of the sacred confidence which ought to prevail between the commanding General of the army and the Commander-in-Chief." Buchanan, "Answer to General Scott" (10/28/1862), Buchanan (1908–1911) 11:279, 283; [Buchanan] (1866) 99–106. Scott had in fact distributed copies of this "confidential" memo in his native Virginia at the time he gave it to Buchanan and Floyd. While Virginians would applaud Floyd for refusing Scott's request to reinforce the Southern forts, Scott, himself a Virginian, could also be praised, the *Richmond Examiner* in 1863 stating, "Had Scott been able to have got these forts in the condition he desired them to be, the Southern Confederacy would not now exist." Quoted in F. Moore (1861–1866) 1:387, W. Scott (1864) 2:615–16; M. Wright 298.

3. *OR* 3/1:22–26, 47–48; Buchanan (10/28/1862), W. Scott (1862) 11, 12; H. Scott 47–51; Peskin 239; Reid 341; Chadwick 186.

4. Richard Delafield/Totten (4/29/1844), U.S. Cong., Sen., Public Documents (28/2) 1:211; *Army and Navy Chronicle* 9:392 (12/19/1839); Morrison 18; *Appleton* 26; U.S. Const. Art. II. § 1; Samuel Cooper, *Concise System of Instructions and Regulations for the Militia and Volunteers* (Philadelphia, 1836), 68–69; Edward M. Coffman, *The Old Army* (New York: Oxford University Press, 1986), 42–103; Weigley (1962) 10–78. See also Gordon Wood, *Empire of Liberty* (New York: Oxford University Press, 2009), 292–98.

5. See, for example, Goodheart 169; C. F. Adams Jr. (1903) 63–70. Over the winter of 1860–1861, seventy-four West Point cadets either resigned or were dismissed for refusing the oath of allegiance. James L. Morrison, "The Struggle between Sectionalism and Nationalism at Ante-bellum West Point" (1973), Hubbell 19–21. Most enlisted men were foreign-born Northerners. As Anderson had been warned by Captain Ord, some switched sides for higher pay. See chapter 2, notes 85–87 above and accompanying text.

6. See, for example, William Plum, *Military Telegraph during the Civil War in the United States* (Chicago, 1881), 1:35–48.

7. John A. Hamilton, "An Incident of Fort Sumter," *South. Hist. Soc. Papers* 9/6:265 (6/1881); W. W. Harllee/Pickens (3/26/1861), *Convention Journal* 533. Robert Gourdin, a friend of both Anderson and Alfred Huger, sometimes volunteered to handle Anderson's outgoing and incoming mail. See, for example, D. F. Jamison/L. M. Hatch (1/15/1861), *OR* 1/53:119; S.C. Executive Council minutes (1/5/1861), Blair (1881) 361.

8. Rhoades 24–25.

9. Pickens/Anderson (1/11/1861), *Appleton* 656; Anderson/Pickens (1/11/1861), id.; Pickens/Buchanan (1/11/1861), id.; Magrath/Hayne (1/12/1861), Hayne et al. 9, *NYT* (2/7/1861) 8; Pickens/Buchanan (1/12/1861), "Seizure of Forts, Arsenals, Revenue Cutters, and Other Property of the United States" 70, *Select Committee Reports*; Curtis 2:465; H.R. no. 88, "Relative to the Correspondence between the President and the Commissioners" (2/27/1861) 7–12, *Select Committee Reports*; Rhoades 23–24.

10. Davis/Hayne (1/15/1861), J. Davis (1971–) 7:10, 11; Davis/Pickens (1/20/1861), J. Davis (1923) 5:39, 40. See also Edmunds (1986) 159; Crawford (1915) item 142.

11. R. Anderson/Crittenden (1/12/1861), Crittenden 2:253; Anderson/Crawford (n.d.), quoted in Crawford (1915) [5]. See also Crittenden/Anderson (2/12/1861), H.R. Rpt. no. 441 (50/1) 2 (2/14/1888).

12. Davis/Hayne (1/15/1861), J. Davis (1971–) 7:10, 11. See also Hayne/Wigfall (1/17/1861), "Seizure of Forts, Arsenals, Revenue Cutters, and Other Property of the United States," 60, *Select Committee Reports*; Haynes/Wigfall (after 1/23/1861), *Correspondence and Other Papers Relating to Fort Sumter*, 2nd ed. (Charleston, 1861), 19; Hayne/Pickens (1/16, 22/1861), *Pickens Papers* Reel 2.

13. Buchanan (1/16/1861), Buchanan (1908–1911) 11:109. Clay resigned from the U.S. Senate five days later. See also T. J. Judge/Clay (2/4/1861), *OR* 1/52 Pt. II:21.

14. Henry Adams/Charles Francis Adams Jr. (1/17/1861), H. Adams (1982–1986) 1:221, 223–24. See also "From Fort Sumter," *NYT* (2/7/1861).

15. Holt/Hayne (1/22/1861), "Seizure of Forts, Arsenals, Revenue Cutters, and Other Property of the United States," 61, *Select Committee Reports*. A draft is in *Holt Papers* Box 100, Folder "Personal Correspondence 1861–69." See also Holt/Benjamin Fitzpatrick (1/22/1861), Hayne et al. 15; McClintock (2008) 134–35; *Globe* (36/2) 1256–57 (2/21/1861); *NYT* (9/16/1865) 8.

16. Hayne/Buchanan (1/31/1861), Buchanan (1908–1911) 11:132; Buchanan (10/28/1862), W. Scott (1862) 11, 22.

17. Pickens/Davis (1/23/1861), J. Davis (1971–) 7:23. See also Pickens/Davis (2/27/1861), Davis/Pickens (3/1/1861), J. Davis (1923) 5:58.

18. "Unionist"/Scott (1/24/1861), "Alleged Hostile Organization against the Government within the District of Columbia" (2/14/1861) 72, *Select Committee Reports*.

19. Pickens/Davis (1/23/1861), J. Davis (1971–) 7:23. See also Pickens/Davis (2/27/1861), J. Davis (1923) 5:58; Davis/Pickens (3/1/1861), id. 5:58.

20. Scott/Lincoln (3/11/1861), *Lincoln Papers*. Cf. Pierre G. T. Beauregard, "Defense of Charleston, South Carolina" (I), *North Am. Rev.* 143:419, 423 (5/1886). The view that Sumter could have been supplied and reinforced even in December was borne out by South Carolina's internal reports of its forces at that time. See, for example, James Simons/Pickens (1/1/1861), W. A. Harris 14.

21. A South Carolina militiaman assigned to Fort Johnson noted to his sister that Buchanan and Scott "may find it very easy to plan Coercion, but I'm afraid that by the time they are ready to execute they will find the whole Southern Country" lined up. (1/5/1861), Abbott and Puryear 62, 64; Morrison 8.

22. *Globe* (37/4) 1445 (3/7/1861).

23. (2/1/1861), *Home Letters of General Sherman*, ed. M. A. DeWolfe Howe (New York: C. Scribner's Sons, 1909), 195.

24. *NYT* (2/7/1861).

25. *Richmond Daily Dispatch* (2/9/1861); Tenney 22. See also G. W. Snyder, T. Seymour/Anderson (3/24/1861), *OR* 1/1:213, 214; Crawford (1887) 206–7.

26. Anderson quoted in Holt/Lincoln (3/5/1861), *Lincoln Papers*; H. King (1895) 126–28.

27. "Militia of the United States," H.R. Rep. no. 58 (1/30/1861) 3–4.

28. Holt/Hayne (2/6/1861), *OR* 1/1:166, 167; [Buchanan] (1866) 194–205. A draft of Holt's response is in *Holt Papers* Box 101, "Personal Correspondence 1861–69" File. See also Gorham 1:167–68; T. M. Cooley, *Treatise on the Constitutional Limitations*, 3rd ed. (Boston, 1874), 525–26n; Fort Leavenworth R.R. v. Lowe, 114 U.S. 525, 528–29 (1885).

29. Attorney General Jeremiah Black informed Buchanan that a president may administer an owner's right "of keeping exclusive possession and repelling exclusion," a right exercised to take back Harpers Ferry from John Brown. (11/20/1860), *Att'y-Gen. Ops.* 9:517, 520–21.

30. *The Federalist*, ed. Jacob E. Cooke (Middletown, CT: Wesleyan University Press, 1961), 288.

31. United States v. Railroad Bridge Co., 6 McLean 517, 526 (Cir. N.D. Ill. 1855) (dictum). See also Fort Leavenworth R.R. v. Lowe, 114 U.S. 525, 528–33 (1885).

32. *Sen. J.* (36/2) 69 (1/2/1861); *Globe* (36/2) 328 (1/11/1861). See also Victor 155–56.

33. On the difficult issue of delegation of powers between branches of the federal government, see, for example, Field v. Clark, 143 U.S. 649, 692–93 (1892).

34. (2/6/1861), Blair (1881) 367–68; Memminger/Pickens (2/4/1861), id. 368. See also Hayne/Magrath (2/7/1861), Blair (1881) 369. Regarding Fort Pickens, see, for example, Crawford (1887) 401–16.

35. Pickens/Dunovant (2/6/1861), Blair (1881) 368.

36. See, for example, South Carolina v. Pinckney, 22 S.C. 484, 488 (1883) ("The state at the close of the revolutionary war succeeded to the territorial rights of the British crown, and became the owner in fee of all the lands within her limits vacant at the time ... by right of discovery and conquest"). Post–Revolutionary War treaties memorialized that certain land ownership by and debts owed to British subjects were not extinguished by the war. See, for example, Martin v. Hunter's Lessee, 14 U.S. 304 (1816). While consonant with principles of international law, these were merely part of negotiations arising from the results on the battlefield.

37. Holt/Hayne (2/6/1861), *OR* 1/1:166, 167.

38. Act of March 20, 1794, ch. 9 §§ 1–3, 1 Stat. 345–46.

39. Act of 12/19/1805, no. 1856, §§ I [para. 5], III, *SLSC* 5:501. See also "Revised Report of the Board of Engineers on the Defence of the Seaboard" (3/24/1826), "Permanent Fortifications and Sea-Coast Defences," H.R. Rpt. no. 86 (37/2) 23, 42,43 (4/23/1862); Robert Preston, "Title of Governors Island," *NYT* (5/9/1926) X14; Paul Graham, "The Invasions of Fort Sumter," *Palmetto Partisan* (2/2010) 1; Swanberg 7; Emanuel Raymond Lewis, *Seacoast Fortifications of the United States* (Washington, DC: Smithsonian Institution Press, 1970).

40. (11/24/1832), Jackson 4:490. Poinsett had brought back from his tenure as minister to Mexico the beautiful red flower that would bear his name.

41. See, for example, Poinsett/Jackson (11/16/1832), id. 4:486, 487 and n2; (11/27/1841), *Journal of the Proceedings of the Senate and House of Representatives of South Carolina* (Columbia, SC, 1841), 44; *Acts and Resolutions of the General Assembly of the State of South Carolina, Passed in December, 1837* (Columbia, 1838), 2; J. Moore (1981B) 18. See also James H. Hammond/Calhoun (4/29/1840), Calhoun 15:188, 190–91.

42. Francis Pickens, then in the House, contemplated a constitutional amendment to limit tariffs if Congress attempted to raise them. J. Van Deusen 59–71.

43. *Niles' Weekly Reg.* 47:296n (1/3/1835); *Am. State Papers* (Military Affairs) 5:463–72; *HABS* 10–11; Crawford (1896) 4. The Committee on Federal Relations of South Carolina's lower chamber "Resolved, That this State do cede to the United States, all the right title and claim of South Carolina to the site of Fort Sumter" and assigned a commission of prominent Carolinians to examine Laval's claim, with a view either to appraise its

dollar value or to have it vacated. (12/21/1836), *Military Reservations, National Military Parks, and National Cemeteries* comp. James B. McCrellis (Washington, 1898), 214–15. The state house of representatives subsequently resolved that the attorney-general should move a competent court to vacate Laval's claim. (12/20/1837), *Acts and Resolutions of the General Assembly of the State of South Carolina, Passed in December, 1837* (Columbia, 1838), 59. See also M. Patrick Hendrix, *History of Fort Sumter* (Charleston: History Press, 2014), 15–23.

44. Deed (11/22/1841), SC Dep't of Archives and Hist.
45. See, for example, Chauncey S. Boucher, "The Annexation of Texas and the Bluffton Movement in South Carolina," *Miss. V. Hist. Rev.* 6/1:3 (6/1919). Nullifiers felt betrayed when the 1842 tariff law reinstituted much from the 1832 law. See, for example, Robert W. Barnwell/Barnwell Rhett (10/1/1842), John Barnwell, "Hamlet to Hotspur," *S.C. Hist. Mag.* 77/4:236, 245–46 (10/1976).
46. See, for example, Wheaton 332–43: "Treaties of cession . . . or those which create a permanent servitude in favor of one nation within the territory of another" are "perpetual in their nature, so that, being once carried into effect, they subsist independent of any change in the sovereignty and form of government of the contracting parties." As authority, Wheaten quotes Society for the Propagation of the Gospel in Foreign Parts v. New-Haven, 21 U.S. 464 (1823). "Where treaties contemplate a permanent arrangement of territorial, and other national rights," Justice Washington there wrote, "it would be against every principle of just interpretation to hold them extinguished by the event of war." Justice Washington further said, "If real estate be purchased or secured under a treaty, it would be most mischievous to admit, that the extinguishment of the treaty extinguished the right of such estate. In truth, it no more affects such rights, than the repeal of a municipal law affects rights acquired under it." 21 U.S. at 493–94. See also Wheaton 369 ("Property of the enemy found within the territory of the belligerent State . . . at the commencement of hostilities, are not liable to be seized and confiscated as [a] prize of war"); William Sutherland, *Notes on the Constitution of the United States* (San Francisco: Bancroft-Whitney, 1904), 205–12.
47. Compare Pollard's Lessee v. Hagan, 44 U.S. 212, 221–23 (1845) with United States v. Ames, 1 Woodb. & Minot 76, 79–80 (1st Cir. 1846). See also Fort Leavenworth R.R. v. Lowe, 114 U.S. 525 (1885); Shively v. Bowlby 152 U.S. 1, 26 (1894); United States v. Jones, 109 U.S. 513, 519 (1883); People v. Godfrey, 17 Johns. 225 (New York, 1819).
48. See, for example, United States v. Ames, 1 Woodb. & Minot 76, 81 (1st Cir. 1846). See also Green v. Biddle, 21 U.S. 1, 12 (1823) (Story, J.); *Globe* (36/2) 136 (12/19/1860) (Sen. Andrew Johnson).
49. *Annals* (15/1) 1236–43 (3/10/1818); Kohl v. United States, 91 U.S. 367 (1875).
50. *Annals* (16/2) 1042 (2/2/1820). South Carolina thus reserved in the deed the power of state constables and process servers to enter the deeded acreage to arrest or serve process upon any person "who may be implicated in law," including accused criminals, fugitives from justice, fugitive slaves, and debtors, depriving them of the right to claim being outside the state's jurisdiction. Nor could one go there to commit any act (e.g., dueling) unlawful in the state. Deed (11/22/1841) 2, SC Dep't of Archives and Hist. And while the state might conceivably pass a statute declaring that its secession itself caused Anderson's garrison to be "implicated in law" and thus subject to state jurisdiction, that would be a clear misapplication of the one authority South Carolina had reserved.

51. 48 U.S. 185, 194 (1849). See also Wilcox v. Jackson, 38 U.S. 498 (1839). In 1820, Joseph Story sat as a federal circuit judge in reviewing a criminal case. "The place where the crime was committed," he noted, "was a fort, ceded to and within the exclusive jurisdiction of, the United States. Strictly speaking, it was not within the body of any county of Rhode Island, for the state had no jurisdiction there. It was as to the state as much a foreign territory, as if it had been occupied by a foreign sovereign." United States v. Cornell, 25 Fed. Cases 650, 653, no. 14,868 (Cir. D.R.I. 1820). See also Scott v. United States, 1 Wyo. 40 (1871). But see United States v. Bevans, 16 U.S. 336, 386–91 (1818) (Marshall, C.J.) (murder occurring on U.S. ship in Boston Harbor is not cognizable in federal court).

52. Even if the federal government paid no cash, it contributed substantially to the local economy, and South Carolina obtained the ample benefit of federal protection of its harbor. See also Fletcher v. Peck, 10 U.S. 87, 136–37 (1810).

53. See Pollard's Lessee v. Hagan, 44 U.S. (3 How.) 212, 220–29 (1845); Martin v. Lessee of Waddell, 41 U.S. (16 Pet.) 367, 410 (1842). See John Norton Pomeroy and Henry Campbell Black, *Treatise on the Law of Water Rights* (St. Paul, MN, 1893), 465–66; Emory Washburn, *Treatise on the American Law of Easements and Servitudes* (1863; 3rd ed. Boston, 1873), 514; Leonard Augustus Jones, *Treatise on the Law of Easements* (New York, 1898), 636–37.

54. (12/18, 19/1860), *Public Proceedings* 37, 38. See also Rhett 19.

55. *Convention Journal* 64.

56. Magrath and dozens of other lawyers involved in secession had been less than fastidious or objective in their legal research. See, for example, Rhett 19–21. A cursory perusal of legislative records would have revealed, for example, the Act of 12/18/1846, *SLSC* 11:390, granting to the United States "all the right, title, and interest of the State to the lands, forts, fortification and sites for the erection of forts on Sullivan's Island, James Island and Shute's Folly Island." See also (11/28/1848), *Journal of the Senate of South Carolina* 25–26 (Columbia, SC, 1848). Even if the deed had not been searched first, this statement would reasonably stimulate inquiry into Sumter's status.

57. Whether the Court would go beyond that narrow holding and decide whether secession was constitutional was a separate question, one whose answer would not be easy to predict. If the Court decided that issue in the negative, secession would be viewed by those in the nation and the world qualified to weigh such matters as an insurgency, something Jefferson Davis and other Confederate leaders denied. For the Court instead to decide that disunion was constitutional would require, in essence, a skewed interpretation of constitutional history. As *Dred Scott* demonstrated, this was possible.

58. Hayne/Pickens (2/7/1861), Blair (1881) 369. See also P. Klein 393–95.

59. Hayne/Buchanan (2/7/1861), Crawford (1887) 230, 231. Hayne's letter was published as *Correspondence between Isaac W. Hayne, Special Envoy, and the President, Relating to Fort Sumter*, its editor describing it as actually to Holt. (Charleston, 1861) 15. Neither Buchanan in his later memoir nor his biographers acknowledged it or discussed its contents. See Buchanan (1908–1911) 12:185; Curtis 2:460.

60. Tyler/Pickens (2/9/1861), Blair (1881) 370; Buchanan (10/28/1862), W. Scott (1862) 11, 20. See also Holt/Hayne (2/6/1861), Buchanan (1908–11) 11:138.

61. *Globe* (36/2) 601 (1/28/1861).

62. See, for example, Crafts J. Wright, *Official Journal of the Conference Convention, Held at Washington City* (Washington, 1861); L. E. Chittenden, *Report of the Debates and*

Proceedings in the Secret Sessions of the Conference Convention (New York, 1864), 18–19; [Buchanan] (1866) 145–52; McClintock (2008) 183–85; *Appleton* 562–68; W. W. Hoppin, *The Peace Conference of 1861* (Providence, RI, 1891); Robert Gunderson, *The Old Gentlemen's Convention* (Madison: University of Wisconsin Press, 1961); Reid 280–90; J. Sherman 213; Bancroft (1891) 413–18.

63. Welles (9/1876) 307.
64. Seward/Lincoln (1/27/1861), *Lincoln Papers*; (2/4/1861), C. F. Adams Sr. See, for example, *Showdown in Virginia*, ed. William W. Freehling and Craig M. Simpson (Charlottesville: University Press of Virginia, 2010), xi; Link 226–27; Denton (2014).
65. C. F. Adams Jr. (1916) 71; C. F. Adams Jr. (1903) 60–62; *National Republican* (2/6/1861) 2 ("The tide has turned, and secession can no longer be mistaken for the popular side. We believe that Virginia is for the Union . . . through and through"); id. (2/5/1861) 2; id. (2/6/1861) 2; *NYT* (2/13/1861); Torget 20–21; Chalfant 223–24; Potter (1976) 507–8; (2/4/1861), C. F. Adams Sr. But see Reuben Hitchcock/Peter Hitchcock Jr. (2/6/1861), "Letters from the Washington Peace Conference of 1861," ed. Robert Gray Gunderson, *J. South. Hist.* 17/3:382, 385, 386 (8/1951) ("The election in Virginia furnishes no real encouragement—Although so called Union men are elected, they are simply such provided such guarantees are given as will satisfy them—If not . . . [Virginia] will go, & the rest of the slaveholding States will follow her").
66. Potter (1976) 508–11; Wooster (1962) 3–4. Missouri, too, convened no meeting of delegates. See also Potter (1976) 442–43.
67. (12/23/1860), Ruffin (1972–1989) 1:514. See also Craven (1932) 79–80, 108–19, 156–57, 195–204.
68. "Constitution for the Provisional Government" (2/8/1861), Richardson (1905) 1:3; "Election of President and Vice President" (2/9/1861), id. 1:29; Inaugural (2/18/1861), J. Davis (1971–) 7:46, 49–50; Stephens (1910) 62, 147–49, 165–66; Stephens (1866) 721–23; Stephens (1868–1870) 2:357. See also *OR* 4/1:92; R. B. Rhett, "The Confederate Government at Montgomery," Buel and Johnson 1:99; Rable 49–77; Bruce Collins, "Southern Secession in 1860–1861," *Themes of the American Civil War*, ed. Susan-Mary Grant and Brian Holden Reid, 2nd ed. (New York: Routledge, 2010), 39. Texas joined the Confederacy on March 2. Richardson (1905) 1:14.
69. W. C. Davis 99–101; David Wallace, *South Carolina* (Columbia: University of South Carolina Press, 1951), 534.
70. *New-York Daily Tribune* (3/16/1861) 3 cols. 2, 5, 6.
71. SC Executive Council minutes (2/12/1861), Blair (1881) 371, 372; Pickens/Cobb (2/12/1861), id. 373. See also Pickens/Memminger (2/13/1861), quoted in Crawford (1915) item 348.
72. Pickens/Cobb (2/13/1861), *OR* 1/1:254, 257. See also Crawford (1915) items 349, 350.
73. Pickens/J. T. Mason (2/7/1861), *Goodyear Collection* vol. 1. See also Crawford (1915) item 347. A Washington correspondent of the *Charleston Courier* agreed that by taking Washington, the Confederacy would be internationally recognized as the legitimate government. At first it would "treat the disorganized and demoralized Northern States as insurgents, and deny them recognition," but then it could condescend to recognize one or more confederacies to be formed among these states, thus giving them their own chance to "take a place among nations." *NYT* (2/12/1861).

74. Pickens/Toombs (3/18/1861) quoted in Crawford (1915) item 355; (2/28/1861), *Confederate Congress* 1:859. See also id. 909; Davis, Inaugural (2/18/1861), J. Davis (1971–) 7:46, 49–50.

75. Pickens/Cobb (2/13/1861), *Confederate Congress* 1:56–58. See also Randall (3/1940) 14.

76. Tyler/Pickens (2/7/1861), Blair (1881) 369.

77. *Globe* (36/1) 1301 (3/22/1860). See also Grayson 146.

78. A. Porter 120, 122; Trescot (1908) 545–46, 552–53; *New-York Daily Tribune* (12/29/1860) 3; Buchanan/Robert Barnwell (12/31/1860), *OR* 1/1:115; [Buchanan] (1866) 181–83; Crawford (1887) 2–7, 125; Holt/J. B. Henry (5/26/1884), Buchanan (1908–1911) 11:84, 85.

79. (2/12/1861), *Confederate Congress* 1:46, 47. See also (2/14/1861), id. 53; Pickens/Memminger [undated], Crawford (1887) 248.

80. Memminger/Pickens (2/10/1861), Call no. AMS 778/4, Rosenbach Museum & Library, Philadelphia.

81. Yancey/J. S. Slaughter (6/15/1858), DuBose 1:376; Yancey/Pickens (2/27/1861) quoted in Crawford (1915) item 481. See also Austin Venable, "William L. Yancey and the League of United Southerners" (1946) in Bonner and Hamer 43.

82. (2/13/1861), *Confederate Congress* 1:48; Resolution (2/15/1861), id. 1:55; Blair (1881) 376. See also Josiah Gorgas (4/20/1861), *OR* 4/1:227.

83. Davis/Howell Cobb (2/25/1861), Richardson (1905) 1:55; Seward memorandum (3/15/1861), id. 1:85; Faulkner 84; L. Johnson 445–48; Toombs/Crawford et al. (2/27/1861), *Commissioners* 5, 9. The collective cache of heavy and field artillery, rifles, muskets, ammunition, and powder taken from Union facilities is laid out in Josiah Gorgas (4/20/1861), *OR* 4/1:227.

84. See, for example, Seward/C. F. Adams (4/10/1861), *Foreign Relations* 71, 77; *Globe* (36/2) 721 (2/4/1861); Foreman 63–64, 77; Victor 493–96; Huston 63–64; E. Adams 1:1–75; Ferris (1976) 19–41.

85. Walker/Pickens (3/1/1861), *Pickens Papers* Reel 2 p. 287. The same letter went to the other six Confederate states.

86. See Buchanan, "Answer to General Scott" (10/28/1862), Buchanan (1908–1911) 11:279, 291–92.

87. Quoted in Holt/Lincoln (3/5/1861), *Lincoln Papers*.

88. *Burlington (VT) Free Press* (2/8/1861) 3 cols. 3, 4.

89. *Reminiscences of James A. Hamilton* (New York, 1869), 460–62.

90. *NYT* (2/8/1861) 2. See also *NYT* (2/22/1861) 1.

91. Derby/Toucey (1/16/1861), *ORN* 1/4:221. See also Sondhaus 73–74; Bernardo and Bacon 183.

92. *Blair Family Papers* Box 70, "Fox, Gustavus Vasa" File; Hoogenboom (2008) 47; Gibson and Gibson 1:28; George Taylor, *The Transportation Revolution 1815–1860* (New York: M. E. Sharpe, 1951), 120–21.

93. Hoogenboom (2008) 51–53, 59; [Buchanan] (1866) 190; Buchanan/Toucey (9/15/1865), Buchanan (1908–1911) 11:397; Toucey/Buchanan (9/18/1865), id. 11:398n1; *Porter Journal* 62. Fox must have wondered whether he would have attempted to complete the journey to Fort Sumter and thus avoid the accusations of cowardice suffered by McGowan. He might also have wondered whether any plaudits for his bravery would have been issued posthumously.

94. *HABS* 13–14; *American Coast Pilot*, 18th ed. (New York, 1857, with Aug. 1859 appendix), 54, 55, 350–55; G. W. Blunt obit., *NYT* (4/20/1878); Fox (2/24/1865); Hoogenboom (2008) 59–60; Maffitt in Bache et al. 17–21; *Hunt's Merchants' Mag. & Commercial Rev.* 37:353, 492, 493 (10/1857); *Coast Survey 1855* 60; *Charleston Yearbook* 498; George Putnam, *Lighthouses and Lightships of the United States* (Boston: Houghton Mifflin, 1917) 17, 100; *National Intelligencer* (1/18/1861) 3. See also W. G. Blunt (2/27/1866), *Fox Collection*, Series X, Bound Volume 2, p. 26; Douglas Bostick, *The Morris Island Lighthouse* (Charleston: History Press, 2008).
95. William Allen Butler, *Memorial of Charles H. Marshall* (New York, 1867), 36–38; Hunt's *Merchants' Mag. and Commercial Rev.* (1/1860) 111; Scott/Fox (1/30/1861), *Fox Collection* Series I, Box 4, Folder 11, Fox (1920) 1:3; Blair/Fox (1/31/1861), Fox (1920) 1:3; George Swede, *The Steam Tug* (n.p.: Xlibris, 2010), 109, 156. Welles at one point ascribed the idea of using tugs to Commodore Silas Stringham. Welles (2014) 643.
96. Fox stated that *Pawnee* "has seven heavy guns," with a pivot gun possibly constituting an eighth. Fox (2/6/1861), *ORN* 1/4:223, 224; Fox/Scott (2/8/1861), *ORN* 1/4:223, Fox (1920) 1:7. *Pawnee* was elsewhere reported to have six guns. Toucey/W. A. Howard (1/24/1861), "Naval Force" 17, 21. See also Fox/Blair (3/31/1861), Fox (1920) 1:13.
97. *DANFS* lists *Pawnee's* draft as ten feet, while Fox stated that it drew twelve feet. Fox (2/6/1861), *ORN* 1/4:223, 224.
98. Id.; "Mem. for the Relief of Fort Sumter, by G. V. Fox," *Fox Collection* Box 14, Folder 10, Fox (1920) 1:8; Porter/Fox (3/11/1862), Fox (1920) 1:73, 84; Welles (2014) 643; Silverstone 41, 82, 187; Paine 69. A later variant featured three tugs. Fox/Blair (2/23/1861), *ORN* 1/4:224. See also Fox/Scott (2/8/1861), *Fox Collection* Series I, Box 4 Folder 11, *ORN* 1/4:223, *OR* 1/1:203, Fox (1920) 1:7.
99. Holt/Anderson (2/23/1861), *OR* 1/1:182, 183, Crawford (1887) 293; Scott endorsement of Holt/Lincoln (3/5/1861), *Lincoln Papers*.
100. Fox/Scott (2/6/8/1861), *ORN* 1/4:223; Fox (2/24/1865), *ORN* 1/4:246. See also Hoogenboom (2008) 60. Scott and Holt had approved Fox's plan, only to have President Buchanan disapprove it on February 8. Fox (2/24/1865). See also Welles (2014) 640–43.
101. Fox/Blair (2/23/1861), *ORN* 1/4:224; Scott endorsement of Holt/Lincoln (3/5/1861), *Lincoln Papers*; W. S. Thayer/Bancroft Davis (2/28/1861), Thayer 244. Cf. Symonds (2008) 8.
102. Scott/H. L. Scott (2/20/1861), *OR* 1/1:177; Buchanan/Joseph Holt (1/30/1861), *Holt Papers* 27:3573; [Buchanan] (1866) 209–11; *Appleton* 748; *Cincinnati Commercial* (2/2/1861), *NYT* (2/5/1861) 8; Lorenzo Thomas/H. L. Scott (2/21/1861), *OR* 1/1:179; "Result of G. V. Fox's Plan," Fox (1920) 1:38, 41. See also H. L. Scott/Lorenzo Thomas (2/22/1861), *OR* 1/1:180; Welles (2014) 640–41.
103. (2/22/1861), *OR* 1/1:183–84. See also Ratner and Teeter 22; Crawford (1887) 292n; Ostaus 77–94.
104. In an undated manuscript, Coast Survey superintendent Alexander Dallas Bache wrote, "Capt. [William] Budd called this morning to say to me confidentially that he had been invited by Capt. Ward . . . to take part in an expedition to relieve Fort Sumter," to be ready on ten hours' notice." Crawford (1915) item 174.

105. Fox/Blair (2/23/1861), *ORN* 1/4:224; Hoogenboom (2008) 50–51. Captain Ward's *Manual of Naval Tactics* discusses the use of steam tugs, but only in defense of a harbor. (New York, 1859), 121, 122. It has only a short section on tactics using steam. Howard Douglas's authoritative *On Naval Warfare with Steam*, 2nd ed. (London, 1860), does not discuss the tactical use of tugs.
106. See, for example, "Canister-Shot," Edward S. Farrow, *Farrow's Military Encyclopedia* (New York, 1885), 1:274; Bartleson 115–20.
107. J. D. Brandt, *Gunnery Catechism, as Applied to the Service of Naval Ordnance* (New York, 1864), 150–51; Roberts 98–99. See also Dahlgren (1852) 51–75; Totten (1857) 44–64; *Ordnance Manual*; Bartleson 5–13, 135, 146.
108. George T. Atkins/"Friend Service" (3/3/1861), *OR* 1/53:128. Although the source was not named, the correspondent noted that the officer initially approached to command the expedition was Navy Lieutenant Charles M. Fauntleroy of Virginia, who "declined the honor," reportedly remarking that the Administration "could take his ship, &c. . . . or words to that effect." Fauntleroy resigned shortly thereafter and joined the Confederate navy. Just why this secret project was first broached to a Southern officer of questionable loyalty was not apparent. *Crusader's* prior commander, Lieutenant John N. Maffitt, was, of course, an expert on the channels. In short order, Maffitt, too, would resign his commission and join the Confederacy, using his skills as a coastal navigator by becoming a blockade runner. Command of *Crusader* was passed in this period to Commander T. A. M. Craven. Compare Totten/Toucey (2/13/1861), *ORN* 1/4:83 with J. H. Strong/Toucey (3/4/1861), *ORN* 1/4:89 and Welles/Craven (3/11/1861), *ORN* 1/4:89. See also *Globe* (36/1) 3068 (6/16/1860).
109. John Adams Dix, *Memoirs of John Adams Dix*, comp. Morgan Dix (New York, 1883), 1:365, 2:8.

Chapter 6: "Hold, Occupy, and Possess"

1. Seward/Frances Seward (5/30/1861), F. Seward (1891) 455.
2. Rudolph Schleiden (2/18/1861), in E. Adams 1:116.
3. Quoted in Bancroft (1894) 603. See also Saunders 145; Connor 116–17.
4. Adam I. P. Smith, *No Party Now: Politics in the Civil War North* (New York: Oxford University Press, 2006), 25–31.
5. *NYT* (2/26/1861) 1. See also *National Republican* (3/21/1861) 2; *Raleigh Weekly Standard* (2/27/1861) 2; id. (3/27/1861) 1; *Nashville Patriot* (3/29/1861) 2; Crofts (1977–1978) 352–62; Rufus S. King Jr./Lincoln (3/19/1861), *Lincoln Papers*.
6. C. F. Adams Jr./Frederic Bancroft (10/11/1911), quoted in Burlingame (2008) 2:98; Rothschild 134–37.
7. Lyons/Russell (2/4/1861), Barnes and Barnes 27, 28.
8. Morehead/John Crittenden (2/23/1862), Crittenden 2:338; David Barbee and Milledge Bonham Jr., "Fort Sumter Again," *Miss. Valley Hist. Rev.* 28/1:65, 66 (6/1941); McClintock (2008) 174.
9. Henry Adams/Charles Francis Adams Jr. (1/17/1861), H. Adams (1982–1986) 1:221, 223; H. Adams (1910) 678–79; H. Adams/C. F. Adams Jr. (1/2/1861), H. Adams (1982–1988) 1:216, 218. See also Burlingame (2008) 1:745–53.

10. Welles (1959–1960) 2:35, Welles (10/1876) 440.
11. See, for example, Beckert 243.
12. E. Adams 2:6–7; Lyons/Russell (2/4/1861), Barnes and Barnes 1:27, 28. See also C. F. Adams Jr. (1915) 193n; Lyons/Russell (3/26/1861), id. 219, 221; Stahr 232–33; "Blockade," *Appleton* 70; "Dis-union of United States," *L. Mag. & Quart. J. Juris.* 3rd ser. 12:359, 377 (1861–1862).
13. *Globe* (36/2) 1284 (2/28/1861). See also W. Cooper (2012) 68; Freehling (2007) 2.
14. Seward/Lincoln (12/26/1860), *Lincoln Papers*; Freehling (1994) 212. For the respective roles of Seward and Lincoln in the amendment, see Mark J. Stegmaier annot., H. Adams (2012) 58–61n11. Cf. "Resolutions Drawn Up for Republican Members of Senate Committee of Thirteen" (12/20/1860), Basler et al. 4:156–57 and n1. After the war, several Southerners would comment that the war was to be blamed on the Republicans' failure to embrace Crittenden's compromise. See, for example, M. T. Hunter, "Origin of the Late War," *South. Hist. Soc. Papers* 1:1, 8–9 (1/1876).
15. Campbell (1917) 43, 45; Connor 117. Although Seward might have been at greater risk if the amendment preserving slavery bore his name, it was instead associated with its House sponsor, Thomas Corwin, who could afford record authorship of a bill hated by the party's radical wing because Lincoln and Seward would be dispatching him to a post in Mexico. (2/1861), Campbell (1917) 43, 45; Henry Adams/*Boston Daily Advertiser* (3/3/1861), H. Adams (2012) 213, 214; Mark J. Stegmaier annot., id. 209–10; John Forsyth/Jefferson Davis (3/20/1861), J. Davis (1971–) 7:74, 76n2; *Globe* (36/2) 1284 (2/28/1861). The proposed amendment is at 12 Stat. 251 (approved 3/2/1861).
16. See, for example, J. Davis (1971–) 7:62n12; Henry Adams/C. F. Adams Jr. (1/2/1861), H. Adams (1982–1988) 1:216, 217. Gideon Welles believed that Seward had lost the confidence of most Republicans, and of the public generally, and that Lincoln was himself diminished by having appointed Seward. Welles narrative, *Welles Papers/LC* Reel 2. See also Hendrick 72; Ashley 2–3.
17. Senator Crittenden tried to withdraw his own bill in favor of the Peace Convention's, failed, and then had his own defeated in the Senate 19–20, with all Republicans against it, none for it. Senator John Cabell Breckinridge (D/KY) recalled that although "the leading statesmen of the lower southern States were willing to accept" Crittenden's compromise package, that became irrelevant once Southern senators resigned rather than press the merits of an argument—slavery in the West—that the Republicans had been elected to defeat. *Globe* (37/1) 142 (7/16/1861). While a positive Senate vote might at least have preserved some hope for further negotiation, the theoretical right to settle slaves in the West became the Southerners' nonnegotiable demand, vehemently pressed even though (1) that right had already been vouchsafed to them by *Dred Scott* and (2) climate, soil, distance to markets, and the high price of slaves combined to make gang labor uneconomical in the West, rendering the benefits of having "equal" political rights there unattainable.
18. In the House, 110 Republicans and three others voted it down, with no Republicans among the eighty in its favor. *Globe* (36/2) 1254–55, 1269–74, 1284–85 (2/27, 28/1861); id. 1305–18, 1402–3, 1374–1405 (3/1, 2 [3]/1861); Holt/Joshua Speed (5/31/1861), Joseph Holt, *The Fallacy of Neutrality: An Address by the Hon. Joseph Holt* (New York, 1861), 15, 21.
19. Lincoln/Duff Green (12/28/1860), Basler et al. 4:162.

20. "No amendment shall be made to the Constitution which will . . . give to Congress the power to abolish or interfere, within any State, with the domestic institutions thereof, including that of persons held to labor or service by the laws of said State." See *Globe* (36/2) 1269–74, 1285, 1305–1318, 1403 (2/28, 3/1, 2/1861); Jt. Res. no. 13, 12 Stat. 251 (3/2/1861); Lee Benson, "Explanations of American Civil War Causation," *Toward the Scientific Study of History* (Philadelphia: Lippincott, 1972), 246. See also Stampp (1950) 181–82.

21. *Globe* (36/2) 1285 (2/28/1861), 1403 (3/2/1861); Lincoln/Seward (2/1/1861), Basler et al. 4:183; H. Adams (1910) 682–83. Seward, having taken a head count indicating that his own bill would pass and that Crittenden's would fail, chose not to cast a vote on either, thus avoiding the ire of both pro- and antislavery interests.

22. If this amendment had been proposed by Seward or Buchanan a year earlier, and then backed by candidate Lincoln, it might have been effective. By March 2, however, seven of the thirty-four states had seceded, bringing the number of states that would vote on any amendment down to twenty-seven. Because the Constitution did not recognize secession, the number of states needed to ratify an amendment remained at twenty-six. While eight of these were slave states, passage of this amendment, or one allowing the secession of states, or any other measure (e.g., making slavery permanent, or banning it, or expanding it westward, or confining it to where it was), would require ratification by all but one state.

23. Gwin and Coleman (1891) 469.

24. See, for example, Seward/Lincoln (3/2/1861), *Seward Papers* Reel 62; Lincoln/Seward (3/4/1861), Basler et al. 4:273; Henry C. Whitney ([1887?]), *Herndon* 647; W. S. Thayer/Bancroft Davis (2/28/1861), Thayer 244; McClintock (2008) 193–99; Duberman 252–54; Crofts (1989) 254–55; Bigelow 1:339; Hendrick 72.

25. Seward/Lincoln (3/2/1861), Basler et al. 4:273n1.

26. [Ruffin] (1860) 1–2, 33; A. L. Mitchell/Seward (2/27/1861), *Seward Papers* Reel 62; W. Smith 1:510; *New Orleans Daily Crescent* (9/13/1860) 2; Denton (2009) 113–14; Craven (1932) 188–89; Sowle 449–50.

27. Lincoln/Seward (3/4/1861), Basler et al. 4:273. Lincoln, choosing the metaphor of a card game, told his secretary, "I can't afford to let Seward take the first trick." Nicolay and Hay (1917) 3:371; Hendrick 32–42, 117–22; Donald 281; Hearn (2010) 44–45. See also Welles (10/1876) 439; G. Van Deusen (1967) 253.

28. Seward/Lincoln (3/5/1861), *Lincoln Papers*. See also Frederick Seward's "Notes and transcriptions for *Seward in Washington*," *Seward Papers* Box 3, Folder 2; Stahr 219, 228, 241–48; Burlingame (2008) 2:57.

29. Stephen Fisk quoted in Rothschild 456n20.

30. Nicolay memorandum (12/22/1860), Nicolay (2000) 21. On December 24, Lincoln's friend Lyman Trumbull, upon hearing that Buchanan might give up the Charleston forts, suggested to Lincoln that "if we are ever in a position to mete out justice" to Buchanan, he should be hanged. Trefousse 145. See also R. White 337–38, 352.

31. Nicolay memo (11/10/1860), Nicolay (2000) 9; Scott/Lincoln (10/29/1860) cited, id. 193n48; Lincoln/Scott (11/9/1860), *Lincoln Papers*; Lincoln/E. B. Washburne (12/21/1860), Basler et al. 4:159; Lincoln/Francis Blair (12/21/1860), id. 4:157; Scott/Lincoln (1/5/1861), *Lincoln Papers*; Scott/Lincoln (1/4/1861), id. See also

Nicolay memorandum (12/22/1860), Nicolay (2000) 21; Peskin 235–36; Catton 169–70.

32. Lincoln/David Hunter (12/22/1860), Basler et al. 4:159; Lincoln/Trumbull (12/24/1860), id. 4:162; "Seizure of Forts, Arsenals, Revenue Cutters, and Other Property of the United States," 80–94, *Select Committee Reports*.

33. Basler et al. 4:194, 195.

34. Proclamation (12/10/1832), Richardson (1897–1903) 2:640; *Register* (21/1) 11–93 (1/12–27/1830); *Globe* (31/1) App. 115–27 (2/5–6/1850); Holzer 256; Donald 270; Francis Newton Thorpe, *The Constitutional History of the United States* (Chicago: Callaghan, 1901), 2:396.

35. Browning/Lincoln (2/17/1861), *Lincoln Papers*. See also Basler et al. 4:261n41.

36. Seward/Lincoln (1/27/1861), *Lincoln Papers*.

37. Seward/Lincoln (2/24/1861), *Seward Papers* Box 1, Folder 7; Basler et al. 4:261n40. See also *Herndon* 705; Stahr 239–41; R. White 383.

38. Dozens of statesmen from all parties had been pushing for reconciliation. On January 3, nine days prior to Seward's conciliation speech, Stephen Douglas had said, "I prefer compromise to war. I prefer concession to a dissolution of the Union." *Globe* (36/2) (1/3/1861) App. 35, 41. See also W. Smith 1:509–10; Nevins (1950) 2:193–98; McClintock (2008) 121.

39. Basler et al. 4:261n41, 266. See Stampp (1945) 304–5; Catton 489n9; Burlingame (2008) 2:45–46.

40. See, for example, Totten/C. M. Conrad (11/1/1851), H.R. Exec. Doc. No. 5 (32/1) 42, 52–53; Weaver 150–57; R. Browning 73.

41. *Globe* (36/2) 1372 (3/2/1861). Wigfall would stay until March 23 and would not be formally expelled until July 11. Forts Jefferson, Taylor, and Pickens would all remain in Union hands throughout the war.

42. Anderson/Samuel Cooper (2/28/1861), *Lincoln Papers*; OR 1/1:197. Anderson had sought the views of his officers. Doubleday opined that since the Confederate troops opposing any amphibious landing would be within the range of Sumter's guns, the landing force need not exceed ten thousand against all positions, and a force of only two or three thousand might suffice if the invading commander chose to attack only Sullivan's Island or only Morris Island. Doubleday/Anderson (2/28/1861), *Lincoln Papers*. See also T. Anderson 60; Crawford (1915) item 447.

43. Anderson had stated on February 5 that Confederate preparations were so advanced as to make it "impossible for any hostile force, other than a large and well appointed one, to enter this Harbor and the chances are that it will then be at a great sacrifice of life." Anderson quoted in Holt/Lincoln (3/5/1861), *Lincoln Papers*; H. King (1895) 126–28.

44. Crawford (1915) item 248; Crawford (1887) 284.

45. John Hay, "The Heroic Age in Washington" (1872), Hay (2000) 113, 119.

46. Perhaps Holt had no time to recite the numbers to Buchanan. Crawford (1915) item 248; Crawford (1887) 284.

47. (3/4/1861), Basler et al. 4:262, 271. Seward's comments to Lincoln's draft inaugural included the following: "The argument is strong and conclusive, and ought not to be in any way abridged or modified. But something besides or in addition to argument is needful to meet and remove prejudice and passion in the South and despondency and

fear in the [North]. Some words of affection—some of calm and cheerful confidence."
Seward/Lincoln (2/24/1861), "Notes and transcriptions for *Seward in Washington*,"
Seward Papers Box 3, Folder 2. See also Madison, *Federalist* 43. It was in fulfilling
Seward's suggestion that Lincoln summoned such beautiful phrases as "mystic chords
of memory" and "better angels of our nature." Lincoln's "curious vein of sentiment"
was—Seward told Charles Francis Adams Jr. on March 3—his "most valuable mental
attribute." See also C. F. Adams Jr. (1916) 96; Basler et al. 4:261n99, 271; Charles Dick-
ens, *Barnaby Rudge* (1841; London, 1911), 307; Shakespeare, *Othello* 5.2.208.

48. See, for example, *Dawson's Fort Wayne (IN) Daily Times* (3/9/1861) 2.

49. Lyons/Russell (3/12/1861), Barnes and Barnes 36, 37.

50. A Virginia Unionist wrote to Winfield Scott that because "here we have no press to
sustain us," Lincoln's speech had been "distorted" and used to hurt the Unionist group
in the Commonwealth's pending secession convention. Williams C. Wickham/Scott
(3/11/1861), *Lincoln Papers*.

51. *New-York Daily Tribune* (3/9/1861) 6. The *New York Times* charged that the *Tribune's*
reporter had fled Charleston and was filing his stories in the North. (3/23/1861) 4. See
also *Northern Editorials on Secession*, ed. Harold Cecil Perkins (New York: American
Historical Association, 1942), 2:607–64; Reid 306–9.

52. (3/5/1861), Dumond (1931B) 474. See also Torget 24.

53. Cauthen (1941) 360–62; *Madison (WI) Daily Argus and Democrat* (3/7/1861) 3.

54. (3/4/1861), Daniel, *The Richmond Examiner during the War* (New York, 1866), 5, 6;
(3/19/1861), id. 7; Peter Bridges, *Pen of Fire* (Kent, OH: Kent State University Press,
2002), 166–68. See also Ida Tarbell, "The Later Life of Lincoln," *McClure's Mag.*
12/3:259, 262 (1/1899); Maihafer 32–33.

55. Pryor (3/18/1861) quoted in *Bull. Va. State Lib.* 15/2–4:178 (9/1925).

56. Campbell/Mary Campbell (3/6/1861) 2, http://digital.archives.alabama.gov; Saunders
145–46.

57. Huger/Anderson (3/5/1861), *Anderson Papers* 11:2391.

58. Elmer Wright/Chase (3/7/1861) quoted in Scrugham 88. Douglas saw fit to tell disgruntled Southern senators still in their places that the inaugural had been not a declaration of war but a peace offering. *Globe* (37/4) 1436–40 (3/6, 7/1861).

59. Buchanan memorandum (3/4/1861), Buchanan (1908–1911) 11:156; Holt/Lincoln
(3/5/1861), *Lincoln Papers*; Lincoln, Message to Congress (7/4/1861), Basler et al. 4:423;
McClintock (2008) 200–201; Holt/Crawford (8/3/1885), quoted in Crawford (1915)
item 248.

60. Seward/Frances Seward (3/8/1860), F. Seward (1891) 518, 519.

61. Anderson/Cooper (12/26/1861), *OR* 1/1:2.

62. See Henry Adams/C. F. Adams Jr. (1/17/1861), H. Adams (1982–1986) 1:221; Black/
Scott (1/16/1861), *OR* 1/1:140, 141; Spaulding 187.

63. Alfred Huger/Benjamin Huger (12/25/1860), Rhoades 17. See also id. 11.

64. (Washington, 1851). See also Trescot (1908) 533; [Anderson et al.], *Instruction for Field
Artillery, Horse and Foot* (1839; Baltimore, 1845); *Evolutions of Field Batteries of Artillery*,
trans. Anderson (1860) in A. W. Stark et al., *Instruction for Field Artillery* (Richmond,
VA, 1864), 185; William Edward Birkhimer, *Historical Sketch of the Organization, Administration, Matériel and Tactics of the Artillery, United States Army* (Washington, 1884),
305–23.

65. W. Scott (1864) 1:512, 519, 534.
66. Benjamin Huger/Alfred Huger (1/3/1861) (draft), Rhoades 21, 22 (italics omitted).
67. Roman 1:13–25; H. King (1895) 55–58.
68. For Beauregard's relationship with Scott's daughter—worthy of a novel—see T. H. Williams (1954) 7–8. Cf. M. Klein 118.
69. Roman 1:29–30.
70. See, for example, Gibbon; J. C. Tidball, *Manual of Heavy Artillery Service*, 2nd ed. (Washington, 1881), 37–38.
71. Roman 1:36; Beauregard/S. W. Crawford (7/16/1870), *Goodyear Collection* vol. 2, item 18. See also Crawford (1915) [10]; Josiah Gorgas (4/20/1861), *OR* 4/1:227; Gordon 39; Spaulding 188.
72. Edwin Stanton, after being introduced to Lincoln in 1855 as one of his possible co-counsel in a significant and complex patent case, reportedly asked, "Where did that long-armed creature come from?" Herndon and Weik (1921) 2:356.
73. Scott/Seward (3/3/1861), *Lincoln Papers*; Buchanan (1908–1911) 11:300; Crofts (1989) 271. See also E. Townsend 6–7; L. E. Chittenden, *Recollections of President Lincoln* (New York, 1891), 96; McClintock (2008) 194; Welles (1960) 1:171–72; Eisenhower 356–57.
74. See, for example, Elliott 696–99; Ashley 6; Charles Stone, "Washington in March and April, 1861," *Mag. of Am. Hist.* 14/1:1, 10 (7/1885).
75. Scott/John J. Crittenden (11/12/1860), Crittenden 1:219.
76. Edmund Ruffin voiced the common concern that Virginia would sell off so many slaves to the south and southwest that it would evolve into a free state like its neighbors directly to the north. See Ruffin (1859) 651–52.
77. See, for example, Daniel Dickinson/J. M. Mason, R. M. T. Hunter (1/4/1861), D. Dickinson 2:539; Gary Gallagher, introduction, Ayers, Gallagher, and Torget 1, 3; Link 3–13; Torget 9; Harrold 5.
78. See, for example, Henry Ruffner, *Address to the People of West Virginia* (Lexington, KY, 1847).
79. Torget 10; Lightner 157.
80. *The Border States: Their Power and Duty* [12/17/1860] (Philadelphia, 1861), 4–5, 34.
81. See, for example, Charles Morehead (10/12/1862), [Hiram Fuller], *North and South* (London, 1863), 257, 261; Ralph Haswell Lutz, "Rudolf Schleiden and the Visit to Richmond, April 25, 1861," *Ann. Report of the Am. Hist. Ass'n for the Year 1915* (Washington, 1917), 207, 210–11; Morehead/J. J. Crittenden (2/23/1862), Crittenden 2:336, 337–38; Fehrenbacher and Fehrenbacher 538n340; Nevins (1959) 46–47; McClintock (2008) 196–97; J. McPherson (2008) 14, 275n9; W. Cooper (2012) 200–201, 305n78; Denton (2009) 147–48.
82. See, for example, Sumner 7:76–77; Summers/J. C. Welling (3/19/1861), J. C. Welling, "The Proposed Evacuation of Fort Sumter," *Nation* 29:383, 384 (12/4/1879).
83. Seward/Lincoln (3/9/1861), *Lincoln Papers*.
84. Seward quoted in Forsyth, Crawford/Toombs (3/8/1861), Crawford (1887) 322:

> I have built up the Republican party. I have brought it to triumph, but its advent to power is accompanied by great difficulties and perils. I must save the party and save the government in its hands. To do this, war must be averted; the negro

question must be dropped; the "irrepressible conflict" ignored; and a Union party to embrace the border slave states inaugurated. I have already whipped [Senator James M.] Mason and [Robert M. T.] Hunter in [Virginia]. I must crush out [Jefferson] Davis, Toombs and their colleagues in sedition in their respective states. Saving the border states to the Union by moderation and justice, the people of the cotton states, unwillingly led into secession, will rebel against their leaders, and [reunification] will follow.

See also *Globe* (36/2) 658–60 (1/31/1861); Gwin and Coleman (1891); McClintock (2008) 207; Barbee 29–33; Crofts (2010) 10n5, 16; Crofts (1977–1978) 339; L. Johnson 450.

85. J. McPherson (1988) 267–69. See also Lincoln, Message to Congress (7/4/1861), Basler et al. 4:421, 424.

86. F. Seward (1891) 527; C. W. Seaton/Lincoln (4/9/1861), *Lincoln Papers*; J. A. McCaffrey/Lincoln (4/9/1861), id. See also I. J. Baxter/Welles (4/9/1861), *ORN* 1/4:241–42.

87. Buchanan/Dix (3/18/1861), *Memoirs of John Adams Dix*, comp. Morgan Dix (New York, 1883), 2:3; [Buchanan] (1866) 210–11. But see Holt/Anderson (2/23/1861), *OR* 1/1:182, 183; Scott endorsement of Holt/Lincoln (3/5/1861), *Lincoln Papers*.

88. Anderson/R. B. Duane (3/11/1861), Crawford (1915) [2]–[5], *Goodyear Collection* vol. 1.

89. See W. Scott (1862) 6–7; Scott/Lincoln (3/12/1861), *OR* 1/1:197. Cf. [Buchanan] (1866) 177–78. See also chapter 5, note 87 above.

90. "Naval Force" 24. By 6/3/1861, of 671 U.S. Navy officers from the South, 321 had resigned or been dismissed. William Harwar Parker, "The Confederate States Navy," Evans 12:1, 4; Welles (1861) 239. See also Victor 116–17.

91. Fox had requested the same two. Since the United States was not at war with the Confederacy, Sturgis would have been within his rights to sell tugs to Hartstene.

92. Fox/Blair (3/1/1861), *ORN* 1/4:225, *OR* 1/1:205.

93. (3/9/1861), *OR* 1/1:272.

94. See, for example, Jordan 134–35.

95. Anderson (2/5/1861) quoted in Holt/Lincoln (3/5/1861), *Lincoln Papers*, Buchanan (1908–11) 11:158, 12:192; Scott endorsement of Holt/Lincoln (3/5/1861), *Lincoln Papers*; Hoogenboom (2008) 324n7. See also Welles (2014) 640.

96. Lincoln had wanted a New Englander whose pre-Republican record was as a Democrat rather than a Whig. Welles (1911) 1:1:21; Welles (1959–1960) 2:41; Charles Eugene Hamlin, *Life and Times of Hannibal Hamlin* (Cambridge, MA, 1899), 369–70, 375; W. M. Fowler 36.

97. See, for example, *Hartford Daily Courant* (1/5/1861) 2; Welles diary (8/22/1841), *Welles Papers/LC* Reel 1. See also *New York Evening Post* (12/1, 7/1860); Niven (1973) 306–8, 326; R. West (1943) 99; Welles (1877) 8–10; Abbatt 35; Catton 279; William E. Gienapp and Erica L. Gienapp, "Brief Biography of Gideon Welles," Welles (2014) xxiii, xxv–xxvii.

98. See, for example, *Vermont Phoenix* (Brattleboro) (1/10/1861) 2; William Spooner/Welles (1/17/1861), *Welles Papers/NYPL* Box 3, Reel 2; West (1943) 91–94; Nicolay memo (12/12/1860), Nicolay (2000) 16; Welles (1925) 19, 32; Hendrick 127; *NYT* (9/14/1865). Blair had lobbied heavily to be secretary of war. See also Ben Perley Poore, *Perley's Reminiscences of Sixty Years in the Metropolis* (Philadelphia, 1886), 2:68.

99. Welles (1/1871) 95; Welles (11/1870) 616–17; Symonds (2008) 8; Fox (2/24/1865); Tucker (2011) 1:25; "Bates, Edward. Diary (incomplete copy) 1861," *Nicolay Papers* Box 12, Nicolay and Hay (12/1887) 431; Bates 177. The term "Commodore" was an honorific for a captain of considerable years who had commanded a squadron. Alfred Thayer Mahan, *Admiral Farragut* (New York, 1892), 101. Stewart alluded to a similar feat performed by the British in the Peninsular War, perhaps their landing at the mouth of the Maceira or of the Montego River. See, for example, *Dispatches of Field Marshal the Duke of Wellington*, comp. John Gurwood (London, 1844), 3:148; Charles William Vane, *Story of the Peninsular War*, rev. ed. (London, 1848), 63–64, 71.
100. Fox/Scott (2/6/8/1861), *ORN* 1/4:223–24; Fox/Blair (2/23/1861), *ORN* 1/4:224; Fox (2/24/1865). See also Soady 154–56.
101. Fox/Blair (2/23/1861), *ORN* 1/4:224, 225; Fox/Blair (3/31/1861), Fox (1920) 1:12; Fox (2/24/1865); Fox/Scott (2/6–8/1861), *ORN* 1/4:223–24; Silverstone 82; "Bates, Edward. Diary (incomplete copy) 1861," *Nicolay Papers* Box 12, Nicolay and Hay (12/1887) 431; Bates 177. See also Welles/Rowan (4/5/1861), Fox (1920) 1:26; Hoogenboom (2008) 324n1.
102. Montgomery Meigs wrote that on March 29, Lincoln told him that on March 5 he had "verbally directed Gen. Scott to hold all these forts and make arrangements to reinforce them." Meigs (3/31/1861), Meigs (2001) 775, Meigs (1921) 299, 300. In 1882, Montgomery Blair wrote, "I do not recollect what took place in relation to Fort Sumter in Cabinet on the 5th of March of '61[;] I only recollect that from the inauguration of Lincoln, an order for the reinforcement of Sumter was given." Blair/Crawford (6/6/1882) quoted in Crawford (1915) [12]. The March 5 date was also mentioned by Scott's assistant, Lieutenant Colonel Keyes, in a purported journal entry of 3/31/1861, although Keyes's credibility is marred by his having doctored other journal entries prior to publication. Keyes 379. See also chapter 7, notes 3, 10, and 11 below and accompanying text.
103. Scott endorsement of Holt/Lincoln (3/5/1861), *Lincoln Papers*.

Chapter 7: "Mr. Seward Has Triumphed"

1. (9/16/1862), Welles (2014) 45, 48, Welles (1911) 1:136. The 1909–1911 edition contains changes and additions made in the years since the original writing.
2. Crawford/Toombs (3/6/1861), *Commissioners* 19–21; Crawford/Toombs (3/3/1861), *Commissioners* 15.
3. Lincoln/Scott (3/9/1861), *Lincoln Papers*. See also Scott/Lincoln (3/11/1861), id.
4. Scott/Lincoln (3/12/1861), *OR* 1/1:197.
5. "Bates, Edward. Diary (incomplete copy) 1861," *Nicolay Papers* Box 12, Nicolay and Hay (12/1887) 431; Bates 177. See also Welles (2014) 643.
6. *NYT* (3/11/1861) 1.
7. [Hurlbert] (1879) 493; Hall 263. See also James Welling, "The Proposed Evacuation of Fort Sumter," *Nation* 29/:383, 384 (12/4/1879).
8. Forsyth, Crawford/Toombs (3/9/1861), *Commissioners* 199; Wigfall/Davis (3/11/1861), *OR* 1/1:273; Wigfall/Beauregard (3/11/1861), id.; Crawford, Forsyth/Toombs (3/12/1861), id. 59.
9. [Hurlbert] (1879) 489.

10. Lincoln/Scott (3/9/1861), Basler et al. 4:279; Lincoln, Cameron/Scott (3/9/1861), id. 4:280; Welles (1/1871) 95; Bancroft (1900) 2:125. See also [Nicolay]/Scott ([3/9/1861]), *Lincoln Papers*; Nicolay and Hay (1917) 4:22, 41; Meigs (3/31/1861), Meigs (2001) 776, Meigs (1921) 300; Nicolay (2000) 30, 198n35; Elliott 700–701.

11. E. D. Townsend/Vogdes (3/12/1861); *OR* 1/1:360; *ORN* 1/4:90; Welles letterbook 1:88, 90; *Welles Papers/CHS*; Randall (3/1940) 15; Boynton 1:302; Scharf 605. Nicolay and Hay in their postwar account noted that Lincoln "gave [Scott] a verbal order, touching his future general public policy, which a few days later was reduced to writing." Nicolay and Hay (12/1887) 430–31. The words in the March 9 written order were more general and ambiguous than the oral order, characterized in Lincoln's March 29 comment to Meigs as a reinforcement order, and exemplifying Blair's postwar recollection of how things were in the new administration's first days. See also chapter 6, note 102 above and accompanying text. Perhaps Lincoln was concerned that disloyal officers might see it, and so, if necessary, he could later plausibly deny that it was a reinforcement order. But Townsend's order supports the view that Lincoln on March 5 specifically told Scott to transfer Vogdes's men to Fort Pickens, despite the truce established in January regarding that facility. See also Scott (3/30/1861), W. Scott (1862) 3, 9; Meigs journal (3/31/1861), Meigs (1921) 300.

12. See Lincoln/Bates (3/18/1861), Basler et al., 4:291. Regarding the taking of Fort Pickens and giving up Fort Sumter, see, for example, J. G. Winter/Andrew Johnson (3/18/1861), A. Johnson 4:407.

13. See, for example, Slemmer/Thomas (2/5/1861), *OR* 1/1:334, 341; Ryan 14–16; Chadwick 247–48; Russell (1863) 1:314–15; Erben. See also Slemmer/Holt (2/1861), *OR* 1/1:358. Cf. William Maynadier/Holt (1/3/1861), *OR* 1/1:349.

14. Quart. Gen. Joseph E. Johnston/Col. D. D. Tompkins (3/21/1861), Nat. Arch. and Rec. Admin., Rec. Group (RG) 92, Office of the Quartermaster General, "letters sent," entry 9. See also H. L. Scott/L. Thomas (2/22/1861), *OR* 1/1:180; Winfield Scott/H. L. Scott (4/4/1861), *ORN* 1/4:233; Bearss (1983) 539–41, 564–67.

15. Francis Blair/Montgomery Blair (3/12/1861), *Lincoln Papers*; Crawford (1887) 364; Welles (1911) 1:13–14; Welles (1877) 11; Welles (1874) 57–60; W. Smith 2:9–10; Burlingame (2008) 1:101. Cf. McClintock (2008) 329n6. Before Lincoln's election, Senator Douglas had reportedly said that the Blairs wanted a "civil war. They are determined, first, on seeing slavery abolished by force, and then on expelling the whole negro race from the continent." Quoted in [Hurlbert] (1879) 261. See also Fox, Boynton 1:254; Hendrick 115–16; Crawford (1887) 364–65; McClintock (2008) 202–3; Nevins (1959) 47–48.

16. *NYT* (3/13/1861). See also (3/12/1861), C. F. Adams Sr.

17. Webb/Lincoln (3/12/1861), *Lincoln Papers*. Webb, publisher of the traditionally Whig *Morning Courier and New-York Enquirer*, essentially replicated one of the plans actually under discussion: the use of three steamers, the first to contain no soldiers or supplies, its purpose being to draw fire.

18. Mark Howard/Welles (3/11/1861), *Welles Papers/NYPL* Box 3, Reel 2. Joseph R. Hawley, another founding member of the Republican Party, wrote to Welles, "I can see the possible necessity for evacuating Fort Sumter. But it brings the tears to my eyes. . . . I will gladly be one of the volunteers to sail into that harbor past all the guns of hell, rather than see the flag dishonored and the government demoralized." (3/12/1861), Goodyear Collection vol. 2, item 38. See also Welles (1924) 37.

19. Quoted in Stahr 260–61, McClintock (2008) 203, Bowman 273.

20. Scott/Anderson (3/11/1861), *Lincoln Papers*; W. Scott (1862). Scott wrote on the outside, "<u>Project</u> of a letter that I wish to send to Major A." See also Ethan Hitchcock/Scott (3/1861), *Lincoln Papers*; J. McPherson (2008) 15–16.

21. Harvey/Magrath et al. (3/11/1861), *Globe* (40/2) 1402 (2/25/1868); Crofts (1979) 186. The March 11 date was referred to in the congressional discussion in 1868. The letter is reproduced in *OR* 1/1:287, but there bears a date of 4/6/1861.

22. Harvey/Magrath (3/13/1861), *Globe* (40/2) 1402 (2/25/1868); Harvey/Cameron (7/4/1861), *Globe* (37/1) 432 (8/3/1861). See also Crofts (1979) 186.

23. *NYT* (3/13/1861).

24. *National Republican* (3/11/1861) 2.

25. Crawford, Forsyth/Toombs (3/12/1861), *Commissioners* 57–59. See also Crawford, Forsyth/Toombs (3/13/1861), id. 199: "You are advised of Seward[']s policy. It is strongly sustained by Genl Scott & commercial men North. Struggle in the Cabinet."

26. Crawford (3/13/1861), *Fort Sumter Diary* 67.

27. Forsyth/Pickens (3/14/1861), *OR* 1/1:260, 275.

28. William Browne/Crawford, Forsyth (3/12/1861), *Commissioners* 49; Toombs/Crawford, Forsyth (3/11/1861), id. 199. See also Crawford, Forsyth/Toombs (3/12/1861), id. 57.

29. Harvey/McGrath ([ca. 3/14/1861]), *Globe* (40/2) 1402 (2/25/1868); Crofts (1979) 186.

30. See, for example, Fox/M. Blair (2/23/1861), *OR* 1/1:204; Fox/M. Blair (3/1/1861), *ORN* 1/4:225; Fox, Boynton 1:253; Fox (1920) 1:8; Crawford (1887) 248–50; Hoogenboom (2008) 61; M. Klein 283, 331–33.

31. Welles/Lincoln (3/15/1861), *Lincoln Papers, Goodyear Collection* vol. 1.

32. "Result of G. V. Fox's Plan," Fox (1920) 1:38, 39. Totten also laid out the many problems to be encountered in any attempt to reach Fort Sumter. *OR* 1/1:198, 199.

33. Andrew Lambert, *The Crimean War* (Manchester, UK: Manchester University Press, 1990), 261–62.

34. Boynton 1:252; Fox/Blair (2/23/1861), *ORN* 1/4:224, 225; Fox (2/24/1865); Dahlgren (1856B) 378–81, 388–415; W. H. Russell, *The British Expedition to the Crimea*, rev. ed. (London, 1858), 512, 518–34; Hoogenboom (2008) 59; W. M. Fowler 32.

35. J. C. Dobbin, Rpt. of the Sec. of the Navy, *Globe* (34/3) App. 27, 29 (12/1/1856); *Naval Encyclopædia* (Philadelphia, 1884), 622.

36. See Dahlgren, "Form of Exercise and Maneuvre for the Boat Howitzers of the U.S. Navy," *Ordnance Instructions* lxxxii; *Ordnance Manual* 386; Hazlett, Olmstead, and Parks 141–43; Ryan 68–69; Dahlgren (1856A) 172–81; William A. Graham, General Order (12/17/1850), id. 20, Madeleine Vinton Dahlgren, *Memoir of John A. Dahlgren* (Boston, 1882), 148–49; J. C. Dobbin, Rpt. of the Sec. of the Navy (12/1/1856), *Globe* (34/3) App. 27, 28–29 (12/1/1856); Tucker (2011) 1:141.

37. See *New-York Daily Tribune* (10/20/1855) 6; "The Naval Expedition against the Kulan Pirates," *U.S. Naut. Mag. & Naval J.* 3/3:190 (12/1855); Clowes 6:389–90. Frigates were supposed to have available for their launches one 24-pound and one 12-pound gun. Dahlgren (1856A) 35.

38. See James St. Clair Morton, *Memoir on the Dangers and Defences of New York City* [9/30/1858] (Washington, 1858), 30, *Message from the President of the United States*, H.R. Exec. Doc. no. 2 (35/2) 2:494, 520–21; T. H. Williams (1954) 16; George Eaton, "Surfboats," *Encyclopedia of the Mexican-American War* (Santa Barbara, CA: ABC-CLIO, 1990). See also Dahlgren (1856A); Sondhaus 44; Grady 111.

39. Lincoln, "Application for Patent on an Improved Method of Lifting Vessels over Shoals" (3/10 1849), Basler et al. 2:32–35; Zenas C. Robbins/Lincoln (4/13/1849), *Lincoln Papers*; U.S. Patent 6469 (5/22/1849).

40. Lincoln/Welles (5/14/1861), Basler et al. 4:370. See also Helen Nicolay, *Personal Traits of Abraham Lincoln* (New York, 1912), 317–25.

41. See, for example, Herndon and Weik 3:540; Bates 178. Another who believed that boats could reinforce Sumter at night, although not present at the meeting, was Commodore Charles Stewart, commandant of the Philadelphia Navy Yard, with a distinguished naval career beginning in the 1790s. Fox (2/24/1865).

42. *Globe* (37/4) 1452–53, 1457–60 (3/13–15/1861).

43. (3/15/1861), *Lincoln Papers*. See also Lincoln/Seward (3/15/1861), Basler et al. 4:284; Stahr 261.

44. See, for example, Weaver 57.

45. Seward/Lincoln (3/15/1861), *Lincoln Papers*; Cameron/Lincoln (3/17/1861), *OR* 1/1:196. Regarding Cameron, see, for example, McClure (1892) 147–68; Hendrick 51–60.

46. Bates 179.

47. See, for example, Hearn (2010) 12–13.

48. Compare Chase/Alphonso Taft (4/28/1861), Crawford (1887) 366 (indicating support for Seward's policy) with Chase/J. S. Black (7/4/1870), id. 367 ("I never voted for the surrender of Fort Sumter. My grounds of opposition were not perhaps the same, nor so absolute as Mr. Blair's, but I was against [surrender], and so voted").

49. See Blair, "Brief for Plaintiff," Scott v. Sandford, 60 U.S. (19 How.) 393 (1857), *Landmark Briefs and Arguments of the Supreme Court of the United States*, ed. Philip B. Kurland et al. (Washington, DC: University Publications of America, 1978), 3:167; *Southern Slaves in Free State Courts*, ed. Paul Finkelman (New York: Garland, 1988), 3:17; Fehrenbacher (1978) 281–313. After Lincoln failed to attract a Southern Unionist to the cabinet, Blair's residence in one border state (Maryland) and family connections in another (Missouri) afforded Lincoln no credit among Southerners, since he had represented Dred Scott and was Francis Blair's son. See Donald 262–64.

50. See Blair/Lincoln (3/15/1861), *OR* 1/53:62, 63; Seward, "Reinforcement of Fort Sumter" (3/15/1861), W. Seward (1884–1890) 5:606, 608; Lincoln (1905) 192, 198–220, 227–31; O. Browning 1:475–76; Goodwin 334–37; Nevins (1959) 44. See also Welles (11/1870) 617; Current (1963) 67–68; James Welling, "The Proposed Evacuation of Fort Sumter," *Nation* 29/:383 (12/4/1879).

51. Seward/R. M. T. Hunter (3/12/1861), *Commissioners* 65; Seward/Frances Seward (3/16/1861), F. Seward (1891) 530.

52. Forsyth, Crawford/Seward (3/12/1861), *Commissioners* 61, Richardson (1905) 1:84; Seward memorandum (3/15/1861), id. 1:85, *Anti-Slavery Bugle* (5/4/1861) 1; F. Moore (1861–1866) 1:42; Seward/Forsyth (3/15/1861), F. Moore (1861–1866) 1:43; Potter (1995) 343–45.

53. See Campbell (7/10/1865), Connor 138; [Campbell], "The Rights of the Slave States," *South. Quart. Rev.* n.s. 3/5:101, 141 (1/1851); [Campbell], "Slavery in the United States," *South. Quart. Rev.* 12/23:91, 133 (7/1847); George W. Duncan, "John Archibald Campbell," *Alabama Hist. Soc. Trans.* 5:107, 120–21, 129 (1904); Saunders

66–68, 128–34, 147; M. Blair (1865) 14. See also Jefferson Davis (5/8/1861), Richardson (1905) 1:82, 83.

54. Scott v. Sandford, 60 U.S. 393, 493 (1857) (Campbell, J. concurring). Blair might have felt otherwise if he had known that in siding with Taney and the other Southerners on the Court, Campbell directly contradicted the judicial philosophy he had espoused nine years earlier. At that time, he wrote: (1) Congress *was* empowered to govern territories, (2) it *could* thus "decide what shall be held and enjoyed as property" in territories, (3) "persons should not be held as property," and (4) the Constitution "does not sanction the [title] of a master in his slaves" and does not provide either (5) "that the rights of the slave owner shall be protected in all the territories" or (6) "that the master shall be free" to take people there "as slaves." Campbell/Calhoun (3/1/1848), Calhoun 25:213. See also Campbell/Calhoun (11/20/1847), id. 24:666. Since Campbell made these statements not in an off-hand, unprepared speech but in a long, detailed, and considered letter, and since Campbell knew that his addressee, John C. Calhoun, differed fundamentally from him on each of these points, the missive is all the more remarkable, and Campbell's hypocrisy nine years later all the more disappointing. See also E. I. McCormac, "Justice Campbell and the Dred Scott Decision," *Miss. Valley Hist. Rev.* 19/4:565, 567–70 (3/1933).

55. See, for example, Austin Allen, *Origins of the "Dred Scott" Case* (Athens: University of Georgia Press, 2006), 151–58.

56. Campbell (1874) 22–23.

57. Campbell (1917) 32. Seward at the time convinced an editor of the *National Intelligencer* both that his belief in imminent abandonment was bona fide and that it was on the authority of the president. J. C. Welling/E. L. Godkin (11/21/1879), *Nation* 29:383 (12/4/1879). See also McClintock (2008) 216 and 324n69; McClintock (2011) 31.

58. Campbell/Seward (3/15/1861), *Seward Papers* Reel 62. See also Campbell/Seward (4/13/1861), F. Moore (1861–1866) 1:427. With a politician's rather than a statesman's instinct, Seward ended the conversation with flattery, congratulating Campbell on a compromise that "might prevent a civil war." See also Crawford (1887) 328n; Rhodes (1892–1906) 3:329–30; Connor 123–25; M. Klein 334; Randall (1956) 322–24.

59. Campbell/[Crawford] (3/15/1861), *Commissioners* 73; Crawford, Forsyth/Toombs (3/15/1861), id. 199.

60. Stanton/Buchanan (3/16/1861), Curtis 2:534; Stanton/Buchanan (3/14/1861), Stanton 473. To the same effect is Holt/Buchanan (3/20/1861), id. 536; John A. Dix/Buchanan (3/28/1861), id. 537. See also P. Klein 406–7.

61. A. L. Washington/L. P. Walker (3/17/1861), *OR* 1/53:133.

62. See Starr 19–21.

63. *Easton Sentinel* in *Bloomsburg (PA) Star of the North* (3/20/1861) 2.

64. Stephens (1866) 718, 726–27.

65. Summers/James Welling (3/19/1861), *Nation* 29:384 (12/4/1879); Shanks 191–92.

66. Welling/E. L. Godkin (11/21/1879), Summers/Welling (3/19/1861), *Nation* 29:383, 384 (12/4/1879); Crofts (1989) 275–77, 289. See also Stahr 262.

67. See, for example, T. Barnes 2:273–90; Denton (2009) 13–14; Nichols 1:330–31.

68. *New-York Daily Tribune* (3/20/1861) 5. See also id. (3/18/1861) 6.

69. Beauregard/Crawford, Forsyth, Roman (3/21/1861), *OR* 1/53:136.

70. Campbell/Crawford, Forsyth, Roman (3/21/1861), Crawford (1887) 331; Campbell (3/21/1861), *Commissioners* 73; Campbell (3/22/1861), id. 75.

71. See, for example, *Sacramento Daily Union* (3/28/1861) 3. See also Starr 26.

72. F. Seward (1891) 528.

73. Campbell (3/22/1861), Crawford (1887) 331–32; Welles (11/1870) 628–31; Lamon 52–53, 69; [Hurlbert] (1879) 271; J. McPherson (1988) 268; Stampp (1945) 315–16. See also Campbell/Seward (4/13/1861), *Seward Papers* Reel 63; Campbell in Connor 126–27; Campbell (3/31/1861), Rhodes (1892–1906) 3:332; Leonard Swett/Herndon (1/17/1866), Herndon and Weik (1921) 3:528, 537.

74. *New-York Tribune* (3/20/1861) 4.

75. Campbell/Crawford, Forsyth, Roman (3/22/1861), Crawford (1887) 331–32; Rhodes (1892–1906) 3:332. See also Roman, Crawford, Forsyth/Toombs (3/22/1861), *Commissioners* 77.

76. Roman, Crawford, Forsyth/Toombs (3/22/1861), *Commissioners* 201. See also id.: "If there is faith in man we may rely on the assurance we have as to the status. Time is essential to a peaceful issue of this mission—in the present posture of affairs, precipitation is war. We are all agreed." Later that afternoon, Forsyth confirmed his optimism to Governor Pickens, advising that Sumter would be evacuated "if there is faith in man." Forsyth/Pickens (3/22/1861), *Pickens Papers* Reel 2.

Chapter 8: A Sea of Troubles

1. Fox (1880) 42–43. See also Fox (2/24/1865); W. Smith 2:12, Boynton 1:255; Hoogenboom (2008) 61.

2. Fox, Boynton 1:255. In another version of this conversation, the man with whom they were speaking was ex-congressman Laurence M. Keitt, although here, too, the name of the "highest authority" did not find its way into Fox's account. Fox (2/24/1865); W. Smith 2:12.

3. Fox (2/24/1865); Detzer 227; Chester G. Hearn, *Lincoln, the Cabinet, and the Generals* (Baton Rouge: Louisiana State University Press, 2010), 51; E. Milby Burton, *The Siege of Charleston, 1861–1865* (Columbia: University of South Carolina Press, 1970), 30; Hoogenboom (1963) 385. Although Fox's New York contacts had informed him on March 1 that Hartstene was trying to purchase two New York tugs, Fox and Hartstene had no contact at that time. Fox/Blair (3/1/1861), *ORN* 1/4:225, *OR* 1/1:205.

4. Cameron/Scott (3/19/1861), *Anderson Papers* vol. 11, *OR* 1/1:208. See also Scott/Fox (3/19/1861), *ORN* 1/4:227; Fishel 10–11.

5. Hoogenboom (2008) 62; Fox/Crawford (5/16/1882), Crawford (1915) item 200; Crawford (1887) 372n.

6. The journalist's report indicated that Fox represented himself as a physician inquiring into the health of the garrison:

> When Commander Hartstene visited Fort Sumter with Surgeon [*sic*] Fox . . . the Doctor [*sic*] remarked that "it rested altogether with the Major how to leave." Major Anderson replied very promptly, "put that in writing, Doctor, as coming from Gen. Scott and the whole Cabinet, including the President, and I will leave

tomorrow." Dr. Fox had to reply that although he was authorized verbally to state as much, he had no official permission to write it.

"Our Southern Correspondence," *NYT* (4/2/1861). See also *New-York Daily Tribune* (3/26/1861) 6. While it would have been sensible, given the wording of Cameron's order, to send a military physician, Fox would not have falsely identified himself as a surgeon in Hartstene's presence, nor—if he had—would Hartstene, a sworn officer of the Confederacy, fail to report such a lie to Beauregard and Pickens. The journalist undoubtedly consulted an official navy directory, found there that the only officer named Fox was a physician, and thus tainted his report of what the principals actually said with his own erroneous background research. See Fox/Virginia Fox (3/27/1861), Fox (1920) 1:11; (3/21/1861), Holmes 19.

7. Fox (2/24/1865).
8. Crawford (1887) 372n. Captain Foster in a letter to General Totten mentioned that Fox had a "confidential interview" with Anderson—that is, they at some point evaded Captain Hartstene's monitoring. (3/22/1861), *OR* 1/1:211. See also Hoogenboom (2008) 62–63; Beauregard/Walker (3/22/1861), *OR* 1/1:280.
9. Anderson would admit only that Fox did briefly allude to a possible relief plan. Fox maintained that he "made no arrangement with Major Anderson for reinforcing or supplying the fort nor did I inform him of my plan." In 1882, one of Sumter's officers, Samuel Wylie Crawford, M.D., sought out Fox's recollections. Although more than twenty years had passed, Fox was adamant that he did not suggest to Anderson or anyone that the president was considering a reinforcement plan, much less that he was authorized to coordinate it with Anderson. Fox told Crawford that his purpose "was to See the condition of things generally, moral and physical and to know how long the provisions would last," adding that he "wished to be able to say to those who opposed the proposal I had made, that I was acquainted with the ground by personal observation," but he would not have told Major Anderson "that there was even a probability of reinforcements," since as of March 21 "Mr Lincoln had not made up his mind to attempt the relief." Thus, "when I entered Sumter there was nothing to concoct" with Anderson. Fox must have assumed, however, that one of Anderson's subordinates, Lieutenant Norman J. Hall, who had been present when Fox outlined his plan in Washington on February 5, had already informed Anderson that Fox (and others) had presented relief plans. "I did intend," Fox added, to give Anderson "a complete history of the conditions of things at Washington, and the dilemma Mr Lincoln was in on account of contrary counsels, but as I found [Anderson] to be on the other side, politically as well as in [a] military point of view, I refrained," having been "fighting this kind of opposition" in Washington already. Fox/Crawford (5/10/1882), *Goodyear Collection* vol. 1 item 28. See also Crawford (1887) 370–71; Fox (2/24/1865), *ORN* 1/4:246; Crawford (1915) item 199.
10. Hartstene/Beauregard (4/10/1861), *OR* 1/1:299; Beauregard/R. G. M. Dunovant (4/10/1861), *OR* 1/1:300; Scharf 659; *HABS* 16; Konstam 26–27.
11. Anderson/Thomas (3/22/1861), *OR* 1/1:211.
12. Fox's plan was premised on that being unnecessary, and as he and Anderson together "looked out upon the water from the parapet," a stealthy entrance at night "seemed very feasible, more especially as we heard the oars of a boat near the Fort, which the sentry

hailed, but we could not see through the darkness until she almost touched the landing." Fox (2/24/1865). See also Crawford (1887) 370–71. Cf. M. Klein 341–43.

13. *New-York Daily Tribune* (3/27/1861) 4.

14. *Boston Daily Courier* (3/29/1861).

15. Seward/Lincoln (3/15/1861), W. Seward (1884–1890) 5:606, 608; Hurlbut/Nicolay (5/4/1876), Nicolay (1996) 62. See also McClintock (2008) 213.

16. *Lamon Papers*, Box 4, File 36; Lamon/Seward (3/25/1861), *Seward Papers* Reel 62. See also Lash 10–35, 56–60; McClintock (2008) 326n78; Henry Whiting/William Henry Herndon (8/27/1887), *Herndon* 627–36.

17. Lamon 74. See also "Our Charleston Correspondence," *NYT* (4/2/1861).

18. Lamon, a man not easily intimidated, might nevertheless have been disconcerted when several locals told him at the Charleston Hotel that they were looking for a "sneaking attorney, named Lamon, reported to be in the city," because they intended to kill him. Quoted in Lash 58. Pickens issued a pass on March 25: "The Bearer, Mr. Lamon, has business with Mr Huger Post Master of Charleston and must not be interrupted by any one, as his business in Charleston is entirely pacific." *Lamon Papers*, Box 4, File 484, Lamon 78–79. See also Hurlbut/Nicolay (5/4/1876), Nicolay (1996) 62, 64.

19. Lamon 71; Hurlbut/Lincoln (3/27/1861), *Lincoln Papers*; Hurlbut/Nicolay (5/4/1876), Nicolay (1996) 62. See also [De Forest] 495–96; Marc Egnal, "Rethinking the Secession of the Lower South," *Civil War Hist.* 50/3:261, 287–89 (9/2004); Jane H. Pease and William H. Pease, *James Louis Petigru* (Athens: University of Georgia Press, 1995), 157. Whether Petigru's fear was justified is unclear, although certainly secession, like nullification earlier, attracted some rough people of the kind who talked to Lamon. But another Northern visitor said locals indulged Petigru because his Unionist notions "were rather to be pitied than resented," the wisdom of secession being "so far above dispute." Lathers 124.

20. Hurlbut/Lincoln (3/27/1861), *Lincoln Papers*. See also *NYT* (9/11/1872) 9.

21. C. F. Adams Jr. (1916) 69–70, 105; Hurlbut/Nicolay (5/4/1876), Nicolay (1996) 62, 63; Brauer 149. See also Dew 60–61.

22. On the day Lamon arrived in Charleston, Bancroft Davis, a lawyer and New York correspondent for the *Times* of London, was informed that Lamon had in fact brought the evacuation order with him. W. S. Thayer/Davis (3/25/1861), Thayer 245.

23. S. W. Crawford (3/25/1861), *Fort Sumter Diary* 40, 69.

24. Beauregard/Anderson (3/26/1861), *Anderson Papers* 9:1972, OR 1/1:222. See also Pickens/Forsyth (3/18/1861), *Commissioners* 215 ("I understand it is said at Washington that Maj Anderson will not be permitted to vacate Sumter peaceably &c. It is doing great injustice to the Military here to say any such thing as it is utterly false and you can say so"); Fox/Blair (3/31/1861), Fox (1920) 1:12, 13.

25. Anderson, others in his command, and Governor Pickens, too, were all apparently told by Lamon that he had come to help negotiate the garrison's withdrawal. Pickens, Message No. 1 (11/5/1861), *Journal of the Senate of the State of South Carolina* (Columbia, SC, 1861), 10, 22; Randall (1956) 329–30. On March 31, Crawford wrote to his brother that the garrison awaited Lamon's return with the evacuation order. S. W. Crawford (3/31/1861), *Crawford Papers* 1:38, 40. Petigru would tell a confidant, "There is no doubt that Anderson will be off in a few days and I don't see why the order was not given weeks ago." Lash 228n72.

26. W. S. Thayer/Bancroft Davis (3/25/1861), Thayer 245.
27. Joseph Lesesne/Calhoun (9/12/1847), "Correspondence of John C. Calhoun," ed. J. Franklin Jameson, *Ann. Rpt. Am. Hist. Assoc. for the Year 1899* (Washington, 1900), 2:1133, 1134–35. See also Thomas Prentice Kettell, *Southern Wealth and Northern Profits* (New York, 1860), 91–98; "Southern Wealth and Northern Profits," *De Bow's Rev.* 19/1:197 (7/1860); [Stephen Colwell], *The Five Cotton States and New York* ([Philadelphia?], 1861), 10–11.
28. J. Davis (1938) 1:251–58; Horace Greeley, "Going to Go," *New-York Daily Tribune* (11/9/1860) 4. See also William C. Wright, *The Secession Movement in the Middle Atlantic States* (Rutherford, NJ: Fairleigh Dickinson University Press, 1973).
29. P. Foner 218–32, 302–3; Robert G. Gunderson, *The Old Gentlemen's Convention* (Madison: University of Wisconsin Press, 1961), 27–29; W. S. Thayer/Bancroft Davis (1/6/1861), Thayer 237. See also J. Wells 61.
30. See Nichols 2:317; P. Foner 135–48, 215–23.
31. Belmont/Forsyth (12/19/1860), Belmont 36, 39. See also Goodheart 74; Jordan 32.
32. (1/6/1861), E. McPherson 42, 43–44; Victor 504–5; W. Cooper (2012) 55–56; J. McPherson (1988) 247. See also Greeley (1864) 450; Stampp (1990) 208–9.
33. See, for example, Richard Bensel, *Yankee Leviathan* (Cambridge: Cambridge University Press, 1990), 60–63.
34. See, for example, *NYT* (3/26/1861) 4. See also *NYT* (3/22/1861) 4.
35. Act of 3/3/1857, chs. 98 &101, 11 Stat. 192. See, for example, Jane Flaherty, "'The Exhausted Condition of the Treasury' on the Eve of the Civil War," *Civil War Hist.* 55/2:244, 261 (6/2009).
36. Act of 3/2/1861, ch. 68 §§ 5–27, 12 Stat. 178, 179–97; Richard Hofstadter, "The Tariff Issue on the Eve of the Civil War," *Am. Hist. Rev.* 44/1:50, 54 (10/1938); Nevins (1950) 1:455–57, 2:192–93, 253–54; Stampp (1990) 19; J. McPherson (1988) 191–93; Currie 3:117–18.
37. See, for example, F. M. Robertson/Samuel J. Anderson (2/7/1861), *OR* 2/2:610–11.
38. See, for example, Welles (10/1876) 438; Heather Cox Richardson, *The Greatest Nation of the Earth* (Cambridge, MA: Harvard University Press, 1997), 31–32, 104–12; Huston 43–67, 203–67; Victor 41–43, 78–79; P. Klein 345–46.
39. *Charleston Mercury* (2/23/1861) 1; Martin Crawford, "Anglo-American Perspectives: J. C. Bancroft Davis," *New-York Hist. Quart.* 62/3:191, 203–4 (7/1978); Sowle 5–6; E. Adams 2:6–7; *NYT* (3/30/1861) 4; *New-York Daily Tribune* (4/12/1861) 4; *Times* (London) 3/8/1861 in *NYT* (3/26/1861) 5; *NYT* (3/27/1861) 4. See also Stanton/Buchanan (3/16/1861), Curtis 2:534; Crofts (1989) 284; McClintock (2008) 216; Rhodes (1913) 82–83. Jefferson Davis nevertheless initiated an export duty on cotton to fund the Confederate government. Callahan 32.
40. Roman/Toombs (3/29/1861), *Commissioners* 121. See also Ferris (1976) 6.
41. See W. Cooper (2000) 336; Callahan 108–16.
42. See, for example, Lyons/Russell (3/30/1861), Barnes and Barnes 42; William R. Garrett, "The South as a Factor in the Territorial Expansion of the United States," Evans 1:59, 241–43; Beckert 243. Mercier's belief proved misguided.
43. Black (2/28/1861), *Foreign Relations* 31.
44. Seward (3/9/1861), id. 32, 33. See also Ferris (1976) 42–45.
45. Crawford, Roman/Toombs (3/26/1861), *Commissioners* 111–17.

46. L. Q. Washington/Walker (3/20/1861), *OR* 1/52 Pt. II p. 27.

47. Crawford, Roman/Toombs (3/29/1861), *Commissioners* 205; *Tribune* (3/28/1861) 5, 6.

48. Russell (1863) 1:61, 64; Goodheart 151–53; Scott/Lincoln (3/26/1861), *Lincoln Papers*.

49. "General Scott's memoranda for the Secretary of War" (undated), *OR* 1/1: 200–201. See also Hoogenboom (1963) 387n14; W. Cooper (2012) 249, 312n14; McClintock (2008) 229–31 and n9; Stahr 266–67; K. Williams 1:387–88n55; Hoogenboom (2008) 325n14.

50. Blair/Samuel Crawford (5/6/1882), Crawford (1887) 365; Crawford (1915) [12]. Several days later, Blair told Lincoln, "As regards Genl Scott—I have no confidence in his judgment in the questions of the day—His political views control his judgt—& his course as remarked on by [you] shows that whilst no one will question his patriotism, the results are the same as if he was in fact traiterous—." *Lincoln Papers* Series 1; Potter (1976) 574–76.

51. Amy Greenberg, *A Wicked War* (New York: Knopf, 2012), 257–58.

52. See, for example, Mitchell 61–65. Some ascribed to Seward the idea that Catholics would flock to the Whig Party from the Democrats because Scott had been careful not to destroy churches in the Mexican War and had two daughters raised in a convent.

53. Seward/James Taylor (6/26/1852), *New-York Tribune* (6/29/1852), 4; H. J. Carman and R. H. Luthin, "The Seward-Fillmore Feud and the Crisis of 1850," *NY Hist.* 24/2:163, 168–70 (4/1943); Susan Dixon, *True History of the Missouri Compromise* (Cincinnati, OH, 1899), 414; Waugh (2003) 38–40; Arthur Cole, *The Whig Party in the South* (1912; Gloucester, MA: P. Smith, 1962), 224–76; Anthony Carey, *Parties, Slavery, and the Union in Antebellum Georgia* (Athens: University of Georgia Press, 1997), 176–79; W. Cooper (1978) 280–81, 324–41; G. Van Deusen (1947) 172–74; Holt (1978) 221–59; J. McPherson (1988) 67; Ayers (2005) 137–38; Nevins (1947) 2:34–38; Gienapp (1987) 16–33. A Southerner wrote:

> The voice of abolition no longer is confined to the distance, but now rings throughout the halls of Congress, and drowns in its din every thing that may be said against it. . . . The whig party . . . endorse the sentiments of William H. Seward, and boldly proclaim that the constitution . . . so far as it tends to the protection of slavery, is against the law of God, and the "higher law" absolves them from all obligation to enforce the provisions of the constitution, which they have sworn to protect and defend. What candidate for the presidency dares to disregard the voice of the abolition party? What candidate for Congress, is safe unless he caters for their vote?

"To the Hon. W. J. Grayson" (n.p., [1850?]), 9; G. Van Deusen (1947) 191–93.

54. Holt (1999) 682–767; T. Johnson 212–17; Gienapp (1987) 23–35; Arthur Cole, *The Whig Party in the South* (1912; Gloucester, MA: P. Smith, 1962), 152, 224–31, 258–76. In the end (a radical Republican later wrote), "the Whig party finally sacrificed both its character and its life on the altar of slavery." Julian 182. Antislavery Whigs were in discussion about a new party within fifteen months of Scott's defeat, well prior to passage of the Kansas-Nebraska Act, which essentially destroyed the Whigs as a national force and thrust the Republican Party to national prominence. Since Seward was politically astute, while Scott's showing was abominable, it is not surprising to see

Frederick Bancroft assert that Seward had used Scott's candidacy in pursuit of his own political purposes. Scott's poor electoral showing left room for a new party initially dominated by Seward. See Bancroft (1900) 2:124; Holt (1978) 96–97, 117–40; Welles narrative, *Welles Papers/LC* Reel 2; T. Johnson 136–37; Eisenhower 204–6, 324–32, 428n3; Holt (2004) 89–90.

55. Buchanan, "Answer to General Scott" (10/28/1862), Buchanan (1908–1911) 11:279, 283; [Buchanan] (1866) 99–106.

56. Bancroft (1900) 2:123–24.

57. Welles (11/1870) 618; Welles (1911) 2:514–16. When Scott during the Mexican War wanted to court-martial several senior officers whom he had already promoted for their service, President Polk ascribed the incident to Scott's "vanity and tyrannical temper." (12/30/1847), *Diary of James K. Polk during His Presidency*, ed. Milo Quaife (Chicago: A. C. McClurg for Chicago Historical Society, 1910), 3:266.

58. See, for example, Lincoln's Peoria speech (9/17/1852), Basler et al. 2:158.

59. Bancroft (1900) 2:124; Welles narrative, *Welles Papers/LC* Reel 2; Hendrick 170–71; T. Johnson 136–37; Eisenhower 204–6, 324–32, 428n3.

60. Bancroft (1900) 2:124–26. A Scott biographer wrote that Seward "changed his mind and turned on his old friend." T. Johnson 225.

61. (3/31/1861), Keyes 379. Keyes's "diary," not published and perhaps not composed until well after the events depicted, is demonstrably untrustworthy on a variety of issues. According to Keyes, Scott, in submitting his memo to Lincoln, assumed that Lamon, upon his return from Charleston, had told the president what he had allegedly told Scott: that Governor Pickens had voiced a desire to return South Carolina to the Union. Keyes 378. A suggestion to give up both forts would make sense if Lincoln were to receive that in return. But Governor Pickens (of all people) would never have proposed such a thing, nor would Lincoln credit such a story by the hard-drinking Lamon. See, for example, "A Friend"/Lincoln (2/1861), *Lincoln Papers*.

62. See Lincoln, Message to Congress (7/4/1861), Basler et al. 4:421, 424–25.

63. (3/16/1861), Curtis 2:534.

64. Although this was later ascribed to Scott's sudden recommendation to abandon Fort Pickens, the real problem was Scott's failure to carry out the reinforcement ordered previously. See Meigs journal (3/31/1861), Meigs (1921) 300. See also Meigs's entries for 3/29, 31/1861, *Nicolay Papers* Box 11; Meigs (2001).

65. Keyes 377–79. See Eisenhower 360–61; Weigley (1959) 139–40.

66. See Montgomery Blair/Wylie Crawford (ca. 1882), *Goodyear Collection* vol. 1. item 18.

67. Welles/Lincoln (3/29/1861), *Lincoln Papers*; Chase/Lincoln (3/29/1861), id.; Bates/Lincoln (3/29/1861), id.; Smith/Lincoln (3/29/1861), id.; Seward/Lincoln (3/29/1861), id.

68. Welles (1911) 1:14.

69. Nicolay and Hay (1917) 2:26–28, 3:432; Lincoln (1922) 27; Blair/Crawford (ca. 1882) quoted in Crawford (1915) [12].

70. Welles (1911) 1:13; Randall (1956) 321; *Selections from the Speeches and Writings of Hon. Thomas L. Clingman* (Raleigh, NC, 1877), 564; W. Smith 2:9. See also McClintock (2008) 330n14.

71. John Andrew/Lincoln (1/20/1861), *Lincoln Papers*; Smith/Lincoln (3/29/1861), *Lincoln Papers*.

72. Roman/Toombs (3/29/1861), *Commissioners* 121, 123. See also "The Policy of Forbearance," *New-York Daily Tribune* (3/27/1861) 4; Scrugham 95–96.

73. Lincoln/Cameron (3/29/1861), *OR* 1/1:226–27; Lincoln/Welles (3/29/1861), Basler et al. 4:301–2.

74. See Fox/Blair (3/31/1861), Fox (1920) 1:12; Nicolay and Hay (2/1888) 611; Welles/Rowan (4/4/1861), Welles letterbook vol. 1, *Welles Papers/CHS*. Fox later wrote that the plan first presented to Scott and Holt on February 6–7 involved anchoring "three small men-of-war off the entrance to the Swash Channel." Fox (2/24/1865).

75. *Pocahontas* "has been remodeled and provided with a new engine, and is an efficient vessel." Isaac Toucey, "Report of the Sec. of the Navy," *Globe* (36/2) App. 20 (12/1/1860). See also id. 348, 843, 1035 (1/12, 2/11, 19/1861).

76. Fox/Blair (3/31/1861), Fox (1920) 1:12. See also Nicolay and Hay (1917) 2:25; Blair/Crawford (5/6/1882), Crawford (1887) 365–66; Silverstone 89; Lorenzo Thomas/D. D. Tompkins (4/4/1861), *OR* 1/1:236.

77. Nicolay and Hay (1917) 3:434.

78. Fox/Blair (3/31/1861), Fox (1920) 1:13.

79. George R. Harrington (1815–1892), assistant treasury secretary, later asserted in a manuscript memoir that he was present at the White House when Lincoln, Welles, Fox, and Blair "decided to attempt [to reprovision Sumter] at once" and agreed upon "the method to accomplish it." When Harrington, who reportedly considered Seward an "older brother," went directly to him to reveal the plan, Seward was shocked. George R. Harrington, "President Lincoln and His Cabinet: Inside Glimpses," Missouri History Museum, http://collections.mohistory.org/archive/ARC:A0653_1. See, for example, introduction 32–33 (handwritten version), 22–23 (typed version); introduction 14–16 (typed version); text 36 (handwritten version). Harrington in this memoir recounts that these events took place on April 7. In this he was undoubtedly mistaken, since April 7 was well after Lincoln, Fox, and Welles made such a plan, and by April 7 Seward would not have been shocked to hear of it. It was on March 29, following the cabinet meeting, that Lincoln issued written orders to Welles and Cameron to proceed with the Charleston operation and "the method to accomplish it," including, for example, the specific vessels to be used, as set forth in the memo reportedly written by Fox that day. In his history of the war, Samuel Wylie Crawford purported to quote Harrington as follows: "I was at the White House one evening, and found there with the President Mr. Welles, Mr. Fox and Mr. Montgomery Blair, and ere they separated it was determined to relieve and provision Fort Sumter. I went to Mr. Seward, and informed him of the fact," Seward answering that he found it "difficult to believe." The authority Crawford cites for this quotation is "Harrington's *Reminiscences*." Crawford (1887) 368. If Crawford is accurately quoting Harrington, it is not from "Inside Glimpses." Perhaps Harrington sent Crawford a letter summarizing "Inside Glimpses." Crawford does not say that the events took place on April 7, either because the source he quoted did not include a date or because he saw that Harrington used the date April 7 and, believing Harrington mistaken, he decided to omit it. Alternatively, the document Crawford read may have been "Inside Glimpses," and he then accurately wrote out the gist but erred by putting quotation marks around it. See also Harrington Papers, Huntington Library, San Marino, CA.

80. Nevins (1959) 58; Crofts (1989) 297; McClintock (2011) 32.
81. Crawford, Roman/Toombs (3/30/1861), *Commissioners* 205.
82. Crawford/Pickens (3/30/1861), *Pickens Papers* Reel 2 p. 325, Blair (1881) 380; Ramsdell 270–71.
83. Lamon 71, 74–79; Campbell in Connor 127; Rhodes (1892–1906) 3:333 and n3, 336; L. Johnson 464; Lash 56–60.
84. Crawford/Toombs (4/1/1861), *Commissioners* 145; Roman, Crawford, Forsyth/Toombs (3/27/1861), id. 203. See also P. Foner 243, 300; Heather Cox Richardson, *The Greatest Nation of the Earth* (Cambridge, MA: Harvard University Press, 1997), 34–39; William Allen Butler, *Retrospect of Forty Years 1825–1865*, ed. Harriet Butler (New York: C. Scribner's Sons, 1911), 343.
85. Crawford/Toombs (4/1/1861), *Commissioners* 145. Aspinwall and Marshall told Fox that Wall Street would not buy the loan if word leaked out of a Union expedition against Charleston. Fox/Blair (3/31/1861), Fox (1920) 1:13, 14; Fox/Blair (3/31/1861), id. 1:12.
86. One of the participants at the March 15 cabinet meeting, perhaps Lincoln himself, noted that if nothing was done and the Confederates attacked Sumter in its "enfeebled condition," the administration's opponents would be merciless. "Some Considerations in Favor of Withdrawing the Troops from Fort Sumter, by President Lincoln" (n.d. [3/18/1861?]), *Welles Papers/LC* Reel 28, Basler et al. 4:288. See also Nicolay and Hay (1917) 3:434.
87. Lamon/Seward (3/25/1861), *Seward Papers* Reel 62. See also Gwin and Coleman (1891) 468; Potter (1995) 340n13. Charlestonians would have told Lamon that they would look favorably on a voluntary evacuation, but if Lincoln did nothing, Sumter might be attacked even before Anderson ran out of food. A reporter in Charleston noted that if Lincoln did not announce a withdrawal soon, local sentiment was "entirely in favor of action." *New-York Daily Tribune* (4/1/1861) 5.
88. March 23d.—The President yesterday issued an order to Major Anderson to put his command in readiness to evacuate Fort Sumter upon the arrival at that place of a U. S. war Steamer. Colonel Lamon of Illinois, the confidential friend of the President, was sent [as] bearer of [the] despatches to Major Anderson. The evacuation will take place upon the arrival of the steamer which has been despatched by the Secretary of the Navy.

     Bedford (PA) Gazette (3/29/1861) 2; *Baltimore Daily Exchange* (3/26/1861) 1. See also *Lamoille (VT) Newsdealer* (3/29/1861) 3. Nor did Lamon, upon his return to Washington, care to remain circumspect. Edwin Stanton wrote to ex-president Buchanan, "There has been a rumor for the last two or three days that, notwithstanding all that has been said, there will be an effort to reinforce Fort Sumter. But I do not believe a word of it. The special messenger, Colonel Lamon, told me that he was satisfied it could not be done." (4/3/1861), Stanton 475. See also McClure (1892) 305–6.
89. Welles later wrote that Lincoln had "never proposed or intended to order" Fort Sumter to be evacuated and that "certain assurances and committals which had been made embarrassed him." Welles (7/1870) 114. The assurances referred to were by Lamon. Although Seward repeatedly assured the commissioners, there is no evidence that Lincoln was aware of these statements until later. See chapter 14, note 66.

90.	Several leading naval officers express the belief that the batteries which guard the entrances to Charleston harbor might be run under steam without more than ordinary risk. They agree, however, that unless such an experiment could be successfully executed at night, the boats or tugs which might be used for this purpose would be exposed to the fire of Fort Moultrie, in an attempt to land the troops and supplies. That contingency must be regarded as nearly inseparable from the enterprise, and it almost necessarily involves the commencement of actual war, for any movement looking toward that object would be certainly resisted. This view is sustained by all the official information on the subject, and by the opinion of an agent [Lamon] sent to make a personal inspection for the satisfaction of the Administration.

New-York Tribune (4/1/1861) 5.
91. "The Last Report about Sumter," *NYT* (4/2/1861).
92. *Lamon Papers* Box 4, File 503.
93. See, for example, *National Intelligencer* (4/5/1861) 3; id. (4/8/1861) 2.
94. Welles (11/1870) 616; Cauthen (1950) 128–29; Stampp (1950) 84–98, 264–86; Furgurson 6–10.
95. Koerner/Lincoln (3/28/1861), *Lincoln Papers*.
96. John W. B. Autram/Lincoln (4/2/1861), *Lincoln Papers*; "A Republican"/Lincoln (4/3/1861), id. (underscoring omitted). See also Frederick J. Blue, *Salmon P. Chase* (Kent, OH: Kent State University Press, 1987), 136; Marvel (2006) 15.
97. (4/1/1861), Nicolay and Hay (1917) 2:29, 3:445. See also F. Seward (1916) 149–50; Ferris (1991); B. Thomas 253–54; Denton (2009) 140–45; Carroll 55n; Bemis 7:33–36; Lynn M. Case, "La Sécession aux Etats-Unis," *Rev. d'Hist. Diplomatique* 77:290, 304–5 (10–12/1963); G. Van Deusen (1967) 281–84; Ferris (1976) 10–12; Mark E. Brandon, *Free in the World: American Slavery and Constitutional Failure* (Princeton, NJ: Princeton University Press, 1998), 172.
98. Changing the rhetoric from slavery to Unionism had been an argument of Thurlow Weed as well as Seward. See, for example, McClintock (2008) 111, 236, 331–32n30; T. Barnes 2:305–7; Lyons/Russell (2/4/1861), Barnes and Barnes 26, 28.
99. Villard 160.
100. H. Adams/C. F. Adams Jr. (1/24/1861), H. Adams (1982–1988) 1:225.
101. *Globe* (36/2) 1373 (3/2/1861). See also (2/24/1861), C. F. Adams Sr.
102. Of 1,520 federal civilian jobs subject to presidential authority, Lincoln replaced 1,194 incumbents. Holzer 235. Cf. Guelzo 127.
103. Lyons/Russell (3/18/1861), Barnes and Barnes 40, 41.
104. C. F. Adams Jr. (1900) 145–46. See also (3/10, 28/1861), C. F. Adams Sr. Even before meeting him, Adams had written, "I am afraid that in this lottery we may have drawn a blank." (2/16/1861), C. F. Adams Sr. The Chicago position was hardly insignificant and on March 28 went to John Locke Scripps of the pro-Lincoln *Chicago Press & Tribune*, author of the longest Lincoln campaign biography. Lincoln (ca. June 1860), Basler et al. 4:60; John Locke Scripps, *John Locke Scripps' 1860 Campaign Life of Abraham Lincoln* (Peoria, IL: E. J. Jacob, 1931); J. Seymour Currey, *Chicago: Its History and Its Builders* (Chicago: S. J. Clarke, 1912), 3:358.
105. Lincoln later told Swett that the war effort required Northern unanimity and, with "more horses than oats," he tended to dispense more to his political enemies than to

friends like Swett, on whose support he could rely without incentives. Swett/Herndon (1/17/1866), Herndon and Weik (1921) 3:528, 533–34.

106. See, for example, C. F. Adams Jr. (1900) 167–68, 178–99; Brauer 148; Crofts (1989) 299–300; Foreman 65–67, 76–77. But see Ferris (1991).

107. See, for example, Crawford, Forsyth, Roman/Toombs (4/4/1861), *Commissioners* 209; Crawford, Roman, Forsyth/Toombs (4/5/1861), id. 209; Manuel D. Crugat/S. R. Mallory (3/241861), *Records of the Confederate States of America 1861–1865,* Microfilm Shelf no. 13,744, container 24, Library of Congress Manuscript Div.; Brauer 155.

108. See, for example, Welles (1960) 1:136–37.

109. See, for example, C. F. Adams Jr. (1916) 88–89; Edward Chase Kirkland, *Charles Francis Adams, Jr. 1835–1915: The Patrician at Bay* (Cambridge, MA: Harvard University Press, 1965), 20–21; [Buchanan] (1866) 57.

110. Seward's desperate attempt at a palace coup was all the worse for not having been the spontaneous impulse of one febrile moment, but rather an odd playing out of the so-called Albany Plan, hatched by Thurlow Weed back when Seward lost the nomination, in which Lincoln would be the rail-splitting figurehead and Seward the actual ruler. See, for example, Hendrick 86–98, 174–77.

111. Lincoln drafted a memo of his own but either did not deliver it to Seward or delivered it with instructions that it be returned to him without any copy being made. Lincoln/Seward (4/1/1861), Basler et al. 4:316–17, Nicolay and Hay (2/1888) 616; Nicolay and Hay (1917) 2:30, 3:448. See also Welles (10/1876) 439; Symonds (2008) 18; Basler et al. 4:317n1; David Herbert Donald, *"We Are Lincoln Men"* (New York: Simon & Schuster, 2003), 153; Stahr 270–72; Brauer 134–36; W. Smith 2:5, 11.

112. See, for example, H. W. Johnstone, *Truth of the War Conspiracy of 1861* (Curryville, GA: McGregor, 1921), 20.

113. While the Blairs, Gideon Welles, and others so distrusted Seward that they would entertain almost any charge made against him, little of substance ever emerged, and in the end all Welles could say with assurance was that the other cabinet members did not at first know anything, then heard rumors that Southern commissioners were in town talking to "the Administration," and then learned that Seward was talking to the commissioners through Justice Campbell. "A strange state of things," Welles wrote, "when the first officer of the cabinet and one of the judges of the highest court were in communication with rebels discussing measures having in view a disruption of the union." Brauer 143–44; Welles narrative, *Welles Papers/LC* Reel 2.

114. See Ratner and Teeter 21, 31; Brown 185–89; William E. Huntzicker, *The Popular Press, 1833–1865* (Westport, CT: Greenwood, 1999), 42–43. The *Times* had already adopted Seward's position, declaring that "the true policy of the Government" would be to use force only in absolute self-defense, while appealing to Southerners' intellect so effectively that "with every day of reflection" they "will become more and more unwilling to precipitate such an issue." *NYT* (3/21/1861) 4. When in the November 1860 election Virginia rejected the disunionist Breckinridge, Raymond had prophesized "that we shall speedily hear of Union meetings in nearly all the Southern States." *NYT* (11/7/1860). See also Carl F. Krummel, "Henry J. Raymond and the *New York Times* in the Secession Crisis, 1860–61," *NY Hist.* 32/4:377 (10/1951); Samuels 97.

115. Swain/Hay (2/21/1888) excerpted in Patrick Sowle, "A Reappraisal of Seward's Memorandum of April 1, 1861, to Lincoln," *J. Southern Hist.* 33/2:234, 235 (5/1967). See also Denton (2009) 145.

116. "Wanted—a Policy," *NYT* (4/3/1861) 4; Brauer 150.

117. (4/1/1861), Russell (1861A) 12, 14. See also Russell (1863) 1:99–100; Foreman 72–73.

118. Quoted in *Yorkville (SC) Enquirer* (4/11/1861) 1.

119. Campbell (1917) 34; Russell (1863) 1:86–87; Crawford, Roman, Forsyth/Toombs (4/5/1861), *OR* 1/1:286. See also Crawford, Forsyth, Roman/Toombs (4/4/1861), *Commissioners* 209; (4/3/1861), *OR* 1/1:286; (4/6/1861), Roman 1:35; *Cleveland Morning Leader* (4/5/1861) 1; Russell (1863) 1:97; Bemis 7:30–32; Brauer 148.

120. Campbell, "Facts of History" [before 7/10/1865], *Goodyear Collection* vol. 2 item 5; Connor 132, quoted in Campbell/Seward (4/13/1861), *Seward Papers* Reel 63; F. Seward (1891) 538; Bancroft (1900) 2:131; L. Johnson 465; Seward quoted in, for example, Campbell (1917) 34–35.

121. Campbell (1874) 24–25. Seward wrote out, "I am satisfied the Govt. will not undertake to supply Fort Sumter without giving notice to Gov. P[ickens]." Campbell (1917) 38.

122. Roman, Crawford/Toombs (4/1/1861), *Commissioners* 205–7. See also Crawford/Walker, Pickens (4/1/1861), Nicolay and Hay (1917) 4:25–26; Beauregard/Walker (4/1/1861), *OR* 1/1:283; Foster/Totten (4/5/1861), *OR* 1/1:242.

123. Fox/Archibald Lowery (4/3/1861), Fox (1920) 1:19.

124. Campbell/Davis (4/3/1861), J. Davis (1971–) 7:88.

125. Seward/Frances Seward (4/1/1861), F. Seward (1891) 534.

126. M. J. Crawford/L. P. Walker (4/1/1861), Nicolay and Hay (1917) 4:25–26; Crawford (1887) 391; Campbell in Connor 227–28. Crawford added, "Would it not be well to aid in this by cutting off supplies?" See also Campbell/Seward (4/13/1861), *Seward Papers* Reel 63.

Chapter 9: Captain Meigs and Lieutenant Porter

1. Seward/Lincoln (3/29/1861), *Lincoln Papers*; Bancroft (1900) 2:128.

2. Meigs (ca. 9/30/1853), Sen. Exec. Doc. no. 1 (33/1) 576; Ways; D. Miller 1, 18–79; Weigley (1959) 59–70. West Point provided Meigs with the best engineering training available. Morrison 23–26.

3. *Meigs Papers* Reel 15; Meigs/Davis (10/22/1853), Sen. Exec. Doc. no. 1 (33/1) 69; Davis/Meigs (1/15/1860), J. Davis (1971–) 6:6; Davis/Floyd (1/23/1858), id. 6:167; Weigley (1959) 63–77. Davis had also served on the Committee on Public Buildings. James Q. Howard, "Architects of the American Capitol," *International Rev.* 1/6:736, 750 (11/1874).

4. See Meigs (2001) xxxiv–xxxv; Davis/Floyd (1/23/1858), id. 791; Harry C. Ways, "Montgomery C. Meigs and the Washington Aqueduct," W. Dickinson et al. 21, 35–39; Nevins (1950) 2:199–200; D. Miller 31–54; Weigley (1959) 78–112; P. Klein 349.

5. See, for example, Meigs/Davis (6/13/1860), Meigs letterpress book 110, *Meigs Papers* Reel 18; Meigs/Toombs (7/19/1861), id. Reel 18; Meigs/Seward (7/2/1860), Meigs letterpress book 164; Davis/Meigs (7/25/1860), J. Davis (1971–) 6:360. For Seward's

responses, see Meigs letterpress book 181 and *Meigs Papers* Reels 12 and 18. In late July, Meigs sent to Seward a published order by Floyd regarding the aqueduct, jotting on the side that Floyd "grasps the money + the patronage" in the project. *Seward Papers* Reel 60.

6. Meigs/Buchanan (7/24/1860), East 121; Ways 34–41. Meigs's papers include numerous letters describing the controversy. See, for example, "Extracts from . . . Diary" (8/13/1860): "Presdt. returned my letter, declining to receive it except through the regular channel." Meigs on August 29, 1860, noted that Buchanan had quipped that he "did not know whether to court martial or send me away." *Meigs Papers* Reel 12. See also id. Reel 17.

7. "Memorial of Captain Meigs" (7/31/1860), *Att'y-Gen. Ops.* 9:462, 468, 472, 473; East 128–32.

8. Meigs statement (11/2/1859), Meigs (2001) 807; Buchanan/Black (9/8/1860), Auchampaugh (1923) 383; L. G. Arnold/Lorenzo Thomas (1/23/1861), *OR* 1/1:346; Meigs/Arnold (1/23/1861), *OR* 1/1:347; D. Miller 55–79; Weigley (1956) 163–315; Weigley (1959) 108–29; East 132–43.

9. Meigs/Scott (11/10/1860), *OR* 1/52 Pt. I:3, 4. See also Ways 40; Johns 25; Weigley (1956) 317, 324; Weigley (1959) 121–26. Meigs had told Israel Vogdes that he would gladly help prepare Fort Pickens. Vogdes/L. Thomas (2/7/1861), *OR* 1/1:357, 358.

10. Albert Gallatin Riddle, *Recollections of War Times* (New York, 1895), 9; Herman Melville, "The Conflict of Convictions" (1861), *Battle-Pieces and Aspects of the War* (New York, 1866), 16; Meigs (2001) 778–79; D. Miller 33–54, 78–79.

11. Louisa Meigs/Montgomery Meigs (1/6, 17/1861), *Meigs Papers* Reel 7; Weigley (1959) 128–29.

12. (2/21/1861), Meigs (2001) 771; Meigs quoted in Weigley (1959) 130. Meigs's biographer noted that he "had the talent of the self-righteous for hating his enemies." Weigley (1956) 241.

13. Meigs/J. F. Meigs (3/4/1861), *Meigs Papers* Reel 7; Meigs (2001) 771–74; Weigley (1956) 334–42; Weigley (1959) 131–32.

14. Meigs/Thomas Anderson (10/21/1881), T. Anderson 43, 44. In 1865, Meigs stated that in his interview with Lincoln on the evening of March 29, "the President did not inform me that he intended to attempt to relieve Fort Sumter, but questioned me as to the possibility of doing it." *NYT* (9/14/1865), Meigs (1921) 299.

15. Meigs/T. M. Anderson (10/31/1881), T. Anderson 43–44, 48–49. Meigs would later claim that he heard nothing about the Sumter operation until he received news that Sumter had been attacked and had fallen. Id. Lincoln's secretaries, perhaps relying solely upon Meigs's statement, accepted it. Nicolay and Hay (1917) 4:439. However, Meigs was often in the Brooklyn Navy Yard when the expedition was being prepared and, like Porter and Seward, would never express all that he knew about the venture in which he was involved. See chapter 11.

16. Meigs (3/29, 31/1861), Meigs (2001) 775, 776; Meigs (1921) 299, 300; Nicolay and Hay (2/1888) 611–12; Nicolay and Hay (1917) 3:434; H. A. Adams/Welles (3/22/1861), *ORN* 1/4:100; *Richland County (WI) Observer* (4/9/1861) 2; *Raleigh Weekly Standard* (4/10/1861) 1; *Anderson (SC) Intelligencer* (4/4/1861) 4.

17. Keyes 380–81.

18. Meigs (3/31/1861), Meigs (2001) 776, Meigs (1921) 300; Meigs diary (3/31/1861), *Meigs Papers* Reel 2; Keyes 382–83.

19. Quoted in Nicolay and Hay (1917) 3:436–37; Scott/Seward (4/1/1861), *Lincoln Papers*. See also F. Seward (1891) 534; Crawford (1887) 408–9; Elliott 705–6; Meigs journal (3/31/1861), *Meigs Typescript* D-11.
20. Scott/Lincoln (3/29/1861), *Lincoln Papers*.
21. Scott/Lincoln (4/1/1861), *Lincoln Papers*.
22. Totten/Cameron (4/3/1861), *OR* 1/1:232.
23. In the *Dictionary of National Biography*, Southerners tended to be prominent for military achievement, Northerners for medicine, education, and the humanities. J. McPherson (1988) 40. See also Huntington 211–21.
24. As Charles Francis Adams prepared to become U.S. minister in London, Seward instructed him to explain that in the unusual U.S. system of owing allegiance to both a national government and a state government, "no provision had ever been made, perhaps none ever could have been made, to anticipate" the "strange and unprecedented disturbance" whereby the two allegiances diverged. (4/10/1861), *Foreign Relations* 71, 72.
25. *Globe* (36/2) 1065, 1095–97, 1423–24 (2/20, 21, 3/2/1861); "Naval Force" 6–10, 23–26; *National Republican* (2/25/1861) 2; id. (2/26/1861) 2; Reagan 124–26; Jeremiah Black/ Henry Wilson (ca. Feb. 1861), J. Black 245, 256–58; W. M. Fowler 34; Paullin 216. See also Raphael Semmes, *Memoirs of Service Afloat, during the War Between the States* (Baltimore, 1869), 76–80.
26. West (1943) 99; U.S. Cong., Sen. (38/1), "Report of the Secretary of the Navy Transmitting . . . a List of Officers," Ex. Doc. no. 3 (1/5/1864); William S. Dudley, *Going South: U.S. Navy Officer Resignations & Dismissals on the Eve of the Civil War* (Washington, DC: Naval Historical Foundation, 1981), 5.
27. W. R. Hopkins/Welles (3/9/1861), *Welles Papers/NYPL* Box 3, Reel 2. Cf. William Harwar Parker, *Recollections of a Naval Officer 1841–1865* (New York, 1883), 201.
28. Blunt/Blair (3/4/1861), *Welles Papers/NYPL* Box 3, Reel 2. See also James Ward/Welles (3/13/1861), *ORN* 1/4:92; Welles/Mercer (3/28/1861), *ORN* 1/4:227; Wesley Millet and Gerald White, *The Rebel and the Rose* (Nashville, TN: Cumberland House, 2007), 75.
29. Keyes/Seward (2/7/1861), *Seward Papers* Reel 61. See also Keyes/Lincoln (11/26/1860), Keyes 429, 430 (asking Lincoln to appoint as secretary of war a Northerner who will "build up Northern officers and place them in commands proportionate with the population of the North").
30. F. Seward (1916) 144. "The people," Seward wrote, "were shocked by successive and astounding developments of what the statute book distinctly pronounced to be sedition and treason," leaving Buchanan's administration "demoralized" and the laws "powerless." Seward had no tolerance for traitors within the State Department. Seward/C. F. Adams Sr. (4/10/1861), W. Seward (1884–1890) 5:199, 202; *Message of the President of the United States to the Two Houses of Congress at the Commencement of the Second Session of the Thirty-Seventh Congress* (Washington, 1861), 1:71, 72; F. Seward (1891) 520; F. Seward (1916) 144; *Appleton* 258–59. An anonymous letter to Lamon dated 4/14/1861, alleged that "a large majority of the police force" in Washington were "Disunionists and Secessionists." *Lamon Papers* Box 6 File 871.
31. W. Sherman (1889) 1:195.
32. Bulloch 1:31–32; Porter/Fox (7/5/1861), Fox (1920) 1:73, 75; Blair/Fox (4/26/1861), id. 1:37; [Matthew Fontaine Maury], "Scraps from the Lucky Bag," *South. Lit. Messenger* 6/4:233, 235–37 (4/1840). See also Headley 326–27; *Autobiography of George Dewey*

(New York: Charles Scribner's Sons, 1913), 41–43; Bernardo and Bacon 167–70; Morrison 20–21; Skelton 192–97; Symonds (2008) 19; Paul Lewis [pseud., Noel Bertram Gerson], *Yankee Admiral: A Biography of David Dixon Porter* (New York: D. McKay, 1968), 52, 73–74; S. L. Southard/James Monroe (1/24/1824), *Am. State Papers* (Naval Affairs) 1:907; Paullin 189–90, 202, 239–43; James Dobbin, "Report of the Secretary of the Navy," *Globe* (33/2) App. 19, 22 (12/4/1854).

33. *Porter Journal* 51–55. See also D. Porter (1885) 13.
34. See Bearss (1957–1961) 36:125.
35. D. Porter (1886) 100.
36. Scott had been "an old fogy years before in 1846, when I knew him at the Siege of Vera Cruz. Fifteen years and the gout . . . had not improved his abilities or his temper." *Porter Journal* 68.
37. Meigs/T. M. Anderson (10/21/1881), T. Anderson 43, 49.
38. D. Porter (1885) 14.
39. Commodore Porter's career was not without controversy. See, for example, *Minutes of Proceedings of the Courts of Inquiry and Court Martial, in Relation to Captain David Porter* (Washington, 1825). His works include *Journal of a Cruise Made to the Pacific Ocean* (1815), the second edition of which (New York, 1822) begins with seventy-six pages dealing with what its author thought unfair criticisms. Regarding his son, perhaps the frustration of stymied careers and the pent-up hunger for feats of daring-do lay behind the theatened duel in 1840 between D. D. Porter and Stephen C. Rowan, future commander of *Pawnee* in the expedition to relieve Fort Sumter. Paullin 193.
40. Meigs/T. M. Anderson (10/31/1881), T. Anderson 43, 47 ("All the orders for the expedition were drawn up by Keyes and myself, and they were signed in effect exactly as we advised"); Meigs journal (4/1/1861), *Meigs Typescript* D-11 ("Hard at work all day making orders for the signature of the President and others"); Soley 102, 104 ("The orders . . . were drawn in official form at the interview by Porter copied by Captain Meigs, and signed by the President [and] bear upon their face the obvious marks of Porter's authorship"). Soley is probably correct. See notes 41–50, 60 and accompanying text.
41. Lincoln/Porter (4/1/1861), *ORN* 1/4:108–9, Soley 102–3. Meigs in his journal characterized this as directing Porter to "proceed to sea and not draw rein until he was inside of Pensacola harbor," where his task would be "to prevent any boat crossing the harbor with troops" to attack Fort Pickens. Meigs journal (4/1/1861), Meigs (2001) 776, Meigs (1921) 301, Meigs journal (3/31/1861), *Meigs Typescript* D-11.
42. Porter's biographer, his former subordinate in the navy, would write that Porter had cleverly made a "request" of "cooperation" from whatever naval officer was at Pensacola. Because that officer (probably Captain Adams) would be senior to Lieutenant Porter, Porter could not order him to do anything, although Adams could hardly ignore an order from the commander in chief. Soley 102–4.
43. If one strained to find a rationale, it was that by successfully entering Pensacola Harbor, a warship could fire upon any small Confederate boats attempting to cross the harbor to attack Fort Pickens before or while a transport was unloading troops on the ocean side of Santa Rosa Island, beyond the range of the Confederate artillery. See Scott/Seward (4/1/1861), *Lincoln Papers*.
44. (4/1/1861), Basler et al. 4:315.

45. Lincoln/Commandant, Navy Yard (4/1/1861), *ORN* 1/4:109; Lincoln/Commandant, Navy Yard (4/1/1861), id. In February 1865 it fell to Meigs to respond to a War Department request for Lincoln's original orders to Porter, by saying that neither the army nor the president had retained copies. Meigs/E. D. Townsend (2/27/1865), T. Anderson 42. Those originals were never found. See Welles's handwritten note following Lincoln's letter to him of March 18, Welles letterbook vol. 1, *Welles Papers/CHS*. See also Basler et al. 4:313–14n.

46. Porter asserted that a man working directly under Welles, Charles W. Welsh, through whose hands as chief clerk all key communications passed, was a secessionist traitor. (In fact, Porter's allegation against Welsh, a Massachusetts man first appointed in 1845, was groundless. *Officers' Register* 15.) Porter noted in a later memoir that at this time Welles was "fitting out [Fox's] expedition for the relief of Fort Sumter" and his orders, issued "in the usual way," were almost immediately telegraphed to Charleston by disloyal members of the Navy Department. D. Porter (1885) 14–15. Porter suggested that "the telegraph wires around Washington ought all to be cut." Meigs/T. Anderson (10/31/1881), T. Anderson 43, 45. See also Symonds (2008) 19, 372n30.

47. D. Porter (1885) 15. See also Crawford (1915) item 370; William E. Gienapp and Erica L. Gienapp, "Brief Biography of Gideon Welles," Welles (2014) xxiii.

48. See, for example, [Welles?], "Comment upon the Autobiographical Sketch of Thurlow Weed Relating to the Formation of the Lincoln Cabinet," *Welles Papers/NYPL*, Box 7, Reel 4 ("He admits his disappointment and dejection over the defeat of his friend Seward at Chicago . . . which he attributed at the time, and not without reason perhaps, in a measure to Gideon Welles"); A Democratic-Republican [pseud., Welles], *New York Evening Post* (11/15/1858) 1; Symonds (2008) 5–6; R. Wilson 339; West (1943) 78–90. See also Welles (1874) 51; Niven (1973) 283–86, 304; Timothy S. Good, *Lincoln for President* (Jefferson, NC: McFarland, 2009), 21–23. Welles, in a slightly shorter and unpublished "Review of William H. Seward's Speech at Rochester," stated that Seward's "irrepressible conflict" speech revealed that he was more an "Imperialist" than a Republican, "the advocate of a consolidated empire rather than an admirer and supporter of a confederate republic of distinct and Independent States with limited and specified powers." *Welles Papers/LC* Reel 31.

49. Welles (1925) 19, 25, 32–33; Weed 1:611. See also Welles (9/1876) 302. Seward had undoubtedly been pleased to hear Porter's unflattering recollections of Welles's tenure as chief of the navy's Bureau of Provision and Clothing under President Polk in 1846–1849. Weed 1:611; Hendrick 75. Welles's responsibilities in that office are described in *Welles Papers/NYPL* Folder 1, Reel 4. See also R. White 316.

50. Lincoln/Mercer (4/1/1861), *ORN* 1/4:109, Soley 101–3. As Porter later wrote, he considered the order to Mercer "a salve for any sensitiveness Captain Mercer might feel." *Porter Journal* 67. See also D. Porter (1885) 16.

51. *ORN* 1/16:xx; *Narrative of the Expedition of an American Squadron to the China Seas and Japan*, comp. Francis L. Hawks (Washington, 1856), 1:328–490, 2:410–14; Silverstone 24; M. C. Perry/J. C. Dobbin (3/20 1854), U.S. Cong., Sen., Ex. Doc. no. 34, "Correspondence Relative to the Naval Expedition to Japan" (33/2) 116; Perry (4/4/1854), Dahlgren (1856A) 167; *DANFS* vol. 5. See also Frank M. Bennett, *Steam Navy of the United States*, 2nd ed. (Pittsburgh, 1897), 1:104–9; "The United States War Steamer *Powhatan*," *U.S. Naut. Mag. & Naval J.* 3/1:28 (10/1855); id. 4/2:104 (5/1856); James D. Johnston, *China*

and Japan: Being a Narrative of the Cruise of the U.S. Steam-Frigate "Powhatan" (Philadelphia, 1861); *Officers' Register* 105; Sondhaus 41, 57.

52. J. S. Saunders/Joseph Holt (1/23/1861), *OR* 1/1:353; *Globe* (36/2) 1095 (2/21/1861); G. J. Prendergast/Toucey (2/20 [21]/1861), *ORN* 1/4:86, 87; Chadwick 248–49; Tucker (2011) 2:542. See also *National Republican* (2/26/1861) 2; *Globe* (36/2) 1095 (2/21/1861). Although the February 5 *National Intelligencer* reported (p. 3) that *Powhatan* had been ordered on January 19 to protect Union interests at Pensacola, no such order has emerged.

53. Meigs, *NYT* (9/14/1865), *Daily National Republican* (9/16/1865) 1, Welles (1/1871) 104; Meigs/T. M. Anderson (10/31/1881), T. Anderson 43, 44.

54. Welles/Mercer (3/28/1861), *ORN* 1/4:227. See also Foote/Welles (3/14/1861), *ORN* 1/4:226; Crawford (1887) 405; Soley 98; Mercer/Welles (3/13/1861), *ORN* 1/4:265.

55. Blair/Fox (4/1/1861), Fox (1920) 1:16. Relevant orders are, for example, Cameron/Fox (4/4/1861), *Fox Collection* Series I, Box 4, Folder 11, *ORN* 1/4:232; Winfield Scott/ Henry L. Scott (4/4/1861), *OR* 1/1:236.

56. Compare Welles/Commandant (4/1/1861), *ORN* 1/4:229 with Lincoln/Commandant (4/1/1861), *ORN* 1/4:109. The only difference is that Welles, in telegraphic style, omitted "the" before "earliest."

57. Welles/[S. L. Breese] (4/1/1861), *Fox Collection* Series I, Box 4, Folder 11, *ORN* 1/4:229; Welles/[S. L. Breese] (4/1/1861), Fox (1920) 1:17; Lincoln/Foote (4/1/1861), Basler et al. 4:313; Lincoln/Foote (4/1/1861), id. 4:314.

58. Welles (1911) 1:17–18. See also Nicolay and Hay (1917) 4:440–41.

59. In a draft for a published article on this topic, Welles wrote that Stringham was his "assistant in detaching," suggesting that he helped Welles identify disloyal officers. "Detaching" is crossed out in the draft, and the published article describes Stringham's position as assisting Welles "in detailing officers of fidelity and patriotism," a positive articulation of the same task. Compare Welles, "History of the Expedition to Relieve Fort Sumter with Special Reference to the Activities of William H. Seward, Who Opposed the Expedition," p. 7, *Welles Papers/NYPL* Reel 4 with Welles (11/1870) 617, 625.

60. Lincoln/Welles (4/1/1861), Basler et al. 4:318–19. The order was partially in Meigs's handwriting, and partially in Porter's. Id.; Barron/Toucey (2/2/1861), *ORN* 1/4:76; S. R. Mallory/V. M. Randolph (1/28/1861), *ORN* 1/4:212; William H. Chase/Barron (1/29/1861), *ORN* 1/4:77; Tamara Moser Melia, "David Dixon Porter," Bradford 227, 245n3. In January, Barron had helped arrange the truce in Pensacola. See also J. H. Ward/ Welles (3/13/1861), *ORN* 1/4:91.

61. See Welles's pencil notation on the Barron/Stringham order, Welles (1924) 3. See also Lincoln/Welles (4/1/1861), id. 4; Welles (11/1870) 624–26. Welles indicated that Stringham had requested a seagoing command and Welles was considering it, although he would never have chosen Barron to replace him. A revised directive from Lincoln to Welles states, "You will select some other officer in whom implicit confidence may be placed to relieve Capt. Stringham." Lincoln/Welles (4/1/1861). It is found in, for example, Emanuel Hertz, *Abraham Lincoln: A New Portrait* (New York: H. Liveright, 1931), 2:827, but not in Basler's edition of Lincoln's works, nor in *Lincoln Papers*. See also Basler et al. 4:313–14n.

62. Welles (1911) 1:1:17. "At first, when I would take up to the president a paper for his signature," Seward's son Frederick later recalled, "he would spread it out and carefully

read the whole of it. But this usage was speedily abandoned, and he would hastily say, 'Your father says this is all right does he? Well, I guess he knows. Where do I put my name?'" F. Seward (1916) 148.

63. Welles (1911) 1:17–18; Welles (2014) 649.

64. In a later memoir, Porter stated that he wished to go to California because he believed that the Confederates would take over Washington following Lincoln's inauguration, and he had a large family and despaired of the situation between North and South. *Porter Journal* 41, 51.

65. C. F. Adams Jr. /Frederic Bancroft (10/11/1911), quoted in Burlingame (2008) 2:98.

66. Welles diary (12/20/1862), Welles (2014) 100, 106 (2/25/1863), id. 141, 143; J. McPherson (2012) 16–17.

67. Quoted in D. Porter (1885) 16. See also Symonds (2008) 20.

68. See Henry B. Stanton, *Random Recollections* (Johnstown, NY, 1885), 70–71.

69. Welles (1911) 1:5, 19–21; Niven (1973) 324–25; *Porter Journal* 42–47.

70. Welles (11/1870) 626; Welles (1911) 1:35–36; Symonds (2008) 21n; Tucker (2011) 1:25–26.

71. L. Q. Washington/Walker (4/4/1861), *OR* 1/53:139; L. Q. Washington/Walker (4/6/1861), *OR* 1/52 Pt. I:37.

Chapter 10: Under Siege

1. William G. Shade, *Democratizing the Old Dominion* (Charlottesville: University Press of Virginia, 1996), 176.

2. J. C. G. Kennedy, *Preliminary Report on the Eighth Census: 1860* (Washington, 1862), clxxii, 247; Wooster (1969) 27–28, 33–37, 146–48; Wooster (1962) 18–19.

3. Baldwin 3–4; Magruder 439–40; "Statement of Allen B. Magruder," Baldwin 22.

4. Baldwin recalled seeing nine governors, while Magruder counted (at least) seven: the governors of Illinois, Indiana, Iowa, Michigan, Ohio, Pennsylvania, and Wisconsin. Magruder 445. The *New York Herald* reported that "Governors [Andrew Gregg] Curtin, of Penn; [Israel] Washburn, of Maine, and [Oliver P.] Moore, of Indiana, severally had interviews with the President this morning, and the principle subject discussed was the present unsettled condition of the country and the best mode to meet it." (4/5/1861) 1. See also *Sacramento Daily Union* (4/20/1861) 4 ("Governors Morton of Indiana and Washburn of Maine have had a long interview with the President, urging the holding of all forts at the South and the speedy adoption of a definite policy"); *Life, Speeches, State Papers and Public Services of Gov. Oliver P. Morton*, ed. William M. French (Cincinnati, OH, 1864), 117, 132–33; William Dudley Foulke, *Life of Oliver P. Morton* (Indianapolis, IN, 1899), 1:113–14. Citing to the *New York Herald* and *New York World* of April 5, the historian James Ford Rhodes stated that "the President's interview with Governors Curtin of Pennsylvania, Morton of Indiana, and Washburn of Maine, must have confirmed him in his decision" to succor Anderson's garrison. Rhodes (1892–1906) 3:346n3. After the war, an unnamed friend of Seward allegedly recounted that ultra-Republican governors, joined by Representative Thaddeus Stevens (R/PA), had invoked "great wrath" in talking to Lincoln. Dabney 443, 450–54. See also W. Cooper (2012) 79. The *New York Herald* also reported that a secret government

agent arrived from the South and was "closeted with the President for over an hour" discussing Charleston. (4/5/1861) 1. Whatever happened that day, Carl Sandburg was incorrect in stating that no New York or Washington newspaper reported Northern governors visiting the White House, thus undermining his conclusion that "the nine governors with whom Baldwin shook hands were his own invention." Sandburg 195. *Lincoln Day by Day* lists no meeting with governors on April 4. Edited by Earl S. Miers (Washington, DC: Lincoln Sesquicentennial Comm'n, 1960). Rather, citing as authority the April 9 *Baltimore Sun*, it states that Lincoln met with the governors of Indiana, Maine, Ohio, and Pennsylvania on April 6 "about military status of militia." See also *Baltimore Daily Exchange* (4/9/1861) 1; Baldwin (2/10/1866), *JCR* 102, 105; Magruder 445; Ramsdell 275–76; Pollard (1862) 55; Crofts (1977–1978) 329; Stampp (1945) 316–17; Rosen 63; Robert N. Rosen, *Short History of Charleston* (San Francisco: Lexikos, 1982), 109; Curry 124–25; William B. Hesseltine, "Lincoln's War Governors," *Abraham Lincoln Quart.* 4/4:153 (12/1946); Hesseltine 141; Barbee 50–52; Cook, Barney, and Varon 7.

5. Nicolay and Hay (2/1888) 610.

6. Even Scott, a native Virginian, was concerned, warning Lincoln that "machinations against the Government & this Capital are secretly going on, all around us—in Virginia, in Maryland & here, as well as farther South." Scott/Lincoln (4/5/1861), *Lincoln Papers*.

7. Baldwin's resolution provided that any attempt by the federal government to subject the people of any state, "against their will, to Federal authority . . . would inevitably result in civil war." (3/11/1861), *Virginia Journal* App. [n.p.].

8. See, for example, Baldwin (2/10/1866), *JCR* 102; Baldwin 7, 9–10; Dabney; Magruder 440; Hall; J. M. Howard/W. H. Herndon (11/18/1866), *Herndon* 400. Cf. Botts 194–200; H. White 158–64; Crawford (1887) 311–12; William Harris (1985) 49–51; Randall (1956) 326–28; Ramsdell 276–78; Nevins (1959) 64–65; Burlingame (2008) 2:121–23; Current (1958) 120–23; Donald 290; B. Thomas 251–52, 540; Crofts (1989) 301–7; McClintock (2008) 241–44; Nelson D. Lankford, *Cry Havoc!* (New York: Viking, 2007), 59–74; Reid 333; Grady 188; Stahr 275. Lincoln's secretaries, perhaps to assure posterity that Lincoln's negative intuition about Virginia's loyalty was accurate, called its secession convention "little else than a warming-pan for the rebellion," with Baldwin "an embryo secessionist." Nicolay and Hay (2/1888) 610. As of April 4, however, the Commonwealth's Unionism was strong but conditioned upon Lincoln's abandoning both forts and not otherwise "coercing" the Confederacy. Another version of the Baldwin/Lincoln interview is that Baldwin told Lincoln that Virginia would not tolerate any attempt to coerce any of the seceded states and that it was to this statement that Lincoln responded "too late" (since plans were under way regarding Fort Sumter and Fort Pickens). Dabney 446–47. See also Shanks 192–95.

9. In August 1860, Botts forwarded to Lincoln a note to the effect that he would vote for him, although he could not say so publicly, forwarded the note to an intermediary, and had Lincoln return it to that intermediary. Lincoln/John B. Fry (8/15/1860), Basler et al. 4:95. Upon reading the note, Lincoln told the intermediary that it was one of "many assurances" from the South indicating that its people were not likely to "break up the Union," since they "have too much of good sense, and good temper, to attempt the ruin of the government," when the alternative was to "see it administered [by him, if he won] as it was administered by the men who made it."

10. Botts (2/15/1866), *JCR* 114–15. See also Baldwin 5–7; Arthur Cole, "The South and the Right of Secession in the Early Fifties," *Miss. V. Hist. Rev.* 1/3:376, 392–93 (12/1914).

11. Smith/John Hay (1/9/1863), *Lincoln Papers*; Hay/Smith (draft) (1/10/1863), id.; Fehrenbacher and Fehrenbacher 25, 37, 409–10.

12. See Freehling (2007) 324–25. Smith later recalled Lincoln saying, "I talked to [Baldwin] till late, gave him a bed," and continued to talk "nearly all next day." Smith/Nicolay (3/5/1878). See also Fehrenbacher and Fehrenbacher 20–21, 410. But this did not happen; Baldwin was not at the White House for more than several hours and was in Alexandria that night, back in Richmond on April 5. Wilmer L. Hall, "Lincoln's Interview with John B. Baldwin," *South Atl. Quart.* 13/3:260, 268 (7/1914).

13. Fox (2/24/1865); Boynton 1:256–57.

14. Baldwin states that the vote could not have taken place until at least 2:30 p.m. Baldwin 4–5. In support, he accurately quotes and characterizes the official minutes for April 4, as printed in *Virginia Journal* 21–33. A subsequent iteration of the Virginia proceedings suggests that the vote could have taken place shortly after 12:00 p.m. Reese 3:162–63, 774n8. See also id. 155–56. Even accepting, hypothetically, this earlier time, news of the vote in Richmond did not reach Lincoln and Baldwin during their meeting, and thus Lincoln could not have cited it.

15. According to Botts, Lincoln told Baldwin that he had issued a letter to Governor Pickens indicating that an attempt would be made to provision Fort Sumter in an unarmed vessel, making clear in the letter that if that vessel was fired upon, an armed fleet would enter the harbor. Lincoln did send Governor Pickens such a letter, but because it was not drafted until April 6, Lincoln would not have been citing it to Baldwin even on April 5 (the date erroneously urged by Botts), much less on the morning of April 4 (the actual date of the Lincoln/Baldwin meeting). Although Lincoln had certainly been thinking about the notice letter for some days prior to sending it, Botts's account treats the letter as already written, and it was not.

16. Baldwin 3.

17. Dabney 444–45.

18. *Globe* (40/2) 1207 (2/17/1868). See also Fox (2/24/1865); Fox, "My Plan for Reinforcing Fort Sumter Was This," *Fox Collection*, Box 14, Folder 10, pp. 2–8; Boynton 1:256–57.

19. (4/8/1861), *Lincoln Papers*, Basler et al. 4:329–30. See also *Virginia Journal* 137–45, 155; *NYT* (4/8/1861).

20. Quoted by J. P. Usher in *Reminiscences of Abraham Lincoln*, comp. Allen Thorndike Rice (Edinburgh, 1886), 77, 81.

21. Floyd/Anderson (12/21/1860), Lawton (1911) [opp. 6]; *OR* 1/1:103.

22. Among the courses at West Point was topographical drawing, in which Truman Seymour ('46) demonstrably excelled. See Morrison 91, 93, 97; Skelton 168.

23. Quoted in "Robert N. Gourdin to Robert Anderson, 1861" [ca. 2/2/1861?], contrib. Samuel G. Stoney, *S.C. Hist. Mag.* 60/1 (1/1959) 10, 11, Racine 445–47.

24. See, for example, *Woodsfield (OH) Spirit of Democracy* (2/20/1861) 2.

25. See, for example, *Cincinnati Daily Press* (2/27/1861) 3. See also F. M. Robertson/Samuel J. Anderson (2/7/1861), *OR* 2/2:610; Thomas Heard Robertson Jr., *Resisting Sherman* (Eldorado Hills, CA: Savas Beatie, 2015).

26. "Robert N. Gourdin to Robert Anderson, 1861" [ca. 2/2/1861?], contrib. Samuel G. Stoney, *S.C. Hist. Mag.* 60/1 (1/1959) 10, 11, Racine 445–47.

27. Gourdin/Anderson (ca. 2/2/1861?), Racine 448.
28. Huger/Gourdin (2/6/1861), Racine 438.
29. Beauregard attended West Point from 7/1/1834 to 7/1/1838. From 9/10/1835 to 11/6/1837, Anderson served as West Point's (only) artillery instructor. Cullum 1:22, 348, 697; *Register of the Officers and Cadets of the U.S. Military Academy, June 1836*, p. 4. Cf. T. H. Williams (1954) 8; Current (1963) 72–74.
30. Beauregard/Anderson (3/26/1861), *OR* 1/1:222; Anderson/Beauregard (3/26/1861), *OR* 1/1:222. A handwritten version is in *Goodyear Collection* vol. 1.
31. Beauregard/Walker (3/27/1861), *OR* 1/1:282, 283.
32. Anderson/Thomas (3/27/1861), *OR* 1/1:221; Nicolay and Hay (1917) 4:20–21.
33. Anderson/Beauregard (3/28/1861), *OR* 1/1:226; Beauregard/Anderson (3/29/1861), *OR* 1/1:226.
34. Anderson/Huger (3/4/1861), Racine 447.
35. *Anderson Diary.*
36. Lamon 75.
37. Scott/Anderson (3/29/1861), *Anderson Papers*, vol. 11. See also Detzer 223.
38. Quoted in Lawton (1911) 10–11.
39. Reproduced in *New-York Daily Tribune* (3/26/1861) 7.
40. *Globe* (37/4) 1461 (3/15/1861).
41. Anderson/E. B. Washburne (5/10/1870), *J. Ill. State Hist. Soc.* 10/2:422, 423 (9/1917). See also Isaac N. Arnold, *Life of Abraham Lincoln*, 3rd ed. (Chicago, 1885), 35–36; Swanberg 34; R. Anderson (1888) 169–70, 175–76; Burgess 1:2; "Editorial Comment," *Midland Monthly Mag.* 6/1:93 (7/1896).
42. Mary Doubleday/Lincoln ([April 1861]), *Lincoln Papers*; Abner Doubleday/Mary Doubleday (3/29/1861), id.; Detzer 215–16. Although the garrison's health had been good, three cases of dysentery appeared and Doubleday said Dr. Crawford feared the disease would spread. Doubleday/Mary Doubleday (4/2/1861), *Lincoln Papers*.
43. Surrounded by a force "so superior," Anderson wrote, that a battle would probably end "in the destruction of our force before relief could reach us, with only a few days' provisions on hand, and with a scanty supply of ammunition . . . in hourly expectation of receiving definite instructions from the War Department, and with [Holt's February 23 orders] so explicit and peremptory as those I am acting under, I deeply regret that I did not feel myself at liberty to resent the insult thus offered to the flag of my beloved country." Anderson/Lorenzo Thomas (4/4/1861), *OR* 1/1:236; Foster (1866) 8. See also Holt/Anderson (2/23/1861), *OR* 1/1:182 quoting Holt/Anderson (1/10/1861), Crawford (1887) 177 *and citing* Buell/Anderson (12/11/1860), *OR* 1/1:89.
44. Crawford/Pickens (4/1/1861), Blair (1881) 380, quoted in Beauregard/Walker (4/1/1861), *OR* 1/1:283.
45. *Anderson Diary* quoting G. W. Snyder/Anderson (4/4/1861), *OR* 1/1:241, 242; Nicolay and Hay (1917) 4:25–26.
46. Anderson/Thomas (4/5/1861), *OR* 1/1:241, Nicolay and Hay (1917) 4:26–27, Crawford (1887) 391–92. Regarding Anderson's knowledge of Crawford's April 1 telegram, see Anderson/Thomas (4/8/1861), T. Anderson 71–72, 83–84.
47. *Anderson Diary.*
48. *Anderson Diary.*
49. Floyd/Anderson (12/21/1860), Lawton (1911) [opp. 6]; *OR* 1/1:103.

50. S. W. Crawford (4/6/1861), *Fort Sumter Diary* 45. See also S. W. Crawford (4/4/1861), id. 70.

51. John Thompson/Robert Thompson (4/28/1861), Thompson 101, Lee and Chepesiuk 9, Johnston 417.

52. [Lincoln], Cameron/Anderson (4/4/1861), *Lincoln Papers*. See also Crawford (1887) 382, 384–86; T. Anderson 70–72; Nicolay and Hay (3/1888) 708; Current (1963) 195.

53. (4/5/1861), Russell (1861A) 18, 20. See also *Spectator* (4/27/1861) reproduced in *The Living Age* 69/888:629, 630 (6/8/1861).

54. Scott/Lincoln (4/8/1861), *Lincoln Papers*. Scott suggested that one cause of Anderson's "nervousness" was that Anderson had been refused the brevet promotions Scott had requested from both Buchanan and Lincoln. Since Fox would be bringing with him Anderson's brevets as lieutenant colonel and colonel, either Scott was misinformed or it was his letter to Lincoln that caused Lincoln to award the promotions.

Chapter 11: "Sail On, O Ship of State!"

1. Scott/Brown (4/1/1861), *ORN* 1/4:107; Tilley 40–41, *Meigs Papers* Reel 12. See also Lincoln/Officers of the Army and Navy (4/1/1861), Basler et al. 4:315. Although Seward failed to obtain for Meigs either command of the expedition or a promotion in rank or pay raise, Meigs felt "deeply the honor which your confidence has brought, and I cheerfully depart though in a position of less distinction and authority than you expected to be able to bestow upon me, intending to give my best efforts to the success of an expedition important to the Administration and the country." Meigs/Seward (4/3/1861), *Seward Papers* Reel 63.

2. Soley 101; Crawford (1887) 411–12; Meigs journal (4/2/1861), Meigs (1921) 301; Meigs journal (4/3, 5/10/1861), *Meigs Typescript* D-12, D-70; Meigs entry for 4/3/1861, *Nicolay Papers* Box 11; Meigs diary (4/3/1861), *Meigs Papers* Reel 2. See also *Porter Journal* 68; *New-York Daily Tribune* (4/2/1861) 8. Meigs, who was not obliged to account for the money, later returned $6,300. Meigs (1921) 201n31; Meigs journal (5/10/1861), *Meigs Typescript* D-70.

3. Lincoln/Porter (4/1/1861), *ORN* 1/4:108; Lincoln/Porter (4/1/1861), *ORN* 1/4:108–9; Lincoln/Commandant (4/1/1861), *ORN* 1/4:109. See also Lincoln/Commandant (4/1/1861), id. ("without delay").

4. See Welles (11/1870) 634; Welles (1911) 1:345–46; Welles/J. M. Hoppin (10/8/1873), Hoppin 391; id. 23; Hoogenboom (2008) 66; Tucker (2000) 3–4, 107; Andrew Hull Foote, *The African Squadron* (Philadelphia, [1855?]). See also [Leonard Bacon], "Andrew Hull Foote," *Hours at Home* 1/1:83 (5/1865); John Milligan, "Andrew Foote," Bradford 115, 116, 124; William E. Gienapp and Erica L. Gienapp, "Brief Biography of Gideon Welles," Welles (2014) xxiii, xv.

5. See D. Porter (1885) 17; Foote/Welles (4/1/1861), *ORN* 1/4:229; D. Porter (1885) 15–17; Crawford (1887) 410–12; Soley 108.

6. Foote/Welles (4/2/1861), *ORN* 1/4:230. See also Foote/Welles (4/3/1861), *ORN* 1/4:231, 232.

7. Hobart Berrien/Foote (4/3/1861), *ORN* 1/4:231; Foote/Welles (4/3/1861), *ORN* 1/4:232.

8. Foote/Welles (4/4/1861), *ORN* 1/4:234; Hearn (1996) 43.
9. *NYT* (4/4/1861) 1.
10. Foote/Welles (4/5/1861), *ORN* 1/4:236; Foote/Welles (4/5/1861), *ORN* 1/4:237.
11. See Soley 109; Tucker (2000) 109.
12. Welles/Foote (4/5/1861), *ORN* 1/4:237; Welles/Breese (4/5/1861), *ORN* 1/4:237. See also *Memphis Daily Appeal* (4/18/1861) 3; Hearn (2010) 57; Symonds (2008) 25–26.
13. On the afternoon of April 4, Lincoln had told Fox to proceed; the next day, Welles told Foote to use "all dispatch." Berrien/Foote (4/5/1861), *ORN* 1/4:234.
14. Porter's biographer would note that when on April 1 Porter, Meigs, and Seward had prepared orders for Lincoln's signature, none of them knew that Welles was also ordering that *Powhatan* be made ready. Soley 101–2. Although Lincoln's confidentiality order excused Foote's refusal to inform Welles about Porter's requisition of *Powhatan*, Foote had no good reason not to advise Porter—at the start—about Welles's requisition.
15. Meigs journal (4/5/1861), Meigs (1921) 301. *Meigs Typescript* D-12 erroneously lists the entry as April 4.
16. At 8:00 p.m. on Friday, April 5, Porter telegraphed Foote from New York's Astor House hotel, declaring Welles's telegram bogus. "Would he, think you, dare to countermand [a written order] of the president? Meigs and myself (knowing all the circumstances) think it impossible." Porter/Foote (4/5/1861), *ORN* 1/4:111–12.
17. Meigs/Seward (4/5/1861), *Seward Papers* Reel 63.
18. Welles (2014) 654; Welles (1911) 1:23–24.
19. Welles/Mercer (4/5/1861), Welles (2014) 652.
20. Apparently no one suggested that *Powhatan* could proceed to Charleston under Mercer's command and, if it remained battle ready thereafter, Porter could take command and continue on to Pensacola.
21. Welles (1911) 1:24–25; Welles (11/1870) 628. Welles and—upon later being informed—Cameron were furious that Seward had been puppeteering a military operation behind their backs. Meigs (1921) 301–2; Welles (11/1870) 627–34; Boynton 1:251–52, 258, 261; M. Klein 378–90; Current (1963) 103–7. See also Welles/Mercer (4/5/1861), *ORN* 1/4:235; Foote/Welles (4/6/1861), *ORN* 1/4:238; West (1943) 106.
22. Lincoln/Welles (3/29/1861), *ORN* 1/4:227, 228.
23. *NYT* (9/14/1865), *Daily National Republican* (9/16/1865), 1, Meigs (1921) 299, Welles (1/1871) 104, Boynton 1:300–301.
24. Welles/[Foote] (4/1/1861), *ORN* 1/4:229.
25. On March 20, in response to Lincoln's desire to know how many navy vessels could be reassigned to collect tariff duties outside Southern harbors, Welles listed forty-eight vessels, including twelve with Indian-sounding names, five of these beginning with "P." Welles/Lincoln (3/20/1861), *Lincoln Papers*. See also *Officers' Register* 104–5; Hoogenboom (2008) 325–26n20.
26. Soley 101–2.
27. Welles (11/1870) 629, Welles (1911) 1:24.
28. *New York Herald* (4/5/1861) 1.
29. Quoted in E. Tidball 325–26. See also J. Tidball 120. Newspapers knew the public hunger for details about military preparations and movements, and some newspapers were delivered so quickly by train that the departure of a ship from New York might be

printed in a Southern newspaper the next morning. *NYT* (4/10, 861) 1; *Anderson (SC) Intelligencer* (4/11/1861) 2.

30. The quartermaster in New York had no sense of priority, putting nonessentials on board and leaving essentials behind. Bearss (1983) 539–41, 564–67.

31. *Richmond Daily Dispatch* (4/9/1861) 1.

32. See Toombs/Crawford, Forsyth (3/20/1861), *Commissioners* 67, 69–71.

33. See, for example, *New-York Daily Tribune* (4/8/1861) 5.

34. *New York World* (4/6/1861) 4; id. (4/8/1861) 3.

35. Crawford/Toombs (4/6/1861), *OR* 1/1:287. See also Crawford/Toombs (4/3/1861), *OR* 1/1:286.

36. The version in the text was transliterated from Meigs's phonetic shorthand by Meigs himself in 1888, but not published for another thirty-three years. Meigs (1921) 302. In the 1990s, William D. Mohr, an expert on this shorthand, with Meigs's own sensible 1888 version in hand, apparently opted for literal accuracy, which perhaps better reflects Meigs's freneticism that day, albeit Meigs's own transliteration makes more sense. Compare *Meigs Typescript* D-12.

37. *New York World* (4/8/1861) 3; *Daily Dispatch* (4/9/1861) 1.

38. Foote wrote to Welles, "I handed Captain Mercer your orders of yesterday; also a telegram, this afternoon" signed by Navy Department clerk Hobart F. Berrien, indicating that Foote would receive an additional dispatch on the evening of April 6. "But Captains Meigs, Porter, and Mercer, after a consultation," decided not to wait for the Berrien telegram and instead "concluded to have Porter go in *Powhatan*." Foote/Welles (4/6/1861), *ORN* 1/4:237. "A few minutes before the *Powhatan* sailed," Foote told Welles in a separate communication, "I delivered a telegram to Captain Mercer, signed by Mr. [Berrien], saying that [Navy Paymaster John S. Gulick] will deliver a dispatch to me this evening [April 6]. But at 2:30 o'clock, the *Powhatan* sailed." Foote/Welles (4/6/1861), *ORN* 1/4:238; Foote/Welles (4/8/1861), *ORN* 1/4:238, 241.

39. Foote/Welles (4/6/1861), *ORN* 1/4:237.

40. See, for example, Weigley (1959) 148.

41. Foote/Welles (4/6/1861), *ORN* 1/4:237. To secure protection for himself in the event of any subsequent inquiry, Foote again wrote to Welles:

> Your orders of the 5th were received by Captain Mercer to-day. Captain Meigs, Lieutenant Porter, and Captain Mercer, after consultation, concluded that Lieutenant Porter should go out in the *Powhatan*, as the arrangements were vital to success; at least so I was informed, not being present at the consultation. . . . At 2:30 o'clock, the *Powhatan* sailed; at 3 o'clock, when the *Powhatan* was out of sight, I received a dispatch directed to Lieutenant Porter from Mr. Seward, telling him to proceed [to Pensacola] without the *Powhatan*. . . . I have sent . . . a lieutenant, with orders to . . . chase the *Powhatan*, unless there is no hope of overtaking her.

Foote/Welles (4/6/1861), *ORN* 1/4:238. See also Foote/Welles (4/6/1861), *ORN* 1/4:238–39. In a later memoir, Porter suggested that Foote knew a telegram was coming from Washington and kept steam up in a fast vessel to deliver it to Porter if he had not yet departed. D. Porter (1885) 21–22.

42. See, for example, *Porter Journal* 83–84; D. Porter (1885) 21. In yet another report to Welles, Foote wrote, "There are but few persons who are yet aware of Lieutenant Porter's going out in the *Powhatan*." Foote/Welles (4/8/1861), *ORN* 1/4:240, 241.

43. Seward/Porter (4/6/1861), *ORN* 1/4:112. Compare D. Porter (1885) 22.

44. See, for example, Hamilton, *Federalist* 78.

45. Seward/Porter (4/6/1861), *ORN* 1/4:112; Porter/Seward (4/6/1861), *ORN* 1/4:112; Hearn (1996) 45. Cf. version in D. Porter (1885) 22. Seward's biographer chose not to opine on whether Seward calculated the result obtained. Bancroft (1900) 2:144.

46. Porter/Foote (4/6/1861), *ORN* 1/4:112.

47. D. Porter (1885) 22; Porter/Foote (4/6/1861), *ORN* 1/4:112. See also Crawford (1887) 415; R. S. McKay/B.F. Butler (2/1/1865), *Private and Official Correspondence of Gen. Benjamin F. Butler* (Norwood, MA: Plimpton, 1917) 5:541: "If justice could have been properly meted out, Adm'l. D. Porter would according to the marine laws of the United States have been convicted and hung."

48. Porter/Lincoln (4/6/1861), *Seward Papers* Reel 63. See also Stahr 277, 609n53.

49. A second handwritten telegraph slip from April 6, also in Seward's files, was from Porter to Seward, stating, "Mr. Welles has altered the destination of the *Powhattan*[,] the ship selected to carry out the orders given to me by the President. Is the President's order of April first to be obeyed or Mr Welles['s] orders of today[?] If the latter Col. Brown [in command of land forces at Pensacola] will be entirely crippled." Porter/Seward (4/6/1861), *Seward Papers* Reel 63. Porter was here making a record (again, a false record) that as a mere lieutenant he would not take it upon himself to choose between Lincoln's order and Welles's, but rather was looking to the president and the secretary of state for direction.

50. D. Porter (1885) 22.

51. F. A. Roe/Foote (4/6/1861), *ORN* 1/4:239; F. Moore (1861–1866) 1:49.

52. See Harvey Brown/E. D. Keyes (4/12/1861), *OR* 1/1:372; Meigs journal (4/6, 7/1861), Meigs (1921) 302, *Meigs Typescript* D-12 (*Atlantic* "got to sea at 3 A.M. with order to . . . pass the Light Ship about 7 A.M."); *New York World* (4/8/1861) 3. Meigs had himself seen Seward's telegram when it arrived at the navy yard before he boarded *Atlantic* and could have caught up with Porter, just as Foote's lieutenant had done. E. Tidball 326. He chose not to.

53. (4/8/1861) 3.

54. (4/9/1861) 1; E. Tidball 326.

55. *National Intelligencer* (4/8/1861) 3.

56. Meigs journal (4/19/1861), Meigs Typescript D-37. See, for example, Dennis Hart Mahan, *Elementary Treatise on Advanced-Guard, Out-Post, and Detachment Service of Troops* (New York, 1847), 45–47, 83–104; Edward Hagerman, "From Jomini to Dennis Hart Mahan" (1967), Hubbell 31, 35–37; Edward Hagerman, *The American Civil War and the Origins of Modern Warfare* (Bloomington: Indiana University Press, 1988), 7–14, 18–26; Weigley (1962) 42–45; J. Tidball 120. See also Totten/Cameron (4/3/1861), *OR* 1/1:232, 234; Skelton 168.

57. Keyes/Seward (4/7/1861), Keyes 389–93. Lincoln's April 3 order to Keyes contained the same Prussian absolutism that Porter had used in Lincoln's orders to himself: "You will proceed forthwith to . . . New York. . . . All requisitions made upon officers of the staff by your authority, and all orders given by you to any officer of the Army in my name, will be instantly obeyed." Basler et al. 4:320.

58. Welles (2014) 643. Keyes in his later memoir stated that as participants in the enterprise, he and Meigs both regarded Seward as its "chief patron and originator." Keyes 389–94. See also Keyes/Seward (4/10/1861), id. 396.
59. Meigs/Seward (4/10/1861), OR 1/1:368, 369, Keyes 389. See also T. Anderson 49, 50.
60. Nichols 2:317.
61. *Presbrey's Information Guide to Transatlantic Travelers*, 7th ed. (New York: Frank Presbrey, 1911), 95; Francis Bradlee, "Old Transatlantic Steam Liners," *Int'l Marine Engineering* 15/12:503, 506 (12/1910); Fox/Blair (3/31/1861), Fox (1920) 1:13, 14; Hoogenboom (2008) 47–48, 64; Boynton 1:59. See also *Hunt's Merchants' Mag.* 29:633–35 (7–12/1853); id. 31:251 (7–12/1854); John H. Morrison, *History of American Steam Navigation* (New York: Stephen Daye, 1903), 410–19, 504; Royal Meeker, "History of Shipping Subsidies," *Pubs. Am. Econ. Ass'n* 6/3:507, 655–63 (8/1905).
62. Fox/Blair (4/8/1861), *Lincoln Papers*; Fox/Virginia Fox (4/[8]/1861), Fox (1922) 1:26; Fox/Cameron (4/19/1861), OR 1/1:11. Compare Fox/Blair (4/17/1861), Fox (1920) 1:31 with Foote/Welles (4/6/1861), id. 1:27, 28.
63. Fox/Blair (4/8/1861), *Lincoln Papers*; Crawford (1887) 419; Fox/Blair (4/17/1861), Fox (1920) 1:31; Fox (2/24/1865), F. Moore (1861–1866) 9:212.
64. Russell/Seward (4/8/1861), *Seward Papers* Reel 63; Fox/Cameron (4/19/1861), OR 1/1:11.
65. Welles (2014) 658–60.

Chapter 12: "At the First Favorable Moment"

1. Meigs/Seward ([4/1/1861]), *Lincoln Papers*. See also Cullum 2:3–4.
2. Lincoln/Scott (4/1/1861), *Lincoln Papers*; Scott/Lincoln (4/1/1861), id.; Meigs/Seward ([1/1/1861]), id. On March 21, Vogdes wrote to Scott that *Brooklyn* would go to Key West or Havana for supplies on March 22 but would leave Vogdes's troops behind on *Sabine*. Vogdes/Scott (3/21/1861), OR 1/1:363, 364. Since, however, Scott cited Tower's memo as the source of this news, Vogdes's letter must have arrived later.
3. Scott/Lincoln (4/1/1861), *Lincoln Papers*. On March 30, Scott had similarly written that his March 12 order, "in duplicate, left New York, by two naval vessels, about the middle of March, as the mail & the wires could not be trusted. And two detached officers could not be substituted; for two had already been arrested & paroled, by the authorities of Pensacola; despatches taken from one of them, & a third, to escape like treatment, forced to turn back when near that city." Scott/Lincoln (3/30/1861), id.
4. A Union officer engaged in readying Fort Pickens for defense had died of "brain fever" in the middle of the afternoon on April 2, and a notice thereof appeared in a New York newspaper on April 4. *Wyandotte* abstract log (4/2/1861), ORN 1/4:211; *New-York Daily Tribune* (4/4/1861) 5. Cf. H. A. Adams/Welles (4/2/1861), ORN 1/4:104 (the officer had "fallen a victim to his zeal and anxiety of mind in the discharge of his duties"); Adams/Samuel Francis Du Pont (4/30/1861), ORN 1/4:125, 126 ("died a victim to anxiety and overwork").
5. Even if a suitable code were developed and instituted, disloyal clerks and/or officers in the War Department would forward it to Montgomery. Scott had been concerned that because Fort Sumter was isolated, secessionists might forge and deliver to Major Ander-

son some telegram with dire news that he would accept as official and, in obedience to its instruction, initiate armed conflict, thus putting the North "in the wrong." Scott/ Buchanan (12/31/1860), *Lincoln Papers*.

6. G. W. Lay/Slemmer (1/3/1861), *OR* 1/1:334.

7. Samuel Barron/Toucey (1/29/1861), *ORN* 1/4:71; Chase/Randolph (1/31/1861), *ORN* 1/4:214. The Confederates had sometimes blocked mail prior to the truce, other times letting it through. See, for example, W. H. Chase/Slemmer (1/26/1861), *OR* 1/1:340; Slemmer/Chase (1/26/1861), id.; Slemmer/L. Thomas (3/18/1861), id. 361, 363.

8. Holt, Toucey/Glynn, W. S. Walker, Slemmer (1/29/1861), *Welles Papers/NYPL* Box 3 Reel 2, *ORN* 1/4:74, 75. See also Holt/Slemmer (1/29/1861), *ORN* 1/4:74; Erben 213.

9. Scott endorsement of Holt/Lincoln (3/5/1861), *Lincoln Papers*.

10. Scott was apparently confusing it with the disputed oral understanding between Buchanan and the South Carolinian congressmen in early December, and/or with the de facto standstill in place while Buchanan and Holt were negotiating with Hayne in January.

11. Regarding staff officers, see, for example, Skelton 221–37.

12. Holt/Buchanan (1/29/1861), Buchanan (1908–1911) 12:197–98n; Buchanan (10/28/1862), id. 11:279, 284–85; Scott/Lincoln (3/30/1861), *Lincoln Papers*; Nicolay and Hay (1917) 3:169–70. See also Scott (3/30/1861), W. Scott (1862) 3, 8–9; Keyes 375–76; Winfield Scott, "Communicated to the Editors [of the *National Intelligencer*] for Publication" (10/21/1862), Buchanan (1908–1911) 11:293, 298, 299; Scott, "Rejoinder of Lieutenant-General Scott to Ex-President Buchanan" (11/12/1862), id. 11:304, 306–7; Stanton 481; P. Klein 417–18; T. Johnson 239–40.

13. See, for example, Scott/Lincoln (1/11/1861), *Lincoln Papers*. See also Soady 12. Because the transition between administrations was so haphazard, there would be no certainty of Seward or Cameron knowing of the truce at the time Lincoln told Scott to reinforce Fort Pickens. Lincoln, his secretary Nicolay, and Gideon Welles all claimed that the cabinet as a whole knew nothing of the truce. See, for example, Lincoln (7/4/1861), Basler et al. 4:421, 424; Welles (1/1871) 101; Nicolay (1881) 51, 54. But see H. A. Adams/Welles (3/18/1861), *ORN* 1/4:97, 98. Although Welles's files contained a copy of the truce, it is unknown when he first saw it. Holt, Toucey/Glynn, W. S. Walker, Slemmer (1/29/1861), *Welles Papers/NYPL* Box 3, Reel 2.

14. References to "messengers" are made in various pieces of correspondence at the time, with no indication that messengers would be stopped. See, for example, J. H. Gilman/ Armstrong (1/11/1861), *ORN* 1/4:12. See also Prime/Totten (1/17, 18/1861), quoted in Bearss (1983) 501, 522–24.

15. V. M. Randolph (1/14/1861), *ORN* 1/4:18. See also Keyes journal (1/20/1861), Keyes 356.

16. Scott/Tower (1/4/1861), *OR* 1/1:350.

17. Scott/Lincoln (4/1/1861), *Lincoln Papers*; Meigs/Seward ([4/1/1861]), *Lincoln Papers*; Vogdes/Scott (3/21/1861), *OR* 1/1:363, 364; McWhiney 1:154–57; Bragg/Henry A. Adams (4/8/1861), *ORN* 1/4:112; Bragg/Adams (4/10/1861), *ORN* 1/4:113; J. Davis (1971–) 7:97–98n10. See also Bragg/Slemmer (3/13/1861), *ORN* 1/4:93; Bragg/ Slemmer (3/13/1861), id. 92; Slemmer/Bragg (3/13/1861), id. Perhaps Bragg wished to interpret the truce in this hyperastringent way so that when his men were ready to violate it with an assault, he could claim that they were merely reacting to some prior violation by Union officers.

18. J. Tidball 118; Vogdes/Scott (3/21/1861), *OR* 1/1:363, 364; Bearss (1983) 543–45. Regarding Major Tower, see, for example, Scott/Tower (1/4/1861), *OR* 1/1:350; E. Tidball 329; Bragg/Davis (4/7/1861), J. Davis (1971–) 7:94, 96, 97–98n10; George Hartsuff, Gen. Orders no. 2 (4/14/1861), *OR* 1/52 Pt. 1:136.

19. One of Scott's aides, Keyes, mentioned that Lincoln issued his oral order on March 5. This was in a purported journal entry of 3/31/1861. Keyes 379. By that time, Keyes and Scott were at odds. In subsequent weeks, Keyes's service was both negligent and impudent, and Scott eventually fired him. Keyes did not publish the alleged journal entry until 1884, as part of a memoir that was not entirely reliable. One might have expected from Keyes, a career officer serving as an aide to the nation's most senior military commander, some sense of personal responsibility or even remorse for Scott's failure to carry out an order issued by the president. But Keyes's memoir reveals no such sense.

20. While it is possible that Seward enlisted the disaffected Keyes to help slow down delivery of the Pensacola order, the mere incompetence of Scott, Keyes, and Townsend constitutes a sufficient explanation for the delay.

21. Scott/Lincoln (4/1/1861), *Lincoln Papers*; Welles/Lt. T. A. Craven (3/11/1861), *ORN* 1/4:89; Craven/Welles (3/29/1861), *ORN* 1/4:102; Welles/Foote (3/12/1861), *ORN* 1/4:90. See also Johns 45.

22. Welles/Craven (3/11/1861), *ORN* 1/4:89.

23. Welles/Foote (3/12/1861), *ORN* 1/4:90–91.

24. Scott/Vogdes (3/12/1861), *ORN* 1/4:90. Scott's communication apparently arrived at Welles's office only after Welles finished his March 12 letter to Foote, necessitating a postscript. While the compiler of the *Official Records* indicated that Scott's communication was not found and no copy exists in Welles's letterpress book, it undoubtedly related to Scott's March 12 transfer order to Vogdes; *ORN* 1/4:91.

25. Foote/Welles (3/13/1861), *ORN* 1/4:91.

26. *Mohawk* arrived at Matagorda Bay, Texas, on the morning of March 29. J. H. Strong/ Welles (3/30/1861), *ORN* 1/4:103.

27. Foote/Welles (3/14/1861), *ORN* 1/4:89; Foote/Welles (3/14/1861), *ORN* 1/4:94; Welles (3/14/1861), *ORN* 1/4:94.

28. Foote/Welles (3/16/1861), *ORN* 1/4:96.

29. Foote/Welles (3/16/1861), *ORN* 1/4:96. Welles's original order to *Crusader*'s commander, marked "Confidential," was to provide passage to a messenger and deposit him on *Brooklyn*, which he "supposed to be off Fort Pickens." Welles/Craven (3/11/1861), *ORN* 1/4:89. Subsequent missives stated that *Crusader* should expect only an order, and deliver it to *Brooklyn*.

30. Vogdes/Scott (3/21/1861), *OR* 1/1:363, 364; T. A. Craven/Welles (3/29/1861), *ORN* 1/4:102; Bancroft (1900) 2:125; H. A. Adams/Samuel Francis Du Pont (4/30/1861), *ORN* 1/4:125, 126; Foote/Welles (3/16/1861), *ORN* 1/4:96. See also Scott/Lincoln (4/1/1861), *Lincoln Papers*; Burlingame (2008) 2:110.

31. Vogdes/[Adams] (2/8/1861), *ORN* 1/4:80.

32. Scott, *Infantry-Tactics* (New York, 1835), 3 vols. New editions appeared subsequently. Scott's earlier work states, "Military compliments are to be paid to officers of the navy, when in uniform, agreeable to their relative rank with the officers of the army." Pierce Darrow, *Scott's Militia Tactics*, 2nd ed. (Hartford, CT, 1821), 278. This concerned social graces, not operational cooperation.

33. Vogdes/Lorenzo Thomas (3/17/1861), *OR* 1/1:360, 361. That this important letter went by messenger is suggested in Slemmer/Thomas (3/18/1861), *OR* 1/1:361, 363.

34. Vogdes/Scott (3/21/1861), *OR* 1/1:363. See *Globe* (32/2) App. 47 (12/21/1852).

35. Vogdes/H. A. Adams (4/1/1861), *ORN* 1/4:110, Welles letterbook vol. 1, *Welles Papers/CHS*; H.A. Adams/Welles (4/1/1861), *ORN* 1/4:109, 110, Welles letterbook vol. 1, *Welles Papers/CHS*; Adams/S. F. Du Pont (4/30/1861), *ORN* 1/4:125; Bearss (1983) 551–52.

36. J. Davis (1971–) 7:97n4.

37. See Adams/Welles (4/1/1861), *ORN* 1/4:109, 110. As Welles would later note, Adams's refusal to follow an order issued by another service branch was no treasonous act, but only a strict interpretation of interservice procedure in a situation where presuming to make an exception would end a truce and start a war. Welles (1/1871) 98. On March 18, Adams had written to Welles that, "as you are aware," a truce between Southern forces and the U.S. government "binds us not to reenforce Fort Pickens unless it is attacked or threatened," adding that Bragg had assured him "that he will respect the engagement . . . and will make 'no disposition for the attack on Fort Pickens.'" Adams/Welles (3/18/1861), *ORN* 1/4:97, 98. In fact, Welles had not known about the truce.

38. See Lincoln's 7/4/1861 speech to Congress, Basler et al. 4:421, 423–24; Niven (1973) 337–38.

39. H. A. Adams/Welles (4/1/1861), *ORN* 1/4:109–10; Welles (1/1871) 93–97; Welles (1911) 1:29; Niven (1973) 614n18; "Welles, Gideon. Diary (extracts) 1860–62" Folder, p. 11, *Nicolay Papers*.

40. Scott/Lincoln (4/6/1861), *Lincoln Papers*.

41. Welles/Adams (4/6/1861), *ORN* 1/4:110; Welles (1911) 1:29–30; James Pickett Jones, "John L. Worden and the Fort Pickens Mission," *Ala. Rev.* 21/2:113 (4/1968).

42. Lincoln (7/4/1861), Basler et al. 4:421, 424.

43. *Globe* (37/1) 206 (7/19/1861); Welles/Lincoln (7/26/1861), *OR* 1/1:23; Lincoln/Senate (7/30/1861), Basler et al. 4:465.

44. See Nicolay and Hay (1917) 4:33–34; Welles (11/1870) 620; Chase/Lincoln (3/29/1861), *Lincoln Papers*; Welles/Lincoln (3/29/1861), id. See also Paris 137; Bancroft (1900) 2:128; Stahr 274.

45. Crawford, Roman/Toombs (4/2/1861), *OR* 1/1:284; Crawford/Beauregard (4/8, 3 P.M.), *OR* 1/1:239.

46. [Lincoln], Cameron/Talbot (4/6/1861), Basler et al. 4:4:323.

47. Justice Campbell later related that on April 11 or 12, William L. Hodge, a pro-South Unionist with good (although obviously imperfect) contacts in Washington, told him that the fleet included no warships, its only purpose being "to ascertain whether unarmed vessels carrying supplies to the soldiers of the United States in their own fort would be molested." Campbell (1874) 26. Campbell recalled that Hodge told him this on Thursday, April 12. Since he refers to this as a day before the bombardment commenced, he undoubtedly meant Thursday, April 11. See also Hodge.

48. See Scott/Lincoln (4/11/1861), *Lincoln Papers*.

49. Campbell, "Facts of History" [before 7/10/1865], Campbell (1917) 35.

50. See, for example, Pollard (1867A) 234; George W. Duncan, "John Archibald Campbell," *Alabama Hist. Soc. Trans.* 5:107, 128 (1904). Thomas Dixon, author of the books from which D. W. Griffith's film *Birth of a Nation* would be made, wrote that Lincoln sent

a messenger to give Governor Pickens notice of the expedition because his "sense of personal honor was too keen to permit this crooked piece of diplomacy" by his "wily Secretary of State." *The Victim: A Romance of the Real Jefferson Davis* (Toronto: D. Appleton, 1914), 154.

51. See F. Seward (1891) 538; Stahr 278–79. In order to give Seward a chance for further clarification, Campbell forwarded to him for review a copy of what he had just told the commissioners, derived from what Seward had told him. Seward did not respond, thus neither confirming nor denying. Campbell/Commissioners (4/7/1861), Nicolay and Hay (1917) 4:37; Campbell/Seward (4/7/1861), *Seward Papers* Reel 63.

52. Cooper/Bragg (4/6/1861), *ORN* 1/4:134. See also Bearss (1957–1961) 39:243.

53. Davis/Bragg (4/3/1861), J. Davis (1971–) 7:85.

54. Slidell/M. S. Perry (1/18/1861), *OR* 1/1:445.

55. Russell (1863) 1:307–9; Keyes/Seward (4/14/1861), Keyes 397, 398.

56. Bragg was asked on March 10 what artillery and munitions he needed to conquer Fort Pickens, but he was never properly supplied. William Harris (1962) 41–52; McWhiney 1:160; Bearss (1957–1961) 39:232–34.

57. While he might annoy any such landing by placing some of his guns on that beach, he would not do so, telling Montgomery that this would stretch his meager assets too far. Walker/Bragg (4/5/1861), *OR* 1/1:456; Bragg/Walker (4/6/1861), id.

58. Some were in good order, others without uniforms, long bearded and undisciplined, although Bragg, known for scrupulous drilling, was the appropriate commander to make of them a credible force. See, for example, Walker/A. B. F. Moore (3/9/1861), *OR* 3/5:691; J. Davis (1971–) 7:87n5; Davis/Bragg (4/3/1861), id. 7:85; Scott/Lincoln (4/1/1861), *Lincoln Papers*; Bragg/Davis (4/7/1861), J. Davis (1971–) 7:94 and 97nn1 and 2; McWhiney 1:161–67; *Washington Evening Star* (4/24/1861) 4; Bearss (1983) 533, 559. See also James Morton, *Letter to the Hon. John B. Floyd, Secretary of War* (Washington, 1858), 81; Fred Robertson, *Soldiers of Florida in the Seminole Indian-Civil and Spanish-American Wars* (Live Oak, FL: Democrat Print, 1903), 35–37.

59. See, for example, Bragg/Davis (4/7/1861), J. Davis (1971–) 7:94, 95–96; Samuel Cooper/Bragg (4/3/1861), Bragg/Walker (4/5/1861), Walker/Bragg (4/5/1861), Bragg/Walker (4/6/1861), Bragg/Walker (4/6/1861), Bragg/Walker (4/14/1861), *OR* 1/1:455–61; Slemmer/Lorenzo Thomas (2/5/1861), *OR* 1/1:334, 341–42; Dibble 236–37; Grady McWhiney, "The Confederacy's First Shot," *Civil War Hist.* 14/1:5, 8–9 (3/1968); Fishel 17.

60. Bragg/Cooper (4/5/1861), *OR* 1/1:455; Walker/Bragg (4/5/1861), *OR* 1/1:456; Bragg/Walker (4/6/1861), *OR* 1/1:456; Cooper/Bragg (4/6/1861), *OR* 1/1:456; Bragg/Walker (4/6/1861), *OR* 1/1:456, 457; Bragg/Walker (4/6/1861), *OR* 1/1:457; Walker/Bragg (4/6/1861), *OR* 1/1:458. While Montgomery would allow Bragg to open fire if the Union tried to land reinforcements at the dock within the harbor, the Union would not do that, and the oceanfront beaches of Santa Rosa were beyond Bragg's range.

61. *NY Daily Tribune* (4/8/1861) 5, *Wheeling (VA) Daily Intelligencer* (4/10/1861) 1.

62. The couriers were State Department clerk Robert S. Chew and one of Anderson's officers, Theodore Talbot, who had been in Washington after delivering one of Anderson's letters there. [Lincoln], Cameron/Talbot (4/6/1861), Basler et al. 4:323; Chew memo (4/8/1861), Nicolay and Hay (1917) 4:34, 35; *Appleton* 573; Foreman 77. See also Basler et al. 4:324n1; Detzer 42. Talbot, though suffering from tuberculosis, wished to return to Sumter following the recitation, but Beauregard refused.

63. Bragg/Walker (4/14/1861), *OR* 1/1:461.
64. *Cincinnati Daily Press* (4/25/1861) 1; Adams/Welles (4/14/1861), *Welles Papers/LC* Reel 19, *ORN* 1/4:115. See also Bragg/Walker (4/13/1861), *OR* 1/1:460–61.
65. *Mercury* (dateline 4/15/1861), *Washington Evening Star* (4/24/1861) 4; *Mobile Mercury* (4/15/1861), *Baltimore Daily Exchange* (4/24/1861) 1.
66. *Cincinnati Daily Press* (4/25/1861) 1; Welles (1/1871) 100.
67. See Walker/Bragg (4/12/1861), *OR* 1/1:459; Bragg/Walker (4/12/1861), *OR* 1/1:459.
68. Worden/Walker (4/16/1861), *OR* 1/1:462. See also Tilley 60–61.
69. Welles/Adams (4/6/1861), *ORN* 1/4:110. See also Worden/Fox (9/20/1865), *ORN* 1/4:111; Bragg/Walker (4/12/1861), *OR* 1/1:459; Walker/Bragg (4/12/1861), *OR* 1/1:459; Hubert/Walker (4/12/1861), *OR* 1/1/460; Walker/Bragg (4/13/1861), *OR* 1/1/460; Welles (1/1871) 99.
70. William J. Lemon, "A Little More Grape Captain Bragg" (Philadelphia, 1847); *All the Letters of Major General Zachary Taylor* (New York, 1848), 13; Bartleson 121; Russell (1863) 1:308; G. Van Deusen (1947) 164.
71. *Diary of the War for Separation* (Vicksburg, MS, 1862), 62. Colonel C. C. Chesney, professor of military history at Sandhurst, later wrote that Bragg, "with whose vacillation and weakness the misfortunes of the Confederate arms are largely identified, was not of a character to take upon himself the responsibility of commencing active hostilities." [Chesney] 190–91.
72. *Sabine* abstract log, *ORN* 1/4:208–9; Slemmer/Townsend (4/12/1861), *OR* 1/1:389; Johns 46; Vogdes/Adams (4/141861), *ORN* 1/4:117. See also McWhiney 1:vii–ix; Grady McWhiney, "Controversy in Kentucky: Braxton Bragg's Campaign of 1862," *Civil War Hist.* 6/1:5 (3/1960); David M. Sullivan, *The United States Marine Corps in the Civil War—First Year* (Shippensburg, PA: White Mane, 1997), 74–76; introduction, Hubbell vii, xi. Nor did one "violate" an at-will truce by ending it.
73. See, for example, William Gregg, *Essays on Domestic Industry* (Charleston, 1845).
74. See Vicki Vaughn Johnson, *The Men and the Vision of the Southern Commercial Conventions, 1845–1871* (Columbia: University of Missouri Press, 1992); Harold Wilson xvii–xxii; E. Channing 27–31; J. McPherson (1988) 258; J. McPherson (2014) 20; Nichols 2:301. Regarding the Confederacy's considerable achievements in quickly developing industrial capacity, however, see, for example, David Goldfield, *Urban Growth in the Age of Sectionalism* (Baton Rouge: Louisiana State University Press, 1977); Beringer.
75. J. McPherson (1988) 40. See also Tom Downey, *Planting a Capitalist South* (Baton Rouge: Louisiana State University Press, 2006).
76. Karp 199.
77. See, for example, *Globe* (36/1) 1301–2 (3/22/1860).
78. Sherman/D. F. Boyd (12/24/1860), Foote 1:58–59; Egerton 12. See also W. Sherman (1889) 1:181; Bateman/Weiss 15–69. Regarding the North's industrial advantage, see, for example, Fred Bateman et al., "Large-Scale Manufacturing in the South and West, 1850–1860," *Bus. Hist. Rev.* 45/1:1 (Spring 1971); Robert Fogel and Stanley Engerman, *Time on the Cross* (Boston, 1974), 256.
79. *Mary Chesnut's Civil War*, ed. C. Vann Woodward (New Haven, CT: Yale University Press, 1981), 3–4. See also J. McPherson (1988) 239–40.
80. [Leonidas Spratt] (1/12/1861), *Appleton* 653.

81. Quoted in, for example, *Yorkville (SC) Enquirer* (4/11/1861) 1, *National Republican* (4/9/1861) 2, E. McPherson 112.
82. [De Forest] 496.
83. (4/6, 8/1861), Ruffin (1972–1989) 1:582. See also J. H. Jordan/Chase (3/27/1861): "Will reinforcing & holding [Fort Sumter] cause the rebels to attack it, and thus bring on 'civil war'? What of it? That is just what the government . . . ought to do." Quoted in Ramsdell 272n.
84. Rhodes (1892–1906) 3:347–48; Pleasant A. Stovall, *Robert Toombs* (New York, 1892), 226; Lathers 164–65; W. C. Davis 4–8. But see L. Johnson 475–76.
85. Quoted in Thomas Sturgis, "Prisoners of War" (2/1/1911), *Personal Recollections of the War of the Rebellion*, ed. Alexander Noel Blakeman, 4th Series (New York: G. P. Putnam's Sons, 1912), 266, 320. See also Ramsdell 283.
86. Lincoln (2/22/1861), Nicolay and Hay (12/1887) 268; (3/4/1861), Basler et al. 4:262, 271.
87. Hurlbut/Lincoln (3/27/1861), *Lincoln Papers*; Welles/Lincoln (3/29/1861), id. See also J. McPherson (1988) 272n78.
88. Fox/Pickens (4/12/1861), Fox (1920) 1:18; Fox/Jackson (undated), id.; Hoogenboom (2008) 69.
89. Fox/Jackson (undated), Fox (1920) 1:18. Cameron had instructed Fox that if the resupply attempt was turned back or fired upon, Fox should "report . . . to the senior naval officer" present, who would at that point "use his entire force to open a passage" to deliver both supplies and troops. Cameron/Fox (4/4/1861), *OR* 1/1:235.
90. J. Davis (1938) 1:294–95.
91. (4/8/1861), Holmes 17.
92. Pollard (1867A) 234.
93. (4/5/1861), Russell (1861A) 18, 21. On whether Lincoln guessed that the Confederates would choose to open fire upon the fort prior to the squadron's arrival, see, for example, K. Williams 1:56–57.
94. See, for example, Nathaniel W. Stephenson, *The Day of the Confederacy* (New Haven, CT: Yale University Press, 1920) 24–26.
95. Wigfall/Davis (4/10/1861), L. Wright (1905) 452.
96. (7/4/1861), Basler et al. 4:421, 425–26.
97. Davis/Wigfall (4/12/1861), id. See also Beauregard/L. P. Walker (4/27/1861), *OR* 1/1:30, 31; J. Davis (1861), *OR* 4/1:256; Current (1961) 367.
98. Beauregard/Walker ([4/8/1861]), *OR* 1/53:163. See also Beauregard/Crawford (4/8/1861), *Commissioners* 217: "Special messenger from Lincoln, Mr Chew, informs us Sumter to be provisioned peaceably otherwise forcibly." The *New-York Daily Tribune* described the Talbot/Chew dispatch as stating "that Fort Sumter would be supplied with provisions at any cost." (4/10/1861) 6. See also Walker/Beauregard (4/8/1861), *OR* 1/1:289.
99. Seward (3/15/1861), *Commissioners* 159; [Pickett] (4/8/1861), *Commissioners* 167.
100. Forsyth, Crawford, Roman/Seward (4/9/1861), F. Moore (1861–1866) 1:49, 50.
101. Message No. 1 (11/5/1861), *Journal of the Senate of the State of South Carolina* (Columbia, 1861), 10, 22.

Chapter 13: "We Have the Honor to Notify You"

1. Faulkner 84. Cf. id. 46.
2. Gordon 39; Spaulding 202.
3. See, for example, *OR* 1/1:25–58; Jamison/Pickens (3/25/1861), *Convention Journal* 519; *Vermont Phoenix* (Brattleboro) (4/25/1861) 1; Spaulding 202; Roman 1:39; (4/11/1861), Ruffin (1972–1989) 1:586; (4/15/1861), Russell (1861A) 32, 29; Ripley 148–60, 364, 372–73; Gordon 39; Alexander L. Holley, *Treatise on Ordnance and Armor* (New York, 1865), 36, 50; S. Jones 34–35; Hazlett, Olmstead, and Parks 196–204; Spaulding 187, 196; Wise 4–6. See also Bartleson 24–29.
4. See, for example, Ryan 28–31, 53–54; Hendrickson 259–61.
5. *OR* 1/1:43; D. F. Jamison/Pickens (3/25/1861), *Convention Journal* 519; Roman 1:38–39; Spaulding 202; J. G. Foster, "Engineer Journal of the Bombardment," *OR* 1/1:16; Gordon 40; Ryan 54–55.
6. Spaulding 202; Gibbon 460; (4/11/1861), Ruffin (1972–1989) 1:586; Katcher 56, 62.
7. Spaulding 191, 202; Crawford (1879) 325. Regarding enfilading batteries, see, for example, Dennis Hart Mahan, *Summary of the Course of Permanent Fortification* (Charleston, 1862), 309–10; *Richmond Daily Dispatch* (4/11/1861) 1. After the battle, the *Charleston Mercury* reported that the Enfilade Battery fired six hundred solid shot and no shells. Quoted in J. Abbott 569n.
8. Anderson/Thomas (3/22/1861), *OR* 1/1:211; Hartstene/Beauregard (4/10/1861), *OR* 1/1:299; Beauregard/R. G. M. Dunovant (4/10/1861), *OR* 1/1:300; Scharf 659; *HABS* 16.
9. J. McPherson (2012) 8.
10. See, for example, Dahlgren (1856B) 178; H. J. Paixhans, *Account of Experiments Made in the French Navy for the Trial of Bomb Cannon*, trans. J. A. Dahlgren (Philadelphia: Dorsey, 1838), 29–32.
11. See *Glossary of Military Terms* (London, 1855), 41; F. Parker 66n2; Ryan 47. But see *Ordnance Manual* 387 (range = 1,955 yards). The *Charleston Mercury* reported that the Floating Battery fired 470 shot and no shells. J. Abbott 569n.
12. Of significant patented inventions since the nation's founding, only 7 percent came from slave states.
13. Regarding ancillary equipment, see, for example, Alfred Mordecai, *Artillery for the United States Land Service* (Washington, 1849), Pt. 10.
14. The 4,836-yard range, with fifteen pounds of powder, was said to consume 27.5 seconds. *Ordnance Manual* 388–89. With a ten-inch siege mortar at forty-five degrees, two pounds of powder would project a ninety-pound shell one thousand yards. H. Scott 65–69; *Ordnance Manual* 390. See also Straith 692–95; Hyde 9; Ryan 106; Roberts 67, 77–78; *Ordnance Papers* 2:133; Lewis 33.
15. *Harper's Weekly* 5:101 (2/16/1861); Gibbon 460; Chester 56; Ryan 62–63. See also Katcher 56.
16. Chester 56–57; Spaulding 192. While mortars were used to fire shells, not solid shot, the columbiad was not a mortar.
17. Cooper/Beauregard (3/29/1861), *OR* 1/1:283.
18. Nicolay and Hay (3/1888) 709; Nicolay and Hay (1917) 4:38; Crawford (1887) 383.

19. While the transcribed text in *Anderson Diary* bears the date of April 9, the content indicates that it was written prior to Anderson's opening the Lincoln/Cameron letter on April 7.

20. See also Louisa Rodgers Meigs/Montgomery Meigs (1/6/1861), *Meigs Papers* Reel 7.

21. Beauregard/Anderson (4/7/1861), *OR* 1/1:248.

22. [Lincoln], Cameron/Anderson (4/4/1861) 1, *Lincoln Papers*. See also J. Davis (1971–) 7:99–100n2.

23. But see *Charleston Daily Courier* (4/17/1861) 1.

24. Anderson/Thomas (4/8/1861), *OR* 1/1:294, W. A. Harris 37; Nicolay (1881) 50–59; Lamon 68–70; Stampp (1950) 284–85. See also Doubleday (1876) 91.

25. Crawford, *Fort Sumter Diary* 59–60.

26. As Beauregard told Montgomery, Anderson's letter "discloses the fact that Mr. Fox who had been allowed to visit Major Anderson, on the pledge that his purpose was pacific, employed his opportunity to devise a plan for supplying the fort by force," a plan which—as Anderson's letter revealed—has been "adopted by the Government in Washington." Montgomery released Beauregard's comment to the press. Beauregard/Walker (4/12/1861), republished in, for example, *Shreveport Daily News* (4/19/1861) 2. See also *Fremont (OH) Journal* (4/13/1861) (Extra) 1.

27. Beauregard/Anderson (4/8/1861), *OR* 1/1:250; Walker/Beauregard (4/9/1861), *OR* 1/1:291; Beauregard/Anderson (4/9/1861), *OR* 1/1:248; Pickens/Davis (4/9/1861), J. Davis (1971–) 7:99. See also Pickens/Davis (4/9/1861), J. Davis (1923) 5:61, 62; Crawford (1915) item 357; Fox/Crawford (2/16/1882), Crawford (1915) item 195.

28. See, for example, Rep. William W. Boyce (D/SC) (8/3/1860), *Anderson (SC) Intelligencer* (8/14/1860) 4; *Newbern (NC) Weekly Progress* (3/26/1861) 2.

29. Seward/C. F. Adams Sr. (4/10/1861), *Message of the President of the United States to the Two Houses of Congress at the Commencement of the Second Session of the Thirty-Seventh Congress* (Washington, 1861), 1:71, 73.

30. Baldwin (2/10/1866), *JCR* 102, 104. See also Wigfall/Davis (4/10/1861), L. Wright (1905) 36; Shanks 193, 267n21.

31. Robert K. Krick, *Civil War Weather in Virginia* (Tuscaloosa: University of Alabama Press, 2007), 21–23.

32. John Beauchamp Jones, *A Rebel War Clerk's Diary at the Confederate Capital* (Philadelphia, 1866), 1:15–16. See also Russell (1863) 1:111–12; Barton Wise, *Life of Henry A. Wise of Virginia* (New York, 1899), 274–80; Gallagher 103; Link 233–34; Sheehan-Dean 13–15.

33. *Richmond Daily Dispatch* (4/11/1861) 1. See also Sheehan-Dean 13–15, 25–28.

34. C. F. Adams Jr. (1916) 73–74. See also C. F. Adams Jr. (1900) 128. Charles Francis Adams Sr. so overestimated Seward's abilities that in his eulogy he likened him to Pericles. *An Address on the Life, Character and Service of William Henry Seward* (Albany, NY, 1873), 14, 52. See also H. Adams/C. F. Adams Jr. (1/17/1861), H. Adams (1982–1986) 1:221, 224; H. Adams/C. F. Adams Jr. (12/29/1860), H. Adams (1982–1986) 1:214, 215; H. Adams (1918) 106; *Speech of Charles Francis Adams, of Mass. Delivered in the House of Representatives, January 31, 1861* (n.p., n.d.); Henry Adams/C. F. Adams Jr. (1/8/1861), H. Adams (1982–1986) 1:218.

35. S. Pryor (1904) 120.

36. *Charleston Mercury* (4/11/1861) quoted in, for example, S. Pryor (1909) 158–59. See also Botts 203–4; Holzman 56; Walther 251; Detzer 241; Eicher 29–31; Link 169–70.

In old age, Mrs. Pryor would claim that it was her husband's speech that pushed the Confederacy to open fire upon Fort Sumter, and if he had not given that speech and the South had not (thus) commenced hostilities, the Republican promise to protect slavery where it already existed would have prevailed, and slavery "would exist to-day [1909] as a recognized institution of the republic." By a tortured logic, she could thus praise her husband for having started the Civil War, since "but for his act the nation would not now be free from the reproach of human slavery." By 1909, Mr. and Mrs. Pryor had spent forty years in the North, rising from the postwar poverty common to Southern firebrands to professional and personal success. Her perspective was perhaps her way to salute and excuse—as a sort of felix culpa—a speech that she might instead have wished to forget. S. Pryor (1909) 160–61; Roger Pryor obituary, *NYT* (3/15/1919).

37. *Newbern (NC) Weekly Progress* (9/18/1860) 3.
38. Walker/Beauregard (4/10/1861), *OR* 1/53:163; Nicolay (1881) 60; Beauregard/Roman, Crawford, Forsyth (4/11/1861), *Commissioners* 219.
39. Forsyth/Pickens (4/10/1861), Pickens/Forsyth (4/10/1861), Blair (1881) 381; Pickens/Davis (4/9/1861), J. Davis (1923) 5:61, 62.
40. Hartstene/William Dozier (4/6/1861), *ORN* 1/4:260–61; Hartstene/Dozier (4/11/1861), *ORN* 1/4:261, 262. See also A. C. Garlington/Pickens (3/26/1861), *Convention Journal* 528, 531; Pickens/L. M. Hatch (1/10/1861), *OR* 1/53:118; Charlotte Wigfall/Louis Wigfall Wright (4/11/1861), L. Wright (1905) 37–38; J. Johnson 18; J. T. Scharf, *History of the Confederate States Navy* (New York, 1887), 658; Silverstone 240.
41. Beauregard/Dunovant (4/10/1861), *OR* 1/1:300. He and Hartstene apparently guessed that the Union would choose the Swash Channel because, as Fox later wrote, from the eastern edge of the bar to Fort Sumter it was said to be "four miles in a straight line with no shoal spots less than nine feet at high water." "Result of G. V. Fox's Plan for Reinforcing Fort Sumter," Fox (1920) 1:38. But see Maffitt in Bache et al. 16, 20; *Appleton* 99.
42. J. G. Foster, "Engineer Journal of the Bombardment," *OR* 1/1:16, 20; (4/10/1861), Ruffin (1972–1989) 1:585; Gordon 42.
43. Beauregard/Walker (3/26/1861), *OR* 1/1:282; Roman 1:38; S. Jones 35; Stephen Lee/W. G. De Saussure (4/10/1861), *OR* 1/53:142. Captain Lee, a recent West Point graduate now in the South Carolina army, wrote to Colonel De Saussure, commandant of the batteries on Morris Island, that Captain Hartstene had set up "a system of lights on flat-boats . . . lighting up the channel to show any small boats that may attempt to reach Fort Sumter with supplies and re-enforcements." See also Lee/Maxcy Gregg (4/8/1861), *OR* 1/53:140.
44. F. Parker 65.
45. Charlotte Wigfall/Louise Wright (4/11/1861), L. Wright (1904) 452.
46. Nathaniel Hawthorne, "English Note-Books" (entry for 1/9/1855), *Works of Nathaniel Hawthorne* (Boston, 1882–1896), 7:552; Thomas W. L. Newton, *Lord Lyons: A Record of British Diplomacy* (New York: Longmans, Green, 1913), 1:24; Virginia Clay-Clopton, *A Belle of the Fifties*, comp. Ada Sterling (1904; New York: Doubleday, Page, 1905), 114–15.
47. *Visit of His Royal Highness The Prince of Wales*, comp. Robert Cellem (Toronto, 1861), 367–404; Elizabeth Fries Ellet, *Court Circles of the Republic* (Hartford, CT, 1869), 502–9.
48. Osbon 96, 115. See also *NYT* (1/1/1861).
49. Fox first encountered the gale soon after leaving Sandy Hook on the morning of April 9. Fox (2/24/1865), *ORN* 1/4:249. Scott told Lincoln he feared that the weather would delay or even disable some of the vessels. Scott/Lincoln (4/10/1861), *Lincoln*

Papers; S. C. Rowan/Welles (4/10/1861), *ORN* 1/4:243; J. P. Gillis/Welles (4/10/1861), *ORN* 1/4:243; Fox/Cameron (4/19/1861), *ORN* 1/4:244. See also *New York Herald* (4/17/1861) 4.

50. Meigs/Louisa Meigs (4/9/1861), *Meigs Papers* Reel 7; Meigs journal (4/9/1861), *Meigs Typescript* D-14.

51. John Tidball quoted in E. Tidball 326; Brown/Keyes (4/12/1861), *OR* 1/1:372; Meigs/ Totten (4/25/1861), *OR* 1/1:393, 394. Cf. an alleged citing of *Atlantic* near Rattle- snake Shoals, east of Charleston, at 5:00 p.m. on April 11. *Baltimore Daily Exchange* (4/24/1861) 1.

52. Osbon 117.

53. (4/11/1861), Holmes 25.

54. Beauregard/Anderson (4/11/1861), *OR* 1/1:13; Anderson/Beauregard (4/11/1861), *OR* 1/1:13; Beauregard/Anderson (4/11/1861), *OR* 1/1:13–14; Anderson quoted in Beauregard/Walker (4/11/1861), *OR* 1/1:301; S. Lee 75. But see Beauregard/Crawford (5/12/1882), quoted in Crawford (1915) [11]: "My impression is the same as yours, that Major Anderson made the remark, as to himself." See also Catton 493n11.

55. (4/10/1861), Ruffin (1972–1989) 1:584; Craven (1932) 201.

56. (4/11/1861), *Anderson Diary*.

57. Beauregard/Walker (4/11/1861), *OR* 1/1:301.

58. Walker/Beauregard (4/11/1861), F. Moore (1861–1866) 1:52; Beauregard/Anderson (4/11/1861), id., *OR* 1/1:13, 14.

59. D. F. Jamison/Beauregard (4/11/1861), *OR* 1/1:304; *Charleston Mercury* (4/12/1861) 2; *Battle of Fort Sumter* 20.

60. Crawford (1887) 424–25. See also Waugh (2002) 85–88.

61. See, for example, Welles (2014) 640.

62. Fox, Boynton 1:258.

63. Anderson/Beauregard (4/12/1861), *OR* 1/1:14; K. Williams 1:47–48.

64. Beauregard's aide-de-camp, Colonel Alexander Chisolm, wrote that in handing over the message, Anderson reportedly stated "that we had twice fired on his flag, and that if we did so again he would open his fire on our batteries." Chisolm 82. By thus alluding to the earlier firings upon *Star of the West* and a schooner, Anderson was apparently trying, orally, as in his written response to Beauregard's proposal, to retain the right to fire upon the Confederates if they fired upon ships.

65. See Chesnut, Lee/D. R. Jones (4/12/1861), *OR* 1/1:60; Chesnut, Lee/Anderson (4/12/1861), *OR* 1/1: 14; Chisolm 82. Decades later, Pryor reportedly claimed that he, Chesnut, and Lee so feared that Davis was attempting a resolution with Seward that they gave the order to open fire without communicating with Beauregard. William E. Dodd, *Statesmen of the Old South* (1911; New York: Macmillan, 1936), 220–21. See also Beauregard/Walker (4/11/1861), *OR* 1/1:301; letters and reports collected in *OR* 1/1:13–67; M. Klein 401. Since, however, Anderson clearly did not comply with Beaure- gard's terms, Chesnut, no mere junior officer, would have been authorized to decide the issue without further consultation.

66. Regarding the order, the pulling of the lanyard, witnesses, and so on, see Ryan 55; Robert Lebby, M.D., "The First Shot on Fort Sumter," *S.C. Hist. & Gen. Mag.* 12/3:141 (7/1911); Stephen Lee and Julian Ruffin, "Who Fired the First Gun at Sumter?" *South.*

Hist. Soc. Papers 11/11:501, 502 (11/1883); Martin Abbott, "The First Shot at Fort Sumter," *Civil War Hist.* 3/1:41–45 (3/1957); S. Lee 76; Roman 1:42; *American* 5/116:40 (10/28/1882); W. H. Gibbes/John Thomas (4/2/1902), *Thirty-Fifth Annual Reunion of the Association of the Graduates of the United States Military Academy* (Saginaw, MI, 1904), 102; Bruce Catton, "The Shot That Began the Civil War," *NYT Mag.* (4/9/1961) SM13; Waugh (2002) 91–97; Hendrickson 183–85; Ashley Halsey Jr., *Who Fired the First Shot?* (New York: Hawthorn Books, 1963), 27–28; Mathew 226–27n97; Marvel (1998).

67. John Thompson/Robert Thompson (4/28/1861), Thompson 101; Lee 76.

68. (4/12/1861), Ruffin (1972–1989) 1:588; Roman 1:42. Officers and men of the several Confederate batteries are listed in, for example, Ellison Capers, "South Carolina," Evans 5:18–19.

69. Dickert 24–25; S. Pryor (1904) 120–21; Roman 1:42–43; J. G. Foster, "Engineer Journal of the Bombardment," *OR* 1/1:16, 18.

70. Spaulding 196, 201; F. Barnes (1962) 9; Ryan 46–47.

71. *Assessment* III.01-5.

72. (4/12/1861), Ruffin (1972–1989) 1:588–89; Young 29; Roman 1:43.

73. *Battle of Fort Sumter* 16; Gibbon 233–37; G. B. Cuthbert (4/17/1861), *OR* 1/1:54; (4/12/1861), Ruffin (1972–1989) 1:590–91.

74. Chester.

75. [De Fontaine] 36–37, 89; Ellison Capers, "South Carolina," Evans 5:16–17; *History of South Carolina*, ed. Yates Snowden (Chicago: Lewis, 1920), 2:682; Roman 1:37, 41; L. T. Wigfall/Charlotte Wigfall (4/12/1861), Charlotte Wigfall/D. Giraud Wright (4/12/1861), L. Wright (1905) 38–40; (4/11/1861), Ruffin (1972–1989) 1:586; (4/15/1861), Russell (1861A) 32, 38; F. Moore (1862) 218. See also "Iron-Clad Ships of War," *Blackwood's Edinburgh Mag.* 88:616, 633 (11, 12/1860); Straith 693–94; J. G. Benton, *Course of Instruction in Ordnance and Gunnery* (New York, 1862), 471–81; James Ward, *Elementary Instructions in Naval Ordnance and Gunnery* (New York, 1861), 189–94; Edward Simpson, *Treatise on Ordnance and Naval Gunnery*, 2nd ed. (New York, 1862), 436–39; F. Parker 66n1; H. Scott 371; Hyde 10.

76. Samuel Wylie Crawford (1/18/1861), *Fort Sumter Diary* 19; *OR* 1/1:12–25; Foster (1866) 8; Detzer 276–77; Gibbon 301–2, 446–49. See also *Ordnance Instructions* 147.

77. Spaulding 196.

78. Fox recorded *Pawnee's* first appearance as 6:00 a.m. or 7:00 a.m. on April 12. *Compare* Fox/Cameron (4/19/1861), *OR* 1/1:11, *ORN* 1/4:244 with Fox (2/24/1865), F. Moore (1861–1866) 9:211.

79. Fox/Blair (4/17/1861), Fox (1920) 1:31, 33.

80. Accounts of damage to ships in the gale and loss of life are in, for example, *Baltimore Daily Exchange* (4/15/1861) 4; *New York Herald* (4/16/1861) 7; *Alexandria Gazette* (4/16/1861) 2.

81. *Charleston Daily Courier* (4/17/1861) 1; *NYT* (4/24/1861) 1.

82. Osbon 119.

83. Fox had indicated that *Baltic* had ten boats and that these would be sufficient to resupply Sumter with food in desiccated form. Fox/Blair (3/31/1861), Fox (1920) 1:13, 14.

84. Fox/Cameron (4/19/1861), *OR* 1/1:11.

85. Osbon 119–20. See also J. Perry 92–93.

86. Two days later, *Nashville* would hoist South Carolina's flag and become a privateer. Osbon 118; *New-York Daily Tribune* (4/19/1861) 1; *DANFS*; Bradley Osbon, *Hand Book of the United States Navy* (New York, 1864), 71.

87. *Charleston Mercury* (4/12/1861) 2. Emma Holmes was told that seven Union vessels were seen late in the evening of April 8. (4/9/1861), Holmes 24. A Confederate infantryman, years later, said he saw "some half-dozen or more U.S. men-of-war." Powe 8. William Jewett Tenney, editor of Appleton's *Annual Cyclopædia*, vastly overstated the number of ships. See Tenney 26.

88. Contemporary accounts of this phenomenon include G. G. Stokes, "On the Effect of Wind on the Intensity of Sound," *Report of the Twenty-Seventh Meeting of the British Ass'n for the Advancement of Science: Miscellaneous Communications to the Sections* (London, 1858), 22. See also W. H. C. Bartlett, *Elements of Natural Philosophy II. Acoustics III. Optics* (New York, 1852), 35–36.

89. Brackett 947; Ann S. Stephens, *Pictorial History of the War for the Union* (New York, 1866), 1:36; Detzer 273; Ellen Elmore, "A Southern Household during the Years 1860 to 1865" (12/1901), T. Taylor 1:196, 197.

90. [De Fontaine] 39. See also Roman 1:43; Starr 28–29.

91. *Reminiscences of Charleston* (Charleston, 1866), 6.

92. A. Porter 123–24. Abner Doubleday later joked that "the landlord had given me a wretched room there one night" and here was an opportunity to get even. Doubleday (1876) 162. While retaining his earlier policy of avoiding civilian targets, Anderson unavoidably damaged houses near Fort Moultrie. F. Moore (1861–1866) 1:82.

93. Hagood 32.

94. Lincoln/W. B. Preston, A. H. H. Stuart, George Randolph (4/13/1861), Basler et al. 4:329–31.

95. See in this regard a memorandum dictated by Mrs. Anderson to Benson J. Lossing on 8/7/1863, as well as related correspondence, in *Goodyear Collection* vol. 2. See also *Harper's Encyclopædia of United States History* (New York, 1907), 468–69.

96. F. Moore (1861–1866) 1:55.

97. Straith 695; Chester 55, 62, 69–70; Foster (1866) 8. Years later, a Confederate veteran told an audience that Anderson had ordered "an immense Dahlgren gun" to open fire upon Charleston, but it misfired and burst. Powe 10. No evidence supports this.

98. Beauregard/Whiting (4/12/1861), *Goodyear Collection* vol. 1, item 13; Beauregard/Whiting (4/12/1861), id. item 14. See also Paltsits 726; Crawford (1915) [6].

99. [De Fontaine] 42; "Details of the Taking of Sumter," *NYT* (4/14/1861). Cf. Dan Bauer, *The Long Lost Journal of Confederate General James Johnston Pettigrew* (Lincoln, NE: Writers Club, 2001), 95.

100. F. Parker 67–68; Young 30.

101. Hartstene/Beauregard (4/13/1861), *ORN* 1/4:262; Roman 1:45; C. M. C. Wigfall/Louise Wigfall Wright (4/13/1861), L. Wright (1904) 453; *Stroudsburg (PA) Jeffersonian* (4/11/1861) 2. Stories proliferated in the Southern press that rough seas had made reinforcement impracticable. See, for example, *Memphis Daily Appeal* (4/14/1861) 1.

102. Francis Parker, M.D., in *Vital Signs in Charleston*, ed. Carolyn B. Matalene and Katherine E. Chaddock (Charleston: History Press, 2009), 44, 45; *Charleston Mercury* (4/12/1861) 1.

103. "Details of the Taking of Sumter," *NYT* (4/14/1861).

104. See, for example, Gibbon 240–42; Halleck 282–83; *Ordnance Manual* 403–4; Bartleson 147–55.

105. John Thompson/Robert Thompson (4/28/1861), Thompson 101; Spaulding 197; Greeley (1864) 447.

106. Lincoln/Mercer (4/1/1861), *ORN* 1/4:109.

107. Welles/Mercer (4/5/1861), *ORN* 1/4:235, Welles (2014) 652.

108. Welles/Rowan (4/5/1861), Welles/Faunce (4/5/1861), Welles/Gillis (4/5/1861), *ORN* 1/4:235–36. See also Fox/Cameron (4/19/1861), *OR* 1/1:11; Act of 1/16/1857, ch. 12 § 5, 11 Stat. 154; "The Navy Register," *Southern Lit. Messenger* 27/2:81, 87 (2/1858).

109. Mercer/Faunce (4/7/1861), *Goodyear Collection*, vol. 2, p. 34 (copy).

110. See Rowan/Welles (4/19/1861), *ORN* 1/4:253; Welles/Mercer (4/5/1861), *ORN* 1/4:235, Welles (2014) 652. Mercer in his April 7, 1861, note had instructed Faunce, "Report yourself to the Senior Naval Officer you may meet [off Charleston], showing him your instructions from the Navy Department of the 5th April." Mercer/Faunce (4/7/1861), *Goodyear Collection* 2:34 (copy). This would naturally mean Welles's April 5 order to Faunce, *ORN* 1/4:236. To Faunce, a Revenue Marine captain now under navy orders, it would have been logical to report to the senior naval officer present pending Mercer's arrival. Although Fox, in overall charge, was commonly addressed in relevant orders as "Captain Fox," this title was an honorific from earlier days, making him at present a civilian. See, for example, Cameron/Fox (4/4/1861), *ORN* 1/4:232; W. Scott/H. L. Scott (4/4/1861), *ORN* 1/4:233. Thus, Rowan, although only a commander, was the "Senior Naval Officer." See also Mercer/Foote in Foote/Welles (4/6/1861), *ORN* 1/4:238; Gillis/Welles (4/16/1861), *ORN* 1/4:251, 252.

111. Welles/Rowan (4/5/1861), *ORN* 1/4:235, 236. See also Welles/Gillis (4/5/1861), *ORN* 1/4:236.

112. Fox (2/24/1865), *ORN* 1/4:245, 249; F. Moore (1861–1866) 9:211.

113. Whether *Harriet Lane* accompanied *Baltic* at this time was variously reported.

114. Fox/Welles (2/24/1861), F. Moore (1861–1866) 9:211; Fox (2/24/1865), *ORN* 1/4:249; Fox/Cameron (4/19/1861), *OR* 1/1:11.

115. Welles's letterbook at the Connecticut Historical Society contains a variant, possibly a draft, of Welles's April 5 letter ordering Faunce to wait for Mercer. In the variant, Faunce is to "wait a reasonable time for [Mercer's] arrival." Because the *Official Records* and other sources did not publish the variant, the inference is reasonable that it was never sent and that Faunce and the others were not given discretion to decide that they had waited long enough.

116. Hagood 32; Chester 67–69; Greeley (1864) 446; F. Parker 67.

117. Rowan/Welles (4/19/1861), *ORN* 1/4:253; *Pawnee* abstract log (4/12/1861), *ORN* 1/4:254. See also J. D. Brandt, *Gunnery Catechism, as Applied to the Service of Naval Ordnance* (New York, 1864), 133–50.

118. Rowan later stated that Fox, who was not Welles's subordinate and was not ordered to wait offshore for Mercer, attempted to cross the bar on the morning of April 13 but was grounded on Rattlesnake Shoal. Rowan/Welles (4/19/1861), *ORN* 1/4:253.

119. Fox/Cameron (4/19/1861), *ORN* 1/4:244, 249–50; Fox (2/24/1865), F. Moore (1861–1866) 9:211; Hoogenboom (2008) 326n28.

120. Mercer/Senior Naval Officer off Charleston Harbor (4/7/1861), *Goodyear Collection*, vol. 2, p. 35 (copy). Mercer apparently included a copy of Welles's April 5 order to him, *ORN* 1/4:235, Welles (2014) 652.

121. In his account of *Harriet Lane's* voyage down the coast, the newspaperman Osbon wrote:

> When we left New York Harbour, on the morning of the 9th of April, 1861, not a soul on board knew positively whither she was bound, for she was despatched with "sealed orders," not to be opened until twelve hours had elapsed. The only sailing orders given were to steer south.... Toward evening, when the twelve hours were up, the official envelope was opened, and all hands learned that we were on our way to a rendezvous off the Charleston Bar, where we would meet other vessels and "report to the senior naval officer present" for further instructions. Further, we were to haul down the revenue cutter ensign and pennant, and hoist in their stead the national ensign and navy pennant.

Osbon 115. If Osbon was correct that the orders Faunce opened were to "report to the senior naval officer present," Faunce was not reciting Welles's April 5 order to him, since Welles did not use that language, telling Faunce instead to report to Mercer specifically. Welles/Faunce (4/5/1861), *ORN* 1/4:236. While Mercer's cover letter did use that language, he said nothing about displaying a naval pennant. Nor, of course, would Faunce be reciting to his men—even if he had it—a letter Mercer addressed not to him but to the senior officer off Charleston. Osbon sometimes opted for drama over reportorial accuracy, and he might have been eliding what happened that night with orders he saw subsequently. Alternatively, the order Faunce opened and read aloud that evening may not even have come from Welles, but rather from the service to which Faunce and his men belonged: the Revenue Marine.

122. Commander Gillis did not bring the letter, because his ship, *Pocahontas*, did not arrive at the rendezvous until 2:00 p.m. on the thirteenth, too late for the meeting on *Pawnee* that morning.

123. Lyons/Russell (4/9/1861), Barnes and Barnes 46, 48.

124. Fox, "My Plan for Reinforcing Fort Sumter Was This," *Fox Collection*, Box 14, Folder 10, pp. 2–8. See also Fox (2/24/1865), F. Moore (1861–1866) 9:211; Boynton 1:256–57. The unpublished memoir appears to have been written before the end of the war. Fox here urged that the "last card" Seward played in trying to prevent Sumter's reinforcement was to bring Baldwin to Washington, a visit Lincoln called "too late."

125. See Pickens/C. G. Memminger (4/13/1861), *OR* 1/53:144.

126. Rowan; Welles/Mercer (4/5/1861), *ORN* 1/4:235.

127. In 1865, Fox stated in a memorandum that he learned in the meeting "that Captain Rowan had received a note from Captain Mercer, of the Powhatan, dated at New-York the sixth, the day he sailed." Fox (2/24/1865), F. Moore (1861–1866) 9:211. See also *ORN* 1/4:245, 250; Rowan/Welles (4/19/1861), *ORN* 1/4:253. Fox's memoranda commonly contain minor errors, inconsistencies, and ambiguities that undercut his credibility. Rowan could not have received Mercer's letter "the day he [i.e., Rowan] sailed,"

because Rowan sailed not from New York but Washington. See, for example, Welles/ F. Buchanan (3/30/1861), *ORN* 1/4:228. And if "he sailed" refers to Mercer, Mercer did not sail anywhere.

128. Mercer/Senior Naval Officer off Charleston Harbor (4/7/1861), *Goodyear Collection* 2:35. Among Fox's comments about the letter are two complaints written during *Baltic's* voyage from Charleston to New York, one to Blair, one to Cameron. When writing them, Fox knew that a "superior authority" had ruined the operation by diverting *Powhatan* and Mercer, but he did not know who it was. Fox/Blair (4/17/1861), Fox (1920) 1:31, 33; Fox/Cameron (4/19/1861), *ORN* 1/4:244, 249–50; Fox (2/24/1865), F. Moore (1861–1866) 9:211.

129. See Rowan/Welles (4/19/1861), *ORN* 1/4:253.

Chapter 14: "We Have Humbled the Flag of the United States"

1. Brackett 948; (4/13/1861), Holmes 26.
2. Whiting/Beauregard (4/13/1861), *OR* 1/1: 313, 314.
3. "Details of the Taking of Sumter," *NYT* (4/14/1861).
4. Hagood 32.
5. A. Porter 124.
6. See, for example, E. Porcher Miles/Beauregard (1/23/1878), *Goodyear Collection* vol. 2; unsigned pencil letter (4/13/1861), id.; Young 31–33; John Thompson/Robert Thompson (4/28/1861), Thompson 101; J. G. Foster, "Engineer Journal of the Bombardment," *OR* 1/1:16, 18, 23; R. D. Jones et al./Beauregard (4/15/1861), *OR* 1/1:64; Beauregard/ Walker (4/13/1861), *OR* 1/1:309; Walther 160; L. Wright (1905) 41–46; Chester 76–79; Chisolm 82–83; Roman 1:46–47; Willard Glazier, *Battles for the Union* (Hartford, CT, 1875), 26–29. Wigfall smoothed over the irregularity of his visit in Wigfall/D. R. Jones (4/13/1861), L. Wright (1904) 453.
7. Pickens/C. G. Memminger (4/13/1861), *OR* 1/53:144. See also Beauregard Gen. Order no. 20, F. Moore (1861–1866) 1:63.
8. *New-York Daily Tribune* (4/19/1861) 1.
9. (4/13, 15/1861), C. F. Adams Sr.
10. D. R. Jones/Beauregard (4/15/1861), *OR* 1/1:64, 65, Roman 1:47; S. Lee 78–79; Beauregard, *General Orders*, no. 20 (4/14/1861), *Goodyear Collection* vol. 1. See also Crawford (1915) [9].
11. Abbott 569n; Guernsey and Alden 66. Compare, for example, Spaulding 192, 198–202; *OR* 1/1:43. See also Bartleson 5–13.
12. See, for example, H. Scott 164; Hazlett, Olmstead, and Parks 191; Dennis Hart Mahan, *Elementary Course of Military Engineering Part II Permanent Fortifications* (New York, 1867), 16, 64; Dennis Hart Mahan, *Descriptive Geometry* (New York, 1864), 14–16; Alexander Moncrieff, "Sea Coast Defence," *Van Nostrand's Eclectic Engineering Mag.* 1/10:870, 873 (10/1869). Cf. Roman 1:44. The exposed tier had two 10-inch columbiads, six 8-inch columbiads, and four 8-inch seacoast howitzers, as well as six 42-pounders, three 32-pounders, and six 24-pounders. Although two men of spirit did steal upstairs and fire

heavier-bore guns from the right gorge angle aimed at Cumming's Point, this was merely a prank.

13. A New York merchant who claimed to have been at Fort Moultrie said that at least two hundred Confederate soldiers died there, their deaths hushed up by authorities. *Burlington (VT) Free Press* (5/10/1861) 2. See also Hazlett, Olmstead, and Parks 191.

14. (4/21/1861), Russell (1861A) 32, 34.

15. Spaulding 196, 198; *Battle of Fort Sumter* 23; Chester 53, 67–69; J. G. Foster, "Engineer Journal of the Bombardment," *OR* 1/1:16, 18, 20; Gordon 40. War journalist W. H. Russell, after visiting Fort Sumter a few days later, told Lord Lyons that Anderson's defense had been passive but "exceedingly creditable." (4/19/1861), Russell (1992) 42.

16. "Fort Sumter," *War Songs of the Blue and the Gray*, ed. H. L. Williams (New York: Hurst, 1905), 152, 153; John A. Wagner, "Carolina: April 14, 1861," *War Songs and Poems of the Southern Confederacy 1861–1865*, comp. H. M. Wharton (Philadelphia: American Book and Bible House, 1904), 58–59.

17. Hayne/Lincoln, Holt (4/13/1861), *Lincoln Papers*. See also H. W. Denslow/Lincoln (4/13/1861), id.

18. Russell (1863) 1:125.

19. *Battle of Fort Sumter* 23. See also *Middletown (NY) Banner of Liberty* (4/17/1861) 123; Pollard (1862) 52.

20. John P. Gillis/Gideon Welles (4/16/1861), *ORN* 1/4:251, 252.

21. *Battle of Fort Sumter* 11–12.

22. See, for example, S. Jones 45; *Ordnance Instructions* 87–89, 147–49; R. W. Gibbes, M.D. (4/16/1861), *OR* 1/1:66; Frederick H. Dyer, *Compendium of the War of the Rebellion* (Des Moines, IA: Dyer, 1908), 588–89. Cf. (4/14/1861), Ruffin (1972–1989) 1:599; Daniel J. Hacker, "A Census-Based Count of Civil War Dead," *Civil War Hist.* 57/4:307 (12/2011); Thomas Fleming, *A Disease in the Public Mind* (New York: Da Capo, 2013), ix.

23. Roman 1:48; Crawford (1915) [9].

24. W. A. Harris 44, 47; *Appleton* 657. See also Edmunds (1986) 163.

25. Petigru/Jane Petigru North (4/16/1861), Petigru 378.

26. Pickens/W. P. Miles (4/9/1861) quoted in Crawford (1915) item 356; L. P. Walker/ Jefferson Davis (4/27/1861), *OR* 4/1:247, 250–51. See also Resolution (5/10/1861), *OR* 4/1:309. Down in Georgia, a diarist ended her April 14 entry about attending a sermon on war by noting that "Fort Sumter had surrendered to the Carolinians." (4/14/1861), *Diary of Dolly Lunt Burge 1848–1879*, ed. Christine Jacobson Carter (Athens: University of Georgia Press, 1962), 117.

27. S. Pryor (1904) 159; *NYT* (4/24/1861) 1. See also Torget 27–28; Link 240–41.

28. Roman 1:48.

29. Beauregard/L. Pope Walker (4/17/1861), *OR* 1/1:28. See also (4/16/1861), Ruffin (1972–1989) 1:604–5.

30. Petigru/Jane Petigru North (4/16/1861), Petigru 378.

31. *Punch* 40:188 (5/4/1861).

32. Ellen Call Long, *Florida Breezes* (Jacksonville, FL, 1883), 311.

33. C. M. C. Wigfall/Louise Wigfall Wright, L. Wright (1904) 453.

34. Powe 7. As between Anderson's and Beauregard's forces, the dueling analogy was rendered complete by featuring controlled violence and release without inflicted death.

35. Compare Foster, "Engineer Journal of the Bombardment," *OR* 1/1:16, 25 with *New-York Daily Tribune* (4/19/1861) 1. The garrison's larder as of March 21 had included twenty-six barrels of pork, three barrels of sugar, six barrels of flour, six barrels of hard bread, and one and a half barrels of rice. Norman J. Hall/Anderson (3/21/1861), *OR* 1/1:211. See also S. Jones 43.
36. Chisolm 83.
37. Fox/Virginia Fox (2/6/1861), *Fox Collection* Series I, Box 4, Folder 11, Fox (1920) 1:5, 6.
38. Anderson/Cameron (4/18/1861), F. Moore (1861–1866) 1:76; *Fox Collection*, Box 17, Folder 2; Boynton 1:252; Crawford (1887) 449, T. Anderson 87, Lawton (1911) 14; Osbon 123–24; Hoogenboom (2008) 70. A notation, probably by Mrs. Fox, states, "Maj A. was unable to write or compose—was depressed + overcome." *Fox Collection*, Series X, Bound Volume 2.
39. Campbell/Seward (4/13/1861), *Seward Papers* Reel 63, Richardson (1905) 1:93, Campbell 38, Connor 133, J. Davis (1938) 1:683, E. McPherson 110, 111.
40. See, for example, Littleton v. Richardson, 32 N.H. 59, 62–63 (1855). See also Francis Hilliard, *Law of Torts or Private Wrongs* (Boston, 1859), 2:503n.
41. Roman later wrote that Seward's "unofficial but positive assurances . . . of an early evacuation" of Fort Sumter were intended to "gain time for the reinforcement of Sumter before it could be reduced by the South Carolina troops under General Beauregard." Roman 1:32–33. That was not Seward's intention, however.
42. Davis/Pickens (1/13/1861), J. Davis (1923) 5:36. See also Crawford (1915) item 140.
43. Davis/Pickens (2/20/1861), J. Davis (1971–) 7:55; Roman 1:25–30.
44. Crawford/Toombs (3/6/1861), *Commissioners* 19, 21; Current (1961) 359; Bancroft (1900) 2:118.
45. Crawford, Forsyth (3/8/1861), Bancroft (1900) 2:118; Acts of 3/6/1861, chs. 26, 29, *Stats. at Large of the Provisional Gov. of the Confed. States of America* (Richmond, VA, 1864), 45, 47; *New-York Daily Tribune* (3/20/1861) 4.
46. On March 5, Lincoln's first full day in office, a Confederate spy in Washington told Confederate Secretary of War Walker that Seward's postures of conciliation were "idle" "pretenses" because he in fact concurred in Lincoln's inaugural undertaking to hold the Southern forts. Lucius Quinton Washington/Walker (3/5/1861), *OR* 1/1:263.
47. Forsyth/Walker (3/14/1861), *OR* 4/1:165.
48. Crawford, Roman/Toombs (3/26/1861), *Commissioners* 115.
49. Toombs/Crawford, Forsyth, Roman (4/2/1861), *Commissioners* 133; Forsyth/Crawford (1870) quoted in Rhodes (1892–1906) 3:340. See also Pleasant Stovall, *Robert Toombs* (New York, 1892), 224; L. Johnson 468n80.
50. Forsyth/Walker (3/14/1861), *OR* 4/1:165.
51. Stephenson 111.
52. Before Davis resigned as senator, Seward told him that South Carolina should not attack Fort Sumter prior to Lincoln's inauguration because, among other things, the new administration, within its first sixty days, would declare a constitutional right to secede. Since Lincoln did not believe in such a right, Seward was lying. "I had to deceive Davis," Seward reportedly admitted, "and I did it." Quoted in *Reminiscences of Abraham Lincoln*, ed. A. T. Rice (Edinburgh, 1886), 77, 85–86. See also Crofts (1989) 251. But Davis was not deceived. Varina Davis noted a conversation with Seward in 1859. Her husband had been indisposed with a serious ocular inflammation, and Seward, a sincere friend, visited him daily. She one day asked, "Mr. Seward, how can you make, with a

grave face, those piteous appeals for the negro that you did in the Senate; you were too long a schoolmaster in Georgia to believe the things you say." Seward "looked at me quizzically, and smilingly answered, 'I do not, but these appeals, as you call them, are potent to affect the rank and file of the North.'" Her husband, "very much shocked at Mr. Seward's answer," said, "'But, Mr. Seward, do you never speak from conviction alone?' 'Nev—er,' answered he." V. Davis 1:581. See also Susan Dixon, *True History of the Missouri Compromise* (Cincinnati, OH, 1899), 239–42; Welles diary (1/2/1864), Welles (2014) 339, 340; [Buchanan] (1866) 57 ("Without strong convictions," Seward "aroused passions, probably without so intending, which it was beyond his power afterwards to control"). Seward wanted peace, but in the "polished cynicism of a diplomat who had been known to deny that he was ever entirely serious." Stephenson 111.

53. Davis/Pickens (3/18/1861), J. Davis (1923) 5:60, 61. See also (3/18/1861), J. Davis (1971–) 7:74; Pickens/Davis (3/17/1861), id. 7:70; Crawford (1915) items 353 and 354; note 52 above.

54. Walker/Beauregard (3/15/1861), *OR* 1/1:276.

55. Walker/Beauregard (4/2/1861), *OR* 1/1:285.

56. Campbell/Seward (4/20/1861), Campbell (1917) 42; J. L. M. Curry, "Legal Justification of the South in Secession," Evans 1:3, 52. Handwritten versions of Campbell's two letters are in *Goodyear Collection* vol. 2, items 2 and 3. See also Crawford (1915) [17].

57. Quoted in Saunders 136, 153. See also id. 153–60.

58. Stanton/Buchanan (5/11/1861), Stanton 476–77. Stanton later softened, telling Buchanan that although Seward's refusal to respond to Campbell's published accusations would leave many convinced that what Campbell had written was true, Seward "believed that Sumter would be evacuated, as he stated it would be," but "the war-party overruled him with Lincoln, and he was forced to give up." Stanton/Buchanan (5/19/1861), Stanton 478. Buchanan would remain so defensive about his presidency that he tried to inject into his 1866 memoir a false air of objective truth by writing it in the third person and not naming himself on the title page as the work's author. Scott (3/30/1861), W. Scott (1862) 3, 8–9; Scott, "Communicated to the Editors [of the *National Intelligencer*] for Publication" (10/21/1862), Buchanan (1908–1911) 11:293, 298, 299; Scott, "Rejoinder of Lieutenant-General Scott to Ex-President Buchanan" (11/12/1862), id. 11:304, 306–7; Holt/Buchanan (1/29/1861), id. 12:197–98n; Blair (1865). See also Stanton 481; Nicolay and Hay (1917) 3:169–70; Scott/Cameron (10/31/1861), F. Moore (1862) 10.

59. J. Davis (1861), *OR* 4/1:256; Richardson (1905) 1:63, 71.

60. *Nashville Union and American* (4/18/1861), Dumond (1931B) 498; id. (5/18/1861) 2. E. A. Pollard of the *Richmond Daily Examiner* referred to Seward's "policy of perfidy." Pollard (1862) 47. See also *Nashville Union and American* (5/14/1861) 2. J. L. M. Curry wrote that "the annals of diplomacy contain no chapter so full of duplicity, insincerity and deception as that which record the conduct and utterances" of Seward regarding his dealing with Campbell and the commissioners. Curry 121–24. "Mr. Seward stands in the history of this transaction unrelieved from the charge of duplicity." "Civil History of the Confederate States," Evans 1:247, 379.

61. On April 5, the British journalist W. H. Russell dined with the Southern commissioners and others at Gautier's Restaurant on Pennsylvania Avenue, finding a "fixed principle in their minds" to be "disbelief of anything a Northern man" (which they equated with "a Republican") said. When the conversation turned to "the duplicity of Mr. Seward, and

the wickedness of the Federal government," however, instead of charging Seward with perfidy, they told Russell that the promises Seward made "must be of very little consequence" since "not the least reliance was to be placed on his word." Russell (1863) 1:94. Perhaps the commissioners, seeing that they had been duped, now tried to make the case that they put no more faith in Seward than the leaders in Montgomery did.

62. [J. W. Jones?], *South. Hist. Soc. Papers* 7/:98 (2/1879) (emphasis deleted).
63. *The Heritage of the South* [ca. 1865–1870] (Lynchburg, VA: Press of Brown-Morrison, 1915), 100.
64. J. Davis (4/29/1861), *OR* 4/1:256.
65. James Williams, *The South Vindicated* (London, 1862), 334.
66. Gideon Welles later wrote that when Lincoln found out about Seward's conduct, his reaction was to keep "a more watchfull . . . attention over occurrences," as if he blamed himself for not monitoring sufficiently the vices of the talents around him. Welles narrative, *Welles Papers/LC* Reel 2.
67. (5/20/1861) 2.
68. Quoted in *NYT* (5/25/1861) 2, Greeley (1864) 632. See also Campbell/J. W. Jones (12/11/1878), *South. Hist. Soc. Papers* 7/2:97 (2/1878).
69. Seward/Frances Seward (5/17/1861), F. Seward (1891) 575. The letter began as a mixture of self-pity with delusions of grandeur: "A country so largely relying on my poor efforts to save it, had refused me the full measure of its confidence, needful to that end. I am a chief reduced to a subordinate position, and surrounded with a guard, to see that I do not do too much for my country, lest some advantage may revert indirectly to my own fame."
70. Seward/Frances Seward (6/5/1861), F. Seward (1891) 590. See also "Why Sumter Was Not Reinforced," *Army and Navy J.* 3/4:53 (9/16/1865).

Chapter 15: "Wavering Hearts Were Turned to Iron"

1. Lincoln/Fox (5/1/1861), Basler et al. 4:350–51.
2. In his message to Congress of July 4, 1861, Lincoln said that Sumter "was attacked, and bombarded to its fall, without even awaiting the arrival of the provisioning expedition." Basler et al. 4:421, 425.
3. "The calculation was thus coolly made by President Lincoln and Captain Fox that the mere attempt itself to reinforce Sumter would accomplish a desired political result." "Civil History of the Confederate States," Evans 1:247, 391. There is no evidence that Fox was part of this calculation.
4. For years, Fox would expend substantial energy blaming the operation's failure on Seward having diverted *Powhatan*, most often mentioning not its firepower but its boats and oarsmen. See, for example, Fox/Blair (4/19/1861), *ORN* 1/4:244; Fox (2/24/1865), F. Moore (1861–1866) 9:211. But Fox had first proposed the incursion before he knew of *Powhatan*'s availability, relying upon *Pawnee*. See, for example, Fox (2/6/1861), *ORN* 1/4:223, 224. Fox had criticized Ward's competing plan by saying that in bad weather no oarsmen could pull the men and provisions the required five miles from beyond the bar to the fort. Fox/Blair (2/23/1861), *ORN* 1/4:224. The other ships had boats, and while several were lowered into the water, they were never used because of the gale. The gist of Fox's plan was to use tugs, but they never arrived.

5. T. Anderson 57–58.
6. Villard 161. Villard's friendship with Lincoln did not disqualify him for work on James Gordon Bennett's proslavery, anti-Lincoln *New York Herald*. In 1899, James Schouler, in a history otherwise so favorable to Lincoln as to skip over or "harmonize" almost all inconvenient facts, wrote that Lincoln, "most likely, had never expected the Fox expedition to accomplish its immediate ends." *History of the United States of America, Under the Constitution* (New York, 1880–1899), 6:31. Cf. Jordan 278–79.
7. See, for example, the summary in Niven (1973) 613n11.
8. See, for example, William Tecumseh Sherman, "The Grand Strategy of the War of the Rebellion," *Century Mag.* 35/4:582, 585 (2/1888); J. McPherson (2008) 3–4.
9. This was not a hurricane, these being extremely rare in April. See, for example, I. A. Lapham, "List of the Great Storms, Hurricanes, and Tornadoes," *Report of the Secretary of War*, H. R., Exec. Doc. 1, Pt. 2 (42/3) 1:682 (1872–1873). The track of a nor'easter from southwest to northeast was first posited by Franklin in May 1760. The sciences of meteorology and climatology advanced substantially in the next century. See, for example, William Reid, *Attempt to Develop the Law of Storms* (London, 1838), 4–9, 13–25; Reid, *Progress of the Development of the Law of Storms* (London, 1849); Matthew Fontaine Maury, *Maury's Wind and Current Charts: Gales in the Atlantic* (Washington, 1857); *Lord Wrottesley's Speech in the House of Lords . . . on Lieut. Maury's Plan*, 2nd ed. (London, 1853). But Fox had no way to contact anyone in the South competent to observe a nor'easter in its early stages and then telegraph the forecast to Washington or New York in time to scrub the mission, even if there had been any time left to reschedule it. See, for example, William Blasius, *Storms* (Philadelphia, 1875), 29–42, 53, 72–89. In Washington, while noon measurements in barometric pressure dropped below thirty on April 9 and did not climb to thirty again until April 20, that drop was insufficient to show the severity of the storm. *Astronomical and Meteorological Observations Made at the United States Naval Observatory, during the Year 1861* (Washington, 1862). Nor was there any means to contact the expedition already under way.
10. Villard 161. Cf. Jordan 278–79. See also Starr 24–25.
11. Lowell 762.
12. Holt/Buchanan (5/24/1861), Buchanan (1908–1911) 11:195, 196–97; Buchanan/Holt (5/21/1861), id. 11:194.
13. See, for example, Crofts (1989) 312–33.
14. In Frost 33.
15. *War Songs of the Blue and the Gray*, ed. H. L. Williams (New York: Hurst, 1905), 73; Frederick Douglass, "Sudden Revolution in Northern Sentiment," *Douglass' Monthly* (5/1861), *Frederick Douglass: Selected Speeches and Writings*, ed. Philip S. Foner (Chicago: University of Chicago Press, 1999), 445–46; Douglass, "The Fall of Sumter," id. 443–44. See also William H. C. Hosmer's untitled poem: "Avengers, full of prowess, woke / To hear his clarion call, 'to arms!' / Forsaking, for the roar and smoke / Of battle-fields, their shops and farms." *Poetical Tributes to the Memory of Abraham Lincoln* (Philadelphia, 1865), 76.
16. Act of 7/29/1861, ch. 25 § 1, 11 Stat. 281; Act of 2/28/1795, ch. 36, 1 Stat. 424.
17. Anderson (10/8/1861) OR 1/4:296. In November 1861, a Kentuckian wrote to Jefferson Davis that "secession" was impossible in his state because its legislature was "enslaved" to the "despotism" of an occupying army, and thus a pro-South provisional government

was being declared under "a doctrine universally recognized by all nations"—that is, "the right of revolution," the right "to destroy any government whose existence is incompatible with the interests and liberty of society," there being in his view nothing incompatible between a state's right to secede and the people's right to revolt. George W. Johnson/ Davis (11/21/1861), *OR* 4/1:743, 744.

18. *Porter Journal* 80–82. See also Powe 10.
19. Huger/Anderson (4/14/1861), *Anderson Papers* 12:2502.
20. Lincoln/Anderson (5/1/1861), Basler et al. 4:350; Boynton 1:265; Welles (11/1870) 635; Fox (1920) 1:43. See also Cameron/Anderson (4/20/1861), *OR* 1/1:16.
21. See, for example, Crofts (1989) 297; Current (1963) 192–94; Stampp (1950) 262–86; J. McPherson (1988) 272–73.
22. Anderson/Thomas (4/8/1861), *OR* 1/1:294, W. A. Harris 37; Crawford (1887) 373–78; T. Anderson 67. See also Doubleday (1876) 9; Nicolay (1881) 50–59; Lamon 68–70; Stampp (1950) 284–85.
23. J. Davis (1938) 1:283–84.
24. T. Anderson 69. See also McClintock (2008) 248.
25. Lawton (1911) 9.
26. Pollard (1863) 55.
27. T. Anderson 57–58, 69–70.
28. Cf. Ellis Merton Coulter, writing in 1950, "The question which has troubled subsequent generations is whether Lincoln was the marplot and bungler or the cunning villain and provocateur; whether he stumbled into war at Sumter or whether he planned it." *The Confederate States of America 1861–1865* (Baton Rouge: Louisiana State University Press, 1950), 37. See also Carl N. Degler, "One Among Many: The United States and National Unification," Boritt (1992) 89, 107–8; Kenneth M. Stampp, "One Alone? The United States and National Self-Determination," id. 123, 135.
29. See Harry V. Jaffa, *Crisis of the House Divided* (1959; Seattle: University of Washington Press, 1973), 19–27. Lincoln lost in the vote of the Illinois legislature but won the popular vote.
30. Walter B. Stevens, *A Reporter's Lincoln* (St. Louis: Missouri Historical Society, 1916), 27–30, 65.
31. Henry C. Whiting/William Henry Herndon (8/27/1887), *Herndon* 627, 636; Leonard Swett/Herndon (1/17/1866), Herndon and Weik (1921) 3:528, 535–38. Fox, after knowing Lincoln well, wrote that Lincoln's policy with regard to Fort Sumter was "profound and secretive." Although many, "even those close to him, thought him to be a 'simple-minded man,'" he was in fact "the deepest, the closest, [the most acute] and the most ambitious man American politics produced." (3/29/1883), Forbes 2:104, 105. The South Carolina poet and writer Archibald Rutledge noted Lincoln's "devious acuteness." "Abraham Lincoln Fights the Battle of Fort Sumter," *S. Atl. Quart.* 34/4:368 (10/1935).
32. Swett/Herndon (1/17/1866), Herndon and Weik 3:528.
33. Marx (2008) (emphasis in original).
34. Swett/Herndon (1/17/1866), Herndon and Weik (1921) 3:528; Proclamation (1/1/1863), Richardson (1897–1903) 6:157. In 1862, Lincoln suggested to Congress that it aid slave states in a schedule of gradual emancipation, in order to send a message to the cotton states. Id. 6:68. See also Second Annual Message (12/1/1862), id. 6:126, 133–41; Third Annual Message (12/8/1863) id. 6:179, 188–91. Lincoln thought slavery immoral and

called for a "national policy . . . which deals with it *as a wrong.*" Basler et al. 3:226, 433, 440.

35. O. Browning 1:476.

36. Nicolay and Hay (1917) 4:62. See also Stampp (1980) 184–85; Potter (1995) xlv, 373–74 and n. 89.

37. See Paullin 254–59.

38. Welles (1/1871) 101; Nicolay (1881) 54.

39. Montgomery Meigs/Louisa Rodgers Meigs (4/12/1861), *Meigs Papers* Reel 7.

40. Meigs/Seward (4/13/1861), *OR* 1/1:374, 375.

41. Meigs journal (4/13/1861), *Meigs Typescript* D-14 (4/14/1861), id. D-15.

42. Meigs journal (4/15/1861), *Meigs Typescript* D-15.

43. Meigs journal (4/14, 5/9/1861), *Meigs Typescript* D-15, D-67/D-69.

44. William French/L. G. Arnold (4/20/1861), *OR* 1/1:389; Brown/Keyes (4/15/1861), *OR* 1/1:376, 377; *National Republican* (5/10/1861) 2; Ernest Dibble, "Slave Rentals to the Military," *Civil War Hist.* 23/2:101 (6/1977).

45. Meigs journal (4/16/1861), *Meigs Typescript* D-22. See also Adams/Welles (4/18/1861), *ORN* 1/4:118; J. Tidball 120–21. The gale apparently did not unduly delay passage. See Matthew Fontaine Maury, *Explanations and Sailing Directions to Accompany the Wind and Current Charts*, 8th ed. (Washington, 1859), 2:7.

46. *New York World* (4/6/1861) 4.

47. *Powhatan* abstract log, *ORN* 1/4:207; Adams/Welles (4/22/1861), *ORN* 1/4:143; *Sabine* abstract log, *ORN* 1/4:209.

48. See, for example, Meigs/T. M. Anderson (10/31/1881), T. Anderson 43, 44–45.

49. D. Porter (1875) 1. See also Charles Benedict Davenport, *Naval Officers: Their Heredity and Development* (Washington, DC: Carnegie Institution, 1919), 175–80.

50. Lincoln/Porter (4/1/1861), *ORN* 1/4:108–9, Soley 102–3.

51. Meigs/Porter (4/17/1861), *ORN* 1/4:123. See also Meigs/Brown (4/19/1861), *OR* 1/1:385. Rather than try to cancel Porter's opportunity, Meigs asked him "to postpone entering the harbor for the present," citing the necessity of avoiding a useless battle while Meigs was still "landing stores, horses, and artillery"—a process far from complete, with additional troops and supplies due soon on *Illinois*. Montgomery Meigs/Louisa Rodgers Meigs (4/18/1861), *Meigs Papers* Reel 7.

52. Brown/Meigs (4/17/1861), *ORN* 1/4:123; Brown/E. D. Keyes (4/18/1861), *OR* 1/1:378, 379; Johns 49. See also Nicolay and Hay (1917) 4:16; *Porter Journal* 90. Brown, not knowing that the war had already started at Charleston, guessed that Bragg would not open fire unless *Powhatan* attempted to enter the harbor. Brown/Keyes (4/19/1861), *OR* 1/1:380; Brown/Keyes (4/22/1861), *OR* 1/1:390; D. Miller 85–86.

53. It undoubtedly came within a few inches of scraping the bottom. See, for example, *Globe* (34/3) App. 271 (1/20/1857) (Pensacola reported as twenty-three feet at high water, twenty-one feet, six inches at low water, and twenty-three feet, eight inches at spring tides).

54. See, for example, *ORN* 1/4:118–32; Meigs/T. M. Anderson (10/31/1881), T. Anderson 43, 47; Meigs journal (4/18/1861), *Meigs Typescript* D-36, Tilley 74–77; Nicolay and Hay (1917) 4:16–17; Meigs/Brown (4/19/1861), *OR* 1/1:385. See also Meigs/Totten (4/25/1861), *OR* 1/1:393, 397.

55. Porter/Brown (4/18/1861), *ORN* 1/4/124. See also Meigs/Porter (4/17/1861), *ORN* 1/4:123; Porter/Brown (4/18/1861), *ORN* 1/4:124; Brown/Keyes (4/19/1861), *OR* 1/1:380; Brown/Keyes (4/22/1861), *OR* 1/1:390.

56. Porter quoted in Meigs journal (4/18/1861), *Meigs Typescript* D-36; Porter/[H.A. Adams] (8/24/1862), *ORN* 1/4:130. See also *Porter Journal* 65. Porter may not have known that the Charleston operation had been led by Gustavus Fox, his old navy friend. Fox felt that by being deprived of *Powhatan*, he had been robbed of his chance for glory, and now Porter, having taken that ship, felt that Meigs and Brown had robbed him of his own chance by not letting *Powhatan* engage the enemy. See, for example, Hoogenboom (2008) 21. In his initial meeting with Lincoln, Porter had virtually guaranteed that he would steam into Pensacola Harbor and fight. In a letter to Seward, he now wanted to make clear that the only reason he was not inside the harbor—as promised—was that his advance had been blocked by Meigs's ship. Porter/Seward (4/21/1861), *ORN* 1/4:122.

57. *Daily National Republican* (9/16/1865), 1, *NYT* (9/18/1865) 5. See also *NYT* (9/11/1865); *NYT* (9/16/1865) 4.

58. Adams/Welles (4/18/1861), *ORN* 1/4:118, 119.

59. See, for example, *National Republican* (4/26/1861) 2. See also *NYT* (4/24/1861) 1; H. A. Adams/S. F. Du Pont (4/30/1861), *ORN* 1/4:125, 127. "The *Powhatan* was not needed either to convoy the transports or to land the troops, and she did neither. . . . Besides, if there was so great an anxiety in regard to Fort Pickens, what more natural than to have stepped into the office of the Secretary of the Navy to ascertain the actual condition of things? A single inquiry would have disclosed the facts that all needed measures had already been taken, and no second expedition was required." Boynton 1:304. Seward, Porter, Meigs, and (of course) Lincoln could each have stepped into Welles's office, and his response would have been just as Boynton suggested. Welles (11/1870) 621. Kenneth Stampp called *Powhatan*'s arrival at Pensacola "irrelevant." Stampp (1945) 314. See also Nicolay and Hay (1917) 4:16–17; Soley 115; Crawford (1887) 415–16; Welles (1/1871) 102–3; Welles (1911) 1:25–26, 31–32; F. Moore (1861–1866) 1:162; Symonds (2008) 31.

60. The shipment of crucial supplies from New York would be a perpetual problem, due to ineptitude in the Quartermaster Department. Bearss (1983) 564–67.

61. Porter/Meigs (5/23/1861), *Meigs Papers* Reel 12. Pensacola would remain a strategic backwater. In November 1861, Fort Pickens and two Union ships exchanged artillery fire with Fort McRee. In January 1862, Fort Pickens damaged Fort McCree and used "hot shots" to burn the navy yard.

Conclusion

1. *Mary Chesnut's Civil War*, ed. C. Vann Woodward (New Haven, CT: Yale University Press, 1981), 48.

2. Hagood 32; Lincoln, "If a house was on fire," Basler et al. 3:503.

3. Russell (1863) 1:140, 169–70, 197–98; (4/16/1861), Russell (1992) 38; (4/18/1861), id. 40, 41. See also Ford; Foreman 78–79; M. Klein 3–14, 349–53, 365–66, 421–30. Petigru would embrace secessionism prior to his death.

4. "Charleston," *Poems of Henry Timrod*, ed. Paul H. Hayne, rev. ed. (New York, 1873), 97.

5. Lathers 124. See also Nichols 2:298.

6. Esther Alden (6/20/1863), *"Our Women in the War"* (Charleston, 1885), 355.
7. See, for example, Garth W. James, "The Assault on Fort Wagner," *War Papers Read before the Commandery of the State of Wisconsin* (Milwaukee, WI, 1891), 1:9; M. A. Smith 194–99; *NY Tribune* in F. Moore (1861–1866) 7:211, 213–14.
8. John T. Luck (10/21/1865), *Army and Navy Journal* 3/11:171 (11/4/1865); John Lothrop Motley/Mary Motley (6/14/1861), *Correspondence of John Lothrop Motley*, ed. George William Curtis (London, 1889), 1:371, 376; William Swinton, *History of the Seventh Regiment, National Guard* (New York, 1870), 451–52. See also French/Cary 24; Hondon B. Hargrove, *Black Union Soldiers in the Civil War* (Jefferson, NC: McFarland, 1988), 159–60; Lorien Foote, *Seeking the One Great Remedy* (Athens: Ohio University Press, 2003), 119–23; Rosen 112. The Citadel's football stadium bears Hagood's name.
9. "Robert Gould Shaw," Lodge and Theodore Roosevelt, *Hero Tales from American History* (1895; New York: Century, 1902), 249, 258. See also Phillips Brooks, "Dedicatory Address," *Annual Report of the School Committee of the City of Boston, 1892* (Boston, 1893), 444, 449; Rosen 104–15. While Hagood in 1881 denied having made these comments, another Confederate officer confirmed that he had. See Hagood/Thomas Wentworth Higginson (9/21/1881), *Proc. Mass. Hist. Soc.* 47:341 (4/1914); 2nd Lt. H. W. Henricks, 27th Reg., S.C. Volunteers/Luis F. Emilio, in Emilio, *History of the Fifty-Fourth Regiment of the Massachusetts Volunteer Infantry*, 2nd ed. (Boston, 1894), 98.
10. Arguments for the essential benignity of the slave regime would survive the Civil War and the civil rights amendments that ended the system, and for many decades they would be part of the sentimental "Lost Cause" argument. See, for example, Reagan 83; Mitchell Snay, *Gospel of Disunion: Religion and Separatism in the Antebellum South* (Chapel Hill: University of North Carolina Press, 1997); Curry; Elizabeth Fox-Genovese and Eugene D. Genovese, *The Mind of the Master Class* (New York: Cambridge University Press, 2005), 249–304; Stephanie McCurry, *Masters of Small Worlds* (New York: Oxford University Press, 1995), 210–14; Bryan 7–12 ("the oldest, and most time-honoured institution of society"). Pollard described slavery as "a convenient ground of dispute" but "merely an incident" of the war and not its cause. Pollard (1867B) 47, 49. Alexander Stephens described the war as arising from the issue of whether the general government should be federal or consolidated, slavery being "but the question on which these antagonistic principles . . . were finally brought into actual . . . collision . . . on the field of battle." Stephens (1868–1870) 1:10. But see Paris 79 (slavery was "not the pretext nor the occasion, but the sole cause" of the Civil War); Gaines M. Foster, "Guilt over Slavery: A Historiographical Analysis," *J. South. Hist.* 56/4:665 (11/1990).
11. Francis Shaw/Edward Pierce (7/31/1863) quoted in, for example, Willie Lee Rose, *Rehearsal for Reconstruction* (Indianapolis, IN: Bobbs-Merrill, 1964), 259.
12. Nichols 2:300.
13. Alvin Voris, "Charleston in the Rebellion," *Sketches of War History 1861–1865* (Cincinnati, OH, 1883–1908), 2:293, 307.
14. French/Cary 91–92, Spicer 34.
15. Quoted in Draper 1:564.
16. Andrews 1–2; Henry Wadsworth Longfellow, "Retribution," *Poems of Henry Wadsworth Longfellow* (New York, 1846), 114. Compare Plutarch, "On Those Who Are Punished by the Deity Late," *Plutarch's Morals*, trans. Arthur Richard Shilleto (London, 1898), 335.

17. Stanton (3/27/1865), *Fort Sumter Memorial* 35. A handwritten version is in *Goodyear Collection* vol. 2, item 48. Lincoln suggested, unsuccessfully, that the commemoration take place on the anniversary of the capitulation (4/13) rather than the formal evacuation. Lincoln/Stanton (3/27/1865), Basler et al. 8:375.
18. (4/14/1861) 2. See also E. Townsend 210–11. Among Virginians serving under Major Anderson was R. K. Meade, who after leaving Fort Sumter would join the Provisional Army of the Confederate States as a major, dying of typhoid in July 1862.
19. Abbatt 39.
20. Quoted in *Fort Sumter Memorial* 38.
21. In id. 45.
22. *Daily National Republican* (4/14/1865) 4.
23. John W. Forney (1872) in Forney, *Anecdotes of Public Men* (New York, 1873), 272.
24. John Hay, "Life in the White House in the Time of Lincoln" (1890), Hay (2000) 131, 137.
25. Lamon 116–17, 279–80.
26. Lincoln/Scott (6/5/1861), Basler et al. 4:394; Ways 62–63.
27. *Daily National Republican* (4/15/1861) 2; id. (4/17/1861) 2; F. Seward (1916) 258–61.
28. Abbatt 40.
29. Sidney Andrews, *The South since the War* (Boston, 1866), 39, 50–56, 94; *Journal of the Convention of the People of South Carolina, Held in Columbia, S.C., September, 1865* (Columbia, SC, 1865), 4, 27.

Bibliography

Additional sources are cited in the notes.

[Abbatt, William]. "Gideon Welles and Lincoln." *Mag. of Hist.* 20/1:34 (1/1915).

Abbot, Henry L. *Course of Lectures upon the Defence of the Sea-Coast of the United States.* New York: D. Van Nostrand, 1888.

Abbott, John S. C. "Heroic Deeds of Heroic Men." *Harper's New Monthly Mag.* 32/191:567 (4/1866).

Abbott, Martin, and Elmer L. Puryear. "Beleaguered Charleston: Letters from the City, 1860–1864." *S.C. Hist. Mag.* 61/2:19 (4/1960).

Abrahamson, James L. *Men of Secession and Civil War, 1859–1861.* Wilmington, DE: SR Books, 2000.

Adams, Charles Francis, Jr. "The British Proclamation of May, 1861." *Proc. Mass. Hist. Soc.* 48:190 (1/1915).

———. *Charles Francis Adams 1835–1915: An Autobiography.* Boston: Houghton Mifflin, 1916.

———. *Charles Francis Adams by His Son Charles Francis Adams.* Boston: Houghton Mifflin, 1900.

———. *"The Constitutional Ethics of Secession"* [1902] *and "War Is Hell."* Boston, 1903.

———. "A Crisis in Downing Street." *Proc. Mass. Hist. Soc.* 47:372 (5/1914).

———. "The Golgotha Year." *Proc. Mass. Hist. Soc.* 47:333 (4/1914).

[———]. "Reign of King Cotton." *Atlantic Monthly* 7/42:451 (4/1861).

———. "Shall Cromwell Have a Statue?" *University [of Chicago] Record* 7/2:52 (June 1902).

Adams, Charles Francis, Sr. *The Civil War Diaries.* Boston, 2015. Available online at www .masshist.org/publications/cfa-civil-war/view?id=DCA61d090.

Adams, Ephraim Douglass. *Great Britain and the American Civil War.* London: Longmans, Green, 1925. 2 vols.

Adams, Henry. *The Education of Henry Adams: An Autobiography.* 1906; 1907; Boston: Houghton Mifflin, 1918.

———. "The Great Secession Winter" [ca. April 1861]. *Proc. Mass. Hist. Soc.* 43:660 (June 1910).

———. *Henry Adams in the Secession Crisis.* Edited and annotated by Mark J. Stegmaier. Baton Rouge: Louisiana State University Press, 2012.

———. *Letters of Henry Adams.* Edited by J. C. Levenson et al. Cambridge, MA: Belknap Press of Harvard University Press, 1982–1988. 6 vols.

———. *Letters of Henry Adams*. Edited by Worthington Chauncey Ford. Boston: Houghton Mifflin, 1930–1938. 2 vols.

Adams, Michael C. C. *Our Masters the Rebels*. Cambridge, MA: Harvard University Press, 1978.

Adams, Nehemiah. *South-Side View of Slavery*. Boston: J. C. Derby, 1854.

Allmendinger, David F., Jr. *Ruffin: Family and Reform in the Old South*. New York: Oxford University Press, 1990.

Amar, Akhil Reed. "Abraham Lincoln and the American Union." *U. Ill. L. Rev.* 2001:1109 (2001).

———. *America's Constitution: A Biography*. New York: Random House, 2005.

———. "Of Sovereignty and Federalism." *Yale L.J.* 96:1425 (1987).

Ambler, Charles Henry. *Life and Diary of John Floyd*. Richmond, VA: Richmond Press, 1918.

———. *Sectionalism in Virginia from 1776 to 1861*. Chicago: University of Chicago Press, 1910.

Anderson, Lawrence M. *Federalism, Secession, and the American State*. New York: Routledge, 2013.

Anderson, Robert. *An Artillery Officer in the Mexican War 1846–7*. Edited by Eba Anderson Lawton. New York: G. P. Putnam's Sons, 1911.

———. "Reminiscences of the Black Hawk War" (5/10, 6/20/1870). *Collections of the State Hist. Soc. of Wisc.* 10:167 (1888).

Anderson Diary. Copies of extracts of diary of Robert Anderson and letters in "Anderson, Robert Diary & Letters (copies)" folder. *Nicolay Papers*, Box 12.

Anderson Papers. Robert Anderson Papers, Library of Congress. MSS 10967, bound volume [box] 1.

Anderson, Thomas M. *Political Conspiracies Preceding the Rebellion*. New York, 1882.

Andrews, Sidney. *The South since the War*. Boston, 1866.

Appleton. American Annual Cyclopædia and Register of Important Events of the Year 1861. New York, 1864.

Ashley, J. M. "Calhoun, Seward and Lincoln II." *Mag. of Western Hist.* 13/1:1 (11/1890).

Ashworth, John. *Slavery, Capitalism, and Politics in the Antebellum Republic*. Cambridge: Cambridge University Press, 1996–2007. 2 vols.

Assessment. National Park Service. *Fort Sumter Historic Structure Assessment Report*. 11/30/1992.

Att'y-Gen. Ops. United States Attorney General. *Official Opinions of the Attorneys General of the United States*. Compiled by Benjamin F. Hall. Washington, 1852–1870. 12 vols.

Auchampaugh, Philip Gerald. *James Buchanan and His Cabinet on the Eve of Secession*. Lancaster, PA: privately printed, 1926.

———. "John B. Floyd and James Buchanan." *Tyler's Quart. Hist. & Geneal. Mag.* 4/4:381 (4/1923).

Austin, George Lowell. "The Conspiracy of 1860–61." *Bay State Monthly* 3/4:233 (9/1885).

Ayers, Edward L. *In the Presence of Mine Enemies: War in the Heart of America 1859–1863*. New York: Norton, 2003.

———. *What Caused the Civil War? Reflections on the South and Southern History*. New York: Norton, 2005.

Ayers, Edward L., Gary W. Gallagher, and Andrew J. Torget. *Crucible of the Civil War*. Charlottesville: University Press of Virginia, 2006.

Bache, Alexander Dallas, et al. *Report on the Harbor of Charleston*. Charleston, 1852. Reprinted in, for example, U.S. Cong. Sen. Ex. Doc. no. 1 (33/1) App. MM, 435.

Baldwin, John B. *Interview between President Lincoln and Col. John B. Baldwin, April 4, 1861*. Staunton, VA, 1866.

Bancroft, Frederic. "The Final Efforts at Compromise, 1860–61." *Pol. Sci. Quart.* 6/3:401 (9/1891).

———. *The Life of William H. Seward*. New York: Harper & Brothers, 1900. 2 vols.

———. "Seward's Attitude toward Compromise and Secession, 1860–61." *Atlantic Monthly* 74/445:597 (11/1894).

Barbee, David Rankin. "The Line of Blood: Lincoln and the Coming of the War." *Tenn. Hist. Quart.* 16/1:3 (3/1957).

Baringer, William E. *House Dividing: Lincoln as President Elect*. Springfield, IL: Abraham Lincoln Ass'n, 1945.

Barnes, Frank. *Fort Sumter: National Monument South Carolina*. 1952, rev. ed. Washington, DC: U.S. Dep't of the Interior, National Park Service, 1962.

[Barnes, Frank, et al.]. *Fort Sumter: Anvil of War*. Washington, DC: National Park Service, Division of Publications, U.S. Department of the Interior, 1984 [rev. ed. of Barnes, Frank, supra].

Barnes, James J., and Patience P. Barnes, eds. *The American Civil War through British Eyes: Dispatches from British Diplomats*. Kent, OH: Kent State University Press, 2003[?]–2005. Vol. 1.

Barnes, Thurlow Weed. *Memoir of Thurlow Weed*. Boston, 1884. 2 vols.

Barney, William L. *The Road to Secession*. New York: Praeger, 1972.

———. *The Secessionist Impulse*. Princeton, NJ: Princeton University Press, 1974.

Bartleson, John D., Jr. *Field Guide for Civil War Explosive Ordnance*. Indian Head, MD: U.S. Naval School, Explosive Ordnance Disposal, Naval Ordnance Station, 1972.

Basler, Roy P., et al., eds. *Collected Works of Abraham Lincoln*. New Brunswick, NJ: Rutgers University Press, 1953–1955. 9 vols. Supplement. Westport, CT: Greenwood, 1974.

Bateman, Fred, and Thomas Weiss. *Deplorable Scarcity*. Chapel Hill: University of North Carolina Press, 1981.

Bates, Edward. *Diary of Edward Bates 1859–1866*. Edited by Howard K. Beale. Washington, DC: U.S. Gov't Printing Office, 1933.

Battle of Fort Sumter. Battle of Fort Sumter and the First Victory of the Southern Troops. Charleston, 1861.

Baxter, Maurice G. *One and Inseparable*. Cambridge, MA: Harvard University Press, 1984.

Bayard, James A., Jr. *Brief Exposition of the Constitution of the United States*. Philadelphia, 1833.

Beard, Charles A. *Economic Interpretation of the Constitution of the United States*. 1913; New York: Macmillan, 1921.

Beard, Charles A., and Mary R. Beard. *The Rise of American Civilization*. New York: Macmillan, 1927. 2 vols.

Beckert, Sven. *Empire of Cotton: A Global History*. New York: Knopf, 2014.

Bearss, Edwin C. "Civil War Operations in and around Pensacola." *Fla. Hist. Quart.* 36/2:125 (10/1957), 39/3:234 (1/1961).

———. *The First Two Fort Moultries*. Washington, DC: Division of History, U.S. Office of Archeology and Historic Preservation, 1968.

———. "Fort Pickens and the Secession Crisis: January-February 1861." *Gulf Coast Hist. Rev.* 4/2:6 (Spring 1989).

———. *Historic Structure Report/Fort Pickens/Historical Data Section/1821–1895*. Denver, CO: U.S. Dep't of the Interior, Historical Preservation Division, Denver Service Center, National Park Service, 1983.

Beeman, Richard, Stephen Botein, and Edward C. Carter II, eds. *Beyond Confederation*. Chapel Hill: University of North Carolina Press, 1987.

Bell, Jack. *Civil War Heavy Explosive Ordnance*. Denton: University of North Texas Press, 2003.

Belmont, August. *Letters[,] Speeches and Addresses of August Belmont*. [New York?], 1890.

Bemis, Samuel Flagg, ed. *American Secretaries of State and Their Diplomacy*. New York: Knopf, 1927–1929. 10 vols.

Beringer, Richard E., et al. *Why the South Lost the Civil War*. Athens: University of Georgia Press, 1986.

Berlin, Ira, and Herbert G. Gutman. "Natives and Immigrants, Free Men and Slaves." *Am. Hist. Rev.* 88/5:1175 (12/1983).

Bernardo, C. Joseph, and Eugene H. Bacon. *American Military Policy*. 1955; 2nd ed. Harrisburg, PA: Military Service, 1961.

Bigelow, John. *Retrospections of an Active Life*. New York: Baker & Taylor, 1909–1913. 5 vols.

Birkner, Michael J. *James Buchanan and the Political Crisis of the 1850s*. Selinsgrove, PA: Susquehanna University Press, 1996.

[Black, Chauncey F.]. *Life of Abraham Lincoln by Ward H. Lamon*. Boston, 1872.

Black, Jeremiah S. *Essays and Speeches of Jeremiah S. Black*. Compiled by C. F. Black. New York, 1886.

Blackett, R. J. M. *Divided Hearts: Britain and the Civil War*. Baton Rouge: Louisiana State University Press, 2001.

Blaine, James G. *Twenty Years of Congress*. Norwich, CT, 1884. 2 vols.

Blair, Montgomery. "The Rebellion—Where the Guilt Lies: Speech of the Hon. Montgomery Blair, Delivered at Clarksville, Howard County, Md., on August 26, 1865."

———. "The Republican Party as It Was and Is." *N. Am. Rev.* 288:422 (11/1880).

———, comp. "Confederate Documents Relating to Fort Sumter." *United Service* 4:358 (3/1881).

Blair Family Papers. Blair Family Papers, Library of Congress.

Bledsoe, Albert Taylor. *Essay on Liberty and Slavery*. Philadelphia, 1856.

———. *Is Davis a Traitor?* Baltimore, 1866.

Blumenthal, Sidney. *A Self-Made Man: The Political Life of Abraham Lincoln, 1809–1849*. New York: Simon & Schuster, 2016.

Bonner, Michael, and Fritz Hamer, eds. *South Carolina in the Civil War and Reconstruction Eras*. Columbia: University of South Carolina Press, 2016.

Boritt, Gabor S., ed. *Lincoln, The War President*. New York: Oxford University Press, 1992.

———, ed. *Why the Civil War Came*. New York: Oxford University Press, 1996.

Botts, John Minor. *The Great Rebellion: Its Secret History, Rise, Progress, and Disastrous Failure*. New York, 1866.

Bowman, Shearer Davis. *At the Precipice*. Chapel Hill: University of North Carolina Press, 2010.

Boynton, Charles B. *History of the Navy During the Rebellion*. New York, 1867–1868. 2 vols.

Brackett, Anna C. "Charleston, South Carolina (1861)." *Harper's* 88:941 (5/1894).

Bradford, James C., ed. *Captains of the Old Steam Navy*. Annapolis, MD: Naval Institute Press, 1986.

Brauer, Kinley J. "Seward's 'Foreign War Panacea': An Interpretation." *NY Hist.* 55/1:132 (1/1974).

Bridges, Peter. *Donn Piatt: Gadfly of the Gilded Age*. Kent, OH: Kent State University Press, 2012.

Brown, Ernest Francis. *Raymond of the "Times."* New York: Norton, 1951.

Browning, Orville Hickman. *Diary of Orville Hickman Browning*. Edited by Theodore Calvin Pease and James G. Randall. Springfield: Trustees of the Illinois State Historical Society, 1925–1933. 2 vols.

Browning, Robert S., III. *Two If by Sea: The Development of American Coastal Defense Policy*. Westport, CT: Greenwood, 1983.

Bruce, Robert V. "The Shadow of a Coming War." In Boritt (1992) 1.

Bryan, Edward B. *The Rightful Remedy*. Charleston, 1850.

[Buchanan, James]. *Mr. Buchanan's Administration on the Eve of the Rebellion*. New York, 1866.

———. *Works of James Buchanan*. Edited by John Bassett Moore. Philadelphia: J. B. Lippincott, 1908–1911. 12 vols.

Buel, Clarence C., and Robert U. Johnson, eds. *Battles and Leaders of the Civil War*. 1884–1887; New York, 1887. 4 vols.

Bulloch, James D. *The Secret Service of the Confederate States in Europe*. New York, 1884. 2 vols.

Burgess, John William. *The Civil War and the Constitution 1859–1865*. New York: C. Scribner's Sons, 1901. 2 vols.

Burlingame, Michael. *Abraham Lincoln: A Life*. Baltimore: Johns Hopkins University Press, 2008. 2 vols.

———. *Lincoln and the Civil War*. Carbondale: Southern Illinois University Press, 2011.

Burton, E. M. *The Siege of Charleston, 1861–1865*. Columbia: University of South Carolina Press, 1970.

Calhoun, John C. *Papers of John C. Calhoun*. Edited by Robert L. Meriwether et al. Columbia: University of South Carolina Press, 1959–2003. 28 vols.

Callahan, James Morton. *Diplomatic History of the Southern Confederacy*. Baltimore: Johns Hopkins Press, 1901.

Campbell, John A. "Facts of History" [before 7/10/1865]. In Connor 122.

———. Letter to G. W. Munford (12/20/1873). *Trans. South. Hist. Soc.* 1:22 (1874).

———. "Papers of Hon. John A. Campbell—1861–1865." *South. Hist. Soc. Papers.* n.s. 4:3 (10/1917).

Capers, Henry D. *Life and Times of C. G. Memminger*. Richmond, VA, 1893.

Carroll, Daniel B. *Henry Mercier and the American Civil War*. Princeton, NJ: Princeton University Press, 1971.

Cartwright, David E. *Tides: A Scientific History*. Cambridge: Cambridge University Press, 1999.

Castel, Albert. "Fort Sumter—1861." *Civil War Times Ill.* 15/6:3 (10/1976).

Catton, Bruce. *The Coming Fury. The Centennial History of the Civil War*. Vol. 1. Garden City, NY: Doubleday, 1961.

Catton, William, and Bruce Catton. *Two Roads to Sumter*. New York: McGraw-Hill, 1963.

Cauthen, Charles Edward. *South Carolina Goes to War 1860–1865*. Columbia: University of South Carolina Press, 1950.

———. "South Carolina's Decision to Lead the Secession Movement." *N.C. Hist. Rev.* 18/4:360 (10/1941).

Chadwick, French Ensor. *Causes of the Civil War 1859–1861*. New York: Harper & Brothers, 1906.

Chalfant, Edward. *Both Sides of the Ocean: A Biography of Henry Adams*. Hamden, CT: Archon Books, 1982.

Channing, Edward. *The War for Southern Independence*. Vol. 6 of *History of the United States*. New York: Macmillan, 1925.

Channing, Steven A. *Crisis of Fear: Secession in South Carolina*. New York: Simon & Schuster, 1970.

Charleston Yearbook. Year Book—1883 City of Charleston, So. Ca. Charleston, [1883].

[Chesney, Charles C.]. "The American Navy in the Late War." *Edinburgh Rev.* no. 253, vol. 124:185 (7/1866).

Chester, James. "Inside Sumter in '61." In Buel/Johnson 1:50.

Chestnutt, David R., and Clyde N. Wilson, eds. *The Meaning of South Carolina History: Essays in Honor of George C. Rogers, Jr.* Columbia: University of South Carolina Press, 1991.

Chisolm, Alexander Robert. "Notes on the Surrender of Fort Sumter." In Buel/Johnson 1:82.

Clowes, William L. *The Royal Navy: A History from the Earliest Times to the Present*. London, 1897–1903. 7 vols.

Coast Survey 1851. U.S. Cong. H.R. Exec. Doc. 3: Annual Rpt. of the Superintendent of the Coast Survey . . . During the Year Ending November, 1851. 32/1. Washington, 1851.

Coast Survey 1855. U.S. Cong., Sen. Exec. Doc. 22: Rpt. of the Superintendent of the Coast Survey . . . During the Year 1855. 34/1. Washington, 1856.

Coast Survey 1859. U.S. Cong. H.R. Exec. Doc. 41: Rpt. of the Superintendent of the Coast Survey . . . During the Year 1859. 36/1. Washington, 1860.

Coast Survey 1860. U.S. Cong. H.R. Exec. Doc. 14: Rpt. of the Superintendent of the Coast Survey . . . During the Year 1860. 36/2. Washington, 1861.

Coletta, Paolo E., ed. *American Secretaries of the Navy*. Annapolis, MD: Naval Institute Press, 1980. Vol. 1.

Commissioners. Transcripts of the "Correspondence of the Southern Commissioners . . . with certificate . . . signed by J. H. Saville . . . June 10, 1873." [Copies by Col. John Pickett.] Rosenbach Museum & Library, Philadelphia.

Confederate Congress. Journal of the Congress of the Confederate States of America. Washington, DC: Government Printing Office, 1904–1905. 3 vols.

Connor, Henry G. *John Archibald Campbell: Associate Justice of the Supreme Court*. Boston: Houghton Mifflin, 1920.

Convention Journal. Journal of the Convention of the People of South Carolina, Held in 1860, 1861 and 1862. Columbia, SC, 1862.

Cook, Robert J., William L. Barney, and Elizabeth R. Varon. *Secession Winter*. Baltimore: Johns Hopkins University Press, 2013.

Cooper, Edward S. *Traitors: The Secession Period; November 1860–July 1861*. Madison, NJ: Fairleigh Dickinson University Press, 2008.

Cooper, William J., Jr. *Jefferson Davis, American*. New York: Knopf, 2000.

————. *The South and the Politics of Slavery 1828–1856*. Baton Rouge: Louisiana State University Press, 1978.

————. *We Have the War upon Us: The Onset of the Civil War, November 1860–April 1861*. New York: Knopf, 2012.

Crafts, William A. *The Southern Rebellion*. Boston, 1869. 2 vols.

Craven, Avery. *The Coming of the Civil War*. 2nd ed. Chicago: University of Chicago Press, 1957.

————. *Edmund Ruffin: Southerner*. New York: Appleton, 1932.

Crawford, Samuel Wylie. "The First Shot Against the Flag." In McClure (1879) 319.

————. *Fort Sumter Diary*. In *Crawford Papers*.

————. *The Genesis of the Civil War*. New York, 1887.

————. *History of the Fall of Fort Sumter*. New York, 1896.

————, comp. *Illustrated Catalogue of the Unique and Valuable Collection of Autographs, Manuscripts and Documents of Persons Intimately Connected with the Civil War and Fort Sumter.* New York: n.p.: 1915.

Crawford Papers. Papers of Samuel Wylie Crawford, Library of Congress.

Crittenden, John J. *Life of John J. Crittenden*. Edited by Chapman Colman. Philadelphia, 1873. 2 vols.

Crofts, Daniel W. "James E. Harvey and the Secession Crisis." *Penn. Mag. of Hist. & Biog.* 103/2:177 (4/1979).

————. *Reluctant Confederates: Upper South Unionists in the Secession Crisis*. Chapel Hill: University of North Carolina Press, 1989.

————. *Secessionist Crisis Enigma*. Baton Rouge: Louisiana State University Press, 2010.

————. "The Union Party of 1861 and the Secession Crisis." *Perspectives in Am. Hist.* 11:327 (1977–1978).

Cullum, George W. *Biographical Register of the Officers and Graduates of the U.S. Military Academy*. 3rd ed. Boston, 1891. 3 vols.

Current, Richard N. "Confederates and the First Shot." *Civil War Hist.* 7/4:357 (12/1961).

————. *Lincoln and the First Shot*. Philadelphia: Lippincott, 1963.

————. *The Lincoln Nobody Knows*. New York: McGraw-Hill, 1958.

Currie, David P. *The Constitution in Congress*. Chicago: University of Chicago Press, 1997–2005. 4 vols.

Curry, J. L. M. *Civil History of the Government of the Confederate States*. Richmond, VA: B. F. Johnson, 1901.

Curtis, George Ticknor. *Life of James Buchanan, Fifteenth President of the United States*. New York, 1883. 2 vols.

Dabney, Robert Lewis. "Memoir of a Narrative Received of Colonel John B. Baldwin, of Staunton, Touching the Origin of the War." *South. Hist. Soc. Papers* 1/6:443 (6/1876).

Dahlgren, John A. *Boat Armament of the U.S. Navy*. 2nd ed. Philadelphia, 1856 ("1856A").

————. *Shells and Shell-Guns*. Philadelphia, 1856 ("1856B").

————. *System of Boat Armament in the United States Navy*. Philadelphia, 1852.

DANFS. *Dictionary of American Naval Fighting Ships*. Washington, DC: U.S. Printing Office, 1959–1981. 8 vols. www.history.navy.mil/danfs.

Davis, George B., et al. *Atlas to Accompany the Official Records of the Union and Confederate Armies*. Washington, 1891–1895.

Davis, Jefferson. Address to C.S.A. Congress (4/29/1861). In *OR* Ser. 4, vol. 1, p. 256.

———. *Jefferson Davis Constitutionalist*. Edited by Dunbar Rowland. Jackson: Mississippi Dep't of Archives and History, 1923. 10 vols.

———. *Papers of Jefferson Davis*. Edited by Haskell M. Monroe Jr. and James McIntosh. Baton Rouge: Louisiana State University Press, 1971–. 14 vols. to date.

———. *The Rise and Fall of the Confederate Government*. 1881; Richmond, VA: Garrett and Massie, 1938. 2 vols.

Davis, Varina. *Jefferson Davis, Ex-President of the Confederate States of America*. New York, 1890. 2 vols.

Davis, William C. *The Union That Shaped the Confederacy*. Lawrence: University Press of Kansas, 2001.

Davis, William Watson. *The Civil War and Reconstruction in Florida*. New York: Columbia University, 1913.

Dawson, Henry B. "The Story of Fort Sumter." *Hist. Mag., and Notes and Queries*. 3rd ser. 1/1:34, 1/3:139 (1, 3/1872).

De Bow, James D. B., and Robert N. Gourdin. "The Non-Slaveholders of the South" (12/5/1860), *De Bow's Rev*. 30:67 (1/1861).

[De Fontaine, Felix Gregory (?)]. "Shoulder to Shoulder: Reminiscences of Confederate Camps and Fields" (1, 2). *XIX Century* 1/1:35, 1/2:85 (6, 7/1869).

[De Forest, John William]. "Charleston under Arms." *Atlantic Monthly* 7/42:488 (4/1861).

Degler, Carl N. *The Other South: Southern Dissenters in the Nineteenth Century*. New York: Harper & Row, 1974.

Denton, Lawrence M. *Unionists in Virginia*. Charleston: History Press, 2014.

———. *William Henry Seward and the Secession Crisis*. Jefferson, NC: McFarland, 2009.

Detzer, David. *Allegiance: Fort Sumter, Charleston, and the Beginning of the Civil War*. New York: Harcourt, 2001.

Dew, Charles B. *Apostles of Disunion*. Charlottesville: University Press of Virginia, 2016.

Dibble, Ernest F. "War Averters: Seward, Mallory, and Fort Pickens." *Fla. Hist. Quart*. 49/3: 232 (1/1971).

Dickert, D. Augustus. *History of Kershaw's Brigade*. Newberry, SC, 1899.

Dickinson, Daniel S. *Speeches, Correspondence, Etc., of the Late Daniel S. Dickinson*. New York, 1867. 2 vols.

Dickinson, W. C., et al., eds. *Montgomery C. Meigs and the Building of the Nation's Capital*. Athens: Ohio University Press, 2001.

Donald, David Herbert. *Lincoln*. New York: Simon & Schuster, 1995.

Doubleday, Abner. "From Moultrie to Sumter." In Buel/Johnson 1:43.

———. *My Life in the Old Army*. Edited by Joseph E. Chance. Fort Worth: Texas Christian University Press, 1998.

———. *Reminiscences of Forts Sumter and Moultrie in 1860–'61*. New York, 1876.

Doyle, Don H., ed. *Secession as an International Phenomenon*. Athens: University of Georgia Press, 2010.

Draper, John William. *History of the American Civil War*. New York, 1868. 3 vols.

Duberman, Martin B. *Charles Francis Adams 1807–1886*. Boston: Houghton Mifflin, 1961.

DuBose, John Witherspoon. *Life and Times of William Lowndes Yancey*. Birmingham, AL, 1892. 2 vols.

Dumond, Dwight Lowell. *The Secession Movement 1860–1861*. New York: Macmillan, 1931 ("1931A").

———. *Southern Editorials on Secession*. New York: Century, 1931 ("1931B").

Durkin, Joseph T. *Confederate Navy Chief: Stephen R. Mallory*. 1954; Columbia: University of South Carolina Press, 1987.

East, Sherrod E. "The Banishment of Captain Meigs." *Rec. Columbia Hist. Soc. of Wash., D.C.* 40:97 (1940).

Edmunds, John B., Jr. "Francis W. Pickens: A Political Biography." PhD diss., University of South Carolina, 1967.

———. *Francis W. Pickens and the Politics of Destruction*. Chapel Hill: University of North Carolina Press, 1986.

———. "Francis W. Pickens and the War Begins." 1970. In Bonner and Hamer 27.

Egerton, Douglas R. *Year of Meteors*. New York: Bloomsbury, 2010.

Egnal, Marc. *Clash of Extremes: The Economic Origins of the Civil War*. New York: Hill and Wang, 2009.

Eicher, David J. *The Longest Night: A Military History of the Civil War*. New York: Simon & Schuster, 2001.

Eisenhower, John S. D. *Agent of Destiny: The Life and Times of General Winfield Scott*. New York: Free Press, 1997.

Elliot, Jonathan, comp. *Debates in the Several State Conventions, on the Adoption of the Federal Constitution*. 2nd ed. Washington, 1836–1845. 5 vols.

Elliott, Charles Winslow. *Winfield Scott: The Soldier and the Man*. New York: Macmillan, 1937.

Erben, Henry. "Surrender of the Navy Yard at Pensacola" (1894). In *Personal Recollections of the War of the Rebellion*, edited by Alexander Noel Blakeman. 2nd Serv. New York, 1897.

Evans, Clement Anselm, ed. *Confederate Military History*. Atlanta, 1899. 12 vols.

Farrand, Max, ed. *The Records of the Federal Convention of 1787*. New Haven, CT: Yale University Press, 1911, 1937. 4 vols.

Farrow, Edward S. *Farrow's Military Encyclopedia*. New York, 1885.

Faulkner, Thomas C. *Faulkner's History of the Revolution in the Southern States*. New York, 1861.

Faust, Drew Gilpin. *James Henry Hammond and the Old South: Design for Mastery*. Baton Rouge: Louisiana State University Press, 1982.

Fehrenbacher, Don E. *The Dred Scott Case: Its Significance in American Law & Politics*. New York: Oxford University Press, 1978.

———. "The New Political History and the Coming of the War." *Pac. Hist. Rev.* 54/2:117 (5/1985).

———. *Prelude to Greatness: Lincoln in the 1850s*. Stanford, CA: Stanford University Press, 1962.

Fehrenbacher, Don E., and Virginia Fehrenbacher, comps. *Recollected Words of Abraham Lincoln*. Stanford, CA: Stanford University Press, 1996.

Ferris, Norman B. *Desperate Diplomacy: William H. Seward's Foreign Policy, 1861*. Knoxville: University of Tennessee Press, 1976.

———. "Lincoln and Seward in Civil War Diplomacy." *J. Abraham Lincoln Ass'n* 12/1:21 (1991).

Finkelman, Paul. "States' Rights, Southern Hypocrisy, and the Crisis of the Union." *Akron L. Rev.* 45:449 (2012).

Fishel, Edwin C. *The Secret War for the Union*. Boston: Houghton Mifflin, 1996.

[Fletcher, A., Miss]. *Within Fort Sumter*. New York, 1861.

Flower, Frank A. *Edwin McMasters Stanton*. Boston: W. W. Wilson, 1905.

Foner, Eric. *Free Soil, Free Labor, Free Men: The Ideology of the Republican Party before the Civil War*. New York: Oxford University Press, 1970.

———, ed. *Our Lincoln: New Perspectives on Lincoln and His World*. New York: Norton, 2008.

Foner, Philip S. *Business & Slavery: The New York Merchants & the Irrepressible Conflict*. Chapel Hill: University of North Carolina Press, 1941.

Foote, Shelby. *The Civil War: A Narrative*. Vol. 1: *Fort Sumter to Perryville*. New York: Random House, 1958.

Forbes, John Murray. *Letters and Recollections of John Murray Forbes*. Edited by Sarah Forbes Hughes. Boston, 1899. 2 vols.

Ford, Lacy K. "James Louis Petigru." In O'Brien and Moltke-Hansen (1986).

Foreign Relations. U.S. Cong. H.R., Exec. Doc., Message of the President of the United States to the Two Houses of Congress (37/2). Vol. 1.

Foreman, Amanda. *A World on Fire: Britain's Crucial Role in the American Civil War*. New York: Random House, 2010.

Fort Sumter Memorial. New York: E. C. Hill, 1915.

Foster, John G. Letter to John H. B. Latrobe (1/10, 1861). In "The Evacuation of Fort Moultrie, 1860," edited by Frank F. White Jr. *S.C. Hist. Mag.* 53/1:1 (1/1952).

———. "Report of Major General J. G. Foster." In U.S. Cong., Jt. Comm. on the Conduct of the War. *Supplemental Report of the Joint Committee on the Conduct of the War*. Washington, 1866. Vol. 2.

Fowler, William Chauncey. *The Sectional Controversy*. 1862. 2nd ed. New York, 1868.

Fowler, William M., Jr. *Under Two Flags: The American Navy in the Civil War*. New York: Norton, 1990.

Fox, Gustavus V. *Confidential Correspondence of Gustavus Vasa Fox*. Edited by Robert Means Thompson and Richard Wainwright. 1918–1919; New York: De Vinne, 1920. 2 vols.

———. "Memorandum of Facts [to Gideon Welles] Concerning the Attempt to Send Supplies to Fort Sumter in 1861" (2/24/1865). In F. Moore (1861–1866) 9:208, *NYT* (9/11/1865), Boynton 1:252.

———. "Memorandum of Facts in Regard to the Attempt to Provision Fort Sumter, in 1861" (1865). In *Contributions of the Old Residents' Hist. Ass'n, Lowell, Mass.* 2/1:38 (11/1880).

Fox Collection. Gustavus Vasa Fox Collection. New-York Historical Society.

Franklin, John Hope. *The Militant South 1800–1861*. Cambridge, MA: Belknap Press of Harvard University Press, 1956.

Fraser, Charles. *Reminiscences of Charleston*. Charleston, 1854.

Fraser, Walter J., Jr. *Charleston! Charleston! The History of a Southern City*. Columbia: University of South Carolina Press, 1989.

Fredrickson, George M. *The Inner Civil War*. New York: Harper & Row, 1965.

Freehling, William W. *The Reintegration of American History*. New York: Oxford University Press, 1994.

———. *The Road to Disunion*. Vol. 1, *Secessionists at Bay, 1776–1854*. New York: Oxford University Press, 1990.

———. *The Road to Disunion*. Vol. 2, *Secessionists Triumphant 1854–1861*. New York: Oxford University Press, 2007.

Freidel, Frank, ed. *Union Pamphlets of the Civil War*. Cambridge, MA: Belknap Press of Harvard University Press, 1967.

[French, J. Clement, and Edward Cary]. *The Trip of the Steamer Oceanus*. Brooklyn, NY, 1865.

Frost, J. Blakeslee. *The Rebellion in the United States*. Hartford, CT, 1862.

Furgurson, Ernest B. *Freedom Rising: Washington in the Civil War*. New York: Knopf, 2004.

Gallagher, Gary W. *The Confederate War*. Cambridge, MA: Harvard University Press, 1997.

[Garrison, William Lloyd (attrib.)]. *The New "Reign of Terror" in the Slaveholding States, for 1859–60*. New York, 1860.

General Orders. General Orders of the War Department Embracing the Years 1861, 1862 & 1863. New York, 1864.

General Regulations. General Regulations for the Army of the United States, 1841. Washington, 1841.

Genovese, Eugene D. *The Slaveholders' Dilemma: Freedom and Progress in Southern Conservative Thought, 1820–1860*. Columbia: University of South Carolina Press, 1992.

Geyle, Pieter. "The American Civil War and the Problem of Inevitability." *New Eng. Quart.* 24/2:147 (6/1951).

Gibbon, John, comp. *The Artillerist's Manual*. 1860; 2nd ed. New York, 1863.

Gibson, Charles Dana, and E. Kay Gibson, comps. *The Army's Navy Series*. Camden, ME: Ensign, 1995. 2 vols.

Gienapp, William E. *Abraham Lincoln and Civil War America: A Biography*. Oxford: Oxford University Press, 2002.

———. "The Crisis of American Democracy." In Boritt (1996).

———. *The Origins of the Republican Party 1852–1856*. New York: Oxford University Press, 1987.

Gillmore, Q. A. *Engineer and Artillery Operations against the Defences of Charleston Harbor in 1863*. New York, 1865.

Gilman, Alfred. "Capt. G. V. Fox in the War of the Rebellion" (8/6/1879). In *Contributions of the Old Residents' Hist. Ass'n, Lowell, Mass.* 2/1:33 (11/1880).

Gilman, Jeremiah H. "With Slemmer in Pensacola Harbor." In Buel/Johnson 1:26.

Globe. Congressional Globe: Debates and Proceedings, 1833–1873. Washington, 1833–1873. 46 vols.

Goodheart, Adam. *1861: The Civil War Awakening*. New York: Knopf, 2011.

Goodwin, Doris Kearns. *Team of Rivals: The Political Genius of Abraham Lincoln*. New York: Simon & Schuster, 2005.

Goodyear Collection. Anson Conger Goodyear Collection (MS 244), Yale University Library.

Gordon, George H. "Major Anderson at Fort Sumter" (1882). *Papers of the Mil. Hist. Soc. of Mass.* 9:1 (1912).

Gorham, George C. *Life and Public Services of Edwin M. Stanton*. Boston, 1899. 2 vols.

Grady, John. *Matthew Fontaine Maury, Father of Oceanography*. Jefferson, NC: McFarland, 2015.

Grayson, William John. *James Louis Petigru: A Biographical Sketch*. New York, 1866.

Greeley, Horace. *The American Conflict: A History of the Great Rebellion*. Vol. 1. Hartford, CT, 1864.

————. *Greeley on Lincoln*. Edited by Joel Benton. 1891; New York, 1893.

Green, Michael S. *Lincoln and the Election of 1860*. Carbondale: Southern Illinois University Press, 2011.

Greenberg, Kenneth S. *Masters and Statesmen: Political Culture of American Slavery*. Baltimore: Johns Hopkins University Press, 1985.

Guelzo, Allen C. *Fateful Lightning: A New History of the Civil War and Reconstruction*. New York: Oxford University Press, 2012.

Guernsey, Alfred H., and Henry Mills Alden. *Harper's Pictorial History of the Civil War*. Chicago, 1894. Vol. 1.

Guess, William Francis. *South Carolina: Annals of Pride and Protest*. New York: Harper, 1960.

Gurowski, Adam. *Diary*. Boston, 1862–1866. Vol. 1.

Gwin, William M., and Evan J. Coleman. "Doctor Gwin and Judge Black." *Overland Monthly* 19:87 (1/1892).

————. "Gwin and Seward.—A Secret Chapter in Ante-Bellum History." *Overland Monthly* 18:469 (11/1891).

HABS. Historic American Buildings Survey, NABS No. SC-194, Fort Sumter. Philadelphia, [various dates].

Hagood, Johnson. *Memoirs of the War of Secession*. Edited by U. R. Brooks. Columbia, SC: State Company, 1910.

Hall, Wilmer L. "Lincoln's Interview with John B. Baldwin." *S. Atl. Quart.* 13/3:260 (July 1914).

Halleck, H. Wager. *Elements of Military Art and Science*. 1846; 2nd ed. New York, 1860.

Halstead, Murat. *Caucuses of 1860: A History of the National Political Conventions*. Columbus, OH, 1860.

Hammond, James H. *Oration on the Life, Character and Services of John Caldwell Calhoun*. Charleston, 1850.

————. *Secret and Sacred: The Diaries of James Henry Hammond, a Southern Slaveholder*. New York: Oxford University Press, 1988.

————. *Selections from the Letters and Speeches of James Henry Hammond*. New York, 1866.

Hammond Papers. James Henry Hammond Papers, Library of Congress.

Harris, W. A., comp. *The Record of Fort Sumter, from Its Occupation by Major Anderson, to Its Reduction by South Carolina Troops*. Columbia, SC, 1862.

Harris, William C. *Leroy Pope Walker*. Tuscaloosa, AL: Confederate, 1962.

————. *Lincoln and the Union Governors*. Carbondale: Southern Illinois University Press, 2013.

————. "The Southern Unionist Critique of the Civil War." *Civil War Hist.* 31/1:39 (3/1985).

Harrold, Stanley. *Border War: Fighting over Slavery before the Civil War*. Chapel Hill: University of North Carolina Press, 2010.

Hay, John. *At Lincoln's Side: John Hay's Civil War Correspondence and Selected Writings*. Edited by Michael Burlingame. Carbondale: Southern Illinois University Press, 2000.

————. *Letters of John Hay and Extracts from Diary*. Washington: privately printed, 1908. Vol. 1.

————. *Life and Letters of John Hay*. Edited by William Roscoe Thayer. Boston: Houghton Mifflin, 1915. 2 vols.

————. *Lincoln's Journalist: John Hay's Anonymous Writings for the Press, 1860–1864*. Edited by Michael Burlingame. Carbondale: Southern Illinois University Press, 1998.

Hayne, Isaac W., et al. *Correspondence and Other Papers Relating to Fort Sumter*. 2nd ed. Charleston, 1861.

Hazlett, James, Edwin Olmstead, and M. Hume Parks. *Field Artillery Weapons of the Civil War*. 2nd ed. Newark: University of Delaware Press, 1988.

Headley, J. T. *Farragut and Our Naval Commanders*. New York, 1867.

Hearn, Chester G. *Admiral David Dixon Porter: The Civil War Years*. Annapolis, MD: Naval Institute Press, 1996.

———. *Lincoln, the Cabinet, and the Generals*. Baton Rouge: Louisiana State University Press, 2010.

Hendrick, Burton J. *Lincoln's War Cabinet*. Boston: Little, Brown, 1946.

Hendrickson, Robert. *Sumter: The First Day of the Civil War*. New York: Promontory, 1990.

Herndon. Herndon's Informants. Edited by Douglas L. Wilson and Rodney O. Davis. Urbana: University of Illinois Press, 1998.

Herndon, William Henry. *Herndon on Lincoln*. Edited by Douglas L. Wilson and Rodney O. Davis. Urbana, IL: Knox College Lincoln Studies Center, 2016.

Herndon, William Henry, and Jesse William Weik. *Herndon's Lincoln: The True Story of a Great Life*. 1888; Springfield, IL: Herndon's Lincoln Publishing, 1921. 3 vols.

Hesseltine, William B. *Lincoln and the War Governors*. New York: Knopf, 1948.

Hodge, William L. *Disunion and Its Results to the South* [2/18/1861]. Washington, 1861.

Hoffer, Peter Charles. *The Free Press Crisis of 1800*. Lawrence: University Press of Kansas, 2011.

Holmes, Emma. *Diary of Miss Emma Holmes 1861–1866*. Edited by John F. Marszalek. Baton Rouge: Louisiana State University Press, 1979.

Holt, Michael F. *The Fate of Their Country*. New York: Hill and Wang, 2004.

———. *The Political Crisis of the 1850s*. New York: Wiley, 1978.

———. *The Rise and Fall of the American Whig Party*. New York: Oxford University Press, 1999.

Holt Papers. Joseph Holt Papers, Library of Congress.

Holzer, Harold. *Lincoln President-Elect*. New York: Simon & Schuster, 2008.

Holzman, Robert S. *Adapt or Perish: The Life of General Roger A. Pryor, C.S.A.* Hamden, CT: Archon Books, 1976.

Hoogenboom, Ari A. "Gustavus Fox and the Relief of Fort Sumter." *Civil War Hist*. 9/4:383 (12/1963).

———. *Gustavus Vasa Fox of the Union Navy*. Baltimore: Johns Hopkins University Press, 2008.

Hoppin, James Mason. *Life of Andrew Hull Foote*. New York, 1874.

Horres, Russell. "'Very Respectfully': Letters from the Ft. Sumter Copy Book." Charleston Museum, 3/28/2011. http://blog.charlestonmuseum.org/2011/03/curator-lecture-series-pt-02-ft-sumter.html.

Howe, Daniel Wait. *Political History of Secession*. New York: G. P. Putnam's Sons, 1914.

Hubbell, John T., ed. *Battles Lost and Won: Essays from "Civil War History."* Westport, CT: Greenwood Press, 1975.

Huger, Alfred, et al. "Letters from Alfred Huger, Edward McCrady and Dr. William H. Huger, of South Carolina." *William & Mary Quart*. 20/1:64 (7/1911).

Huger, Alfred, et al. Letter to Cleland Kinloch Huger. 5/13/1851. In Cleland Kinloch Huger Papers. Manuscripts P1B and Pob. Box 2, folder 30. South Caroliniana Library, University of South Carolina.

Huger Papers. Alfred Huger Letterpress Books, 1853–1859; 1861–1863, Special Collections Library, William R. Perkins Library, Duke University.

Huntington, Samuel P. *The Soldier and the State*. Cambridge, MA: Belknap Press of Harvard University Press, 1957.

Hurd, John Codman. *Law of Freedom and Bondage in the United States*. Boston, 1858–1862. 2 vols.

[Hurlbert, William Henry]. *Diary of a Public Man*. Chicago: Abraham Lincoln Book Shop, 1945.

[———]. "Diary of a Public Man." *North Am. Rev.* 129/273–76:125–497 (8–11/1879).

Huston, James L. *The Panic of 1857 and the Coming of the Civil War*. Baton Rouge: Louisiana State University Press, 1987.

Hyde, John T. *Elementary Principles of Fortification*. London, 1860.

Hyman, Harold M. *A More Perfect Union*. New York: Knopf, 1973.

Jackson, Andrew. *Correspondence of Andrew Jackson*. Edited by John Spencer Bassett. Washington, DC: Carnegie Institution of Washington, 1926–1935. 7 vols.

Jaffa, Harry V. *A New Birth of Freedom: Abraham Lincoln and the Coming of the Civil War*. 2000; Lanham, MD: Rowman & Littlefield, 2018.

JCR. Report of the Jt. Committee on Reconstruction at the First Session Thirty-Ninth Congress. Washington, 1866.

Jervey, Theodore D. *Robert Y. Hayne and His Times*. New York: Macmillan, 1909.

Johns, John E. *Florida during the Civil War*. Gainesville: University of Florida Press, 1963.

Johnson, Andrew. *Papers of Andrew Johnson*. Edited by LeRoy P. Graf and Ralph W. Haskins. Knoxville: University of Tennessee Press, 1967–2000. 16 vols.

Johnson, John. *The Defense of Charleston Harbor*. 2nd ed. Charleston, 1890.

Johnson, Ludwell H. "Fort Sumter and Confederate Diplomacy." *J. South. Hist.* 26/4:441 (11/1960).

Johnson, Timothy. *Winfield Scott: The Quest for Military Glory*. Lawrence: University Press of Kansas, 1998.

Johnston, Edith M., ed. "Inside Sumter: Letters of a Federal Artillerist." *Civil War Hist.* 8/4:417 (12/1962).

Jones, Samuel. *The Siege of Charleston*. New York: Neale, 1911.

Jones, Virgil Carrington. *The Civil War at Sea*. Vol. 1, *The Blockaders*. New York: Holt, Rinehart and Winston, 1960.

Jordan, Thomas. "Beginnings of the Civil War in America." *Mag. of Am. Hist.* 14/1:25, 2:113, 3:269 (1885).

Julian, George W. *Political Recollections 1840 to 1872*. Chicago, 1884.

Karp, Matthew. *This Vast Southern Empire*. Cambridge, MA: Harvard University Press, 2016.

Katcher, Philip. *American Civil War Artillery 1861–1865*. Oxford: Osprey, 2001.

Kendall, Amos. *Autobiography of Amos Kendall*. Edited by William Stickney. Boston, 1872.

———. *Letters on Our Country's Crisis*. Washington, 1864.

———. *Papers, 1835–1909*. Library of Congress.

Kerksis, Sydney C., and Thomas S. Dickey. *Field Artillery Projectiles of the Civil War*. Atlanta: Phoenix, 1968.

———. *Heavy Artillery Projectiles of the Civil War*. Kennesaw, GA: Phoenix, 1972.

Kettell, Thomas P. *History of the Great Rebellion*. Hartford, CT, 1865.

Keyes, Erasmus D. *Fifty Years' Observations of Men and Events, Civil and Military*. New York, 1884.

Kielbowicz, Richard B. "The Telegraph, Censorship, and Politics." *Civil War Hist.* 40/2:95 (June 1994).

King, Alvy L. *Louis T. Wigfall: Southern Fire-Eater.* Baton Rouge: Louisiana State University Press, 1970.

King, Horatio. "Reminiscences of the Early Stages of the Rebellion." *Lippincott's Mag.* 9:402 (4/1872).

———. *Turning On the Light.* Philadelphia, 1895.

Kirwan, Albert D. *John J. Crittenden: The Struggle for the Union.* Lexington: University of Kentucky Press, 1962.

Klein, Maury. *Days of Defiance: Sumter, Secession, and the Coming of the Civil War.* New York: Knopf, 1997.

Klein, Philip Shriver. *President James Buchanan: A Biography.* University Park: Pennsylvania State University Press, 1962.

Klunder, Willard Carl. *Lewis Cass and the Politics of Moderation.* Kent, OH: Kent State University Press, 1996.

Knoles, George Harmon, ed. *The Crisis of the Union 1860–1861.* Baton Rouge: Louisiana State University Press, 1965.

Konstam, Angus. *American Civil War Fortifications (1) Coastal Brick and Stone Forts.* Oxford: Osprey, 2003.

Lamon, Ward Hill. *Recollections of Abraham Lincoln 1847–1865.* Edited by Dorothy Lamon Teillard. 1895; 2nd ed. 1911; Lincoln: University of Nebraska Press, 1994.

Lamon Papers. Papers of Ward Hill Lamon, Huntington Library, San Marino, CA.

Lash, Jeffrey Norman. *Politician Turned General.* Kent, OH: Kent State University Press, 2003.

Lathers, Richard. *Reminiscences of Richard Lathers.* Edited by Alvan F. Sanborn. New York: Grafton, 1907.

Lawton, Eba Anderson. *History of the "Soldiers' Home" / Washington, D.C.* New York: Putnam, 1914.

———. *Major Robert Anderson and Fort Sumter 1861.* New York: Knickerbocker, 1911.

Lee, Elizabeth Blair. *Wartime Washington.* Edited by Virginia Jeans Laas. Urbana: University of Illinois Press, 1991.

Lee, J. Edward, and Ron Chepesiuk, eds. *South Carolina in the Civil War.* Jefferson, NC: McFarland, 2000.

Lee, Stephen D. "The First Step in the War." In Buel/Johnson 1:74.

Leslie, Frank. *Frank Leslie's Illustrated History of the Civil War.* New York, 1895.

Lesser, Charles H. *Relic of the Lost Cause.* 2nd ed. Columbia: University of South Carolina Press, 1996.

Lewis, Emanuel R. *Seacoast Fortifications of the United States.* 1970; Annapolis, MD: Naval Institute Press, 1979.

Lieber, Francis. *Life and Letters of Francis Lieber.* Edited by Thomas Sergeant Perry. Boston, 1882.

Lightner, David L. *Slavery and the Commerce Power.* New Haven, CT: Yale University Press, 2006.

Lincoln, Abraham. *The Collected Works of Abraham Lincoln.* See Basler et al., supra.

———. *Complete Works.* Edited by John G. Nicolay and John Hay. 1894. Vol. 2. New York, 1922.

———. *Life and Works of Abraham Lincoln.* [Edited by John Hay and John G. Nicolay.] [New York, 1905.] Vol. 6, pt. 2.

Lincoln Archives. Lincoln Archives Digital Project, www.lincolnarchives.us.

Lincoln Papers. Abraham Lincoln Papers at the Library of Congress, http://memory.loc.gov/ ammem/alhtml/alhome.html. Series 1, General Correspondence. 1833–1916.

Link, William A. *Roots of Secession: Slavery and Politics in Antebellum Virginia.* Chapel Hill: University of North Carolina Press, 2003.

Lossing, Benson John. *Pictorial History of the Civil War in the United States.* Philadelphia, 1866–1868. 3 vols.

Lothrop, Thornton Kirkland. *William Henry Seward.* Boston: Houghton Mifflin, 1899.

Lowell, James Russell. "The Pickens-and-Stealin's Rebellion." *Atlantic Monthly* 7:757 (6/1861).

Lunt, George. *The Origin of the Late War.* New York, 1866.

Madison, James. *Papers of James Madison.* Edited by William T. Hutchinson and William M. E. Rachal. Charlottesville: University Press of Virginia; Chicago: University of Chicago Press, 1962–1991. 17 vols.

Maffitt, John Newland. "A Descriptive Memoir of Charleston Harbor." In Bache et al. 16.

———. "Harbor of Charleston, S.C." [ca. 1851]. *De Bow's Rev.* 26/6:698 (6/1859).

Magruder, Allan B. "A Piece of Secret History: President Lincoln and the Virginia Convention of 1861." *Atl. Monthly* 35/ 438 (4/1875).

Maihafer, Harry J. *War of Words: Abraham Lincoln and the Civil War Press.* Washington, DC: Brassey's, 2001.

Malanowski, Jamie. *And the War Came: The Six Months That Tore America Apart.* Byliner Ebook, 2011.

Mansfield, Edward D. *Life of General Winfield Scott.* New York, 1846.

Marvel, William. *Five Flags over Fort Sumter.* Conshohocken, PA: Eastern National, 1998.

———. *Mr. Lincoln Goes to War.* Boston: Houghton Mifflin, 2006.

Marx, Karl. "The North American Civil War." *Die Presse* (Vienna), October 25, 1861. Translated 2008. www.tenc.net/a/18611025.htm.

———. *On America and the Civil War.* Edited by Saul K. Padover. New York: McGraw-Hill, 1972.

Mathew, William M. *Edmund Ruffin and the Crisis of Slavery in the Old South.* Athens: University of Georgia Press, 1988.

May, John Amasa, and Joan Reynolds Faunt. *South Carolina Secedes.* Columbia: University of South Carolina Press, 1960.

McCaslin, Richard B. *Portraits of Conflict.* Fayetteville: University of Arkansas Press, 1994.

McClintock, Russell. *Lincoln and the Decision for War: The Northern Response to Secession.* Chapel Hill: University of North Carolina Press, 2008.

———. "The Men & the Hour: Lincoln, Davis, and the Struggle to Avert War." *Civil War Monitor* 1/1:22 (Fall 2011).

McClure, Alexander K. *Abraham Lincoln and Men of War-Times.* Philadelphia, 1892.

[———, comp.]. *Annals of the War Written by Leading Participants North and South.* Philadelphia, 1879.

McDonnell, Lawrence T. *Performing Disunion: The Coming of the Civil War in Charleston, South Carolina.* Cambridge: Cambridge University Press, 2018.

McGinty, Brian. "Robert Anderson: Reluctant Hero." *Civil War Times Ill.* 31/2:44 (5–6/1992).

McPherson, Edward. *Political History of the United States of America.* Washington, 1864.

McPherson, James M. *Battle Cry of Freedom: The Civil War Era.* New York: Oxford University Press, 1988.

———. *Embattled Rebel: Jefferson Davis as Commander in Chief.* New York: Penguin, 2014.

———. *Ordeal by Fire.* 2nd ed. Vol. 1: *The Coming of War.* New York: Knopf, 1993.

———. *This Mighty Scourge: Perspectives on the Civil War.* New York: Oxford University Press, 2007.

———. *Tried by War: Abraham Lincoln as Commander in Chief.* New York: Penguin, 2008.

———. *War on the Waters: The Union & Confederate Navies, 1861–1865.* Chapel Hill: University of North Carolina Press, 2012.

———. *What They Fought For, 1861–1865.* Baton Rouge: Louisiana State University Press, 1994.

McWhiney, Grady. *Braxton Bragg and Confederate Defeat.* New York: Columbia University Press, 1969. Vol. 1.

Meigs, Montgomery C. *Capitol Builder: The Shorthand Journals of Montgomery C. Meigs, 1853–1859, 1861.* Transliterated by William D. Mohr. Edited by Wendy Wolff. Sen. Doc. 106–20. Washington, DC: Government Publishing Office, 2001.

———. "General M.C. Meigs on the Conduct of the Civil War" (1888). *Am. Hist. Rev.* 26/:2:285 (1/1921).

Meigs Diary. "Meigs, Montgomery Diary (copy)." *Nicolay Papers* Box 13, Library of Congress.

Meigs Papers. Montgomery C. Meigs Papers, Library of Congress.

Meigs Typescript. Typescript of Meigs Shorthand Journal for 1861. Transliterated by William D. Mohr using Meigs (1921) as base. In *Meigs Papers* Box 52, vol. 6.

Meneely, A. H. *The War Department, 1861.* Columbia Studies in History, Economics and Public Law no. 300. New York, 1928.

Merchant, Holt. *South Carolina Fire-Eater: The Life of Laurence Massillon Keitt.* Columbia: University of South Carolina Press, 2014.

Meredith, Roy. *Storm over Sumter.* New York: Simon & Schuster, 1957.

Merrens, H. Roy, ed. *The Colonial South Carolina Scene.* Columbia: University of South Carolina Press, 1977.

[Miles, William Porcher, et al.]. *Correspondence between the Commissioners of the State of So. Ca. to the Government at Washington and the President of the United States.* Charleston, 1861.

Miles Papers. William Porcher Miles Papers, Southern Historical Collection, University of North Carolina, Chapel Hill.

Mill, John Stuart. "The Contest in America" (1862). *Dissertations and Discussions* (London, 1867) 3:179.

Miller, David W. *Second Only to Grant: Quartermaster General Montgomery C. Meigs.* Shippensburg, PA: White Mane Books, 2000.

Mitchell, Thomas G. *Antislavery Politics in Antebellum and Civil War America.* Westport, CT: Praeger, 2007.

Moody, Wesley. *The Battle of Fort Sumter.* New York: Routledge, 2016.

Moore, Frank, ed. *Heroes and Martyrs: Notable Men of the Time.* New York, 1862.

———, ed. *The Rebellion Record: A Diary of American Events.* New York, 1861–1866. 11 vols. & supp.

Moore, Jaimie W. *The Fortifications Board 1816–1828 and the Definition of National Security.* Citadel Monog. Series no. 16. Charleston, 1981 ("1981A").

———. *The Lowcountry Engineers: Military Missions and Economic Development in the Charleston District.* [Washington: Superintendent of Documents], 1981 ("1981B").

Morrison, James L., Jr. *The Best School in the World.* Kent, OH: Kent State University Press, 1986.

Motley, John Lothrop. "The Causes of the American Civil War." 1861. In F. Moore (1861–1866) 1:209.

Mottelay, Paul F., and T. Campbell-Copeland. *Frank Leslie's "The Soldier in Our Civil War."* New York, 1893. Vol. 1.

"Naval Force." "Naval Force of the United States—Where Ships Are Now Stationed" (2/21/1861). In *Select Committee Reports.*

Nevins, Allan. *Emergence of Lincoln.* New York: Scribner, 1950. 2 vols.

———. *Ordeal of the Union.* New York: Scribner, 1947. 2 vols.

———. *The War for the Union.* Vol. I. *The Improvised War 1861–1862.* New York: Scribner, 1959.

Nichols, Thomas Low. *Forty Years of American Life.* London, 1864. 2 vols.

Nicolay, John G. *An Oral History of Abraham Lincoln: John G. Nicolay's Interviews and Essays.* Edited by Michael Burlingame. Carbondale: Southern Illinois University Press, 1996.

———. *The Outbreak of Rebellion.* New York, 1881.

———. *With Lincoln in the White House.* Edited by Michael Burlingame. Carbondale: Southern Illinois University Press, 2000.

Nicolay Papers. John G. Nicolay Papers, Library of Congress.

Nicolay, John G., and John Hay. *Abraham Lincoln: A History.* 1890; Los Angeles: William V. Bottom, 1917. 10 vols.

———. "Abraham Lincoln: A History; Lincoln's Inauguration." *Century Mag.* 35/2:265 (12/1887).

———. "Abraham Lincoln: A History; Premier or President." *Century Mag.* 35/4:599 (2/1888).

———. "Abraham Lincoln: A History; The Call to Arms." *Century Mag.* 35/5:707 (3/1888).

Niven, John. *Gideon Welles: Lincoln's Secretary of the Navy.* New York: Oxford University Press, 1973.

———. *John C. Calhoun and the Price of Union.* Baton Rouge: Louisiana State University Press, 1988.

Noll, Mark A. *The Civil War as a Theological Crisis.* Chapel Hill: University of North Carolina Press, 2006.

O'Brien, Michael, and David Moltke-Hansen, eds. *Intellectual Life in Antebellum Charleston.* Knoxville: University of Tennessee Press, 1986.

Officers' Register. Register of the Commissioned and Warrant Officers of the Navy of the United States. Washington, 1860.

OR. [United States. War Dep't.] *War of the Rebellion: A Compilation of the Official Records of the Union and Confederate Armies.* Washington, 1880–1900. 128 vols.

———. Series 1, vol. 1. Washington, 1880.

———. Series 1, vol. 6. Washington, 1882.

———. Series 1, vol. 52, Pt. I. Washington, 1898.

———. Series 1, vol. 52, Pt. II. Washington, 1898.

————. Series 1, vol. 53. Washington, 1898.

————. Series 3, vol. 1. Washington, 1899.

————. Series 4, vol. 1. Washington, 1900.

ORN. Official Records of the Union and Confederate Navies in the War of the Rebellion. Washington, 1874–1922. 30 vols.

————. Series 1, vol. 1. Washington, 1894.

————. Series 1, vol. 4. Washington, 1896.

————. Series 2, vol. 1. Washington, 1921.

Ordnance Instructions. United States. Navy Dep't. Bureau of Ordnance. *Ordnance Instructions for the United States Navy.* 2nd ed. Washington, 1860.

Ordnance Manual. United States. Army Ordnance Dep't. *Ordnance Manual for the Use of the Officers of the United States Army.* 3rd ed. Philadelphia, 1862.

Ordnance Papers. Collection of Annual Reports and Other Important Papers, Relating to the Ordnance Department. Washington, 1878–1890. 4 vols.

Osbon, Bradley Sillick. *A Sailor of Fortune.* Edited by Albert Bigelow Paine. New York: McClure, Phillips, 1906.

Ostaus, Carl R. *Partisans of the Southern Press.* Lexington: University Press of Kentucky, 1994.

Paine, Lincoln P. *Warships of the World to 1900.* Boston: Houghton Mifflin, 2000.

Paltsits. *American Book-Prices Current.* Vol. 21, compiled by Victor Hugo Paltsits. New York: Bancroft-Parkman, 1915.

Paludan, Phillip S. "The American Civil War Considered as a Crisis in Law and Order." *Am. Hist. Rev.* 77/4:1013 (10/1972).

Paris, Louis-Philippe-Albert d'Orléans, comte de. *Histoire de la guerre civile en Amérique.* 1874–1890. Translated by L. F. Tasistro, edited by Henry Coppée. Philadelphia, 1874–1888. Vol. 1.

Parker, F. L. "The Battle of Fort Sumter as Seen from Morris Island." *S.C. Hist. Mag.* 62/2:65 (4/1961).

Parker, Joel. "The Right of Secession." 7/1/1861. In Freidel 55.

Parton, James. *Life of Andrew Jackson.* New York, 1860. 3 vols.

Paullin, Charles Oscar. *Paullin's History of Naval Administration 1775–1911.* 1905–1914. Annapolis, MD: Naval Institute Press, 1968.

Perman, Michael, ed. *The Coming of the American Civil War.* 3rd ed. Lexington, MA: D.C. Heath, 1993.

Perry, Benjamin Franklin. *Biographical Sketches of Eminent American Statesmen.* Philadelphia, 1887.

————. *Letters of Gov. Benjamin Franklin Perry to His Wife.* 2nd Ser. Greenville, SC, 1890.

————. *Letters of My Father to My Mother.* Compiled by Hext McCall Perry, M.D. Philadelphia, 1889 ("1889A").

————. *Reminiscences of Public Men.* Philadelphia, 1883.

————. *Reminiscences of Public Men.* 2nd Ser. Philadelphia, 1889 ("1889B").

Perry, James M. *A Bohemian Brigade: The Civil War Correspondents—Mostly Rough, Sometimes Ready.* New York: Wiley, 2000.

Peskin, Allan. *Winfield Scott and the Profession of Arms.* Kent, OH: Kent State University Press, 2003.

Petigru, James L. *Life, Letters and Speeches of James Louis Petigru.* Edited by James Petigru Carson. Washington, DC: W. H. Lowdermilk, 1920.

Petigru Papers. James Louis Petigru Papers. Southern Historical Collection, University of South Carolina.

Petty, Julian J. *The Growth and Distribution of Population in South Carolina.* Columbia: University of South Carolina Press, 1943.

Phillips, Ulrich B., ed. "Correspondence of Robert Toombs, Alexander H. Stephens, and Howell Cobb." *Am. Hist. Ass'n Annual Report for the Year 1911.* Vol. 2. Washington, 1913.

Piatt, Donn. *Memories of the Men Who Saved the Union.* New York, 1887.

Pickens Papers. Papers of Francis Wilkinson Pickens, Library of Congress.

Pierce, Edward L. *Memoir and Letters of Charles Sumner.* Boston, 1877–1893. 4 vols.

Poinsett Papers. Joel Roberts Poinsett Papers, South Caroliniana Library, University of South Carolina.

Pollard, Edward Alfred. *The First Year of the War.* 2nd ed. 1862; New York, 1863. Vol. 1 of *Southern History of the War.*

———. *Lee and His Lieutenants.* New York, 1867 ("1867A").

———. *The Lost Cause.* 1866; 2nd ed. New York, 1867 ("1867B").

———. *The Lost Cause Regained.* New York, 1868.

Porter, Anthony Toomer. *Led On! Step by Step.* New York, 1898.

Porter, David Dixon. *Incidents and Anecdotes of the Civil War.* New York, 1885.

———. *Memoir of Commodore David Porter.* Albany, NY, 1875.

———. *The Naval History of the Civil War.* New York, 1886.

Porter Journal. Vice Admiral D. D. Porter Private Journal No. 1, p. 90, *Porter Papers* Box 22.

Porter Papers. David Dixon Porter Papers, Library of Congress.

Porter, William D. *State Sovereignty and the Doctrine of Coercion.* [Ca. 1860].

Potter, David M. *The Impending Crisis 1848–1861.* Edited and completed by Don E. Fehrenbacher. New York: Harper & Row, 1976.

———. *Lincoln and His Party in the Secession Crisis.* 1942; 1962; Baton Rouge: Louisiana State University Press, 1995.

Powe, James Harrington. *Reminiscences and Sketches of Confederate Times.* Edited by Harriet Powe Lynch. Columbia, SC: R. L. Bryan, 1909.

Preble, George Henry. *History of the Flag of the United States of America.* 2nd ed. Boston, 1880.

Pressly, Thomas J. *Americans Interpret Their Civil War.* 1954; New York: Free Press, 1962.

Preston, Antony, and John Major. *Send a Gunboat.* 1967; London: Conway, 2007.

Pryor, Dayton E. *The Beginning and the End.* Bowie, MD: Heritage Books, 2001.

Pryor, Sara Agnes Rice. *My Day: Reminiscences of a Long Life.* New York: Macmillan, 1909.

———. *Reminiscences of Peace and War.* New York: Macmillan, 1904.

Public Proceedings. Journal of the Public Proceedings of the Convention of the People of South Carolina, Held in 1860–'61. Charleston, 1860.

Quigley, Paul. *Shifting Grounds: Nationalism & the American South 1848–1865.* New York: Oxford University Press, 2012.

Rable, George C. *The Confederate Republic: Revolution against Politics.* Chapel Hill: University of North Carolina Press, 1994.

Racine, Philip N., ed. *Gentlemen Merchants: A Charleston Family's Odyssey, 1828–1870.* Knoxville: University of Tennessee Press, 2008.

Radan, Peter. "Lincoln, the Constitution, and Secession." In Doyle 56.

Rainwater, Percy Lee. *Mississippi: Storm Center of Secession.* Baton Rouge: Louisiana State University Press, 1938.

Ramsdell, Charles W. "Lincoln and Fort Sumter." *J. South. Hist.* 3/3:272 (8/1937).

Randall, James G. "The Blundering Generation." *Miss. Valley Hist. Rev.* 27/1:3 (6/1940).

———. *Constitutional Problems under Lincoln.* New York: Appleton, 1926.

———. *Lincoln the Liberal Statesman.* New York: Dodd, Mead, 1947.

———. *Lincoln the President.* Vol. 1, *Springfield to Bull Run.* 1945; New York: Dodd, Mead, 1956.

———. "When War Came in 1861." *Abraham Lincoln Quart.* 1/1:3 (3/1940).

Randall, James G., and David Donald. *The Divided Union.* Boston: Little, Brown, 1961.

Ratner, Lorman A., and Dwight L. Teeter Jr. *Fanatics and Fire-Eaters.* Urbana: University of Illinois Press, 2003.

Ravenel, Henry William. *The Private Journal of Henry William Ravenel 1859–1887.* Edited by Arney Robinson Childs. Columbia: University of South Carolina Press, 1947.

Ravenel Papers. Ravenel Family Papers, 1790–1918, Southern Historical Collection, University of North Carolina.

Reagan, John H. *Memoirs with Special Reference to Secession and the Civil War.* Edited by Walter Flavius McCaleb. New York: Neale, 1906.

Reese, George H., ed. *Proceedings of the Virginia State Convention of 1861.* Richmond: Virginia State Library, 1965. 4 vols.

Register. Register of Debates in Congress, Comprising the Leading Debates and Incidents [12/66/1824–10/16/1837]. Washington, 1825–1837. 14 vols.

Reid, Brian Holden. *The Origins of the American Civil War.* London: Longman, 1996.

Reynolds, Donald E. *Editors Make War: Southern Newspapers in the Secession Crisis.* Nashville, TN: Vanderbilt University Press, 1970.

Rhett, Robert Barnwell. *A Fire-Eater Remembers: The Confederate Memoir of Robert Barnwell Rhett.* Edited by William C. Davis. Columbia: University of South Carolina Press, 2000.

Rhoades, Jeffrey L. *Scapegoat General: The Story of Major General Benjamin Huger, C.S.A.* Hamden, CT: Archon Books, 1985.

Rhodes, James Ford. *History of the United States from the Compromise of 1850.* New York: Macmillan, 1892–1906. 7 vols.

———. *Lectures on the American Civil War.* 1912; New York: Macmillan, 1913.

Rich, William J. "Lessons of Charleston Harbor." *McGeorge L. Rev.* 36:569 (2005).

Richards, Leonard L. *The Slave Power: The Free North and Southern Domination.* Baton Rouge: Louisiana State University Press, 2000.

Richardson, James D., comp. *Compilation of the Messages and Papers of the Presidents, 1789–1902.* Washington, DC: Bureau of National Literature, 1897–1903. 10 vols.

———, comp. *Compilation of the Messages and Papers of the Confederacy.* Nashville, TN: United States Publishing, 1905. 2 vols. in 1.

Ripley, Warren. *Artillery and Ammunition of the Civil War.* 1970; 4th ed. Charleston: Battery, 1984.

Roark, James L. *Masters without Slaves: Southern Planters in the Civil War and Reconstruction.* New York: Norton, 1977.

Roberts, Joseph. *Hand-Book of Artillery, for the Service of the United States.* 2nd ed. Charleston, 1861.

Robertson, Ben. *Red Hills and Cotton: An Upcountry Memoir.* New York: Knopf, 1942.

Robinson, Willard B. *American Forts: Architectural Form and Function.* Urbana: University of Illinois Press, 1977.

Roman, Alfred. *Military Operations of General Beauregard.* New York, 1884. 2 vols.

Rosen, Robert N. *Confederate Charleston: An Illustrated History of the City and the People during the Civil War.* Columbia: University of South Carolina Press, 1994.

Rothschild, Alonzo. *Lincoln: Master of Men.* Boston: Houghton Mifflin, 1908.

Rowan, Stephen. Papers of Stephen C. Rowan, Record Group 45, Naval Records Collection of the Office of Naval Records and Library. Vol. 3, "A Journal Kept by Comdr. Stephen C. Rowan December 1859–April 1861." Microfilm.

[Ruffin, Edmund]. *Anticipations of the Future, to Serve as Lessons for the Present Time.* Richmond, VA, 1860.

———. *Diary of Edmund Ruffin.* Edited by William Kauffman Scarborough. Baton Rouge: Louisiana State University Press, 1972–1989. 2 vols.

———. "The Effects of High Prices of Slaves." *De Bow's Rev.* 26/6:647 (6/1859).

Russell, William Howard. *The Civil War in America.* Boston, 1861 ("1861A").

———. *My Diary North and South.* London, 1863. 2 vols.

———. *Pictures of Southern Life.* New York, 1861 ("1861B").

———. *William Howard Russell's Civil War: Private Diary and Letters, 1861–1862.* Edited by Martin Crawford. Athens: University of Georgia Press, 1992.

Ryan, Mike. "The Historic Guns of Forts Sumter and Moultrie." National Parks Service (5/1997).

Saint-Amand, Mary Scott. *A Balcony in Charleston.* Richmond, VA: Garrett and Massie, 1941.

Samuels, Ernest. *The Young Henry Adams.* Cambridge, MA: Harvard University Press, 1948.

Sandburg, Carl. *Abraham Lincoln: The War Years.* New York: Harcourt, Brace, 1939. Vol. 1.

Saunders, Robert, Jr. *John Archibald Campbell, Southern Moderate, 1811–1889.* Tuscaloosa: University of Alabama Press, 1997.

Scharf, J. Thomas. *History of the Confederate States Navy.* New York, 1887.

Schoen, Brian. *The Fragile Fabric of Union.* Baltimore: Johns Hopkins University Press, 2009.

Schöpf, Johann David. *Travels in the Confederation.* Translated by Alfred J. Morrison. Philadelphia: W. J. Campbell, 1911. 2 vols.

Schultz, Harold S. *Nationalism and Sectionalism in South Carolina 1852–1860.* Durham, NC: Duke University Press, 1950.

Scott, Henry L. *Military Dictionary.* New York, 1861.

Scott, Winfield. *Memoirs of Lieut.-General Scott, LL.D.* New York, 1864. 2 vols.

———. *Private Letters of Lieut.-General Scott, and the Reply of Ex-President Buchanan.* New York, 1862.

Scrugham, Mary. *The Peaceable Americans of 1860–1861: A Study in Public Opinion.* Columbia Studies in History, Economics and Public Law, no. 219. New York, 1921.

Seitz, Don. *Braxton Bragg General of the Confederacy.* Columbia, SC: State Company, 1924.

Select Committee Reports. U.S. Cong., H.R., Select Committee of Five. Reports of the Select Committee of Five. 36/2. Washington, 1861.

Seward, Frederick W. *Reminiscences of a War-Time Statesman and Diplomat 1830–1915.* New York: Putnam, 1916.

———. *Seward at Washington, as Senator and Secretary of State.* New York, 1891.

Seward, William Henry. *William H. Seward: An Autobiography.* Edited by Frederick W. Seward. New York, 1891.

———. *Works of William H. Seward*. Edited by George E. Baker. 2nd ed. Boston, 1884–1890. 5 vols.

Seward Papers. William Henry Seward Papers. Rush Rhees Library, Dep't of Rare Books, Special Collections and Preservation, University of Rochester.

Shaffner, Taliaferro P. *The War in America*. London, 1862.

Shanks, Henry T. *The Secession Movement in Virginia 1847–1861*. Richmond, VA: Garrett and Massie, 1934.

Sheehan-Dean, Aaron. *Why Confederates Fought*. Chapel Hill: University of North Carolina Press, 2007.

Sherman, John. *John Sherman's Recollections of Forty Years in the House, Senate and Cabinet*. Chicago, 1895. 2 vols.

Sherman, William Tecumseh. *Memoirs of General William T. Sherman*. 2nd ed. New York, 1889. Vol. 1.

———. *Sherman's Civil War: Selected Correspondence of William T. Sherman*. Chapel Hill: University of North Carolina Press, 1999.

Silverstone, Paul H. *Warships of the Civil War Navies*. Annapolis, MD: Naval Institute Press, 1989.

Simpson, Brooks D., Stephen W. Sears, and Aaron Sheehan-Dean, eds. *The Civil War: The First Year Told by Those Who Lived It*. New York: Library of America, 2011.

Simpson, Lewis P. *Mind and the American Civil War: A Meditation on Lost Causes*. Baton Rouge: Louisiana State University Press, 1989.

Skelton, William B. *An American Profession of Arms*. Lawrence: University Press of Kansas, 1992.

SLSC. *Statutes at Large of South Carolina*. Edited by Thomas Cooper et al. Columbia, SC. 1836–1873. 11 vols.

Smith, Derek. *Sumter after the First Shots*. Mechanicsburg, PA: Stackpole Books, 2015.

Smith, Mark A. *Engineering Security*. Tuscaloosa: University of Alabama Press, 2009.

Smith, Mark M. *The Smell of Battle, the Taste of Siege*. New York: Oxford University Press, 2015.

Smith, William Ernest. *The Francis Preston Blair Family in Politics*. New York: Macmillan, 1933. 2 vols.

Soady, France James. *Lessons of War as Taught by the Great Masters*. London, 1870.

Soley, James Russell. *Admiral Porter*. New York: D. Appleton, 1903.

Sondhaus, Lawrence. *Naval Warfare, 1815–1914*. London: Routledge, 2001.

Sowle, Patrick Michael. "The Conciliatory Republicans during the Winter of Secession." PhD diss., Duke University, 1963.

Spaulding, Oliver Lyman, Jr. "The Bombardment of Fort Sumter, 1861." *Ann. Report of the Am. Hist. Ass'n for 1913* (Washington, 1915), 1:177.

Spicer, William A. *The Flag Replaced on Sumter*. Providence, RI, 1885.

Sprout, Harold H., and Margaret T. Sprout. *The Rise of American Naval Power 1776–1918*. Princeton, NJ: Princeton University Press, 1939.

Stahr, Walter. *Seward: Lincoln's Indispensable Man*. New York: Simon & Schuster, 2012.

Stampp, Kenneth M. *America in 1857: A Nation on the Brink*. New York: Oxford University Press, 1990.

———. *And the War Came: The North and Secession Crisis, 1860–1861*. Baton Rouge: Louisiana State University Press, 1950.

————, ed. *The Causes of the Civil War*. 3rd ed. New York: Simon & Schuster, 1991.

————. *The Imperiled Union: Essays on the Background of the Civil War*. New York: Oxford University Press, 1980.

————. "Lincoln and the Strategy of Defense in the Crisis of 1861." *J. South. Hist.* 11/3:297 (8/1945).

————. "The Southern Refutation of the Proslavery Argument." *N. Carolina Hist. Rev.* 21:35 (1/1944).

Stanton, Edwin M. "A Page of Political Correspondence." *North Am. Rev.* 129/276:473 (11/1879).

Starr, Louis M. *Bohemian Brigade: Civil War Newsmen in Action*. New York: Knopf, 1954.

Stephens, Alexander H. *Alexander H. Stephens, in Public and Private*. Edited by Henry Cleveland. Philadelphia, 1866.

————. *Constitutional View of the Late War between the States*. Philadelphia, 1868–1870. 2 vols.

————. *Recollections of Alexander H. Stephens*. New York: Doubleday, Page, 1910.

Stephenson, Nathaniel Wright. *Lincoln: An Account of His Personal Life*. Indianapolis, IN: Bobbs-Merrill, 1922.

Stern, Philip Van Doren. *Prologue to Sumter*. Bloomington: Indiana University Press, 1961.

Stets, Robert J., and Harvey S. Teal. *South Carolina Postoffices & Postmasters, 1860–1865*. [N.p., n.p.]: 1995.

Stevens, Thaddeus. *Selected Papers of Thaddeus Stevens*. Edited by Beverly Wilson Palmer. Pittsburgh: University of Pittsburgh Press, 1997–1998. 2 vols.

Stillé, Charles J. *Life and Services of Joel R. Poinsett*. Philadelphia, 1888.

Stokely, Jim. *Fort Moultrie: Constant Defender*. Washington, DC: U.S. Government Printing Office, 1985.

Straith, Hector. *Treatise on Fortification and Artillery*. 5th ed. London, 1850.

Sumner, Charles. *Charles Sumner: His Complete Works*. Boston: Lee & Shepard, 1900. 20 vols.

Swanberg, W. A. *First Blood: The Story of Fort Sumter*. New York: Scribner, 1957.

Symonds, Craig L. *Lincoln and His Admirals*. Oxford: Oxford University Press, 2008.

————. "The Sumter Conundrum." *Naval Hist. Mag.* 25/2:18 (4/2011).

Taliaferro, John. *All the Great Prizes: The Life of John Hay, from Lincoln to Roosevelt*. New York: Simon & Schuster, 2013.

Taliaferro, Preston. *The War in America*. London, 1862.

Taylor, John M. *William Henry Seward: Lincoln's Right Hand*. New York: HarperCollins, 1991.

Taylor, Thomas (Mrs.), et al., eds. *South Carolina Women in the Confederacy*. Columbia, SC: State Company, 1903–1907. 2 vols.

Taylor, William R. *Cavalier and Yankee: The Old South and American National Character*. New York: Oxford University Press, 1961.

Telegrams. Telegrams Received by the Confederate Secretary of War 1861–95. Nat'l Arch. & Records Serv. 1966.

Tenney, William Jewett. *Military and Naval History of the Rebellion in the United States*. New York, 1866.

Thayer, William S. "Politicians in Crisis." Edited by Martin Crawford. *Civil War Hist.* 27/3:236 (9/1981).

Thomas, Benjamin P. *Abraham Lincoln: A Biography*. New York: Knopf, 1952.

Thomas, Emory M. *The Confederate Nation 1861–1865*. New York: Harper & Row, 1979.

Thomas, John P., ed. *The Carolina Tribute to Calhoun*. Columbia, SC, 1857.

Thompson, John. "A Union Soldier at Fort Sumter, 1860–1861." *S.C. Hist. Mag.* 67/2:99 (4/1966).

Thorndike, Rachel Sherman, ed. *The Sherman Letters*. New York, 1894.

Tidball, Eugene C. "The Fort Pickens Relief Expedition of 1861: John C. Tidball's Journals." *Civil War Hist.* 42/4:322 (12/1996).

Tidball, John C. "A Distinguished Horse Artilleryman." Comp. John H. Calef. *J. Mil. Serv. Inst. of the U.S.* 43:110 (1908).

Tilley, John Shipley. *Lincoln Takes Command*. Chapel Hill: University of North Carolina Press, 1941.

Tomes, Robert. *The War with the South*. New York, [1865]. Vol. 1.

Torget, Andrew J. "Unions of Slavery: Slavery, Politics, and Secession in the Valley of Virginia." In Ayers, Gallagher, and Torget 9.

Totten, Joseph G. *Report Addressed to the Hon. Jefferson Davis, Secretary of War*. Washington, 1857.

———. *Report of General J. G. Totten, Chief Engineer, on the Subject of National Defences*. Washington, 1851.

Tower, Roderick. *The Defense of Fort Sumter*. Charleston: Walker, Evans & Cogswell, 1938.

Townsend, E. D. *Anecdotes of the Civil War in the United States*. New York, 1884.

Townsend, John. *The South Alone Should Govern the South*. Charleston, 1860.

Trefousse, Hans L. *The Radical Republicans*. New York: Knopf, 1969.

Trescot, William Henry. "Narrative and Letter of William Henry Trescot" [Feb. 1861]. Edited by Gaillard Hunt. *Am. Hist. Rev.* 13/3:528 (4/1908).

———. *The Position and Source of the South*. Charleston, 1850.

Tucker, Spencer C. *Andrew Foote: Civil War Admiral on Western Waters*. Annapolis: Naval Institute Press, 2000.

———, ed. *Civil War Naval Encyclopedia*. Santa Barbara, CA: ABC-CLIO, 2011. 2 vols.

U.S. Army Engineer School. *Sand Movement & Beaches*. Fort Humphreys, VA: U.S. Army Engineer School, 1929.

Van Deusen, Glyndon G. *Thurlow Weed: Wizard of the Lobby*. Boston: Little, Brown, 1947.

———. *William Henry Seward*. New York: Oxford University Press, 1967.

Van Deusen, John G. *Economic Bases of Disunion in South Carolina*. New York: Columbia University Press, 1928.

Varon, Elizabeth R. *Disunion! The Coming of the American Civil War, 1789–1859*. Chapel Hill: University of North Carolina Press, 2008.

Victor, Orville J. *Comprehensive History of the Southern Rebellion and the War for the Union*. New York, 1862. Vol. 1.

Villard, Henry. *Memoirs of Henry Villard: Journalist and Financier*. Boston: Houghton Mifflin, 1904. Vol. 1.

Virginia Journal. Journal of the Acts and Proceedings of a General Convention of the State of Virginia. Richmond, VA, 1861.

Wakelyn, Jon L. *Southern Pamphlets on Secession*. Chapel Hill: University of North Carolina Press, 1996.

Walther, Eric H. *The Fire-Eaters*. Baton Rouge: Louisiana State University Press, 1992.

Warden, Robert B. *Account of the Private Life and Public Services of Salmon Portland Chase*. Cincinnati, OH, 1874.

Watson, Samuel. "Knowledge, Interest and the Limits of Military Professionalism." *War in History* 5/3:280 (7/1998).

Waugh, John C. *On the Brink of Civil War.* Wilmington, DE: Scholarly Resources, 2003.

———. *Surviving the Confederacy.* New York: Harcourt, 2002.

Ways, Harry C. *The Washington Aqueduct 1852–1992.* [Washington?], [1996?].

Weaver, John R., II. *Legacy in Brick and Stone.* Missoula, MT: Pictorial Histories, 2001.

Weed, Thurlow. *Autobiography of Thurlow Weed.* Edited by Harriet A. Weed. Boston, 1884. 2 vols.

Weigley, Russell F. "M. C. Meigs: Builder of the Capitol." PhD diss., University of Pennsylvania, 1956.

———. *Quartermaster General of the Union Army.* New York: Columbia University Press, 1959.

———. *Towards an American Army.* New York: Columbia University Press, 1962.

Weiner, Marli F. *Mistress and Slaves: Plantation Women in South Carolina, 1830–1880.* Urbana: University of Illinois Press, 1998.

Welles, Gideon. "Administration of Abraham Lincoln." *Galaxy* 23:5, 149 (1, 2/1877).

———. *Civil War and Reconstruction: Selected Essays of Gideon Welles.* Compiled by Albert Mordell. New York: Twayne, 1959–1960. 2 vols.

———. *The Civil War Diaries of Gideon Welles.* Edited by William E. Gienapp and Erica L. Gienapp. Urbana: University of Illinois Press, 2014.

———. *Diary of Gideon Welles.* [Edited by Edgar Welles.] Boston: Houghton Mifflin, 1911. 3 vols.

———. *Diary of Gideon Welles.* Edited by Howard K. Beale. New York: Norton, 1960. 3 vols.

———. "Election and Administration of Abraham Lincoln." *Galaxy* 22/3:300 (9/1876).

———. "Fort Pickens: Facts in Relation to the Reinforcement of Fort Pickens, in the Spring of 1861." *Galaxy* 11/1:92 (1/1871).

———. "Fort Sumter: Facts in Relation to the Expedition Ordered by the Administration." *Galaxy* 10/5:613 (11/1870).

———. "Letters of Gideon Welles." *Mag. of Hist.* 27/1, Extra number 105 (1925).

———. Lincoln and Seward: Remarks upon the Memorial Address of Chas. Francis Adams. New York, 1874.

———. "Mr. Lincoln and Mr. Seward" II. *Galaxy* 16/5:687 (11/1873).

———. "Mr. Welles in Answer to Mr. Weed." *Galaxy* 10/1:109 (7/1870).

———. "Nomination and Election of Abraham Lincoln." *Galaxy* 22/4:437 (10/1876).

———. "Report of the Sec'y of the Navy" (7/4/1861). In F. Moore (1861–1866) 2:235.

———. Valuable Papers of the Late Hon. Gideon Welles Secretary of the Navy under Lincoln. Auction Jan. 4, 1924, Stan V. Henkels Catalogue no. 1342.

Welles Papers/CHS. Gideon Welles Papers, Connecticut Historical Society, Hartford.

Welles Papers/Huntington. Gideon Welles Papers, Huntington Library, San Marino, CA.

Welles Papers/LC. Gideon Welles Papers, Library of Congress.

Welles Papers/NYPL. Gideon Welles Papers, New York Public Library.

Wellman, Manly. *They Took Their Stand: The Founders of the Confederacy.* New York: Putnam, 1959.

Wells, Jonathan Daniel. *The Origins of the Southern Middle Class 1800–1861.* Chapel Hill: University of North Carolina Press, 2004.

Wells, T. Tileston. *The Hugers of South Carolina.* New York: privately printed, 1931.

West, Richard S., Jr. *Gideon Welles: Lincoln's Navy Department*. Indianapolis, IN: Bobbs-Merrill, 1943.

———. *The Second Admiral: A Life of David Dixon Porter 1813–1891*. New York: Coward-McCann, 1937.

Weston, George M. *Poor Whites of the South*. 1856; Washington, 1860.

———. *The Progress of Slavery in the United States*. Washington, 1857.

Wheaton, Henry. *Elements of International Law*. 1821; 6th ed. Boston, 1855.

White, Horace. *Life of Lyman Trumbull*. Boston: Houghton Mifflin, 1913.

White, Laura A. *Robert Barnwell Rhett: Father of Secession*. New York: Century, 1931.

White, Ronald C., Jr. *A. Lincoln: A Biography*. New York: Random House, 2009.

Williams, Kenneth P. *Lincoln Finds a General*. New York: Macmillan, 1949–1959. 5 vols.

Williams, T. Harry. *Lincoln and the Radicals*. Madison: University of Wisconsin Press, 1941.

———. *P.G.T. Beauregard: Napoleon in Gray*. Baton Rouge: Louisiana State University Press, 1954.

Wilson, Harold S. *Confederate Industry*. Jackson: University Press of Mississippi, 2002.

Wilson, Henry. *History of the Rise and Fall of the Slave Power in America*. Boston, 1872–1877. 3 vols.

———. "Jeremiah Black and Edwin M. Stanton." *Atlantic Monthly* 26/156:463 (10/1870).

Wilson, Rufus Rockwell, comp. *Intimate Memories of Lincoln*. Elmira, NY: Primavera, 1945.

Wise, Stephen R. *Gate of Hell: Campaign for Charleston Harbor, 1863*. Columbia: South Carolina University Press, 1994.

Woodford, Stewart L. "The Story of Fort Sumter" (1886). In *Personal Recollections of the War of the Rebellion*, edited by James Grant Wilson and Titus Munson Coan. New York, 1891.

Woodman, Harold D. *King Cotton & His Retainers*. Lexington: University of Kentucky Press, 1968.

Wooster, Ralph A. *The People in Power*. Knoxville: University of Tennessee Press, 1969.

———. *The Secession Conventions of the South*. Princeton, NJ: Princeton University Press, 1962.

Wright, Gavin. *The Political Economy of the Cotton South*. New York: Norton, 1978.

Wright, Louise Wigfall. "Memories of the Beginning and End of the Southern Confederacy." *McClure's Mag.* 23/5:451 (9/1904).

———. *A Southern Girl in '61: The War-Time Memories of a Confederate Senator's Daughter*. New York: Doubleday, Page, 1905.

Wright, Marcus Joseph. *General Scott*. New York, 1894.

Wyatt-Brown, Bertram. *Southern Honor: Ethics and Behavior in the Old South*. New York: Oxford University Press, 1982.

———. *Yankee Saints and Southern Sinners*. Baton Rouge: Louisiana State University Press, 1985.

Young, William Gourdin (Sept. 15, 1904). In May Spencer Ringold, "William Gourdin Young and the Wigfall Mission—Fort Sumter, April 13, 1861." *S.C. Hist. Mag.* 73/1:27 (1/1972).

Zeller, Bob. *The Blue and Gray in Black and White: A History of Civil War Photography*. Westport, CT: Praeger, 2005.

Index

abolitionism, 11

act of hostility, term, 73

act of war, term, 73

Adams, Charles Francis, Jr., 98, 137, 228

Adams, Charles Francis, Sr., 12, 14, 29, 78, 149, 250–51, 356n24

Adams, Henry, 12; on Anderson, 81; on Buchanan, 43; on first shot, 51; on Lincoln, 148; and negotiations, 89–90; on Scott, 80; on Seward, 108

Adams, Henry A. (captain), 201, 207, 208, 213, 275, 371n37

Adams, James H., 38

African Americans: and Fort Pickens, 272–73; and harbor defenses, 72; and war, 277. *See also* slavery

Albany Plan, 353n110

Alden, Esther, 278–79

Aldrich, A. P., 3

amphibious landings, 126–27, 169

Anderson, Eliza Bayard Clinch, 31, 51, 179, 241

Anderson, Larz, 46, 89, 114

Anderson, Robert, 49*f*–50*f*; background of, 26; character of, 75, 319n96; communications to, 225–27; and defense of Sumter, 236–37, 241–42; and evacuation prospects, 175–85, 234–35, 363n43; and Fox, 134, 344n6, 345n9, 376n26; health of, 175–76; and Lamon, 137; and Lincoln, 119,

181–83, 185, 266–67, 282, 364n54; military background of, 48–49, 80; and negotiations, 250; and Pickens, 89; on reinforcement, 26–27, 34–35, 68–69, 112; and repossession of Sumter, 281, 282*f*; reputation of, 26, 45–51, 241, 250, 254, 265–66, 312n2; and safe passage proposal, 232–33; Scott correspondence, 123, 124*f*, 180*f*, 180–81; and slaves, 301n37; and *Star of the West*, 71, 73–75; state of mind, 178–85, 226–27, 232–33, 255–56, 308n52, 321n119, 364n54; and transfer from Moultrie, 38–45

Anderson, Thomas M., 264, 267

Armstrong, James, 82–83, 171, 322n131

Army, U.S.: condition of, 87–88; foreign-born enlisted men, 34, 304n86; resignations from, 1, 160, 287n3

Army Corps of Engineers, 21, 40, 61

Aspinwall, William Henry, 135, 144

Atlantic, 192, 197, 198, 271, 273, 275

Bache, Alexander Dallas, 331n104

Baldwin, John B., 171–74, 227–28, 360n4, 361n7, 362nn14–15

Baltic, 105, 198*f*, 199*f*, 199–200, 234, 238

Bancroft, Frederick, 349n54

Barnwell, Robert W., 38

Barrancas Barracks, 82

Barron, Samuel, 85, 167, 169

cotton, 5, 100, 108, 137–39, 289n22
Coulter, Ellis Merton, 389n28
Craven, T. A. M., 332n108
Crawford, Martin J., 101, 121; and
 Anderson, 234, 319n96; and Lincoln,
 152, 153, 183; and negotiations,
 130; and Pensacola rumors, 140; and
 preparation time, 257
Crawford, Samuel Wylie, 27, 50f; on
 evacuation rumors, 125; and Fox,
 345n9; and Lamon, 137
Crimean War, 59–60, 103, 126
Crittenden, John J., 16, 89, 107, 109, 125,
 319n93, 333n17
Cromwell, Ruth N., 265
Crusader, 61, 205, 206
Cuba, 150
Cullum, George W., 34
Cumming's Point, 176f; armaments, 221,
 222f
Curry, J. L. M., 386n60

Dabney, Robert Lewis, 174
Dahlgren, John A., 126–27, 127f
Dahlgren guns, 165, 223
Dana, Charles A., 13
Daniel, John Moncure, 56, 113
Davis, Bancroft, 346n22
Davis, Garrett, 174
Davis, Jefferson, 9, 85, 99, 155; and
 Anderson, 26, 52–53, 266–67; and
 attack on Sumter, 215–19; and
 military, 115; and negotiations, 89,
 101; and preparation time, 257; and
 reinforcement, 37–38; and secession,
 138; and Seward, 118, 259, 385n52
Davis, Jefferson C. (Union lieutenant), 50f
Davis, Varina Howell, 9–10, 385n52
deeds, and facility claims, 94–97, 327n50
Derby, Elias Hasket, III, 103
Dévastation, 103
Dix, John A., 46, 79

Dixon, Thomas, 371n50
Dobbin, James C., 60
Dolphin, 61
Doubleday, Abner, 25, 50f, 74, 237,
 380n92; and Anderson, 266; and
 Crawford, 363n42
Doubleday, Mary, 182
Doubleday, Ulysses, 25, 74
Douglas, Stephen, 13, 268, 335n38; and
 Anderson, 182; and attack on Sumter,
 200; and reinforcement, 91, 122, 128;
 and Seward, 107
Dred Scott decision, 10, 97
Drummond lights, 229
Dry Tortugas, 156, 272
Duane, Richard B., 31
Dunovant, R. G. M., 94

Early, Jubal, 260
economic issues: and Confederacy, 101–2,
 214; and secession, 138–39
Edmondston, Catherine, 72, 74
election of Lincoln, 13–14; reactions to,
 1–5, 14
elites, in South Carolina, and secession,
 3–4, 8
Elliott, J. D., 21
emancipation amendment, 7
Emmons, Alexander H., 4f
Enfilade Battery, 223
erring sister approach, 24, 117
Europe, and Confederacy, 137–40
evacuation of Sumter: Anderson on,
 75, 179; Baldwin and, 171–74; of
 dependents, 90–92; March 15 meeting
 on, 126–29; March 29 meeting on,
 140–45; rumors of, 121–32, 145–47,
 152–53, 175–85, 217, 346n25, 351n89;
 Scott and, 123, 124f; support for, 122

Farragut, David, 60
Farrand, Ebenezer, 85